Ulrich Sieber / Nicolas von zur Mühlen (eds.)

Access to Telecommunication Data in Criminal Justice

Schriftenreihe des Max-Planck-Instituts für
ausländisches und internationales Strafrecht

Strafrechtliche Forschungsberichte

Herausgegeben von Ulrich Sieber

Band S 156

Max-Planck-Institut für ausländisches
und internationales Strafrecht

Access to Telecommunication Data in Criminal Justice

A Comparative Analysis of European Legal Orders

Ulrich Sieber • Nicolas von zur Mühlen (eds.)

Duncker & Humblot • Berlin

Bibliografische Information der Deutschen Nationalbibliothek

Die Deutsche Nationalbibliothek verzeichnet diese Publikation in der Deutschen Nationalbibliografie; detaillierte bibliografische Daten sind im Internet über <http://dnb.ddb.de> abrufbar.

c/o Max-Planck-Institut für ausländisches und internationales Strafrecht
Günterstalstraße 73, 79100 Freiburg i.Br.
http://www.mpicc.de
Vertrieb in Gemeinschaft mit Duncker & Humblot GmbH, Berlin
http://www.duncker-humblot.de

Umschlagbild: © istock.com/kynny
Druck: Stückle Druck und Verlag, Stückle-Straße 1, 77955 Ettenheim
Printed in Germany

ISSN 1860-0093
ISBN 978-3-86113-796-2 (Max-Planck-Institut)
ISBN 978-3-428-15143-1 (Duncker & Humblot)
Gedruckt auf alterungsbeständigem (säurefreiem) Papier
entsprechend ISO 9706 ♾

Preface

Access to telecommunication data is an essential and powerful investigative tool in criminal justice. At the same time, the interception of such data can seriously affect individual privacy. This is true not only with respect to content data but with respect to traffic data as well. The legal instruments and provisions that allow the gathering of these data are primarily the traditional rules on the interception of telecommunication based on the cooperation duties of telecommunication providers. In addition, access to telecommunication data can also be granted by rules on remote forensic software, by search and seizure of – temporarily or permanently – stored data, and (esp. in cases of traffic and subscriber data) by production orders demanding the delivery of stored data.

The rules governing these interception techniques vary considerably among the national legal orders. Differences are found, for example, in the formal requirements for interception orders, in the scope of professional secrecy and privacy protections leading to the exemption from interception, and in the possibilities to access (esp. encrypted) telecommunication data by means of remote forensic software, either to specifically procure telecommunication data or in general. These legal differences are not only most interesting from the perspective of fundamental research in the area of comparative criminal law but also for practical reasons, such as identifying best practices and evaluating the scope of international cooperation.

This publication provides a comparative analysis dealing with the commonalities and differences of these rules on interception and other means of access to telecommunication data. It also includes country reports on the following European legal orders on which this comparison is based: Belgium, Czech Republic (including a comparative presentation of the law of Slovakia), France, Germany, Spain, Sweden, and the United Kingdom. The research undertaken on these countries encompasses not only the law on the books but also the law in action as analyzed in interviews and workshops with specialists in the fields of telecommunication interception and international cooperation in criminal matters. The analysis of law in action also includes the Netherlands, in addition to the above-mentioned countries.

The original incentive to conduct this analysis was an expert opinion prepared for the Centre for Strategy and Research on Telecommunication (SFZ TK) on international cooperation in the interception of telecommunication. International cooperation in this area based on mutual legal assistance was and still is complicated, slow, and – in practice – rare. For these reasons, the goal of the study for the Ministry was to develop legal and technical solutions by means of which telecommunication data could be transmitted from one country to another in real time, by direct transmission, and without violating human rights standards. Since such transmissions are especially problematic due to differences in the laws of the various national orders (esp. professional secrecy and privacy protections), the study also required a specific comparative analysis of these differences. The solutions developed SFZ TK on international cooperation were published in a separate volume (S 157 of this book series) in German.

The wealth of information gathered by this practice-oriented study on international cooperation inspired us to develop our applied research into a general comparative analysis on access to telecommunication data, which is published in this book. In contrast to the above-mentioned study for the Ministry, this general comparative analysis is written in English and addresses not only questions that arise in the context of mutual legal assistance in interception of content data but rather covers all questions implicated in the context of access to telecommunication data. Thus, the scope of this second study extends beyond traditional interception and includes all types of access to telecommunication data that can be used as functional equivalents to traditional interception. Additionally, it is not limited to the interception of content data but rather covers access to traffic and subscriber data as well. In contrast to the above-mentioned study, this publication contains both the results of the comparative study as well as the underlying country reports. As a consequence, the general analysis on access to telecommunication data presented here not only supports our specific study on legal cooperation in interception but can also serve as a general research tool in support of future studies and practical work.

We would like to thank both the academic authors of the country reports for their most valuable support of this study and the many dedicated practitioners who provided us with comprehensive, detailed information about the concrete situation in their countries in interviews in Brussels, Gießen, London, Madrid, Paris, Prague, Stockholm, and Utrecht. Above all, we are most grateful to Mr. *Christian Förster* from SFZ TK as the appointed project manager, who who efficiently organized and made possible these interviews on "the law in action". In addition, sincere thanks are also due to our editing and proofreading teams, especially Ms. *Ines Hofmann*, Ms. *Petra Lehser*, Ms. *Indira Tie*, and Ms. *Anna Riddell* (as external proofreader).

Freiburg, October 2016

Prof. Dr. Dr. h.c. mult. *Ulrich Sieber*
Nicolas von zur Mühlen

Contents

Part 1 – Introduction: Object, Aims, and Research Methods

Ulrich Sieber
Nicolas von zur Mühlen

Contents

I. Subject

The interception of telecommunication is key in the practice of law enforcement. In Germany, 23,382 warrants authorizing an interception of telecommunication in criminal cases were issued in 2014 in the context of 5,625 cases, which translates to 28 warrants per 100,000 residents. In other countries, this investigative tool plays an even greater role. For example, in Belgium, 6,712 warrants were issued in 2012, amounting to 60 warrants per 100,000 residents. In addition to (repressive) measures located in the criminal law authorizing telecommunication interception, all countries also employ (preventive) measures that authorize interception, especially measures of intelligence law.

One of the reasons for the current significance of telecommunication interception is the fact that modern communication techniques have been instrumental in recent decades in inducing a profound change in society, commonly termed "information society." By now, digital interconnectivity permeates almost all aspects of life. Technical media have increasingly replaced the direct and personal exchange of information that used to be the rule. End user devices such as smart phones, tablets, and smartwatches provide uninterrupted connectivity using an array of communication channels. Communication between information systems, aside from the familiar telecommunication between people, has become ever more important. At present, this is particularly true in the context of the transfer of applications, data processing capabilities, and storage into the cloud, and communication between systems is expected to increase even more in the coming years through the so-called internet of things, which links household appliances, vehicles, sensors, and control systems.

As a result of these technical and social changes, law enforcement agencies are facing a host of challenges, not least because criminal offenders are also users of modern communication technologies. The use of such technologies is particularly significant in crimes planned and executed by offender groups operating mostly in a decentralized and trans-national manner, particularly in the areas of organized crime, terrorism, and cybercrime.

In addition, the new risks presented by terrorism, organized crime, economic and business crime, and cybercrime have made it necessary to prevent these offenses as early in the process of commission as possible, which in turn requires intensified information-gathering prior to the actual commission of a crime. The need for these efforts to gather information before actual harm is caused arises not only in the context of preventive information gathering by police and intelligence services but also in criminal investigations. The reason is that recently enacted precursor offenses increasingly criminalize preparatory acts – acts that, for the most part, are value neutral – if the offender has certain offenses in mind or the requisite knowledge. This type of investigation conducted prior to the occurrence of any actual harm and for the purpose of proving criminal intent and knowledge may be accomplished primarily by means of telecommunication interception.

Currently, telecommunication interception is *functionally* linked to new technical and legal problems. *Technical* problems arise primarily from the encryption of communication, from the wealth of telecommunication service providers used, and from the huge number of terminal devices, protocols and applications. These developments generate new *legal* issues and approaches, such as source telecommunication surveillance and the growing number of requirements imposed on service providers. More legal problems arise from the fact that the distinction between access to stored data and access to transmitted data (such as temporarily stored emails) is blurred in the internet. Another question involves the conditions that would permit the authorized interception not only of person-to-person communication but also of communication between persons and machines (such as during interception of the retrieval of websites) and of exchanges of data between technical devices (such as in the internet of things).

These technical and legal problems increase exponentially at the *territorial* level if offenders operate across borders. The interception of the telecommunication of a suspect who travels abroad becomes even more complicated in terms of law because the authority of investigative agencies to engage in telecommunication interception are limited, in principle, to the national territory; as a rule, any interception of telecommunication systems in a foreign state constitutes a violation of that country's sovereignty. However, the required mutual legal assistance in matters involving foreign countries presents additional legal challenges. The main challenge is due to the fact that different national legal systems have different provisions on telecommunication interception, which is why they may conflict with a transfer of data, for example, in terms of the legal problems mentioned above or in terms of the definition of professional secrecy leading to exemption from telecommunication interception. Prosecutors are saddled with more legal and organizational problems: the special, little-known, and complex topic of mutual legal assistance; the ambiguities in the national law of the requested state; and translation issues involved in providing mutual legal assistance. And, above all, the technical difficulties that may arise, for example, if each state involved employs a different system for telecommunication interception, thus creating compatibility issues. These problems are compounded if the interception results need to be transferred not only as "canned" information in data files but in real time over data lines to enable an immediate response on the part of the investigation agencies in the requesting state. For these reasons, national borders within the European Union continue to create major challenges for the efficient interception of transnational telecommunication.

However, these cases create problems not only in terms of the efficiency of criminal justice but also in terms of the protection of the citizens concerned. To take an example: by way of mutual legal assistance, a router's data packets recorded in Germany, which might possibly include communication by a member of the clergy or data from the core area of privacy (which, in Germany, may neither be surveilled nor evaluated) are directly transmitted to France (where no such legal privileges exist). Similarly, in England, telecommunication interception may be issued without court order: what if such a request is transmitted to the German authorities by way of mutual legal assistance? If telecommunication interception results are transmitted to a foreign country in real time, the opportunity to engage in the control and selection of transmitted data is even more limited. Any transmission of telecommunication interception results to a foreign country in real time, which is needed for effective investigations, means a further reduction in the ability to control and select the transmitted data.

II. Research Aims

The first aim of this study is to identify, by way of a comprehensive comparative legal analysis, the concepts employed by the various states to manage the technical and legal problems involved in telecommunication interception. Special focus is on specific deficiencies in existing methods of lawful intervention and on the different approaches developed to address specific problems.

By providing a comprehensive overview of the relevant national legislation of various countries, this study also seeks to provide a foundation for additional research projects that address both the functional as well as the territorial limits of criminal law in the context of the issue at hand. A pertinent example is the study entitled *Rechtshilfe in der Telekommunikationsüberwachung* (Mutual legal assistance in telecommunication interception) mentioned in the Preface. Its aim is to generate an effective system of transnational telecommunication interception that provides an appropriate level of protection for the citizens involved and, as such, is compatible with constitutional and human rights guarantees.

An additional goal of this study is to support law enforcement agencies by presenting national law in a way that helps make international cooperation in the context of telecommunication interception more effective. Requests for telecommunication interception can be successful only if the investigating authorities know the pertinent local rules.

III. Research Method

A. Identifying Relevant Provisions

This research study addresses the national *laws of criminal procedure* and the national *laws on telecommunication* of the participating countries, specifically the powers of intervention involving telecommunication interception provided by the laws of criminal procedure and the specific provisions on the obligations of providers. In most countries, these requirements are enacted as special legislation or as ordinances. In order to create a foundation for further projects on issues involving telecommunication interception (in particular, the study entitled *Rechtshilfe in der Telekommunikationsüberwachung*), this study also covers relevant national provisions on mutual legal assistance.

B. Selecting Legal Systems for the Study

The following eight countries were selected to participate in the study: Belgium, the Czech Republic, France, Germany, the Netherlands, Sweden, Spain, and the United Kingdom. These states are all EU members and all of them have ratified the Council of Europe Convention on mutual legal assistance. By incorporating German, Nordic, and Roman law legal systems as well as the Common Law system, this study reflects the legal diversity in Europe.

C. Obtaining Relevant Country Information

1. Issue

The study involves not only multiple legal systems but also numerous aspects of law in these systems, including the pertinent law of criminal procedure and various aspects of constitutional law, telecommunication law, and the law of mutual legal assistance. Additional expertise is required because the aim of this study, which also includes practical objectives, dictates not only the analysis of the law on the books but also the law in practice.

Obtaining reliable information on the laws of the participating countries, including the "law in action," requires a combination of two methods of data collection: first, country reports by foreign legal scholars who are specialists in telecommunication law or information law, and second, interviews and workshops with members of the police and the judiciary working in the area of prosecution, in particular in organized crime and mutual legal assistance on telecommunication interception.

2. Country reports

The "law on the books" was analyzed on the basis of the responses to a standard questionnaire provided to experts on telecommunication interception in the aforementioned countries. In order to enable a comparative legal analysis, the reports are all organized according to the same outline.

- The country report Belgium was written by Prof. *Paul De Hert* and *Gertjan Boulet*, Vrije Universiteit Brussel.
- The country report Czech Republic was prepared under the leadership of Prof. *Radim Polčák*, University of Brno. This report includes a comparative presentation of the law of Slovakia, which is very similar to the law of the Czech Republic.
- The country report France was written by Dr. *Estelle De Marco*, Inthemis, Montpellier.
- The German country report on telecommunication law was prepared under the leadership of Prof. *Ulrich Sieber* and *Nicolas von zur Mühlen* by staff members Dr. *Benjamin Vogel, Patrick Köppen* and *Thomas Wahl* of the Max Planck Institute for Foreign and International Criminal Law.
- The country report Spain was written by Prof. *Lorena Bachmaier Winter*, University of Madrid.
- The country report Sweden was written by Prof. *Iain Cameron*, University of Uppsala.
- The country report United Kingdom was written by Prof. *Ian Walden*, Queen Mary University London.

3. Workshops with legal practitioners

Primarily in order to incorporate law in action, a one-day workshop was organized in each of the participating legal systems. The main goal of these workshops was to provide an opportunity for questions and discussions on legal and practical issues involving police and judicial practice. Participants in the discussions were investigators and prosecutors experienced in telecommunication interception as well as specialists on mutual legal assistance. The analysis of law in action also includes the Netherlands, in addition to the above-mentioned countries.

4. Questionnaires and scope of analysis

Both the country reports and the interviews with practitioners were based on detailed, highly-structured questionnaires. Both questionnaires were designed by Prof. Dr. *Ulrich Sieber* in cooperation with *Nicolas von zur Mühlen* and can be found in the Appendix, along with the country reports and the summaries of interviews with practitioners.

With regard to the law of criminal procedure, both questionnaires expanded the subject matter over and above the regulatory scope of telecommunication interception to include issues regarding access to stored communication data and additional questions regarding access to computer-stored data (in particular, issues surrounding the distinction between transmitted and stored data). The reasons for this were twofold: First, to leverage the availability of these specialists from academia and legal practice to obtain data for future research on digital investigative measures. Second, the objective for the research issue at hand was to address all types of access to communication data, i.e., both data transmitted and data stored, in order to identify by means of a comprehensive, functional approach any consequences arising from regulations for mutual legal assistance relating to telecommunication interception.

D. Comparative Legal Analysis

The aim of this study is to analyze concepts for the interception of telecommunication. In line with this, a comparative legal analysis was undertaken, based on the information derived from the country reports, to determine where the participating legal systems converge and where they diverge. The resulting findings on common features and differences between national regulations facilitated an assessment, not only in terms of each country under study but also generally and comprehensively, of potential challenges to international cooperation.

The aim of the study determined both subject matter and scope of the comparative legal analysis. Accordingly, the possibilities and limits of telecommunication interception under the rules of criminal procedure and telecommunication law were at the heart of this legal analysis. The comprehensive questionnaires, developed on the basis of a functional approach, made it easy to compare country information. This provided the foundation for Dr. *Tatjana Tropina* of the Max Planck Institute for Foreign and International Criminal Law to prepare a comparative legal analysis that focuses on the national law on telecommunication interception (Part 2).

IV. Subsequent Outline

Part 2 begins with a *comparative* legal outline of the law on criminal procedure and on telecommunication relating to telecommunication interception. The extensive country reports, which serve as the foundation for the comparative legal outline, follow in alphabetical order by country.

Part 2
Comparative Analysis

Tatiana Tropina

Contents

I. Security Architecture and the Interception of Telecommunication

A. Law Enforcement Institutions and Security Services with Powers of Telecommunications Interception

The interception of electronic communications has become one of the major instruments for criminal investigation. At the same time, however, this measure is also being used for the prevention of future dangers and for information gathering by intelligence agencies. While this study analyses the lawful interception of communications in criminal procedure, it is important to understand the role that such interception has for purpose of criminal investigation and criminal prosecution in different interception regimes – such as interception for intelligence purposes, crime prevention, or to address dangers – and whether there is a separation between them. The following chapter attempts to analyse the entire spectrum of different legal regimes that provide coercive powers for the interception of electronic communications in the countries included in this study, with the aim of embedding the interception of communications for the purpose of criminal justice into the broader context of the national security architecture.

1. National security architecture

In all eight countries included in this study, the interception of communications can be carried out by different authorities under various interception regimes provided for in the legislation of their respective jurisdictions. In most of the states, except the **United Kingdom**, distinct laws govern interception for the purpose of the prosecution and prevention of crime.

Security-related legislation at the national level constitutes a system of different legislative acts on the powers of various authorities tasked with security issues for the purpose of crime prevention and safety of the state. In all of the jurisdictions, this architecture includes police forces and various security entities, such as intelligence agencies, the military, and civil defence bodies, and, in some countries, customs authorities.

The structures of security regimes at the national level are usually very complex and are almost incomparable because of the organisational differences and specifics of national laws establishing and governing their security architectures. Even the police agencies, which exist in every country, may be differently set up, complex organisational structures. For example, in **Spain,** the police consists of three different bodies – National Police, Guardia Civil, and municipal police – with only the first two granted the power to intercept communications. While these two Spanish police forces have a number of exclusive responsibilities for the investigation of certain types of crimes, their domains might overlap, depending on the number of inhabitants in a city or the agency that receives information first about a crime.[1] This creates a complex system of application of police regulations in practice. Another illustrative example of a specific regulation is **Sweden**, where two police bodies – national police and security police, which represents internal intelligence services – were separated institutionally, but not legally, in January 2015. The two structures still operate under the same legislation and can both intercept communications and share information.[2]

Further differences in the national security architecture arise from the complexity of the national regimes concerning intelligence agencies and other entities responsible for state security. The framework and design of such systems include various agencies at the national level tasked with state security as well as military and civil defence. For example, in **Germany**, the security system includes offices for the protection of the Constitution, established at both the state and federal levels, and, at the national level, the Federal Intelligence Service (BND) and the Military Counterintelligence Service (MAD).[3] More examples on the national security architecture, including detailed information on police and security services as well as the respective legislation regulating them, can be found in the country reports.

2. Powers for the interception of telecommunications

Most of the national reporters indicated that their respective interception regimes include three pillars: preventive police law, repressive criminal procedural law, and state security legislation, all of them providing the framework for the interception of communications. The national reports also noted that the law of criminal procedure is one of the main regimes regulating interception for the investigation of crime. There are two exceptions to this general model of having three regimes allowing for interception: the **Czech Republic**, where police law does not allow interception for crime prevention, and the **United Kingdom**, which has a different system of interception regulation.

One of the most important issues in this regard is the question of safeguards provided by different regimes allowing for the interception of communications: the level of checks and balances in all the countries, except the **United Kingdom**, can differ for preventive, repressive, and intelligence purposes. The national reporters

---

1 Information obtained at the law enforcement workshop.

2 Swedish country report, Chapter I.A.4 and information from the Swedish law enforcement workshop.

3 German country report, Chapter I.A.1.

from the **Czech Republic** and **France** specifically highlighted that the law of criminal procedure in their countries provides much stricter safeguards for the interception of communications, such as the need for court authorisation, compared to other existing interception regimes.[4] Even stricter regulation concerning the level of safeguards can be found in **Germany**, where interception both for the purpose of prevention and for criminal investigations requires a court order. However, German legislation regulating interception carried out by intelligence services does not require judicial authorisation and establishes "mere factual indication" as a prerequisite instead of requiring a certain degree of suspicion,[5] thus providing fewer safeguards for acquiring communications by means of intelligence agencies.

In contrast, **Belgium** and **Sweden** have the same requirements for judicial authorisation of interception carried out by intelligence services and law enforcement agencies, but fewer checks and balances for capturing communications for the purpose of crime prevention or for certain types of investigations. In **Belgium**, the preventive interception regime has less strict safeguards compared to both the law of criminal procedure and intelligence law: the latter stipulates the same condition for judicial authorisation to intercept as criminal procedure.[6] **Swedish** legislation requires both national police and security police (internal intelligence) to obtain judicial approval for interception; however, exceptions to the requirement of court authorisation are granted to the security police based on special legislation on the investigation of particularly dangerous crimes.[7]

In the **United Kingdom**, the situation differs from all other legal regimes due to the different architecture of the national legal system. The same statute – Regulation of Investigatory Powers Act 2000 (RIPA) – governs communications interception for law enforcement, intelligence, and other agencies. RIPA thus represents an "umbrella" act, a one-size-fits-all legal solution for repressive, preventive, and intelligence purposes. There are, however, also separate, additional pieces of legislation providing for the interception of communications, such as the Intelligence Services Act 1994 and, as indicated in the UK country report, the Police and Criminal Evidence Act 1984. Both acts can be used in certain cases for interception purposes when communication is stored during transmission.[8]

---

4 French country report, Chapter I.A.2.b); Czech country report, Chapter I.A.2.c).

5 German country report, Chapter I.A.2.c).

6 Belgian country report, Chapter I.A.2.c) referring to Article 90*ter* of the Code of Criminal Procedure, and Article 18/2 §2, 7° of the Act of 30 November 1998 on the Intelligence and Security Services.

7 Swedish country report, Chapter I.A.2.a).

8 UK country report, Chapter I.

3. Responsibility for the technical performance of interception measures

In all of the countries included in this study, the general mode of the interception of communications for the purpose of criminal investigations is to order communications providers to extract data and surrender them to the respective agencies responsible for carrying out the interception. However, different approaches to the centralisation of interception lead to divergences in the implementation of this general mode, both technically and functionally, on the national level.

As can be seen from the analysis of the country reports and from information obtained at practical workshops, the bodies responsible for the interception platforms may vary from designated technical units within the police to special departments within the Ministry of Justice. Furthermore, in addition to carrying out interception with the help of communications service providers, law enforcement agencies can use their own technical tools to carry out interception or the acquisition of certain types of communications and other data.

Most of the countries (the **Czech Republic, Belgium**, the **Netherlands, Sweden**, and the **United Kingdom**) have **centralised** interception platforms either within the police unit or within the Ministry of Justice, which use the equipment installed at the communications providers. **France's** centralised interception platform and its organisational structure are currently undergoing a major reform concerning the interception system: while the technical platform itself is still going to be centralised, the major change will be the replacement of the system currently under police supervision with a system under control of the Ministry of Justice.

In two states – **Germany** and **Spain** – interception is **not centralised**. **Germany**, due to its federal state structure, has a multifaceted network of platforms for the interception of communications on it federal territories. In **Spain**, the system is also complex because there are two police units – Guardia Civil and Policia Nacional – responsible for the interception, each of them having its own platform. There are also several platforms on the territories, such as Catalonia, the Basque Country, and Navarra.

Furthermore, in some countries, like the **Czech Republic** and **Belgium**, law enforcement agencies share the technical platform for interception with intelligence agencies. Yet other jurisdictions, like **Spain**, feature a separation of platforms for different agencies.

The **Netherlands** represent a distinct example in the organisation of its centralised platform, because they have an additional link in the chain of interception – a Central Information Desk Telecommunications Research, which represents a point of exchange for specific information between law enforcement agencies and communications providers. Before submitting the request for authorisation of a wiretap, investigators must check whether the phone number or IP address is still in use.

This information has to be verified with the help of the Central Information Desk Telecommunications Research. Communications providers are obliged to refresh identification data every 24 hours, and law enforcement agencies can verify the data with the central desk.[9]

There is a strict separation between responsibility for the technical performance of the interception and actual access to the content of communications. In every country, included in this study, it is only law enforcement agencies that gain knowledge of telecommunication content, even if providers are involved in performing the interception.

4. Legitimacy of data transfers between different security agencies

In most of the countries included in this study, except **Sweden** and the **United Kingdom**, intelligence services and other agencies responsible for crime prevention are separated from the bodies dealing with the interception of communications for the purpose of the investigation and prosecution of crime. However, there are still certain frameworks allowing data resulting from interception to be passed between law enforcement and intelligence. Only in the **Netherlands** did the representatives of the law enforcement agencies at the law enforcement workshop indicate that there is no possibility for such data sharing in practice. Further analysis shows that, in most jurisdictions, information flows between different interception regimes are possible either because of the lack of strict separation between different regimes, as in **Sweden** and the **United Kingdom**, or because of special legal provisions that allow for information sharing. The conditions for information sharing between different agencies might either be provided for by specific laws, like those in **Germany** and **Belgium**, where legislation establishes a complex set of conditions for such information exchange, or be outlined in generic clauses on cooperation between different national agencies as in **France**, **Spain,** and the **Czech Republic**, where information sharing is limited.

– *No strict separation concerning information flows*

Logically, when the intelligence services are not strictly separated, if separated at all, from the agencies dealing with the prevention and investigation of crime, as in **Sweden** and the **United Kingdom,** more flexible rules for information flows between them can be found in the national legal system. In **Sweden**, even after the separation of security services from the police on 1 January 2015, both agencies are still considered to be police organisations: they fall under the same legislation and follow the same rules on how to handle and process information. The Swedish re-

[9] *Odinot et al.*, Summary – The use of telephone and Internet taps in criminal investigations, 2012, available at: https://english.wodc.nl/onderzoeksdatabase/effectiviteit-van-tappen.aspx?cp=45&cs=6798 [last accessed 10/2016].

port points out that the Transparency and Secrecy Act 2009 permits information transfers between different agencies if necessary to carry out their functions, thus making possible the data sharing between different police agencies and the signal intelligence agency (National Defence Radio Establishment).[10] As was shared by law enforcement agency representatives at the workshop in Sweden, in practice in some type of investigations, e.g., in many terrorist cases, both the police and security services work together and share information throughout the course of an investigation. When data are intercepted for the purpose of crime prevention, however, such sharing is not always possible, because preventive police activity is subject to different legal regulation. Nevertheless, as stated by Swedish law enforcement agencies, permission to use such data can be granted by the prosecutor. Another exception is the participation of the signal intelligence agency in criminal investigations: as the Swedish country report points out, while the Swedish National Defence Radio Establishment can be tasked with assisting in the obtaining intelligence information upon request by the police authorities concerning certain crimes, the inclusion of the signal intelligence agency in the investigation of specific offences is prohibited.[11]

The **United Kingdom** is another country in which the interception of communications can entail cooperation between different agencies, such as security services and police divisions. Therefore, intercepted data might be disclosed to other entities when necessary. The information from the law enforcement workshop, however, revealed that the extracted data are shared only in certain cases and never include the entire interception outcome. The exchange of information obtained during the course of interception is regulated in Sections 15 and 16 of RIPA in a very complex way.

– *Strict separation, but information flows are permissible*

In contrast to **Sweden** and the **United Kingdom**, other countries included in this study separate the regimes governing interception carried out by different agencies, thus making information sharing subject to strict rules and procedures. When sharing is possible, it usually falls under one of the two models indicated in this comparative analysis: exchange of the intercepted data either under the specific detailed regulation or under the general rules on information sharing.

Specific regulations on information transfers exist in **Germany** and in **Belgium**. Although police forces and intelligence agencies are separated in **Germany**, the transfer of information gained through the interception of communications are allowed under certain conditions involving the assessment of justification in each individual case of such sharing and the application of the principle of proportionali-

---

[10] Swedish country report, Chapter I.A.4.

[11] *Ibid.*

ty.[12] Therefore, the possibility to share information depends on which authorities are transferring such information and who the recipient is. For example, although passing on data from law enforcement to preventive police authorities in Germany is, in principle, possible under § 481 Para. 1 StPO,[13] the information flows in the other direction – from preventive police authorities to law enforcement – are more limited. These data can be passed and used as evidence only if they could have been legally obtained under the law of criminal procedure.[14] Furthermore, the disclosure of data from intelligence to law enforcement is permissible only under the condition of prevention and prosecution of crimes related to state security and a number of other serious crimes.[15] Passing data from interception the other way around – from law enforcement to intelligence – is also restricted to crimes endangering the security of the state.[16] At the federal state level, such information transfers are also limited, and the police do not regularly share data with intelligence services.[17]

Even more complex specific frameworks govern data transfers between different agencies in **Belgium**. In principle, the exchange of information is enabled by the Law on the Intelligence and Security Services, which provides the obligation for the efficiency of mutual cooperation between intelligence and security services, the police, and the judiciary. However, the system for such information exchanges is outlined in different pieces of legislation. Intelligence and security services have a duty to pass on relevant information to the police under the Act of 18 March 2014.[18] Information transfers to the prosecutors are permitted by virtue of Article 29 of the Belgian Code of Criminal Procedure, which requires intelligence and security agencies to inform a public prosecutor immediately if any information about a crime is obtained. The body responsible for such transfers is a special administrative commission, which has the duty to monitor the data collection methods used by the intelligence and security services (SIM commission).[19] Additional cooperation possibilities are outlined in Article 20 §2 of the Act of 30 November 1998 on the Intelligence and Security Services, which states that, upon receiving a request from judicial authorities, intelligence and security services "*can*[20] cooperate with the judicial and administrative authorities, upon their request, and within the

12 German country report, Chapter I.A.4.

13 Furthermore, some states require cases of threat to life, health, or freedom of persons. For the purpose of investigations into serious crimes, see, for example, Article 38 Para. 2 of the Bavarian Police Code. See German country report, Chapter I.A.4.a).

14 German country report, Chapter I.A.4.a) referring to §161, Section 1 StPO.

15 German country report, Chapter I.A.4.b).

16 German country report, Chapter I.A.4.c).

17 *Ibid*

18 Belgian country report, Chapter I.A.4.

19 *Ibid.*

20 Emphasis added by the national reporter.

limits of a protocol adopted by the relevant ministers." Lastly, the possibility to pass data on to the intelligence agencies also generally falls under the above-mentioned provision on maximally efficient cooperation: police services and judicial authorities can even transfer data at their own initiative.[21] Law enforcement agencies, however, can refuse to provide such requested information to other entities if it might hamper an ongoing investigation and in a number of other circumstances.[22]

Less complex and very general regulation on data sharing exists in **France, Spain,** and the **Czech Republic**, where the possibility for such information transfers is outlined in the generic clauses on cooperation between different national agencies. In **France** (except when a criminal activity has been revealed during the intelligence information gathering), there is no regulation providing for the ways to exchange information between law enforcement and security services. The French report states that the general perception on the national level is that regulation on data transfers from police to intelligence agencies is not necessary, because intelligence services already have a broad discretion to intercept.[23] In contrast, when information sharing goes in the other direction, the **French** law provides for the duty to pass on data from intelligence agencies to the police under the general regulation (Art. 40 of the Penal Procedure Code),[24] obliging any authority, including intelligence agencies, to pass on information about the crime to the prosecutor.

Like **France, Spanish** procedural legislation provides only for the general obligation to report facts on a possible crime to the police, prosecutor, or investigating judge.[25] In addition, there is a general provision on cooperation in Article 4 of the law on the National Intelligence Centre (CNI), which refers to the coordination of action between different government bodies. In practice, as shared by the Spanish law enforcement agency representatives during the workshop, information obtained by the CNI can be used only for the purpose of state security and strictly for the aim of criminal investigation; it cannot be shared with anyone except the Guardia Civil. Intelligence services can share data for the purpose of criminal investigation only as names or addresses or other identifiers, but they are not allowed to hand over the content of intercepted communications. Since all the information obtained by the CNI is classified, the police authority has no possibility to use this data in court.

---

[21] Belgian country report, Chapter I.A.4.c) referring to Article 14 §1–2 of the Act of 30 November 1998 Law on the Intelligence and Security Services.

[22] *Ibid.*

[23] French country report, Chapter I.A.4.b) referring to the Law n° 2015-912 of 24 July 2015.

[24] French country report, Chapter I.A.4.b).

[25] Spanish country report, Chapter I.A.4.a) referring to Articles 259, 262, and 264 of LECRIM.

Corresponding general provisions on cooperation between different agencies in **Czech** law are, however, very limited by court practice in the **Czech Republic** – a country with stricter rules on separation than most and the most restricted possibilities for information sharing among the countries included in this study. The Czech Constitutional Court, in judgement No. I. ÚS 3038/07-1 of 29 February 2008, stated that, since the law of criminal procedure does not provide for the possibility to use intercepted data obtained by any other body than law enforcement (police), the principle of legality prohibits using such information as evidence.[26] However, the intelligence agencies in the Czech Republic are still obliged to provide data to the police pursuant to general provisions in Section 8 Para. 3 of Act No. 153/1994 Sb. on intelligence services if findings fall under police jurisdiction. According to the Czech Constitutional Court, this obligation cannot include sharing too much detailed information. A similar general authorisation is outlined in Section 78 of Act No. 273/2008 Sb. on the Police of the Czech Republic, which allows the police to pass information on to security agencies if it is necessary to perform tasks within the scope of their activities. In both cases, however, the provisions are general and do not specifically regulate the sharing of data gained from the interception of communications.[27] At the law enforcement workshop in the Czech Republic, the Czech representatives stated that sharing data between police and security agencies is almost impossible due to the strict rules and the Constitutional court's practice. There is an ongoing discussion, however, on the need for specific regulation and on possible legal reform allowing data transfers in certain very limited cases.

B. Statistics on Telecommunications Interception

Although the national reporters were initially asked to provide statistics on telecommunications interception in the course of this project, comparison of the statistical data presented in the national reports is not significant for the purpose of the current study due to the different methodologies of collecting and reporting information and the different ways of providing such data. Even at the national level, the analysis of statistics is not always straightforward, and the statistics stem from different sources, e.g., law enforcement agencies and telecommunications providers. For example, the **Swedish** report points out that data on interception warrants and authorisation to obtain metadata might overlap, since one person might be subject to both.[28] Similarly, **Czech** law enforcement agencies confirmed during the workshop that statistics might not always be relevant because (a) they might overlap in some of the cases; or (b) might not fit into the specific calendar year; or (c) a case

---

26 Czech country report, Chapter I.A.4 referring to Paragraph 25 of the decision of the Czech Constitutional Court No. I. ÚS 3038/07-1 of 29 February 2008.

27 *Ibid.*

28 Swedish country report, Chapter I.B.2.

might involve several warrants and involve many requests for data from communications intermediaries that might contribute to the significant increase in the statistical number of requests, especially as reported by the service providers.

At the national level, however, the publication of statistical data serves to make law enforcement work transparent and allows for the indication of at least certain trends in the application of interception measures. The obligation to collect and report statistics on communications interception exists in **Germany, Belgium, France**, and **Sweden**. National reporters from the **United Kingdom** and the **Czech Republic** indicated that, although there is no legally established duty for law enforcement to collect statistics, data is publicly available, e.g., in the United Kingdom, the number of warrants is reported for both police and security services by the respective commissioners.[29] In the **Czech Republic**, despite the absence of such an obligation in the law, the police are required under internal regulations to publish analytical and statistical information, including data on the interception of communications.[30] Some of the country reports, like that from **Belgium**, also referred to statistics in the transparency and disclosure reports from electronic communications service providers, e.g., Google, Vodafone, Microsoft, etc., as to the assessment of the number of requests coming from law enforcement agencies. **Spain** is the only country where such a reporting obligation does not exist and statistical data are not currently available to the public. All the statistics concerning the interception of communications can be found in the respective country reports.

II. Principles of Telecommunications Interception in Constitutional and Criminal Procedural Law

A. Constitutional Safeguards of Telecommunications

Protection of the privacy of communications is one of the fundamental principles of human rights. On the international level, Article 17 of the United Nations International Covenant on Civil and Political Rights protects privacy and correspondance against arbitrary or unlawful interference. On the European level, the safeguards related to private communications can be found in Article 8 of the European Convention on Human Rights and specifically in Article 7 of the Charter of Fundamental Rights of the European Union – "Respect for private and family life," which mentions communications as one of the fundamental rights to respect. The fundamental principles and safeguards of privacy and family life are reflected in the national legislation of the countries included in this study. This chapter ana-

29 UK country report, Chapter I.B.

30 Czech country report, Chapter I.B.1.

lyzes and compares the national approaches to the constitutional safeguards related to the interception of communications.

1. Areas of constitutional protection

a) Secrecy of telecommunication

Among the eight countries included in this report, only one – the **United Kingdom** – has no Constitution. In all other jurisdictions, the secrecy of telecommunications is a matter of constitutional protection. An analysis of the national legislation shows that such protection can either be provided for in the specific constitutional norms related to the secrecy of communications or fall under the general constitutional protection of privacy.

Most of the countries followed the first approach and adopted a **specific provision in their constitutional law**, which either refers only to telecommunications or protects any correspondence in a more general way. In **Germany**, Subsection 2 of Article 10 of the Constitution provides protection for the secrecy of telecommunications (which refers both to content and metadata) by requiring statutory authorisation for any infringements.[31] In the **Czech Republic**, the **Netherlands**, and **Spain**, constitutional laws safeguard the secrecy of communications under the provisions of protection of any correspondence including by telephone, telegraph, and other facilities. These provisions stipulate that interceptions can take place only when provided for in the law and with proper court authorisation.[32] In **Belgium**, the privacy of communications is protected by a special provision in the Belgian Constitution, namely Article 29, which stipulates the right to secrecy of communications and additionally by the constitutional right to privacy in general (Article 22 of the Constitution).[33] Similarly, the **Swedish** constitution has two provisions: one specifically protecting the privacy of correspondence, including telecommunications, and one on privacy, prohibiting significant privacy invasions without consent.[34]

Two of the countries included in this study – **France** and the **United Kingdom** – have no specific constitutional norms related to the secrecy of telecommunications

---

[31] German country report, Chpater II.A.1.a).

[32] Czech country report, Chapter II.A.1.a) referring to Article 13 of the Charter of Fundamental Rights and Freedoms; for Dutch law, see Article 13 of the Constitution of the Kingdom of the Netherlands 2008, available at: https://www.government.nl/documents/regulations/2012/10/18/the-constitution-of-the-kingdom-of-the-netherlands-2008 [last accessed 10/2016]; for Spain, see 3 Article 18 of Spanish Constitution and Spanish Country Report, Chapter II.A.

[33] Belgium country report, Chapter II.A.1.a).

[34] Swedish country report, Chapter II.A. referring to Instrument of Government 2:6 Paras. 1, 2.

and safeguard it under **general privacy provisions**. **French** constitutional law does not explicitly protect electronic communications and refers only to the respect for private and family life.[35] This general rule is considered protection of the secrecy of communications in accordance with the interpretation of the French Constitutional Council, which stated that the provision on respect for private and family life involves protection of the secrecy of "correspondences transmitted by means of electronic communications [and] information consulted using an electronic communications network"[36] and "protection of connection and traffic technical data."[37] The **United Kingdom** has no written constitution and, thus, no constitutional provision on communications secrecy. However, as stated by the country reporter, the Human Rights Act 1998 requires any public bodies to carry out their activities in accordance with the European Convention on Human Rights. In this regard, Article 8 of the European Convention on the right to respect privacy is relevant for the secrecy of communications.[38]

b) Confidentiality and integrity of information systems

In addition to the constitutional protection of the secrecy of communications, the **German** report points out the existence of the constitutional protection of confidentiality and the integrity of information systems as a fundamental right.[39] Other national reports provided no information on the existence of any similar provisions – only the **Czech** country report mentioned that such constitutional protection might theoretically result from fundamental rights but, in general, the systems are protected by special legislation, e.g., the Cybersecurity Act. Thus, it can be assumed that the case of Germany considering the integrity of information systems worthy of protection within the realm of constitutional law is unique up to now.

The constitutional protection of the fundamental right to confidentiality and integrity of information technology systems in **Germany** was developed by the decision of the German Federal Constitutional Court of 27 February 2008 (1 BvR 595/07), which states that this right originates from the "general right of personality," provided for in Article 2.1 in conjunction with Article 1.1 of the German Constitution. The judgment states that, due to the particular intrusiveness of the "secret

[35] French country report, Chapter II.A.1 referring to Articles 2 and 4 of the French Human and Citizens Rights Declaration of 1789 and to the French Constitutional Council, Decision n° 2004-492 DC of 2 March 2004.

[36] French country report, Chapter II.A.1.a) referring to the French Constitutional Council, Decision n° 2015-478 QPC of 24 July 2015.

[37] French country report, Chapter II.A.1.a) referring to the French constitutional Council, Decision n° 2005-532 DC of 19 January 2006.

[38] UK country report, Chapter II.1

[39] German country report, Chapter II.A.1.b).

infiltration of an information technology system by means of which the use of the system can be monitored and its storage media can be read" it can be allowed only when "factual indications exist of a concrete danger to a predominantly important legal interest."[40] In this regard, according to the Court, the predominant interests can involve "life, limb and freedom of the individual or such interests of the public a threat to which affects the basis or continued existence of the state or the basis of human existence." The judgment pointed out that, in order to justify the intrusion, the facts indicating danger should be assessed in each individual case, even if the threat "cannot yet be ascertained with sufficient probability."[41]

c) Core area of privacy

Another unique area of constitutional protection that exists in **German** law is the concept of the "core area of privacy."[42] This notion includes communications related to the innermost private area of life, such as sexuality or the expression of intimate feelings. Constitutional protection of the core area of privacy requires careful consideration, even before and during the interception of communications, with regard to both avoiding the acquisition of such information and deleting all the data collected if they are related to the core area of privacy.[43] The concept itself and the special protection accorded to this kind of information will be further discussed in the chapter of this study on the prohibition on the interception of privileged communications. While all other country reports indicated that privacy falls under constitutional protection or, as in the case of the United Kingdom, under human rights-related safeguards, no reporter indicated a special concept of the core area of privacy similar to that in German legal doctrine.

d) Right to informational self-determination

Two of the country reports – **German** and **Spanish** – pointed to yet one more area of constitutional protection: the right to informational self-determination. The **German** reporters explain this protection as a concept relating to the rights of individuals to take decisions on how they disclose and use their personal data and, in particular, refer to the reasonable faith a person places in the identity of communications partners. Moreover, this principle of guaranteeing informational self-determination safeguards persons against the deliberate collection and analysis of data gathered from publicly available content without a proportional statutory basis. Any infringement of informational self-determination, therefore, has to be

---

[40] *Ibid.*

[41] *Ibid.*

[42] German country report, Chapter II.A.1.c).

[43] *Ibid.*

justified by a prevailing public interest. In this regard, the special factor for consideration is data relevant to personality. Any intrusion during the investigation is deemed to be of significant invasiveness if the data can lead to conclusions about the "the nature and intensity of interpersonal relationships, personal interests, habits and tendencies, or the content of communication."[44]

A similar concept exists in **Spain**, where the decision of the Constitutional Court 292/2000 made a distinction between the notion of privacy and personal data protection, referring to the "fundamental right to data protection" as the right aiming "to guarantee that the individual has the power of control over their personal data, its use and destination, in order to prevent any illicit and damaging transfer of those data, that may affect the dignity and the rights of the affected person."[45] According to the national reporter, this decision allows the conclusion to be drawn that the court recognised the right to informational self-determination as a power and right to "control over the information regarding him/herself, about its use and destination, to avoid an illicit use of it."[46]

2. Proportionality of access to data

The principle of proportionality was referred to in all of the national reports as one of the most important requirements for the interception of communications and any other form of access to data in criminal investigations. The application of the principle of proportionality as one of the substantial prerequisites for any intrusion into the secrecy of communications will be further analyzed in this study, especially with regard to the interception of the content of electronic communications.

3. Consequences for the interception of telecommunication

Different safeguards, e.g., constitutional guarantees for the secrecy of communications, privacy, and informational self-determination, together with the application of the principle of proportionality as one of the substantive requirements for any intrusion into a person's private life, have had a number of consequences for the interception of electronic communications. Except for the United Kingdom, legislation in all other jurisdictions requires interception for the purpose of criminal investigations to be authorised by a court (as further analysis will show), with some exception provided for for urgent circumstances.

Furthermore, national legislation implements various checks and balances, such as limiting the application of the interception to only certain types of crime, limiting the period of validity of the interception order and the possible number of pro-

---

[44] German country report, Chapter II.A.1.d).

[45] Spanish country report, Chapter II.A.2.

[46] *Ibid.*

longations, establishing reporting obligations as well as duties and obligations concerning the destruction of irrelevant information, and many other formal requirements and safeguards. Moreover, since certain types of communication are especially protected at the national level, such as information related to the core area of privacy in Germany or communications related to the attorney-client privilege in some of the countries, the frameworks regulating interception in most of the jurisdictions specifically address this issue by including special rules on protecting this type of communications from interception or by ensuring that such information will not be used in criminal investigations. These issues will be further considered in detail in the following chapters of this study.

4. Statutory protection of personal data

To protect the secrecy of communications, the criminal law in all the countries included in this study have established criminal liability for the unlawful interception of communications. Further regimes of protection at the national level involve the prohibition on access to computer systems and of the interception of computer data, outlined either in the criminal law or in specific cybercrime legislation and other provisions aiming to protect the secrecy of communications and the integrity of data.

As already noted above, another regime of protection includes safeguarding certain information related to professional communications, e.g., those of lawyers, clergymen, medical professionals, journalists, parliamentarians, against the interception of communications, either by imposing a direct prohibition on such interception or by providing for an obligation to delete or not use this information if captured. Additional safeguards in this regard can include the notification of respective professional associations or the technical obligation to filter certain communications. Such obligations and the methods of dealing with privileged information are analyzed further in this study.

Four country reports – the **German, Czech, Belgian**, and **Spanish** reports – also highlighted the application of the principle of purpose limitation of personal data, which stipulates that data may be used only for the purpose of their collection. In accordance with this principle, interception data collected during criminal investigations have to be deleted if they are irrelevant for the investigation or no longer required for the purpose of the criminal prosecution of offences. Other dimensions of this principle might include frameworks limiting the use of collected data in other criminal investigations or rules on the admissibility of evidence resulting from the interception of communications. Detailed comparative reviews of such requirements at the national level are included in Chapter III of the study.

B. Powers in the Code of Criminal Procedure

Most of the country reports stated that the requirement for reasonable clarity of powers in the law of criminal procedure, related to the principle of legality, is one of the basic conditions in their respective legislation. However, although national reporters referred to the prohibition on using the powers by analogy as the underlying basis of this principle, some of the country reports (**Belgian** and **Swedish**) question this principle and point out that, in fact, some of the technology-neutral language in the national laws of criminal procedure allow the new techniques to be used to acquire data under existing legal provisions.[47] According to the **Belgian** report, one example is the application of traditional interception provisions on surfing communications.[48] In this respect, some issues might arise because of the temporary limits of communications and the use of provisions on access to stored data instead of interception. This study will provide insights into how these controversies are solved in the law and in practice at the national level.

The powers provided in the law of criminal procedure related to interception of the content of communications, remote data capture, interception of and access to traffic data, and access to subscriber data in the jurisdictions included in this research study are outlined and analyzed in the following chapters.

III. Powers for Accessing Telecommunication Data in the Law of Criminal Procedure

A. Overview

This chapter aims to provide a comprehensive comparative analysis of powers for accessing telecommunication data under the law of criminal procedure of the countries included in this study. In addition to a detailed evaluation of all the aspects concerning the power of law enforcement agencies to acquire communications in the course of their transmission, this analysis includes a comparison of the national laws related to such investigative measures as collection of traffic data and subscriber data, search and seizure of electronic data, and additional instruments like the use of IMSI catchers.

47 Swedish country report, Chapter II.C; Belgian country report, Chapter II.B.1.

48 Belgian country report, Chapter II.B.1.

B. Interception of Content Data

1. Statutory provisions

The following provisions of the national legislation have been indicated in the country reports as the main legal basis for the power of law enforcement agencies to intercept communications for the purpose of criminal investigations:

- Germany: Section 100a Subsection 1 StPO
- Belgium: Article 90*ter* of the Code of Criminal Procedure
- Czech Republic: Section 88 of the Code of Criminal Procedure
- France: Article 100 of the Penal Procedure Code
- Netherlands: Article 126m of the Code of Criminal Procedure
- Spain: Article 588 of LECRIM
- Sweden: Section 27:20 of CJP
- United Kingdom: Chapter I of the Regulation of Investigatory Powers Act

2. Scope of application

a) Definition of "communication"

Prior to the development of information and communication technologies and the use of digital networks, the interception of voice traffic in circuit-switched telecommunications systems was direct and unsophisticated – compared to today's situation. With the availability of changing communications patterns and the use of different communications channels, however, the scope of the interception of both traffic data and content data has widened. Growing numbers of devices are moving increasing amounts of data across networks by means of different technologies and services. Moreover, with the development of machine-to-machine communications, meaning that technology allows wireless and wired systems to interact with other devices without the involvement of a direct human component, it is very important to understand whether the scope of national legislation covers all types of communication in the interconnected world and whether the law of criminal procedure can address the emerging technical complexity.

National criminal procedure can define the object of interception in different ways, usually by using such generic terms as "telephone communication," "electronic communications," or "electronic communications between persons." The legislation in eight jurisdictions included in this study varies from country to country concerning the use of these generic terms with regard to the object of interception.

The first group of countries uses the term "**telecommunications**." In **Germany**, the object of interception is defined as "telecommunication" and in the **Czech Re-**

public as "telecommunications traffic." The second most common reference is the use of the term "communication" in different variations: for example, the legislation of the **United Kingdom** defines the object of interception as "communication" and **Swedish** law uses the term "electronic communication." Procedural law in the **Netherlands** describes the object of interception by using an additional clause referring to the privacy of communications, namely "communication, which is not meant to be public." In **Belgium**, both generic terms – "communication" and "telecommunication" – are used to outline the scope of the interception provision. Similarly, the **Spanish** law of criminal procedure refers to the interception of "telephone and electronic communications." **French** legislation defines the object of interception as "correspondences transmitted by means of electronic communications."[49]

Most of the national reports refer to the lack or even absence of a definition concerning the generic terms "communications" or "telecommunications" in the law of criminal procedure for the purpose of interception in their respective jurisdictions. As the analysis shows, when a definition exists, it can be found either in the special legislation on telecommunication, as in **Germany** and **Sweden**, or in the law of criminal procedure, as in the **United Kingdom**. The **Belgian, Czech**, and **French** national reporters specifically pointed out the lack of a statutory definition of communications for the purpose of interception and referred to the relevant discussions on this issue in the academic literature.

– *Statutory clarification in special legislation on telecommunications*

Two countries – **Germany** and **Sweden** – reported that, despite the lack of a comprehensive definition in the procedural law, the related terms can be found in the **special legislation on telecommunications or electronic communications**, thus providing the possibility for judicial interpretation. However, even such reference might not be able to solve all the problems related to the possible scope of the object of interception. As highlighted in the **German** national report, the understanding of the term "telecommunications" is established through the interpretation of the special telecommunications regulation in combination with judicial practice. In judicial practice, the meaning of "telecommunication" is understood as "incorporeal transmission of information through electromagnetic or optical signals, following the interpretation in the Telecommunications Act (TKG)."[50] This interpretation, however, does not address all the concerns related to the scope of the interception object. On the contrary, according to the German country report, the lack of an exact meaning and the absence of a proper statutory clarification raise numerous issues related to the application of the interception provision.[51]

---

49 French country report, Chapter III.B.2.a).

50 Cited from German country report, Chapter III.B.2.a).

51 German country report, Chapter III.B.2.a).

A similar definition of the object of interception can be found in **Swedish** law on electronic communications, although no discussion similar to the German debate was mentioned in the Swedish country report. As pointed out in the Swedish national report, the Electronic Communications Act 2003 provides an explanation of the term "communication". Article 6:1 of this act defines it as follows:

> "communication by electronic means any information exchanged or transmitted between a limited number of parties through a publicly available electronic communications service, except information which is transmitted as part of the broadcasting of radio and television programs that are targeted to the general public..."[52]

The national report further notes that this definition, together with Article 1:7 of the same law, which defines "electronic communications network," gives a clear interpretation of the term "communications" for the purpose of defining the scope of the procedural provisions related to interception.

– *Statutory clarification in procedural law*

The **United Kingdom** is the only country among those included in this study, which directly explains to the meaning of the term "communication" within its procedural framework on interception of communications (RIPA) for the purpose of interception, thus precisely defining the scope of interception as follows:

> "Communication includes:
> (a) (except in the definition of "postal service" in section 2(1)) anything transmitted by means of a postal service;
> (b) anything comprising speech, music, sounds, visual images or data of any description; and
> (c) signals serving either for the impartation of anything between persons, between a person and a thing or between things or for the actuation or control of any apparatus".[53]

– *No precise statutory definition*

National reporters from **Belgium**, the **Czech Republic,** and **France** referred to the lack of legal clarity concerning the definition of the object of interception and provided an overview of the discussions in the academic literature. The **Belgian** country report pointed out that the issue of the scope of the interception provision was reflected on in the parliamentary preparatory works documents, which provided that the "term (tele-)communications has a broad scope, understood in its daily use: it includes any linguistic expression, verbal or non-verbal, whether directly or at distance, and irrespective of the number of participants. In this regard, the term conflates monologues, telegrams, telex, telefax and electronic data transfers in

52 Swedish country report, Chapter III.B.1.

53 UK country report, Chapter III.B.2 referring to Section s. 81(1) RIPA.

computers and computer networks."[54] In addition, the Belgian report stated that the scope of the term "communication" in procedural law for the purpose of interception is discussed in the literature from the predominant view that this term covers almost all different types of modern communication in digital networks.[55]

In the **Czech Republic**, according to the national reporter, the special legislation on telecommunications, namely the Act on Electronic Communications,[56] does not provide a statutory clarification of the term "telecommunications traffic" used in procedural law. However, the debates in the academic literature, together with an analysis of the special legislation, enable the conclusion that the object of interception can be interpreted as "content transferred via electronic communications networks, which are defined in the electronic communications legislation as transmission systems and, where applicable, switching or routing equipment and other facilities, including network elements which are inactive and which permit the conveyance of signals."[57]

Like the Czech Republic, legislation on electronic communications and criminal procedure in **France** uses different terms for what can be described as "communication" for the purpose of interception, thus creating a lack of clarity concerning a comprehensive legal definition of the object of interception. In this regard, the French country report refers to the necessity of interpreting the scope of the application of the interception provision by means of analysis of the academic literature together with civil legislation, the French Code on penal procedure, and special legislation on electronic communications. The academic literature in France perceives the object of interception of communications – "correspondence" – as "personal and temporal communication, which allow interactivity, and which are addressed to determined and individualised persons."[58] The protection that French penal law gives to correspondence during the time of transmission relates to the provisions on interception of correspondence in the French law on criminal procedure; however, private correspondence is also the subject of legal protection provided by civil legislation. Furthermore, the term "electronic communications" is defined in the special legislation as "emissions, transmissions or reception of signs,

---

[54] Belgian country report, Chapter III.B.2.a) referring to: Parliamentary preparatory works, regarding the legislative proposal protecting privacy against the interception of communication and telecommunication, Belgian Senate, 1992–1993, 1 September 1993, 843-1, p. 7; Parliamentary preparatory works, regarding the legislative proposal protecting privacy against the interception of communication and telecommunication, Belgian Senate, 1993–1994, 18 May 1994, 843-2, p. 38.

[55] Belgian country report, Chapter III.B.2.a).

[56] Czech country report, Chapter III.B.2.a).

[57] Czech country report, Chapter III.B.2.a) referring to Section 2 of Act No. 127/2005 Sb., on electronic communications.

[58] French country report, Chapter III.B.2.a).

signals, writings, images or sounds, by electro-magnetic means." [59] Based on the analysis of the law and academic literature, the French national reporter defines electronic correspondence as "correspondences emitted, transmitted or received electro-magnetically, in the form of signs, signals, writing, images or sounds."[60]

b) Content of communications: communication between persons

The growing technical complexity of networks and services, on the one hand, and the lack of a precise statutory definition of communications for the purpose of interception in criminal procedure in many countries, on the other, raise a very important question as to the extent to which new types of electronic communication and services are covered by procedural law. All of the national reporters, except the Belgian reporter, stated that the legislation in their respective jurisdictions is technology-neutral enough to cover the interception the following types of communication in addition to "conventional" interception of analogous communication (voice and data communication) via landline:

- IP traffic of a person-to-person-communication;
- IP traffic between a person and an automated information system (e.g., communication with a webserver while downloading a website);
- IP traffic between a person's computer and their data storage in a cloud or other remote storage of data processing systems (if this is covered by "communication," as defined in the main legal provision that clarifies the definition of communications in the respective national law, between the user and the cloud provider or as an internal activity within the private storage devices of the user, which is comparable to the use of a single internal storage device);
- IP traffic between two independent computer systems.

The coverage, however, is not straightforward and simple. The lack of a clear legal definition in some of the jurisdictions raises certain questions related to the new types of information transfer and to the differences between interception of person-to-person and machine-to-machine communications. While such jurisdictions as the **United Kingdom**, where the term "communications" is defined precisely in procedural law, cover every type of traffic in respective legal provisions, other nations, like **German** and **Belgian**, are currently debating the difference between person-to-person, machine-to-machine communications, and Internet surfing as a form of communication. These discussions are generally related to the notion of the "human" component of communications for the purpose of interception as opposed to the "machine-to-machine" interactions. Furthermore, as analysed below, the same concept can be found to a certain degree in **French** legislation.

---

59 French country report, Chapter III.B.2.a) quoting Article L.32-1 of the Post and Electronic Communications Code (PECC).

60 French country report, Chapter III.B.2.a).

The **German** country report points out that, for the purpose of interception, legislation in Germany refers to a person exchanging information via telecommunications equipment; this conflates a wide range of possible ways to transfer information, from the automated arrival of data to voicemail and e-mail boxes to failed attempts to establish a communication connection. The reference to a personal, human component in current court practice, however, means that communication transmissions carried out only between technical devices are covered by the scope of the interception provision only when such data exchanges take place to establish a connection or transfer information with the final aim of facilitating communications between human beings. Consequently, the data transfers occurring between mobile devices in standby mode, for example to convey signals of readiness to operate, do not constitute telecommunication according to a decision of the German constitutional court. So far, however, it neither been clarified on the academic level or in court practice to what extent this interpretation can be applied to IP traffic.[61]

Other difficulties related to the possible coverage of different types of communications are highlighted in the Belgian national report. As was already mentioned in the previous section of this study, in **Belgium**, the question of what constitutes the content of communications for the purpose of interception in criminal investigations, in addition to analogous communications between persons, is a matter of debate in the academic literature. The Belgian reporter states that it is commonly agreed in the literature that, in addition to the conventional analogous communications, Belgian procedural law covers different types of data transfer between persons, e.g., various services related to e-mail, instant messaging via different applications and services (including mobile applications), VoIP traffic, etc.[62] However, according to the report, "IP data of machine-to-machine communications between two independent computer systems do not constitute private communications and therefore doesn't fall under the scope" of the interception provision.[63] The national reporter also refers to the non-inclusion of cases of interception of cloud computing communications and machine-to-machine communications in the annual reports published by the Minister of Justice.[64]

France represents a distinct case due to the existence of several interception-related investigative measures in its legislation on criminal procedure. According to the French national report, the analysis of the scope of the provision on the interception of correspondence, together with special legislation on electronic communications, leads to the conclusion that the object of interception conflates "at least analogous communication (voice and data) via landlines, and IP-traffic of a person-

---

61 Geman country report, Chapter III.B.2.a).

62 Belgian country report, Chapter III.B.2.a) referring to: Kerkhofs/Van Linthout, *Cybercrime*, Politeia, Brussels, 2013, pp. 279, 282, 295.

63 Belgian country report, Chapter III.B.2.a).

64 *Ibid.*

to-person-communication."[65] Thus, French legislation also seems to have the notion of a "human" component in relation to the interception of communications. Furthermore, according to the French country report, interception of other types of information transfer, such as data traffic between human beings and automated systems, including communications with a cloud and also machine-to-machine communications, would instead fall under the scope of provisions of criminal procedure other than the interception of private correspondence. The report lists search and seizure and norms regulating interception with the use of remote forensic software among these procedures.[66]

c) Current matters of dispute

Most of the countries included in this study indicated further challenges related to the definition and scope of the interception of communications provisions in the modern digital era. These challenges involve the temporary limits of communications and the blurring lines between communications in transmission and stored communications as well as issues related to the use of remote forensic software for capturing data and to the possibility of accessing the communication system remotely to install such software. Further matters of dispute include the use of passwords to access e-mail boxes and the interception of communications between computer and storage media. These challenges will be discussed in the respective chapters of this report.

3. Special protection of confidential communication content

a) Privileged communication

The protection of certain types of privileged communication from interception represents one of the most significant divergences in the law and practice of the countries included in this comparative study. Professional confidentiality and the privacy of persons are protected in national laws by systems of different safeguards that regulate which information cannot be captured during the course of interception and regulate how to deal with information obtained in practice if an acquisition takes place. The current state of legal approaches to safeguarding professional secrecy and certain types of other privileged communication against interception can be characterised as a patchwork of various legal rules. These rules range from detailed and extensive protection regimes, such as those existing in Germany and France, to the prohibition on interception of only one particular type of professional secrecy, such as lawyer-client communications in the Czech Republic.

---

65 French country report, Chapter III.B.2.a).

66 *Ibid.*

The divergences in the national laws can be attributed to a number of different matters. First of all, the prohibition on the interception of a certain type of communication is not always straightforward: there are different types of protection. Protection can be conditional or unconditional, or the rules of protection against interception can distinguish between prohibition on recording and prohibition on transcription of certain privileged communications. Secondly, differences exist in the nature of the content that is safeguarded against interception: while the rules on protection of certain types of communication include professional privileges in all of the countries, in Germany there is an additional area of protection that refers to the private nature of communications beyond professional privileges – the core area of privacy. Thirdly, the types of professional communications protected against interception may vary significantly from one country to the next with regard to which professions enjoy special privileges. All these variables contribute to the complexity of the system of protection of privileged communications and can thus become a very complicated issue for cross-border cooperation involving the interception of safeguarded content, especially with regard to the possibility of direct data transfers in the context of mutual legal assistance.

Taking into account the complexity of the national approaches to the interception of privileged communications and the different variables concerning the type and nature of protection, this chapter approaches the comparison of national legislation as follows: Firstly, it analyses various **types of protection**, such as **conditional and unconditional protection**. This comparison is taken further in the second part of the analysis, namely the protection of communication content specifically related to **different types of protected communication**, such as professional communication and the core area of privacy. The combination of both factors – types of protection and types of protected communication – in a comparative analysis enbles the complexity of the legal regimes of privileged communications to be illustrated. Thirdly, the chapter will compare the national legal and practical approaches to dealing with privileged communications in the course of interception, e.g., blocking, deletion, and prohibition on use in court proceedings.

aa) Types of protection

An analysis of the national laws shows that the protection of certain types of communication from interception is not always uncomplicated and cannot always be prescribed. From the national law comparison of the countries included in this study, two diverging factors can be found. The first one is conditional and unconditional protection, which can be found in **Germany,** and the second is the difference between the prohibition on recording of particular communication and protection against transcription when communication is intercepted. The latter regime exists in **Belgium** and **France**. It shall be noted that, as the analysis will point further, both regimes provide no protection in the case of suspicion.

– *Conditional/unconditional protection*

The distinction between conditional and unconditional protection of privileged communications can be found in **German** legislation. These two types of safeguards differ in terms of the object of protection and the consequences of the interception of communications. *Unconditional* protection implies that certain professions are strictly safeguarded from the interception of communications. Any data acquired despite this strict prohibition cannot be used for the purpose of investigation, not even as a mere clue.[67] If records of such communications are made, they have to be destroyed without delay, but the circumstances of the capture of unconditionally protected communications as well as their deletion must be documented. Provisions regulating unconditional privilege also cover cases in which any information related to unconditionally protected communications is obtained accidentally during the interception. This type of privilege is provided for in Section 160a Subsection 1 S. 1 in connection with Section 53 German StPO for certain types of professional communication, e.g., clergymen or attorneys.[68]

The second type of protection – *conditional* protection – refers in Germany to the safeguarding of certain professions from the interception of communications, depending on the gravity of the offence for which interception is used in the criminal investigation. The prohibition on interception here depends on the principle of proportionality and on balancing the interests of the investigation with the protection of professional secrecy of certain types of communication. Conditional protection against interception is provided for by Section 160a Subsection 2 and Section 53 of the German StPO. As far as the interception of conditionally protected communication is concerned, Section 160a Subsection 2 StPO stipulates that the question of whether the measure is applicable or not depends on the proportionality of the intrusion. The key criterion for reviewing proportionality is the significance of the criminal offence being investigated.[69] As stated in the German country report, unless the criminal investigation is carried out in relation to an offence of substantial significance, legal protection from interception is very likely to be granted to the conditionally protected communication or, at least, the execution of the interception might be limited. The principle of proportionality also applies to the analysis of the results of the interception related to conditionally protected professional secrets.

---

67 German country report, Chapter III.B.3.a).

68 For a detailed list of professions, see the comparative table in paragrah bb) of this chapter and German country report, Chapter III.B.3.a).

69 According to the German country report (Chapter III.B.3.a), "a criminal offence of substantial significance can be assumed when the specific offence exhibits at least an intermediate level of criminality, significantly disturbs peace under the law, and is suited to significantly compromise the population's sense of legal security. These prerequisites are usually not met when the offence is punishable by a maximum prison sentence of less than 5 years".

When criminal offences are considered to be of substantial significance in an investigation, the possibility to use interception as an investigative measure depends on balancing the interests of the criminal investigation, on the one hand, and, on the other, the legally protected public interest as well as the interests of the person who entrusted certain information to the professional falling under the privileged category.[70]

– *Prohibition on recording and prohibition on transcription*

This distinction can be found in the interception legislation of **France** and **Belgium**, which differentiate between prohibition on interception concerning certain professions enjoying privileged regimes and prohibition on the transcription of certain types of communication related to specially protected professional secrets. In **France**, the law of criminal procedure provides a complex set of measures protecting privileged communications against interception: Article 100-7 of the French Penal Procedure Code provides for the strict safeguards in relation to several types of professional communications, thus prohibiting their capture. However, addition to such prohibition, Article 100-5 of the Penal Procedure Code stipulates protection against transcription for certain types of professional communication.[71]

Similar provisions can be found in the **Belgian** law of criminal procedure, which distinguishes between interception and the official transcription of communications of certain professions unless special conditions are met. The first type of protection against interception is provided for by Article 90*octies* §1 and §2, 1° of the Belgian Code of Criminal Procedure, which establishes a special regime of privileged communications with a strict prohibition on interception. In addition to this safeguard, Article 90*sexies* §3, 1° Code of Criminal Procedure prohibits the inclusion of several types of professional communications in official transcripts. This prohibition covers a broader range of confidentiality related to professional activity than the legal provision on protection against interception. The Belgian report notes that, although recordings protected by the rules on privileged communications cannot be included in official transcripts, they must be retained in a sealed envelope,[72] because interested parties (e.g., defendant, accused, and others) can lawfully demand access to the investigation material.[73]

---

[70] German country report, Chapter III.B.3.a).

[71] For a detailed list of professions, see the comparative table in paragraph (bb) of this chapter and the French country report, Chapter III.B.3.

[72] Belgian report, Chapter III.B.3.a) referring to Article 90*septies* §3 of the Belgian Code of Criminal Procedure.

[73] Belgian country report, Chapter III.B.3.a) referring to Article 90*septies* §§5–7.

– *Legal regimes of protection with no distinctions between the types of protection*

Other countries have more general and less complex legal regimes of protection of professional secrecy. In **Sweden**, the **Netherlands**, and **Spain**, this protection refers to the exemption from the duty to testify in court or to the right of non-disclosure. In **Sweden**, Article 27:22 of CJP prohibits the interception of communications of persons who cannot be called as a witness in criminal proceedings due to their professional activity.[74] Similarly, in the **Netherlands**, a general provision covering professional secrecy – Article 126aa of the Criminal Procedure Code in conjunction with Articles 218 and 272 of the Dutch Criminal Code – prohibits the interception of information related to professional secrets for persons with a right to non-disclosure. In **Spain**, the provisions on the interception of communications explicitly protect only one category: privileged communication between the suspect and his/her defence lawyer. However, Spanish law on criminal procedure – Article 417 LECRIM and Article 20.1 of the Spanish Constitution – establishes a general protection regime of professional secrecy by exempting journalists from the duty to testify, which is considered a constitutional protection of journalists' professional secrets, namely their source of information.[75]

The least complex set of measures protecting professional secrecy exists in the **Czech Republic**. According to the Czech national report, only communication between the defence council and the accused falls under the privilege and could be the subject of the prohibition on interception.[76]

The model of protection of professional secrecy in **UK** law differs from all of the above. Procedural legislation, namely RIPA, does not provide any regulation on the interception of privileged information. However, the Code of Practice "Interception of Communications" states that "particular consideration should also be given in cases where the subject of the interception might reasonably assume a high degree of privacy, or where confidential information is involved. Confidential information consists of matters subject to legal privilege, confidential personal information or confidential journalistic material" (Chapter 3.2). The Code of Practice gives examples of such confidential information and states that the level of protection from the safeguards depends on whether the information was obtained intentionally or incidentally with some other material being sought.

bb) Protected communications

Most of the countries have legislation providing for the protection of professional secrets against telecommunications interception; however, the types of profes-

---

74 The list of such professions is provided for in Article 36:5 CJP. See: Swedish country report, Chapter III.B.2.

75 Spanish country report, Chapter III.B.3.a) and Chapter II.A.4.b).

76 Czech country report, Chapter III.B.3.a).

sions protected and the conditions for protection can vary significantly. There are various approaches to which communications are to be protected, to the protection of either professional secrecy or privacy or both, and to different practical consequences of such prohibition for criminal investigations. In general, two types of protected communication can be found in the national legislation. The first type of protection refers to different **professions** protected by virtue of law as privileged communications. The second type refers to communications protected on account of their special nature – this type of protection can be found in Germany and concerns information related to the "**core area of privacy**." The following analysis compares the details and divergences of such protection for both types.

– *Privileged professions*

The table on page 41 summarizes the complex system of safeguards related to different professional activities protected against interception of communications in the countries included in this study. Some of the complex protection regimes, like those in **German, French**, or **Belgian** law, provide more sophisticated protection with reference to conditional and unconditional protection or the distinction between recording and transcribing privileged communications. As can be seen from the table, the most commonly protected professions are: lawyers (in particular defence attorneys), medical professionals, clergymen, journalists, public notaries, and members of parliament.

However, even when legislation in different countries refers to the same professional activity, the scope of protection might still differ. These divergences are based on the different types of protection that were explained in the previous part of this chapter, such as conditional and unconditional protection, or the distinction between recording and transcripts. Further analysis will provide insight into these divergences on the national level, with regard to the most common protected professional privileges listed in the table. It shall be noted here that protection against interception deriving from a professional privilege is not absolute: exemption from such protection in a case of suspicion is further analyzed in this chapter.

Lawyers, in particular defence attorneys, are protected in most of the countries, based on the notion of a privileged communication between lawyer and client. In the more complex regimes of privileged communication, this profession enjoys the highest level of safeguards against interception. **German** law (Section 160a Subsection 1 S. 1 in connection with Section 53 German StPO) protects defence counsels of the accused and attorney unconditionally. Furthermore, in **Germany** the unconditional protection provisions also extend to assistants to defence lawyers and attorneys as well as trainees involved in the professional activity.[77] The **French**

[77] German country report, Chapter III.B.3.a).

	Germany		Belgium		Czech Republic	France		The Netherlands	Spain	Sweden	United Kingdom (no prohibition, only greater consideration requirement)
	Conditional Protection	Unconditional Protection	No Recording	No Transcript		No Recording	No Transcript				
Defence lawyer		✓	✓	✓	✓	✓	✓	✓	✓	✓	✓
Judge						✓					
Prosecutor						✓					
Clergymen		✓						✓	✓	✓	✓
Medical professionals	✓		✓	✓		✓		✓		✓	✓
Journalist	✓			✓		✓	✓		✓	✓	✓
Member of parliament		✓				✓					✓
Patent attorney	✓									✓	
Notary	✓					✓		✓			
Certified public accountant	✓										
Sworn auditor	✓										
Tax consultant	✓										
Psychotherapist	✓										
Pharmacist	✓										
Midwife	✓										

and **Belgian** codes of criminal procedure[78] exempt this type of communication from both recording and transcription. **Czech** and **Spanish** laws of criminal procedure protect communications between the defence council and the accused explicitly in the provisions related to communications interception.[79] The **Netherlands** provide such protection under the right of non-disclosure for lawyers;[80] **Swedish** law exempts communication between lawyer and client under the prohibition on interception of communications for persons who cannot be called as a witness in criminal proceedings due to their professional activity and, therefore, their professional communications with the clients are protected against interception.[81] In the **United Kingdom**, where the interception of privileged communications is not prohibited, Chapter 3.3 of the Code of Practice, which refers to Section 98 of the Police Act 1997, requires special approval for the interception of communications between a professional legal adviser and his client, or any person representing his client, which are made in connection with the dispensing of legal advice to the client. Chapters 3.6-3.8 of the Code of Practice establish additional safeguards related to lawyer-client communications, such as special assessment as well as reporting and notification duties.

Five of eight countries included in this study provide special protection for communication of **clergymen**. This type of communications is the subject of unconditional protection under the **German** law.[82] **Swedish**[83] and **Spanish**[84] legislation provides special safeguards against interception of clergymen's communications under the rules of the exemption from duty to testify, and **Dutch**[85] law does so under the right of non-disclosure. In the **United Kingdom**, the Code of Practice "Interception of Communications" provides for the obligation to give particular consideration to cases of such communications, e.g., between a minister of religion and an individual, relating to the latter's spiritual welfare.[86]

---

[78] French country report, Chapter III.B.3 referring to Articles 100-7 and 100-5 of the Penal Procedure Code; Belgian country report, Chapter III.B.3.a) referring to Articles 90*octies* §1 and §2, 1°, Article 90*sexies* §3, 1° Code of Criminal Procedure.

[79] Czech country report, Chapter III.B.3 referring to Section 88 Para. 1 of the Code of Criminal Procedure; Spanish country report, Chapter III.B.3.a) referring to Article 118.4 LECRIM.

[80] Article 126aa in conjunction with Articles 218 and 272 of the Dutch Criminal Code.

[81] Swedish country report, Chapter III.B.2 referring to Article 27:22 of CJP.

[82] German country report, Chapter III.B.3.a) referring to Section 160a Subsection 1 Section 1 in connection with Section 53 German StPO.

[83] Swedish country report, Chapter III.B.2 referring to Article 27:22 of CJP.

[84] Spanish country report, Chapter III.B.3.a) referring to Article 417 LECRIM.

[85] Article 126aa in conjunction with Article 218 of the Dutch Code of Criminal Procedure and Article 272 of the Dutch Criminal Code.

[86] *Home Office*, Interception of Communications Code of Practice, January 2016, Chapter 3.2.

The communication of **medical professionals** is another type of professional secrecy that has been given special protection in many of the national laws: six of eight countries provide special safeguards for this type of communication. In **Germany**, however, compared to the unconditional protection of defence lawyers and clergymen, the communication of doctors is protected only conditionally and is thus subject to assessment in accordance with the principle of proportionality, and it must be balanced with the interests of the investigation.[87] In contrast, in **Belgium**, physicians' communications are protected from both recording and transcription.[88] In **France**, a doctor's premises are explicitly protected against the use of remote forensic software, while the interception of communications without the use of remote forensic software can still be performed.[89] The **Netherlands** and **Sweden** protect doctors under the same provisions as those for lawyers' and clergymen's professional secrets.[90] The **United Kingdom**, again, requires special consideration for communications related to matters of medical confidentiality in accordance with the Code of Practice "Interception of Communications."[91]

Journalists are also the subject of conditional protection in **Germany**[92] and exempted from transcription of interception in **Belgium**.[93] **French** law approaches the protection of journalists differently, depending on whether the use of remote forensic software or the interception of communications is concerned. The law provides a strict ban on the use of remote forensic software on business premises and in company vehicles of media companies, audio-visual communication companies, online public communication companies, and press agencies.[94] With regard to the interception of communication, the French Penal Procedure Code does not prohibit interception but instead establishes additional safeguards against transcription of any correspondence with a journalist, which could enable the identification of "a source in breach of Article 2 of the Law of 29 July 1881 on freedom of the press."[95] In **Spain**, the communications of journalists are protected against interception un-

---

87 German country report, Chapter III.B.3.a) referring to Section 160a Subsection 2 and Section 53 of the German StPO.

88 Belgian country report, Chapter III.B.3.a) referring to Articles 90*octies* §1 and §2, 1°, Article 90*sexies* §3, 1° Code of Criminal Procedure.

89 French country report, Chapter III.B.3.

90 Article 126aa in conjunction with Articles 218 and 272 of the Dutch Criminal Code; Swedish country report, referring to Article 27:22 of CJP.

91 *Home Office*, Interception of Communications Code of Practice, January 2016, Chapter 3.2.

92 German country report, Chapter III.B.3.a) referring to Section 160a Subsection 2 and Section 53 of the German StPO.

93 Belgian country report, Chapter III.B.3.a) referring to Article 90*sexies* §3, 1° Code of Criminal Procedure.

94 French country report, Chapter III.B.3.

95 *Ibid.*

der the general exemption from the duty to testify in court regarding sources.[96] In the **United Kingdom**, the Code of Practice "Interception of Communications" provides, as in other cases, that journalists' communications require additional consideration when interception is concerned.[97]

The communication of **public notaries** is yet another type of privilege protected by virtue of law in several countries. **German** legislation provides conditional protection for this type of professional privilege,[98] **France** protects the premises of notaries against the use of remote forensic software,[99] and the **Netherlands** provide protection of this type of communication under the right of non-disclosure.[100]

Members of parliament are protected against interception in **Germany** and in **France**. The **German** law of criminal procedure provides unconditional protection for communications of the members of the federal parliament, state parliament, or the European Parliament.[101] French legislation prohibits both the interception of electronic communications by parliamentarians and the use of remote forensic software on their office premises, in their vehicles, and in their homes.[102] Furthermore, in the **United Kingdom**, although such interception is not explicitly prohibited, the Code of Practice "Interception of Communications" requires greater consideration to be given to granting interception when the Member of Parliament is involved.[103]

In addition to the most common protection of professional privileges listed above, national legislation can cover **other types of professional secrecy**. In **Germany**, the Code of Criminal Procedure provides conditional protection against interception for information entrusted to or having become known to individuals acting in their capacity as patent attorneys, certified public accountants, sworn auditors, tax consultants, psychotherapists, pharmacists, midwives, members of a pregnancy counselling agency, or drug dependency counsellors in a counselling

---

[96] Spanish country report, Chapters III.B.3.a) and Chapter II.A.4.b) referring to Article 417 LECRIM and Article 20.1 of SC.

[97] *Home Office*, Interception of Communications Code of Practice, January 2016, Chapter 3.2.

[98] German country report, Chapter III.B.3.a) referring to Section 160a Subsection 2 and Section 53 of the German StPO.

[99] French country report, Chapter III.B.3.

[100] Article 126aa in conjunction with Articles 218 and 272 of the Dutch Criminal Code.

[101] German country report, Chapter III.B.3.a) referring to Section 160a Subsection 1 Section 1 in connection with Section 53 German StPO.

[102] French country, report Chapter III.B.3 referring to Article 100-7 of the French Penal Procedure Code.

[103] *Home Office*, Interception of Communications Code of Practice, January 2016, Chapter 3.2.

agency as well as their assistants and trainees.[104] In **France**, legislation protects judges and prosecutors from both interception and data capture by means of remote forensic software.[105]

– *Exemption: no protection for professional secrecy in a case of suspicion*

The protection of professional secrecy in a criminal investigation does not provide absolute immunity against the interception of communications. Five national reports – **Germany, Belgium,** the **Czech Republic, Spain** and the **United Kingdom** – indicated that explicit exemption for such protection is provided in criminal procedure legislation if the person who is the subject of privilege is involved in criminal aid or criminal commission. Furthermore, in **France**, **Sweden**, and **the Netherlands**, even if the rule on exemption in the case of suspicion is not directly provided for in the law of criminal procedure, the interception of privileged communications is also possible under certain circumstances (in law and in practice).

In **Germany**, Section 160a Subsection 4 StPO, stipulates that "when factual indications give rise to the suspicion that the protected person is involved with the offence being investigated, or participated in giving aid to the offender after the crime, in obstructing justice or in dealing with stolen goods," no protection, whether conditional or unconditional, should be given to this type of professional communication.[106] When the suspicion of criminal aid, obstruction of justice, and dealing with stolen goods is not enough to authorise the interception of communications, privileged communications between the accused and the defendant are the only exception in German law.[107] **Belgian** legislation provides for the possibility to authorise the interception of communications falling under professional privilege protection in cases in which the persons who are the subject of such protection are suspected of committing or participating in the criminal offence allowing for the application of the interception of communications.[108] In the **Czech Republic**, an exemption from the special protection of communications between lawyer and defendant is possible if the interception is requested for a criminal act, which is "committed by the defence counsel in cooperation with the accused."[109] A similar provision exists in **Spain**, where the client-lawyer privilege does not apply if the

---

104 German country report, Chapter III.B.3.a) referring to Section 160a Subsection 3 in connection with Section 53a StPO.

105 French country report, Chapter III.B.3. referring to Article 100-7 of the French Penal Procedure Code.

106 German country report, Chapter III.B.3.a).

107 *Ibid.*

108 Belgian country report, Chapter III.B.3.a) referring to the Article 90*octies* §1 and §2, 1° of the Criminal Procedure Code.

109 Czech country report, Chapter III.B.3.

counsel is involved in the offence with the suspect or defendant.[110] Comparably, in the **United Kingdom**, the safeguards related to legal privilege do not apply if there are grounds to believe that the professional legal advisor has the intent of furthering a criminal purpose.[111]

The **Swedish** and **French** reports did not indicate that an exemption such as a case of suspicion is explicitly stipulated in the national law; however, in both countries, the interception of communications that are privileged is possible in criminal investigations. **Swedish** law provides for special circumstances in which people who enjoy professional secrecy protection can nevertheless be called upon as a witness, thus establishing exceptions from the general safeguards for privileged communications.[112] In **France**, the rules that prohibit the recording of privileged communications provide that interception is possible if the respective professional associations are informed.[113] In the **Netherlands**, exceptions from absolute protection are outlined in the Explanatory Memorandum to the Special Investigatory Powers Act, which refers to legal practice and states that, in cases in which the privileged professional is a suspect, the opinion of an authoritative member of the relevant professional group (e.g., the president of the local bar association) is requested as to which conversations or parts thereof contain such incriminating statements.[114]

– *Protection of the core area of privacy*

In addition to the protection of professional communications, there is a distinct model of protection for the "core area of privacy" against the interception of communications in **Germany**. Among the national legislations analysed in this study, it is only only German law that has established this type of special safeguard, provided for by Section 100a Subsection 4 StPO, against the interception of communications concerning the core area of privacy. The notion of the "core area of privacy," according to the German country report, refers to such types of information transfer as, for example, the expression of "innermost feelings or expressions of sexuality." Unless there are serious indications that the information will reveal a direct link to the criminal act, special protection is given to the communications of a person where a particular relationship of trust in connection with the "core area" is concerned. As explained in the German country report, this type of communication

110 Spanish country report, Chapter III.B.3.a) referring to Article 118. 4. LECRIM.

111 Information obtained during the UK law enforcement workshop.

112 Swedish country report, Chapter III.B.2 referring to Article 27:22 of CJP.

113 French country report, Chapter III.B.3. referring to Article 100-7 of the French Penal Procedure Code.

114 Kamerstukken II [Parliamentary Documents Second Chamber] 1996/97, 25 403, no. 3, p. 83 – the Explanatory Memorandum to the Special Investigatory Powers Act, referring to Art. 126aa Criminal Procedure Code.

encompasses such conversations as those with "close family members, priests, telephone pastors, criminal defence attorneys, or – in individual cases – doctors." In accordance with Section 100a Subsection 4 StPO, the consequence of this special protection is the unconditional inadmissibility as evidence of communications related exclusively to the core area of privacy and the prohibition on interception of communications once it is revealed that the information exchange concerns the type of trust and intimacy that is the subject of this special protection. Any data related to the core area of privacy acquired during the course of interception must be immediately destroyed and cannot be used even as a mere clue in the criminal investigation.[115]

b) Privileged communications: practical implications and responsibilities for ensuring protection

While the analysis of legislation shows that at least certain types of professions (e.g., lawyers) enjoy special privileges against interception in almost every country, the way to ensure this protection in practice, both technically and procedurally, might vary from one jurisdiction to another even more than the law in books. This comparative analysis has identified several ways of dealing with interception in the national jurisdictions. The first two possible approaches are based on the deletion or blocking of the privileged content, while the third approach, in contrast, includes no obligation to make the content technical inavailable but implies that privileged communications, when intercepted, cannot be used in criminal proceedings.

The first approach identified *is interruption of interception; deletion of records and filtering*. It can be found in **Germany**, **Sweden**, the **Czech Republic**, and the **Netherlands**. The second way of dealing with privileged communications – *blocking the content but keeping the records* – exists in **Belgium**. The third approach, which does not require deletion of the intercepted content, but *prohibits using it in criminal proceedings*, has been adopted in **France** and **Spain** (and, to some extent, in the **United Kingdom** where the content is generally not used in the court proceedings). Further comparison will yield a detailed analysis of these approaches.

– Interruption of interception, deletion of records, and filtering

The first way of dealing with privileged communications in practice (identified in this study) is when interception of the privileged information must be discontinued, if done in realtime, and the records have to be deleted if any data has been acquired. This model is implemented in **Germany**, the **Czech Republic**, and **Sweden**. Furthermore, the **Netherlands** are also following this approach but with an

---

[115] German country report, Chapter III.B.3.a).

additional very distinct option to use special technology to filter the content of communications of persons enjoying the lawyer-client privilege.

In **Germany**, the corresponding legislation requires a public prosecutor to already consider the protection of privileged communications and the core area of privacy at the stage of application for judicial authorisation to intercept. Furthermore, the court must examine this issue when granting permission to intercept. If protected communication is nonetheless acquired, e.g., when the interception is carried out by means of automated recording without listening in realtime, the wiretapping must be stopped immediately and records destroyed. This obligation has to be performed by an investigator in charge execution of the measure, with the possibility of consulting the public prosecutor, but only if this does not entail unnecessary delays concerning the requirement to destroy information. In any other cases, the decision on what can be used in criminal proceedings is the responsibility of the public prosecutor.[116]

Similar to Germany, in **Sweden**, the person who leads the criminal investigation is responsible for handling communications protected by the rules of legal privilege. Special safeguards are implemented to ensure that this power is not misused: if the decision on the protection of professional secrecy is unjustified, it might entail charges of the abuse of office.[117] When a person whose communication is intercepted is entitled to privilege, the law requires interrupting the ongoing interception immediately and destroying without delay all data obtained. The national reporter especially highlights the fact that Internet providers are not part of the process of assessment or blocking of privileged communications, since their duty is only to capture and transfer data in the process of interception without any power to determine what can be intercepted and handed over to law enforcement agencies.[118] Furthermore, since the interception of real-time monitoring is not possible in some cases of digital communication, the court is responsible for the final assessment of all data, which have not been deleted as irrelevant or privileged in conjunction with the issue of special protection.[119]

Another country requiring deletion of records of privileged communications is the **Czech Republic**. If such communication is captured during the performance of the interception, the police authority is required to delete the records without delay. Furthermore, the law prohibits using such information in the investigation. The destruction of such records shall be logged.[120]

---

[116] German country report, Chapter III.B.3.b).

[117] Swedish country report, Chapter III.B.2.

[118] *Ibid.*

[119] *Ibid.*

[120] Czech country report, Chapter III.B.3 referring to Section 88 (1) of the Czech Code of Criminal Procedure.

A very interesting and distinct approach to interruption of interception and deletion of all records related to privileged communications can be found in the **Netherlands**. The Dutch model of dealing with the protection of professional secrecy in practice represents a hybrid model of deletion of records and filtering and deserves additional attention. As a general rule in The Netherlands, if the conversation of the persons enjoying special privilege is recorded, it has to be deleted. However, this rule has different technical implications, depending on profession. A specific technical solution is implemented for the communications of lawyers.[121] The special system, which holds all telephone and fax numbers used by lawyers in a filter registered with the National Interception Unit, was implemented in 2011. When the interception of communications starts, the traffic data are routed to this filter and, if the system recognises the number as belonging to a lawyer, the data capture ends automatically. If any delay in transfer happens, any information already recorded is deleted. All lawyers in The Netherlands are obliged to register their telephone numbers in this system. However, this filtering rule is applicable, first of all, only to lawyers and, secondly, only to the content of voice (telephone) communications. Conversations of other professions pledged to confidentiality are not the subject of this automatic filtering.[122] Automatic filtering is not performed for IP communications (IP traffic). There are ongoing discussions in The Netherlands on how to ensure the destruction of IP traffic because, although data can be deleted or overwritten, it is still technically possible to find them. All professional communications, such as those of medical professionals and clergymen, which are not automatically filtered, have to be deleted as soon as it is discovered that the communications fall under the non-disclosure rule.

– *Blocking content without deletion*

A second approach towards dealing with the interception of privileged communications among the countries included in this study – making the acquired content unavailable but keeping the records – has only been adopted in **Belgium** due to very specific concerns about the integrity of the evidence. As was revealed at a workshop with Belgian law enforcement agency representatives, the investigators who analyse the intercepted content must issue a notification that a particular communication falls under this privilege and request hiding it such that no one besides the National Tech Support Unit and court can access the communications without credentials, such as password. The content is not deleted, but it is technically hidden and protected after analysis of the intercepted material. Investigators in Belgium always have to go through all the acquired content before issuing a no-

121 For more details, see: *Odinot et al.*, Summary – The use of telephone and Internet taps in criminal investigations, 2012, p. 273 f., available at: https://english.wodc.nl/onderzoeksdatabase/effectiviteit-van-tappen.aspx?cp=45&cs=6798 [last accessed 10/2016].

122 *Ibid.*

tification about protected communications, because criminals can use tricks, e.g., pretending that they are communicating with a lawyer. As a measure of privacy protection, the judge issues an order to appoint a police officer responsible for the selection of the conversations. The right to privacy guarantees that, if the conversation is not related to the investigation or concerns private life (e.g., sexual activities), the officer is allowed to listen to it but has to mark the conversation as irrelevant. This conversation can be further "unpacked" during the proceedings if there is any controversy about its content with regard to what was selected. Previously, there was no possibility to remove irrelevant conversations; however, after Belgium decided to separate the information related to the investigation from other information, the police have to write down what is removed so there is always a possibility to check. No content needs to be deleted and filtered, since the defence lawyers can question the integrity of the records. Furthermore, the Belgian country report noted that judicial practice reinforces the necessity of retaining the records even if the interception is nullified: in a judgment of 18 February 2003, the Supreme Court of Belgium decided that the right to defence justifies access by the defence to the documents resulting from investigation measures that have been declared nullified.[123] Thus, all the records are retained in a special registry allowing for access under certain conditions.

– *No obligation to delete, but the information cannot be used*

In some jurisdictions, the content is neither deleted nor blocked as in **France** or **Spain.** In **France**, however, such content cannot be used in court proceedings because it is considered irrelevant, In **Spain**, the protection of privileged communications is a duty of the court and not of the police performing the interception; thus, the content is neither deleted nor blocked before it goes to court. Furthermore, the **United Kingdom** usually does not use the content in court, so there are no measures by which to interrupt interception of privileged communications or destroy or block the records. This approach seems to have one common component though: information is collected, but it is not used in the court proceedings, the three aforementioned jurisdictions follow this approach in different ways and based on distinctive legal grounds.

In **France**, when the interception of privileged communications is taken into consideration in a criminal investigation, the law requires an application for consent from the respective professional associations before the measure can be authorised. This responsibility is the duty of a judge who grants permission to perform the interception.[124] In general, the police can use only communications related to the purpose of the investigation. As stated by law enforcement agency represent-

---

[123] Belgian country report, Chapter III.B.3.b) referring to Supreme Court, 18 February 2003, P.02.0913.N.

[124] French country report, Chapter III.B.3.

atives at the workshop in France, privileged information is considered irrelevant to the investigation.

In **Spain**, special limitations on the interception of communications between a suspect and a defence lawyer provide that such content will not be used in court, despite having been acquired in practice during the course of an interception.[125] Both the Spanish national report and the law enforcement workshop in Spain revealed that the law there provides no model for dealing with such situations: the police have to record all data during an interception because they technically and legally do not have the capacity to remove this privileged communication. Therefore, all communication content is recorded and the police have to make transcripts, which also include privileged communications. Nothing can be removed from the transcript because the police cannot manipulate the evidence. It is the duty of a judge to ensure special protection of privileged communications.[126] The judge has to decide what has to be removed if the intercepted material contains privileged communications when he/she receives the transcript; thus, investigators are not responsible for handling the issue of professional secrecy. Privileged communications, however, cannot be presented as evidence in court. The new regulation on the interception of communications, adopted in 2015, has not essentially changed this approach and has not outlined any new procedures in the handling of privileged communications, leaving it to the judge to order parts of the conversation containing professional secrecy removed.[127]

In the **United Kingdom**, the intercepted material cannot be used in court; thus, safeguards concerning the deletion of data falling under legal privilege are not as relevant as in those countries where interception can be used as evidence in criminal proceedings. The general rule provided for in Section 15(3) RIPA stipulates that the intercepted information must be destroyed as soon as its retention is no longer necessary. Nevertheless, some safeguards and checks have been implemented to ensure adequate legal protection of privileged information before and after communication is intercepted. According to Chapter 3 of the Code of Practice "Interception of Communications," communications that are subject to legal privilege or contain confidential information require additional safeguards, and any application for a warrant likely to result in the interception of such material should include an assessment of how likely it is that communications subject to legal privilege will be intercepted. The Secretary of State can impose additional safeguards, e.g., special assessment, reporting, and notification duties.[128] If the investigation involves a

---

125 Spanish country report, Chapter III.B.3.a).

126 *Ibid.*

127 Spanish country report, Chapter III.B.3.a) and information obtained at law enforcement workshop.

128 *Home Office*, Interception of Communications Code of Practice, January 2016, Chapter 3.6.

lawyer as the subject of an interception, the Interception of Communications Commissioner must be notified and any material that has been retained be made available to the Commissioner on request. In addition to the general safeguards provided for in Section 15 of RIPA, caseworkers that examine the intercepted material should be warned about any material that might be subject to a legal privilege.[129]

4. Execution of telecommunications interception

a) Interception via communications providers and interception with the use of LEA-own equipment

In all of the countries included in this study, the standard mode of interception is to order telecommunications service providers to extract data and surrender it to the law enforcement agencies. However, despite the existence of a general regime to carry out interception ***by means of orders submitted to the telecommunications providers***, **German**, **Belgian**, **UK**, **Spanish**, and **Swedish** reports indicated that law enforcement agencies are allowed to ***use their own equipment*** to perform the interception.

The **German** report states that "according to prevailing opinion, the law enforcement authorities are permitted to perform the interception by their own means,[130] for instance by gaining access to a wireless network."[131] Similarly, the **Belgian** national reporter points out that the main interception provision in Article 90*ter,* 1° & 2° of CCP does not impose any direct requirement on law enforcement agencies to cooperate with third parties while performing the interception, thus allowing for the use of their own technical tools if necessary.[132] The **Swedish** national report, while highlighting that law enforcement agencies can use their own equipment without relying on service providers to execute the interception, additionally addresses the question of direct access of law enforcement agencies to cables or other parts of telecommunications infrastructure. Access to the signal bearers, such as fibre optic cables, without participation of the communications providers is permitted in Sweden only in the case of signals intelligence collection and cannot be used in criminal investigations.[133]

Two countries indicated that the police's use of their own tools are to be provided for in the interception warrant. In the **United Kingdom** and in **Spain**, the use of special equipment, though permitted, has to be indicated in the interception author-

---

129 *Ibid*, Chapters 3.7-3.8.

130 German country report, Chapter III.B.4.a).

131 *Ibid.*

132 Belgian country report, Chapter III.B.4.a).

133 Swedish country report, Chapter III.B.3.

isation. The United Kingdom's country reporter states that the agencies responsible for the interception can potentially use their own equipment.[134] In **Spain**, lawful interception can be carried out only under the conditions provided for in the court order; the use of any equipment that is not part of the centralised system has to be authorised by the court and explained to the judge who granted authorisation.[135]

b) Accompanying investigative powers

In addition to the interception of communications, the national law can allow for the use of different accompanying investigative powers, such as clandestine access to houses in order to install equipment, hacking techniques, the use of key loggers, etc. One of the major current issues and, at the same time, a source of divergence, is the problem of the use of remote forensic software.

The use of remote forensic software will be discussed in detail in a special chapter on this topic (Chapter III.D.1). Suffice it to briefly mention here that such use is explicitly permitted only in the legislations of two countries: **France** and **Spain**. All other national reports noted the lack of powers concerning such an investigative measure in their respective laws on criminal procedure. The approaches to this issue in the absence of explicitly provided for powers vary from country to country. In the **Czech Republic** and the **United Kingdom**, the use of remote forensic software might be legally permissible. In the United Kingdom, however, it requires additional authorisation; the Czech Republic has no experience in the application of general provisions on the use of such software. In the law of criminal procedure in **Germany**, legal grounds are lacking, at least concerning intrusion into a computer system for clandestine access to stored data that is not part of a communication process. In **Belgium**, the **Netherlands**, and **Sweden**, the law requires physical installation of the remote forensic software. Further analysis as to details and justification for the use of remote forensic software can further be found in this study in Chapter III.D.1.

5. Duties of telecommunications service providers to cooperate

With the development of information and communication networks, which today include various applications and services, the duty of communications providers to cooperate in the interception of communications poses serious challenges for criminal investigations. The duty of cooperation for the purpose of interception of communications is twofold and applies, first, to the communication providers who are subject to telecommucations regulation, and, secondly, to the unregulated entities providing other services related to data transmission. The first type of relation-

---

134 UK country report, Chapter I.A.3.

135 Information obtained during the law enforcement workshop.

ship between law enforcement and communication providers is fairly straightforward as far as the duty to cooperate is concerned. The communications service providers that fall under the scope of telecommunication or electronic communications regulation are commonly subjected to such a duty. They are normally obliged to make communications transmitted through their networks available for interception and provide intercepted data to law enforcement agencies in a readable format.

Nowadays, however, it is not only communications providers falling under the scope of regulation of electronic communications who can transmit information that might be of importance for criminal investigations and needs to be intercepted. The traditional scope of the obligation of interceptability for networks and services does not cover all existing communication and service providers in a sufficient manner. With the development of Voice over IP communications, different messengers and chat applications that can be either integrated into social networks and other services or exist as mobile phone applications, the possibilities for communications transmissions are countless. In many cases, the scope of the "traditional" specific provisions on the duty of communications providers to cooperate cannot adequately cover the new applications and services, not only because many providers are outside the scope of specific duties but also simply because they are not physically present on a country's territory and thus cannot be forced to cooperate even under more general provisions on assistance in criminal investigations.

In most of the countries, the duty to cooperate is provided for either in the rules of criminal procedure, in a special communications regulation, or both. However, when it comes to providers who are not physically present on the national territory or do not fall under the communications regulation, the national law does not fully cover the problem. While some of the countries allow for a broader interpretation of the provisions on the duty to cooperate, others limit them to only regulated entities, such as telecommunication providers or Internet service providers. The following analysis covers three aspects of this issue: first, it examines specific legislation related to cooperation between communication service providers and law enforcement agencies; secondly, it considers the scope of the provisions with regard to the entities falling under the duty to cooperate; and, thirdly, it discusses the problems of limitation of current legislation.

– *Specific legislation on the duty to cooperate*

There are several ways to implement the duty of service providers to cooperate on interception in criminal investigations in the national legislation. It can be provided for either in rules of criminal procedure or in a special communications regulation, or both.

Germany, the **Czech Republic**, and **France** address the issue of providing assistance for the purpose of interception by outlining the general duty to cooperate in a criminal investigation in the law of criminal procedure *and* by using the special telecommunications legislation to provide further details. In **Germany**, Sec. 100b(3) StPO obliges anyone providing, or contributing to the provision of, telecommunication services on a commercial basis to assist the public prosecutor's office in implementing any measures required for the interception/recording of the communication and to supply all necessary information without delay.[136] The measures referred to in the above-mentioned provision are further detailed in the Telecommunications Act (TKG), the Telecommunications Interception Ordinance (TKÜV), and the associated technical guidelines (TR TKÜV). In the **Czech Republic**, the duty to cooperate falls under a general provision – Section 8 of the Code of Criminal Procedure –, which obliges any natural or legal person to comply with requests from law enforcement agencies.[137] Furthermore, the Czech Act on Electronic Communications requires any entities involved in the provision of a public communication network or a publicly available electronic communication service to make their networks interceptable and to provide assistance in the execution of the interception. **French** legislation follows the same approach, providing for a general duty of every citizen to comply with lawful requests from law enforcement entities and courts,[138] detailing specific rules in the French Post and Communications Code.[139]

Two of the countries included in this study – the **Netherlands** and **Sweden** – detail the duty to cooperate in specific legislation. In the **Netherlands**, this duty is stipulated in Article 13.2 of the Telecommunications Act, which requires providers of public telecommunication networks to deliver assistance to law enforcement in the execution of measures provided for in the Dutch Code of Criminal Procedure for the interception of communications, if the interception is executed via their communication networks or concerns communications handled by them.[140] The same approach is taken by **Sweden**, where the Electronic Communications Act and special ordinances stipulate the duty of any regulated providers of electronic communication services to cooperate with law enforcement agencies for the purpose of the interception of communications.[141]

The legislation in **Belgium**, **Spain** and the **United Kingdom** provides for the duty to cooperate in the interception-related provisions of the law of criminal procedure. In **Belgium**, provisions of Article 90*quater* §§2, 4 of the Criminal Procedure Code require natural and legal persons to cooperate in the interception of communications. **Spanish** procedural law also features a broad scope for the duty to coop-

[136] German country report, Chapter III.B.5.a).

[137] Czech country report. Chapter III.B.5.a).

[138] French country report, Chapter III.B.5. referring to Article 10 of the French Civil Code.

[139] French country report, Chapter III.B.5.

[140] *Vodafone*, Law Enforcement Disclosure Report, Legal Annexe, June 2014.

[141] Swedish country report, Chapter III.B.4.

erate in the performance of interception: Article 588*ter* of LECRIM obliges any telecommunication service provider and any persons playing a role in facilitating communications to comply with cooperation orders from a judge, public prosecutor, and the police during the course of the execution of communications interception.[142] In the **United Kingdom**, the duty to cooperate is provided for in Section 11(4) of RIPA.

– *The subjects of the duty to cooperate*

The scope of legal rules that oblige communication providers to cooperate with law enforcement agencies for the purpose of interception of communications is one of the most prevailing and controversial issues, as was pointed out during several workshops with law enforcement agencies during the data collection phase of this study. All of the countries included in this study have legislation requiring "traditional" communications providers to make communications transmitted through their networks interceptable. However, with the development of different applications and services, the interception of many types of communications passing through various devices and networks is difficult, if not impossible, because most of the national laws have their limitations with regard to which entities are regulated or can be forced to cooperate.

Some of the countries, like the **Czech Republic**, **France**, the **Netherlands**, and **Sweden** instead ***limit the duty to cooperate in interception*** to only the entities that are the subject of telecommunication regulation. In the **Czech Republic**, only providers of a network infrastructure or an electronic communications service, which have a license issued by the Czech Telecommunications Office, fall under this obligation. Providers of information society services, e.g., cloud providers, social networks, e-mail service providers, portals, and search engines, are not obliged to cooperate for the purpose of communications interception.[143] In **France**, as is highlighted in the national report, and according to interpretation of the provisions of the French Post and Communications Code, the entities that are subject of the obligation to cooperate are electronic communications operators and Internet access providers.[144] In **the Netherlands**, the literal interpretation of Article 13.2 of the Telecommunications Act shows that only public telecommunications network

---

142 Spanish country report, Chapter III.B.5.a).

143 Czech country report, Chapter III.B.5.a).

144 As the French country report (Chapter III.B.5) points out, the electronic communications operators are defined in Article L.32, 15° of the Post and Electronic Communications Code as "*natural or legal persons who exploit an electronic communications network opened to the public or who provide the public with an electronic communications service*" (the notion of "provision" being understood here as the transmission of electronic communications on a network). Internet access providers are defined in Article 6, I, 1 of Law 2004-575 of 21 June 2004 as "*persons whose activity is to provide an access to online public communication services*".

providers can be the subject of the duty to cooperate.[145] Similarly, in **Sweden**, Section 6:19 of the Electronic Communications Act refers only to "telecommunication services" when it establishes the duty to provide data in an accessible form.[146] Swedish law enforcement representatives during the workshop confirmed that only those services provided by regulated telecommunication companies are considered "communication services."

Other countries, like **Germany**, **Belgium**, and **Spain** ***interpret the provisions on the duty to cooperate in a broader way***. In **Germany**, the TKG provides that the term telecommunications services comprises those addresses consisting wholly or mainly of the conveyance of signals through the telecommunications networks.[147] As explained in the German country report, this definition includes mainly access providers and network providers providing services to the public;[148] however, a broader interpretation basically allows for the inclusion of e-mail services, as long the focus of the service is the transmission of data. In addition, access providers who do not provide an identifier for monitoring purposes but are involved in the transmission of communications may also possibly be subjected to this duty.

In **Belgium**, the scope of the duty to cooperate is quite broad and, according to the national reporter, includes "infrastructure providers working on the IP-transport level (operators of a telecommunications network), Internet Access Providers (IAP's) and Internet Service Providers (ISPs), such as social media providers and cloud computing service providers."[149] Belgian judicial practice also reveals that the duty to cooperate might be interpreted much more broadly for regulated communications providers: for example, the Belgian Supreme Court, in its decision of 18 January 2011, used a broad interpretation of the term "electronic communications provider" for the purpose of Article 46*bis* of the Belgian Code of Criminal Procedure, covering e-mail providers.[150] **Spanish** procedural law also features a broad scope for the duty to cooperate in the performance of the interception: Article 588*ter* of LECRIM obliges any telecommunications service provider and any persons playing a role in facilitating communications to comply with cooperation orders from a judge, public prosecutor, and police during the course of the execution of communications interception.[151]

---

145 *Vodafone*, Law Enforcement Disclosure Report, Legal Annexe, June 2014.

146 Swedish country report, Chapter III.B.4.

147 *Vodafone*, Law Enforcement Disclosure Report, Legal Annexe, June 2014.

148 Other than regulations in the TKG, Section 100b(3) StPO also generally covers not only public telecommunication systems but also closed communication networks, such as corporate networks. See: German country report, Chapter III.B.5.a).

149 Belgian country report, Chapter III.B.5.a).

150 *Ibid.*

151 Spanish country report, Chapter III.B.5.a).

– *Current debates*

Even if national legislation on the duty to cooperate allows, e.g., in Belgium, for a broader interpretation of the term "communications provider" or is general enough to oblige any entity to comply with the interception request, the enforceability of such provisions is not always straighforward if the provider of a particular service is outside of the reach of law enforcement agencies due to jurisdictional issues. As shared by the representatives of national law enforcement agencies during the workshop phase of this study, it is difficult, if not impossible, to intercept communications when they are transmitted via messengers or a few VoIP services, if the service providers use encryption and are not physically present in the particular jurisdiction.

There are different suggestions on how to solve these problems, but all of them raise more questions than provide answers. For example, calls to extend the telecommunication regulation to cover the providers of messenger or Voice-over-IP services might raise the issue of the actual incompatibility of such services with the traditional notion of communications providers and could require reconsideration of the entire concept of the communication infrastructure, networks, and services. A simple extension of the general duty to cooperate in interception matters to these services also would not solve the problem as long as the issue of enforceability of such provisions in the foreign jurisdiction is not addressed. It is outside the scope of this study to analyse different possible solutions to the problem of the duty of providers to cooperate in the interception of communications. With continued development, however, of information technologies, services, and applications, these issues will require attention. Future solutions might require not only national legal reforms but also better international cooperation and coordination.

6. Formal prerequisites of interception orders

a) *Competent authorities*

In all the countries included in this study, except the **United Kingdom**, an interception is normally authorised by the court upon the request of either a police officer or – in most of the countries – a prosecutor. However, some exceptions from the rule of prior court authorisation are possible, among them, as will be analysed further, application for interception in urgent circumstances. The formal prerequisites for granting interception authorisation, however, may vary for both obtaining the warrant under normal circumstances and authorising the interception in urgent situations as regards who the competent authority is and how to apply for permission to intercept. In **Germany**, the **Czech Republic**, the **Netherlands**, **Spain**, and **Sweden** interception is authorised by the court upon application of either the prosecutor or the police; in **Belgium** and **France**, the investigating judge can authorise interception in his or her own investigation. Furthermore, in the **United Kingdom**, there is no requirement for judicial authorisation of interception of communications. Under urgent circumstances, further divergences can be found with regard to how the interception is authorised in cases of emergency. The differences at the national level are outlined in the following analysis: firstly, part (aa) will consider authorisation in normal situations and, secondly, part (bb) will follow with an analysis of applications for urgent warrants.

aa) Authorization in normal situations

– Authorisation upon prosecutor's or police officer's application

Three countries – **Germany**, the **Czech Republic**, and **Sweden** – have a model of authorisation, in which the public prosecutor applies for the judicial authorisation.[152] The **Czech** and **Swedish** reports indicated that a prosecutor closely collaborates with the police to file such an application.[153] In the **Netherlands**, while court approval is required, the role of the prosecutor is different. Judicial permission is granted to a prosecutor to authorise the interception, so it is the prosecutor who authorises the measure and the court confirms it. In **Spain**, while judicial authorisation is necessary, both police and prosecutor are competent to submit an application for judicial authorisation on their own. As stated in the Spanish country report, a judge can also apply for the interception *ex officio*.[154]

– Mixed model of court authorisation

Belgium and **France** have a mixed model of issuing authorisation for the interception of communications due to the existence of the institution of the investigating judge. In **Belgium**, authorisation is an issue for consideration by the investigating judge,[155] but the process of authorisation depends on the body actually investigating the offence. The first possibility for the authorisation occurs when the police requests that a prosecutor apply for the interception, which is granted by the judge. However, as was revealed during the law enforcement workshop in Belgium, the existence of the institution of an investigating judge provides for the second option, when the judge who takes over the investigation of the criminal case can authorise interception for the purpose of investigation in his own capacity. Cases in which a public prosecutor is not involved in the process of authorisation

---

152 German country report, Chapter III.B.6.a) referring to Sec. 100a StPO; Czech country report, Chapter III.B.6.a), Swedish country report, Chapter III.B.5.

153 Czech country report Chapter III.B.6.a); Swedish country report, Chapter III.B.5.

154 Information from Spanish country report, Chapter III.B.6.a) and from Spanish law enforcement workshop.

155 Belgian country report, Chapter III.B.6.a) referring to Article 90*ter* §1 of the Belgian Code of Criminal Procedure.

also include situations in which another identifier (e.g., a second telephone number) is discovered during the same investigation. Under the Belgian system, when a public prosecutor considers cases that need interception and transfers the file to the investigating judge, together with a request to investigate, the judge has to examine the case within this requisition. Thus, the power of the judge is limited to the crimes ordered for investigation in the requisition, and there is no possibility to go outside the borders of investigation of a particular case. Yet, since the duty of an investigating judge is to find the truth via all possible means, he/she can therefore order the interception without the police and prosecutor being involved in the authorisation process if this investigative measure falls within the framework of the requisition. Consequently, in some cases, there is no application for interception but only an order issued by a judge.

A similar model for interception authorisation exists in **France**. As a general rule, in accordance with Article 74-2 of the French Penal Procedure Code, the warrant for the interception is issued upon application by the prosecutor to a liberty and custody judge. Like **Belgium**, an investigating judge can authorise interception himself or herself without the prosecutor's request when the needs of a particular criminal investigation require it or "for the investigation of felonies and misdemeanours where the penalty incurred is equal to or in excess of two years imprisonment,[156] or in case a person has disappeared."[157] This mixed model is applicable only to the interception of correspondence. In order to authorise any other investigative measure that includes the acquisition of communication during transmission, such as remote data capture, an investigating judge must ask for the prosecutor's opinion.[158]

– *No court authorisation needed*

The **United Kingdom** is the only country among those included in this study where the warrant to intercept does not have to be approved by a court. Under normal circumstances, the relevant Secretary of State grants the authorisation to intercept but, in urgent cases, a senior official can perform this task.[159] An application for an interception warrant must be made by or on behalf of the directors or chiefs of the institutions outlines in Section 6(2) of RIPA.

156 Article 100 of the Penal Procedure Code, quoted from the French country report, Chapter III.B.6.a).

157 Article 80-4 of the Penal Procedure Code, quoted from the French country report, Chapter III.B.6.a).

158 French country report, Chapter III.B.6.a).

159 Section 7 RIPA.

bb) Interception in urgent circumstances

The cases of emergency in all of the countries included in this study represent an exemption from the normal process of granting authorisation for interception in order to enable law enforcement to start interception as quickly as possible. These exemptions have divergences, however, with regard to how the applications are *addressed* in urgent situations in the law of criminal procedure and/or in practice. There are two possible approaches to the cases of emergency: first of all, as in **Germany**, **Belgium**, the **Netherlands**, **Sweden**, **Spain**, and the **United Kingdom,** the law of criminal procedure outlines a special procedure for such situations. Secondly, when the law does not address this issue, as in **France** and the **Czech Republic**, special procedures have been developed in practice by the police, prosecutors, and courts to solve the problem of urgent authorisation and issuing the court warrant as early as possible. The two approaches are analysed further in this chapter.

– *Urgent warrants with no court authorisation or with subsequent court approval*

The special procedures to start interception in urgent circumstances via an order by the prosecutor, with subsequent court approval, are provided for in the law of criminal procedure of **Germany**, the **Netherlands**, **Sweden**, and **Spain**. In **Belgium**, for a short period of interception in case of emergency, no court approval is required. Furthermore, in the **United Kingdom**, where court authorisation is not needed in general, the legislation still provides for a procedure of issung emergency warrants.

In **Germany** and **Sweden**, the power to decide whether to start emergency interception is given to the prosecutor. The **German** law of criminal procedure stipulates that, when urgency requires the interception of communications for the purpose of criminal investigation, the public prosecutor's office is empowered to issue an interception authorisation, which must further be approved by the court within three working days after the date of issue. If the authorisation is not subsequently judicially approved, it becomes ineffective.[160] The same approach is found in **Swedish** legislation, which was amended in 2014 to address the issue of interception in urgent cases. This amendment granted a prosecutor the power to temporarily authorise interception in emergency circumstances, providing that the reasons for the decision are stated and the issue of authorisation is forwarded to a responsible judge who can confirm or revoke the interception order without delay.[161] As noted in the Swedish report, before the amendment was introduced in 2014, the emergen-

160 German country report, Chapter III.B.8.a) referring to Sec. 100b(1) of the German StPO.

161 Swedish country report, Chapter III.B.5.

cy procedure was foreseen only for certain types of crimes against national security and, therefore, rarely used in practice, e.g., it was ordered only four times from 2009-2012.[162]

In the **Netherlands**, the power of a prosecutor to start interception in cases of emergency is restricted by the rule that court opinion has to be requested via telephone. Thus, a warrant can be granted in a phone call in urgent cases, and a public prosecutor and a judge authorising the interception must communicate on the phone. When the authorisation is obtained, the interception starts on very short notice. According to the information gained during the workshop with Dutch law enforcement agency representatives, obtaining a warrant in urgent cases takes approximately five minutes: after the telephone call, the phone warrant goes through the interception department of the Dutch police and is then passed directly to the provider. The judge has to issue the warrant in writing within three days of granting of the permission. The law provides that urgent authorisation has the same validity period as a warrant issued under normal circumstances – four weeks; in practice, however, the emergency warrants are granted for approximately two weeks.

Further divergences can be found in **Spanish** legislation. The emergency warrant can be granted under very limited circumstances. This urgent procedure for starting interception without judicial authorisation does not involve the prosecutor as a competent authority and gives the power to grant interception to administrative governmental bodies. Emergency procedures can be used only in case of terrorist crime, and it is the Ministry of Interior or the Director of State Security that has the power to issue the warrant. The court must be subsequently informed within 72 hours in order to revoke or confirm the interception.[163] Up to the adoption of new legislation in 2015, the same power was provided for in Section 3 of Article 579 of the Criminal Procedure Act. However, according to the Spanish law enforcement representatives, this possibility had been never used in practice. In emergency cases, the police and the prosecutor can obtain a warrant from the judge on duty within approximately four hours.[164]

Belgian law, while providing for the possibility to intercept without judicial authorisation in cases of emergency, follows a different approach to subsequent judicial authorisation than the national models analysed above: in a number of exceptional cases, the public prosecutor has the same powers to intercept as the investigating judge and can order an interception for 24 hours without court authorisation.[165] Exceptional cases include "the case of flagrante delicto and as long as

---

162 *Ibid.*

163 Spanish country report, Chapter III.B.6.a) referring to Article 588*ter* c. of LECRIM.

164 Information obtained at the law enforcement workshop.

165 Belgian country report, Chapter III.B.6.a) referring to Article 90*ter* §5 of the Belgian code of criminal procedure.

the flagrante delicto situation lasts"[166] when investigation concerns criminal acts listed in Article 347*bis* (offence of taking hostages) or Article 470 (offence of extortion committed through violence or threats) of the Belgian Criminal Code.[167] As was shared by the Belgian law enforcement agency representatives during the workshop, for any other emergency cases not covered by the provisions on urgent warrants, there is always a judge on duty and the procedure follows all the necessary checks and formalities. The police have to contact the prosecutor who, in turn, must request the authorisation of the investigating judge on 24/7 duty. The interception cannot start immediately because the judge must go to his or her office to stamp the written court order. After the order has been signed, however, the Belgian National Tech Support Unit can launch interception within 15 minutes in urgent cases.

In the **United Kingdom**, where court approval for interception is not needed, there are still special procedures for emergency cases. In an urgent situation, a senior official can sign the warrant instead of the respective Secretary of State.[168] However, in this case, the law requires that the files have to be examined and discussed very carefully.

– *No special procedure for urgent warrants*

Another approach is taken by those countries where the possibility to intercept without a court warrant in urgent circumstances is not provided for in their respective laws. These countries, namely the **Czech Republic** and **France**, have developed certain procedures in practice to address the emergency situation and quickly obtain court authorisation in writing.

In the **Czech Republic**, the law in fact provides for a few exceptions whereby the interception can be carried without a warrant for serious crimes. However, the exceptions listed in Section 88 (5) of the Czech Code of Criminal Procedure require the consent of one of the parties of the intercepted communications in cases of urgent interception. These cases concern such criminal acts as human trafficking, certain types of kidnapping, etc.[169] In any other urgent cases, or in a situation in which a party to the communications does not consent to the interception, the process of interception authorisation strictly follows the normal procedure of obtaining a court warrant. However, as Czech law enforcement agency representatives explained during the workshop, there are procedures to allow the authorisation to be obtained quickly: in urgent cases, there are judges and prosecutors on duty who can be reached 24 hours/7 days a week. Police investigators also have the

---

166 Legislation cited from Belgian country report, Chapter III.B.6.a).

167 Belgium country report, Chapter III.B.6.a).

168 Section 7 RIPA.

169 Czech country report, Chapter III.B.7.f).

possibility to submit an urgent application for interception authorisation. Furthermore, there is also always a person on duty in the interception unit to handle interception orders issued at night.

Similarly, the procedure to obtain a court authorisation quickly was adopted in **France**, where the law requires written warrants to be issued in any case, even in urgent matters. As French law enforcement representatives revealed during the workshop, there is a special procedure for emergency cases, when the crime is serious and the investigation calls for immediate action. If an enquiry or a preliminary investigation is needed for one of the offences falling under the scope of Article 706-73 (which contains a list of serious crimes, such as organised crime, drug trafficking, kidnapping, etc.), the prosecutor can request urgent authorisation of the interception of communications.[170] The judge of liberty *(juge des libertés et de la détention)* can grant this authorisation for a maximum period of one month, and the decision of the judge should be issued in written form. In practice, the situation can be resolved on the phone, with the judge sending the decision in writing, which takes approximately 30 minutes. Each court has a judge on duty to handle such cases. Communication providers do not start intercepting without this decision, but the authorisation is usually submitted to telecommunication providers by fax or e-mail to speed up the process in urgent cases.

b) Formal requirements for applications

The law of criminal procedure and other regulations can establish formal requirements that are to be met in applications for the interception warrant, e.g., written form or the necessity for an oral hearing. Such provisions can be found in the law of criminal procedure in **Sweden** and **Spain**. Other countries have no requirements outlined in the law but, e.g., in the case of the **Czech Republic** or the **United Kingdom**, special regulations, such as a code of practice or binding guidelines.

– No formal requirements outlined in the law of criminal procedure

No special requirements for interception applications exist in **Germany**, **France** and in the **Netherlands**. However, in practice in **Germany**, there are still some substantial prerequisites for the submission of such an application: as pointed out in the German country report, a prosecutor cannot submit a request that merely sums up the circumstances of the case, because the court has a duty to assess all the necessary prerequisites for ordering the investigative measure. It is therefore necessary for the public prosecutor to present all the relevant evidence determining the need for the interception, together with the investigative file, if the case is complex.[171] In

170 Article 706-95 of the French Penal Procedure Code.

171 German country report, Chapter III.B.6.b).

France and the **Netherlands**, criminal procedure law not impose any specific requirements. The French national reporter expressly noted that the form of the interception application is neither regulated nor outlined in the law of criminal procedure.[172] The same approach is taken in The Netherlands. The academic report from France and practical workshops in both countries revealed that no specific regulation exists concerning formal requirements for the application.

– *Formal requirements outlined in the law of criminal procedure*

In **Spain** and **Sweden**, some of the formal prerequisites are provided for in the law of criminal procedure. The **Spanish** law outlines a detailed set of requirements regarding application for the authorisation of interception of communications: the applications must contain a description of facts, among them a detailed statement justifying the application of the measure, the form of execution, the necessary duration, and identifiers concerning the person and connection, to name but a few.[173]

In comparison to Spain, the law in **Sweden** outlines different mandatory requirements for the interception requests: firstly, the application must be made in writing and, secondly, any related oral hearings must be documented.[174] The application for interception is not made on oath; however, it is safeguarded from a possible criminal conviction of misuse of office. As stated in the Swedish report, such cases of conviction have taken place in practice: for example, in 2000, a prosecutor faced criminal charges for submitting a negligent application for interception authorisation because the legal requirements for ordering this measure had not been met.[175] A general procedure in Sweden is to consider the request for interception at the court hearing, with both a police investigator and a public prosecutor present in person. As was stated at the workshop with Swedish law enforcement agency representatives, in practice, this hearing is always a discussion in person, despite the fact that there is no legal requirement for a personal meeting. When it is not feasible to travel to the court – for example, if the court is situated in a remote location – the prosecutor and the judge can arrange a videoconference, or the prosecutor and the police can ask colleagues to represent them at the court hearings. It is impossible to just send a request with a report if secret wiretapping is concerned: a personal meeting is always required in practice. In addition, the Swedish system has the institution of public representatives, who must be present at the interception appli-

---

172 French country report, Chapter III.B.6.b).

173 Spanish country report, Chapter III.B.6.b) referring to Article 588*bis* b.2) and Article 588*ter* d. of LECRIM. A detailed list of formal requirements can be found in the Spanish country report in the respective chapter on the formal requirements of the application for interception.

174 Swedish country report, Chapter III.B.5 referring to Article 21 of the Swedish Code of Criminal Procedure.

175 Swedish country report, Chapter III.B.5.

cation hearings. The representative is usually a retired judge or a lawyer representing public interests. This is an additional safeguard: the public representative is a considered to be an ombudsman.

– *Formal requirements outlined in other regulations*

While the laws in the **United Kingdom** and in the **Czech Republic** contain no specific requirements for the application for interception, they are outlined in the different piece of regulation. The **Czech** national report refers to Article 67 of the binding guideline No. 30/2009 Sb. on the tasks in criminal proceedings,[176]which establishes formal prerequisites for a request for interception of communications, providing that it must contain such information as specific facts about the case, a description of the offence, identifiers for the purpose of interception, and other data.[177] In the **United Kingdom**, Chapter 5, Sec. 5.2 of the Code of Practice "Interception of Communications" outlines a set of requirements on the information that an application for a warrant should contain, such as background information on the operation in question, the person or premises to which the application relates, a description of the communications to be intercepted, details of the communication service provider(s), and an assessment of the feasibility of the interception operation (where relevant), etc.

c) *Formal requirements for interception orders*

In addition to demanding the warrant application to be made in a specific form, the law of criminal procedure can establish formal requirements for interception warrants. All the countries included in this study require the authorisation to be made in writing, except authorisation granted in urgent circumstances, e.g., the telephone authorisation in the **Netherlands**.

In addition to the written form, specific formal requirements in most of the countries refer to identification for the interception (either name, or number, or terminal device), e.g., in **Germany**, **Belgium**, the **Czech Republic**, **France**, **Spain**, and the **United Kingdom.**[178] The law in the **Netherlands** requires the inclusion of identifi-

---

[176] Czech country report, Chapter III.B.6.b) referring to binding guideline no. 30/2009 Sb., on the tasks in criminal proceedings.

[177] Czech country report, Chapter III.B.6.b).

[178] See respective country reports referring to Section 100b Subsection 2 StPO (German country report, Chapter III.B.6.c); Article 90*quater* of Belgian Code of Criminal Procedure (Belgian country report, Chapter III.B.6.c); Section 88 Para. 2 of the Czech Code of Criminal Procedure (Czech country report, Chapter III.B.6.c); Articles 100–100-2 of the French Penal Procedure Code (French country report, Chapter III.B.6.b); Para. 3 of Article 588*bis* c of LECRIM (Spanish country report, Chapter III.B.6.c); Sections 8(1) and (2) of RIPA (UK country report, Chapter III.B.6).

ers "if possible" and the address "if known."[179] The obligation to mention the type of and duration of the measure is yet another formal requirement established in all of the countries' procedural law.[180] In most of the countries – **Germany, Belgium,** the **Czech Republic**, the **Netherlands**, and **Spain**[181] – the legislation provides for the requirement that the warrant should justify the reasons for granting interception. In **France**, in addition to such justification, the law requires the issue of proportionality to be specifically addressed in the interception warrant.[182]

7. Substantive prerequisites of interception orders

Since the interception of communications represents one of the most intrusive investigative measures, which conflicts with the individual's right to privacy, most of the national legislations on interception have established sets of checks and safeguards in order to ensure that interception takes place only when necessary and that it is carried out in a proportionate manner. To counterbalance the intrusiveness of interference, national legislation in most of the countries requires an interception to be granted upon a certain degree of suspicion and to be necessary and proportionate. Furthermore, all the countries included in this study limit the possibility of using interception in criminal investigations to certain types of serious crimes. Despite the fact that these safeguards can be found in every national legal order, they might vary from country to country as to checks, balances, and thresholds for authorising interception, thus also having an effect on cross-border cooperation in the interception of communications.

a) Predicate offences

All of the countries included in this study limit the availability of the interception of communications as an investigative measure by making it possible only for certain types of offences. While this restriction exists in every national legal order, the approaches to imposing this limitation vary. There are three possible ways to restrict interception to only specific types of crime: by creating a ***list of offences*** (**Germany** and **Belgium**), by establishing a ***minimum punishment threshold*** for

---

179 Para. 2 Art. 126m of the Dutch Code of Criminal Procedure.

180 See above-mentioned chapters of respective country reports referring to Section 100b Subsection 2 StPO, Article 90*quater* of Belgian Code of Criminal Procedure; Section 88 Para. 2 of the Czech Code of Criminal Procedure; Articles 100–100-2 of the French Penal Procedure Code; Para. 3 of Article 588*bis* c of LECRIM, Sections 8(1) and (2) of RIPA, also see Para. 2 Art. 126m of the Dutch Code of Criminal Procedure.

181 See above-mentioned chapters of respective country reports referring to Section 34 StPO, Article 90*quater* of the Belgian Code of Criminal Procedure; Section 88 Para. 2 of the Czech Code of Criminal Procedure; 1 Para. 2 Art. 126m of the Dutch Code of Criminal Procedure, Para. 3 of Article 588*bis* c of LECRIM.

182 French country report, Chapter III.B.6.b).

crime through the number of years of imprisonment (**France** and the **United Kingdom**), or by a ***combination of both*** (the **Czech Republic,** the **Netherlands, Spain**, and **Sweden**).

– *List of predicate offences*

The list of predicate offences for the purpose of the application of the interception exists in **Germany** and **Belgium**. In **Germany**, the interception of communications can be granted only in the case of investigations related to certain criminal offences from the list provided in Annex I to the German country report. When interception is considered, this formal requirement is balanced with the need for assessment of the seriousness of the offence in each individual case. In this regard, as pointed out in the German country report, the evaluation of seriousness shall take into account not only the sentencing range but also other considerations, such as the significance of the danger to legally protected interests and other circumstances.[183] Similarly, in **Belgium**, Article 90*ter* §2 of the Code of Criminal Procedure provides an exclusive list of criminal acts that allow interception to be authorised as a measure in criminal investigation. The exclusiveness of the list stipulates that interception is not applicable in criminal investigations dealing with any other offences.[184]

– *Minimum penalty requirement*

The second approach is taken in **France** and the **United Kingdom**. However, even while following the model of establishing the minimum penalty requirement, these two countries have different regulations in this regard. In **France**, the law of criminal procedure establishes a minimum penalty threshold for crimes in order to qualify for the application of interception in criminal investigations. According to Art. 100 of the Criminal Procedure Code, the interception of correspondence can be used for the investigation of offences if the penalty incurred is equal to or exceeds two years of imprisonment.[185] In the **United Kingdom**, legislation refers to "serious offences" and not to the penalty threshold; however, the penalty is one of the requirements for the definition of a serious offence. Pursuant to Section 5(3) of RIPA, the authorisation for interception and recording of telecommunication traffic may only be granted if it is necessary in the interest of national security, for the purpose of preventing or detecting serious crime, to safeguard the economic well-being of the United Kingdom, or to comply with an obligation under any international mutual legal assistance agreement. In accordance with s. 81(2) and (3), serious crimes are defined as offences for which a person who has reached the age of

183 German country report, Chapter III.B.7.b).

184 Belgian country report, Chapter III.B.7.b).

185 French country report, Chapter III.B.1.

twenty-one and has no previous convictions could reasonably be expected to be sentenced to imprisonment for a term of three years or more or that involves the use of violence, results in substantial financial gain, or are perpetrated by a large number of persons in pursuit of a common purpose. The interests of national security or the economic well-being of the UK are not defined in the legislation, but it is generally assumed that the latter is also relevant to the interests of national security.[186]

– *Combination of list of offences and minimum penalty requirement*

A combination of approaches to limiting interception to certain types of offences by both establishing the minimum penalty threshold and providing for a list of offences can be found in the national procedural legislation of the **Czech Republic**, the **Netherlands**, and **Sweden**. The Criminal Procedure Code of the Czech Republic[187] provides that the interception can be authorised for crimes with a minimum penalty threshold of at least eight years of imprisonment. Furthermore, the following offences are listed, in addition to those meeting the minimum penalty requirement:

- "machinations in insolvency proceedings,
- violation of regulations on rules of competition,
- negotiating advantages during public procurement, tender and auction,
- machinations during public procurement and tenders,
- machinations at a public auction,
- misuse of powers of an official person, or
- other intentional criminal offence for which prosecution is stipulated in a declared international treaty."[188]

Dutch law follows the same approach. Interception can be granted only for the investigation of offences listed in Article 67 of the Criminal Procedure Code, which includes crimes allowing pre-trial detention. This means that only crimes involving more than four years of imprisonment can be the subject of interception. However, there are certain specifically mentioned offences (Art. 67 Para. 1 b) for which interception could be granted if a crime involves a less than four-year maximum penalty threshold. For example, most forms of cybercrime are included in the category of specifically mentioned offences. Similarly, the **Swedish** law of criminal procedure – Article 27:18 of CJP – establishes a minimum penalty requirement of two or more years of imprisonment in order for interception to be granted for the purpose of preliminary investigation. In addition to offences falling into this category, Para. 2–7 of Section 2 of the same article provides for a list of crimes allow-

[186] *Home Office*, Interception of Communications Code of Practice, January 2016, Chapter 4.4.

[187] Para. 1 of Section 88, reference from Czech country report, Chapter III.B.7.b).

[188] Quoted from Czech country report, Chapter III.B.7.b).

ing for interception to be authorised in criminal investigations, even if the minimum penalty does not meet the general requirement.[189]

In **Spain**, the same approach was adopted very recently. Up to the enactment of the new legislation in December 2015, interception could be used only in cases of serious crime,[190] meaning crime punished with three or more years of imprisonment. However, the new legislation implemented a combination of the minimum penalty requirement and a list of predicate offences. Article 588*ter* a.1 LECRIM establishes that interception can be ordered for an investigation of intentional offences punishable with a term of imprisonment of at least three years and also for offences committed within a group or criminal organisation as well as for terrorist offences. In addition to these crimes, the law provides that interception of communications can be authorised for the investigation of crimes committed through "computers or IT equipment (*instrumentos informáticos*), or other information technology or communication or communication services."[191]

b) Degree of suspicion

In addition to limiting the interception of communications to certain types of crimes and dangers, most of the countries establish further safeguards to ensure that the intrusion is balanced. The legal requirement to take into account the degree of suspicion is one such safeguard, can be found in the legislation of **Germany**, the **Netherlands**, **Sweden**, and, with some modifications, in **Spain**. The **Czech Republic** follows this principle in practice but without an explicit requirement in the law.

The **German** law of criminal procedure establishes the requirement of "an ordinary degree of suspicion of someone having committed or participated in the commission of a serious criminal offence, or in cases where there is criminal liability for attempt, having attempted to commit such an offence or having prepared such an offence by committing a criminal offence."[192] This degree of suspicion, however, is assessed by taking into account the circumstances of the case, which have to provide enough grounds to assume that a person is actually involved in the commission of the crime.[193] In **Belgium**, the requirement exists for the court to assess whether there are serious indications of commission of a crime.[194] Article 126m of

---

189 Swedish country report, Chapter III.B.6.

190 Spanish country report, Chapter III.B.7.b) referring to Arts. 13 and 33 of the Spanish Criminal Code and Art. 579 of the Criminal Procedure Act.

191 *Ibid.*

192 Cited from German country report, Chapter III.B.7.a) referring to Section 100a Subsection 1 No. 1 of the German StPO.

193 German country report, Chapter III.B.7.a).

194 Belgian country report, Chapter III.B.7.a) referring to Article 90*ter* §1 CCP of the Belgian Code of Criminal Procedure.

the **Dutch** Code of Criminal Procedure refers to suspicion of a particular criminal offence for which interception is possible and which must be a serious infringement of the legal order. In **Sweden**, Article 27:20 of CJP requires reasonable suspicion of an offence for the interception authorisation to be granted.[195]

In two countries – **Spain** and the **Czech Republic** – the degree of suspicion, though not explicitly worded as a necessary prerequisite in the interception provisions, is required in court practice. Spanish legislation uses the terminology "sufficient indications of the existence of the criminal offence".[196] The issue of the degree of suspicion has been addressed in Spanish judicial practice in the decisions of the Supreme Court, in particular Decision 18 June 1992, which stated that "mere affirmation" and "existence of certain suspicions" do not provide enough justification for authorisation of the interception.[197] Similarly, in the **Czech Republic**, the law of criminal procedure does not positively indicate the degree of suspicion requirement. However, this issue is addressed in judicial practice, which stipulates that the degree of suspicion has to be assessed by the court granting interception on a case-by-case basis. As pointed out in the Czech country report, the Constitutional Court has passed judgements referring to the duty of the judge to evaluate the degree of suspicion and to provide the relevant information in the interception order.[198]

c) Principle of subsidiarity

The principle of subsidiarity represents yet another safeguard explicitly implemented in the legislation of several countries, namely, **Germany**, **Belgium**, the **Czech Republic**, **Spain**, and the **United Kingdom**, to ensure the balance between the intrusiveness of the measure and its proportionality. The application of this principle requires the judge to consider whether other – less intrusive – means of investigation first be tried unsuccessfully or considered unlikely to be successful.

In **Germany**, the law of criminal procedure stipulates that interception can be authorised only when the use of any other less intrusive tools would be much more difficult or of no avail. The degree of difficulty in this regard especially means the application of more time-consuming investigative tools that might significantly delay the investigation itself.[199] Similarly, the **Spanish** country report states that the principle of subsidiarity is provided for in the law and means that the investigating authority and the judge have to assess whether other less intrusive measures could

---

195 Swedish country report, Chapter III.B.6.

196 Spanish country report, Chapter III.B.7.a).

197 *Ibid.*

198 Czech country report, Chapter III.B.7.a).

199 German country report, Chapter III.B.7.d).

be applied and whether they are likely to be successful.[200] In **Belgium**, the Criminal Procedure Code requires the court to evaluate whether other investigative tools may be sufficient. Interception can be granted only if there are reasonable grounds to believe that other methods will not help to "reveal the truth."[201] In this regard, however, the national reporter notes that the parliamentary preparatory works especially highlight that there is no necessity for the court to apply other investigative measures unsuccessfully: the assessment of the judge that other tools will not succeed is sufficient to address the issue of subsidiarity.[202] In the **United Kingdom**, an application for an interception warrant must justify why another less intrusive method could not achieve the same results expected to be obtained from the interception.[203]

The law of criminal procedure in the **Czech Republic** also refers to the principle of subsidiarity, though in a more general way. According to the national reporter, interception can be authorised only if there are reasonable grounds to believe that it will yield the facts relevant for investigation and that either there is no other way to obtain these facts or they will significantly reduce the possibility of achieving the aim of investigation.[204] This requirement forces the law enforcement agencies and the court to consider the application of less intrusive measures.[205]

However, not all of the countries follow the approach of establishing subsidiarity requirements. For example, the **French** country report clearly states that the legislation does not establish any obligation to consider or try less intrusive methods of investigation.[206] **Swedish** law does not provide for any specific requirement of reasonable belief that the evidence will be acquired in the course of interception or for consideration of less intrusive measures first, although it does require the measure to be of "particular importance to the investigation."[207] However, as noted in Swedish report, in practice, the principle of proportionally means that the application of less intrusive investigative measures is at least a factor to consider before the authorisation of interception.[208]

---

200 Spanish country report, Chapter III.B.7.d).

201 Belgian country report, Chapter III.B.7.d) referring to Article 90*ter* §1.

202 Belgian country report, Chapter III.B.7.d) referring to parliamentary preparatory works, regarding the legislative proposal protecting privacy against the interception of communications and telecommunication, Belgian Senate, 1992–1993, 1 September 1993.

203 UK Country report, Chapter III.B.7.

204 Czech country report, Chapter III.B.7.d) referring to Section 88 Para. 1 of Act No. 141/1961 Sb., Code of Criminal Procedure.

205 Czech country report, Chapter III.B.7.d).

206 French country report, Chapter III.B.6.b).

207 Swedish country report, Chapter III.B.6.

208 *Ibid.*

d) Proportionality of interception in individual cases

Another principle by which to ensure that interception is applied with checks and balances is a specific requirement to address the issue of the proportionality of the measure in each individual case of the interception. This requirement exists in the national laws of **Germany**, **Belgium**, **Sweden**, **Spain**, and the **United Kingdom**. Even if there is no explicit requirement in the legislation related to interception, the analysis of the national reports shows that a principle of proportionality can be applied in practice, as done in the **Czech Republic** and **France.**

In **Germany**, the approach to interception follows the concept that such an intrusion must be proportionate in each individual case of investigation.[209] Hence, the application of interception in a criminal investigation contradicts the principle of proportionality if the information related to the core area of privacy could possibly be captured in the course of communications acquisition. Another dimension of the principle of proportionally of interception in German legislation is the requirement of assuming that that interception will successfully lead to information related to the particular investigation.[210]

The **Belgian** law of criminal procedure directly obliges the court to assess whether the application of interception in a particular criminal investigation is proportionate to the seriousness of the crime: the investigating judge may authorise interception only if the case is exceptional.[211] A similar requirement can be found in **Swedish** law, which requires interception to be proportionate to the seriousness of the crime in each individual case of criminal investigation: Article 27:21 of CJP imposes a duty to specify the conditions aimed at protecting the integrity of the individual whenever interception is considered.[212] The **Spanish** national reporter states that the law requires the judge to assess the proportionality of the measure in each individual case; however, for crimes with a minimum threshold of three years of imprisonment, this requirement is usually considered fulfilled.[213] In the **United Kingdom**, the warrant must also specifically address the proportionality issue.[214]

The national reports from the **Czech Republic** and **France** highlighted that the legislation in their respective countries does not impose any direct obligations on the authority that grants interception to assess the proportionality of the interception in relation to the seriousness of the crime. In both countries, however, the principle of proportionality is applicable when interception is considered in practice. In

---

209 German country report, Chapter III.B.7.e).

210 *Ibid.*

211 Belgian country report, Chapter III.B.7.e) referring to Article 90*ter* §1 of the Belgian Criminal Procedure Code.

212 Swedish country report, Chapter III.B.6.

213 Spanish country report, Chapter III.B.7.e).

214 UK country report Chapter III.B.7.

the **Czech Republic**, in cases in which law enforcement would apply for too many interception authorisations for one individual case, the court would be very likely to reject the applications pursuant to the "principle of moderation" outlined in Para. 4 of Section 2 of the Czech Code of Criminal Procedure.[215] In **France**, according to the national reporter, requests for interception and justification of the application of such intrusive investigative measures are the subject of the general rules on the principle of proportionality in criminal procedure.[216]

e) Persons and connections under surveillance

All the country reports state that the interception of communications could be directed not only against the accused but also against other persons not suspected of the offence but whose communications might be of importance for the purpose of the criminal investigation. This principle has to be balanced, however, with certain checks and safeguards to avoid proactive monitoring. Consequently, there are certain regulations at the national level as to what kind of connections can be placed under surveillance in criminal proceedings and which identifiers (names, addresses, or specific connections) can be the subject of the interception order.

In **Germany**, the interception measure can be directed either against a suspect or against other persons if there are certain grounds to believe that they are communicating with the suspect or if the person under investigation might use their devices and connections. The order to intercept must always be issued only in relation to specific persons, though there is no need to know the exact identity of the suspicious persons at the time of interception authorisation. When the identity of the suspect is unknown, the authorisation might provide identifiers, such as a phone number or data allowing for identification of devices or connections, e.g., IP addresses or IMEI. As clarified in the German report, device identification is, however, admissible only when it can be proven that the number has not been assigned to another device at the same time.[217] Likewise, in the **Netherlands** and in the **Czech Republic**, there is no need to know the identity of the suspect. According to **Dutch** legislation, an interception order has to take into account the suspect of the crime but can be directed against a "user." The Dutch Code of Criminal Procedure requires either a number to be identified or identification of the user or communication service to be provided and, if known, the name and address of the user.[218] Likewise, in the **Czech Republic**, any user of communication services can be the subject of an interception order as long as all the prerequisites for granting authori-

---

215 Czech country report, Chapter III.B.7.e).

216 French country report, Chapters II.A.2 and III.B.6.b).

217 German country report, Chapter III.B.7.c).

218 Article 126m (2) (a) of the Dutch Code of Criminal Procedure.

sation are fulfilled and the court finds sufficient justification for such interception. As in other countries, the interception order can target a particular number or device but not specific communication content.[219] In **Sweden**, the order to intercept can be issued only for a particular phone number or other identifiers. The suspect is not the only person against whom interception might be ordered if there are reasonable grounds to believe that the accused will contact a particular number at a particular time.[220]

Belgian procedural law, in addition to allowing for the order to be issued against a suspect or persons who are expected to have regular contact with the suspect, explicitly provides for the possibility to direct the warrant to the places where the suspect is expected to stay.[221] Similarly, in the **United Kingdom**, the warrant can be issued not only against persons but also against premises.[222] **Spanish** legislation also has distinct legal provisions: in addition to the possibility of ordering the interception against a suspect, devices belonging to the suspect, and third parties, the law provides for the possibility to intercept devices that are being used by suspects electronically for illegal purposes without the knowledge of the owner.[223]

In all of the countries, the requirements to specifically identify persons or connections under surveillance serve as safeguards against proactive monitoring. For example, as mentioned in the Belgian country report, the issue of proactive monitoring was addressed in the parliamentary preparatory works, which ruled such a measure as unacceptable and referred to the existence of a suspect as one of the necessary prerequisites for the interception order.[224] However, the reports from **Sweden** and the **United Kingdom** specifically addressed the question of the use of interception to target particular content with the use of trigger words. The **Swedish** national reporter points out that, although this measure is not possible in criminal investigations, it exists for the signals intelligence operations carried out by the national signals intelligence agency (National Defence Radio Establishment, FRA) and only in relation to international communications.[225] Similarly, in the **United Kingdom**, the interception of specific communication content is applicable only in cases of a warrant under RIPA, s. 8(4), which involves the interception of "external

---

219 Czech country report, Chapter III.B.7.c).

220 Swedish country report, Chapter III.B.6.

221 Belgian country report, Chapter III.B.7.c) referring to Article 90*ter* §1, 3° of the Criminal Procedure Code.

222 UK country report, Chapter III.B.2.

223 Spanish country report, Chapter III.B.7.c) referring to Articles 588*bis* h and 588*ter* c of LECRIM.

224 Belgian country report, Chapter III.B.7.c) referring to parliamentary preparatory works, regarding the legislative proposal protecting privacy against the interception of communication and telecommunication, Belgian Senate, 1992–1993, 1 September 1993.

225 Swedish country report, Chapter I.A.3.

communications," namely interception for intelligence purposes and not as part of criminal proceedings.[226]

f) Consent of a communication participant to the measure

Another divergence in the national legislation comes from the differences in the approaches to interception when one of the parties agrees to this measure. While, as analysed below, there is no need to issue an interception warrant in this case in **Germany** and **Spain**, in the **Czech Republic**, **Sweden**, and the **United Kingdom**, the law requires a certain authorisation.

– *No authorisation for interception is needed if one communication party consents*

The **German** report clarifies that when one party to the communication exchange permits law enforcement agencies to read or listen to the communication, they do not fall under the scope of the interception provision (Section 100a StPO). The notion behind this is that such interception does not breach the confidentiality of communications: the only breach in this case is that of the trust that one person puts into someone he/she communicates with.[227] In this regard, the interception provision protects the secrecy of communications only against interference by a third party.[228] Similarly, in **Spain**, when consent for the interception is given by one of the communication parties, the interception cannot be considered an unlawful breach of the secrecy of communications, except in cases when an imprisoned person consents to the interception. As the Spanish national reporter points out, the latter requires authorisation in accordance with the European Court of Human Rights judgement.[229]

– *Certain authorisation is needed*

In contrast to the approaches requiring no authorisation when one of the parties agrees to interception, several national reports (**Sweden**, the **United Kingdom**, and the **Czech Republic**) indicated that certain authorisation is still needed. However, the approaches to authorisation in this case vary. The stricter regulation exists in **Sweden**, where an interception order is to be issued even if one of the parties to the communication has given consent to the interception.[230] As clarified in the Swedish country report, this conclusion can be drawn from the judicial practice related to

[226] UK country report, Chapter III.B.2.

[227] German country report, Chapter III.B.7.f).

[228] *Ibid.*

[229] Spanish country report, Chapter III.B.7.f) referring to *M.M. v The Netherlands*, 8 April 2004, no. 39339/98.

[230] Swedish country report, Chapter III.B.6.

the decisions of the European Court of Human Rights, which requires getting court authorisation to permit the use of hidden microphones in order to record a conversation when a party of the conversation agrees to "wearing a wire."[231] The need for court authorisation in cases of consent for interception is outlined in the documents of the Swedish Commission of Inquiry on Certain Police Methods.[232] In the **United Kingdom**, the same situation (when one party consents to the interception of communications) is considered a form of surveillance that still requires authorisation under Part II of RIPA. However, this authorisation does not imply the issuing of a warrant.

A combination of approaches to authorisation of this particular type of interception is taken in the **Czech Republic**, where a court order is always required, even in cases of consent – except for certain urgent cases (as analysed above in the chapter on urgent warrants), in which case the consent of one party is a necessary prerequisite for the interception of communications with no court authorisation.[233] However, as the national reporter points out, this provision is subject to criticism because, according to the opponents of this measure, it infringes the principle of the secrecy of communications concerning the party who did not consent to interception. As a general rule, this principle is counterbalanced with the requirement for the court to consider whether the intrusion is properly justified. But, in the case of consent, this balance is upset.[234]

8. Validity of interception order

a) Maximum length of interception order

The maximum length of the interception order is another issue that highlights differences at the national level and that can affect international cooperation. As revealed by this study, the period of validity of the interception warrants for the purpose of criminal investigation varies from four weeks to four months, depending on the national legislation.

The shortest period of validity of the interception warrant is provided for in **Dutch** law, which restricts the maximum length of interception to four weeks. In **Belgium** and **Sweden**, the validity of the interception order cannot exceed one month. In **Germany** and **Spain**, the maximum period of validity is three months. However, as discussed at the meeting with Spanish law enforcement agencies, warrants in Spain are normally issued for no longer than one month in practice, and the police are obliged to provide the judge with the results of the interception so that

231 Swedish country report Chapter III.B.6.

232 Swedish country report, Chapter III.B.6.

233 Czech country report, Chapter III.B.7.f).

234 *Ibid.*

he/she can decide whether continued interception is necessary. In the **United Kingdom**, the law provides for three months of interception for serious crimes and six months for national security matters.

In the **Czech Republic** and **France**, the general period of interception shall not exceed four months; however, **French** legislation provides additional clauses concerning different lengths of interception orders, depending on the purpose of interception and the authority that grants the authorisation. The maximum duration of four months is established in French legislation for the interception of correspondence authorised by the investigating judge and by the judge responsible for enforcing sentences. If the interception of correspondence is ordered by the liberty and custody judge, the duration of the warrant cannot exceed two months in cases of "search for an escaping person" and one month if the case concerns "flagrancy or preliminary procedure in relation with a restricted list of infringements."[235]

b) Prolongation of authorization

In all of the countries included in this analysis, the interception order can be prolonged for the same period of time with the justification that the conditions for the interception of communications still exist and interception is still required for the purpose of investigation. The prolongation usually follows the same procedure as the initial application for the interception. Legislation in most of the countries, with some exceptions, establishes neither limits for the number of prolongations nor restrictions for a cumulative period of interception. Such provisions, limiting the time for the cumulative interception of communications, can be found only in **Belgian**, **Spanish**, and **French** legislation.

In **Belgium**, the Code of Criminal Procedure provides for a maximum prolongation period of six months. As discussed at the workshop with Belgian law enforcement agency representatives, if the interception is still necessary after this period of time, the investigating judge has to start a new interception case and find new circumstances to justify the interception. In **Spain**, which has a maximum three-month period of validity for the interception warrant, the court can extend it for the same period of time but for no longer than 18 months cumulatively.[236] **French** legislation has established special temporal limits for certain types of interception warrants. There is a limitation on the length of interception of correspondence authorised by the liberty and custody judge: the maximum duration for such authorisation in case of a misdemeanour is six months, including prolongations. No limit, however, was established for crimes that justify the application of the interception. Further limitations refer to interception warrants issued by the same courts with a

---

[235] French country report, Chapter III.B.7.a).

[236] Spanish country report, Chapter III.B.8.a).

maximum duration of one month for cases of flagrancy and a number of other infringements. This authorisation to intercept can be renewed only once under the same conditions.[237] A warrant for the use of remote forensic software devices can be issued for a maximum period of four months and prolonged for another four months only under exceptional circumstances (Article 706-102-2 of the Penal Procedure Code).[238]

In **Sweden**, although the national legislation does not establish limits on the number of possible extensions of interception authorisations, the national report highlighted that the principle of proportionality means that limits are considered in practice when a judge considers authorisation of interception in a particular case. As the national reporter points out, cases such as certain security-related investigations in Sweden in the 1960s, when the warrants were prolonged every month for a period of 16 years, would be unacceptable today, even though security operations and organised crime investigations generally last longer.[239]

c) *Revocation of authorisation*

Most of the countries have the possibility to revoke the authorisation; however, the approaches vary concerning the responsibility to revoke. In **Germany**, **Sweden**, the **United Kingdom**, and **Spain**, the interception order must be revoked under certain circumstances, and revocation is considered a duty of the authority who issues the authorisation. In contrast, the national reports from **Belgium**, the **Czech Republic**, and **France** indicated that their law establishes no obligation to revoke the interception warrant.

– *Revocation as a duty*

In **Germany**, the law of criminal procedure requires termination of the interception without any delay as soon as the prerequisites for authorisation of this measure no longer exist. In this case, both the public prosecutor and the court have the power to revoke the interception order. A revocation is especially essential in cases in which suspicion is proven to be unfounded, the investigation is no longer in need of interception, or it is questionable whether interception will succeed for the purpose of the investigation.[240] In **Sweden**, the law obliges the prosecutor or the court to repeal the authorisation immediately if there is no longer any need for the measure.[241] The same approach is followed by the **United Kingdom**, where legislation

---

237 French country report, Chapter III.B.7.a).

238 French country report, Chapter III.B.7.b).

239 Swedish country report, Chapter III.B.7.

240 German country report, Chapter III.B.8.c).

241 Swedish country report, Chapter III.B.7 referring to Article 27: 23 of CJP.

establishes a mandatory requirement to cancel a warrant when it is no longer necessary for the specified aim of investigation. According to the **Spanish** national report, the national legislation provides that the interception shall be terminated once the grounds for its authorisation cease to exist or when it becomes clear that the measure will produce no results for the investigation.[242]

– *No duty to revoke*

In contrast to the approaches where the obligation of the duty to revoke the interception is explicitly stated, the legislation in **France**, **Belgium**, and the **Czech Republic** does not provide for a duty to revoke a warrant. This does not mean, however, that revocation cannot take place. Only the French country report indicated no discussion on this issue on the national level, where the law of criminal procedure imposes no obligation to revoke the authorisation of the interception.[243]

In **Belgium** and the **Czech Republic**, despite the absence of the duty to revoke provided for in the law, the revocation may still be a result of some other obligations. Article 90quinquies §1 of the **Belgian** Code of Criminal Procedure stipulates that the investigating judge "may" end the interception "as soon as the circumstances that justified the measure have disappeared."[244] As pointed out in the national report, Belgian academic literature argues, however, that the existence of the principle of subsidiarity obliges the judge to revoke the authorisation if interception is no longer necessary.[245] In the **Czech Republic**, the legislation provides no requirements to revoke the authorisation; however, the national report highlights that the revocation might take place when it becomes apparent that there is a lack of substantive grounds for the use of interception. In addition, the report states that, pursuant to Para. 8 of Section 88 of the Criminal Procedure Code, the Constitutional Court may also revoke the interception warrant.[246] Furthermore, the police authority in the Czech Republic is required to perform regular checks as to the existence of the reasons that led to the authorisation of interception. If the grounds for authorisation have ceased to exist, the police have a duty to terminate the interception without delay, even before the end of the period of the interception order. In this case, the court that gave the authorisation has to be notified in writing.[247]

---

[242] Spanish country report, Chapter III.B.8.c) referring to Article 588*bis* j of LECRIM.

[243] French country report, Chapter III.B.7.a).

[244] Belgian country report, Chapter III.B.8.c).

[245] *Ibid*

[246] Czech country report, Chapter III.B.8.c).

[247] Czech country report, Chapter III.B.8.c) referring to Section 88 Para. 3 of the Code of Criminal Procedure.

9. Duties to record, report, and destroy

Additional divergences in the interception procedure can be found in the laws stipulating the duties to produce the interception recording and the duties to report the interception results. Furthermore, there are different approaches to the destruction of the records. These differences will be further analysed in the next part of the study.

a) Duty to record and report

aa) Duty to record interception

Only three country reports (**France**, **Spain,** and the **Czech Republic**) indicated that there is always a duty to produce official records – explicitly provided for in the law. Furthermore, in the **Czech Republic** and **Sweden** (where no duty to record exists), the law imposes a recording duty.

In **France**, although the recording procedure varies slightly, depending on the interception regime, there is always a duty to produce official records. For data acquired under the provisions on electronic correspondence interception, Article 100-4 of the Penal Procedure Code establishes for the official records, which should be kept under closed official seals, that they should always indicate the time and date of the interception and provide information on the beginning and end of the measure. The same requirement under Article 100-5 of the French Penal Procedure Code exists for any transcriptions of correspondence. In the same manner, in case of remote data capture, an official record is compulsory for each device installed and for each data capture carried out in the course of the investigation. Transcription and description of remote data capture are also the subject of the official records requirement.[248] In **Spain**, the duty to record includes the obligation to submit the information, so that it can be verified as authentic. The recording duty is provided for by Article 588*ter* f of LECRIM, which requires the police to submit a transcription of the relevant information and the complete recorded data to the judge in a way that will prove its authenticity.[249]

In the **Czech Republic**, in addition to the obligation to record, there is a recording duty, which is linked to the subsequent presentation of the intercepted material in court as evidence. The police investigator is required to evaluate the content acquired during the interception and to prepare the record, which represents a transcript of those data relevant to the investigation. A protocol is mandatory if this record is going to be presented as evidence in court. The Czech Code of Criminal Procedure establishes a set of formal requirements for this protocol: it must "con-

248 French country report, Chapter III.B.8.a).

249 Spanish country report, Chapter III.B.9.a).

tain information about the place where the interception was conducted, time of interception, manner of the interception, authority, which issued the record, and general information about contents of the record."[250] In addition, the protocol must meet another set of formal requirements, which have been established in Sec. 55 of the Czech Code of Criminal Procedure for any transcript recordings in criminal proceedings.[251]

Another country with a requirement for recording duties is **Sweden**. The internal Swedish regulation of the Prosecuting Authority, namely Section 7 of the Ordinance on Preliminary Investigation (1947:948), stipulates the obligation of the person leading the investigation to log the interception of communications. These records are, however, not attached to the file of the preliminary investigation: as pointed out in the country report, in practice, the interception is usually only noted in the file in case it might be further used as evidence in criminal proceedings.[252]

In **Belgium**, there is no duty to record; however, the national reporter stated that Article 90*sexies* CCP[253] obliges the police officer responsible for the interception in a particular investigation to send the recordings made during the interception to the investigating judge. These recordings should be sent together with the transcripts that the police officer considers relevant for the investigation and include "its possible translation and, what the irrelevantly deemed (tele)-communications concerns, the cited topics and the identification of the telecommunications means to which or from which was called." However, this data does not have to be presented as an official record.[254]

bb) Duty to report the progress of interception to judge / prosecutor

There are different approaches to the duty to report the progress of interception. In several countries, namely **Germany**, the **Czech Republic**, **Sweden**, and the **United Kingdom**, the law imposes no special obligation to report on interception progress during the process of application of this measure. The absence of this duty, however, can still be balanced with additional checks during or after the interception. In **Germany**, there is a requirement to notify the court that granted the authorisation to intercept about the results of the interception.[255] In the **Czech Republic**, as a balancing measure, the record of the interception should be made

[250] Czech country report, Chapter III.B.9.a) referring to Para. 6 of Section 88 of the Czech Code of Criminal Procedure.

[251] Czech country report, Chapter III.B.9.a).

[252] Swedish country report, Chapter III.B.8.

[253] Article 90*sexies* CCP, translation from Belgian country report, Chapter III.B.9.a).

[254] Belgian country report, Chapter III.B.9.a) referring to Article 90*septies* §1 of the Belgian Code of Criminal Procedure.

[255] German country report, Chapter III.B.9.a) referring to in Section 100b Subsection 4 Section 2 StPO.

available to the public prosecutor who is, in turn, obliged to perform regular checks concerning the legality of the interception and its progress.[256] Similarly, in the **United Kingdom**, the official who issued the warrant is required to review the authorisation regularly.[257] In **Sweden**, as stated by the national reporter, the absence of the reporting duty is balanced with the short validity period of the interception warrant, which means that the prosecutor is required to report to the court the circumstances of the interception once the application for the extension has been made.[258]

In contrast, there are formal obligations to report to the court on the progress of interception in **Belgium** and **France**. In **Belgium**, the police are required to submit reports to an investigating judge about the course of interception every five days.[259] As pointed out during the practical workshop with Belgian law enforcement agency representatives, the report usually includes technical details, information about the intercepted person, and details about the progress of the interception. Furthermore, the judge has to be informed by the police in cases in which the phone number or other identification has changed. Similarly, in **France**, the police have to report to the investigating judge about both measures related to the interception of communications: interception of electronic correspondence and remote data capture.[260] Different reporting regulations can be found in the **Netherlands**, where the police do not have to inform the court on the progress of interception; however, there is an obligation to report to the prosecutor who issued the interception requisition.[261]

In **Spain**, although there is no direct legal obligation on the frequency of providing information on the progress of interception, the comprehensive judicial oversight in criminal investigations creates the reporting duties in practice.[262] As shared by Spanish law enforcement agency representatives during the workshop, the judge or the prosecutor can request information on the performance of the interception every week, every 15 days, and at the end of the validity period of the interception warrant. Upon such request, the police have to provide the transcripts and all other information about the interception progress.

---

[256] Czech country report, Chapter III.B.9.a).

[257] UK country report, Chapter III.B.7.

[258] Swedish country report, Chapter III.B.8.

[259] Belgian country report, Chapter III.B.9.a) referring to the Article 90*quater* §3, 2° Criminal Procedure Code.

[260] French country report, Chapter III.B.8 referring to Articles 706-102-1 and 706-102-5 of the Penal Procedure Code.

[261] Information obtained at the law enforcement workshop in The Netherlands.

[262] Spanish country report, Chapter III.B.9.a).

b) Duty to destroy

Another safeguard concerning the interception of communications is the duty to destroy the records provided for by the national law in almost all the jurisdictions covered by this study. The grounds for such destruction and the bodies responsible for it still vary from country to country.

In **Germany**, **France**, the **Netherlands**, and **Sweden,** the decision on record destruction is a power of the prosecutor. **German** legislation requires deletion without delay of the personal data acquired during the course of the interception if they are no longer deemed necessary for the purpose of the investigation and not the subject of a court review of the investigative measure.[263] Both technical recordings and written material are to be destroyed; furthermore, the deletion must be officially documented. When the data represent accidental discoveries that are not related to the main proceedings but can be used as evidence in other criminal proceedings, the requirement to delete is not applicable. The public prosecutor takes into consideration all decisions on deletion of data; however, if the case is pending, it is the court that decides whether the intercepted data shall be destroyed.[264] **French** legislation also leaves the decision on the destruction of records to the public prosecutor; however, Article 100-6 of the French Penal Procedure Code stipulates that the reason for record destruction is "expiry of the limitation period for prosecution."[265] In the **Netherlands**, the information collected by means of interception must be destroyed two months after the intercepted person was notified about the interception. However, the prosecutor in control of the interception can postpone the destruction if the data is needed in another investigation or if data has to be stored in the serious crime register. The destruction must be officially documented in the records. **Swedish** legislation provides for the responsibility of the public prosecutor to order the destruction of all records having no relevance to the aim of the interception authorisation and which will not be used as evidence in criminal proceedings. As pointed out in the national report, the Swedish Commission on Security and Integrity Protection has criticised both the police and prosecutors for significant delays in carrying out the duty to destroy the records of interception and, as a result of these checks, the Chief Public Prosecutor's Office adopted new guidelines in 2012, specifically addressing this issue.[266]

A different approach to the distribution of responsibility to destroy data can be found in **Belgium**, where police authorities are named as the bodies responsible for carrying out this duty. A police officer who is responsible for implementation of

263 German country report, Chapter III.B.9.b) referring to Section 101 Subsection 8 StPO.

264 German country report, Chapter III.B.9.b).

265 French country report, Chapter III.B.8.

266 Swedish country report, Chapter III.B.8 referring to ÅM RättsPM 2012:8.

the interception has to destroy any information that is not kept in an official record.[267] However, the law makes an exception from this rule for the "transcription of the relevantly deemed (tele-)communications of the record, any translation thereof, and what the irrelevantly deemed (tele)-communications concerns, the cited topics and the identification of the telecommunications means to which or from which was called."[268] The destruction must also be officially recorded.[269]

In **Spain** and in the **Czech Republic**, it is also the duty of the police to destroy the records; however, the law provides for the necessary time period between conclusion of the investigation and destruction. According to the law of criminal procedure in the **Czech Republic**, the destruction shall take place three years after final conclusion of the case and only with the consent of the public prosecutor.[270] In **Spain**, a provision on the duty to destroy makes a distinction between original records and preserved copies of the interception data. While the original records are to be destroyed upon court order after the final ruling on termination of criminal proceedings, the preserved copies have to be kept for five years after the penalty was executed or when the time for the prosecution has expired or when the acquittal decision becomes final.[271]

The law in the **United Kingdom** imposes the duty to ensure destruction on the Secretary of State. RIPA requires destruction of any data resulting from interception as soon as they are no longer needed for the purpose for which the authorisation to intercept was granted.[272] The Code of Practice "Interception of Communications"[273] further provides that, if such data is retained, reviews are to be taken at "appropriate intervals" to justify the validity of such retention in accordance with RIPA.

10. Notification duties and remedies

a) Duty to notify persons affected by the measure

– Legislation on the duty to notify

As one of the safeguards, some of the countries demand notification about the interception. Such a requirement can be found in the legislation in **Germany**, **Bel-**

---

267 Belgian country report, Chapter III.B.9.b) referring to Article 90*septies* §1 of the Belgian Code of Criminal Procedure.

268 Article 90*septies* §1 CCP, translation from Belgian country report, Chapter III.B.9.b).

269 Belgian country report, Chapter III.B.9.b).

270 Czech country report, Chapter III.B.9.b) referring to Para. 7 of Section 88 of the Czech code of criminal procedure.

271 Spanish country report, Chapter III.B.9.b) referring to Article 588*bis* k of LECRIM.

272 Section 15 (3) RIPA.

273 *Home Office*, Interception of Communications Code of Practice, January 2016, Chapter 6.8.

gium, the **Netherlands**, **Spain**, and **Sweden**.[274] A different approach is taken in **France** and in the **United Kingdom**: neither country has legislation stipulating the duty to notify affected persons after the interception has ended. In **France**, due to the concept of the secrecy of the interception measures, it is only the accused that can learn about the interception and only after he/she is given access to the case files.[275] In the **United Kingdom**, both RIPA and the Code of Practice contain no requirements to notify affected parties after interception ends.

– *Exemptions from the duty to notify*

While stipulating the obligation to notify affected parties, **Germany**, the **Czech Republic**, the **Netherlands**, and **Sweden** provide in their laws for exceptions from this duty when certain conditions are met. These conditions, as shown below vary, however, depending on the jurisdiction.

In **Germany**, the duty to notify might be relieved in cases in which such notification can damage the protected interests of such persons, e.g., damaging the interests or reputation of the accused after no incriminating evidence has been found or when the person is not significantly affected by the measure and there are reasons to believe that there is no interest in such notification. The latter exception is, therefore, applicable only to those targets that were not a primary subject of the interception.[276] Such notification is to be carried out as soon as possible, unless it is poses a threat to the aim of the criminal investigation or "the life, physical integrity and personal liberty of another person, or significant assets."[277] In cases in which notification was postponed for more than twelve months on the above-mentioned grounds, there is a requirement of court approval for any further delays. In cases in which it can be foreseen that the reasons for the delay will not cease to exist, a court has the power to authorise the permanent dispensation of the notification about interception.[278]

In the **Czech Republic**, the obligation to inform the suspect constitutes an administrative procedure; the duty of notification is not applicable in cases of certain crimes, or when a criminal investigation is being carried out against several persons and has not yet been completed in relation to at least one of them, or when such

274 German country report, Chapter III.B.10.a) referring to Section 101 Subsection 4 StPO; Czech country report, Chapter III.B.10.a) referring to Sections 88(8) and 88(9) of the Czech Code of Criminal Procedure; Spanish country report, Chapter III.B.10.a) Article 588*ter* i.3 of LECRIM; Swedish country report, Chapter III.B.9.

275 French country report, Chapter III.B.9.

276 German country report.

277 Section 101 Subsection 5 StPO, German country report, Chapter III.B.10.a).

278 German country report, Chapter III.B.10.a).

notification can pose threats to "national security, life, health, or the rights and freedoms of individuals, etc."[279]

Similarly, **Dutch** legislation makes exceptions from the rule of notification in cases in which the person has already been granted access to the criminal investigation file or if notification is not feasible for fair reasons. These reasons might include the impossibility of finding out the identity or address of the person or situations when disclosure of the wiretapping constitutes a security risk.[280]

Swedish legislation provides for exemption from the notification requirement in cases in which it is obviously unnecessary, when such notification can damage an ongoing investigation, in certain cases of mutual legal assistance, or when notification can be harmful to the personal or economic integrity of an individual. Other exceptions from the notification duty are provided for offences within the jurisdiction of the security police. In such investigations, notification can be postponed until the secrecy rules are no longer applicable; however, one year after the investigation is complete, the duty to notify expires, even if notification has not been made. As pointed out in the Swedish national report, notification for these types of investigations is very unlikely; all cases of non-notification are under the supervision of the Commission on Security and Integrity Protection.[281]

b) Remedies

Six of eight countries included in this study, have different remedies, which intercepted persons can use against the measure. The set of remedies varies from judicial reviews, like those in **Germany**, the **Czech Republic**, and **Belgium**, to complaints and claiming damages in civil procedures like those in **Sweden**, **Spain**, and the **United Kingdom**.

Two countries – **Germany** and the **Czech Republic** – provide for such an interception-related specific remedy as an opportunity to initiate judicial review for cases of interception. In **Germany**, Section 101 Subsection 7 StPO allows, through a judicial review, any person who has been the subject of communication interception to challenge the legality of the measure and the way it was carried out. The application must be filed two weeks after the notification of interception has been received.[282] In the **Czech Republic**, Para. 8 of Section 88 of the Code of Criminal Procedure stipulates that a person whose communications have been intercepted can apply to the Supreme Court in order to challenge the lawfulness of the authorisation for interception. The procedure for such judicial review is regulated under

---

279 Czech country report, Chapter III.B.10.a) referring to Section 88 Para. 9 of the Criminal Procedure Code.

280 Information obtained at the law enforcement workshop.

281 Swedish country report, Chapter III.B.9.

282 German country report, Chapter III.B.10.b).

the general provisions 314l – 314n of the Code of Criminal Procedure.[283] Another country in which judicial review is generally possible is **Belgium**. However, as pointed out in the national report, there is no specific remedy stipulated specifically for cases of interception. The affected person can file against the performed measure under the general rules provided by the Code of Criminal Procedure to challenge the legality of investigative measures.[284]

In **Sweden**, despite the fact that a person affected by interception theoretically has several possibilities to challenge the measure – either to file a complaint with the Commission on Security and Integrity Protection, or to appeal against the measure to the chief government law officer (the Chancellor of Justice), or to use a civil court procedure to claim damage – the national reporter states that no such cases have been known since the 1980s.[285] **Spanish** legislation also several possible remedies for the third person affected by interception, such as initiating a criminal accusation of unlawful infringement or claiming damage in civil proceedings. However, since the duty to notify third parties was introduced together with the new legislation and had not yet entered into force at the time of writing the Spanish national report, the reporter points out that no practical analysis can be made on this issue.[286] In the **United Kingdom**, where a notification requirement is not provided by RIPA, a person can launch a complaint case with the Investigatory Powers Tribunal.[287]

c) Criminal consequences of unlawful interception measures

In all of the countries included in this study, illegal interception constitutes a criminal offence. However, the national reports from **Germany** and **Spain** especially highlighted that unlawful interception carried out by law enforcement will entail these particular consequences. **German** criminal law prohibits unlawful eavesdropping or recording of non-publicly spoken words under Section 201 StGB, which stipulates higher sentences for public officials. If the interception of communications does not meet the requirements established by the German law of criminal procedure, it entails criminal liability if knowledge and intent for such a crime exist. Furthermore, some cases of unlawful interception in the information systems might theoretically fall under provisions dealing with illegal access (202a StGB) and illegal interception (202b StGB).[288] The **Spanish** report states that the official involved in unlawful interception would face disciplinary sanctions with the possi-

---

[283] Czech country report, Chapter III.B.10.b).
[284] Belgian country report, Chapter III.B.10.b).
[285] Swedish country report, Chapter III.B.9.
[286] Spanish country report, Chapter III.B.10.b).
[287] Section 65 RIPA.
[288] German country report, Chapter III.B.10.c).

bility of dismissal[289] in addition to criminal liability for interference with the secrecy of communications.

In the **Czech Republic**, there is also a general provision on violation of the confidentiality of messages, which stipulates criminal responsibility for unlawful interception – Section 182 of the Penal Code. In addition, as stated in the national report, if a judge authorises interception illegally, criminal liability might also follow under prohibition on the abuse of powers of an official person (Section 329 of the Czech Penal Code).[290] Similarly, the **Swedish** report highlighted that unlawful surveillance operations can entail criminal responsibility for the misuse of office. In this case, the overseeing body – the Commission on Security and Integrity Protection – has to report this offence for further prosecution.[291]

In **Belgium**, the criminal offence of unlawful interception is covered by Articles 314*bis* and 259*bis* of the Criminal Code. The Belgian national reporter stated that, since data on the breach of law concerning the interception of communications is not available, it is impossible to provide information on specific sanctions for infringement of the rules on the investigating procedure. However, as noted in the report, a violation of the duty to notify those who were intercepted about the interception might entail disciplinary or civil sanctions.[292]

The **French** report highlighted that, in addition to the criminal responsibility that might be faced for unlawful interception, there are also consequences for the validity of the evidence in cases when certain requirements outlined in the criminal procedure legislation for the interception are not met. These consequences do not, however, include criminal responsibility and refer mostly to the penalty of nullity, e.g., in the case of interception of privileged communications without following the special procedure of notification of respective chambers and professional associations.[293]

11. Confidentiality requirements

a) Obligations of telecommunication service providers to maintain secrecy

Legislation in most of the countries included in this analysis requires communications service providers to maintain secrecy about the interception of communications. On the national level, this is achieved by the implementation of special provisions to maintain the confidentiality of the interception in either a telecommuni-

289 Spanish country report, Chapter III.B.10.c).

290 Czech country report, Chapter III.B.10.c).

291 Swedish country report, Chapter III.B.9.

292 Belgian country report, Chapter III.B.10.c).

293 French country report, Chapter III.B.9.

cation regulation, as in **Germany** and **Sweden,**[294] or in the procedural law, as in **Belgium**, **Spain**, and the **United Kingdom**.[295] Furthermore, this obligation can fall under the general provisions on the duty to cooperate, as found in **France**[296] and the **Czech Republic**, using a mixed approach: the obligation to maintain secrecy of communications is secured by the virtue of both special legislation and a general prohibition on disclosure.[297]

b) Sanctions against telecommunications service providers and their employees

In most of the countries, a violation of the duty to maintain secrecy entails criminal liability, although the thresholds for sanctions might vary. **Germany**, the **Czech Republic**, and **Sweden** outline criminal responsibility in the special regulation on telecommunications, while **Belgium**, **France**, **Spain**, and the **United Kingdom** provide for criminal sanctions in the criminal code or the law on criminal procedure.

In **Germany**, violation of the obligation to maintain secrecy constitutes a regulatory offence punishable with a fine of up to 500,000 Euro (Section 149 Subsection 1 No. 22, Subsection 2 S. 1 TKG). Furthermore, disclosure of interception entails a punishment of up to two years of imprisonment or a fine (Section 18 G 10 Act).[298] In the **Czech Republic**, violation of the duty of secrecy can be punished either under specific legislation (Art. 118 of the Act on Electronic Communications), with a fine of up to 20,000,000 Czech crowns, or under the general provisions on disclosure of classified information, as an administrative offence with a fine of up to 5,000,000 CZK. Furthermore, Sections 317 or 318 of the Code of Criminal Procedure establish criminal liability for endangering classified information, providing for different imprisonment terms depending on the gravity of the offence.[299] **Swedish** legislation on electronic communications (ECA 7:15) also re-

---

294 German country report, Chapter III.B.11.a) referring to; 5 Subsection 4 Sections 1 and 15 TKÜV; Swedish country report, Chapter III.B.10 referring to Section 6:20-23 of Electronic Communications Act.

295 Belgian country report, Chapter III.B.11.a) referring Article 90*quater* §2 and §4 of the Belgian Code of Criminal Procedure; Spanish country report, Chapter III.B.11.a) referring to Article 588*ter* e of LECRIM; UK country report, Chapter III.B.9 referring to Sec. 19 of RIPA.

296 French country report, Chapter III.B.10 referring to Articles 226-13 and 226-14 of the French Penal Procedure Code.

297 According to the country report, Chapter III.B.11, the special obligation is provided for in para. 8 of Section 97 of the Act on Electronic Communications. In addition, Act no. 412/2005 Sb. prohibits the unauthorised disclosure of classified information and is thus applicable to the obligation to maintain secrecy.

298 German country report, Chapter III.B.11.b).

299 Czech country report, Chapter III.B.11.

fers to criminal sanctions provided by the criminal code and by legislation on the breach of secrecy (the Act on Transparency and Secrecy).[300]

Belgium, **France**, **Spain**, and the **United Kingdom** provide for criminal responsibility for breach of the obligation to maintain secrecy in their criminal codes or in their codes of criminal procedure. In **Belgium**, the violation of secrecy obligations is punished in accordance with Article 458 of the Penal Code.[301] In **Spain**, Article 588*ter* e of LECRIM provides for criminal liability for disobeying a judicial order when persons fail to fulfil the duties outlined in the provisions on the duty to cooperate, including the obligation to maintain secrecy.[302] **French** legislation also provides for penal sanctions in accordance with Articles 226-13 and 226-14 of the Penal Procedure Code.[303] In the **United Kingdom**, breach of the obligation to maintain secrecy under RIPA can be punished with up to five years of imprisonment.[304]

C. Collection and use of traffic data and subscriber data

1. Collection of traffic data and subscriber data

a) Collection of traffic data

aa) Relevant information

The importance nowadays of metadata in criminal investigations can hardly be overestimated. During the practical workshops in every country included in this study, the law enforcement representatives stated that content data and metadata are equally important for the purpose of investigation. Often, the law enforcement agencies have to examine both content and traffic/subscriber data or investigate one type of data before requesting another category of information, e.g., analysis of metadata can precede the interception of communications. The importance of the interception of metadata (not access to stored data) is also increasing because the investigation can benefit from information about communication if the content is encrypted.

All the countries included in this study have legal provisions for traffic data requests. The following regulations have been indicated in the national reports:

– **Germany**: Section 100g StPO

300 Swedish country report, Chapter III.B.10.

301 Belgian country report, Chapter III.B.11.b).

302 Spanish country report, Chapter III.B.11.b).

303 French country report, Chapter III.B.10 referring to the Article 11 of the Penal Procedure Code.

304 UK country report, Chapter III.B.9.

- **Belgium**: Article 88*bis* of the Code of Criminal Procedure
- **Czech Republic**: Article § 88a of the Code of Criminal Procedure
- **France**: 77-1-1 (preliminary investigation), 60-1 (flagrancy) and 99-3 (investigating judge) of the Penal Procedure Code
- the **Netherlands**: Article 126n of the Code of Criminal Procedure
- **Spain**: Article 588*ter* j of LECRIM
- **Sweden**: Section 19 of CJP
- **United Kingdom**: Part I, Chapter II of RIPA

bb) Substantive prerequisites of collection

Substantive prerequisites for orders concerning traffic data vary in the national legislations. Most of the countries, – **Germany**, **Belgium**, the **Czech Republic**, the **Netherlands**, **Spain**, **Sweden**, and the **United Kingdom**, permit the application of this measure only in relation to specific crimes or require a certain degree of suspicion. In contrary, **France** does not provide for such safeguards. The analysis of these requirements is provided below on the basis of distinguishing between these two approaches.

– *Specific crimes and/or degree of suspicion as prerequisites*

German law establishes two substantive prerequisites: the nature of the offence committed and the degree of suspicion concerning the targeted person. Section 100g of the German StPO provides that there must be certain grounds to believe that the person whose traffic data is to be collected has been involved in the commission of the offence, either as a perpetrator or as a participant.[305] In addition, the offence itself must have either substantial significance,[306] meaning that "suspicion goes beyond vague clues or mere conjecture"[307] or have been committed via telecommunication means.[308] The issue of significance is assessed in accordance with court practice, which considers the element of "substantial significance" to be a decisive factor for the infringement of person's rights.[309] The recent judgement of the German Federal Constitutional Court provides that offences with a maximum penalty threshold of five-year imprisonment do not always possess the element of substantial significance, and thus justification of the intrusion into civil rights has

---

305 German country report, Chapter III.C.1.a).

306 German country report, Chapter III.C.1.a) referring to Section 100g Subsection 1 Section 1 No. 1 StPO.

307 German country report, Chapter III.C.1.a).

308 German country report, Chapter III.C.1.a) referring to Section 100g Subsection 1 Sesction 2 No. 2 StPO.

309 German country report, Chapter III.C.1.a).

to be decided based on the circumstances of the individual case. Misdemeanours with a maximum punishment of less than two years of imprisonment cannot be considered offences of substantial significance. For offences committed via telecommunication means, the subsidiarity principle must always be taken into consideration.[310]

Some countries provide for a minimum penalty threshold as a prerequisite for traffic data collection. In the **Czech Republic**, the minimum penalty threshold established in the legislation – Section 88a of the Code of Criminal Procedure – provides that traffic data collection can be ordered for crimes with an upper penalty threshold of a minimum of three years of imprisonment, with the exception of crimes that cannot be investigated without such data, e.g., crimes committed using electronic communications.[311] Furthermore, as in the case of substantive prerequisites for interception, traffic data can be obtained in the investigation of an intentional crime, which the Czech Republic must prosecute by virtue of an international treaty. Ultimately, the substantive prerequisite is the application of the principle of subsidiarity.[312]

Similarly, in **Spain**, the penalty threshold is written in the law. According to the Spanish report, the substantive requirements are the same as those for the interception of communications. Although there have been debates in Spanish academic literature that intrusion in the case of traffic data collection is lower than in the case of interception, and the requirements should therefore have a lower threshold, Spanish law still requires the same degree of suspicion for both measures and limits both of them to offences with a penalty higher than three years of imprisonment, to organised crime or terrorism, and to cybercrime.[313] Furthermore, the law requires the data to be indispensable for the investigation.[314] The same approach concerning offences justifying the collection of traffic data can be found in the **Netherlands**, where, despite the fact that the collection of traffic data does not require judicial approval, it can be applied only to investigations of the same categories of crimes as those for interception.[315] **Swedish** legislation provides that traffic data collection may be ordered for offences with a penalty of at least six months of imprisonment

---

310 *Ibid.*

311 Czech country report, Chapter III.C.1.a) referring to the section of the Penal Code No. 40/2009 Sb., which includes the following list of offences: violating the secrecy of conveyed messages (Sec. 182), fraud (Sec. 209), unlawfully gained access to a computer system or data carrier (Sec. 230), acquisition and receipt of access, equipment, or codes for computer systems or other similar data (Sec. 231), criminal threat (Sec. 353), stalking (Sec. 354), spreading of false news (Sec. 357), incitement (Sec. 364), and criminal connivance (Sec. 365).

312 Czech country report, Chapter III.C.1.a).

313 Spanish country report, Chapter III.C.1.a).

314 *Ibid*, referring to Article 588*ter* j of Spanish LECRIM.

315 Art. 126n and Art. 67 Criminal Procedure Code.

or for some other categories of offences, e.g., hacking, drug trafficking, etc.[316] In **Belgium** the minimum penalty requirement – one year of imprisonment – was introduced in April 2016. The same law establishes the requirements for proportionality and subsidiarity.[317]

In the **United Kingdom**, traffic data collection is also allowed only for specific crimes. RIPA permits the collection of traffic data only if it is necessary for the purposes listed in Section 22(2) of RIPA. This list includes such reasons as national security, public safety, preventing or detecting crime, preventing public disorder, etc.[318]

– *No requirement concerning degree of suspicion or specific crimes*

France has only general provisions allowing for the collection of traffic data without establishing specific requirements concerning the degree of suspicion or specific crimes. French Penal Procedure Code does not establish specific requirements concerning the degree of suspicion and does not limit requests for traffic data to particular types of crime or a minimum penalty requirement.[319]

cc) Formal prerequisites of collection

National laws differ concerning the need for judicial approval for the collection of traffic data. In **France** and the **Netherlands** the court authorisation is not required: the public prosecutor or judicial police officer can make a request for the collection of traffic data on their own without the court approval.[320] Furthermore, in the **United Kingdom**, as with the case of interception, judicial approval is also not required.[321]

In contrast, in **Germany**, the **Czech Republic**, and **Spain**, legislation provides that the request for traffic data collection requires judicial approval.[322] The same requirement exists in **Sweden**; however, according to the national report, there are some exceptions to this rule. Although the collection of traffic data in preliminary investigations requires court authorisation, both the police and the security police may order this measure without judicial authorisation as a part of intelligence work under the Act on the Collection of Data on Electronic Communications in Law

---

316 Swedish country report, Chapter III.C.1.

317 Belgian country report, Chapter III.C.1.a, referring to the Art. 88*bis* CPP and the Data Retention Act of 29 May 2016.

318 UK country report, Chapter III.C.1.

319 French country report, Chapter III.C.1.a).

320 French country report, Chapter III.C.1.a; for the Netherlands: information from the law enforcement workshop.

321 UK country report, Chapter III.C.1.

322 German, Czech and Spanish country reports, Chapters III.C.1.a).

Enforcement Intelligence (2012:278) if the request can be made without court approval on the reasonable suspicion of involvement in a "criminal activity."[323] **Belgium** represents a mixed model concerning judicial authorisation: while the request for traffic data is made by the investigating judge under normal circumstances, a public prosecutor is also empowered to give such an order in case of *flagrante delicto* for specific offences listed in Article 90*ter*, §§2, 3 and 4 of the Belgian Code of Criminal Procedure. However, such an order has to be confirmed by the investigating judge within twenty-four hours. Judicial confirmation is not required for the offences of taking hostages or extortion by force.[324]

dd) Duty of addressees to disclose information

All of the country reports stated that communications providers must supply the necessary information upon receiving an order for traffic data collection. Furthermore, some of the national reporters additionally stated the penalties applicable to those providers who refuse to cooperate. For example, such refusal is punishable in **France** by one year of imprisonment and a fine of 75,000 EUR.[325] The **Swedish** report notes that administrative fines are also applicable.[326]

Two of the reports pointed to the practical problems of addressing the orders for traffic data collection. The **Czech** report mentioned that, in practice, orders for traffic data are carefully evaluated on the part of service providers and, if the request is not specific enough or does not contain all the information required by legislation, the provider might refuse to provide the data.[327] Furthermore, the **Swedish** report also noted that, after the EU Court of Justice had declared the data retention directive null and void, some of the service providers in Sweden refused to comply with requests from law enforcement agencies concerning traffic data handovers for those procedures where requests had not been authorised by the court. Since the Swedish telecommunications regulator (PTS) was unsure of whether such procedures are in compliance with the judgement of the European Court of Justice, the duty to cooperate in these cases was not enforced before the PTS came to the conclusion that the legislation contains enough safeguards for such procedures. After this decision of the PTS, enforcement was resumed; however, two of the intermediaries appealed it: at the time of writing of the Swedish report, one of them was still not cooperating and was thus facing the possibility of an administrative fine.[328]

---

[323] Swedish country report, Chapter III.C.1.

[324] Belgian country report, Chapter III.C.1.a).

[325] French country report, Chapter III.C.1.b) referring to Article 6, VI of law n°2004-575 of 21 June 2004 regarding confidence in the digital economy.

[326] Swedish country report, Chapter III.C.1.

[327] Czech country report, Chapter III.C.1.a).

[328] Swedish country report, Chapter III.C.2.

ee) Automated procedure of disclosure

Most of the country reports either stated that an automatic procedure does not exist (**German**, **Belgian**, **Czech**, and **Swedish** reports) or provided no information concerning the current arrangements regarding automatic data transfers. The **Swedish** report further noted that the security police had attempted to introduce such procedures several times but faced resistance from the communication providers because the Swedish market is highly competitive and the operators consider a high level of data integrity a competitive advantage that can be advertised in order to attract customers.[329]

b) Collection of subscriber data

aa) Relevant information

The collection of subscriber data is regulated in the national jurisdictions in the following provisions:

- **Germany**: Section 100j StPO
- **Belgium**: Article 46*bis* of the Code of Criminal Procedure
- **Czech Republic** – Sections 88a and 8 of the Code of Criminal Procedure
- **France**: Article L. 33-1, V of the Post and Electronic Communications Code, Articles 77-1-1 (preliminary investigation), 60-1 (flagrancy) and 99-3 (investigating judge) of the Penal Procedure Code
- **Spain**: Articles 588*ter* m and 588*ter* k of LECRIM
- **Sweden**: Electronic Communications Act

bb) Prerequisites of data collection

In most of the countries, court approval is not required for orders concerning the provision of subscriber data. In certain jurisdictions, however, such as **Germany**, the **Czech Republic**, and **Spain**, this rule has some exceptions.

National reporters from **Belgium, France, Sweden**, and the **United Kingdom** stated that no judicial approval is needed in every case: in **Belgium**, the request must be authorised by the public prosecutor or, in extremely urgent cases, by any judicial police officer with the "verbal and prior consent of the public prosecutor";[330] in **France,** the order can be issued either by the prosecutor or by a judicial

---

[329] *Ibid.*

[330] Belgian country report, Chapter III.C.1.b) referring to Articles 46*bis* §2 CCP, 46*bis* §1, 3° CCP.

police officer.[331] In **Sweden**, as stated in the country report, the request for subscriber information is not considered a serious intrusion into personal integrity, so no requirements concerning specific offences have been introduced into Swedish law. Access to subscriber information shall be provided to the law enforcement each time it is necessary for the criminal investigation.[332] In the **United Kingdom**, the requirements are the same as those for traffic data, and a court order is not required.[333]

In other states, the requirement for the court approval depends on different circumstances, such as nature of the data or type of communications provider. In **German** law, Article 100j StPO, in contrast to the collection of traffic data, does not specify special requirements for subscriber data orders in relation to the degree of suspicion or particular type of offence. In general, the data can be ordered without court authorisation upon a request made by the public prosecutor, except when such a request is directed at information concerning access control codes. In the latter case, information may only be requested if the statutory requirements for the use of such data have been met, with the consequence that, in some cases, prior court authorisation is required or other prerequisites must be fulfilled.[334]

The **Czech** report further mentions that the necessity for court approval depends on the type of provider that is requested to supply subscriber data. For orders directed to the providers of IP application-level services, there is no need for judicial authorisation unless the data fall under the obligation of secrecy.[335] For requests to providers at the IP transport level, court authorisation is a necessary prerequisite, and the law stipulates the application of the same substantive and formal requirements as for the collection of traffic data.[336]

In **Spain**, in accordance with Article 588*ter* m LECRIM, the public prosecutor or judicial police are allowed to request subscriber data from the telephone or other communication service directly from the company providing such service. However, in accordance with Article 588*ter* k, in cases concerning offences committed through the Internet, court authorisation is required when "the judicial officers have access to an IP that is being used to commit a crime, and nor the equipment or identity of the user is identified nor is the equipment located."[337]

---

331 French country report, Chapter III.C.1.a).

332 Swedish country report, Chapter III.C.1.

333 UK country report, Chapter III.C.1.

334 German country report, Chapter III.C.1.b).

335 Czech country report, Chapter III.C.1.b).

336 *Ibid.*

337 Spanish country report, Chapter III.C.1.b).

cc) Duty of addressees to disclose information in manual and automated procedures

All of the national reports stated that their legislation provides for the duty to cooperate in case of an order to disclose subscriber data. Concerning the possibility of an automatic procedure, some of the country reporters noted that the application of such a technique is possible. For example, in **Germany**, Section 113 TKG stipulates a manual procedure for the transfer of such data; however, automatic data transfers are possible in some cases in accordance with Section 112 TKG concerning the data mentioned in 111 Subsection 1 S. 1, 3, 4 and in Subsection 2 TKG.[338] In such an automatic procedure, the data can be accessed by the Federal Network Agency, which hands them over to the requesting body.[339] The **Belgian** report stated that the automatic procedure was installed "for electronic communications networks that were granted numbering capacity" by Article 3 §2 of the Royal Decree of 9 January 2003 regarding the legal duty to cooperate with judicial requests regarding electronic communication.[340] This automatic procedure involves access via a secure application over the Internet, which sends the request to the communications operator who must then process the request and address it immediately. The **Spanish** report also noted that subscriber data are provided automatically.[341] In contrast, the **Czech** and **Swedish** country reports explicitly stated that there is no automatic procedure.

c) "Data retention"

While Directive 2006/24/EG on data retention (requiring EU Member States to implement the provisions obliging providers to retain certain communication data) was declared invalid by the ECJ in 2014, all of the countries included in this study adopted the provisions on data retention. Concerning the period for such retention, however, the rules vary. The shortest data retention period can be found in **Germany** – recently, approved legislation makes providers retain data for ten weeks (four weeks for location data). In the **Czech Republic** and **Sweden**, the data retention period is six months. Other countries, such as **Belgium** and **Spain**, have longer retention periods – 12 months. **France** established one year as the term for retaining data. In the **United Kingdom**, the Data Retention and Investigatory Powers Act 2014 (DRIPA) and the Data Retention Regulations 2014 establish a maximum pe-

---

[338] German country report, Chapter III.C.1.b).cc).

[339] *Ibid.*

[340] Belgian country report, Chapter III.C.1.b) referring to Royal Decree of 9 January 2003 regarding the legal duty to cooperate with judicial requests regarding electronic communications, Belgian Official Journal, 10 February 2003.

[341] Spanish country report, Chapter III.C.1.b).

riod of retention of 12 months; however, DRIPA was recently challenged in the High Court and ruled unlawful.

The **German** and **Czech** country reports indicated controversies at the national level concerning the legislation on data retention. This includes challenging the respective laws in court and refinements of the legislation. The **German** legislation on data retention was first introduced in 2007 by Section 113a TKG in an effort to implement Directive 2006/24/EG. This provision was later declared unconstitutional by the judgement of the Federal Constitutional Court of 2.3.2010.[342] Recently, however (in October 2015), the German Parliament voted for the new law, which introduced revised data retention rules. According to the new bill, the time period for data retention has been reduced from six months to ten weeks, with four weeks for location data. Furthermore, the law limits the scope of the data that are to be retained as well as the cases in which the law enforcement can use such data.[343]

The **Czech Republic** also encountered problems when legislating data retention. The first law was introduced on the 1st of May 2005 by the Act on Electronic Communications, which was amended by Act No. 247/2008, following the adoption of the EU Directive 2006. Even after the amendments, the legislation went far beyond the requirements of the directive in its scope and was challenged in the Constitutional Court, which declared the legislation anti-constitutional. The revised data retention legislation was passed in 2012 by Act No. 273/2012 Sb., which introduced stricter rules for data retention.[344]

2. Identification of device ID (IMEI), card number (IMSI), and location of mobile terminal devices

a) Identification of device ID with the help of IMSI catchers

Some of the country reports addressed the issue of the use of the procedural law in their respective countries for the identification of device ID (IMEI), card numbers (IMSI), and the location of mobile terminal devices. Most of the national reporters in this case, however, stated that, when/if such measures are used, they either fall under the general provisions on traffic data or geo-location or are not regulated at all.

Two countries indicated that specific provisions exist in their national laws, with **Germany** being the only country where such data acquisition represents a specially designed measure: it is provided for by Section 100i StPO and limited to IMSI catchers.[345] In **France**, according to the national reporter, IMSI catchers fall under

---

342 German country report, Chapter III.C.1.c).

343 *Ibid.*

344 Czech country report, Chapter III.C.1.c).

345 German country report, Chapter III.C.2.a).

the general provisions on real-time geo-location – Articles 230-32 to 230-44[346] of the Penal Procedure Code – and the police is allowed to use any technical means to achieve this goal.[347]

No specific provisions exist in other jurisdictions. In **Belgium**, there is no legislation concerning the identification of IMEI and IMSI; however, the academic literature considers such measures possible in accordance with Article 46*bis* of the Code of Criminal Procedure concerning access to identification data.[348] In **Spain**, there is also no explicit provision covering such investigative measures, although, according to the national reporter, they are applied by the law enforcement agencies.[349] Furthermore, in Spain, the judicial practice of the Supreme Court stipulated that, since such measures are used to track the presence of mobile devices in certain locations and thus do not affect personal data, court authorisation is not necessary.[350] The use of IMSI catchers is not regulated in **Sweden**; however, they are utilised in practice, although rarely, according to the Swedish report. The **Czech** report stated that such measures are not provided for in the legislation.

b) Location determination via "silent SMS"

The use of "silent SMS," which are not visible to the owner of the mobile phone, to determine location is also possible under the current legislation in some countries included in this study: this possibility is indicated in the **German**, **Belgian**, **French**, and **Spanish** country reports. Such SMS can play a significant role, both in intelligence and in criminal investigation. For example, according to **German** statistics, "in the first half of 2014 alone, the Federal Office for the Protection of the Constitution, the Federal Criminal Police Office and the Federal Police sent a combined 156,466 'silent SMS.'"[351]

Despite the use of this tool, according to the **German** country report, the legal basis for such a measure is still under discussion. In this regard, the main issue is whether Sections 100a ff. StPO in conjunction with Sections 163 Subsection 1, 161 Subsection 1 StPO are applicable to the active generation of data.[352]

In **Belgium**, the use of silent SMS has been approved by the Ministry of Justice as one of the measures falling under the scope of the provisions of Article 88*bis* of

---

346 French country report, Chapter III.C.3.

347 *Ibid.*

348 Belgian country report, Chapter III.C.2.a) referring to Kerkhofs/Van Linthout, *Cybercrime*, Politeia, Brussels, 2013, p. 356.

349 Spanish country report, Chapter III.C.2.a).

350 *Ibid.*

351 German country report, Chapter III.C.2.b).

352 *Ibid.*

the Code of Criminal Procedure on tracing traffic data and localisation.[353] In **Spain**, the possibility to use this tool is not explicitly provided for in the current legislation; however, according to the Spanish reporter, the police use silent SMS in criminal investigations.[354] The **Czech** report noted that silent SMS are not covered in Czech legislation.[355]

D. Access to (temporarily) stored communication data

1. Online searches with the help of remote forensic software

Legislation permitting the use of remote forensic software is both a source of divergences in the national laws and a very heated issue in the current discussion on investigative powers. As was briefly discussed in Chapter III.B.4.b) of this study, only two countries – **France** and **Spain** – explicitly permit and regulate the use of remote forensic tools.

All other national reports highlighted that there is a lack of powers concerning such an investigative measure in the law of criminal procedure and that remote forensic software is an issue of current debate. In **Germany**, the **Czech Republic**, and the **United Kingdom**, the use of remote forensic software has not been clearly addressed in the law of criminal procedure, which raises the question as to whether the use of special tools for remote data capture is permissible. In **Belgium**, the **Netherlands**, and **Sweden**, the use of remote surveillance is possible but it requires physical installation and cannot be planted into a computer system remotely. These problems are now discussed in detail.

– *The use of remote forensic software is explicitly permitted*

Two countries out of eights jurisdictions included in this study, namely **France** and **Spain**, have special legal provisions explicitly regulating the use of remote forensic software. In both countries, however, these measures are considered to be separate powers related to the interception of communications rather than accompanying investigative powers.[356] In **France**, the power of law enforcement to use remote forensic tools was introduced into the Code of Criminal Procedure by the LOPPSI 2 Law in March 2011, with changes made in November 2014. This law introduced Article 706-102-1 of the Criminal Procedure Code that permit the judge, after consultation with the prosecutor, to authorise a police officer to set up a

---

353 Belgian country report, Chapter III.C.2.b).

354 Spanish country report, Chapter III.C.2.b).

355 Czech country report, Chapter III.C.2.

356 See French country report Chapter III; Spanish country report, Chapter III.

technical device, without consent of the person affected, in order to remotely access computer data and record, retain, and transmit them. This concerns data from the input or data recorded and transmitted by audio-visual services. These operations should be performed under the control of the judge and can be applied only in the investigation of serious offences.[357]

The use of remote forensic software in **Spain** has a broader scope, because it covers not only serious crimes but also crimes committed with the use of computer tools. The use of remote forensic software was introduced into Spanish criminal procedural law quite recently by the new Law 13/2015 of 5 October 2015 (LECRIM). In accordance with Article 588*septies* a of LECRIM, the court can give permission to "use of identification data and codes, as well as the installation of a software that allow the electronic remote search, without knowledge of the owner or user, of the contents of a computer, and electronic device, a computer system, or instruments for mass storage of computer data, or databases"[358] in investigations concerning offences committed by criminal organizations, terrorist crimes, crimes committed by means of computer tools or other information technology or telecommunications or a communications service, and an number of other serious offences exclusively listed in the same provision.[359]

– *The use of remote forensic software is not explicitly solved in the law*

The **German** national report highlights in this regard that, despite the absence of a legal provision allowing for remote forensic surveillance for law enforcement purposes, the practice deems targeting the integrity of users' devices in the case of interception "legally permissible" and draws the conclusion that the installation of software to collect and process the data for the purpose of bypassing encryption is possible under the current legislation, as long as the surveillance is restricted exclusively to data emanating from an ongoing telecommunication process (so-called "source communication surveillance").[360] As noted in the report, however, the potential problem in this regard is constituted by the lack of legal grounds for intrusion into the personal/private sphere as a preparatory measure for the interception.[361]

Similarly, the opinion that the use of remote tools might be legally possible under the above-mentioned Section 158 of the Code of Criminal Procedure was voiced by the **Czech** law enforcement representatives at the workshop, despite the

---

357 Information obtained during law enforcement workshop: serious offences in this regard are the crimes listed in Article 706-73 of the Criminal Procedure Code (such as organised crime, drug trafficking, kidnapping, etc.).

358 Spanish country report, Chapter III.D.1.

359 *Ibid.*

360 German country report, Chapter III.B.4.b).

361 German country report, Chapters III.B.2.c) and III.D.1.a).

fact that there are no accompanying investigative measures provided for in Czech procedural law concerning the interception of communications. Furthermore, as stated in the Czech country report, the law enforcement agencies can access private places in a clandestine manner under Section 82 of the Criminal Procedure Code[362] or acquire knowledge of persons and items in a classified manner by technical or other means under Section 158d of the respective code.[363] However, the representatives at the law enforcement workshop stated that there is no experience available with the use of remote forensic software in the Czech Republic.

Another country where the question of the use of the remote forensic software has not yet been solved is the **United Kingdom**. Moreover, the remote access to a computer system by means of remote forensic software is considered highly controversial because of the possible breach of the Computer Misuse Act 1990 and interference with the property rights regulated in Part III of the Police Act 1997. Nevertheless, the Security Service, the Intelligence Service, and the GCHQ can obtain a warrant to interfere directly with domestic property (e.g. a cable or computer) under Section 5 of ISA. The police can also obtain authorisation to interfere with property under the Police Act 1997, Part III. When such equipment is used to enable a covert surveillance operation, which is likely to result in the procurement of private information about a person, Chapter 2.3 of the Code of Practice "Equipment Interference" requires an additional surveillance authorisation under Part 2 of RIPA.

– *Physical installation of remote forensic software is required*

Even if the use of remote surveillance techniques is currently allowed under general criminal procedural provisions, like those in Belgium, The Netherlands, and Sweden, the law enforcement agencies may face practical challenges because of the absence of rules allowing remote installation of such software. In both **Belgium** (Article 90*ter* §2) and in the **Netherlands**, legislation allows clandestine access to private places, e.g., houses, for the purpose of installing equipment to carry out the interception of communications as an accompanying measure. However, as the national reporter points out, in **Belgium**, the parliamentary preparatory works outline the strict prohibition on intrusion into a computer system (hacking) for performance of an interception in accordance with Article 90*ter* of the Belgian Code of Criminal Procedure.[364] Similarly, in the **Netherlands**, remote intrusion into a computer system is also impossible under the current interception regime. As was revealed during the workshop with law enforcement agency representatives, the use

---

362 Czech country report, Chapter III.D.1.

363 *Ibid.*

364 Belgian country report, Chapter III.B.4.b) referring to parliamentary preparatory works, regarding the legislative proposal protecting privacy against the interception of communication and telecommunication, Belgian Senate, 1992–1993, 1 September 1993.

of remote forensic software in both countries is considered to be legal and acceptable in general; however, since the law does not allow accessing of the system remotely, it is necessary to install the equipment in a clandestine manner in a house or private place first.[365] This requirement makes remote surveillance problematic, if not impossible, in many cases.

Law enforcement agencies in **Sweden** face the same practical problems. The Swedish report notes that, while is possible to get permission from the court to break into private places to install the interception equipment, and this provision possibly covers such tools as key loggers, the fact that such access entails costs and technical problems makes such cases very rare.[366] The national reporter further explained that the current debate concerning additional powers to use remote forensic software are being initiated by the Swedish Security Police, which argues that the law empowers agencies to use these techniques. This suggestion was supported by the Commission of Inquiry, which suggested implementing such tools.[367]

2. Search and seizure of stored communication data

a) Provisions on search and seizure

Approaches to the search and seizure of stored data differ at the national level concerning the existence of special provisions covering such investigative measures. While some of the states, like **Spain** and the **United Kingdom**, have implemented specific frameworks for such measures, general rules on search and seizure are applicable to electronic data in other jurisdictions, as is the case in **France**, the **Czech Republic**, and **Sweden**. Some countries, like **Germany,** the **Netherlands**, and **Belgium** use both general and specific provisions, depending on the individual case.

– Both general and special provisions are applicable

In **Germany**, Section 94 of StPO provides for the seizure of objects, which also includes electronic data. Furthermore, Section 110 StPO features a special provision in Para. 3 on the examination of an electronic storage medium, permitting the examination of such a medium on the premises of the person affected by the search to be extended to also cover physically separate storage media insofar as they are accessible from the storage medium. In addition, according to the German country report, the general provisions of Articles 102 and 103 StPO also cover the search of computers and other devices.[368] Similarly, in the **Netherlands**, according to the

---

365 Information obtained at the law enforcement workshop.

366 Swedish country report, Chapter III.B.3.

367 *Ibid.*

368 German country report, Chapter III.D.2.

information obtained during the law enforcement workshop, in addition to the application of a special provision regulating the seizure of (access to) stored electronic data – part 2 of Article 126ng – law enforcement agencies can use search and seizure in accordance with general provisions.

In **Spain** and the **United Kingdom**, the search and seizure of electronic data is covered in special provisions. The new **Spanish** legislation 13/2005 of 5 October 2015 introduced special regulation of the search and seizure of electronic data. Articles 588*sexies* a – 588*sexies* c of LECRIM – covers all possible aspects of such search and seizure, from establishing the requirements for judicial authorisation to the process of making copies of relevant information.[369] In the **United Kingdom**, Section 20 of PACE provides that the "powers of seizure can extend to any information 'accessible from the premises' being searched,"[370] which includes data, even if they are stored remotely. Section 10 of the Computer Misuse Act 1990 authorises law enforcement to "access a computer, program or data without the consent of the person entitled to grant access to the computer, program or data."[371]

In **Belgium**, the search and seizure of electronic data is a controversial issue and the subject of considerable discussion concerning the applicability of different legal provisions. While Belgian law contains a special provision on the seizure of data – Article 39*bis* of the Code of Criminal Procedure –, there is no provision on data searches. The network search provision of Article 88*ter* of the Belgian Criminal Procedure Code is distinguished from online searches and the search of stored communication data in Belgian academic literature. As concluded in the Belgian report, the data search falls under the seizure provision of Article 39*bis* CCP instead of under the rules regulating interception (Article 90*ter* CCP) or other investigative methods, with the network search as the only exception. As the Belgian reporter notes, access to data in a cloud represents this exception because, according to Belgian judicial practice, the provisions of Article 88*ter* are applicable in addition to the interception provisions.[372]

– *General provision apply to search and seizure of data*

The **French** report stated that there are no special provisions on the search and seizure of electronic data; thus, general provisions cover such measures with the same safeguards being applicable.[373] In the **Czech Republic**, the law provides no special regulation concerning the search and seizure of stored communication data. Therefore, the general provisions are also applicable. According to the Czech Re-

369 Spanish country report, Chapter III.D.2.a).

370 UK country report, Chapter III.D.2.

371 *Ibid.*

372 Belgian country report, Chapter III.D.2.b).

373 French country report, Chapter III.D.1.

port, the data itself cannot be seized, so the police have to acquire the storage media under the provision on property seizure or the provisions on house and personal searches.[374] According to the **Swedish** report, application of the general provisions on search and seizure is only be possible as an open measure and only for data delivered to the recipient and stored on his/her device. For any data in possession of the service providers, a warrant for the interception is required.[375]

b) Access to communications in transmission and access to stored communications

One of the most important questions concerning the interception of communications is the possible difference in the protection of communication in transmission versus stored data. In the modern-day world, the transmission of communication can take a few seconds and then the data is stored on the servers of the provider or on the user's device. However, in some countries, the safeguards for access to stored data are lower than those for the protection of communications in transmission. This situation raises significant concerns with regard to how access to stored communication is treated in the national laws of criminal procedure. In practice, this issue is solved differently at the national level. In **Germany** and **France**, the search and seizure provisions are applicable to such situations. Some of the countries, such as the **Netherlands** and **Spain**, provide the same safeguards for stored and transmitted communications, thus solving this problem. Others – **Belgium**, the **Czech Republic**, **Sweden**, and the **United Kingdom** – require an interception warrant or a combination of warrants.

– *Seizure provisions are applicable*

In **Germany**, the question of which legal basis may be used to obtain e-mails that are stored on the communications provider's server shows the blurring of the lines between communications in transmission and stored communications. According to the country report, a recent decision of the Constitutional Court has clarified that, within the context of a search and seizure of the suspect's premises, investigators can request the provider to grant a copy of an e-mail account under the normal seizure provision (§ 94 StPO) without judicial authorisation. A former decision by the Federal Court had determined that, if such a production order is executed without the suspect's knowledge, the request could be made with a judicial warrant under the provision admitting the seizure of postal items (§ 99 StPO). This would also include future communication. Nevertheless, according to the country report, after the aforementioned decision of the Constitutional Court, the academic

374 Czech country report, Chapter III.D.2.

375 Swedish country report, Chapter III.D.

literature argues that a request for stored communication content without the suspect's knowledge can only be made under the same conditions as the interception of telecommunications (§ 100a StPO). This means that a judicial warrant is needed and that the investigation must be related to a specific qualified criminal offence listed in § 100a Abs. 2 StPO.[376]

In **France**, although the safeguards for search and seizure are considerably lower than those provided for for the interception of communications,[377] seizure in practice is an applicable measure. As shared by the French law enforcement agency representatives during the workshop, there are several approaches to obtaining access to e-mails stored in mailboxes. When e-mails are stored on the server of the provider, the police can use the production order[378] to obtain the content of stored communications. If the data and e-mails are not stored on the servers of a communications provider – for example, when the suspect uses a program that downloads e-mails and deletes them from the server – one possible option is search and seizure.[379] The French country report states that the practice of using the seizure warrant for e-mails was rendered legal by a decision of the Court of Cassation of 8 July 2015,[380] which states that "collection, registration and transcription of correspondences sent or received by telecommunication means before the date of the written decision of correspondences interception taken by the investigating judge (...) must be performed in compliance with provisions regulating seizure."[381]

– *The same safeguards are established for both types of communications*

In the **Netherlands**, according to the Dutch law enforcement representatives, the safeguards for interception and access to stored communications are the same; thus, it is not easier to obtain access to the content of a communication after transmission has ended. Access to the stored content is provided for by part 2 of Article 126ng and has the same requirements and safeguards as interception of communications, thus requiring authorisation by a judge. Similarly, according to the **Spanish** country report, the new legislation in Spain provides for the same safeguards for both communications in transmission and stored communications. The only issue that might arise in this regard, as the national reporter notes, is the lack of clarity of the

376 German country report, Chapter III.D.2.d).

377 French country report, Chapter III.D.1.

378 Art. 60-1, 77-1-1, 99-3 of the Penal Procedure Code.

379 Art. 56 of the Penal Procedure Code.

380 French country report, Chapter III.B.2.b) referring to Court of Cassation, criminal chamber, 8 July 2015, available at http://www.legalis.net/spip.php?page=jurisprudence-decision&id_article=4696 [last accessed 10/2016].

381 Translated from the French by the country reporter, see French country report, Chapter III.B.2.b).

new legislation, which does not distinguish between ordinary files and stored communications.[382]

– *Interception warrant or combination of warrants is necessary to access certain types of stored communications*

The practice of accessing certain stored communications with either an interception warrant or a combination of warrants, as found from analysis of the country reports and information from the law enforcement workshops in **Belgium**, the **Czech Republic**, **Sweden**, and the **United Kingdom**, results from disputes over the differences between stored communications and communications in transmission and the lack of legal safeguards for the latter. Each country, however, solves this situation in a different way.

In **Belgium**, according to the country report, the difference between a stored e-mail and an e-mail in transmission is a current matter of dispute in the academic literature. While some of the scholars consider certain types of stored e-mails, e.g., those arriving to online mailboxes, as being the subject of an interception warrant, others argue that interception is not possible once transmission has ended.[383] According to the national reporter, the parliamentary preparatory works also stated that a stored e-mail cannot be the subject of interception but falls under the provisions on search and seizure (Article 39*bis* CCP) or on network searches (Article 88*ter* CCP).[384] However, the information gained at the law enforcement workshop revealed that, in practice, the blurring of borders between stored communications and communications in transition require investigators to apply for interception warrants for access to the content of the web e-mail accounts. According to Belgian law enforcement representatives, in order to search mail accounts (e.g., Gmail), two different provisions are used in combination: Article 88*ter* (network search) and Article 90*ter* (interception) because a new e-mail can arrive during the search. If the law enforcement agencies are not sure whether new communication will take place, they are advised to obtain two warrants, because the safeguards for a network search are lower than those for the interception of communications.

The **Czech** country report states that stored data and communication in transmission have different levels of protection, with the latter enjoying a higher degree of applicable safeguards.[385] The Code of Criminal Procedure, according to the national reporter, is too old to be able to address the issue of blurred borders between

---

382 Spanish country report, Chapter III.D.2.b).

383 Belgian country report, Chapter II.B.2.c).

384 Belgian country report, Chapter II.B.2.c, referring to parliamentary preparatory works, regarding the modification of the Act of 30 June 1994 protecting privacy against the interception of communication and telecommunication, Belgian Chamber of Parliament, 1996–1997, 29 May 1998.

385 Czech country report, Chapter II.B.2.b).

stored communications and those in transmission.[386] At the law enforcement workshop, the Czech representatives stated that, because of the high degree of fragmentation of the approaches to accessing stored e-mail content, this issue was addressed in the special recommendations of the Supreme Public Prosecutor's Office for the purpose of unifying legal practice. The application of the legal provisions recommended by this document depends on the nature of the communications that are to be seized or intercepted. When content has been localised on a seized data carrier before the time of its seizure, an interception order is not necessary. For communications that may arrive after seizure of the medium, the use of the seizure order or – as carried out in practice – the order to obtain traffic data is not sufficient in such cases. For such acquisitions of data in mailboxes, the Supreme Public Prosecutor's Office recommends applying for court authorisation of surveillance of persons and items according to Section 158d (1), (3) of the Code of Criminal Procedure.[387]

In **Sweden**, provisions regulating seizure are applicable only to data delivered to the recipient and stored on his/her own device. The interception warrant, according to the national reporter, is required for any data stored on the servers of the providers.[388] Swedish law enforcement representatives at the national workshop confirmed this approach. According to them, this model of authorisation was developed as the result of a long discussion in Sweden on how to prove whether an e-mail has already reached the recipient, and it was intended to solve the problem of read/unread e-mails. Interestingly, the Swedish approach to search and seizure and interception differs, depending on whether a communications provider is a regulated entity or not. Whereas an interception order is always needed for communications stored on the servers of regulated providers, law enforcement agencies can use a search and seizure warrant for access to data stored by information society service intermediaries, because these providers are not considered communication services. Furthermore, Swedish law enforcement representatives noted that, in order to avoid any controversies, the seized device should immediately be disconnected from all networks, so that no new communication can arrive. It should be noted that the requirements for search and seizure in Sweden are also lower than for interception: according to the Swedish representatives, in the case of search and seizure, there is no need for a court order. The requirement for search and seizure is that the offence must be punishable with imprisonment, without a minimum threshold.

---

386 *Ibid.*

387 Supreme Public Prosecutor's Office, 1 SL 760/2014, Collection of Explanatory Opinions of the Supreme Public Prosecutor's Office, Brno, January 26, 2015, File no. 1/2015. Czech representatives provided the document after the law enforcement workshop.

388 Swedish country report, Chapter III.C.

In the **United Kingdom**, according to the information obtained during the law enforcement workshop, the approach to the seizure of stored e-mails is determined by Section 2(7) of RIPA, which defines the time during which a communication is being transmitted as "any time when the system by means of which the communication is being, or has been, transmitted is used for storing it in a manner that enables the intended recipient to collect it or otherwise to have access to it." This means that, in accordance with chapter 2.14 of the Code of Practice "Interception of Communications," a warrant can be used to obtain both communications that are in the process of transmission and those that are being stored in the transmission system. Furthermore, according to the decision of the Court of Appeal,[389] communication continues to be in the course of transmission and is protected by the prohibition on intercepting communications before the intended recipient collects it. Section 1(5)(c) of RIPA also provides that stored communications can be accessed by a lawful authority by means of an existing statutory power other than a RIPA warrant, e.g., a production order (under the Police and Criminal Evidence Act 1984) or a search warrant (Code of Practice "Interception of Communications", chapter 2.15). Such warrants are limited to communication that has already taken place and do not include future communications. All coercive powers to access objects (search, seizure, production) require a court order; additional safeguards are thus applicable.

c) Open and clandestine access to stored data

Some of the national reports also discussed the issue of the openness of the search and seizure provisions. The country reports from **Germany**, **Belgium**, and **Sweden** stated that access to data under the search and seizure rules can be carried out only as an open measure.[390] In **Spain** and **France**, if access is not carried out under the remote forensic software provision, the search is also considered an open measure. French legislation requires a search to be carried out "in presence of the person in whose domicile the search is made or of two witnesses,"[391] and Spanish law stipulates that the inhabitant or owner be present.[392]

Clandestine search and seizure is allowed under the legislation of the **United Kingdom** and the **Czech Republic**. In the **United Kingdom**, according to the national reporter, access to stored data is possible without informing the suspect if it can be proven that such notification "would prejudice the investigation due to a

---

389 *Edmondson & Ors v R.* [2013] EWCA Crim 1026.

390 See German country report, Chapter III.D.2.e); Belgian country report, Chapter III.D.2.d) and Swedish country report Chapter III.C.

391 French country report, Chapter II.D.1.

392 Spanish country report, Chapter III.D.2.c).

realistic threat that the evidence could be destroyed."[393] The **Czech** report stated that the clandestine search and seizure of data is permitted under Section 158d of the Code of Criminal Procedure, which provides for surveillance of persons and items.[394]

3. Duties to cooperate: production and decryption orders

Most of the countries included in this study do not allow an order to provide a decryption key to be addressed to the suspect. The **German** report states that, in this regard, the law of criminal procedure does not provide for any specific rules that would allow requiring the decryption of encrypted data.[395] In **France** and in **Sweden**, provisions on a duty to cooperate are explicitly not applicable to the suspect.[396] In the **Czech Republic**, according to the national reporter, the provision of a decryption order is not regulated and the practice is uncertain; however, it could be assumed that the requirement for the suspect to provide the decryption key would contradict the prohibition on self-incrimination.[397]

In **Belgium**, the duty of the suspect to obey the order to provide the decryption key is a matter of current dispute because, while 88quater §2 CCP in relation to the network search provides that the duty to cooperate is not applicable to the suspect, other provisions requiring assistance do not mention the suspect as an exception. Some practitioners thus argue that other forms of cooperation in which decryption is required are permissible concerning a suspect, too.[398] As noted in the Belgian report, however, even these arguments are made with the reservation that they have to pass the human rights test.[399]

The **United Kingdom** is the only country in which a suspect, in accordance with Part III of RIPA, might be subject to an order requiring him/her to either "provide information in an intelligible format or to disclose the 'key' to access the protected data."[400] This is not considered self-incrimination in the light of judgement *R v S and A* [2008] EWCA Crim 2177.[401]

---

393 UK country report, Chapter III.D.2.

394 Czech country report, Chapter III.D.2.d).

395 German country report, Chapter III.D.3.

396 French country report, Chapter III.D.2.b); Swedish country report, Chapter III.C.

397 Czech country report, Chapter III.D.3.

398 Belgian country report, Chapter III.D.3, referring to Kerkhofs/Van Linthout, *Cybercrime*, Politeia, Brussels, 2013, p. 369.

399 *Ibid.*

400 UK country report, Chapter III.D.3.

401 *Ibid.*

IV. Use of electronic communications data in judicial proceedings

In all of the countries, except the **United Kingdom**, the intercepted material, including data obtained abroad, can be used as evidence in criminal proceedings. However, even in the **United Kingdom**, in accordance with Section 18 of RIPA, data from interception can be used if it is required for the aim of "assessing the fairness of criminal proceedings."[402] In addition, in the **United Kingdom**, interception data received from a foreign law enforcement agency within the framework of mutual legal assistance and data originating from private interception activities may also be admissible.[403]

As far as the issue of the use of preventive or intelligence information in criminal proceedings is concerned, only **Belgian** law explicitly allows data from intelligence services and preventive activities to be used in criminal proceedings.[404] **Spanish** court practice also considers intelligence reports to be admissible as expert evidence in some cases.[405] In **Germany**, the use of such material is generally prohibited under the principle of purpose limitation; however, in some cases, the product of this interception may be admissible if an appropriate measure exists in the law of criminal procedure.[406] In contrast, the **Czech** and **Swedish** reports stated that such data is not admissible.[407]

Formal requirements and the provisions on challenging the admissibility of evidence might vary from detailed requirements to very general rules, depending on the jurisdiction. In most of the countries, such rules either fall under the general provisions regulating evidence in criminal proceedings or have been developed in judicial practice concerning the use of the interception product in the courts.

402 UK country report, Chapter IV.1.

403 UK country report, Chapter IV.1, referring to *R v P and ors* [2001] 2 All ER 58 and Attorney-General's Reference (No 5 of 2002] sub nom *R v W* (2005) 1 AC 167.

404 Belgian country report, Chapter IV.

405 Spanish country report, Chapter IV.

406 German country report, Chapter IV.

407 Czech country report, Chapter IV and Swedish country report, Chapter IV.

V. Exchange of Intercepted Electronic Communications Data between Foreign Countries

A. Legal basis for mutual legal assistance

Mutual legal assistance in lawful interception of electronic communications in the national jurisdictions included in this study is part of a more complex issue of mutual legal assistance in criminal matters. This regime can be governed by international treaties, which a country is a party to, by bilateral agreements on mutual legal assistance, which vary from country to country, and by national legislation in this field.

With regard to the international treaties that provide for mutual legal assistance in the interception of communications, most of the national reports listed such treaties as the European Convention on Mutual Assistance in Criminal Matters of 20 April 1959, the Council of Europe Convention on Cybercrime 2001, the Convention of 29 May 2000 on Mutual Assistance in Criminal Matters between the Member States of the European Union, and the United Nations Convention against Transnational Organised Crime of 15 November 2000. **Belgium** and the **Netherlands** are also parties to the Treaty between the Kingdom of Belgium, the Grand Duchy of Luxembourg, and the Kingdom of The Netherlands concerning extradition and mutual assistance in criminal matters (Benelux Treaty) 1962.[408]

In addition to international instruments, the countries have various bilateral treaties on mutual legal assistance that aim to further strengthen mutual legal assistance. The number and content of such treaties vary from one country to another. Some of them, such as the supplementary treaties between **Germany** and the **Czech Republic** (2000) and between **Germany** and Poland (2003) outline specific rules on the interception of communication, as indicated by the German country report.[409]

The national legislation governing mutual legal assistance in criminal matters includes the following laws:[410]

- **Germany**: Act on International Cooperation in Criminal Matters of 23 December 1982
- **Belgium**: Belgian Act of 9 December 2004 concerning international mutual legal assistance in criminal matters
- **Czech Republic**: Act No. 104/2013 Sb., on Mutual Judicial Assistance in Criminal Matters

408 Belgian country report, Chapter V.A.1.

409 German country report, Chapter V.A.2.

410 German country report, Chapter V.A.1; Belgian country report, Chapter V.A.3; Czech country report, Chapter V.A.3; French country Report, Chapter V.A.1; Swedish country report, Chapter V.A; UK country report, Chapter V.

- **France**: Articles 694 et seq. of the Penal Procedure Code
- **Spain**: Law 23/2014 of 20 November on Mutual Recognition of Criminal Decisions in the European Union
- **Sweden**: Act on International Legal Assistance (2000: 562)
- **United Kingdom**: The Crime (International Co-operation) Act 2003.

Most of the national reporters also indicated that mutual legal assistance in interception of communications is possible without a bilateral or multilateral treaty: in **Germany**, **Belgium**, the **Czech Republic**, and **Sweden**, according to the country reporters, the national laws providing for general rules on mutual legal assistance enable interception requests on the basis of general clauses. The **Czech** national reporter states that the Ministry of Justice, when addressing such a request, needs to confirm reciprocity, which, according to some, might be preferable for the execution of the request because it allows for less formalities in the procedure.[411] In contrast, the **Swedish** country report remarks that, while the state requesting mutual legal assistance in accordance with Swedish national law need not be party to the treaty acceded to by Sweden, accession to treaties facilitates easier procedures for addressing mutual legal assistance requests.[412]

The **United Kingdom** has a very distinct approach to mutual legal assistance in lawful interception compared to other jurisdictions included in this study. As the law enforcement representatives shared during the workshop, as far as the interception of communications is concerned, the incidence of mutual legal assistance is relatively low, because the intercepted material cannot be used in court proceedings. Furthermore, the fact that mutual legal assistance in the United Kingdom is the responsibility of the prosecutor, and interception generally the domain of the police, can influence outgoing requests in this context.

B. Requirements and procedure for EU mutual legal assistance, including direct data transfers

The complex legal regime of international and bilateral treaties, together with the national legislation of a particular country, creates a multifaceted framework of approaches to the incoming and outgoing requests for the interception of communications. The most harmonised procedure among the states included in this study can be found in the cooperation with the Member States of the European Union under the framework established by the Convention on Mutual Assistance in Criminal Matters between the Member States of the European Union of 2000. The for-

---

[411] Czech country report, Chapter V.A.2.

[412] Swedish country report, Chapter V.A.

mal requirements for interception requests are outlined in Art 18 (3) and include the following:

"(a) an indication of the authority making the request;

(b) confirmation that a lawful interception order or warrant has been issued in connection with a criminal investigation;

(c) information for the purpose of identifying the subject of this interception;

(d) an indication of the criminal conduct under investigation;

(e) the desired duration of the interception; and

(f) if possible, the provision of sufficient technical data, in particular the relevant network connection number, to ensure that the request can be met."

On the national level, in most of the countries, the competent authorities include either an investigating judge or a prosecutor or both. In some cases, addressing the EU request can also involve participation on the part of the Ministry of Justice.

In **Germany**, the authority responsible for taking the decision on whether to respond to the request for mutual legal assistance from an EU Member State is the (head of the) prosecutors' offices at the Regional Courts, acting "in lieu" of the federal authorities.[413] Legislation in some of the federal states grants such a competence to the prosecutors' offices only if the international agreement allows for direct transmission of the mutual legal assistance requests, which is the case for requests received in accordance with the EU Convention 2000 or some of the bilateral treaties with the EU Member States, e.g., those between Germany and the Czech Republic or Poland. The enforcement of the intra-EU requests rests with the same authority that would normally enforce it in domestic cases, meaning that, in the case of an interception, the prosecutors' offices at the Regional Courts must ask the investigating judge at the local court for judicial authorisation. When the local court decides that the request does not meet the requirements for the mutual legal assistance, the Higher Regional Court resolves the case on the admissibility of the request.[414]

Like Germany (except for the fact that as a federal state Germany has a more complex system of competence distribution between the federation and the states), the responsible authorities for handling incoming requests in **Belgium** and **Sweden** are the public prosecutor and the investigating judge.[415] Some exceptions from these general rules in Belgium include cases in which regulation requires the request from the EU Member State to be forwarded to the Minister of Justice for consideration if it could be refused under certain conditions provided for in the national law.[416]

---

413 German country report, Chapter V.B.1.a).

414 *Ibid.*

415 Belgian country report, Chapter V.B.1.a, Swedish country report, Chapter V.B.

416 Belgian country report, Chapter V.B.1.a).

In the **Czech Republic**, the legislation defines two stages of the addressing request for mutual legal assistance: pre-trial and trial. In the pre-trial stage, the responsible authority is the Department of International Affairs of the Supreme Public Prosecutor's Office whereas, on the trial stage, the request is processed by the International Department for Criminal Matters of the Ministry of Justice of the Czech Republic.[417] In **Spain**, despite the fact that incoming requests from EU Member States fall under the authority of the competent investigating judge, in practice, the requesting authority might forward it to the National Court, which has jurisdiction over the entire territory. Sometimes, the mutual legal assistance requests also land in the International Cooperation Unit of the Public Prosecutor's Office, which forwards it to the investigating judge.[418]

As regards outgoing requests, the national system mirrors the regulation for addressing incoming requests. For example, in **Germany** and the **Czech Republic**, preparation of a request for the interception of communications in another EU Member State is completed by the public prosecutor but, in **Spain**, where many responsibilities for addressing mutual legal assistance requests rest with judiciary authorities, it is up to the investigating judge who is responsible for sending the request.[419]

One of the most complex issues related to EU cooperation on the interception of communications concerns direct data transfers. While Articles 18 and 19 of the EU Convention on Mutual Assistance in Criminal Matters 2000 enable such transmissions, more than a decade after the adoption of this instrument, direct transfers are rarely used in practice, and the national approaches to this matter vary significantly. While the **German** and **Czech** national reporters refer to the possibility of direct data transfers in accordance with their national legislations,[420] the **Spanish** and **Belgian** country reports state otherwise. The **Belgian** reporter directly indicates that such transfers are currently considered impossible, as stated in a circular of 28 December 2005 from the Board of Prosecutors General.[421] The **Spanish** national report notes that the current national legal framework and technical regulations do not enable law enforcement agencies from another EU Member State to "accede directly to the data resulting from the telecommunications interception."[422] Other countries, like **Sweden**, still require "legal, and organisational national reform measures" to perform direct data transfers. Although, according to the national re-

---

[417] Czech country report, Chapter V.B.1.

[418] Spanish country report, Chapter V.B.1.

[419] German country report, Chapter V.B.2; Czech country report, Chapter V.B.2; Spanish country report, Chapter V.B.2.

[420] German country report, Chapter V.B.4.a; Czech country report, Chapter V.B.4.

[421] Belgian country report, Chapter V.B.3.

[422] Spanish country report, Chapter V.B.4.

porter, the required reforms the Swedish law has to undergo to enable direct transfers are "relatively little", they still shall be "assuming there is mutual trust."[423]

Thus, despite the existence of the international framework and – in some countries – national regulation enabling direct transfers, both the national reports and the workshops with law enforcement agency representatives revealed that, in practice, such transfers rarely take place. For example, the Czech national reporter commented that, although the law permits direct transfers, the "Czech Republic is poorly prepared for such a solution and subsequent transfers are mostly used."[424] Most of the jurisdictions included in this study do not execute such transfers on a regular basis or, even if they are performed, the law enforcement authorities still encounter problems, e.g., an unexpected cut in direct transfers in the middle of an intercepted conversation. Instead of direct data transmissions, the national law enforcement authorities use different ways of handling intercepted material – from downloading it safely to the FTP servers to sending it to hard drives or other mediums.

C. European Investigation Order

One of the major issues addressed by several of the national reporters is the question of whether Directive 2014/41/EU regarding the European Investigation Order in criminal matters would significantly change mutual legal assistance in the interception of communications. At the time of writing this comparative report, the European Investigation Order directive had yet to be implemented into the national legislation of most of the jurisdictions included in this study. Several national reporters – **Czech**, **German**, and **Swedish** –, expressed the opinion that the new regulation will not significantly challenge or influence the current complex regime of mutual legal assistance in the matter of interception requests, since it will not fundamentally change the current legal system of judicial approval or the grounds for refusal of a request for the interception of communications.[425]

---

[423] Swedish country report, Chapter V.B.

[424] Czech country report, Chapter V.B.4.

[425] Czech country report, Chapter V.C.; German country report, Chapter V.C; Swedish country report, Chapter V.B.

List of Abbreviations

BND	Bundesnachrichtendienst (German Federal Intelligence Service)
CCP	Belgian Code of Criminal Procedure
CJP	Swedish Code of Judicial Procedure
CNI	Centro National de Inteligencia (Spanisch National Intelligence Centre)
DRIPA	Data Retention and Investigatory Powers Act
ECA	Swedish Electronic Communications Act
ECJ	European Court of Justice
FRA	Försvarets radio anstalt (Swedish National Defence Radio Establishment)
GCHQ	Government Communications Headquarters (British signal intelligence service)
IAP	Internet Access Provider
ICT	Information and Communication Technology
IMEI	International Mobile Equipment Identity
IMSI	International Mobile Subscriber Identity
IP	Internet Protocol
ISP	Internet Service Provider
LEA	Law Enforcement Agency
LECRIM	Ley de Enjuiciamiento Criminal (Spanish Criminal Procedure Code)
LOPPSI	Loi d'orientation et de programmation pour la sécurité intérieure (French Law on Orientation and Programming Performance of Homeland Security)
MAD	Miltärischer Abschirmdienst (German Military Counterintelligence Service)
PACE	British Police and Criminal Evidence Act
PTS	Post och telestyrelsen (Swedish Post and Telecom Authority)
RIPA	Regulation of Investigatory Powers Act
SIM	Intelligence and security services
SMS	Short Message Service

SOU	Statens offentliga utredningar (Swedish Government Official Reports)
StGB	Strafgesetzbuch (German Criminal Code)
StPO	Strafprozessordnung (German Code of Criminal Procedure)
TKG	Telekommunikationsgesetz (German Telecommunications Act)
TKÜV	Telekommunikations-Überwachungsverordnung (German Telecommunications Interceptions Ordinance)
TR TKÜV	Technische Richtlinie TKÜV (Technical Directive TKÜV)
VoIP	Voice over Internet Protocol

Part 3
Country Reports

Belgium*

National Rapporteurs:
Gertjan Boulet
Paul De Hert

* This report reflects legislation and case law as of September 2016.

Contents

I. Security Architecture and the Interception of Telecommunication

A. Law Enforcement Institutions and Security Services with Powers of Telecommunication Interception

1. National security architecture

The Belgian national security architecture includes (preventive) police law, (preventive and reactive) criminal law, and intelligence (state security) law. All of these legal regimes provide coercive powers for the interception of electronic communications.

The prerequisites under general police law for the interception of electronic communications differ from the other legal regimes, which contain stricter rules and authorization, more particularly: in criminal law, prior authorization by the public prosecutor (during the preliminary investigation/inquiry phase, or during the investigation/instruction phase) or by the investigating judge (during the investigation/instruction phase); in intelligence law, prior authorization (for exceptional intelligence collection methods) or *a posteriori* authorization (for specific intelligence collection methods) by the administrative commission responsible for monitoring the specific and exceptional intelligence collection methods used by the intelligence and security services (SIM commission).

The prerequisites for the interception of the content of communication in transmission under criminal law and intelligence law are largely similar.[1] However, the interception powers under intelligence law provide special protection for journalists, unlike the interception powers under criminal law.

[1] Article 90*ter* of the Code of Criminal Procedure, and Article 18/2 §2, 7° of the Act of 30 November 1998 on the Intelligence and Security Services.

2. Powers for the interception of telecommunication[2]

a) Law of criminal procedure

aa) Normal investigation methods

The legal provisions for intercepting electronic communications under (reactive) criminal law are provided in the Code of Criminal Procedure (hereinafter: CCP): data seizure (Article 39*bis* CCP), the collection of identification data of electronic communications (Article 46*bis* CCP), tracing of traffic data, and localization of electronic communications (Article 88*bis* CCP), the network search (Article 88*ter* CCP), and wiretapping/monitoring, including direct monitoring/eavesdropping[3] (Article 90*ter* §1 CCP).

bb) Special investigation methods and any other methods of investigation

The Act of 6 January 2003 concerning special investigation methods and any other methods of investigation[4] introduced three *special investigation methods* and five *other investigation methods* into the CCP.

The two *special investigation methods* relevant for the interception of electronic communications are observation (Article 47*sexies* CCP) and infiltration (Article 47*octies* CCP).

The two *other investigation methods* relevant for the interception of electronic communications are looking-in operations (Article 46*quinquies* and 89*ter* CCP), and the power to enter a house or a private place to enable eavesdropping with technical means (Article 90*ter* §1, 2° CCP). Hereinafter, we use the term monitoring measure to refer to both the general wiretapping measure under Article 90*ter* §1, 1° CCP and the measure to enter a house or a private place to enable eavesdropping with technical means under Article 90*ter* §1, 2° CCP.

---

2 The answers to the questions under this section are partially based on Gertjan Boulet's contribution to an EU-funded project on surveillance: Gertjan Boulet, "Regulating Surveillance: The Belgian case," Deliverable 2.3 (The Legal Perspective) for the EU-funded project Increasing Resilience in Surveillance Studies (IRISS), pp. 49–52, 31 January 2013, available at http://irissproject.eu/wp-content/uploads/2013/04/Legal-perspectives-of-surveillance-and-democracy-report-D2.3-IRISS.pdf.

3 The monitoring measure in Article 90*ter* §1, 1° CCP also covers direct eavesdropping from outside a home or private place. Article 90*ter* §1, 2° CCP, however, describes the power to enter a house or a private place to enable eavesdropping by technical means. See Chris Van den Wyngaert, *Strafrecht, Strafprocesrecht & Internationaal Strafrecht in hoofdlijnen* (An Outline of Criminal Law, Criminal Procedural Law & International Criminal Law), Antwerp-Apeldoorn, Maklu, 2006, p. 982, footnote 4012.

4 Act of 6 January 2003 concerning special investigation methods and any other methods of investigation, *Belgian Official Journal*, 12 May 2003, entry into force on 22 May 2003.

cc) Cooperation with individuals and the private sector

For the execution of the above-mentioned investigation operations, Belgian law enforcement agencies can cooperate with individuals and the private sector (Article 39*bis*, Article 46*bis*, Article 88*bis*, Article 88*quater*, Article 90*quater* §§2, 4 CCP). Belgian law enforcement agencies can also cooperate with so-called closed user groups,[5] on the basis of Articles 122, 125, and 127 of the Electronic Communications Act,[6] and with service providers acting as a mere conduit, catching, and hosting on the basis of Articles XII.17 to XII.20 of the Code of Economic Law.[7] Furthermore, in specific cases, judicial authorities can order a temporary surveillance period for Internet service providers acting as a mere conduit, catching, and hosting (Article XII.20 of the Code of Economic Law).

dd) Data retention

The general data retention (preservation) provision is Article 126 of the Electronic Communications Act of 13 June 2005.[8] However, on 11 June 2015, the Belgian Constitutional Court invalidated Article 126 of the Electronic Communications Act. A new Belgian data retention law of 29 May 2016 entered into force on 28 July 2016.[9]

A Royal Decree of 19 September 2013 lists the types of data subject to data retention.[10] Article 9 §7 of the Electronic Communications Act provides that a specific Royal Decree shall address the matter of data retention for closed user groups.

---

5 Article 9 §5-6 of the Electronic Communications Act provides that the duty to notify the Belgian Institute for Postal Services and Telecommunications does not apply to providers and resellers of electronic communications networks or services not exceeding the public domain (§5), or to providers and resellers of electronic communications networks or services either exclusively targeted at legal entities in which the provider or seller has a controlling interest, or provided to a natural or legal persons as mere support and accessory (§6).

6 Article 9 §7 of the Electronic Communications Act of 13 June 2005 provides that a specific Royal Decree shall address the matter of the cooperation between law enforcement agencies and closed user groups: Act of 13 June 2005 on electronic communications, *Belgian Official Journal*, 20 June 2005, entry into force on 30 June 2005.

7 The Code of Economic Law of 28 February 2013, *Belgian Official Journal*, 29 March 2013, entry into force on 12 December 2013.

8 As amended by the Belgian Communication Act of 30 July 2013 amending Articles 2, 126, and 145 of the Act of 13 June 2005 on electronic communications and Article 90*decies* of the Code of Criminal Procedure, *Belgian Official Journal*, 23 August 2013, entry into force on 2 September 2013.

9 Act of 29 May 2016 on the collection and retention of data in the electronic communications sector, *Belgian Official Journal*, 18 July 2016, entry into force on 28 July 2016.

10 Royal Decree of 19 September 2013 regarding the execution of Article 126 of the Act of 13 June 2005 on electronic communications, *Belgian Official Journal*, 8 October 2013, entry into force on 19 September 2013.

Federal Magistrate Jan Kerkhofs and Investigating Judge Philippe Van Linthout argue that Belgian providers of electronic communication services or networks, with no notification duty, are currently released from data retention obligations, taking into account the lack of a specific Royal Decree.[11] For the same reason, the service providers that act as a mere conduit or provide caching and hosting activities under the Code of Economic Law are currently released from data retention obligations.

Finally, notaries, bailiffs, and accountants are subject to specific data retention and production obligations, provided in Article 7 and under chapter III of the Law of 11 January 1993 on preventing misuse of the financial system for purposes of laundering money and terrorism financing.[12]

b) Preventive law

The legal provisions for intercepting electronic communications under (preventive) police law are the general provision on crime detection and evidence gathering by the police (Article 8 CCP), and a specific provision on access by the police to publicly accessible places (Article 26 of the Act on the Police Function).[13]

The legal provision for intercepting electronic communications under (preventive) criminal law is the provision on proactive investigation (Article 28*bis* §2 CCP), which reads as follows:[14]

> §2. The preliminary investigation extends to proactive investigation. This is understood, in order to prosecute perpetrators of criminal offences, the detection, collection, recording and processing of data and intelligence on the basis of a reasonable presumption of punishable acts yet to be committed or already committed but not yet discovered, and that are or would be committed in the framework of a criminal organization as defined by law, or constitute or would constitute crimes or misdemeanours referred to in Article 90ter, §§2, 3 and 4. The use of proactive investigation requires prior written approval by the public prosecutor, the labour prosecutor (or the federal prosecutor) given under their respective jurisdiction, without prejudice to compliance with the specific legal provisions that regulate special investigative methods and other methods.

Delbrouck (attorney-at-law) underlines that the coercive powers of wiretapping, observation, and entering private places within the framework of a looking-in operation cannot be used by the public prosecutor during the preliminary investigation

[11] Jan Kerkhofs and Philippe Van Linthout, *Cybercrime*, Brussels, Politeia, 2013, p. 396.

[12] Act of 11 January 1993 on preventing use of the financial system for purposes of laundering money and terrorism financing, *Belgian Official Journal*, 9 February 1993, entry into force on 1 December 1993, available at http://www.imolin.org/doc/amlid/Belgium_law_11_January_1993.pdf

[13] Act of 5 August 1992 on the Police Function, *Belgian Official Journal*, 22 December 1992, entry into force on 1 March 1993.

[14] Author's own translation of the Belgian law related to the interception of electronic communications. All subsequent translations of statutory texts are the author's own.

phase, hence also not during proactive investigation, on the basis of Article 28*septies* CCP, which explains the so-called legal notion of mini-instruction:[15]

> The public prosecutor can request the investigating judge, without the initiation of a judicial investigation, to perform any investigative measure for which only the investigating judge is competent, with the exception of an arrest warrant provided in Article 16 of the Law of 20 July 1990 on remand custody, the fully anonymous testimony referred to in Article 86bis, the monitoring measure referred to in Article 90ter [interception], the investigative measures referred to in Article 56bis, second paragraph [observation] and 89ter [looking-in operations] and the house search. After the execution of the investigative measure carried out by the investigating judge, he shall decide whether to return the file to the public prosecutor responsible for the continuation of the investigation or to continue the whole investigation himself, in which case one shall further act in accordance with the provisions of Chapter VI of this book. This decision cannot be appealed.

Furthermore, Kennes (attorney-at-law) notes that, whereas the proactive investigation can be activated following a "reasonable presumption of punishable acts," the monitoring measure (Article 90*ter* CCP) is reserved for cases in which there are "serious indications that the offense is a criminal offense."[16]

Van den Wyngaert, however, notes that the distinction between proactive and reactive investigation is not always an easy one to draw and that the European Court of Human Rights (ECtHR) in the case *Lüdi v. Switzerland*[17] held that a proactive wiretapping measure, if based on law, is not incompatible with the European Convention on Human Rights (ECHR).[18]

c) Law of intelligence agencies

The legal provisions for intercepting electronic communications under intelligence law are provided in the Act of 30 November 1998 on the Intelligence and Security Services.[19] Ordinary collection methods include: intelligence collection with private actors (Article 16), observation and search without technical means of public places and private places accessible to the public (Article 16/1).

---

[15] Luk Delbrouck, "De proactieve recherche: een nieuw middel in de strijd tegen de georganiseerde criminaliteit?" (The proactive investigation: a new method in the fight against organized crime), *Jura Falconis*, 1999-2000, no. 1, pp. 121–158, available at https://www.law.kuleuven.be/jura/art/36n1/delbrouck.htm#N_136_

[16] Laurent Kennes, *Manuel de la preuve en matière pénale* (Manual on evidence in criminal matters), Mechelen, Kluwer, 2009, p. 209.

[17] ECtHR, *Lüdi v. Switzerland*, 15 June 1992, Grand Chamber, no. 12433/86, via http://hudoc.echr.coe.int/

[18] Chris Van den Wyngaert, *Strafrecht, Strafprocesrecht & Internationaal Strafrecht in hoofdlijnen* (An Outline of Criminal Law, Criminal Procedural Law & International Criminal Law), Antwerp-Apeldoorn, Maklu, 2006, pp. 683, 843, 986, footnote 4399.

[19] Act of 30 November 1998 Law on the Intelligence and Security Services, *Belgian Official Journal*, 18 December 1998, entry into force on 1 February 1999.

Specific collection methods include: observation or searches with technical means of public places and private places accessible to the public, observation with or without technical means of private places not accessible to the public (Article 18/2 §1, 1° and 2°; specified in Articles 18/4, 18/5), collection of identification data of electronic communications (Article 18/2 §1, 4°; specified in Article 18/7), the tracing of traffic data, and localization of electronic communications (Article 18/2 §1, 5°; specified in Article 18/8).

Exceptional collection methods include: observation with or without technical means *in* private places not accessible to the public, or in houses (Article 18/2 §2, 1°; specified in Article 18/11), a search with or without technical means of private places not accessible to the public, or houses (Article 18/2 §2, 2°; specified in Article 18/12), the collection of banking data (Article 18/2 §2, 5°; specified in Article 18/15), intrusion into a computer system (Article 18/2 §2, 6°; specified in Article 18/16), and wiretapping (Article 18/2 §2, 7°; specified in Article 18/17).

An additional collection method concerns the power for the (military) General Intelligence and Security Service of the Armed Forces (GISS) to intercept communications transmitted from abroad (Article 44*bis*).

For the execution of the above-mentioned intelligence operations, Belgian intelligence agencies can cooperate with individuals and the private sector (Article 16, Article 18/7, Article 18/8, Article 18/16, Article 18/17 of the Act of 30 November 1998 on the Intelligence and Security Services).

d) Customs Investigation Service

Belgian Customs Investigation Services have no powers to intercept electronic communications under Belgian law. Cybersquad, falling under the investigation services of the General Administration Customs and Excise (Federal Public Service Finance),[20] has powers, among others, to block websites offering illegal goods.[21] The Belgian Internet Service Center (BISC), established in 2011 under the Federal Public Service Finance's General Administration's Special Tax Inspectorate,[22] has powers to investigate Internet fraud: it detects infringements of Belgian law by

[20] Federal Overheidsdienst Financiën, Algemene Administratie der douane en accijnzen (in Dutch), Service Public Fédéral Finances, Administration générale des doaunes et accises (in French).

[21] A project leader at Cybersquad presented the functions of Cybersquad in a presentation (September 2012): available at https://www.b-ccentre.be/wp-content/uploads/2012/04/Cybersqu@d-28maart2012-v005.pdf

[22] Bijzondere Belastinginspectie (BBI, in Dutch), Inspection spéciale des impôts (ISI, in French).

online shops offering goods in Belgium and controls domain names with the extension .be. BISC also possesses software to map suspicious websites.[23]

3. Responsibility for the technical performance of interception measures

a) Material competence

The responsibility for the technical performance of interception measures under police law lies with the judicial police.

The responsibility for the technical performance of interception measures under (preventive) criminal law lies with the public prosecutor.

The responsibility for the technical performance of interception measures under (reactive) criminal law lies with the investigating judge, the public prosecutor, and judicial police officers.

The responsibility for the technical performance of interception measures under intelligence law lies with both the Director-General of the intelligence and security agencies and the administrative commission responsible for monitoring the specific and exceptional intelligence collection methods used by the intelligence and security services (SIM commission).

b) Territorial competence

The police and law enforcement agencies are structured at the federal and local levels. The intelligence agencies are structured at the federal level. There is one federal public prosecutor. The local public prosecutor's offices are situated at the same level as the Courts of First Instance: the judicial districts. The 2014 judicial reform reduced the judicial arrondissements (districts) from 27 to 12, of which the boundaries overlap with nine of the 10 provinces (West Flanders, East Flanders, Antwerp, Limburg, Hainaut, Namur, Walloon Brabant, Liège, Luxembourg) and the cities Leuven (province Flemish Brabant), Brussels (province Flemish Brabant), and Eupen for German-speaking Belgium (part of the province Liège).[24]

---

23 Christina Bourlet, "La lutte contre la fraude de mass: développements récents" (the fight against mass fraud: recent developments), in Dominique Grisay (ed.), *De la lutte contre la fraude à l'argent du crime: État des lieux*, Brussels, Groupe De Boeck, 2013, pp. 83–98.

24 The rationale behind the division into 27 districts, dating back to the foundation of Belgium in 1831, is that every capital city in each district be reachable by horse in one day. On the judicial reform in Belgium, see Stefaan Voet, "Belgium's new specialized judiciary," *Russian Law Journal*, 2014, vol. II, issue 4, pp. (129) 130, 138, available at http://www.russianlawjournal.org/index.php/jour/article/view/14/10

The law of 19 July 2012 on the reform of the judicial arrondissement Brussels[25] split up the public prosecutor's office covering the area Brussels-Halle-Vilvoorde.[26] The law of 19 July 2012 created, on the one hand, a public prosecutor's office covering the administrative arrondissement of Brussels-Capital and, on the other hand, a public prosecutor's office covering the administrative arrondissement Halle-Vilvoorde. In other words, a public prosecutor's office was created for the administrative district of Brussels-Capital, which covers the bilingual (French and Dutch) 19 municipalities of the Brussels-Capital Region (better known as Brussels); another public prosecutor's office was created for the administrative district Halle-Vilvoorde, which surrounds Brussels and consists of 35 Dutch-speaking municipalities that have language facilities.

The local Prosecutor General's offices are situated at the same level as the courts of appeal, more particularly at the five judicial areas (Ghent, Brussels, Antwerp, Mons, Liège).

The federal Prosecutor General's office is situated at the level of the Supreme Court.

The investigating judges are situated at the Courts of First Instance and are appointed by the King from among the judges at the Courts of First Instance.

c) Cooperation with individuals and the private sector

As mentioned above (section I.A.2.), for the execution of investigation and intelligence operations, Belgian law enforcement agencies and intelligence agencies can cooperate with individuals and the private sector.

4. Legitimacy of data transfers between different security agencies

There is a separation between the various institutions responsible for the interception of electronic communications under the police law, criminal law, and intelligence law. Thus, there are no joint agencies that carry out interception.

However, the results of interception measures under these different legal regimes can be exchanged between the competent authorities.

---

25 Law of 19 July 2012 on the reform of the judicial district Brussels, *Belgian Official Journal*, 22 August 2012, entry into force (almost two years later) on 31 March 2014.

26 The area Brussels-Halle-Vilvoorde was not only covered by the "judicial district" of Brussels, but also by the "electoral district" of Brussels.

a) Exchange of data between law enforcement authorities and preventive police authorities

There are several provisions that imply data exchanges from police authorities to law enforcement authorities.

First, Article 29 CCP provides that any authority shall immediately inform the public prosecutor of a crime or misdemeanour that comes to its knowledge. This article also applies to the intelligence and security services (see I.A.4.b. below) and is echoed by Article 44/1 §3 of the Act of 5 August 1992 on the Police Function.

Second, Article 28*bis* §1 CCP provides that preliminary investigations be conducted under the direction and authority of the competent public prosecutor. This is confirmed by Article 6 of the Act of 5 August 1992 on the Police Function.

Third, Article 15, 1° of the Act of 5 August 1992 on the Police Function reads as follows:

> In the performance of their judicial police functions, the police have the task: 1° to detect the crimes, misdemeanours and contraventions, to gather evidence thereof, to notify the competent authorities thereof, to apprehend and arrest the perpetrators, to bring them at the disposal of the competent authorities, in the manner and forms provided by law;

Article 53 CCP adds that the judicial police officers shall immediately send the reports (of an offense), official records,[27] and any other acts drafted under their competence to the public prosecutor. This provision is echoed by Article 40 of the Act of 5 August 1992 on the Police Function, which provides that police officers shall send official records on complaints, reports of offenses, and intelligence and any detections to the competent judicial authorities.

Article 54 CCP adds that the judicial police officers shall also immediately send any reports of crimes and misdemeanours they are not competent to detect to the public prosecutor.

Article 5/3 of Act of 5 August 1992 on the Police Function adds that, for the performance of judicial police functions, the police shall maintain regular *service relations* with the local public prosecutors, the federal public prosecutor, and the Prosecutors General.

Third, the project "Autonomic Police Treatment" (APT)[28] allows for independent police treatment in specific cases. Article 28*bis* §1, 2° CCP provides that the

---

[27] Proces-verbaal (in Dutch), procès-verbal (in French).

[28] Previously called Autonome Politionele Afhandeling (APA, in Dutch), or le Traitement Policier Autonome (in French); currently called Ambtshalve Politioneel Onderzoek (APO), or Enquête Policière d'Office (in French). For a government-funded research project on the opportunity of APT and the evaluation of its effectiveness, see Federal Science Policy Office (BELSPO), "Stated goals van autonome afhandeling door de politie (APA): zijn ze opportuun en worden ze bereikt?" (Stated goals of the Autonomic Police Treatment: are they opportune and are they achieved?), SO/02/016, research project from 1 De-

law and special rules issued via circular by the Board of Prosecutors General[29] determine the general principles for APT. The circular of 15 June 2005 issued by the Board of Prosecutors General lays down the rules on APT and the simplified official record (see below under this section).[30]

Although Article 28*bis* §1, 3° CCP confirms that the preliminary investigations are conducted under the direction and authority of the competent public prosecutor, Ponsaers and other members of a research project on APT explain that APT "breaks with the tradition of the public prosecutor as a mere sender and receiver of instructions (a 'letter-box'); all necessary police research should be finished before the file can be sent to the public prosecutor's office."[31] The authors further refer to the wording of Article 28*ter* §2 CCP, which provides that judicial police officers and agents acting on their own initiative shall inform the public prosecutor of the conducted investigations *within the time and in the manner provided by the public prosecutor in a directive (circular)* (italics added). They see APT as a *manner* for the public prosecutor to realize investigation policy. In this manner, Article 28*ter* §4 CCP provides that the police, designated by the public prosecutor to perform judicial police functions, shall immediately inform the latter of the information and intelligence in its possession, and of every conducted investigation *in the manner provided by the public prosecutor* (italics added). The authors also refer to a judgment of the Supreme Court of 21 August 2001,[32] which confirms the possibility of APT without prior notification of the public prosecutor. The Supreme Court also held that the notification duty laid down in Article 28*ter* CCP is not substantial and not prescribed under penalty of nullity.

Fourth, the police principally do not forward simplified official records, which are used for relatively non-serious offenses,[33] to the public prosecutor. The police only send a monthly list to the public prosecutor, which contains the number of the simplified official records; a short description of the offense; the qualification,

---

cember 2000 till 28 February 2003, available via http://www.belspo.be/belspo/fedra/proj.asp?l=nl&COD=SO%2F02%2F016

29 The Board of Prosecutors General (*College van procureurs-generaal* in Dutch; *Collège des procureurs généraux* in French) can take measures to ensure a coherent implementation and coordination of criminal policy as determined in ministerial directives and the well general and coordinated functioning of the public prosecutor's office (Article 143*bis* §2 of the Judicial Code).

30 Board of Prosecutors General, Circular of 15 June 2005 regarding the Autonomic Police Treatment and the simplified official records, COL 8, available (in Dutch and French) at http://www.om-mp.be/omzendbrief/4016820/omzendbrief_col_8_d_d__15_06_2005.html

31 See the English summary of the APT project: "Policing: Relative Autonomy? An empirical research into Autonomic Police Action," available at http://www.belspo.be/belspo/organisation/publ/pub_ostc/SoCoh/rSO02016_en.pdf

32 Supreme Court, 21 August 2011, P.01.1203.F/1, available via http://jure.juridat.just.fgov.be/

33 Vereenvoudigd proces-verbaal (in Dutch), procès-verbal simplifié (in French).

place, and time of the offense; and the identity of the implicated persons. As mentioned earlier under this section, the circular of 15 June 2005 issued by the Board of Prosecutors General lays down the rules on APT and simplified official records.[34]

b) Passing on of data by intelligence agencies

Regarding information transfers from the intelligence and security services to the police services, Article 20 §1 of the Act of 30 November 1998 on the Intelligence and Security Services lays down a general obligation of maximum efficient mutual cooperation between intelligence and security services, police services, and administrative and judicial authorities.

Furthermore, the Act of 18 March 2014 inserted a new Article 44/11/9 into the Act of 5 August 1992 on the Police Function, §4 of which lays down a duty for the intelligence and security services and other services to transfer data and information, which are processed within the framework of their functions and that are sufficient, relevant, and not excessive in view of police functions, to the police services.

Regarding information transfers from the intelligence and security services to the judicial authorities, there are three ways to transfer information.

First, Article 19/1 §1 of the Act of 30 November 1998 on the Intelligence and Security Services provides that, in view of the application of Article 29 CCP, these services shall immediately inform the administrative commission responsible for monitoring the specific and exceptional intelligence collection methods used by the intelligence and security services (SIM commission) if the performance of specific or exceptional collection methods reveals serious indications of the commission of a crime or misdemeanor, or, in case of reasonable suspicion, of unrevealed or future offenses. As said, Article 29 CCP provides that any authority shall immediately inform the public prosecutor of a crime or misdemeanor that comes to its knowledge (see section I.A.4.a. above). This article also applies to the intelligence and security services.

Article 19/1 §2 of the Act of 30 November 1998 on the Intelligence and Security Services provides that, if the SIM commission confirms the findings of the intelligence and security services, then the president of the SIM commission shall draft an *unclassified* official record and immediately send it to the public prosecutor or the federal prosecutor after having heard the Director-General of the intelligence and security agencies regarding the conditions of the transfer.

---

34 Board of Prosecutors General, Circular of 15 June 2005, COL 8, available (in Dutch and French) at http://www.om-mp.be/omzendbrief/4016820/omzendbrief_col_8_d_d__15_06_2005.html

Second, Article 20 §1 of the Act of 30 November 1998 on the Intelligence and Security Services lays down a general obligation of maximum efficient mutual cooperation between intelligence and security services, police services, and administrative and judicial authorities. Article 20 §2 of the Act of 30 November 1998 on the Intelligence and Security Services provides that the intelligence and security services *can* cooperate with the judicial and administrative authorities, upon their request, and within the limits of a protocol adopted by the relevant ministers.

Article 19 provides that the intelligence and security services shall *only* transfer intelligence to the concerned ministers or judicial and administrative authorities, the police services, and all competent organizations and persons according to the purposes of their functions and in relation to threatened organizations and persons.

A service note of the Federal Prosecutor of 17 December 2012 on the written information exchanges between the intelligence and security services and the public prosecutor is based on the unpublished circular COL 9/2012 of 21 June 2012 of the Board of Prosecutors General regarding the Act of 30 November 1998 on the Intelligence and Security Services; it determines the principles regarding the use and preservation of classified information at the federal public prosecutor's office.[35]

For the data transfer from intelligence agencies to judicial authorities, there is no similar provision to Article 14 §1-2 of the Act of 30 November 1998 on the Intelligence and Security Services, which allows information transfers from judicial authorities and police service, *on their own initiative*, to intelligence and security services (see I.A.4.c. below).

Third, there is an additional information flow from the oversight body of the intelligence agencies, i.e., the Belgian Standing Intelligence Agencies Review Committee (Standing Committee I), to the judicial authorities. The Standing Committee I acts as a prejudicial advisor in case the Council Chamber[36] (Article 131*bis* CCP) or the court dealing with the substance of the case (Article 189*quater* CCP) or the Court of Assize (Article 279*bis* CCP), when confronted with an unclassified official record as referred to in Article 19/1 of the Act of 30 November 1998 on the Intelligence and Security Services, requests the advice of the Standing Committee I on the legality of the collection methods used by the intelligence services.

---

[35] Federal Prosecutor's Office, Annual report of the Public Prosecutor's Office to the Board of Prosecutors General for the period 1 January 2012 till 23 December 2012, 2012, p. 124, available (in Dutch) at http://www.om-mp.be/images/upload_dir/jaarverslag2012.pdf

[36] The Council Chamber (*Raadkamer* in Dutch; *Chambre du conseil* in French) supervises the investigation phase at the Court of First Instance. The Indictment Chamber or Court of Indictment (*Kamer van Inbeschuldigingstelling* in Dutch; *Chambre des mises en accusation* in French) supervises the investigation phase at the Court of Appeal.

c) Passing on of data to intelligence agencies

Regarding the transfer of information from the police services and judicial authorities to the intelligence and security services, first, Article 20 §1 of the Act of 30 November 1998 on the Intelligence and Security Services lays down a general obligation of maximum efficient mutual cooperation between intelligence and security services, police services, and administrative and judicial authorities.

Second, Article 14 §1-2 of the Act of 30 November 1998 on the Intelligence and Security Services provides that the civil servants and agents of public services (including police services) and judicial authorities, can transfer information that is useful for the functions of the intelligence and security services, on their own initiative or upon request, while considering the law, and on the basis of potentially concluded agreements or hierarchical rules. Article 14 §2 of the Act of 30 November 1998 on the Intelligence and Security Services provides that the civil servants and agents of public services (including police services) and judicial authorities can refuse to transfer information, if they deem that such a transfer would compromise an ongoing (preliminary) investigation or the collection of information according to the law of 11 January 1993 on preventing misuse of the financial system for purposes of laundering money and terrorism financing, or if it could harm someone in his or her personal physical integrity.

B. Statistics on Telecommunication Interception

1. Obligation to collect statistics

There is an obligation for law enforcement authorities and courts to report statistics to the Ministry of Justice. Article 90*decies* CCP provides that the Minister of Justice will report annually to the Parliament on the application of some but not all investigation methods:

> The Minister of Justice will report annually to the Parliament on the application of Articles 90ter to 90novies.
>
> He informs the Parliament of the number of investigations which gave rise to the measures referred to in those articles, the duration of these measures, the number of persons involved and the results obtained.
>
> He also reports on the application of Articles 40bis, 46ter, 46quater, 47ter to 47decies, 56bis, 86bis, 86ter, 88sexies and 89ter.
>
> He informs the Parliament of the number of investigations which gave rise to the measures referred to in these articles, the number of affected persons, the offenses to which they relate and the results obtained.
>
> He also reports on the application of Articles 102 to 111 and 317 and notifies the Federal Parliament of the number of cases involved, persons and crimes.
>
> This report is also complemented by the report prepared pursuant to Article 126, §6, third paragraph, of the Act of 13 June 2005 on electronic communications.

This report is also complemented by the report prepared pursuant to Article 126, §5, fourth paragraph, of the Act of 13 June 2005 on electronic communications.

The annual reports of the Minister of Justice in implementation of Article 90*decies* CCP[37] provide that data collection and processing is determined via the confidential circular COL 17/2006 of the Board of Prosecutors General. The annual reports of the Minister of Justice in implementation of Article 90*decies* CCP disclose some explanations about the general procedure and the data collection. The reports provide details about the providers of information: the federal police provides data regarding the power to enter a house or a private place in order to enable eavesdropping with technical means and looking-in operations; the National Informants Administrator, which functions at the judicial police's Directorate-General level under the supervision of the federal prosecutor (Article 47*decies* §2 CCP),[38] provides data on informants; the investigating judge (via the public prosecutors) provides data on anonymous witnesses and other investigation methods; the federal prosecutor provides data on anonymous witnesses, the protection of threatened witnesses, special investigation methods, and the other investigation methods.

The annual reports add that all information, except information regarding the wiretapping method, is provided via uniform forms and sent to the Criminal Policy Service of the Ministry of Justice.[39] For information regarding the wiretapping methods, the reports mention two ways of data gathering: first, an automatic transfer for users of the programme "Phoobs" developed by the federal police in view of standardized data collection with the different operators.[40] Phoobs creates an access file which is sent to the Federal Computer Crime Unit (FCCU) of the Federal Judicial Police (Directorate for Combating Economic and Financial Crime). Second, for non-Phoobs users, the FCCU requires an Excel spreadsheet to be completed by the investigating judge. The annual reports add that the FCCU also receives data from the federal police's unit that technically implements the wiretapping measure: the "Commissariat-general Special Units – National Technical and Tactical Support Unit – Central Technical Interception Facilities."

---

37 The reports in implementation of Article 90*decies* CCP are available at the website of the Criminal Policy Service of the Ministry of Justice: http://www.dsb-spc.be/web/index.php?option=com_content&task=view&lang=nl&id=55

38 Nationale Informantenbeerder (in Dutch), Gestionnaire des indicateurs (in French).

39 Dienst voor het Strafrechtelijk Beleid (in Dutch), Service de la Politique Criminelle (in French).

40 Belgian Institute for Postal Services and Telecommunications, "Synthese van de raadpleging door de raad van het bipt op verzoek van de minister voor ondernemen en vereenvoudigen van 29/04/2010 betreffende de praktische uitvoering van richtlijn 2006/24/EG van 15 maart 2006 (richtlijn betreffende de bewaring van gegevens)" (Summary regarding the implementation of the data retention directive 2006/24/EG of 15 March 2006), 2010, p. 14, available at http://www.bipt.be/public/files/nl/1259/3344_nl_2010-10-01_bipt-verslag_consultatie_data_retention-publieke_versie_v20101001_nl.pdf

Ultimately, the Criminal Policy Service of the Ministry of Justice processes the data and drafts the report for the Minister of Justice and, in copy, for the Board of Prosecutors General.

2. Current data

Below we provide, first, current data for law enforcement methods provided by the Ministry of Justice; second, current data for intelligence collection methods provided by the Belgian Standing Intelligence Agencies Review Committee (Standing Committee I); and, third, current data for government access provided by electronic communication companies.

a) Current data for law enforcement methods provided by the Ministry of Justice

aa) Overview

As stated above (section I.B.1.), the Minister of Justice will report annually to the Parliament on the application of some but not all investigation methods. Article 90*decies* CCP requires reporting for only two electronic communications interception methods: the wiretapping measure (Article 90*ter* §1, 1° CCP) and the power to enter a house or a private place to enable eavesdropping with technical means (Article 90*ter* §1, 2° CCP). Hence, there are no reporting obligations for the collection of identification data of electronic communications (Article 46*bis* CCP), tracing of traffic data, and localization of electronic communications (Article 88*bis* CCP), and the network search (Article 88*ter* CCP). Although the reporting obligation also applies to looking-in operations (Article 46*quinquies* and 89*ter* CCP) and the special investigation methods observation (Article 47*sexies* CCP) and infiltration (Article 47*octies* CCP), the annual reports of the Minister of Justice – in implementation of Article 90*decies* CCP – do not specify the cases in which these measures were used in the context of the interception of electronic communications.

The annual reports of the Minister of Justice – in implementation of Article 90*decies* CCP – refer to the productive cooperation with the federal public prosecutor's office and the federal police, which resulted in accurate statistics on looking-in operations and the special investigation methods (observation and infiltration). But for the other investigation methods, the annual reports refer to the incomplete data collection and lacking coordination between the investigating judges and the public prosecutors. The annual reports therefore use the term indications rather than statistics. Furthermore, for the wiretapping measure, the annual reports mention the lack of general cooperation between the federal judicial police and local police services, such as failure to complete the evaluation forms and return them to the Ministry of Justice.

bb) Wiretapping

The first table below under this section gives an overview of the number of wiretapping measures performed by law enforcement agencies (Article 90*ter* §1, 1° CCP). The table also provides statistics regarding the object of the wiretapping measures:

The 2004 annual report contains figures in relation to the following categories for the wiretapping measure: 117 interceptions of landline numbers; 1390 interceptions of mobile numbers; nine interceptions of fax numbers; five interceptions of Internet (modems); and 136 non-specified interceptions. Regarding the eavesdropping measure, the 2004 annual report indicates that only one public prosecutor's office provided data, which more specifically noted two cases of eavesdropping. The 2005 annual report, however, provides more specific data on eavesdropping for 2004: 38 cases.

Since 2005, the annual reports have been using different categories: landline numbers, mobile numbers, IMEI numbers, and e-mails. As the 2011, 2012, and 2013 reports (for the years 2010, 2011 and 2012) only present a non-numerical marked line chart, the numbers provided below are an estimate based on the author's reading of these charts.

Wiretapping (Article 90*ter* §1, 1° CCP)					
Year	**Number (#)**	**Object (#, estimate)**			
		Landline	**GSM**	**IMEI**	**Mail**
2005	2569#	373#	1660#	536#	0
2006	3036#	511#	2089#	436#	0
2007	3603#	495#	2473#	632#	3#
2008	4881#	686#	3133#	1062#	0
2009[41]	5653#	114#	2818#	531#	3#
2010	6031#	631# (estimate)	4200# (estimate)	1200# (estimate)	0
2011	6671#	621# (estimate)	4800# (estimate)	1250# (estimate)	0
2012	6712#	712# (estimate)	4700# (estimate)	1300# (estimate)	0

41 The total number exceeds the sum of the numbers provided per category. This could be due to an error in the 2009 annual report.

cc) Power to enter a house or a private place to enable eavesdropping with technical means

The second table concerns the power to enter a house or a private place in order to enable eavesdropping with technical means performed by law enforcement agencies (Article 90*ter* §1, 2° CCP): the reports of the Ministry of Justice do not indicate the number of measures executed but only the annual number of case files in which they were applied.

Power to enter a house or a private place to enable eavesdropping with technical means (Article 90*ter* §1, 2° CCP)	
Year	**Number of case files in which measure applied (#)**
2004	38#
2005	29#
2006	24#
2007	24#
2008	40#
2009	40#
2010	48#
2011	54#
2012	71#

b) Current data for intelligence collection methods provided by the Belgian Standing Intelligence Agencies Review Committee (Standing Committee I)

aa) Overview

The next tables show the number of authorizations granted by the two intelligence agencies for the interception of electronic communications. The data are found in the activity reports of the Belgian Standing Intelligence Agencies Review Committee (Standing Committee I),[42] which has been providing data on the specific collection methods since 2010 and, since 2011, also for the exceptional collection methods. Thus, contrary to the lack of reporting obligations for law enforcement authorities regarding electronic communications methods other than the monitoring measure, the Standing Committee I provides statistics on *all* electronic communications interceptions collection methods.

[42] Belgian Standing Intelligence Agencies Review Committee (Standing Committee I), "Activity reports", available (in Dutch and French) at http://www.comiteri.be/index.php?option=com_content&view=article&id=40&Itemid=74&lang=EN. The Standing Committee I also produced three activity reports in English for the periods 2006-2007, 2008-2009, and 2010–2011.

The relevant specific collection methods are the collection of identification data of electronic communications (Article 18/2 §1, 4° and Article 18/7 of the Act of 30 November 1998), tracing of traffic data, and localization of electronic communications (Article 18/2 §1, 5 and Article 18/8 of the Act of 30 November 1998).

The relevant exceptional collection methods are the intrusion into a computer system (Article 18/2 §2, 6° and Article 18/16 of the Act of 30 November 1998) and wiretapping (Article 18/2 §2, 7° and Article 18/17 of the Act of 30 November 1998).

Of note is that the Standing Committee I did not provide any statistics regarding ministerial approval, and review by the Committee itself, of the interception of communications transmitted from abroad by the General Intelligence and Security Service of the Armed Forces (GISS) (Article 44*bis* of the Act of 30 November 1998).

Again, we only provide statistics that exclusively address the interception of electronic communications. The reason is, again, the lack of specification by the Ministry of Justice regarding cases in which other law enforcement measures (not explicitly created for the interception of electronic communications) were used in view of the interception of electronic communications.

The Standing Committee I provides separate statistics for the (civil) State Security[43] and the (military) General Intelligence and Security Service of the Armed Forces (GISS).[44] The 2010 activity report notes that the Standing Committee I could not could not give an indication of the number of measures actually implemented by the State Security, as the latter used its legal power to send these listings to the SIM commission only. The GISS, however, gave an indication of the results delivered by the various methods and, even more, showed the lack of implementation of a large number of methods authorized by the GISS in the reference period.[45]

bb) Collection of identification data of electronic communications

The first table below refers to the specific collection method of collecting identification data of electronic communications (Article 18/2 §1, 4° and Article 18/7 of the Act of 30 November 1998). Of note is that, before 2013, the Standing Committee I did not show the number of measures but instead the annual number of case files in which they were applied.

In the 2012 activity report, the Standing Committee I explains that the decreasing frequency of this method, and also of the method of tracing traffic data of electronic communications, followed from its decision that these methods can no longer

---

[43] De Veiligheid van de Staat (VSSE, in Dutch), La Sûreté de l'Etat (VSSE, in French).

[44] De Algemene Dienst Inlichtingen en Veiligheid (ADIV, in Dutch), le Service général du Renseignement et de la Sécurité (SGRS, in French).

[45] See the 2010-2011 activity report (in English), pp. 68–69.

automatically result in the transfer of localization data (Article 18/2 §1, 5 and Article 18/8 of the Act of 30 November 1998).[46] In the 2013 activity report, the Standing Committee I confirmed an increasing number of localizations of electronic communications by both the State Security and the GISS.[47]

Although, since January 2013, identification data can no longer be authorized by the same authorization for the tracing of traffic data,[48] the decrease in identification data collection remained.

Collection of identification data of electronic communications (Article 18/2 §1, 4° and Article 18/7 Act of 30 November 1998)		
Year	Number of case files in which measure applied (#)	
	State Security	GISS
2010	15#	8#
2011	355#	23#
2012	254#	25#
2013	243# (613# measures)	16# (66# measures)

cc) Tracing of traffic data, and localization of electronic communications

The next table concerns the specific collection method of tracing of traffic data of electronic communications, and localization of electronic communications (Article 18/2 §1, 5 and Article 18/8 of the Act of 30 November 1998).

Tracing of traffic data, and localization of electronic communications (Article 18/2 §1, 5 and Article 18/8 Act of 30 November 1998)				
Year	Tracing of traffic data (#)		Localization (#)	
	State Security	GISS	State Security	GISS
2010	30#	7#	6#	7#
2011	237#	17#	46#	13#
2012	147#	30#	176#	4#
2013	136#	15#	244#	36#

46 See the 2012 activity report of the Standing Committee I, p. 49.

47 See the 2013 activity report of the Standing Committee I, p. 69 (footnote 129), p. 71 (footnote 135), and p. 72.

48 See the English 2010–2011 activity report of the Standing Committee I, p. 148; the 2012 activity report of the Standing Committee I, p. 49; and the 2013 activity report of the Standing Committee I, p. 68.

dd) Intrusion into a computer system

The next table concerns the specific collection method of intrusion into a computer system.

Intrusion into a computer system (Article 18/2 §2, 6° and Article 18/16 Act of 30 November 1998)		
Year	Number (#)	
	State Security	GISS
2011	3#	0
2012	10#	2#
2013	12#	0

ee) Wiretapping

In the 2013 activity report, the Standing Committee I refers to an increasing number of wiretapping measures by both the State Security and the General Information and Security Service.[49]

Wiretapping (Article 18/2 §2, 7° and Article 18/17 Act of 30 November 1998)		
Year	Number (#)	
	State Security	GISS
2011	11#	2#
2012	50#	14#
2013	81#	17#

c) Current data provided by electronic communication companies

aa) Vodafone

The 2014 law enforcement disclosure report of the telecommunications company Vodafone contains a legal annex providing an overview of law enforcement and intelligence powers in several countries, including Belgium.[50] In its analysis for Belgium, Vodafone refers to two demands for the disclosure of communication

49 See the 2013 activity report, p. 72.

50 Vodafone, "Law Enforcement Disclosure Report," 2014, available at http://www.vodafone.com/content/sustainabilityreport/2014/index/operating_responsibly/privacy_and_security/law_enforcement.html

data, saying that it has not implemented the technical requirements necessary to enable lawful interception and therefore did not receive any agency or authority demands for lawful interception assistance.[51]

bb) Google

The following table shows the number of requests for user data that the technology company Google received, the number of users/accounts specified in the requests, and the percentage of request that Google complied with.[52]

User data requests to Google			
Period	**Number (#)**	**Users/accounts (#)**	**Compliance rate (%)**
July to December 2009	67#	No data provided	No data provided
January to June 2010	71#	No data provided	No data provided
July to December 2010	85#	No data provided	73%
January to June 2011	90#	111#	67%
July to December 2011	99#	124#	67%
January to June 2012	107#	127#	67%
July to December 2012	120#	153#	63%
January to June 2013	194#	289#	66%
July to December 2013	162#	206#	73%
January to June 2014	213#	513#	73%
July to December 2014	214#	297#	67%

cc) Microsoft

The following table shows the number of law enforcement requests made to the technology company Microsoft.[53] Like Google, Microsoft provides the number of requests for user data it has received, the number of users/accounts specified in the requests, and the percentage of requests it complied with. Unlike Google's trans-

[51] *Ibid.*, p. 71; see also Vodafone's "country-by-country disclosure of law enforcement assistance demands," available at http://www.vodafone.com/content/sustainabilityreport/2014/index/operating_responsibly/privacy_and_security/law_enforcement/country_by_country.html

[52] Google, "Transparency Reports," available via http://www.google.com/transparencyreport/?hl=en_US

[53] Microsoft, "Law Enforcement Requests Reports," available at https://www.microsoft.com/about/corporatecitizenship/en-us/reporting/transparency/

parency reports, Microsoft breaks the compliance rate into three percentages: provided subscriber/transactional data; provided content data; or no data provided because no data were found. In addition, Microsoft provides a rejection rate showing the percentage of rejected requests for reasons of not meeting legal requirements. The law enforcement request reports cover requests for all Microsoft services, except for the 2012 report, which does not include the voice-call service Skype.

User data requests to Microsoft						
Period	Number (#)	Rejection rate (#, %)	Users/ accounts (#)	Subscriber/ transactional data (#, %)	Content data (#, %)	No data found (#, %)
January to December 2012	727#	0%	1140#	629# 86,5%	0%	98# 13,5%
January to June 2013	500#	0%	784#	406# 81,2%	0%	94# 18,8%
July to December 2013	378#	12# 3,2%	520#	287# 75,9%	0%	79# 20,9%
January to June 2014	433#	66# 1%	922#	360# 83,1%	0%	66# 15,2%
July to December 2014	481#	17# 3,5%	765#	394# 81,9%	0%	70# 14,6%

A brief comparison of the Google and Microsoft statistics shows that, prior to the latest Microsoft law enforcement request report (from 2012 till June 2014) the rejection rate was zero. The rejection rate of 3,5% for the period July to December 2014 is, however, still significantly lower than Google's rejection rate, which has remained stable at around 30% since 2010. Nevertheless, the number of requests to Microsoft has generally decreased, in contrast to the increasing number of requests to Google.

As the statistics of Microsoft show that no content data were provided to Belgian authorities, there is a high probability that Articles 46*bis* (identification data of electronic communications) and 88*bis* CCP (tracing of traffic data, and localization of electronic communications) were the legal bases for the data transfers.

dd) Twitter

The transparency reports of the social networking service Twitter show almost no information requests from Belgium.[54]

---

[54] Twitter, "Transparency reports," available via https://transparency.twitter.com/

User data requests to Twitter			
Period	Number (#)	Compliance (%)	Accounts (#)
January to June 2012	No data provided	No data provided	No data provided
July to December 2012	0	Not applicable	Not applicable
January to June 2013	0	Not applicable	Not applicable
July to December 2013	2#	50%	2#
January to June 2014	0	Not applicable	Not applicable
July to December 2014	1#	0%	1#

ee) Facebook

The government request reports of the social media service Facebook show an increasing number of requests (like Google).[55] Whereas Google's compliance rate has remained stable at around 70%, Facebook's compliance rate has gradually decreased.

User data requests to Facebook			
Period	Number (#)	Compliance (%)	Users/accounts (#)
January to June 2013	150#	70%	169#
July to December 2013	154#	64,94%	196#
January to June 2014	209#	56,94%	246#
July to December 2014	239#	59%	319#

ff) Verizon

The transparency reports of the US telecommunications provider Verizon do not provide the total number of requests received, nor compliance or rejection rates.[56]

Until the report for the second half of 2014, the transparency reports did not provide details regarding the number of requests for subscriber information and transactional information.

The 2013 transparency report specifies customer selectors (number of users/accounts specified in the requests) for all requests complied with. The transparency

---

[55] Facebook, "Government requests reports," available via https://govtrequests.facebook.com/

[56] Verizon, "Transparency Reports," available via http://transparency.verizon.com/

report for the first half of 2014 breaks the customer selector rates into numbers for subscriber information and transactional information.

User data requests to Verizon				
Period	Number (#)		Customer selectors (#)	
	Subscriber information	Transactional information	Subscriber information	Transactional information
2013	No data available		473#	
1st half of 2014	No data available		362#	0
2nd half of 2014	173#	0	193#	0

II. Principles of Telecommunication Interception in Constitutional and Criminal Procedure

A. Constitutional Safeguards of Telecommunication

1. Areas of constitutional protection[57]

a) Secrecy of telecommunication

Private communications are protected by the constitutional right to privacy (Article 22 of the Belgian Constitution)[58] and the constitutional right of secrecy of communications (Article 29 of the Constitution).[59]

Article 22 of the Constitution reads as follows:

> Everyone has the right to the respect of his private and family life, except in the cases and conditions determined by the law.
>
> The laws, decrees, and rulings alluded to in Article 134 guarantee the protection of this right.

Article 29 of the Constitution reads as follows:

> The confidentiality of letters is inviolable.
>
> The law determines which nominated representatives can violate the confidentiality of letters entrusted to the postal service.

---

[57] The Belgian Constitution neither contains an explicit right to the confidentiality and integrity of information systems nor an explicit right to informational self-determination.

[58] An English version of the Constitution is available via www.legislationline.org

[59] See Paul De Hert and Serge Gutwirth, *Anthologie privacy/Anthologie de la vie privée* (Anthology of privacy), Academic and Scientific Publishers, 2013, p. 28, available at http://www.anthologieprivacy.be/sites/anthology/files/documents/anthologie-privacy-asp_0.pdf

b) Core area of privacy

Private communications are protected by the constitutional right to the inviolability of the home (Article 15 of the Constitution), the constitutional right to privacy (Article 22 of the Constitution), and the constitutional right of secrecy of communications (Article 29 of the Constitution, see II.A.1.a. above). The constitutional right to privacy protects against secret surveillance as well as monitoring and searching of computer data.

2. Proportionality of access to data

a) Belgian Constitution

The Belgian Constitution does not contain a constitutional principle of proportionality and necessity.

b) Data Protection Act of 8 December 1992

The Belgian Data Protection Act of 8 December 1992[60] includes the duty of observance of the principles of transparency and proportionality. Article 4 §1, 3° of the Act provides that personal data must be "adequate, relevant and not excessive in relation to the purposes for which it is collected or further processed." However, as mentioned below (see II.A.2.c.), the act contains certain exemptions, for instance in case of information gathering for police purposes.

c) Act of 5 August 1992 on the Police Function

Until 7 April 2014 (the date of entry into force of the Act of 18 March 2014),[61] Article 44/1 §1 of the Act of 5 August 1992 on the Police Function was phrased in general terms, allowing the police to gather information and intelligence on persons and groups that showed a concrete interest for the exercise of police functions. Professor De Hert and Vermeulen observed the general nature of this provision and its silence regarding systematic data collection.[62] The Act of 5 August 1992 on the

---

[60] Act of 8 December 1992 concerning the protection of privacy in relation to the processing of personal data, *Belgian Official Journal*, 18 March 1993, available at http://www.privacycommission.be/sites/privacycommission/files/documents/Privacy_Act_1992.pdf

[61] Act of 18 March 2014 regarding police information management and modifying the Act of 5 August 1992 on the Police Function, the Data Protection Act of 8 December 1992, and the Code of Criminal Procedure, *Belgian Official Journal*, 28 March 2014, entry into force on 7 April 2014.

[62] Paul De Hert and Mathias Vermeulen, "Toegang tot sociale media en controle door politie. Een eerste juridische verkenning vanuit mensenrechtelijk perspectief" (Access to

Police Function only mentioned the principle of proportionality and subsidiarity in relation to coercive police powers, more particularly in Article 37 which provides that any use of violence by the police services should be reasonable and in proportion to the pursued goals.

The Act of 18 March 2014 inserted a new Article 44/1 into the Act of 5 August 1992 on the Police Function, the first paragraph of which provides that the police services shall only process information and personal data insofar as sufficient, relevant, and not excessive in view of police purposes. Hence, this provision also applies to the powers for interception of electronic communications under (preventive) police law (see section I.A.2.b.): the general provision on crime detection and evidence gathering by the police (Article 8 CCP) and the specific provision on access by the police to publicly accessible places (Article 26 of the Act on the Police Function).

Furthermore, the Act of 18 March 2014 created a new Article 44/11/9, the fourth paragraph of which lays down a duty for the intelligence and security services, the Belgian Financial Intelligence Processing Unit (CTIF-CFI),[63] the Home Affairs Federal Public Service – Immigration Office,[64] and the prosecution and investigation services of the Federal Public Services Finance's General Administration Customs and Excise to transfer to the police services data and information that are processed within the framework of their functions and that are sufficient, relevant, and not excessive in view of police functions.

d) Normal investigation methods

Regarding the legal regime of criminal law, the principle of proportionality and necessity is found in relation to most, but not all, of the legal provisions for intercepting electronic communications. The principle is, first of all, foreseen for all normal investigation powers, except for the data seizure (Article 39*bis* CCP). The investigation methods to which the principle applies are thus the following: the collection of identification data of electronic communications (Article 46*bis* CCP), the tracing of traffic data, and localization of electronic communications (Article 88*bis* CCP), the network search (Article 88*ter* CCP), and the monitoring measure (Article 90*ter* §1 CCP).

social media and control by the police: a first legal exploration from the human rights perspective), *Panopticon*, 2012, vol. 33(2), p. (258) 261.

63 The CTIF-CFI is the Belgian preventive anti-money laundering and counter-terrorist financing system. De Cel voor Financiële Informatieverwerking (CFI, in Dutch), La Cellule de Traitement des Informations Financières (CTIF, in French).

64 Federale Overheidsdienst (FOD) Binnenlandse Zaken – Vreemdelingenzaken (in Dutch), Service Public Fédéral (SPF) Intérieur – Office des étrangers (in French).

e) Special investigation methods and any other methods of investigation

The Act of 6 January 2003 concerning special investigation methods and any other methods of investigation[65] introduced three *special investigation methods* and five *other investigation methods* into the CCP. Only the use of the special investigation methods is subject to the conditions of subsidiarity and proportionality.

The *special investigation methods* are observation (Article 47*sexies* CCP), infiltration (Article 47*octies* CCP), and the use of informants (Article 47*decies* CCP). The two *special investigation methods* relevant for the interception of electronic communications are observation and infiltration.

The *other investigation methods* are the postponed intervention (Article 40*bis* CCP), the interception and opening of classical mail (Article 46*ter* CCP), the collection of data regarding bank accounts and bank transactions (Article 46*quater* CCP), looking-in operations (Articles 46*quinquies* and 89*ter* CCP), and the power to enter a house or a private place to enable eavesdropping with technical means (Article 90*ter* §1, 2° CCP). The two *other investigation methods* relevant for the interception of electronic communications are looking-in operations and the power to enter a house or a private place to enable eavesdropping with technical means.

f) National collective agreement on the protection of the private lives of employees with respect to controls on electronic on-line communications data

The national collective agreement on the protection of the private lives of employees with respect to controls on electronic on-line communications data, signed by Belgium's National Labour Council on 26 April 2002,[66] covers all on-line technologies, such as the Internet, e-mail, and Wireless Application Protocol (WAP), and has been drafted in sufficiently broad terms to also cover future developments. The agreement seeks to clarify and complement Article 8 of the ECHR, Article 22 of the Constitution (constitutional right to privacy), and the Act of 8 December 1992 on the protection of personal data. The obligations of the employer must respect the principle of proportionality: the controls impinging on an employee's private life must be kept to a minimum (Article 6); only data that are necessary for the control purpose may be collected or processed, i.e., as little possible data that affect the private life of the employee.

---

[65] Act of 6 January 2003 concerning special investigation methods and any other methods of investigation, *Belgian Official Journal*, 12 May 2003, entry into force on 22 May 2003.

[66] National Labour Council, "National collective agreement no. 81 of 26 April 2002 on the protection of the private lives of employees with respect to controls on electronic on-line communications data," 26 April 2002, available via www.cnt-nar.be. For a discussion of the agreement, see Paul De Hert, "C.A.O. no. 81 en advies no. 10/2000 over controle van Internet en e-mail" [Labour law: Soft law on e-mail and Internet practices], *Rechtskundig weekblad*, 2002-2003, vol. 66/33, 19 April 2003, pp. 1281–1294.

3. Consequences for the interception of telecommunication

The effective protection of the secrecy of telecommunications and the core area of privacy is guaranteed in several ways.

First, the right to privacy (Article 22 of the Constitution) applies to several spheres in the law of criminal procedure, including:[67]

- The secrecy of correspondence: Article 28*septies* §1 and Article 57 §1 CCP require the secrecy of correspondence on the part of everyone who contributes to the preliminary investigation respectively the investigation. Any breach of secrecy shall be punished in accordance with Article 458 of the Criminal Code. The following articles recall the principle of the secrecy of correspondence: Article 46*bis* CCP, Article 88*bis* CCP, Article 88*quater* CCP, Article 90*quater* CCP, Article 47*septies* CCP,[68] and Article 47*novies* CCP;[69]
- Wiretapping (Article 90*ter* CCP);
- The respect for professional secrecy: Article 90*sexies* §3, and Article 90*octies* CCP (see below, section II.A.4.b.).

Second, data collection by police services and law enforcement authorities is subject to control mechanisms (see also below on remedies against interception orders, section III.B.10.b.).

The Act of 18 March 2014[70] inserted a new Article 44/6 into the Act of 5 August 1992 on the Police Function, which foresees the establishment of a monitoring body for police information.[71]

The Courts in Chambers (a court of instruction in first instance)[72] and the Indictment Chamber (a court of instruction in appeal)[73] evaluate the legality of the

---

[67] Brigitte Pesquié (revised by Yves Cartuyvels), "The Belgian system", in Mireille Delmas-Marty and John R. Spencer, *European Criminal Procedures*, Cambridge Studies in International and Comparative Law, Cambridge University Press, 2002, p. (81) 89.

[68] Article 47*septies* CCP concerns the observation measure (Article 47*sexies* CCP).

[69] Article 47*novies* CCP concerns the infiltration measure (Article 47*octies* CCP).

[70] Act of 18 March 2014 regarding police information management and modifying the Act of 5 August 1992 on the Police Function, the Data Protection Act of 8 December 1992, and the Code of Criminal Procedure, *Belgian Official Journal*, 28 March 2014, entry into force on 7 April 2014.

[71] Het Controleorgaan op de politionele informatie (in Dutch), L'Organe de contrôle de l'information policière (in French).

[72] Raadkamer (in Dutch), Chambre du conseil (in French).

[73] Kamer van Inbeschuldigingstelling (in Dutch), Chambres des mises en accusation (in French).

evidence collection during the investigation phase (Articles 131, 135 §2, and 235*bis* §6 CCP).[74]

Third, exclusionary rules demand the exclusion of illegally obtained evidence (see section IV.2. below).

Finally, criminal liability exists for the unlawful infringement of telecommunications (see section II.A.4.a. below).

4. Statutory protection of personal data

a) Criminal liability for the unlawful infringement of telecommunication[75]

This section only addresses criminal liability for unlawful infringements that directly target telecommunications.[76] Neither does it discuss *non-criminal* liability for the unlawful infringement of telecommunication.[77]

---

[74] Brigitte Pesquié (revised by Yves Cartuyvels), "The Belgian system", in Mireille Delmas-Marty and John R. Spencer, *European Criminal Procedures*, Cambridge Studies in International and Comparative Law, Cambridge University Press, 2002, (81) 87, 97.

[75] This section is partially based on the authors' earlier work: Paul De Hert and Gertjan Boulet, "Cybercrime report for Belgium," *International Review of Penal Law (RIDP / IRPL)*, 2013, issue 84, no. 1-2, pp. 12–59, available at http://www.penal.org/IMG/pdf/RIDP_2013_1_2_CD_Annexe.pdf, and *Electronic Review of the International Association of Penal* Law, 2013, http://www.penal.org/sites/default/files/files/RV-2.pdf; see also Paul De Hert and Frédéric Van Leeuw, "Cybercrime Legislation in Belgium," in Eric Dirix and Yves-Henri Leleu (eds.), *The Belgian reports at the Congress of Washington of the International Academy of Comparative Law*, Brussels, Bruylant, 2011, pp. 867–956, available at http://www.vub.ac.be/LSTS/pub/Dehert/389.pdf

[76] The following unlawful infringements do not necessarily directly target telecommunications: child pornography (Articles 383 and 283*bis* CC); grooming (Article 380*ter* §2 CC); stalking (Article 442*bis* CC for normal stalking, and Article 145 §3*bis* of the Act of 13 June 2005 on electronic communications for online stalking); defamation (libel, slander) (Article 443 CC); online gambling (see the Act of 10 January 2010 on gambling, *Belgian Official Journal*, 1 February 2010, entry into force on 1 January 2011); infringements of copyright (see the Act of 19 April 2014 inserting a book XI on 'intellectual property' into the Code of Economic Law, *Belgian Official Journal*, 12 June 2014, entry into force on 1 January 2014; the Act repealed the copyright Act of 30 June 1994, *Belgian Official Journal*, 27 July 1994, entry into force on 1 August 1994); the protection of databases and the rights of the producers of the databases (the Act of 19 April 2014 also repealed the Act of 31 August 1998 transposing the European directive from 11 March 1996 on the juridical protection of databases, *Belgian Official Journal*, 14 November 1998, entry into force on 14 November 1998); abuse registration of a domain name (see the Act of 15 December 2013 inserting book XII on " Law of the electronic economy" in the Code of Economic Law, *Belgian Official Journal*, 14 January 2014, entry into force on 31 May 2014. The Act repealed the Act of 26 June 2003 about the abuse of registration of a domain name, *Belgian Official Journal,* 9 September 2003, entry into force on 19 September 2003); provisions criminalizing racism and holocaust denial (see, for instance, the Act of 30 July 1981 to suppress certain acts inspired by racism and xenophobia, *Belgian Official Journal*, 8 August 1981, entry into force on 18 August 1981); and press crimes (judicial interpreta-

aa) Traditional offenses in the Belgian Criminal Code

The Belgian Criminal Code (CC) traditionally criminalizes identity theft (Article 231), trespassing (Article 439), violations of professional secrecy (Article 458), and the secrecy of communications (Article 460).

bb) The protection and interception of electronic communications: the Act of 30 June 1994

The Act of 30 June 1994 protecting privacy against the interception of communication and telecommunication[78] regulates both the protection and the interception of electronic communications. The Act introduced Article 314*bis* into the Belgian Criminal Code, which lays down the prohibition, applicable to everyone, of taking cognisance of the contents of electronic communications one does not participate in during the transfer of the electronic communications. A similar prohibition was introduced for public officials in Article 259*bis* CC. However, it should be noted that the monitoring exception in Article 90*ter* CCP provides an exception to the theoretical prohibition of the interception of electronic communications.

cc) The Computer Crime Act of 28 November 2000

The Computer Crime Act of 28 November 2000[79] introduced new penal legislation concerning computer crimes in Belgium. The Act introduced new provisions into the Code of Criminal Law and the Code of Criminal Procedure. The law created the crime of computer forgery[80] (Article 210*bis*), computer fraud[81] (Arti-

---

tion of the right to freedom of expression and freedom of the press as shaped by Articles 19, 25, and 150 of the Constitution).

77 Non-criminal liability for the unlawful infringement of telecommunication follows from infringements of the national collective agreement of 26 April 2002 on the protection of the private lives of employees with respect to controls on electronic on-line communications data (see section II.A.2. above). The collective agreement of 26 April 2002 was declared legally binding by Royal Decree of 12 June 2002 declaring legally binding the national collective agreement of 26 April 2002 on the protection of the private lives of employees with respect to controls on electronic on-line communications data, *Belgian Official Journal*, 29 June 2002, entry into force on 9 July 2002.

Article 189 of the Social Criminal Code of 6 June 2010 (*Belgian Official Journal*, 1 July 2010, entry into force on the same day) provides that infringements of generally legally binding, declared collective agreements shall be punished by a level 1 sanction, to be multiplied by the total number of employees involved. Article 100 of the Social Criminal Code provides that a level 1 sanction consists of an administrative fine of 10 to 100 euro.

78 Act of 30 June 1994 protecting privacy against the interception of communication and telecommunication, *Belgian Official Journal*, 24 January 1995, entry into force on 3 February 1995.

79 Wet inzake informaticacriminaliteit (in Dutch), Loi sur la criminalité informatique (in French), *Belgian Official Journal,* 3 February 2001, entry into force on 13 February 2002.

80 Valsheid in informatica (in Dutch), faux en informatique (in French).

cle 540*quater*), hacking (Article 550*bis*), and sabotage of computer data/data and system interference[82] (Article 550*ter*).

dd) The Act of 13 June 2005 on electronic communications

Article 124 §§1 and 3 of the Act of 13 June 2005 on electronic communications protects the content of e-mails. Under Article 124 of the Act, the following actions are regarded as crimes unless the consent of all parties directly or indirectly involved has been given:

1. Intentionally taking note of the existence of signs, signals, writings, images, sounds, or data of any nature that originate from and are addressed to others;
2. Intentionally modifying or deleting this information by any technical means or identifying the other persons;
3. Intentionally taking note of telecommunication data that relate to other persons;
4. Disclosing, using in any way, modifying, or destroying the information, identification, and data set forth in 1, 2, and 3 above.

The Act of 13 June 2005 on electronic communications also contains a special penal provision in Article 145 §3, 1° that punishes anyone who carries out fraudulent electronic communications through a network of electronic communication. The provision can be used to prosecute hacking.

ee) The Belgian Data Protection Act of 8 December 1992

The Belgian Data Protection Act of 8 December 1992 imposes obligations on data controllers both in the public and in the private sector, although certain exemptions do exist, for instance in the case of information gathering for police purposes. The criminal provisions of the Act (Articles 37 to 39) provide a whole range of sanctions for the data controller who, if failing to meet his obligations, would jeopardize the confidentiality of data. These sanctions will undoubtedly apply to certain uses of personal data threatening the identity data of a person. Especially Article 39 of the Act is, in theory at least, a very suitable instrument to combat identity theft, hacking, secret surveillance, and websites with sensitive data hosted by individuals without permission, such as websites about suspected sex offenders.

Article 39 of the Belgian Data Protection Act of 8 December 1992 punishes with a fine of one hundred to one hundred thousand francs

1) any controller, his representative in Belgium, appointee or agent who processes personal data in violation of the principles and requirements imposed in Article 4 §1 (finality principle, proportionality principle, etc.);

---

[81] Informaticabedrog (in Dutch), fraude informatique (in French).

[82] Informaticasabotage (in Dutch), sabotage de données informatiques (in French).

2) any controller, his representative in Belgium, appointee or agent who processes personal data in cases other than those permitted in Article 5 (consent, contract, legal ground);

3) any controller, his representative in Belgium, appointee or agent who processes personal data in violation of the Articles 6, 7 and 8 (regarding the so-called sensitive data);

4) any controller, his representative in Belgium, appointee or agent who has failed to comply with the obligations laid down in Article 9 (duty to inform the data subject);

5) any controller, his representative in Belgium, appointee or agent who fails to communicate the information referred to in Article 10 §1 within forty five days upon receipt of the request, or who knowingly communicates inaccurate or incomplete data;

6) any person who resorts to acts of violence or threat with the purpose to force another person to disclose information that is obtained through the exercise of the right as defined in Article 10 §1 or to give his consent for the processing of personal data relating to him;

7) any controller, his representative in Belgium, appointee or agent who starts, manages, continues to manage or terminates an automatic processing operation of personal data without compliance with the requirements of Prior notification to the National Data Protection Authority (Article 17);

8) any controller, his representative in Belgium, appointee or agent who communicates incomplete or inaccurate information in the notifications prescribed in Article 17;

[…]

10) any controller, his representative in Belgium, appointee or agent who, in violation of Article 19, refuses to communicate to the Commission the information relating to the non-automatic processing of personal data that are contained in a filing system or that are intended to be contained therein;

[…]

12) any person who transfers personal data, brings about or permits such transfer to a country outside the European Community that has been entered on the list referred to in Article 21 §2 in violation of the requirements of Article 22;

13) any person who prevents the Commission, its members or the experts who have been deployed by it from making the verifications referred to in Article 32.

b) Protection of professional secrets in criminal procedural law

Article 89*ter* CCP (looking-in operations) provides a special rule for measures targeted at lawyers and doctors: In case the private place is a home, a part of a home, or the office of a lawyer of doctor, then the investigating judge (instead of the public prosecutor) has to authorize the measure.

The data retention Act of 29 May 2016 added a new paragraph 3 on professional secrecy to Article 88*bis* CCP (tracing of traffic data, and localization of electronic communications). The new paragraph 3 reflects Article 90*octies* CCP (wiretapping), and reads as follows:

The measure may only cover the electronic communications of a lawyer or a doctor, who themselves are suspected of having committed or participated in one of the criminal offenses referred to in the first paragraph, or if specific facts suggest that third parties

> suspected of having committed a criminal offense referred to in the first paragraph, use their electronic communications.
>
> The measure may not be implemented if, depending on the case, the president of the Bar or the representative of the provincial council of the order of physicians have not been informed of it. They will be informed by the investigating judge of what according to him shall be covered by professional secrecy. These data shall not be recorded in the official record.

Articles 90*sexies* and 90*octies* CCP provide special rules for wiretapping measures targeted at lawyers and doctors.

Article 90*sexies* §3 provides the following:

> The official record shall not include (tele-)communications covered by professional secrecy. Such (tele-)communications shall be kept at the Registry in a sealed envelope.[83] If it concerns persons referred to in Article 90octies, first paragraph, then shall be acted on the matter as provided in Article 90octies, second paragraph.

Article 90*octies* CCP reads as follows:

> The measure may only cover the premises used for business purposes, the domicile or the (tele-)communications means of a lawyer or a doctor, who themselves are suspected of having committed or participated in one of the criminal offenses referred to in article 90ter, or if specific facts suggest that third parties suspected of having committed a criminal offense referred to in Article 90ter, use their premises, domicile or (tele-)communications.
>
> The measure may not be implemented if, depending on the case, the president of the Bar or the representative of the provincial council of the order of physicians is not aware of it. They will be informed by the investigating judge of which according to him shall be considered as (tele-)communications covered by professional secrecy and not recorded in the official record under Article 90sexies, third paragraph.

c) Principle of "purpose limitation of personal data"

Article 15, 1° of 5 August 1992 on the Police Function reads as follows:

> In the performance of their judicial police functions, the police have the task: 1° to detect the crimes, misdemeanours and contraventions, to gather evidence thereof, to notify the competent authorities thereof, to apprehend and arrest the perpetrators, to bring them at the disposal of the competent authorities, in the manner and forms provided by law;

Furthermore, as mentioned above (section II.A.2.c.), the Act of 18 March 2014 inserted a new Article 44/1 into the Act of 5 August 1992 on the Police Function, which provides that the police services shall only process information and personal data insofar as sufficient, relevant, and not excessive in view of police purposes.

Similarly, the data gathering practices of public prosecutors and investigating judges should be seen in light of their functions in conjunction with the prosecution

---

[83] The Act of 5 February 2016 added the specification that "[s]uch (tele-)communications shall be kept at the Registry in a sealed envelope." Act of 5 February 2016 regarding the modification of criminal law and criminal procedure and regarding diverse provisions on criminal policy, *Belgian Official Journal*, 19 February 2016, entry into force on 29 February 2016.

and investigation of criminal offenses. Article 28*bis* §1 CCP provides that "[t]he preliminary investigation is the whole of actions aimed at the detection of crimes, their perpetrators and evidence, and to collect the information relevant for the purposes of criminal proceedings." Article 55 CCP provides that "the investigation is the whole of action aimed at the detection of the perpetrators of crimes, to collect evidence and to take measures that allow the courts to pass informed judgments."

The Belgian Data Protection Act of 8 December 1992 imposes data protection obligations, including the principle of purpose limitation, on data controllers in the public and private sectors. However, as noted earlier (section II.A.2.c.), the Privacy Act contains some exemptions, e.g., for police purposes.

B. Powers in the Code of Criminal Procedure

1. Requirement of (reasonable) clarity for powers in the law of criminal procedure

The *nullum crimen sine lege* principle also applies in the area of criminal procedure.[84] Article 12(2) of the Constitution reads as follows:

> The freedom of the individual is guaranteed.
>
> No one can be prosecuted except in the cases provided for by the law, and in the form prescribed by the law.
>
> Except in the case of a flagrant offence, no one can be arrested except on the strength of a reasoned judge's order, which must be served at the time of arrest or at the latest within twenty-four hours.

In his doctoral thesis on police powers and human rights, Goossens (former attorney-at-law, now member of the Standing Police Monitoring Committee[85]) uses the definition of the legality principle in the criminal procedural sense as proposed by Professor Traest:[86] a legal basis, which moreover should specify the competent authorities as well as the conditions under which the exercise of the investigation method may involve the infringement of human rights protected by the ECHR.[87]

---

[84] The principle also applies in the area of preventive police law. Article 1, §3 of the Act of 5 August 1992 on the Police Function provides that the police services shall only use coercive methods under the conditions determined by law.

[85] Vast Comité van toezicht op de politiediensten (*Comité P*, in Dutch), Comité permanent de contrôle des services de police (in French).

[86] Franky Goossens, *Politiebevoegdheden en mensenrechten in België. Rechtsvergelijkend en internationaal onderzoek* (Police powers and human rights in Belgium. Comparative and international research), doctoral thesis, Leuven, 2006, pp. 28–29, available at https://lirias.kuleuven.be/bitstream/1979/420/2/frankydoctoraat.pdf

[87] Philip Traest, "Rechts(on)zekerheid in materieel en formeel strafrecht en strafrechtelijk legaliteitsbeginsel" (Legal uncertainty in material and formal criminal law, and the

Goossens further embraces Professor Dupont's description of the legality principle as one of the most fundamental principles of criminal law and as a legal protective principle that finds its historic roots in a reaction against government arbitrariness in the criminal justice system of the ancien régime.[88]

The principle of strict interpretation of criminal law, and thereto related the prohibition of an analogous application of criminal law, is closely related to the principle of legality.[89] Legal doctrine traditionally discusses the prohibition of analogous application under criminal law rather than under the law of criminal procedure. In reality, we observe that law enforcement authorities apply the traditional monitoring measure (Article 90*ter* CCP) to electronic communications and thus allow the analogy between the wiretapping of traditional telecommunications and contemporary electronic communications (see below, section III.B.2.).[90] However, the annual reports of the Minister of Justice in implementation of Article 90*decies* CCP express the need for a modernization of the laws regarding wiretapping on the Internet (see below, section III.B.c.).[91]

2. Differentiation and classification of powers in the law of criminal procedure

The preliminary investigation methods in the Belgian law of criminal procedure are based on the distinction between the preliminary investigation/inquiry phase, under the responsibility of the public prosecutor, and the investigation/instruction phase, under the responsibility of the investigating judge who can also use coercive investigation methods.[92] Article 28*bis* §3 CCP provides that:

> [s]ubject to statutory exceptions, the preliminary investigation measures cannot involve coercive measure nor involve violation of individual rights and freedoms.

All reactive criminal law powers mentioned under section I.A.2.a. are principally reserved for the investigation phase, except for data seizure (Article 39*bis* CCP) and the collection of identification data of electronic communications (Article 46*bis* CCP).

---

principle of legality in criminal law), *Rechtskundig Weekblad*, 1993-1994, pp. (1190) 1192.

88 Goossens, *op. cit.*, pp. 28, 30; Lieven Dupont, *Beginselen van strafrecht Deel 1* (Principles of criminal law vol. 1), Leuven, Acco, 2004, pp. 28, 29.

89 Chris Van den Wyngaert, *Strafrecht, Strafprocesrecht & Internationaal Strafrecht in hoofdlijnen* (An Outline of Criminal Law, Criminal Procedural Law & International Criminal Law), Antwerp-Apeldoorn, Maklu, 2006, p. 80.

90 Jan Kerkhofs and Philippe Van Linthout, *Cybercrime*, Brussels, Politeia, 2013, pp. 396, 244 and following.

91 See above, section I.B.2.a. See, for instance, the 2013 report in implementation of Article 90*decies* CCP, pp. 18, 47, 48.

92 Brigitte Pesquié (revised by Yves Cartuyvels), "The Belgian system", in Mireille Delmas-Marty and John R. Spencer, *European Criminal Procedures*, Cambridge Studies in International and Comparative Law, Cambridge University Press, 2002, (81) 87.

III. Powers for Accessing Telecommunication Data in the Law of Criminal Procedure

A. Overview

In this section, we briefly explain the legal provisions for intercepting electronic communications under (reactive) criminal law that are also listed under section I.A.2.a.

1. Normal investigation methods

Article 39*bis* CCP (data seizure) provides that the rules in the CCP on seizure apply to the copying, making inaccessible, and deleting of data stored in a computer system.

Article 46*bis* CCP (collection of identification data of electronic communications) empowers the public prosecutor to identify 1) the subscriber or the habitual user of an electronic communications service, 2) the electronic communication means used, and 3) the electronic communications services to which a particular person is a subscriber or that are habitually used by a particular person.

Article 88*bis* CCP (tracing of traffic data, and localization of electronic communications) empowers the investigating judge, and in specific cases the public prosecutor, to 1) trace traffic data of electronic communications means from which or to which electronic communications are or were made, 2) locate the origin or the destination of electronic communications.

Article 88*ter* CCP (the network search) empowers the investigating judge, when ordering a search of a computer system or a part thereof, to expand this search to a computer system or a part thereof at a place other than that at which the search takes place.

Article 90*ter* §1 CCP (wiretapping/monitoring) empowers the investigating judge, and in specific cases the public prosecutor, to wiretap, take cognizance of, and record private (tele-)communications during transmission.

2. Special investigation methods and any other methods of investigation

The Act of 6 January 2003 concerning special investigation methods and any other methods of investigation[93] introduced three *special investigation methods* and five *other investigation methods* into the CCP. The two *other investigation methods* relevant for the interception of electronic communications are looking-in opera-

[93] Act of 6 January 2003 concerning special investigation methods and any other methods of investigation, *Belgian Official Journal*, 12 May 2003, entry into force on 22 May 2003.

tions (Articles 46*quinquies* and 89*ter* CCP) and the power to enter a house or a private place to enable eavesdropping with technical means (Article 90*ter* §1, 2° CCP). The two *special investigation methods* relevant for the interception of electronic communications are observation (Article 47*sexies* CCP) and infiltration (Article 47*octies* CCP).

Articles 46*quinquies* and 89*ter* CCP (looking-in operations) empowers the public prosecutor to authorize police officers to enter a private place without the knowledge or consent of the owner.

Article 90*ter* §1, 2° CCP (the power to enter a house or a private place to enable eavesdropping with technical means) empowers the investigating judge, and in specific cases the public prosecutor, to directly monitor (eavesdropping), take cognizance of, or record private electronic communications with technical means.

Article 47*sexies* CCP (observation) empowers the public prosecutor and the investigating judge to order systematic observation by police officers of one or more persons; their presence or behavior; or of certain items, places, or events.

Article 47*octies* CCP (infiltration) empowers the public prosecutor and the investigating judge to authorize a police officer to maintain contact, under a false identity, with one or more persons for whom serious indications exist that they have committed or will commit either offenses within a criminal organization or offenses that are of a certain seriousness.

3. Cooperation with individuals and the private sector

For the execution of the above-mentioned investigation operations Belgian law enforcement agencies can cooperate with individuals and the private sector (Article 39*bis*, Article 46*bis*, Article 88*bis*, Article 88*quater*, Article 90*quater* §§2, 4 CCP).

Article 39*bis* §3 CCP (data seizure) allows public prosecutors to request an Internet Service Provider (ISP) to delete the domain name of a site that violates the law from their Domain Name Server (DNS).

Article 46*bis* CCP (collection of identification data of electronic communications) obliges operators of an electronic communications network and providers of an electronic communications service to provide identification data upon request of the public prosecutor.

Article 88*bis* CCP (tracing of traffic data, and localization of electronic communications) obliges operators of an electronic communications network and providers of an electronic communications service to provide traffic or localization data upon request of the public prosecutor.

Article 88*quater* CCP (network search) allows the public prosecutor to impose on certain individuals the obligation to cooperate during an investigation. These individuals are persons of whom the investigating judge thinks that they have special capacities/knowledge concerning the computer system that is the object of an investigation or concerning services used to store, process, encrypt, or transfer data.

Article 90*quater* §2 CCP (wiretapping) obliges operators of an electronic communications network and providers of an electronic communications service to provide technical assistance to a data tapping measure upon request of the investigating judge.

Article 90*quater* §4 (wiretapping) echoes Article 88*quater* CCP.

Belgian law enforcement agencies can also cooperate with so-called closed user groups on the basis of Articles 122, 125, and 127 of the Electronic Communications Act[94] and with service providers acting as a mere conduit, catching and hosting on the basis of Articles XII.17 till XII.20 of the Code of Economic Law.[95]

Furthermore, in specific cases, judicial authorities can order a temporary surveillance period for Internet service providers acting as a mere conduit, catching and hosting (Article XII.20 of the Code of Economic Law).

4. Data retention

The general data retention (preservation) provision is Article 126 of the Electronic Communications Act,[96] which provides, among others, the providers that are subject to data retention obligations, the purposes of data retention, the obligations of the network and service providers, and the data retention periods. However, on 11 June 2015, the Belgian Constitutional Court invalidated article 126 of the Electronic Communications Act. A new Belgian data retention law of 29 May 2016 entered into force on 28 July 2016.

A Royal Decree of 19 September 2013 lists the types of data that are subject to data retention.[97]

Article 9 §7 of the Electronic Communications Act of 13 June 2005 provides that a specific Royal Decree shall address the matter of data retention for closed user

---

[94] Article 9 §7 of the Electronic Communications Act of 13 June 2005 provides that a specific Royal Decree shall address the matter of the cooperation between law enforcement agencies and closed user groups.

[95] Code of Economic Law of 28 February 2013, *Belgian Official Journal*, 29 March 2013, entry into force on 12 December 2013.

[96] As amended by the Belgian Communication Act of 30 July 2013 amending Articles 2, 126, and 145 of the Act of 13 June 2005 on electronic communications and Article 90*decies* of the Code of Criminal Procedure, *Belgian Official Journal*, 23 August 2013, entry into force on 2 September 2013.

[97] Royal Decree of 19 September 2013 regarding the execution of Article 126 of the Act of 13 June 2005 on electronic communications, *Belgian Official Journal*, 8 October 2013, entry into force on 19 September 2013.

groups. Federal Magistrate Jan Kerkhofs and Investigating Judge Philippe Van Linthout state that it could be said that Belgian providers of electronic communication services or networks with no notification duty are currently released from data retention obligations, taking into account the lack of a specific Royal Decree.[98] For the same reason, service providers that act as a mere conduit or provide caching and hosting activities under the Code of Economic Law are currently released from data retention obligations.

B. Interception of Content Data

1. Statutory provision

Article 90*ter* CCP is the main provision in the law of criminal procedure dealing with the interception of the content of communications in transmission. Article 90*ter*, 1° CCP contains its core meaning:

> §1 The investigating judge may, in exceptional cases, when the investigation so requires, wiretap, take cognizance and record private (tele-)communications, during transmission, if there are serious indications that the offense for which he is seized is a criminal offense, as referred to in any of the provisions listed in §2, and if the other investigation methods are not sufficient to reveal the truth.
>
> In order to enable direct monitoring (eavesdropping), taking cognizance or recording of private (tele-)communications with technical means, the investigating judge may order, at any time, also without the knowledge or without the consent of either the resident or the owner or his rightful claimant, to enter a house or a private place.

2. Scope of application

a) Object of interception

Kerkhofs and Van Linthout say that the application of the wiretapping measure depends on three conditions pertaining to the nature of communications:

1) active communications;
2) private communications (see the text of Article 90*ter* CCP);
3) communications in transmission (see below, section III.B.2.).

The following facts show that electronic telecommunication falls under the material scope of the application of Article 90*ter* CCP.

First, we referred to the annual reports of the Minister of Justice in implementation of Article 90*decies* CCP, which provide statistics on the subjects of the wire-

98 Jan Kerkhofs and Philippe Van Linthout, *Cybercrime*, Brussels, Politeia, 2013, p. 396.

tapping measures: landline numbers, mobile numbers, IMEI numbers, and e-mail (see section I.B.2.).

Second, the parliamentary preparatory works provide that the term (tele-)communications has a broad scope, as understood in its daily use: the term includes any linguistic expression, verbal or non-verbal, whether directly or from a physical distance, and irrespective of the number of participants. The term includes monologues, telegrams, telex, telefax, and electronic data transfers in computers and computer networks.[99]

Third, Kerkhofs and Van Linthout further specify that Article 90*ter* CCP covers the following forms of communication:[100]

- Classical telecommunications: analogous communication (voice and data) via landlines (landline numbers) and mobile communications;
- Pop-mail: e.g., Microsoft Outlook, Mozilla Thunderbird, Apple Mail;
- Webmail: e.g., Yahoo, Gmail, MSN, Hotmail;
- Voiceover IP (VoIP): e.g., Viber, Skype;
- Instant Messaging (IM) via
  - private chatrooms: e.g., Paltalk.com;
  - online gaming applications: e.g., World of Warcraft;
  - virtual gaming worlds: e.g., Second Lige;
  - mobile applications: e.g., WhatsApp, Google Talk, Blackberry Messenger.

It should be noted that IP data do not constitute private communications and therefore do not fall under the scope of Article 90*ter* CCP.

The available annual reports of the Minister of Justice as regards the implementation of Article 90*decies* CCP (until 2013) show no cases of wiretapping clouds or communications between two independent computer systems (e.g., between an automated machine and its computer-based automated control center, especially in the "Internet of things").

---

[99] Parliamentary preparatory works, regarding the legislative proposal protecting privacy against the interception of communication and telecommunication, Belgian Senate, 1992–1993, 1 September 1993, 843-1, p. 7, available at http://www.senate.be/lexdocs/S0539/S05390297.pdf; Parliamentary preparatory works, regarding the legislative proposal protecting privacy against the interception of communication and telecommunication, Belgian Senate, 1993–1994, 18 May 1994, 843-2, p. 38, available at http://www.senate.be/lexdocs/S0539/S05390364.pdf

[100] Jan Kerkhofs and Philippe Van Linthout, *Cybercrime*, Brussels, Politeia, 2013, pp. 279, 282, 295.

b) Temporal limits of telecommunication

aa) Access to ongoing telecommunication

Article 90*ter* §1 CCP provides that the wiretapping measure only applies to (tele-)communications "during transmission."[101] For Kerkhofs and Van Linthout, the end of the transmission phase is the so-called "indicated necessary terminal," i.e., the place where an e-mail is deemed to arrive considering its nature and the e-mail configuration. They specify that, whereas the indicated necessary terminal of "pop-mail" is principally the user's own computer, the indicated necessary terminal of "webmail" is principally the user's online webmail account. Hence, pop-mail that arrives in an online web mailbox is still deemed to be in transmission, whereas webmail that arrives in an online web mailbox will be deemed to be out of transmission and therefore beyond the scope of the monitoring measure of Article 90*ter* CCP. In the latter case, law enforcement authorities will have to use a network search (Article 88*ter* CCP) to access the data. Hence, the use of a monitoring measure or a network search will depend on the specific e-mail configuration set by the user. In practice, however, pop-mail may *de facto* be configured as webmail, and vice versa. In case of doubt, law enforcement authorities issue a combined warrant: "90*ter* CCP versus 88*ter* CCP," or vice versa.

Kerkhofs and van Linthout also say that a wiretapping measure is possible in case of misuse of webmail, such as the sharing of one webmail account to exchange messages via e-mails stored in the draft folder. In this case, the transmission phase ends after login and reading of the draft e-mail by the recipient. Thus, in this case the end of the transmission phase seems conditioned by the "reading" of e-mails.

bb) Access after the end of telecommunication transmission

As said in the previous section, Article 90*ter* §1 CCP provides that the monitoring measure only applies to (tele-)communications *during transmission*. Hence, the monitoring measure does not apply when the respective data are stored before or after the transmission process.

c) Current matters of dispute

A first current matter of dispute is the determination of the transmission phase. As previously said, for Kerkhofs and Van Linthout, pop-mail arriving in an online web mailbox is still deemed to be in transmission and therefore can be intercepted on the basis of Article 90*ter* CCP. Former attorney-at-law Dewandeleer confirmed

---

[101] Jan Kerkhofs and Philippe Van Linthout, *Cybercrime*, Brussels, Politeia, 2013, p. 288.

this view, which is based on a judgment of 4 December 2007 of the Correctional Court of Leuven.[102]

Arnou (attorney-at-law), however, says that the wiretapping measure is not possible for e-mails stored on the server of the service provider.[103] His reasoning echoes the parliamentary preparatory works of 1998 modifying Act of 30 June 1994 protecting privacy against the interception of communication and telecommunication, which state that e-mails stored on the server of a service provider do not enjoy the privacy protection against the interception of (tele-)communications (Article 314*bis* and Article 259*bis* CC, see section II.A.4. above) but are possibly protected by other criminal laws. Therefore, the parliamentary preparatory works say such e-mails cannot be intercepted on the basis of Article 90*ter* CC but on the basis of other investigation methods, such as the powers of search and seizure (Article 39*bis* CCP) and the network search (Article 88*ter* CCP).[104]

The foregoing shows that constitutional reasoning regarding the scope of privacy and criminal law protection, such as the protection against the interception of (tele-)communications offered by Article 314*bis* and Article 259*bis* CC, could influence the discussions regarding the scope of the wiretapping measure.

An additional current matter of dispute is the difficulty of determining the transmission phase on social media, considering for instance the potential impact of status messages on Facebook. Kerkhofs and Van Linthout have therefore proposed a rewriting of the laws on wiretapping.[105] As said earlier, the annual reports of the Minister of Justice in implementation of Article 90*decies* CCP also express the need for a modernization of the laws regarding wiretapping on the Internet.[106]

---

[102] Dirk Dewandeleer, "De kennisname van e-mails 'tijdens de overbrenging ervan', een verduidelijking van het telecommunicatiegeheim" (Taking knowledge of e-mails during the transmission phase. A clarification of the secrecy of telecommunications), annotation to the judgment of the Correctional Court of Leuven, 4 December 2007), *Tijdschrift voor Strafrecht*, 2008, vol. 3, p. [226] 226.

[103] Luc Arnou, "Afluisteren tijdens het gerechtelijk onderzoek" (Wiretapping during the investigation); in Commentaar Strafrecht en strafvordering (Commentary criminal law and criminal procedural law), Gent, Kluwer, 2008, vol. 59, pp. 13–14, no. 12.

[104] Parliamentary preparatory works, modifying the Act of 30 June 1994 protecting privacy against the interception of communication and telecommunication, Belgian Chamber of Parliaments, 1996-1997, 29 May 1998, no. 49K1075/017, p. 10, available at http://www.dekamer.be/FLWB/PDF/49/1075/49K1075017.pdf

[105] Jan Kerkhofs and Philippe Van Linthout, *Cybercrime*, Brussels, Politeia, 2013, p. 246.

[106] See I.B.2.a. above. See, for instance, the 2013 annual report of the Minister of Justice in implementation of Article 90*decies* CCP, pp. 18, 47, 48.

3. Special protection of confidential communication content

a) Privileged communication

aa) Professional secrets

(1) Conditional protection of lawyer's and doctor's secrets against the monitoring measure: in case of suspicion only and after notification of the Bar and the order of physicians

Article 90*octies* §1 and §2, 1° read as follows:

> The monitoring measure may only cover the premises used for business purposes, the domicile or the (tele-)communications means of a lawyer or a doctor, who themselves are suspected of having committed or participated in one of the criminal offenses referred to in article 90ter, or if specific facts suggest that third parties suspected of having committed a criminal offense referred to in Article 90ter, use their premises, domicile or (tele-)communications.
>
> The monitoring measure may not be implemented if, depending on the case, the president of the Bar or the representative of the provincial council of the order of physicians is not aware of it. […]

Accordingly, the conditions of "suspicion" and "notification of the Bar and the order of physicians" only hold for a monitoring measure that covers premises used for business purposes, the domicile, or the (tele-)communications means of a lawyer or a doctor.

Arnou and public prosecutor Freyne hold that compliance with the notification duty follows from a written notification or confirmation of an oral notification in an official record.[107] Although notification of the Bar and the order of physicians is not prescribed under sanction of nullity (see below on the exclusionary rules, section IV.2.), the parliamentary preparatory works underline that the public order nature of this provision implies that failure to do so will entail the nullity of the monitoring measure.[108] As said below, in a judgment of 18 February 2003,[109] the Supreme Court held that the rights of the defense may justify access by the defense to the documents resulting from a nullified investigation method. In fact, these

---

[107] Luc Arnou, "Afluisteren tijdens het gerechtelijk onderzoek" (Wiretapping during the investigation); in Commentaar Strafrecht en strafvordering (Commentary criminal law and criminal procedural law), Gent, Kluwer, 2008, vol. 59, p. 36, no. 33; Thierry Freyne, "De bewaking van privécommunicatie en –telecommunicatie in strafonderzoeken: een stand van zaken" (The monitoring of private communications and telecommunications in criminal proceedings: a state of affairs), *Tijdschrift voor Strafrecht*, 2008, vol. 3, p. 177, no. 33.

[108] Parliamentary preparatory works, regarding the legislative proposal protecting privacy against the interception of communication and telecommunication, Belgian Senate, 1993–1994, 18 May 1994, no. 843-2, p. 189, available at http://www.senate.be/lexdocs/S0539/S05390364.pdf

[109] Supreme Court, 18 February 2003, P.02.0913.N.

documents are not deleted but kept at the Registry in a sealed envelope (Article 235*bis* §6 CCP).

(2) Unconditional protection of professional secrets against inclusion in official records

Article 90*sexies* §3, 1° CCP protects *all* possible professional secrets, such as communication between an attorney-at-law and a client, a medical practitioner and a patient, journalists' communications, communication under the law regulating financial and banking secrecy, etc. The provision provides that "[t]he official records shall not include (tele-)communications covered by professional secrecy."

Article 90*sexies* §3, 2° CCP, read in conjunction with Article 90*octies* §2, 2° CCP, provides additional protection for lawyers and doctors:

> Article 90sexies §3 CCP: If it concerns persons referred to in Article 90octies, first paragraph, then shall be acted on the matter as provided in Article 90octies, second paragraph.
>
> Article 90octies §2, 2° CCP: They [the president of the Bar or the representative of the provincial council of the order of physicians] will be informed by the investigating judge of what according to him shall be considered as (tele-)communications covered by professional secrecy and shall not be recorded in the official record under Article 90sexies, third paragraph.

Although the recordings protected by professional secrecy are not recorded in the official record, they are kept at the Registry in a closed and sealed envelope on the basis of Article 90*septies* §3 CCP.[110] Article 90*septies* §§6–8 CCP provides cases in which the investigating judge or the court *may* upon request allow access to the whole or parts of the recordings deposited at the Registry:[111]

> The defendant, the accused, the civil party, the civilly liable party or their counsel shall receive upon request a copy of all the records of the (tele-)communications of which relevantly deemed parts were transcribed and recorded in an official record to which they have access.
>
> The judge shall decide on the request of the defendant, the accused, the civil party or their counsel, to consult the whole or parts of the other recordings deposited at the Registry, and transcripts that are not recorded in an official record, as well as on their request to transcribe additional parts of the recordings.

---

110 Thierry Freyne, "De bewaking van privécommunicatie en -telecommunicatie in strafonderzoeken: een stand van zaken" (The monitoring of private communications and telecommunications in criminal proceedings: a state of affairs), *Tijdschrift voor Strafrecht,* 2008, vol. 3, p. 177, no. 30.

111 The Act of 5 February 2016 added a new (fifth) paragraph to Article 90*septies* CCP, laying down a right for some parties to access a copy of all the records of the (tele-) communications of which relevantly deemed parts were transcribed and recorded in an official record to which they have access. Act of 5 February 2016 regarding the modification of criminal law and criminal procedure and regarding diverse provisions on criminal policy, *Belgian Official Journal*, 19 February 2016, entry into force on 29 February 2016.

The request addressed to the investigating judge, is treated in accordance with Article 61quinquies. The investigating judge may also refuse this request for reasons connected with the protection of other individual rights or interests.

bb) Protection of the core area of privacy

Article 90*ter* CCP provides no additional protection for the core area of privacy.

b) Responsibility for ensuring protection

The articles discussed in the previous section show that the responsibility for ensuring the protection of professional secrets lies with the investigating judge, thus the magistrate that issues the warrant.

The investigating judge, however, has no complete discretion to determine the stage of the interception phase in which, and the way in which, these privileges have to be conducted. It is recalled, first, that, according to Article 90*octies* §2, 1° CCP, a monitoring measure in respect of the premises used for business purposes, the domicile, or the (tele-)communications means of a lawyer or a doctor may only be implemented *after* notification, depending on the case, of the president of the Bar or the representative of the provincial council of the order of physicians. Second, according to Article 90*octies* §2, 2° CCP, the investigating judge shall inform the president of the Bar or the representative of the provincial council of the order of physicians of what, according to him, shall be considered (tele-)communications covered by professional secrecy and thus not be recorded in the official record under Article 90*sexies*, third paragraph.

However, the investigating judge seems to have more discretion as regards the analysis of the captured information. In fact, the president of the Bar or the representative of the provincial council of the order of physicians does not have the right to be consulted prior to assessment by the investigating judge of what, according to him, shall be considered (tele-)communications covered by professional secrecy. Neither do they have any right of co-decision or contradiction.[112]

4. Execution of telecommunication interception

a) Execution by the authorities with or without the help of third parties

As said, the monitoring measure is laid down in Article 90*ter*, 1° and 2° CCP. A literal reading of the law shows that the Belgian law enforcement authorities do not necessarily need to cooperate with third parties. For instance, law enforcement

---

[112] Raf Verstraeten, *Handboek strafvordering* (Manual on criminal procedure), Antwerp, Maklu, 2007, p. 472, no. 948.

authorities can use their own technical equipment to execute an eavesdropping measure (see below III.B.4.b.).

Article 90*quater* §§2, 4 CCP lays down the cooperation duties for individuals and the private sector.

Article 90*quater* §2, 1° CCP reads as follows:

> §2. If the measure involves an operation on a communications network, then is the operator of this network or the provider of the telecommunications service obliged to provide technical cooperation, if the investigating judge requests so directly or via a by the King designated police service.[113] […]

Article 90*quater* §4, 1-2° CCP reads as follows:

> The investigating judge can order, directly or via a by the King designated police service, persons of whom he thinks that they have special knowledge of the telecommunications service subject to the monitoring measure, or of services used to protect or encrypt data that are stored, processed, encrypted or transferred via a computer system, to provide information on the operation of the system and on the way to get access to the content of the telecommunication, that is or has been transferred, in an understandable format.
>
> He can order persons to make the content of telecommunications accessible in the format requested by him. These persons are obliged to comply with the order, to the extent of their capabilities. […]

Media reports have also alleged direct access by Belgian law enforcement agencies to the servers of operators and service providers.[114] Vodafone's online presentation of its 2014 law enforcement disclosure report confirms this practice but does not specify which countries allow such direct access:

> However, in a small number of countries the law dictates that specific agencies and authorities must have direct access to an operator's network, bypassing any form of operational control over lawful interception on the part of the operator. In those countries, Vodafone will not receive any form of demand for lawful interception access as the relevant agencies and authorities already have permanent access to customer communications via their own direct link.[115]

In our view, it should be kept in mind that the monitoring measure in Article 90*ter* CCP cannot be applied to proactive investigations, and that the modalities

---

[113] The Act of 5 February 2016 amended Article 90*quater* §2, 1° CCP and Article 90*quater* §4, 1-2° CCP, and added the possibility for the investigating judge to request technical cooperation via a police service appointed by the King. Act of 5 February 2016 regarding the modification of criminal law and criminal procedure and regarding diverse provisions on criminal policy, *Belgian Official Journal*, 19 February 2016, entry into force on 29 February 2016.

[114] Cf. The Washington Post, "Do France and Belgium have direct wiretap access to telecom switches?," 7 June 2014, available at http://www.washingtonpost.com/news/volokh-conspiracy/wp/2014/06/07/do-france-and-belgium-have-direct-wiretap-access-to-telecom-switches/

[115] Vodafone, "Law Enforcement Disclosure Report," via https://www.vodafone.com/content/sustainabilityreport/2014/index/operating_responsibly/privacy_and_security/law_enforcement.html

of the cooperation duties under Article 90*quater* §2 and §4 CCP are laid down in the Royal Decree of 9 January 2003 regarding the legal duty to cooperate with judicial requests regarding electronic communications.[116] The Royal Decree installs a Coordination Cell Justice responsible for handling the information requests by Belgian legal authorities. According to Article 4 of the Royal Decree, the Coordination Cell Justice shall transfer the data in real time after receipt of the warrant in Article 90*ter* §1 or §5 CCP. Hence, direct access by law enforcement to the servers of operators and service providers seems questionable, considering the installation of the Coordination Cell Justice for cooperation with law enforcement.

In this regard, the following standard set by the European Telecommunications Standards Institute may also be considered:[117]

> [T]he result of interception shall only be transmitted to the Law Enforcement Monitoring Facility [LEMF] as indicated in the lawful authorization when proof of the authority to receive of the LEMF, and proof of the authority to send of the interface, has been furnished;

b) Accompanying powers for the execution of interception

Article 90*ter* §2 CCP allows clandestine access to a house in order to install equipment to carry out the eavesdropping measure:

> In order to enable direct monitoring (eavesdropping), taking cognizance or recording of private (tele-)communications with technical means, the investigating judge may order, at any time, also without the knowledge or without the consent of either the resident or the owner or his rightful claimant, to enter a house or a private place.

Article 90*ter* CCP does not explain the meaning of the term technical means as to whether or not it can also include technical means falling under the definition of technical means for a looking-in operation and observation (see below, section III.D.1.). Furthermore, the parliamentary preparatory works deliberately give no definition of technical means under Article 259*bis* CC (protection of telecommunications) because any such definition would risk beoming outdated due to techno-

---

[116] Royal Decree of 9 January 2003 regarding the legal duty to cooperate with judicial requests regarding electronic communications, *Belgian Official Journal*, 10 February 2003, entry into force on 10 May 2003; The Royal Decree of 9 January 2003 was amended by the Royal Decree of 8 February 2011: Royal Decree of 8 February 2011 modifying Royal Decree of 9 January 2003 regarding the execution of the Royal Decree of 9 January 2003 regarding the execution of Article 46*bis* §2, paragraph 1, 88*bis* §2, paragraphs 1 and 3 and 90*quater* §2 paragraph 3 CCP and of Article 109*ter* E §2 of the Act of 21 March 1991 on the reform of certain economic public enterprises, *Belgian Official Journal*, 23 February 2011, entry into force on 5 March 2011.

[117] European Telecommunications Standards Institute, "TS 101-331 Lawful Interception (LI); Requirements of Law Enforcement Agencies," V1.1.1 (2001-08), 4.7.g, available at http://www.etsi.org/deliver/etsi_TS/101300_101399/101331/01.01.01_60/ts_101331v0101 01p.pdf

logical developments.[118] However, the parliamentary preparatory works prohibit the intrusion into a computer system (hacking) for the monitoring measure of Article 90*ter* CCP.[119]

Professor De Valkeneer, who is also a Prosecutor General, explains that technical means under Article 90*ter* CCP can include micro-spies, key-loggers, and parabolic microphones outside a home or private place.[120] As said earlier (section I.A.2.), the general wiretapping measure under Article 90*ter* §1, 1° CCP includes direct monitoring/eavesdropping and can therefore also be executed with technical means outside a home or a private place. The eavesdropping measure under Article 90*ter* §1, 2° CCP, however, concerns the power to enter a house or a private place in order to enable eavesdropping with technical means.

Dr. De Wolf asks himself whether viruses could also be used for the monitoring measure.[121]

5. Duties of telecommunication service providers to cooperate

a) Possible addressees of duties of cooperation

As said above (section III.B.5.a.), the cooperation duties for individuals and the private sector, provided in Article 90*quater* §§2, 4 CCP apply to the operators of a communications network, the provider of a telecommunications service, and any persons of whom the investigating judge thinks that they have special knowledge of the telecommunications service subject to the monitoring measure. They also apply to the operators/providers of services used to protect or encrypt data that are stored, processed, encrypted, or transferred via a computer system.

Hence, the personal scope of application of the cooperation duty is quite broad and includes infrastructure providers working at the IP-transport level (operators of a telecommunications network), Internet Access Providers (IAPs) and Internet Service Providers (ISPs), such as social media providers and cloud computing service providers.

---

118 Parliamentary preparatory works, regarding the legislative proposal protecting privacy against the interception of communication and telecommunication, Belgian Senate, 1992-1993, 1 September 1993, no. 843-1, p. 6, available at http://www.senate.be/lexdocs/S0539/S05390297.pdf

119 Parliamentary preparatory works, regarding the legislative proposal protecting privacy against the interception of communication and telecommunication, Belgian Senate, 1992-1993, 1 September 1993, no. 843-1, p. 11, available at http://www.senate.be/lexdocs/S0539/S05390297.pdf

120 Christian De Valkeneer, *Manuel de l'enquête pénale* (Manual on criminal investigation), Brussels, Larcier, 2006, p. 334.

121 Daniel De Wolf, "Rapport Belge" (Belgian report on criminal procedure), *Electronic Review of the International Association of Penal Law*, 2014, p. 23, available at http://www.penal.org/sites/default/files/files/RA%20-%203.pdf

Of note in this regard is a judgment of the Belgian Supreme Court of 18 January 2011 (see section III.C.1.dd.), in which the court gave an autonomous (broad) interpretation of the term "electronic communications provider" mentioned in Article 46*bis* CCP (the collection of identification data of electronic communications).

b) Content of duties to cooperate

Article 90*quater* §§2, 4 CCP lays down the cooperation duties for individuals and the private sector.

Article 90*quater* §2, 1° CCP reads as follows:

> §2. If the measure involves an operation on a communications network, then is the operator of this network or the provider of the telecommunications service obliged to provide technical cooperation, if the investigating judge requests so directly or via a by the King designated police service.[122] [...]

Article 90*quater* §4, 1° and 2° CCP reads as follows:

> §4 The investigating judge can order, directly or via a by the King designated police service, persons of whom he thinks that they have special knowledge of the telecommunications service subject to the monitoring measure, or of services used to protect or encrypt data that are stored, processed, encrypted or transferred via a computer system, to provide information on the operation of the system and on the way to get access to the content of the telecommunication, that is or has been transferred, in an understandable format.
>
> He can order persons to make the content of telecommunications accessible in the format requested by him. These persons are obliged to comply with the order, to the extent of their capabilities.

The modalities of the cooperation duties under Article 90*quater* §§2, 4 CCP are laid down in the Royal Decree of 9 January 2003 regarding the legal duty to cooperate with judicial requests regarding electronic communications.[123] The Royal Decree installs a Coordination Cell Justice responsible for handling the information requests from Belgian legal authorities.

---

[122] The Act of 5 February 2016 amended Article 90*quater* §2, 1° CCP and Article 90*quater* §4, 1° and 2° CCP, and added the possibility for the investigating judge to request technical cooperation via a by the King appointed police service. Act of 5 February 2016 regarding the modification of criminal law and criminal procedure and regarding diverse provisions on criminal policy, *Belgian Official Journal*, 19 February 2016, entry into force on 29 February 2016.

[123] Royal Decree of 9 January 2003 regarding the legal duty to cooperate with judicial requests regarding electronic communications, *Belgian Official Journal*, 10 February 2003; The Royal Decree of 9 January 2003 was amended by the Royal Decree of 8 February 2011 modifying the Royal Decree of 9 January 2003 regarding the execution of the Royal Decree of 9 January 2003 regarding the execution of Article 46*bis* §2, paragraph 1, 88*bis* §2, paragraph 1 and 3 and 90*quater* §2 paragraph 3 CCP and of Article 109*ter* E §2 of the Act of 21 March 1991 on the reform of certain economic public enterprises, *Belgian Official Journal*, 23 February 2011, entry into force on 5 March 2011.

A circular of the Board of Prosecutors General of 17 December 2009 explains the criminal policy regarding violations of the cooperation duties under Article 46*bis* §2 CCP (the collection of identification data of electronic communications), Article 88*bis* §2 CCP (tracing of traffic data, and localization of electronic communications), and Article 90*quater* §2 CCP.[124]

c) *Duties to provide technical and organizational infrastructure*

aa) Obligated parties

Article 1, 5° of the Royal Decree of 9 January 2003 regarding the legal duty to cooperate with judicial requests regarding electronic communications defines its personal scope of application in terms of the "Internet sector," i.e., the entirety of operators of electronic communications networks and providers of electronic communications services.

bb) Individual technical obligations

Article 6 §3 of the Royal Decree of 9 January 2003 regarding the legal duty to cooperate with judicial requests regarding electronic communications provides that the technical requirements for the data transfer need to comply with the following updated standards and reports of the European Telecommunications Standards Institute:

1) TS 101-331: Lawful Interception (LI); Requirements of Law Enforcement Agencies;
2) TS 101-671: Lawful Interception (LI); Handover interface for the lawful interception of telecommunications traffic;
3) TS 101-909-20-1: AT Digital. Digital Broadband Cable Access to the Public Telecommunications Network; IP Multimedia Time Critical Services; Part 20: Lawful Interception; Sub-part 1: CMS based Voice Telephony Services;
4) TS 101-909-20-2 AT Digital. Digital Broadband Cable Access to the Public Telecommunications Network; IP Multimedia Time Critical Services; Part 20: Lawful Interception; Sub-part 2: Streamed multimedia services;
5) TR 101-943: Lawful Interception (LI); Concepts of Interception in a Generic Network Architecture;

---

[124] Board of Prosecutors General, "Telecommunicatierichtlijn inzake het opsporings- en vervolgingsbeleid betreffende inbreuken op de medewerkingsverplichtingen vervat in de artikelen 46bis § 2, 88bis § 2 en 90quater § 2 van het wetboek van strafvordering" (Telecommunications Circular regarding the investigation and prosecution of violations of the cooperation duties under Articles 46*bis* §2, 88*bis* §2 and 90*quater* §2 CCP), COL 14/2009, 17 December 2009, available (in Dutch and French) at http://www.om-mp.be/omzendbrief/4420834/col_14-2009_dd__17_12_2009.html

6) TR 101-944: Lawful Interception (LI); Issues on IP Interception;
7) TR 102-053: Lawful Interception (LI); Notes on ISDN LI functionality;
8) TS 102-232: Lawful Interception (LI); Handover Specification for IP Delivery;
9) TS 102-233: Service-specific details for e-mail services;
10) TS 102-234: Lawful Interception (LI); Service-specific details for internet access services;
11) TS 102-815: Lawful Interception (LI); Service-specific details for Layer 2 Lawful Interception;
12) TS 133-10: Universal Mobile Telecommunication System (UMTS); "Lawful interception requirements (3GPP TS 33.106 version 5.1.0 Release 5) [3GPP SA3];
13) TS 133-107: Universal Mobile Telecommunication System (UMTS); 3G security; Lawful interception architecture and functions (3GPP TS 33.107 version 5.5.0 Release 5) [3GPP SA3];
14) TS 133-108: Universal Mobile Telecommunications System (UMTS); 3G security; Handover interface for Lawful interception (LI) (3GPP TS 33.108 version 5.4.0 Release 5) [3GPP SA3];
15) ES 201-158: Lawful Interception (LI); Requirements for Network Functions;
16) ES 201-671: Lawful Interception (LI): Handover Interface for the Lawful Interception of Telecommunications traffic;
17) Digital cellular telecommunications system (Phase 2+); Lawful interception requirements for GSM (GSM 01.33 version 8.0.0 Release 1999) [TC SMG] TR 101 514;
18) Digital cellular telecommunications system (Phase 2+); Lawful interception – Stage 1 (GSM 02.33 version 8.0.1 Release 1999) [TC SMG] TR 101 507;
19) Digital cellular telecommunications system (Phase 2+); Lawful interception – Stage 1 (3GPP TS 43.033 version 5.0.0 Release 5) [3GPP SA3] TR 143 033;
20) Digital cellular telecommunications system (Phase 2+); Lawful interception – Stage 1 (3GPP TS 42.033 version 5.0.0 Release 5) [3GPP SA3] TR 142 033;
21) Digital cellular telecommunications system (Phase 2+); Lawful interception requirements for GSM (3GPP TR 41.033 version 5.0.0 Release 5) [3GPP SA3] TR 141 033;
22) Digital cellular telecommunications system (Phase 2+) (GSM); Lawful interception – Stage 2 (3GPP TS 03.33 version 8.1.0 Release 1999) [3GPP SA3] TS 101 509.

cc) Organizational obligations

Article 2 of the Royal Decree of 9 January 2003 regarding the legal duty to co-operate with judicial requests regarding electronic communications requests operators of electronic communications networks and providers of electronic communications services to install a Coordination Cell Justice, individually or jointly, to handle the information requests from Belgian legal authorities.

d) Security requirements for data transfers by communication service providers

The following, rather broad, norms exist concerning the technical aspects of the transfer of intercepted data.

aa) Format

Article 90*quater* §4 CCP provides that the investigating judge can order persons to make the content of telecommunications accessible in the format requested by him, to the extent of their capabilities.

Article 10*bis*, 1° of the Royal Decree of 9 January 2003 provides that the Coordination Cell Justice shall transfer the data to the requesting authority via an easy-to-use form.

Article 10*bis*, 2° of the Royal Decree of 9 January 2003 provides that the Minister of Justice and the minister competent for electronic communications shall determine the specific format.

In this regard, the "format requirements" set by the European Telecommunications Standards Institute in its TS 101-331 "Lawful Interception (LI); Requirements of Law Enforcement Agencies" may also be considered:[125]

a) The technical handover interfaces shall provide the results of interception for the entire duration of the interception measure.

   NOTE: If a lawful authorization is received during ongoing communication, depending on the intercept implementation, some operational problems might be experienced.

b) These handover interfaces need to be implemented in those telecommunication networks for which the interception capability is required by national laws.

c) The configuration of the handover interface shall ensure that it provides the results of interception.

d) The configuration of the handover interface shall ensure that the quality of service of the telecommunications traffic provided at the handover interface is not inferior to that offered to the target service for each particular call.

---

125 European Telecommunications Standards Institute, "TS 101-331 Lawful Interception (LI); Requirements of Law Enforcement Agencies," V1.1.1 (2001-08), 4.10.h, available at http://www.etsi.org/deliver/etsi_TS/101300_101399/101331/01.01.01_60/ts_101331v010101p.pdf

e) The configuration of the handover interface shall be such that that the transmission to the LEMF of the result of interception provided at the interface can be implemented with standard, generally available transmission paths, protocols and coding principles.
f) Each interception target shall be uniquely associated with a single instance of the handover interface. This could be achieved by separate channels or the use of identifiers.
g) The correlation between the content of communication and intercept related information shall be unique.
h) LEAs require that the format for transmitting the intercepted telecommunications to the monitoring facility be a generally available format.
i) If network operators/service providers/access providers initiate encoding, compression or encryption of telecommunications traffic, LEAs require the network operators/service providers/access providers to provide intercepted telecommunications en clair.
j) LEAs require network operators/service providers/access providers to be able to transmit the intercepted telecommunications to the LEMF via landline or switched connections.
k) The LEMF/LEA will be informed of: 1) the activation of an intercept measure; 2) the deactivation of the intercept measure; 3) any change of the intercept measure; 4) the temporary unavailability of the intercept measure.

bb) Transport channels

Article 10*bis*, 1° of the Royal Decree of 9 January 2003 provides that the Coordination Cell Justice shall transfer the data *lege artis* (according to the law of the art), through efficient technical means available on the market.

The European Telecommunications Standards Institute, in its "TS 101-331 Lawful Interception (LI); Requirements of Law Enforcement Agencies," refers to generally available transmission paths:[126]

> The configuration of the handover interface shall be such that that the transmission to the LEMF of the result of interception provided at the interface can be implemented with standard, generally available transmission paths, protocols and coding principles.

cc) Protocol

Article 10*bis*, 2° of the Royal Decree of 9 January 2003 provides that the Minister of Justice and the minister competent for electronic communications shall determine the transfer modus of data.

---

126 European Telecommunications Standards Institute, "TS 101-331 Lawful Interception (LI); Requirements of Law Enforcement Agencies," V1.1.1 (2001-08), 4.10.e, available at http://www.etsi.org/deliver/etsi_TS/101300_101399/101331/01.01.01_60/ts_101331v010101p.pdf

In this regard, the reference to "generally available protocols" by the European Telecommunications Standards Institute in its "TS 101-331 "Lawful Interception (LI); Requirements of Law Enforcement Agencies" may be considered:[127]

> The configuration of the handover interface shall be such that that the transmission to the LEMF of the result of interception provided at the interface can be implemented with standard, generally available transmission paths, protocols and coding principles.

dd) Time limits

Article 126 §2 of the Electronic Communications Act provides that the operators and services shall *immediately* transfer the requested data to the requesting authorities.

Article 5 of the Royal Decree of 9 January 2003 regarding the legal duty to cooperate with judicial requests regarding electronic communications provides that the Coordination Cell Justice shall transfer the data in real time to the National Technical & Tactical Support Unit – Central Technical Interception Facility (NTSU-CTIF) after receipt of the warrant pursuant to Article 90*ter* §1 or §5 CCP. Article 1, 4° of the Royal Decree defines "real time" as the "minimum time necessary for executing a certain performance according to the rules of art, without interruption and with deployment of *adequate means* and personnel" (emphasis added).

Article 6 §1 of the Royal Decree of 9 January 2003 lays down five functional requirements for the data transfer, established in a Council Resolution of 17 January 1995 on the lawful interception of telecommunications.[128] The second functional requirement in Article 6 §1 of the Royal Decree of 9 January 2003 concerns the transfer of interception communications in real time.

In this regard, the reference to "time constraints" by the European Telecommunications Standards Institute in its "TS 101-331 Lawful Interception (LI); Requirements of Law Enforcement Agencies" may also be considered:[129]

> a) A network operator/service provider/access provider shall make the necessary arrangements to fulfil[l] his obligation to enable the interception and delivery of the result of interception from the point in time when the telecommunication installation commences commercial service.

---

127 European Telecommunications Standards Institute, "TS 101-331 Lawful Interception (LI); Requirements of Law Enforcement Agencies," V1.1.1 (2001-08), 4.10.e, available at http://www.etsi.org/deliver/etsi_TS/101300_101399/101331/01.01.01_60/ts_101331v010101p.pdf

128 Council of the European Union, Council Resolution of 17 January 1995 on the lawful interception of telecommunications, COM 96/C329/01, OJ C 4 November 1996, pp. 1–6.

129 European Telecommunications Standards Institute, "TS 101-331 Lawful Interception (LI); Requirements of Law Enforcement Agencies," V1.1.1 (2001-08), 4.5, available at http://www.etsi.org/deliver/etsi_TS/101300_101399/101331/01.01.01_60/ts_101331v010101p.pdf

b) The above requirement applies accordingly to the introduction of modifications to the telecommunication installation or to new operational features for existing telecommunications services to the extent of their impact on existing interception capabilities.

NOTE 1: It is a national implementation (issue for negotiation) whether the operator does this proactively or passively upon request by the LEA.

c) When a lawful authorization is presented a network operator/service provider/access provider shall co-operate immediately.

NOTE 2: If a lawful authorization is received during an ongoing call, depending on the interception implementation, some operational problems might be experienced.

d) After a lawful authorization has been issued, provision of the results of interception of a target identity shall proceed on a real-time or near real-time basis. In the case of near real-time the LEA should be able to force real-time (by means of emptying any buffers involved) if necessary.

ee) Encryption

The data retention Act of 29 May 2016[130] retained the security measures laid down in Article 125 §5 of the Electronic Communications Act, and complemented them with three additional security measures, including an obligation "to put in place technological protection measures that make the retained data unreadable for any unauthorized individual from the moment of their registration."

ff) Security measures

The previous version of Article 125 §5 of the Electronic Communications Act laid down the following technical and security measures for providers and operators:

– To guarantee that the retained data are of the same quality and subject to the same security and protection measures as the network data;
– To implement appropriate technical and organizational measures to protect the data against accidental or unlawful destruction, accidental loss or alteration, or unauthorized or unlawful storage, processing, access or disclosure;
– To ensure that data may be accessed by specially authorized personnel only, i.e., the "Coordination Cell Justice," as provided for in Article 2 of the Royal Decree of 9 January 2003 regarding the legal duty to cooperate with regard to judicial requests involving electronic communications;
– To destroy the data at the end of the applicable data retention period.

130 Act of 29 May 2016 on the collection and retention of data in the electronic communications sector, *Belgian Official Journal*, 18 July 2016, entry into force on 28 July 2016.

The Data Retention Act of 29 May 2016[131] retained the security measures laid down in Article 125 §5 of the Electronic Communications Act and complemented them with three additional security measures:

- To store the data on the territory of the EU;
- To put in place technological protection measures that make the retained data unreadable for any unauthorized individuals from the moment of their registration;
- To subject the use of retained data to an efficient traceability process.

Furthermore, the Data Retention Act of 29 May 2016 also requires the appointment of a data protection officer, to ensure that:

- All data processing made by the Coordination Cell Justice complies with the law;
- The operator or operators concerned collect and retain only the data that may be legally retained;
- Only the legally competent authorities have access to the retained data.

The fifth functional requirement in Article 6 §1 of the Royal Decree of 9 January 2003 concerns the secure transfer to prevent data interception by third parties.

Article 10*bis*, 1° of the Royal Decree of 9 January 2003 provides that the Coordination Cell Justice shall transfer the data via a secure transfer.

In this regard, the "information protection requirements" set by the European Telecommunications Standards Institute in its "TS 101-331 Lawful Interception (LI); Requirements of Law Enforcement Agencies" may be considered:[132]

> The technical arrangements required within a telecommunication installation to allow implementation of the interception measures shall be realized with due care exercised in operating telecommunication installations, particularly with respect to:
>
> a) the need to protect information on which and how many target identities are or were subject to interception and the periods during which the interception measures were active;
>
> b) the restriction to a minimum of staff engaged in implementation and operation of the interception measure;
>
> c) to ensure the clear delimitation of functions and responsibilities and the maintenance of third-party telecommunications privacy, interception and recording shall be carried out in operating rooms accessible only by authorized personnel;
>
> d) the result of interception shall be delivered through a handover interface;

[131] Act of 29 May 2016 on the collection and retention of data in the electronic communications sector, *Belgian Official Journal*, 18 July 2016, entry into force on 28 July 2016.

[132] European Telecommunications Standards Institute, "TS 101-331 Lawful Interception (LI); Requirements of Law Enforcement Agencies," V1.1.1 (2001-08), 4.5, available at http://www.etsi.org/deliver/etsi_TS/101300_101399/101331/01.01.01_60/ts_101331v010101p.pdf

e) no access of any form to the handover interface shall be granted to unauthorized persons;

f) network operators, service providers and access providers shall take all necessary measures to protect the handover interface against misuse;

g) the result of interception shall only be transmitted to the LEMF as indicated in the lawful authorization when proof of the authority to receive of the LEMF, and proof of the authority to send of the interface, has been furnished;

h) authentication and proof of authentication shall be implement subject to national laws and regulations;

i) if no dedicated routes to the LEMF are used, such proof shall be furnished for each communication set-up;

j) depending on certain interception cases, LEAs may require confidentiality measures to protect the transmission of the results of such interception. The use of encryption shall be possible;

k) in order to prevent or trace misuse of the technical functions integrated in the telecommunication installation enabling interception, any activation or application of these functions in relation to a given identity shall be fully recorded, including any activation or application caused by faulty or unauthorized input. The records, which are subject to national regulation, shall cover all or some of:

   1) the target identity of the target service or target services concerned;
   2) the beginning and end of the activation or application of the interception measure;
   3) the LEMF to which the result of interception is routed;
   4) an authenticator suitable to identify the operating staff (including date and time of input);
   5) a reference to the lawful authorization.

l) the network operator/service provider/access provider shall ensure that the records are tamper-proof and only accessible to specific nominated staff.

e) Checks, filtering, and decryption obligations of communication service providers

Under Belgian law, there are no checks and filtering obligations that must be performed (automatically or manually) by Internet providers before or during the execution of the interception process. Of note, however, are the checks and filtering standards set by the European Telecommunications Standards Institute in its "TS 101-331 Lawful Interception (LI); Requirements of Law Enforcement Agencies":

4.2. General requirements […]

e) The results of interception relating to a target service shall be provided by the network operator, access provider, service provider in such a way that any telecommunications that do not fall within the scope of the lawful authorization shall be excluded by the network operator, access provider, service provider.

NOTE 5: It is assumed that the intercepting system exercises best effort to exclude non-authorized interception patterns (e.g. transferred communication).[133]

---

[133] European Telecommunications Standards Institute, "TS 101-331 Lawful Interception (LI); Requirements of Law Enforcement Agencies," V1.1.1 (2001-08), 4.2, available at

4.3. Results of interception

The network operator, access provider or service provider shall, in relation to each target service:

a) provide the content of communication;

b) remove any service coding or encryption which has been applied to the content of communication (i.e. en clair) and the intercept related information at the instigation of the network operator or service provider;

NOTE 1: If coding/encryption cannot be removed through means that are available in the network or service for the given communication, the receiving agencies should be provided with keys, etc. to access the information *en clair*, cf. next clause

[...]

e) intercept related information shall contain:
   1) the identities that have attempted telecommunications with the target identity, successful or not;
   2) identities used by or associated with the target identity;
   3) details of services used and their associated parameters;
   4) information relating to status;
   5) time stamps.[134]

The third functional requirement in Article 6 §1 of the Royal Decree of 9 January 2003 concerns the transfer of encrypted information in a generally accessible format.

The fourth functional requirement in Article 6 §1 of the Royal Decree of 9 January 2003 concerns the transfer of data content in plain language in case the operator of an electronic communications network or the provider of electronic communications introduced encoding, compression, or encryption of the electronic communications traffic. Hence, the transfer takes place without the use of encryption.

6. Formal prerequisites of interception orders

a) Competent authorities

Under normal circumstances, the investigating judge authorizes the monitoring measure (Article 90*ter* §1 CCP).

Article 90*ter* §5 CCP provides that, in a *flagrante delicto* case and as long as the *flagrante delicto* situation lasts, the public prosecutor can order the monitoring measure for the criminal offenses referred to in Article 347*bis* CC (on crimes re-

---

http://www.etsi.org/deliver/etsi_TS/101300_101399/101331/01.01.01_60/ts_101331v010101p.pdf

134 European Telecommunications Standards Institute, "TS 101-331 Lawful Interception (LI); Requirements of Law Enforcement Agencies," V1.1.1 (2001-08), 4.3, available at http://www.etsi.org/deliver/etsi_TS/101300_101399/101331/01.01.01_60/ts_101331v010101p.pdf

garding the taking of hostages) or Article 470 CC (on extortion committed through violence or threats).

Both under normal circumstances, as in the case of *flagrante delicto*, a judicial police officer is designated for the implementation of the measure (Article 90*quater* §1, 5° CCP).

b) Formal requirements for applications

According to Article 61*quinquies* §1 CCP, the suspect and the civil party have the right to request the investigating judge to perform additional investigation methods.

According to Article 61*quinquies* §2 CCP, the suspect and the civil party shall submit their petition for an additional investigation method in writing to the Registry of the Court of First Instance. The petition must be substantiated and give a detailed description of the requested investigation method.

According to Article 61*quinquies* §3 CCP, the judge may reject the request if he considers the measures unnecessary in order to reveal the truth or if, at that moment, he considers the measures prejudicial to the investigation. According to Article 61*quinquies* §4 CCP, rejection by the investigating judge is subject to appeal before the Indictment Chamber (see I.A.4.b.), in which case the investigating judge shall hear the Prosecutor General, the suspect, and his or her attorney (Article 61*quater* §5 CCP).

c) Formal requirements for orders

Article 90*quater* CCP reads as follows:

> §1 The investigating judge authorizes each monitoring measure under Article 90ter by a reasoned decision, and communicates the warrant to the public prosecutor.
>
> The warrant shall be dated and mentions:
>
> 1) the indications and concrete facts specific to the case, which justify the measure under Article 90ter;
> 2) the reasons why the measure is necessary to reveal the truth;
> 3) the person, the (tele-)communications method or the place that is the subject of the monitoring measure;
> 4) the period during which the monitoring measure can be carried out, which should not be longer than one month counting from the decision by which the measure is ordered;
> 5) the name and the capacity of the judicial police officer designated for the implementation of the measure.

The Act of 5 February 2016 deleted the prescription of this provision on penalty of nullity.[135]

7. Substantive prerequisites of interception orders

a) Degree of suspicion

According to Article 90*ter* §1 CCP, the investigating judge may wiretap, take cognizance of, and record private (tele-)communications if there are "serious indications" of a criminal offense.

b) Predicate offences

In the wake of the terrorist attacks against the French satirical magazine Charlie Hebdo on 7 January 2015, the Belgian legislator extended the list of terrorism crimes that can justify an interception measure. Thereto, the Law of 20 July 2015[136] amended Article 90*ter* §2, 1°*ter* CCP to include *all*, and not just three, terrorism crimes, provided in Book II, title I*ter* of the Criminal Code:[137]

- Article 137 – on the execution of terrorism crimes;
- Article 138 – on penalties for terrorism crimes;
- Article 139 – on the definition of a terrorist group;
- Article 140 – on participating in or financing the activities of a terrorist group, supplying information or material resources to a terrorist group, and leading a terrorist group;
- Article 140*bis* – on publicly spreading a message in order to incite to terrorism crimes;
- Article 140*ter* – on recruiting persons for the execution of terrorism crimes;
- Article 140*quater* – on giving instructions or education to fabricate explosives, firearms or other weapons or harmful or dangerous substances;
- Article 140*quinquies* – on taking instructions or education to fabricate explosives, firearms or other weapons or harmful or dangerous substances;
- Article 140*sexies* – on leaving or entering the territory to commit terrorism crimes in Belgium or abroad;

---

135 Act of 5 February 2016 regarding the modification of criminal law and criminal procedure and regarding diverse provisions on criminal policy, *Belgian Official Journal*, 19 February 2016, entry into force on 29 February 2016.

136 Act of 20 July 2015 to strengthen the fight against terrorism, *Belgian Official Journal*, 5 August 2015, entry into force on 15 August 2015.

137 The previous version of Article 90*ter* §2, 1°*ter* CCP referred to only three articles in Book II, title I*ter* of the Criminal Code (Article 137, Article 140, and Article 141).

- Article 141 – on supplying material resources, including financial support, to commit one of the terrorist crimes provided in Article 137;
- Article 141*bis* – on the non-application of this title to the acts of armed forces during armed conflict or in the fulfillment of their official duties insofar governed by other rules of international law;
- Article 141*ter* – on the non-derogation from fundamental rights protection.

One month after the terrorist attacks in Brussels on 22 March 2016, the Belgian legislator once more extended the list of terrorism crimes that can justify an interception measure. The Act of 27 April 2016[138] retained the reference in Article 90*ter* §2, 10° CCP to the six articles under Book II, title IX, chapter I, section II*bis* of the Criminal Code; and, in addition, it included reference in the same Article 90*ter* §2, 10° CCP to *all*, and not just one of the, nuclear crimes in Book II, title IX, chapter I*bis* of the Criminal Code.[139]

- Article 488*bis* – on the unlawful delivery, possession, use, modification, cession, leaving behind, transport or distribution of, or committing an act against, nuclear materials;
- Article 488*ter* – on the unlawful preservation, fabrication, use of, or committing an act against, radioactive materials other than nuclear materials;
- Article 488*quater* – to demand – via threats that seem credible in the circumstances, or on the basis of violence – the transfer of nuclear materials, nuclear instruments or nuclear installations;
- Article 488*quinquies* – on unlawful intrusion (or attempt thereto) into a nuclear installation.

The same Act of 27 April 2016 also complements Article 90*ter* §2, 16° CCP with the following list of Belgian laws:

- Article 16 of the Decree of the Flemish Parliament of 15 June 2012 on the import, export, transit and transfer of defense-related products, other material for military use, law enforcement equipment, civilian firearms, parts and ammunition;
- Article 20 of the Decree of the Walloon Region of 21 June 2012 on the import, export, transit and transfer of civil weapons and defense-related products;
- Article 42 of the Ordonnance of the Brussels Capital Region of 20 June 2013 on the import, export, transit and transfer of defense-related products, other material

---

138 Act of 27 April 2016 on additional measures to fight terrorism, *Belgian Official Journal*, 9 May 2016, entry into force on 19 May 2016.

139 The previous version of Article 90*ter* §2, 10° CCP also referred to the six articles under Book II, title IX, chapter I, section II*bis* of the Criminal Code (Articles 477, 477*bis*, 477*ter*, 477*quater*, 477*quinquies*, 477*sexies* – on the theft and extortion of nuclear materials). But it referred to only article under Book II, title IX, chapter I*bis* of the Criminal Code (Article 488*bis*).

for military use, law enforcement equipment, civilian firearms, parts, accessories and its ammunition;

- Articles 8 to 11, 14, 16, 19, 1°, 2°, 3°, 5° and 6°, 20, 22, 27 and 33 of the Act of 8 June 2006 on the regulation of economic and individual activities with weapons, also called the "Arms Act";
- The Act of 28 May 1956 on explosives and the deflagration substances and mixtures and thereby loaded vehicles;
- Articles 21 to 26 of the Cooperation Agreement between the Federal State, the Flemish Region, the Walloon Region and the Brussels Capital Region concerning the implementation of the Convention on the prohibition of the development, production, stockpiling and use of chemical weapons and on their destruction, Paris 13 January 1993.

The current version of Article 90*ter* §2 CCP provides the following list of offences that can justify a monitoring measure:

- 1° Articles 101 to 110 of the Criminal Code [on the attack and conspiracy against the King, the royal family and the form of government];
- 1°*bis* Articles 136*bis* [on genocide], 136*ter* [on crimes against humanity], 136*quater* [on war crimes], 136*sexies* [on producing, keeping or transporting a tool, a device or any object, and constructing a building or changing a building to commit one of the crimes provided in Article 136*bis*, 136*ter*, and 136*quater*] and 136*septies* of the same Code [on ordering, proposing, accepting, inciting, attempting to commit one of the crimes provided in Article 136*bis*, 136*ter*, and 136*quater*, as well as participating in, and the failure to prevent, the commission of these crimes], and Article 41 of the Law of 29 March 2004 regarding the cooperation with the International Criminal Court and the international criminal tribunals [crimes against the administration of justice of the International Criminal Court];
- 1°*ter* Book II, title I*ter* of the same Code [on terrorism crimes]: Article 137 [on the execution of terrorism crimes]; Article 138 [on penalties for terrorism crimes]; Article 139 [on the definition of a terrorist group]; Article 140 [on participating in or financing the activities of a terrorist group, supplying information or material resources to a terrorist group, and leading a terrorist group]; Article 140*bis* [on publicly spreading a message in order to incite to terrorism crimes]; Article 140*ter* [on recruiting persons for the execution of terrorism crimes]; Article 140*quater* [on giving instructions or education to fabricate explosives, firearms or other weapons or harmful or dangerous substances]; Article 140*quinquies* [on taking instructions or education to fabricate explosives, firearms or other weapons or harmful or dangerous substances]; Article 140*sexies* [on leaving or entering the territory to commit terrorism crimes in Belgium or abroad]; Article 141 [on supplying material resources, including financial support, to commit one of the terrorist crimes provided in Article 137];

Article 141*bis* [on the non-application of this title to the acts of armed forces during armed conflict or in the fulfillment of their official duties insofar governed by other rules of international law]; Article 141*ter* [on the non-derogation from fundamental rights protection];

- 1°*quater* Article 210*bis* of the same Code [forgery through entering, changing or deleting computer data or through altering their potential use, if this causes a change in the legal scope of such data];
- 1°*quinquies* Articles 246, 247, 248, 249, 250 and 251 of the same Code [on the bribery of persons exercising a public function];
- 1°*sexies* Article 259*bis* of the same Code [on wiretapping, taking cognizance and recording of private (tele-)communications by public officials];
- 1°*septies* Article 314*bis* of the same Code [on the prohibition, applicable to everyone, of taking knowledge of the content, during the transfer, of private (tele-) communications one does not participate in];
- 1°*octies* Articles 324*bis* and 324*ter* of the same Code [on criminal organisations].
- 2° Articles 327, 328, 329 or 330 of the same Code [on threating to attack persons or property and giving false information on serious attacks], to the extent that a complaint has been filed;
- 3° Article 331*bis* of the same Code [on the harmful use of radioactive materials or instruments];
- 4° Article 347*bis* of the same Code [on crimes regarding the taking of hostages];
- 4°*bis* [...]
- 5° Articles 379 and 380 of the same Code [on the decay of youth and prostitution].
- 6° Article 393 of the same Code [on manslaughter];
- 7° Articles 394 [on murder] or 397 [on intoxication] of the same Code;
- 7°*bis* Articles 428 and 429 of the same Code [on kidnapping of minors];
- 7°*ter* Articles 433*sexies*, 433*septies* and 433*octies* of the same Code [on human trafficking];
- 8° Articles 468, 470, 471 or 472 of the same Code [on theft committed through violence or threats, and extortion];
- 9° Article 475 of the same Code [on manslaughter to facilitate or ensure the impunity of theft or extortion];
- 10° Book II, title IX, chapter I, section II*bis*, and chapter I*bis* of the Criminal Code: Articles 477, 477*bis*, 477*ter*, 477*quater*, 477*quinquies*, 477*sexies* [on the theft and extortion of nuclear materials]; Article 488*bis* [on the unlawful delivery, possession, use, modification, cession, leaving behind, transport or distribution of nuclear materials] of the same Code; Article 488*ter* [on the unlawful

preservation, fabrication, use of, or committing an act against, radioactive materials other than nuclear materials]; Article 488*quater* [to demand – via threats that seem credible in the circumstances, or on the basis of violence – the transfer of nuclear materials, nuclear instruments or nuclear installations]; Article 488*quinquies* [on unlawful intrusion (or attempt thereto) into a nuclear installation];

- 10°*bis* Articles 504*bis* and 504*ter* of the same Code [on private commercial bribery];
- 10°*ter* Article 504*quater* of the same Code [on computer fraud];
- 11° Article 505 (first paragraph, 2°, 3° and 4°) of the same Code [on receiving of, and other transactions relating to, objects resulting from a criminal offense];
- 12° Articles 510, 511, first paragraph or 516 of the same Code [on arson];
- 13° Article 520 of the same Code [on the destruction of constructions by causing an explosion], if the circumstances referred to in Articles 510 or 511, first paragraph, of the same Code are united;
- 13°*bis* Articles 550*bis* [on hacking] and 550*ter* [on data and system interference] of the same Code;
- 14° Article 2*bis*, §3, b [on offences regarding narcotics or stupefying substances, other psychotropic substances that may cause dependency, or cultivating of plants to extract these substances, that consist in the participation in the activities of an association] or §4, b [on the same offences but committed in the capacity of a leading person] of the Law of 24 February 1921 concerning the trafficking of poisonous, narcotic, stupefying, psychotropic, disinfectant and antiseptic substances;
- 15° Article 145 §3 [on the fraudulent making of electronic communications through a network of electronic communications, in order to provide oneself or another an unlawful benefit] and §3*bis* [on the use of an electronic communications network or provider, or of other electronic communication methods, to cause nuisance to his correspondent or to cause harm, or setting up a device intended to commit the previous offences] of the Law of 13 June 2005 on electronic communications;
- 16° Article 10 of the Law of 5 August 1991 on the import, export and transit of arms, ammunition and materials specifically intended for military use and the associated technology [on illegal trade in weapons, ammunition and materials specifically intended for military use and the associated technology];
- 16°*bis* Article 16 of the Decree of the Flemish Parliament of 15 June 2012 on the import, export, transit and transfer of defense-related products, other material for military use, law enforcement equipment, civilian firearms, parts and ammunition;

- 16°*ter* Article 20 of the Decree of the Walloon Region of 21 June 2012 on the import, export, transit and transfer of civil weapons and defense-related products;
- 16°*quater* Article 42 of the Ordonnance of the Brussels Capital Region of 20 June 2013 on the import, export, transit and transfer of defense-related products, other material for military use, law enforcement equipment, civilian firearms, parts, accessories and its ammunition;
- 16°*quinquies* Articles 8 to 11, 14, 16, 19, 1°, 2°, 3°, 5° and 6°, 20, 22, 27 and 33 of the Act of 8 June 2006 on the regulation of economic and individual activities with weapons, also called the "Arms Act";
- 16°*sexies* of the Act of 28 May 1956 on explosives and the deflagration substances and mixtures and thereby loaded vehicles;
- 16°*septies* Articles 21 to 26 of the Cooperation Agreement between the Federal State, the Flemish Region, the Walloon Region and the Brussels Capital Region concerning the implementation of the Convention on the prohibition of the development, production, stockpiling and use of chemical weapons and on their destruction, Paris 13 January 1993;
- 17° Articles 77*ter*, 77*quater* and 77*quinquies* of the Law of 15 December 1980 on access to the territory, residence, establishment and removal of foreigners [on human trafficking];
- 18° Article 10, §1, 2° of the Law of 15 July 1985 regarding the use in animals of substances with hormonal, anti-hormonal, beta-adrenergic or production stimulating effects [on the offences relating to the administration of substances, and the trade in animals to which substances were unlawfully administered];
- 19° Article 1 of the Royal Decree of 12 April 1974 with respect to some actions relating to materials with a hormonal, anti-hormonal, anabolic, beta-adrenergic, anti-infectious, anti-parasitic and anti-inflammatory effect, which concerns criminal offenses for which criminal sanctions are provided by the Law of 24 February 1921 concerning the trafficking of poisonous, narcotic, stupefying, psychotropic, disinfectant and antiseptic substances [on the licence for the actions relating to these materials].

Article 90*ter* §4 CCP provides that:

> [a] criminal offense, referred to in Articles 322 or 323 of the Criminal Code [on associations with a view to commit an attack on persons or property] may also justify a monitoring measure, to the extent that the association is formed with the aim to commit an attack against the persons or properties referred to in §2, or to commit the criminal offence referred to in article 467, first paragraph, of the Criminal Code [on theft though burglary, climbing through, false keys, or by a public official through his ministry].

The potential or the likely sentencing range for the offenses listed in Article 90*ter* §§2 and 4 does not serve as additional mitigating criteria.

c) Persons and connections under surveillance

Article 90*ter* §1, 3° CCP provides that the monitoring measure can be ordered in respect of:

1) the (tele-)communications methods that are regularly used by a suspected person
2) or in respect of places where he is suspected to stay
3) or in respect of persons who are suspected, on the basis of specific facts, to have regular communications with a suspected person.

The parliamentary preparatory works specify that proactive monitoring is prohibited (cf. supra I.A.2.b.), for instance in relation to a reputed criminal: the application of Article 90*ter* CCP depends on the existence of a suspect.[140]

d) Principle of subsidiarity

According to Article 90*ter* §1 CCP, the investigating judge may only carry out a wiretapping measure if the other investigation methods are not sufficient to reveal the truth. The parliamentary preparatory works note, however, that there is no need for a prior unsuccessful application of the other investigation methods by the investigating judge: it suffices that the investigating judge considers the other measures unlikely to be successful.[141]

e) Proportionality of interception in individual cases

There is an obligation for the investigating judge to verify that the interception is proportionate to the seriousness of the offense in the individual case. According to Article 90*ter* §1 CCP, the investigating judge may wiretap, take cognizance of, and record private (tele-)communications only in *exceptional cases*.

Van den Wyngaert relates the proportionality principle to the list of offenses provided in Article 90*ter* §2 CCP, which can justify a monitoring measure (see section III.B.7.b.).[142] Hence, monitoring measures that are ordered for other offenses than the ones listed in Article 90*ter* §2 violate the principle of proportionality.

---

[140] Parliamentary preparatory works, regarding the legislative proposal protecting privacy against the interception of communication and telecommunication, Belgian Senate, 1992-1993, 1 September 1993, no. 843-1, p. 15, available at http://www.senate.be/lexdocs/S0539/S05390297.pdf

[141] Parliamentary preparatory works, regarding the legislative proposal protecting privacy against the interception of communication and telecommunication, Belgian Senate, 1992-1993, 1 September 1993, no. 843-1, p. 14, available at http://www.senate.be/lexdocs/S0539/S05390297.pdf

[142] Chris Van den Wyngaert, *Strafrecht, Strafprocesrecht & Internationaal Strafrecht in hoofdlijnen* (An Outline of Criminal Law, Criminal Procedural Law & International Criminal Law), Antwerp-Apeldoorn, Maklu, 2006, p. 983.

Freyne distinguishes three subcriteria of the proportionality principle: the seriousness of the offense, the finality/purpose of the monitoring measure (the protection of public order or public security), and the breach of the legal order.[143] Hence, there is no specific requirement regarding the likelihood that the anticipated evidence will actually be obtained by means of the requested monitoring measure.

f) Consent by a communication participant to the measure

As said earlier (section III.B.6.b.), according to Article 61*quinquies* §3 CCP, the judge may reject the request by the suspect or a civil party if he considers the measures unnecessary in order to reveal the truth or if, at that moment, he considers the measures prejudicial to the investigation. Hence, the consent by a communication participant to the measure is not a decisive prerequisite for the interception order.

8. Validity of interception order

a) Maximum length of interception order

Article 90*quater* §1, 4° CCP provides that, on penalty of nullity, the warrant shall be dated and mention "the period during which the monitoring measure can be carried out, which should not be longer than one month counting from the decision by which the measure is ordered."

b) Prolongation of authorization

In both normal circumstances and cases of emergency, Article 90*quinquies* CCP allows prolongation and renewal of the monitoring warrant:

> The investigating judge may extend the effect of its warrant one or more times by a period not longer than one month, with a maximum of six months, without prejudice to its decision to end the measure as soon as the circumstances that justified the measure have disappeared. The provisions in article 90quater, §1, are applicable to the extension referred to in the preceding paragraph. The warrant shall also mention the precise circumstances, which justify the extension of the measure.
>
> If new and serious circumstances necessitate the measures referred to in Article 90*ter*, then the investigating judge may order a new measure, in compliance with the formalities set out in Articles 90*ter* and 90*quater*. In that case, the warrant must state the precise new and serious circumstances that necessitate and justify a new measure.

Hence, the prolongation or renewal of the monitoring measure follows the same procedure as the initial application for a monitoring measure.

---

143 Thierry Freyne, "De bewaking van privécommunicatie en -telecommunicatie in strafonderzoeken: een stand van zaken" (The monitoring of private communications and telecommunications in criminal proceedings: a state of affairs), *Tijdschrift voor Strafrecht*, 2008, vol. 3, p. 172, no. 17.

c) Revocation of authorization

In both normal circumstances and cases of emergency, Article 90*quinquies* §1 CCP allows revocation of the monitoring warrant:

> The investigating judge may extend the effect of its warrant one or more times by a period not longer than one month, with a maximum of six months, without prejudice to its decision to end the measure as soon as the circumstances that justified the measure have disappeared.

Freyne holds that the investigating judge has a duty to revoke the authorization during the monitoring measure in case it becomes apparent that other investigation methods are sufficient to reveal the truth (principle of subsidiarity, see section III.B.7.d. above).[144]

9. Duties to record, report, and destroy

a) Duty to record and report

As said above, a set of articles regulates the general exchange of data between the police service and law enforcement authorities (section I.A.4.a.).

Article 15, 1° of the Act of 5 August 1992 on the Police Function reads as follows:

> In the performance of their judicial police functions, the police have the task: 1° to detect the crimes, misdemeanours and contraventions, to gather evidence thereof, to notify the competent authorities thereof, to apprehend and arrest the perpetrators, to bring them at the disposal of the competent authorities, in the manner and forms provided by law;

Article 53 CCP adds that the judicial police officers shall immediately send the reports (of an offense), official records, and any other acts drafted under their competence to the public prosecutor. This provision is echoed by Article 40 of the Act of 5 August 1992 on the Police Function, which provides that police officers shall send the official records on complaints, reports of offenses, the intelligence and any detections to the competent judicial authorities.

Article 54 CCP adds that the judicial police officers shall also immediately send any reports of crimes and misdemeanours they are not competent to deal with to the public prosecutor.

Article 5/3 of the Act of 5 August 1992 on the Police Function adds that, in order to perform judicial police functions, the police shall maintain regular *service relations* with the local public prosecutors, the federal public prosecutor, and the Prosecutors General.

---

[144] Thierry Freyne, "De bewaking van privécommunicatie en -telecommunicatie in strafonderzoeken: een stand van zaken" (The monitoring of private communications and telecommunications in criminal proceedings: a state of affairs), *Tijdschrift voor Strafrecht*, 2008, vol. 3, p. 173, no. 18.

More specifically regarding the monitoring measure, first, Article 90*quater* §3, 2° CCP provides that "[t]he designated judicial police officers report at least every five days in writing to the investigating judge on the implementation of the warrant."

Second, Article 90*sexies* CCP reads as follows:

> §1 The designated judicial police officers shall provide the investigating judge with:
>
> 1° the file with the recordings made as a result of the measures taken in application of Articles 90ter, 90quater and 90quinquies;
>
> 2° the transcription of the parts[145] of the (tele-)communications that the designated judicial police officer deems relevant for the investigation, and its possible translation;
>
> 3° what the irrelevantly deemed (tele-)communications concerns, the cited topics and the identification of the (tele-)communications means to which or from which was called.

According to Article 90*septies* §1 CCP, the data mentioned in Article 90*sexies* CCP do not necessarily need to be recorded in an official record (see the following section).

b) Duty to destroy

With regard to the monitoring measure on the part of the Belgian investigating judge, Article 90*septies* §1 CCP reads as follows:

> Every record in the context of the implementation of the measures referred to in the preceding paragraph by the designated persons, which is not recorded in an official record, is destroyed, except for the transcription of the parts of the relevantly deemed (tele-) communications of the record, any translation thereof, and what the irrelevantly deemed (tele-)communications concerns, the cited topics and the identification of the telecommunications means to which or from which was called. The judicial police offer designated for the implementation of the measure undertakes the destruction and states this in an official record.

Hence, both relevantly deemed parts of (tele-)communications and irrelevantly deemed (tele-)communications are not destroyed.

With regard to the monitoring measure by foreign authorities, Article 90*ter* §6, 1° CCP provides that:

> [a] competent foreign authority may, within the framework of a criminal investigation, temporarily wiretap, take cognizance of, and record private telecommunications during transmission, if the person to whom this measure applies is located on the Belgian territory,

---

145 The Act of 5 February 2016 amended Article 90*sexies* CCP by deeming it sufficient that the designated judicial police officers shall provide the investigating judge with only *parts* of (tele-)communications that the designated judicial police officer deems relevant for the investigation. Act of 5 February 2016 regarding the modification of criminal law and criminal procedure and regarding diverse provisions on criminal policy, *Belgian Official Journal*, 19 February 2016, entry into force on 29 February 2016.

under certain conditions provided in its paragraph 2 including the notification of the measure to a Belgian judicial authority.

Article 90*ter* §7 *in fine* CCP provides that:

> [i]f the investigating judge does not allow the measure referred to in §6, it shall also notify the foreign government that the gathered data must be destroyed and cannot be used.

10. Notification duties and remedies

a) Duty to notify persons affected by the measure

Article 90*sexies in fine* CCP reads as follows:

> The warrants of the investigating judge, the reports of the judicial police officers referred to in Article 90quater, §3, and the official records relating to the implementation of the measure, are included in the file at the latest by the end of the measure.

Van den Wyngaert specifies that these documents are included in the file at the latest 15 days after the end of the measure, which is also the deadline for notifying the persons subject to a monitoring measure (see below in this section).[146] The suspect has access to the judicial file (Article 61*ter* CCP).

As third parties do not have access to the judicial file, Article 90*novies* CCP lays down a notification duty towards *any* person subject to a monitoring measure:

> Not later than fifteen days after the decision on the administration of justice becomes final, or after the deposit of summons referred to in Article 524b, §6 at the Registry of the tribunal or the court, the Registrar shall, at the request of the public prosecutor or where appropriate the Prosecutor General, inform in writing any person against whom a measure was taken under Article 90ter, of *the nature of the measure and the days on which the measure was executed.* (italics added)

Arnou notes that the duty of notification of the nature of measure and the days on which it was executed is not prescribed under sanction of nullity (see below, section IV.2.). Nor do the parliamentary preparatory works provide any clarity in this regard. In any case, no exclusion will follow on the basis of an alleged violation of the rights of defense because, as said, the suspect has access to the judicial file on the basis of Article 61*ter* CCP. Arnou says further that, at most, a disciplinary sanction or civil sanction will be allowed.[147]

Unfortunately, the Board of Public Prosecutors could not positively respond to our request of 2 April 2015 to obtain data on infringements of the laws on intercep-

---

146 Chris Van den Wyngaert, *Strafrecht, Strafprocesrecht en internationaal strafrecht in hoofdlijnen* (An Outline of Criminal Law, Criminal Procedural Law & International Criminal Law), Antwerp-Apeldoorn, Maklu, 2009, p. 1058.

147 Luc Arnou, "Afluisteren tijdens het gerechtelijk onderzoek" (Wiretapping during the investigation); in Commentaar Strafrecht en strafvordering (Commentary criminal law and criminal procedural law), Gent, Kluwer, 2008, vol. 59, pp. 80–81, no. 83.

tion of telecommunications. Hence, it not possible to report on the notification practices.

b) Remedies

Article 90*ter* and following of the CCP are silent regarding the remedies available to the suspect during the interception. As said in the previous section, Article 90*novies* CCP lays down a notification duty towards any person subject to a monitoring measure fifteen days after the end of the measure.

However, the general rules of criminal procedure apply as regards the remedies that are available to a person who becomes aware that he/she was subject to an illegally performed monitoring measure. As already said (see section II.A.3.), the Courts in Chambers (court of instruction in first instance) and the Indictment Chamber (court of instruction in appeal) evaluate the legality of the evidence collection during the investigation phase (Article 131 CCP, Article 135 §2 CCP, and Article 235*bis* §6 CCP). Both the Courts in Chambers[148] and the Indictment Chamber determine the grounds for finding a nullity on the basis of the so-called Antigoon criteria (see below, section IV.2.). The lack of rationale may give rise to an appeal against the decision of the Courts in Chambers before the Chamber of Indictment (Article 135 §2 CCP) and against the decision of the latter before the Supreme Court (Article 235*bis* §6 CCP *versus* Article 416 CCP). The proceedings before the Courts in Chambers and the Indictment Chamber are public and adversarial (Article 127 §4 CCP, respectively Article 135 §3 CCP).

If the Courts in Chambers finds no illegality, and the parties do not appeal this decision before the Court of Indictment, then they can raise this point again before the trial judge. If the parties do appeal this decision before the Indictment Chamber decides, then they cannot raise this point again before the trial judge except when the alleged nullity concerns the weighing of evidence, which is an exclusive task of the trial judge (Article 235*bis* §5 CCP).

It is of note that illegally obtained files are not destroyed but instead removed from the judicial file and kept at the Registry of the Court of First Instance (Article 235*bis* §6 CCP). The Indictment Chamber decides who can have access to the removed files in light of the right of defense. In this regard, the Supreme Court also

---

148 Unlike the Indictment Chamber (Article 235*bis* CCP), the Courts in Chambers can only evaluate evidence during the investigation phase and not during the preliminary investigation phase: more particularly, the Courts in Chambers evaluates the evidence during the formal closure of the investigation phase during the so-called settlement of proceedings (*Regeling van de rechtspleging* in Dutch; *règlement de la procédure* in French). See Brigitte Pesquié (revised by Yves Cartuyvels), "The Belgian system", in Mireille Delmas-Marty and John R. Spencer, *European Criminal Procedures*, Cambridge Studies in International and Comparative Law, Cambridge University Press, 2002, (81) 109.

held that the trial judge may allow parties access to the removed documents that are essential for the right of defense.[149]

c) Criminal consequences of unlawful interception measures

The Board of Public Prosecutors could not positively respond to our request of 2 April 2015 to obtain data on the infringements of the laws on interception of telecommunications. Hence, it is not possible to list specific sanctions imposed on officials for wrongfully conducting a monitoring measure, nor to provide the frequency with which such cases occurs or sanctions are imposed.

As noted earlier (section III.B.10.a.), at most, a disciplinary sanction or civil sanction would be allowed for violations of the notification duty.[150]

We also recall that the monitoring measure in Article 90*ter* CCP provides an exception to the general prohibition of the interception of (tele-)communications (Article 314*bis* CC and Article 259*bis* CC, see section II.A.4.a.).

11. Confidentiality requirements

a) Obligations of telecommunication service providers to maintain secrecy

As said above (section III.B.5.b.), Article 90*quater* §2 and §4 CCP lays down the cooperation duties for individuals and the private sector. Both provisions lay down a specific obligation for Internet providers and individuals to keep their support measures confidential.

Article 90*quater* §2, 1° CCP reads as follows:

> §2. If the measure involves an operation on a communications network, then is the operator of this network or the provider of the telecommunications service obliged to provide technical cooperation, if the investigating judge requests so directly or via a by the King designated police service.[151]

Article 90*quater* §4, 1-2° CCP reads as follows:

> §4 The investigating judge can order, directly or via a by the King designated police service, persons of whom he thinks that they have special knowledge of the telecommunications service subject to the monitoring measure, or of services used to protect or en-

[149] Supreme Court, 18 February 2003, P020913N.

[150] Luc Arnou, "Afluisteren tijdens het gerechtelijk onderzoek" (Wiretapping during the investigation); in Commentaar Strafrecht en strafvordering (Commentary criminal law and criminal procedural law), Gent, Kluwer, 2008, vol. 59, pp. 80–81, no. 83.

[151] The Act of 5 February 2016 amended Article 90quater §2, 1° CCP and Article 90*quater* §4, 1-2° CCP, and added the possibility for the investigating judge to request technical cooperation via a by the King appointed police service. Act of 5 February 2016 regarding the modification of criminal law and criminal procedure and regarding diverse provisions on criminal policy, *Belgian Official Journal*, 19 February 2016, entry into force on 29 February 2016.

crypt data that are stored, processed, encrypted or transferred via a computer system, to provide information on the operation of the system and on the way to get access to the content of the telecommunication, that is or has been transferred, in an understandable format.

He can order persons to make the content of telecommunications accessible in the format requested by him. These persons are obliged to comply with the order, to the extent of their capabilities.

b) Sanctions against telecommunication service providers and their employees

Both articles discussed in the previous section lay down specific sanctions for infringements of their obligations.

Article 90*quater* §2, 2° and 3° CCP reads as follows:

§2 […]

Any person, who by virtue of his office is informed of the measure or cooperates thereto, is bound by secrecy. Any violation of secrecy shall be punished in accordance with Article 458 of the Penal Code.

Any person who refuses technical cooperation to the requests referred to in this article, of which the modalities are determined by the King, is punished with a fine of twenty six francs to ten thousand francs on the proposal of the Minister of Justice and the Minister competent for Telecommunications.

Article 90*quater* §4, 3-5° CCP reads as follows:

§4 […]

He who refuses to provide the cooperation ordered in accordance with the preceding paragraphs shall be punished with imprisonment of six months to one year and a fine of twenty six francs to twenty thousand francs or one of these penalties.

Any person who by virtue of his ministry receives notification of the measure or who is called to granting technical cooperation is bound to the secrecy of the judicial investigation.

Any person, who by virtue of his office is informed of the measure or is called to grant technical cooperation, is bound to secrecy. Any violation of secrecy shall be punished in accordance with Article 458 of the Criminal Code.

A circular of the Board of Prosecutors General of 17 December 2009 explains the criminal policy regarding violations of the cooperation duties under Article 46*bis* §2 CCP (collection of identification data of electronic communications), Article 88*bis* §2 CCP (tracing of traffic data, and localization of electronic communications), and Article 90*quater* §2 CCP.[152] An investigation follows from manifest

---

[152] Board of Prosecutors General, "Telecommunicatierichtlijn inzake het opsporings- en vervolgingsbeleid betreffende inbreuken op de medewerkingsverplichtingen vervat in de artikelen 46bis § 2, 88bis § 2 en 90quater § 2 van het wetboek van strafvordering" (Telecommunications Circular regarding the investigation and prosecution of violations of the cooperation duties under Articles 46*bis* §2, 88*bis* § 2 and 90*quater* § 2 CCP), COL 14/2009, 17 December 2009, available (in Dutch and French) at http://www.om-mp.be/omzendbrief/4420834/col_14-2009_dd__17_12_2009.html

refusals to cooperate. In other cases, an adequate reaction will depend on the seriousness of the infringement or the specific circumstances.

No specific sanctions are foreseen for violations of the earlier discussed security requirements for data transfers by communication service providers (section III.B.5.d.).

C. Collection and Use of Traffic Data and Subscriber Data

1. Collection of traffic data and subscriber data

a) Collection of traffic data

aa) Relevant information

The Data Retention Act of 29 May 2016 added eight amendments to Article 88*bis* CCP:

1) Replacement of the term "telecommunications" with the term "electronic communications";
2) An additional application requirement for the measure: in addition to the already existing requirement that the investigating judge find circumstances that necessitate the application of the measure, from now on serious indications also need to exist that the criminal facts can result in the imposition of a correctional penalty of one-year imprisonment or a higher penalty;
3) The investigating judge can now also request cooperation via a police service designated by the King;
4) Inclusion of the principles of proportionality and subsidiarity;
5) The possibility to order the measure orally in case of emergency, in which case the measure must be confirmed as soon as possible in the form set out in the third and fourth paragraph of Article 88*bis* CCP.
6) If the measure applies to the traffic or localization data retained under Article 126 of the Act of 13 June 2005 on electronic communications, then the warrant also needs to mention the past period to which the warrant refers.
7) A new paragraph 2 on the application of the measure to the traffic or localization data retained under Article 126 of the Act of 13 June 2005 on electronic communications. The following rules apply:

   For a criminal offense referred to in Book II, Title I*ter* of the Criminal Code [terrorism crimes], the investigating judge in his warrant may request the data for a period of twelve months prior to his warrant;

   For another criminal offense referred to in Article 90ter, §§2 to 4, which is not referred to in the first indent, or a criminal offense which was committed within the framework of a criminal organization as defined in Article 324bis of the Criminal Code, or a criminal offense that may result in five years imprisonment or a more severe penalty, the investigating judge in his warrant may request the data for a period of nine months prior to the warrant;

For other offenses, the investigating judge may only request the data for a period of six months prior to the warrant.

8) A new paragraph 3 on professional secrecy, which reflects Article 90*octies* (wiretapping). New paragraph 3 reads as follows:

The measure may only cover the electronic communications of a lawyer or a doctor, who themselves are suspected of having committed or participated in one of the criminal offenses referred to in the first paragraph, or if specific facts suggest that third parties suspected of having committed a criminal offense referred to in the first paragraph, use their electronic communications.

The measure may not be implemented if, depending on the case, the president of the Bar or the representative of the provincial council of the order of physicians have not been informed of it. They will be informed by the investigating judge of what according to him shall be covered by professional secrecy. These data shall not be recorded in the official record.

Article 88*bis* CCP refers to the tracing of traffic data, and localization of electronic communications. Article 88*bis* §1 CCP describes the relevant information:

- tracing traffic data of electronic communications means from which or to which electronic communications are or were made.
- locating the origin or the destination of electronic communications

Article 88*bis* §1 CCP lays down the prerequisites for the tracing of traffic data, and localization of electronic communications:[153]

§1. In case of serious indications that the criminal facts can result in the imposition of a correctional penalty of one year imprisonment or of a higher penalty, and the investigating judge finds circumstances that necessitate the tracing of electronic communications or the localisation of the origin or the destination of electronic communications in order to find the truth, then he can, directly or via a police service designated by the King request the cooperation of an operator of an electronic communications network or the provider of an electronic communications service, to proceed or initiate to proceed to

- tracing traffic data of electronic communications means from which or to which electronic communications are or were made.
- locating the origin or the destination of electronic communications.

In the cases provided for in the first paragraph, the day, time, duration, and, if necessary, the place of the call for each telecommunications method of which the call data are detected or of which the destination of the telecommunications is localized, shall be determined and included in an official record.

In a reasoned warrant, the investigating judge states the factual circumstances of the case that justify the measure, and the proportionality in relation to the privacy and the subsidiarity in relation to any other investigatory act.

He also mentions the duration of the measure, which shall not be longer than two months starting from the warrant, without prejudice to a renewal, and if applicable, the period in the past to which the warrant extends in accordance with paragraph 2.

---

153 Annex 2 provides the future version of Article 88*bis* CCP.

In case of *flagrante delicto*, the public prosecutor can order the measure for the offences provided in Article 90ter, §§2, 3 and 4 [linguistic reformulation in future law but without any change in content: "*In case of flagrante delicto, the public prosecutor can order the* measure for the offences enumerated in Article 90*ter*, §§2, 3 and 4"]. In this case, the investigating judge must confirm the measure within twenty-four hours. However, if it concerns an offense referred to in Article 347*bis* [taking of hostages] and 470 [extortion by force] of the Criminal Code, the public prosecutor can order the measure during the situation *flagrante delicto*, without requirement of confirmation by the investigating judge.

The public prosecutor can order the measure upon request of the complainant, if the measure seems essential for establishing an offense referred to in Article 145 §3 and §3a of the Electronic Communications Act of 13 June 2005.[154]

In cases of emergency, the measure can be ordered orally. The measure must be confirmed as soon as possible in the form set out in the third and fourth paragraphs.

bb) Duty of addressees to disclose information in manual procedures

Article 88*bis* §4 CCP reads as follows:

§4. Any operator of an electronic communications network and any provider of an electronic communication service shall communicate the requested data within a period to be determined by the King, on the proposal of the Minister of Justice and the Minister responsible for Telecommunications.

Any person, who by virtue of his office is informed of the action or cooperates thereto, is bound to secrecy. Any breach of secrecy is punishable in accordance with Article 458 of the Criminal Code.

Any person who refuses technical cooperation with the request mentioned in this article, of which the King determines the modalities, shall be punished with a fine of twenty-six euro to ten thousand euros, on the proposal of the Minister of Justice and the Minister responsible for Telecommunications.

The modalities of the cooperation duties under Article 88*bis* CCP are laid down in the Royal Decree of 9 January 2003 regarding the legal duty to cooperate with judicial requests regarding electronic communications.[155] Article 4 of the Royal Decree provides that the traffic data of telecommunications, meaning from where or to where calls are or were made and that are more than 30 days old, shall be provided as soon as they are available and, at the latest, on the next working day at the same hour as the receipt of the request, unless the request provides otherwise.

---

[154] Article 145 §3, 1° of the Law of 13 June 2005 on electronic communications punishes anyone who carries out fraudulent electronic communications through a network of electronic communication in order to gain for himself/herself or another an unlawful advantage; Article 145 §3*bis* of the Law of 13 June 2005 on electronic communications incriminates "the person who uses an electronic communications network or an electronic communications service or other electronic means to annoy or cause damage to his correspondent and the person installing any device intended to commit the offence and the attempt to commit it."

[155] Royal Decree of 9 January 2003 regarding the legal duty to cooperate with judicial requests regarding electronic communications, *Belgian Official Journal*, 10 February 2003.

No automated procedure is prescribed for data transfers under Article 88*bis* CCP.

We refer to our earlier discussion regarding the duties to provide a technical and organizational infrastructure (section III.B.5.c.), the security requirements for data transfers by communication service providers (section III.B.5.d.) as well as checks, filtering, and decryption obligations of communication service providers (section III.B.5.e.).

b) Collection of subscriber data

aa) Relevant information

Article 46*bis* CCP is on the collection of identification data of electronic communications. Article 46*bis*, §1, 1° and 2° CCP describes the relevant information:

> 1) the identification of the subscriber or the habitual user of an electronic communications service or of the used electronic communication means;
>
> 2) the identification of electronic communications services to which a particular person is a subscriber or that are habitually used by a particular person. The reasoning reflects the proportionality in relation to the privacy and the subsidiarity in relation to any other investigatory act.

bb) Substantive prerequisites of collection

(1) Degree of suspicion

According to Article 46*bis* §1 CCP, the public prosecutor may proceed or initiate to proceed with the collection of identification data of electronic communications "on the basis of any information in his possession".

(2) Predicate offenses

Article 46*bis* CCP does not contain a list of offenses that can justify a monitoring measure. According to Article 46*bis* §1 CCP, the measure can only be ordered for crimes and misdemeanours; hence, *a contrario*, not for contraventions.

(3) Persons and connections under surveillance

Article 46*bis* §1, 1° CCP refers to "the subscriber or the habitual user of an electronic communications service or of the used electronic communication means."

Article 46*bis* §1, 2° CCP refers to "electronic communications services to which a particular person is a subscriber or that are habitually used by a particular person."

(4) Principle of subsidiarity

Article 46*bis* §1, 2° CCP provides that the reasoning of the public prosecutor reflects the proportionality in relation to privacy and the subsidiarity in relation to any other investigatory act.

(5) Proportionality of interception in individual cases

Article 46*bis* §1, 2° CCP provides that the reasoning reflects the proportionality in relation to privacy and the subsidiarity in relation to any other investigatory act.

(6) Consent by a communication participant to the measure

As said earlier (section III.B.6.b.), according to Article 61*quinquies* §3 CCP, the judge may reject the request by the suspect or a civil party if he considers the measures unnecessary in order to reveal the truth or if, at that moment, he considers the measures prejudicial to the investigation.

cc) Formal prerequisites of collection

(1) Competent authorities

Under normal circumstances, the public prosecutor authorizes the measure (Article 46*bis* §1, 3° CCP).

Under circumstances of emergency, also a judicial police officer can authorize the measure, but only after consent of the public prosecutor. Article 46*bis* §2 CCP reads as follows:

> [i]n cases of extreme urgency, any judicial police officer can, after verbal and prior consent of the public prosecutor, in a reasoned and written decision order the production of these data.

(2) Formal requirements for applications

As said earlier (section III.B.6.b.), according to Article 61*quinquies* §3 CCP, the judge may reject the request by the suspect or a civil party if he considers the measures unnecessary in order to reveal the truth or if, at that moment, he considers the measures prejudicial to the investigation.

(3) Formal requirements for orders

Article 46*bis* §1 CCP provides that the public prosecutor issues a reasoned and written decision in order to proceed or initiate to proceed with the collection of identification data.

The Data Retention Act of 29 May 2016 added a new paragraph to Article 46*bis* §1 CCP:

> For criminal facts that cannot result in the imposition of a correctional penalty of one-year imprisonment or of a more severe penalty, the public prosecutor – or in case of extreme emergency, the judicial police officer – can only request the data referred to in the first paragraph, for a period of six months prior to its decision.

dd) Duty of addressees to disclose information

Article 46*bis* §2 CCP reads as follows:

> §2. Any operator of an electronic communications network and any provider of an electronic communications service that is required to communicate information referred to in paragraph 1, provides the public prosecutor or judicial police officer the data that were requested within a period to be determined by the King, on the proposal of the Minister of Justice and the Minister competent for Telecommunications.
>
> The King determines, upon advice of the Privacy Commission and based on the proposal of the Minister of Justice and the Minister competent for Telecommunications, the technical conditions for the access to the information referred to in §1, which is available to the public prosecutor and to the police services designated in the same paragraph.
>
> Any person, who by virtue of his office is informed of the measure or cooperates thereto, is bound by secrecy. Any breach of secrecy shall be punished in accordance with Article 458 of the Criminal Code.
>
> Refusal to disclose the information shall be punished with a fine of twenty-six euro to ten thousand euros.

Of note in this regard is a judgment of the Belgian Supreme Court of 18 January 2011, in which the court gave an autonomous interpretation of the term "electronic communications provider" as mentioned in Article 46*bis* CCP (the collection of identification data of electronic communications). The Supreme Court held that:

> the obligation to cooperate under article 46bis of the Code of Criminal Procedure is not restricted to operators of an electronic communications network or to providers of an electronic communications service that are also operators within the meaning of the Electronic Communications Act of 13 June 2005, or that only provide their electronic communications services through their own infrastructure. This obligation also applies to anyone who provides a service, which consists wholly, or mainly in the conveyance of signals on electronic communications networks. The person who provides a service which consists of enabling its customers to obtain, or to receive or distribute information through an electronic network, can also be a provider of an electronic communications service.[156]

---

[156] Supreme Court, 18 January 2011, P.10.1347.N, available via http://jure.juridat.just.fgov.be/

ee) Automated procedure of disclosure

The modalities of the cooperation duties under Article 46*bis* CCP are laid down in the Royal Decree of 9 January 2003 regarding the legal duty to cooperate with judicial requests regarding electronic communications.[157]

Article 3 §1 of the Royal Decree provides that the Coordination Cell Justice of the operators of electronic communications networks that were not granted numbering capacity in the national numbering plan by the Belgian Institute for Postal Services and Telecommunications (BIPT),[158] and the electronic communications providers shall communicate in real time according to the rules provided in Article 10*bis* of the same Royal Decree (see section III.B.5.d. and e.).

Article 3 §2 of the Royal Decree prescribes an automated procedure of disclosure for electronic communications networks that were granted numbering capacity in the national numbering plan by the BIPT. The access is granted via a secure Internet application, by means of which the operator receives a request, which he is required to process and reply to immediately. The National Technical & Tactical Support Unit – Central Technical Interception Facility (NTSU-CTIF) determines further technical details of the procedure and shall only consult the database after receipt of a request based on Article 46*bis* CCP. The NTSU-CTIF shall keep a log file of every access to and consultation of the database and take the necessary physical and software-based measures in order to install an adequate security level.

In addition, we refer to our earlier discussion about the duties to provide a technical and organizational infrastructure (section III.B.5.c.), the security requirements for data transfers by communication service providers (section III.B.5.d.) as well as checks, filtering, and decryption obligations of communication service providers (section III.B.5.e.).

c) Data retention[159]

As said earlier (section I.A.2.a.dd.), the general data retention (preservation) provision is Article 126 of the Electronic Communications Act.[160] However, on

---

[157] Royal decree of 9 January 2003 regarding the legal duty to cooperate with judicial requests regarding electronic communications, *Belgian Official Journal,* 10 February 2003.

[158] On the basis of Article 11 §1 of the Electronic Communications Act of 13 June 2005.

[159] For further details, see the authors' country report for the Cybercrime Research Centre at Nicolaus Copernicus University (Poland): Paul De Hert and Gertjan Boulet, "The cooperation between Internet service/access providers and law enforcement authorities," February 2015, 29 pp., available at http://www.cybercrime.umk.pl/files/files/Report%20Belgium_De%20Hert%20Boulet.docx

[160] As amended by the Belgian Communication Act of 30 July 2013 amending Articles 2, 126, and 145 of the Act of 13 June 2005 on electronic communications and Article

11 June 2015, the Belgian Constitutional Court invalidated Article 126 of the Electronic Communications Act.[161] A new Belgian data retention law of 29 May 2016 entered into force on 28 July 2016.

Article 126 §1 of the Electronic Communications Act of 13 June 2005 provided that the following providers of *publicly available* services are subject to data retention obligations:

- Landline telephony services;
- Mobile telephony services;
- Internet access services;
- Internet e-mail services;
- Internet telephony services;
- Providers of underlying public electronic communication networks;
- Resellers in own name and on own behalf.

The Data Retention Act of 29 May 2016 retains these categories in the new version of Article 126, with the exception of resellers in own name and on own behalf.

The former version of Article 126 §3 of the Electronic Communications Act of 13 June 2005 established a data retention period of 12 months. The former version of Article 126 §4 of the Electronic Communications Act provided that the King could extend the data retention periods for certain categories of data, without exceeding 18 months, as well as install a temporary data retention period of more than 12 months. If the data retention period in the latter case exceeded 24 months, then the minister competent for telecommunications could inform the other EU Member States and the European Commission (EC).

The Data Retention Act of 29 May 2016 deletes paragraph 4 of Article 126 and lays down a uniform data retention period of 12 months in Article 126 §3, without the possibility of renewal.

The new version of Article 126 Data Retention Act of the Electronic Communications Act 29 May 2016 retains the requirement that the following statistics shall be added to the annual reports of the Minister of Justice in implementation of Article 90*decies* CCP:

1° the cases in which data have been provided to the competent authorities in accordance with the applicable legal provisions;

2° the time elapsed between the date on which the data were retained and the date on which the competent authority requested the transfer;

3° the cases in which the data requests could not be met.

90*decies* of the Code of Criminal Procedure, *Belgian Official Journal*, 23 August 2013, entry into force on 2 September 2013.

161 Constitutional Court of Belgium, 11 June 2015, no. 84/2015, available at http://www.const-court.be/public/n/2015/2015-084n.pdf

A Royal Decree of 19 September 2013 lists the types of data that are subject to data retention.[162]

Article 3 §1 of the Royal Decree of 19 September 2013 provides that landline telephony services retain the following identification data:

1) the number allocated to the user;
2) the user's personal data;
3) the subscription's starting date or the registration data;
4) the type of landline telephony service used and the types of other services with which the user is registered;
5) in case of number transfer, the identity of the transferring provider and of the receiving provider;
6) the data relating to the payment method, the identification of the payment instrument, and the time of payment for the subscription or for the use of the service.

Article 3 §2 of the Royal Decree of 19 September 2013 provides that landline telephony services retain the following traffic and localization data:

1) the identification of the calling number and the number called;
2) the location of the network connection point of the calling party and of the called party;
3) the identification of all lines in case of group calls, call forwarding, or call transfer;
4) data and time of the start and end of the call;
5) description of the telephony service used.

Article 4 §1 of the Royal Decree of 19 September 2013 provides that mobile telephony services retain the following identification data:

1) the number allocated to the user and his International Mobile Subscriber Identity (IMSI);
2) the user's personal data;
3) the date and location of the user's registration or subscription;
4) the date and time of the first activation of the service and the cell ID from which the service is activated;
5) the additional services to which the user has subscribed;
6) in case of number transfer, the identity of the transferring provider;

---

[162] Royal Decree of 19 September 2013 regarding the execution of Article 126 of the Act of 13 June 2005 on electronic communications, *Belgian Official Journal*, 8 October 2013, entry into force on 19 September 2013.

7) the data relating to the payment method, the identification of the payment instrument, and the time of payment for the subscription or for the use of the service;
8) the ID number of the user's mobile equipment (IMEI).

Article 4 §2 of the Royal Decree of 19 September 2013 provides that mobile telephony services retain the following traffic and localization data:

1) the identification of the telephone number of the calling party and of the called party;
2) the identification of all lines in case of group calls, call forwarding, or call transfer;
3) the IMSI of the calling and called participants;
4) the IMEI of the mobile equipment of the calling and called participants;
5) the data and time of the start and end of the call;
6) the location of the network connection point at the start and the end of each connection;
7) the identification of the geographic location of cells, via reference to the cell ID, at the time of connection;
8) the technical characteristics of the telephony service used.

Article 5 §1 of the Royal Decree of 19 September 2013 provides that Internet access services retain the following identification data:

1) the user ID allocated;
2) the user's personal data;
3) the data and time of the user's registration or subscription;
4) the IP-address, source port of the connection used for subscribing or registering the user;
5) the identification of the network connection point used for subscribing or registering the user;
6) the additional services to which the user has subscribed with the provider concerned;
7) the data relating to the payment method, identification of the payment instrument, and the time of payment of the subscription fee or for the use of the service.

Article 5 §2 of the Royal Decree of 19 September 2013 provides that Internet access services retain the following traffic and localization data:

1) the user's ID;

2a) the IP-address;

2b) in case of shared use of an IP-address, the ports allocated to the IP-address and the data and time of allocation;

3) the identification and location of the network connection point used when logging-in and logging-off;
4) the data and time of an Internet access service session's log-in and log-off;
5) the data volume uploaded and downloaded during a session;
6) the data necessary to identify the geographic location of cells, via reference to the cell ID, at the time of the connection.

Article 6 §1 of the Royal Decree of 19 September 2013 provides that Internet e-mail services and Internet telephony services retain the following identification data:

1) the user ID;
2) the user's personal data;
3) the data and time of creation of the e-mail or Internet telephony account;
4) the IP-address and source port used for the creation of the e-mail or Internet telephony account;
5) the data relating to the payment method, the identification of the payment instrument, and the time of payment of the subscription fee or for the use of the service.

Article 6 §2 of the Royal Decree of 19 September 2013 provides that Internet e-mail services and Internet telephony services retain the following traffic and localization data:

1) the user's ID relating to the e-mail or Internet telephony account, including the number of the ID code of the intended recipient of the communication;
2) the telephony number allocated to each communication entering the telephony network within the framework of an Internet telephony service;
3a) the IP-address and the source port used by the user;
3b) the IP-address and the source port used by the addressee;
4) the data and time of the log-in and log-off of a session of the e-mail service or Internet telephony service;
5) the data and time of a connection made by means of the Internet telephony account;
6) the technical characteristics of the service used.

Article 9 §7 of the Electronic Communications Act of 13 June 2005 provides that a specific Royal Decree shall address the matter of data retention for closed user groups. Federal Magistrate Jan Kerkhofs and Investigating Judge Philippe Van Linthout state that it could be said that Belgian providers of electronic communication services or networks with no notification duty are currently released from data retention obligations, taking into account the lack of a specific Royal Decree.[163] For the same reason, service providers that act as a mere conduit or provide caching and hosting activities under the Code of Economic Law are currently released from data retention obligations.

Ultimately, it should be noted that notaries, bailiffsn and accountants are subject to specific data retention and production obligations, provided in Article 7 and under chapter III of the Law of 11 January 1993 on preventing misuse of the financial system for purposes of laundering money and terrorism financing).[164]

2. Identification of device ID (IMEI), card number (IMSI), and location of mobile terminal devices

a) Identification of IMEI and IMSI

The Belgian CCP does not have a specific provision for the identification of the device ID (IMEI)[165] and the card number (IMSI).[166] Kerkhofs and Van Linthout say that such identification activities are justified on the basis of Article 46*bis* CCP on the collection of identification data of electronic communications (see section III.C.1.).[167]

b) Location determination via "silent SMS"

In a reply of 9 June 2011 to a parliamentary question regarding the use of "stealth" (silent SMS) technology, the Minister of Justice confirmed that such activities are justified on the basis of Article 88*bis* §1 CCP regarding the tracing of traffic data, and localization of electronic communications.[168]

---

163 Jan Kerkhofs and Philippe Van Linthout, *Cybercrime*, Brussels, Politeia, 2013, p. 396.

164 Act of 11 January 1993 on preventing misuse of the financial system for purposes of laundering money and terrorism financing, *Belgian Official Journal*, 9 February 1993, entry into force on 1 December 1993, available at http://www.imolin.org/doc/amlid/Belgium_law_11_January_1993.pdf

165 International Mobile Station Equipment Identity.

166 International Mobile Subscriber Identity.

167 Jan Kerkhofs and Philippe Van Linthout, *Cybercrime*, Brussels, Politeia, 2013, p. 356.

168 Belgian Chamber of Representatives, *Schriftelijke vragen en antwoorden* (Written questions and answers), 2010–2011, no. 53-032, pp. 35–36, available at http://www.dekamer.be/QRVA/pdf/53/53K0032.pdf; see also Jan Kerkhofs and Philippe Van Linthout, *Cybercrime*, Brussels, Politeia, 2013, p. 258.

D. Access to (Temporarily) Stored Communication Data

1. Online searches with the help of remote forensic software

a) Looking-in operations and observation

As noted earlier (section III.B.4.b.), the use of "technical means" is allowed for the looking-in operations power (Articles 46*quinquies* and 89*ter* CCP) and observation power (Article 47*sexies* CCP).

The power of looking-in operations allows the public prosecutor to authorize police officers to enter a private place, without knowledge of the owner or consent of the owner, in case there are serious suspicions that the punishable acts constitute or would constitute a crime referred to in Article 90*ter* §§2–4 CCP (on wiretapping, see section III.B.7.b.), or are committed or would be committed in the context of a criminal organization as referred to in Article 324*bis* CC, and when no other investigation means suffice to reveal the truth. In case the private place is a home, a part of a home, or the office of a lawyer of doctor, then the investigating judge has to authorize the measure (Article 89*ter* CCP).

Kerkhofs and Van Linthout view private cyber areas as a private place in the meaning of Article 46*quinquies* §1 CCP.[169]

Article 46*quinquies* §2 CCP lays down the limited cases in which looking-in operations may be used:

1) to record the place and to assess the potential presence of goods that are the object of the crime, or that were used to commit the crime, or that result from the crime, or of the presence of profits gained from committing the crime;
2) to collect evidence of the presence of those items;
3) to install technical means within the framework of the observation power (Article 47*sexies* CCP).

In the latter case, the authorization of the looking-in operation and all official reports shall be added to the judicial file at the latest after completion of the observation (see Article 46*quinquies* §1 *in fine* CCP). The suspect has access to the judicial file (Article 61*ter* CCP).

The observation power empowers the public prosecutor and the investigating judge to order systematic observation by police officers of one or more persons, their presence or behavior, or of certain items, places, or events. An observation is systematic when:

1) it is longer than five consecutive days or five non-consecutive days within a period of a month;

---

[169] Jan Kerkhofs and Philippe Van Linthout, *Cybercrime*, Brussels, Politeia, 2013, pp. 242–243.

2) it involves the use of technical means;
3) it has an international character;
4) it is performed by special units of the federal police.

The authorization of the observation and all official reports shall be added to the judicial file at the latest after completion of the observation (Article 47*septies* CCP).

The term "technical means" appears twice in Article 46*quinquies* CCP. First, Article 46*quinquies* §2, 3° CCP mentions the use of looking-in operations to install technical means within the framework of the observation power (Article 47*sexies* CCP) and refers to the meaning of the term technical means provided in Article 47*sexies* §1, 3° (observation):

> technical means is a configuration of components that detects and transmits signals, activates their recording and records the signals, with the exception of technical means used to perform a measure under Article 90ter [CCP].

Hence, the meaning of the term technical means in relation to the observation power is not identical to the meaning of the same term in Article 90*ter* §1, 2° (see section III.B.4.b.). In fact, microphones are a traditional example of technical means that can be used for the eavesdropping measure but not for the looking-in operation and observation.[170] Bockstaele, Chief Commissioner with the Ghent judicial police, gives as examples of technical means for the observation measure: a video camera, motion detectors, or a tracking system[171] on a container.[172]

Second, Article 46*quinquies* §4 CCP mentions the use of technical means for *all* purposes provided in Article 46*quinquies* §2 CCP, thus not only for the purpose to use the observation power (see section III.D.1.). The parliamentary preparatory works explain that this category is actually unlimited, including an infrared camera, an endoscope, and a drill to make a hole in the roof.[173]

For Kerkhofs and Van Linthout, technical means include key loggers, cameras, spyware, hacking, etc.[174] Legal doctrine, however, questions the extraterritorial scope of these powers, considering the significant cross-border reach of technical

---

170 Christine Van den Wyngaert, (An Outline of Criminal Law, Criminal Procedural Law & International Criminal Law), Antwerp-Apeldoorn, Maklu, 2006, pp. 963, 982 and 991.

171 Peilzender (in Dutch).

172 Marc Bockstaele and others (eds.), *De Zoeking onderzocht* (An analysis of the search), Antwerp-Apeldoorn, Maklu, 2009, p. 87.

173 Parliamentary preparatory works, Belgian Chamber of Representatives, regarding the special investigation methods and any other methods of investigation, 2001-2002, no. 50 1688/001, pp. 87–88, available via http://www.senate.be/www/?MIval=dossier&LEG=2&NR=1260&LANG=nl

174 Jan Kerkhofs and Philippe Van Linthout, *Cybercrime*, Brussels, Politeia, 2013, pp. 241, 243.

means, such as botnet crawlers, i.e., a technique "used for gathering intelligence on a P2P botnet, a decentralized network of infected computers under the control of a bot master".[175]

b) Network search

Article 88*ter* CCP referts to the network search, which empowers the investigating judge, when ordering the search of a computer system or a part thereof, to expand this search to a computer system or a part thereof at a place other than where the search takes place:

> §1. When the investigating judge orders a search in a computer system or part therefore, this search can be expanded to a computer system or a part thereof at a place other than where the search takes place:
>
> – If such expansion is necessary to reveal the truth concerning the investigated offense which is the object of the search; and
>
> – If other measures would be disproportional, or if there is a risk that without such expansion evidence would be lost.
>
> §2. The expansion of the search in an information system may not extend further than to information systems or the parts to which the persons that have the rights to use the searched information system, have specific access.
>
> §3. Regarding the data gathered by expanding the search in an information system, and that are useful for the same purposes as the seizure, one shall operate as specified in Article 39bis. The investigating judge shall inform the responsible of this computer system, unless his identity or domicile cannot be reasonably found.
>
> If it appears that these data are not situated on the national territory, then only copying is allowed. In that case, the investigating judge shall promptly notify, through the public prosecutor, the Minister of Justice, who will subsequently notify the competent authority of the State concerned, if it can be reasonably determined.
>
> §4. Article 89bis [on the designation of judicial police officers for the home search and seizure] applies to the expansion of the search in a computer system.

Conings and Oerlemans say that the use of hacker tools seems possible when the investigating judge does not have access to the computer system, and that the use of these tools would not violate the prohibition of hacking provided in Article 550*bis* CC.[176]

---

175 Karine Silva and Ruben Roex, "Zombie alert: Assessing legitimacy of P2P botnet mitigation techniques," 2014, conference paper, 25th European Regional Conference of the International Telecommunications Society (ITS), Brussels, Belgium, 22–25 June 2014, p. 1, available at http://econstor.eu/bitstream/10419/101402/1/795035411.pdf

176 Charlotte Konings and Jaap-Jan Oerlemans, "Van een netwerkzoeking naar online doorzoeking: grenzeloos of grensverleggend" (From a network search to an online search: borderless or groundbreaking?), *Computerrecht*, 2013, vol. 5, pp. 23–32, available at https://www.b-ccentre.be/download/b-ccentre_legal/B-CCENTRE%20Van%20een%20netwerkzoeking%20naar%20online%20doorzoeking.pdf

2. Search and seizure of stored communication data

a) Special provisions

The CCP contains a specific provision for data seizure, but not for the search of stored communication data. Article 39*bis* CCP is on data seizure and reads as follows:

§1. Without prejudice to specific provisions of this Article, the rules in this Code on the seizure, including Article 28 sexies, apply to the copying, making inaccessible and deleting data stored in a computer system.

§2. If the public prosecutor or the labour prosecutor encounters stored data in a computer system that are useful for the same purposes as the seizure, but when the seizure of their carrier is not desirable, these data and the data necessary for reading them, are copied on carriers belonging to the government. In case of urgency or for technical reasons, use can be made of carriers, which are available to persons who are entitled to use the computer system.

§3. He uses the appropriate technical means to prevent the access to and to guarantee the integrity of these data in the computer system, as well as the copies thereof which are available to persons who are entitled to use the computer system.

If the data are the subject of the offence or have been produced by the offence and if they infringe public order or public decency or constitute a danger to the integrity of computer systems or data stored, processed or transmitted through such system, the public prosecutor or the labour prosecutor shall use all appropriate technical means to make these data inaccessible.

Except in the case referred to in the preceding paragraph, he may, however, allow the further use of all or part of these data, when it does not endanger the prosecution.

§4. If the measure specified in §2 is not possible for technical reasons or because of the size of the data, he uses the appropriate technical means to prevent the access to the data and to guarantee the integrity of these data in the computer system, as well as the copies thereof which are available to persons who are entitled to use the computer system.

§5. The public prosecutor or the labour prosecutor informs the responsible of the computer system of the search in the computer system, and communicates to him a summary of the data copied, made inaccessible or deleted.

§6. The public prosecutor or the Labour prosecutor uses the appropriate technical means to ensure the integrity and confidentiality of the data.

Appropriate technical resources are used for the preservation of these data on the Registry.

The same applies if data stored, processed or transmitted through a computer system, are seized along with their carrier, pursuant to the previous articles.

b) Applicability of seizure provisions to electronic data

The foregoing shows that the data seizure (Article 39*bis* CCP) applies to electronic data. A current matter of dispute, however, is to what extent this data "seizure" power also includes information "search" powers.

Konings and Oerlemans distinguish the network search (Article 88*ter* CCP) from both the online search and the information search (search of stored communication data).[177] Moreover, they find that Belgian law does not contain any legal basis at all for the latter two investigation methods.

Regarding the online search, Belgian law enforcement agencies do access the cloud on the basis of the network search.[178]

Regarding the information search, Kerkhofs and Van Linthout read this power in the (data) seizure provisions (Article 35 CCP, Article 39*bis* CCP, etc.).[179] Their view was echoed by the Supreme Court in its judgment of 11 February 2015, in which it held that the data seizure from a mobile (Article 39*bis* CCP) empowers the police officers to analyze the data stored in the information memory. The Court referred to Article 35 CCP (the standard seizure provision) and Article 39*bis* §2 CCP (the data seizure provision): the latter article provides that the public prosecutor can copy stored data on a computer system if these data are useful for the same purposes as the seizure and if the seizure of the data carrier is not desirable.

Hence, the information search is covered by the seizure provision of Article 39*bis* CCP rather than by the general monitoring measure (Article 90*ter* CCP) or the other investigation methods to access stored communication data: looking-in operations (Article 46*quinquies* CCP), observation (Article 47*sexies* CCP), and the network search (Article 88*ter* CCP).

However, the Supreme Court held that, for data access to the cloud, the power of the network search (Article 88*ter* CCP) needs to be applied.[180] As noted earlier (section III.B.2.c.), webmail that arrives in an online web mailbox is deemed out of transmission and therefore can no longer be intercepted on the basis of Article 90*ter* CCP. In these cases, only a network search is possible (Article 88*ter* CCP) or a data seizure (Article 39*ter* CCP). However, it is debated whether or not pop-mail arriving in an online web mailbox is still deemed to be in transmission and therefore whether or not it could be intercepted on the basis of Article 90*ter* CCP.

---

177 Charlotte Konings and Jaap-Jan Oerlemans, "Van een netwerkzoeking naar online doorzoeking: grenzeloos of grensverleggend" (From a network search to an online search: borderless or groundbreaking?), *Computerrecht*, 2013, vol. 5, pp. 23-32, available at https://www.b-ccentre.be/download/b-ccentre_legal/B-CCENTRE%20Van%20een%20netwerkzoeking%20naar%20online%20doorzoeking.pdf. On the network search, see section III.D.1.

178 Jan Kerkhofs and Philippe Van Linthout, *Cybercrime*, Brussels, Politeia, 2013, pp. 263, 268 and 295.

179 Jan Kerkhofs and Philippe Van Linthout, *Cybercrime*, Brussels, Politeia, 2013, p. 167.

180 Supreme Court, 11 February 2015, P.14.1739.F, available at http://www.legalworld.be/legalworld/uploadedFiles/Rechtspraak/De_Juristenkrant/P.14.1739.F%20(11.02.2015)%20(gsm%20-%20pdk).pdf?LangType=2067

c) Different standards of protection for stored and for transmitted data

As noted earlier (sections II.A.4.a. and III.B.10.c.), the monitoring measure in Article 90*ter* CCP provides an exception to the general prohibition of the interception of (tele-)communications provided in Article 314*bis* and Article 259*bis* CC. Article 314*bis* CC lays down the prohibition, applicable to everyone, of taking cognizance of the contents of a telecommunication one does not participate in *during the transfer* of the telecommunication. A similar prohibition was introduced for public officials in Article 259*bis* CC. Hence, the standards provided in Article 90*ter* CCP for interception data in transmission are higher than the standards for accessing stored data on the basis of other provisions.

d) Open and clandestine access to stored data

Article 39*bis* §5 CCP provides that "[t]he public prosecutor or the labour prosecutor informs the responsible of the computer system of the search in the computer system, and communicates to him a summary of the data copied, made inaccessible or deleted".

3. Duties to cooperate: production and decryption orders

As noted (sections I.A.2.a., III.B.5., III.C.1.), the CCP contains production and decryption orders in connection with the collection of identification data of electronic communications (Article 46*bis* CCP), tracing of traffic data, and localization of electronic communications (Article 88*bis* CCP), the network search (Article 88*ter* CCP), and wiretapping (Article 90*ter* CCP).

With regard to Article 46*bis*, Article 88*bis*, and Article 90*ter* CCP, the fourth functional requirement in Article 6 §1 of the Royal Decree of 9 January 2003 concerns the transfer of content of data in plain language in case the operator of an electronic communications network or the provider of electronic communications introduced encoding, compression, or encryption of the electronic communications traffic.

With regard to Article 88*ter* CCP, Article 88*quater* §1 CCP reads as follows:

> §1. The investigating judge, or on his behalf a judicial police officer, assistant officer of the public prosecutor and of the labour prosecutor, can order persons of whom the investigating judge thinks that they have special knowledge concerning the computer system that is the object of a search, or of services to protect or encrypt data that are processed, encrypted or transferred through a computer system, to provide information concerning its functioning or the ways to get access to it, or to get access in an understandable format to the data that are processed, encrypted or transferred through it. The investigating judge specifies the factual circumstances of the case that justify the measure in a substantiated warrant that he communicates to the public prosecutor or the labour prosecutor.

All these cooperation duties also apply to the suspect, with the exception of the specific cooperation duty laid down in Article 88*quater* §2 CCP in relation to the network search:

> §2. The investigating judge, or on his behalf a judicial police officer, assistant officer of the public prosecutor and of the labour prosecutor, can order any suitable person to operate the computer system himself or, as appropriate, to search, to make accessible, to copy, to make inaccessible or to delete the relevant data that are processed, encrypted or transferred through it. These persons are obliged to comply with the order, to the extent of their capabilities.
>
> The order referred to in the first paragraph cannot be given to the accused and to the persons referred to in Article 156.

Kerkhofs and Van Linthout explain that, whereas Article 88*quater* §2 CCP concerns actions to be taken by the suspect, the other articles concern the provision of mere intelligence or existing evidence. They refer to the case *Saunders v. the United Kingdom* in which the ECtHR held that:

> [t]he right not to incriminate oneself, in particular, presupposes that the prosecution in a criminal case seek to prove their case against the accused without resort to evidence obtained through methods of coercion or oppression in defiance of the will of the accused.[181]

Thus, Kerkhofs and Van Linthout accept the practice of requesting cooperation from suspects.

Yet, they add as a side remark that it is still to be seen whether this solution will pass the human rights test by the ECtHR.[182]

Article 39*bis* CCP does not lay down production and decryption orders. However, Article 39*bis* §3 CCP allows the public prosecutor to order the seizure of alleged illegal data (e.g., a computer virus). The public prosecutor can use all technical means to make data inaccessible that:

> are the subject of the offence or have been produced by the offence and if they infringe public order or public decency or constitute a danger to the integrity of computer systems or data stored, processed or transmitted through such system.

This power is used, for example, by prosecutors to request an Internet Service Provider (ISP) to delete from their Domain Name Server (DNS) the domain name of a site that violates the law.

---

181 ECtHR, *Saunders v. the United Kingdom*, Grand Chamber, 17 December 1996, No. 19187/91, §68, available via http://hudoc.echr.coe.int/

182 Jan Kerkhofs and Philippe Van Linthout, *Cybercrime*, Brussels, Politeia, 2013, p. 369.

IV. Use of Electronic Communication Data in Judicial Proceedings

1. Use of electronic communication data in the law of criminal procedure

There are no rules specifically designed for using intercepted or stored electronic data as evidence in court proceedings.

In Belgium, the use of evidence is free. Hence there are no limits regarding the form by which intercepted material shall be introduced as evidence in criminal proceedings.[183]

2. Inadmissibility of evidence as a consequence of inappropriate collection

In Belgium, illegally obtained evidence follows from:

1) the commission of a criminal offense;
2) a violation of the law of criminal procedure;
3) a violation of the right to privacy;
4) a violation of the right of defense;
5) a violation of the right to human dignity.[184]

However, an illegality committed during evidence collection does not automatically result in the exclusion of the illegally obtained evidence. In its judgment of 14 October 2003, the Supreme Court developed three exclusionary rules, the so-called Antigoon criteria for excluding illegally obtained evidence.[185] More particularly, evidence has to be excluded in three cases:

1) if compliance with procedural rules is legally prescribed under penalty of nullity;
2) if the illegality has compromised the reliability of the evidence;
3) if the use of the illegally obtained evidence violates the right to a fair trial.

In a judgment of 23 March 2004,[186] the Supreme Court held that the violation of the right to a fair trial has to be assessed on the basis of all aspects of the case as a whole, and proposed a number of factors that the judge can take into consideration:

---

183 Raf Verstraeten, *Handboek strafvordering* (Manual on criminal procedure), Antwerp, Maklu, 2007, p. 859; Chris Van den Wyngaert, *Strafrecht, Strafprocesrecht & Internationaal Strafrecht in hoofdlijnen* (An Outline of Criminal Law, Criminal Procedural Law & International Criminal Law), Antwerp-Apeldoorn, Maklu, 2006, p. 1127.

184 Raf Verstraeten and Frank Verbruggen, *Straf- en strafprocesrecht voor bachelors* (Criminal law and criminal procedural law for bachelors), Antwerp-Apeldoorn, Maklu, 2007, p. 336.

185 Supreme Court, 14 October 2003, P030762N, available via http://jure.juridat.just.fgov.be/

186 Supreme Court, 23 March 2004, P040012N, available via http://jure.juridat.just.fgov.be/

1) whether or not the authorities intentionally committed the illegality;
2) whether the seriousness of the criminal offense exceeds the seriousness of the illegality committed;
3) whether or not the illegality only concerns a material element of the criminal offense;
4) the impact of the illegality on the protected fundamental right;
5) the mere formal nature of the illegality.

The Act of 24 October 2013[187] laid down the Antigoon exclusionary rules in Article 32 of the Preliminary Title of the CCP. However, the Belgian legislator did not incorporate a fourth exclusionary rule developed by the Supreme Court in a judgment of 26 January 2011: an illegality that concerns "a substantial procedural rule that affects the organization of the courts," i.e., an illegality concerning the *material* jurisdiction of the courts.[188] The Supreme Court held that this fourth exclusionary rule does not apply if the illegality concerns the *territorial* jurisdiction of the courts: in this case, exclusion of evidence can only be based on the three traditional Antigoon criteria. In a judgment of 24 April 2013, the Supreme Court effectively applied the fourth exclusionary rule to evidence found during a home search[189] that was authorized by a judge in a police court instead of by the investigating judge.[190]

Regarding the investigation methods referred to in this report, only the formal requirements for monitoring measures (Article 90*quater* §1 CCP) are prescribed under sanction of nullity (see section III.B.6.b. above):

> §1 The investigating judge authorizes each monitoring measure under Article 90ter by a reasoned decision, and communicates the warrant to the public prosecutor.
>
> On penalty of nullity, the warrant shall be dated and mentions:
>
> 1° the indications and concrete facts specific to the case, which justify the measure under Article 90ter;
>
> 2° the reasons why the measure is necessary to reveal the truth;
>
> 3° the person, the (tele-)communications method or the place that is the subject of the monitoring measure;

[187] Act of 24 October 2013 amending the Preliminary Title of the Code of Criminal Procedure, *Belgian Official Journal*, 12 November 2013, entry into force on 22 November 2013.

[188] Supreme Court, 26 January 2011, P.10.1321.F, available via http://jure.juridat.just.fgov.be/ ; See also the report of the law firm Eubelius: "Legal Embedment of the Antigoon case law", December 2013, available at http://www.eubelius.be/en/spotlight/legal-embedment-antigoon-case-law

[189] On the basis of the Act of 16 November 1972 concerning the Labour Inspectorate, *Belgian Official Journal,* 8 December 1972, entry into force on the same date.

[190] Supreme Court, 24 April 2013, P.12.1919.F.

4° the period during which the monitoring measure can be carried out, which should not be longer than one month counting from the decision by which the measure is ordered;

5° the name and the capacity of the judicial police officer designated for the implementation of the measure.

Regarding Article 90*quater* §1n 5° CCP, i.e., the duty to mention in the warrant the name and the capacity of the judicial police officer designated for the implementation of the measure, the Supreme Court held in a judgment of 19 June 1967 that another agent than the one mentioned in the warrant can implement the monitoring measure. In fact, implementation by the judicial police officer only concerns a measure of implementation of the warrant, not the legality of the warrant itself.[191]

As said earlier (section III.B.3.a.aa.), although notification of the Bar and the order of physicians for a monitoring measure that covers premises used for business purposes or domicile, or the (tele-)communications means of a lawyer or a doctor (Article 90*octies* §2 CCP), is not prescribed under sanction of nullity, the parliamentary preparatory works underline that the public order nature of this provision implies that failure to do so will entail the nullity of the monitoring measure.[192]

Apart from the exclusionary rules discussed above, the issue of "admissibility" emerges when a court potentially cannot admit evidence because its legality cannot be determined.[193] With regard to a foreign wiretapping measure, the Supreme Court held on 30 March 2010 that the non-availability of sufficient data to assess the legality of *one piece* of evidence can result in the non-admissibility of that piece; and that the non-availability of sufficient data to assess the legality of *all* evidence can result in the non-admissibility or the exclusion of the evidence but not in the discontinuance of the proceedings.[194]

On 3 April 2012, the Supreme Court found a violation of the right of defense, as the defense did not have the possibility to assess the legality of evidence resulting from a Dutch wiretapping measure: more specifically, the Court of Appeal of Antwerp had assessed the legality of the evidence merely on the basis of the evidence itself and a letter of the Dutch public prosecutor (officier van justitie).[195] The Su-

---

191 Supreme Court, 19 June 1967, P.07.0311.

192 Parliamentary preparatory works, regarding the legislative proposal protecting privacy against the interception of communication and telecommunication, Belgian Senate, 1993–1994, 18 May 1994, no. 843-2, p. 189, available at http://www.senate.be/lexdocs/S0539/S05390364.pdf

193 Raf Verstraeten, *Handboek strafvordering* (Manual on criminal procedure), Antwerp, Maklu, 2012, p. 1015.

194 Supreme Court, 30 March 2010, P.09.1789.N/1, available via http://jure.juridat.just.fgov.be/

195 Supreme Court, 3 April 2012, P.10.0973.N, available via http://jure.juridat.just.fgov.be/

preme Court clarified that the assessment of the legality of the evidence can be based on the authorization of the wiretapping measure.

3. Use of data outside the main proceedings

a) Data from other criminal investigations

The judge does not have a right of injunction against the public prosecutor and thus cannot order the public prosecutor to request the judicial files of other criminal investigations.[196]

In this regard, it is of note that intercepted data can be used for the prosecution of individuals who were not the subject of the underlying interception order, but if so, only in another criminal investigation. Verstraeten and Verbruggen hold that the monitoring measure may not be halted if it reveals information pointing to the commission of offenses not anticipated by or not mentioned in the monitoring order.[197] These offenses are lawfully established only insofar as the execution of the monitoring measure does not exceed the limits of the authorization. The investigating judge cannot extend the investigation to these offenses if no action was brought before him/her in relation to these offenses. The investigating judge must inform the public prosecutor of these offenses on the basis of Article 56 §1 *in fine* CCP.

b) Data from preventive investigations

Data obtained from intelligence services and non-judicial police forces are admissible as evidence in criminal proceedings. We refer to our earlier discussion regarding the data exchanges between preventive police authorities/intelligence agencies and law enforcement authorities (section I.A.4.).

c) Data obtained from foreign jurisdictions

Article 6 of the Act of 9 December 2004 concerning international mutual legal assistance in criminal matters lays down the general rules on international legal assistance in criminal matters (see below, section V.A.3.).

---

[196] Court of Appeal of Antwerp, 13 March 2002, annotated by Bart De Smet, "Voeging van strafdossiers op verzoek van de verdediging" (Adding a file at the request of the defense), *Rechtskundig Weekblad*, 2002-2003, p. 1022; see Chris Van den Wyngaert, *Strafrecht, Strafprocesrecht & Internationaal Strafrecht in hoofdlijnen* (An Outline of Criminal Law, Criminal Procedural Law & International Criminal Law), Antwerp-Apeldoorn, Maklu, 2006, p. 615.

[197] Raf Verstraeten and Frank Verbruggen, *Straf- en strafprocesrecht voor bachelors* (Criminal law and criminal procedural law for bachelors), Antwerp-Apeldoorn, Maklu, 2007, pp. 209 and 220, nos. 873 and 933.

Article 13 of the Act of 9 December 2004 regarding mutual assistance in criminal matters[198] lays down the rules on the admissibility of intercepted data obtained from foreign jurisdictions. These rules match the Antigoon criteria discussed above (section IV.2.). Article 13 of the Act of 9 December 2004 reads as follows:

> Within the framework of criminal proceedings conducted before a Belgian court, no use shall be made of evidence:
>
> 1° which was illegally obtained in a foreign country if the illegality:
>
> – follows from the infringement of procedural requirements prescribed under sanction of nullity according to the law of the state where the evidence was obtained
>
> – compromises the reliability of the evidence;
>
> 2° of which the use would imply a violation of the fundamental right of a fair trial.

4. Challenging the probity of intercepted data

a) Duty to ensure the integrity and confidentiality of the recorded (tele-)communications

Article 90*septies* §5 CCP provides that:

> [t]he appropriate means are used to ensure the integrity and confidentiality of the recorded (tele-)communications, and where possible, to ensure the transcription or translation. The same applies to the custody at the Registry of the records and the transcription or translation thereof, and to the entries in the special register. The King determines, after consulting the Privacy Commission, these means as well as the time when they replace the custody in a sealed envelope or the special register, referred to in the third and the fourth paragraph.

In relation to the data seizure measure (Article 39*bis* CCP), Kerkhofs and Van Linthout explain the need for regulating the chain of custody and for expert reports about the integrity of the evidence.[199] Similar concerns could arguably be raised regarding the integrity and reliability of intercepted data.

b) Access of parties to the judicial file

Article 90*sexies in fine* CCP (monitoring measure) provides that:

> [t]he warrants of the investigating judge, the reports of the judicial police officers referred to in Article 90quater, §3, and the official records relating to the implementation of the measure, are included in the judicial file at the latest by the end of the measure.

The suspect has access to the judicial file (Article 61*ter* CCP). As said (section IV.2.), Article 90*quater* §1 CCP provides that the warrant shall mention:

---

[198] Act of 9 December 2004 regarding mutual assistance in criminal matters and modifying Article 90ter of the Code of Criminal Procedure, *Belgian Official Journal*, 24 December 2004, entry into force on 3 January 2005.

[199] Jan Kerkhofs and Philippe Van Linthout, *Cybercrime*, Brussels, Politeia, 2013, p. 184.

1) the indications and concrete facts specific to the case, which justify the measure under Article 90ter;
2) the reasons why the measure is necessary to reveal the truth;
3) the person, the (tele-)communications method or the place that is the subject of the monitoring measure;
4) the period during which the monitoring measure can be carried out, which should not be longer than one month counting from the decision by which the measure is ordered;
5) the name and the capacity of the judicial police officer designated for the implementation of the measure.

As said earlier, third parties do not have access to the judicial file (III.B.10.a.).

c) Access of the defense to non-official reports

According to Article 90*septies* §§6-8, the investigating judge or the court may allow the defendant, the accused, the civil party or their counsel upon request access to the whole or parts of the recordings deposited at the Registry (section III.B.3.a.aa.(1)).

d) Right to request additional investigation methods

As said above (section III.B.6.b.), on the basis of Article 61*quinquies* §1 CCP, the suspect and the civil party have the right to request the investigating judge to carry out additional investigation methods, such as the appointment of an expert or performance of a second test.[200]

According to Article 61*quinquies* §2 CCP, the suspect and the civil party shall submit their petition for an additional investigation method in writing to the Registry of the Court of First Instance. The petition should be substantiated and give a detailed description of the requested investigation method.

According to Article 61*quinquies* §3 CCP, the judge may reject the request if he considers the measures to be unnecessary in order to reveal the truth or if, at that moment, he considers the measures prejudicial to the investigation. According to Article 61*quinquies* §4 CCP, rejection by the investigating judge is subject to appeal before the Indictment Chamber (see section I.A.4.b.), in which case the investigating judge shall hear the Prosecutor General, the suspect, and his or her attorney (Article 61*quater* §5 CCP).

---

[200] Cf. Philip Traest, "Judicial control on the gathering and reliability of technical evidence in a continental criminal justice system", conference paper for the 16th International Conference of the International Society for the Reform of Criminal Law, 2002, p. 10, available at http://www.isrcl.org/Papers/Traest.pdf

Even though there is no explicit legal basis, the trial judge can also order the appointment of an expert or a second test at his own request or at the request of the parties. This power is included in the judge's general task of the finding of truth.[201]

e) Non-disclosure of technical means

In a reply of 9 June 2011 to a parliamentary question (see section III.C.2.b.), the Minister of Justice explained that the use of "stealth" technology is allowed under Article 88*bis* CCP (tracing of traffic data, and localization of electronic communications). However, at the same time, the Minister of Justice recalled that the traditional prohibition of disclosure of the technical means used for special investigation methods, such as observation (Article 47*sexies* CCP; Article 47*octies* CCP), also holds for Article 88*bis* CCP, even though this measure concerns other investigation methods "in the area of the interception of telecommunications."[202] Hence, it could be asked to what extent the same rationale holds for the powers of looking-in operations (Articles 46*quinquies* and 89*ter* CCP) and the monitoring measure (Article 90*ter* CCP).

f) Exclusion of unreliable evidence

Regarding the probity of intercepted data, the second Antigoon criterion is relevant, according to which illegally obtained evidence has to be excluded if the illegality has compromised the reliability of the evidence.

As noted above, both the Courts in Chambers, the Indictment Chamber, and the trial judge determine the grounds for finding a nullity on the basis of the so-called Antigoon criteria (see sections III.B.10.b. and IV.2.). If the Courts in Chambers finds no illegality and the parties do not appeal against this decision before the Court of Indictment, then they can raise this point again before the trial judge. If the parties appeal against this decision before the Indictment Chamber, then they cannot raise this point again before the trial judge, except if the alleged nullity concerns the weighing of evidence, which is an exclusive task of the trial judge (Article 235*bis* §5 CCP).

---

201 Raf Verstraeten and Frank Verbruggen, *Straf- en strafprocesrecht voor bachelors* (Criminal law and criminal procedural law for bachelors), Antwerp-Apeldoorn, Maklu, 2007, p. 322.

202 Belgian Chamber of Representatives, *Schriftelijke vragen en antwoorden* (written question and answers), 2010-2011, no. 53-032, p. 36, available at http://www.dekamer.be/QRVA/pdf/53/53K0032.pdf; see also Jan Kerkhofs and Philippe Van Linthout, *Cybercrime*, Brussels, Politeia, 2013, p. 258.

V. Exchange of Intercepted Electronic Communication Data between Foreign Countries

A. Legal Basis for Mutual Legal Assistance

1. International conventions

Belgium has ratified the following international conventions on mutual assistance applicable to the interception of electronic communications:

a) UN conventions

United Nations Convention against Transnational Organized Crime of 15 November 2000:[203] signature on 12 December 2000, ratification on 11 August 2004.[204] According to Article 38 §1 of the Convention (on entry into force), "[t]his Convention shall enter into force on the ninetieth day after the date of deposit of the fortieth instrument of ratification, acceptance, approval or accession." Hence, the Convention entered into force in Belgium on 9 November 2001.

Belgium made no declarations, reservations, or notifications specifically regarding the interception of electronic communications.[205]

b) Council of Europe conventions

European Convention on Mutual Assistance in Criminal Matters of 20 April 1959 (CETS No. 030):[206] signature on 20 April 1959, ratification on 13 August 1975.[207] Article 27 §3 of the Convention provides: "As regards any signatory ratifying subsequently the Convention shall come into force 90 days after the date of

---

[203] United Nations Convention against Transnational Organized Crime, General Assembly Resolution 55/25 of 15 November 2000, the conventions and the protocols thereto are available at http://www.unodc.org/documents/treaties/UNTOC/Publications/TOC%20 Convention/TOCebook-e.pdf

[204] Act of 24 June 2004 regarding the approval of the Convention against Transnational Organized Crime and its protocols, *Belgian Official Journal*, 13 October 2004, entry into force on 23 October 2004.

[205] The declarations and notifications by Belgium at the time of depositing (11 August 2004) the instrument of ratification of the United Nations Convention against Transnational Organized Crime are available here https://treaties.un.org/Pages/ViewDetails.aspx?src= TREATY&mtdsg_no=XVIII-12&chapter=18&lang=en#EndDec

[206] European Convention on Mutual Assistance in Criminal Matters, Strasbourg, 20 April 1959, available at http://conventions.coe.int/treaty/en/Treaties/Html/030.htm

[207] Act of 19 July 1975 regarding approval of the European Convention on Mutual Assistance in Criminal Matters of 20 April 1959, *Belgian Official Journal*, 23 October 1975, entry into force on 11 November 1975.

the deposit of its instrument of ratification." Hence, the Convention entered into force in Belgium on 11 November 1975.

Of note are the following reservations made by Belgium, at the time of depositing the instrument of ratification with the Secretary General of the Council of Europe, which cover the period since the entry into force of the Convention on 11 November 1975:

Concerning Article 2 of the Convention (on the refusal of assistance, under chapter I on general provisions):[208]

> The Government of the Kingdom of Belgium reserves the right not to comply with a request for assistance
>
> a. if there are good grounds for believing that it concerns an inquiry instituted with a view to prosecuting, punishing or otherwise interfering with an accused person because of his political convictions or religion, his nationality, his race or the population group to which he belongs;
> b. is so far as it concerns a prosecution or proceedings incompatible with the principle non bis in idem;
> c. in so far as it concerns an inquiry into acts for which the accused person is being prosecuted in Belgium.

Concerning Article 22 of the Convention (single article under chapter VII on the exchange of information from judicial records):

> The Government of the Kingdom of Belgium will not notify the subsequent measures referred to in Article 22 except in so far as the organisation of its judicial records allows of so doing.

Concerning Article 26 of the Convention (relation of the Convention to other legal instruments, under chapter VIII on final provisions):

> By reason of the special arrangements between the Benelux countries, the Government of the Kingdom of Belgium does not accept Article 26, paragraphs 1 and 3 in respect of its relations with the Netherlands and Luxembourg.
>
> The Government of the Kingdom of Belgium reserves the right to derogate from these provisions in respect of its relations with other member States of the European Economic Community.

Belgium also signed the two additional protocols to the *European Convention on Mutual Assistance in Criminal Matters:*

The *Additional Protocol to the European Convention on Mutual Assistance in Criminal Matters*, 17 March 1978:[209] signature on 11 July 1978, ratification on

---

[208] The reservations and declarations made by Belgium at the time of depositing (13 August 1975) the instrument of ratification of the Convention on Mutual Assistance in Criminal Matters of 20 April 1959 are available here: http://conventions. coe.int/Treaty/Commun/ListeDeclarations.asp?CL=ENG&NT=030&VL=1

[209] Additional Protocol to the European Convention on Mutual Assistance in Criminal Matters, Strasbourg, 17 March 1978, available at http://conventions.coe.int/treaty/en/Treaties/Html/099.htm

28 February 2002.[210] The additional protocol entered into force in Belgium on 29 May 2002.

The Second Additional Protocol to the European Convention on Mutual Assistance in Criminal Matters, 8 November 2001:[211] signature on 8 November 2011, ratification on 9 March 2009.[212] The additional protocol entered into force in Belgium on 1 July 2009.

Convention on Cybercrime (CETS No. 185):[213] signature on 23 November 2001, ratification on 20 August 2012.[214] According to Article 36 §4 of the Convention:

> the Convention shall enter into force on the first day of the month following the expiration of a period of three months after the date of the expression of its consent to be bound by the Convention.

Hence, the Convention entered into force in Belgium on 1 December 2012.

Belgium made no reservations or declarations specifically regarding the interception of electronic communications.[215]

c) EU conventions

Treaty between the Kingdom of Belgium, the Grand Duchy of Luxembourg and the Kingdom of the Netherlands concerning extradition and mutual assistance in criminal matters (Benelux Treaty), 27 June 1962:[216] signature on 27 June 1962, ratification on 30 July 1964.[217] Article 49 §2 of the Convention provides that "[t]he

---

210 Act of 29 January 2002 regarding approval of the Additional Protocol to the European Convention on Mutual Assistance in Criminal Matters, *Belgian Official Journal*, 1 June 2002, entry into force on 11 June 2002.

211 Second Additional Protocol to the European Convention on Mutual Assistance in Criminal Matters, Strasbourg, 8 November 2001, available at http://conventions.coe.int/treaty/en/Treaties/Html/182.htm

212 Act of 8 November 2001 regarding approval of the Second Additional Protocol to the European Convention on Mutual Assistance in Criminal Matters, *Belgian Official Journal*, 19 June 2009, entry into force on 1 July 2009.

213 Cybercrime Convention, Budapest, 23 November 2001, available at http://conventions.coe.int/Treaty/EN/Treaties/Html/185.htm

214 Act of 3 August 2012 regarding approval of the Cybercrime Convention, *Belgian Official Journal*, 21 November 2012, entry into force on 1 December 2012.

215 The declaration of Belgium at the time of depositing (20 August 2012) the instrument of ratification of the Cybercrime Convention is available at http://conventions.coe.int/Treaty/Commun/ListeDeclarations.asp?NT=185&CM=&DF=&CL=ENG&VL=1

216 Treaty between the Kingdom of Belgium, the Grand Duchy of Luxembourg and the Kingdom of the Netherlands concerning extradition and mutual assistance in criminal matters, Brussels, 27 June 1962, available at https://www.consilium.europa.eu/ueDocs/cms_Data/docs/polju/en/EJN220.pdf

217 Act of 27 June 1962 regarding the approval of the Treaty between the Kingdom of Belgium, the Grand Duchy of Luxembourg and the Kingdom of the Netherlands concern-

Treaty shall enter into force two months after the deposit of the last instrument of ratification." Hence, the treaty entered into force on the same date for Belgium, Luxembourg, and the Netherlands. The Netherlands deposited the last instrument of ratification on 11 October 1967. Hence, the treaty entered into force two months later, on 11 December 1967.

Belgium made no declarations specifically regarding the interception of electronic communications.[218]

Convention on Mutual Assistance in Criminal Matters between the Member States of the European Union, 29 May 2000:[219] signature on 29 May 2000, ratification on 25 May 2005.[220] Article 27 §§2–3 of the Convention read as follows:

> 2. Member States shall notify the Secretary-General of the Council of the European Union of the completion of the constitutional procedures for the adoption of this Convention. 3. This Convention shall, 90 days after the notification referred to in paragraph 2 by the State, member of the European Union at the time of adoption by the Council of the Act establishing this Convention, which is the eighth to complete this formality, enter into force for the eight Member States concerned.

Hence, the Convention entered into force in Belgium on 23 August 2005.

Belgium made no declarations specifically regarding the interception of electronic communications.[221]

Belgium also signed the additional protocol to the European Convention on Mutual Assistance in Criminal Matters:

Protocol to the Convention on Mutual Assistance in Criminal Matters between the Member States of the European Union, 16 October 2001:[222] signature on

---

ing extradition and mutual assistance in criminal matters, *Belgian Official Journal*, 24 October 1967, entry into force on 11 December 1967.

218 The declarations of Belgium under the Benelux Treaty are available at the end of the Treaty: https://www.consilium.europa.eu/ueDocs/cms_Data/docs/polju/en/EJN220.pdf

219 Council Act of 29 May 2000 establishing, in accordance with Article 34 of the Treaty on European Union, the Convention on Mutual Assistance in Criminal Matters between the Member States of the European Union, OJ C 197, 12.7.2000, pp. 1-23.

220 Act of 11 May 2005 regarding approval of the Convention on Mutual Assistance in Criminal Matters between the Member States of the European Union, *Belgian Official Journal*, 22 June 2006, entry into force on 2 July 2005.

221 The declaration of Belgium of 23 March 2011 under the Convention on Mutual Assistance in Criminal Matters between the Member States of the European Union is available at https://www.ejn-crimjust.europa.eu/ejn/libdocumentproperties.aspx?Id=18

222 Protocol established by the Council in accordance with Article 34 of the Treaty on European Union to the Convention on Mutual Assistance in Criminal Matters between the Member States of the European Union, OJ C 326, 21.11.2001, pp. 2–8.

16 October 2001, ratification on 25 May 2005.[223] The additional protocol entered into force in Belgium on 5 October 2005.

2. Bilateral Treaties

Article 25 §2 of the European Convention on Mutual Assistance in Criminal Matters of 20 April 1959 provides that "[t]he Contracting Parties may conclude between themselves bilateral or multilateral agreements on mutual assistance in criminal matters only in order to supplement the provisions of this Convention or to facilitate the application of the principles contained therein."

Accordingly, via letters signed on 6 March and 18 July 1975, Belgium and Germany concluded an additional bilateral agreement for cases in which the request for assistance concerns the following:

1) a civilly liable person who is involved in a criminal case, or
2) criminal investigations in fiscal matters (customs and excise, direct or indirect taxation, and exchange control).[224]

These cases were already provided in the provisions 2a-b of the additional protocol to the extradition and mutual legal assistance treaty between Belgium and Germany of 17 January 1958.[225]

3. National Regulation

Beyond the ratified treaties, Article 6 of the Act of 9 December 2004 concerning international mutual legal assistance in criminal matters lays down the general rules on international legal assistance in criminal matters (see above, section IV.3.c.):[226]

> §1. Requests for mutual legal assistance in criminal matters from the competent foreign authorities are implemented in accordance with Belgian law and, where appropriate, in

---

[223] Act of 11 May 2005 regarding approval of the Protocol to the Convention on Mutual Assistance in Criminal Matters between the Member States of the European Union, *Belgian Official Journal*, 22.6.2005, entry into force on 2 July 2005.

[224] See Point 1.A of the agreement. An extract of the agreement is available on the website of the online legal database Vlex: http://vlex.be/vid/wisseling-brieven-belgi-bonds republiek-strafbare-30519154

[225] See the doctoral thesis of Professor Gert Vermeulen, *Wederzijdse rechtshulp in strafzaken in de Europese Unie* (mutual legal assistance in criminal matters in the European Union), Antwerp-Apeldoorn, Maklu, 1999, pp. 70–71, footnote 266; see also Gert Vermeulen, Tom Vander Beken, Els De Busser, Chris Van den Wyngaert, Guy Stessens, Adrien Masset, and Christophe Meunier, *Een nieuwe Belgisch wetgeving inzake internationale rechtshulp in strafzaken* (New Belgian legislation regarding international legal assistance in criminal matters), Antwerp-Apeldoorn, Maklu, 2002, p. 122, footnote 87.

[226] Act of 9 December 2004 regarding mutual assistance in criminal matters and modifying Article 90ter of the Code of Criminal Procedure, *Belgian Official Journal*, 24 December 2004, entry into force on 3 January 2005.

accordance with applicable international legal instruments that bind the requesting State and Belgium.

§2. However, if provided in the request for mutual legal assistance and if an international instrument that binds Belgium and the requesting State provides for such an obligation, the request shall be implemented in accordance with the procedural rules of the foreign authorities, provided that those rules do not restrict fundamental rights and without prejudice to any other principle of Belgian law.

§3. In the absence of an international instrument, that binds Belgium and the requesting State, and that provide for such an obligation, a request for mutual legal assistance may also, within the limits specified in §2, be implemented according to the procedural rules explicitly set out by the foreign authorities.

§4. If a request for mutual legal assistance cannot be implemented for legal reasons, then the responsible Belgian authorities immediately notify the competent foreign authorities with a reasoned decision and mention, where appropriate, the conditions under which implementation could still occur.

If a request for mutual legal assistance cannot be implemented within the timelines set, then the responsible Belgian authorities immediately notify the competent foreign authority, with a clear description of the reasons for the delay and the time within which implementation can take place.

Hence, Article 6 §4 of the Act of 9 December 2004 concerning international mutual legal assistance in criminal matters enables non-treaty based assistance for the interception of electronic communications.

B. Requirements and Procedure (Including the Handling of Privileged Information)

1. Incoming requests

a) Designation of authorities on the basis of Belgian law: no consent needed from the Belgian Minister of Justice for requests from EU Member States

Article 5 §1 of the Act of 9 December 2004 concerning international mutual legal assistance in criminal matters provides that the consent of the Minister of Justice is not required for the implementation in Belgium of requests for mutual assistance from EU Member States.

However, Article 5 §2 of the Act of 9 December 2004 provides that the consent of the Minister of Justice is required when the request can be refused on the basis of one of the three reasons provided in Article 4 §1 of the same Act:

1) to reduce the risk that the death penalty will be imposed;
2) in case the suspect requests refusal of the mutual legal assistance request;
3) in case the requesting state does not give sufficient guarantees that the death penalty will not be pronounced or executed.

In these cases, Article 5 §3 of the Act provides that the Belgian judicial authorities, or the Prosecutor General in case the public prosecutor and the investigating judge received the request, shall send the foreign request to the Minister of Justice.

An *a contrario* reading of Article 5 §1 of the Act of 9 December 2004 means that the consent of the Minister of Justice is required for the implementation in Belgium of requests for mutual assistance from non-EU Member States.

Article 7 §1, 2° of the Act prescribes that requests for mutual assistance from foreign authorities shall be addressed to the Belgian judicial authorities via diplomatic channels. Belgium shall send the records relating to the implementation of the measure to the requesting state in the same way.

b) Designation of authorities on the basis of international instruments

Article 7 §2 of the Act of 9 December 2004 provides that an international instrument may prescribe that mutual legal assistance takes place either between the foreign authority and the Belgian judicial authorities or between the Ministries of Justice of the requesting state and Belgium.

However, Article 7 §4 of the Act of 9 December 2004 provides that, in case the foreign request concerns a case that can seriously harm the public order or essential interests of Belgium, the federal prosecutor, or the Prosecutor General in case the public prosecutor and the investigating judge received the request, shall immediately send an information report to the Minister of Justice.

Below, we apply this rule to the conventions on mutual legal assistance, mentioned earlier (section V.A.1.).

Two of the conventions regarding mutual legal assistance determine the competent authorities for implementing mutual legal assistance requests:

Article 15 of the *European Convention on Mutual Assistance in Criminal Matters of 20 April 1959* and Article 30 of the *Treaty between the Kingdom of Belgium, the Grand Duchy of Luxembourg and the Kingdom of the Netherlands concerning extradition and mutual assistance in criminal matters (Benelux Treaty) of 27 June 1962* determine the competent authorities for implementing mutual assistance requests.

The other two conventions allow the parties to designate the relevant authorities.

Belgium designated the Directorate-General legislation, fundamental rights and freedoms[227] of the Federal Public Service Justice as the competent authority under Article 18(13) of the United Nations Convention against Transnational Organized

[227] Directoraat-generaal Wetgeving en Fundamentele Rechten en Vrijheden (DG WL, in Dutch), Direction générale de la Législation et des Libertés et Droits fondamentaux (DG WL, in French).

Crime of 15 November 2000 and under Article 24 of the Convention on Mutual Assistance in Criminal Matters between the Member States of the European Union.[228]

Belgium designated the International Criminal Cooperation Department[229] of the Federal Public Service Justice as the competent authority under Article 24.7.a (making or receiving requests for extradition or provisional arrest) and Article 27.2 (sending and answering requests for mutual assistance) of the Cybercrime Convention:[230]

Belgium designated the Federal Computer Crime Unit (FCCU) of the Federal Judicial Police (Directorate for Combating Economic and Financial Crime) as the competent authority under Article 35 (24/7 point of contact) of the Cybercrime Convention.

c) *Reporting duties to the Ministry of Justice*

Article 7 §3 of the Act of 9 December 2004 provides that the Belgian judicial authorities shall send a copy of every received request for mutual assistance to the Federal Public Service Justice.[231]

d) *No filtering duties*

Belgian law does not subject the Belgian authorities to a duty to filter out or delete privileged information before transmitting the results of an interception measure to a foreign country (see section B.3.A.). As said above under this section, in special cases, the Minister of Justice will decide whether or not to respond to a foreign mutual legal assistance request.

---

228 See the declaration of Belgium of 23 March 2011 under the Convention on Mutual Assistance in Criminal Matters between the Member States of the European Union, available at https://www.ejn-crimjust.europa.eu/ejn/libdocumentproperties.aspx?Id=18

229 Dienst Internationale Samenwerking in Strafzaken (in Dutch), Service de la coopération internationale pénale (in French).

230 See the declaration of Belgium at the time of depositing (20 August 2012) the instrument of ratification of the Cybercrime Convention, available at http://conventions.coe.int/Treaty/Commun/ListeDeclarations.asp?NT=185&CM=&DF=&CL=ENG&VL=1

231 Federale Overheidsdienst Justitie (in Dutch), Service Public Fédéral Justice (in French); see the notification by Belgium at the time of depositing (11 August 2004) the instrument of ratification of the United Nations Convention against Transnational Organized Crime, available at https://treaties.un.org/Pages/ViewDetails.aspx?src=TREATY&mtdsg_no=XVIII-12&chapter=18&lang=en#EndDec

2. Outgoing requests

a) Designation of authorities on the basis of Belgian law: consent needed from the Belgian Minister of Justice for requests from Belgium

The principle of no consent by the Minister of Justice for requests from EU Member States, set forth in Article 5 §1 of the Belgian Act of 9 December 2004 concerning international mutual legal assistance in criminal matters, does not apply to mutual assistance requests from Belgian to EU Member States. Article 7 §1, 1° of the Act provides that the Belgian judicial authorities shall use diplomatic channels, via the Minister of Justice, to send the mutual assistance request as well as the records relating to the implementation of the measure to the foreign state.

b) Designation of authorities on the basis of international instruments

Article 7 §2 of the Act of 9 December 2004 concerning international mutual legal assistance in criminal matters (regarding the designation of authorities by international instruments), as well as the exceptions thereto provided in Article 7 §4 of the same Act, also apply to cases of foreign requests for mutual assistance to Belgium (see section V.B.1.b.).

c) Exclusion of foreign evidence

As said above (section IV.3.c.), Article 13 of the Act of 9 December 2004 regarding mutual assistance in criminal matters lays down the rules on the admissibility of intercepted data obtained from foreign jurisdictions. The first ground for excluding foreign evidence under Article 13 is the infringement of procedural requirements prescribed under sanction of nullity according to the law of the state where the evidence was obtained. Hence, there is no duty for Belgian authorities to delete information from foreign countries, which could not be intercepted according to Belgian laws.

3. Real-time transfer of communication data

Article 14, 2° of the Act of 9 December 2004 concerning international mutual legal assistance in criminal matters inserts §§6–7 into Article 90*ter* CCP (monitoring measure) (see also above: III.B.9.b.):

> §6. A competent foreign authority may, within the framework of a criminal investigation, temporarily wiretap, take cognizance of, and record private telecommunications during transmission, if the person to whom this measure applies is located on the Belgian territory and if the following conditions are fulfilled:
>
> 1° this measure requires no technical intervention of a body which is established in Belgium;
>
> 2° the foreign government has notified the measure to a Belgian judicial authority;

3° this possibility is provided in an international legal instrument between Belgium and the requesting State;

4° the decision of the investigating judge referred to in §7 has not yet been communicated to the foreign government concerned.

The information gathered under this paragraph can only be used on condition that the competent Belgian authority has agreed to the measure.

§7. Once the public prosecutor receives the notice referred to in paragraph 6, first section, 2 ° he immediately brings the notice to the investigating judge.

The investigating judge to whom a notice referred to in §6, first section, 2 ° is brought approves the measure if it is permissible in accordance with this article.

He informs the foreign government on his decision within ninety-six hours from its receipt by the Belgian judicial authorities.

In the event that additional time is necessary, the investigating judge may postpone its decision and its notification to the competent foreign authorities with a maximum of eight days. He shall immediately notify the competent foreign authority of this delay, stating the reasons.

If the investigating judge does not allow the measure referred to in §6, it shall also notify the foreign government that the gathered data must be destroyed and cannot be used.

The parliamentary preparatory works clarify that this provision implements Article 20 of the Convention on Mutual Assistance in Criminal Matters between the Member States of the European Union (see above, section V.A.1.).[232] Article 20 of the Convention refers to the interception of telecommunications without the technical assistance of another Member State and addresses situations in which the suspect either is situated in border areas where the networks of Belgian and foreign operators intertwine or uses satellite communication. In these cases, the requesting state can wiretap the communications as long as the requested state has not given a negative answer.

In a circular of 28 December 2005, the Board of Prosecutors General referred to the impossibility of applying the scenarios described in Article 18 of the Convention on Mutual Assistance in Criminal Matters between the Member States of the European Union, which deals with wiretapping and immediate or subsequent transmission of telecommunications to the requesting state, and in Article 19 of the same Convention, which concerns access by foreign authorities to telecommunications services operated via a gateway on national territory via the intermediary of a designated service provider.[233]

---

232 Parliamentary preparatory works, Chamber of Representatives, regarding international mutual assistance in criminal matters, 2003–2003, no. 51 1278/001, pp. 21–22, available at http://www.dekamer.be/FLWB/pdf/51/1278/51K1278001.pdf

233 Board of Prosecutors General, Circular of 28 December 2005 on European Union the Convention on Mutual Assistance in Criminal Matters between the Member States of the European Union, COL 15/2005, pp. 15–17, available (in Dutch and French) at http://www.om-mp.be/extern/getfile.php?p_name=3505798.PDF&pid=4226362

C. European Investigation Order

The European Investigation Order[234](EIO) will pose challenges regarding electronic communications interception measures.

First, the EIO order will increase cases in which foreign law applies to evidence gathering on Belgian territory. We recall that Article 6 §2 of the Belgian Act of 9 December 2004 concerning international mutual legal assistance in criminal matters allows the implementation of foreign mutual assistance requests in accordance with foreign procedural law:

> if provided in the request for mutual legal assistance and if an international instrument that binds Belgium and the requesting State provides for such an obligation […], provided that those rules do not restrict fundamental rights and without prejudice to any other principle of Belgian law.

Furthermore, we noted that the annual reports of the Minister of Justice in implementation of Article 90*decies* CCP call for a modernization of the laws regarding the monitoring measures prescribed in Article 90*ter* (see section III.B.).[235] This call may resonate well with the observation of the Board of Prosecutors General that it is currently impossible for Belgium to realize immediate or subsequent transmission of electronic communications to a requesting state and to allow the latter state to access electronic communications services operated via a gateway on Belgian territory via the intermediary of a designated service provider (see the previous section V.B.3.).[236]

D. Statistics

We did not receive a reply from the Ministry of Justice to our request to gain access to statistics or information on the extent of mutual legal assistance requests for electronic communications interception.

---

[234] The European Parliament and the Council of the European Union, Directive 2014/41/EU of the European Parliament and of the Council of the European Union of 3 April 2014 regarding the European Investigation Order in criminal matters, OJ L 130, 1.5.2014, pp. 1–36.

[235] See I.B.2.a. above. See, for instance, the 2013 annual report of the Minister of Justice in implementation of Article 90*decies* CCP, pp. 18, 47–48.

[236] Board of Prosecutors General, Circular of 28 December 2005 on European Union the Convention on Mutual Assistance in Criminal Matters between the Member States of the European Union, COL 15/2005, pp. 15–17, available (in Dutch and French) at http://www.om-mp.be/extern/getfile.php?p_name=3505798.PDF&pid=4226362

Bibliography*

Arnou, Luc, "Afluisteren tijdens het gerechtelijk onderzoek" (Wiretapping during the investigation); in Commentaar Strafrecht en strafvordering (Commentary criminal law and criminal procedural law), Gent, Kluwer, 2008, vol. 59, 95 pp.

Belgian Chamber of Representatives, *Schriftelijke vragen en antwoorden* (written questions and answers), 2010-2011, no. 53-032, 79 pp., available at http://www.dekamer.be/QRVA/pdf/53/53K0032.pdf

Belgian Institute for Postal Services and Telecommunications, "Synthese van de raadpleging door de raad van het bipt op verzoek van de minister voor ondernemen en vereenvoudigen van 29/04/2010 betreffende de praktische uitvoering van richtlijn 2006/24/EG van 15 maart 2006 (richtlijn betreffende de bewaring van gegevens)" (Summary regarding the implementation of the data retention directive 2006/24/EG of 15 March 2006), 2010, p. 14, available at http://www.bipt.be/public/files/nl/1259/3344_nl_2010-10-01_bipt-verslag_consultatie_data_retention-publieke_versie_v20101001_nl.pdf

Belgian Standing Intelligence Agencies Review Committee (Standing Committee I), "Activity reports", available (in Dutch and French) at http://www.comiteri.be/index.php?option=com_content&view=article&id=40&Itemid=74&lang=EN

Board of Prosecutors General, "Telecommunicatierichtlijn inzake het opsporings- en vervolgingsbeleid betreffende inbreuken op de medewerkingsverplichtingen vervat in de artikelen 46bis §2, 88bis §2 en 90quater §2 van het wetboek van strafvordering" (Telecommunications Circular regarding the investigation and prosecution of violations of the cooperation duties under *Articles 46bis §2, 88bis §2 and 90 quater §2 CCP),* COL 14/2009, 17 December 2009, 11 pp., available (in Dutch and French) at http://www.om-mp.be/omzendbrief/4420834/col_14-2009_dd__17_12_2009.html

Board of Prosecutors General, Circular of 28 December 2005 on European Union the Convention on Mutual Assistance in Criminal Matters between the Member States of the European Union, COL 15/2005, 26 pp., available (in Dutch and French) at http://www.om-mp.be/extern/getfile.php?p_name=3505798.PDF&pid=4226362

Board of Prosecutors General, Circular of 15 June 2005 regarding the Autonomic Police Treatment and the simplified official records, COL 8, available (in Dutch and French) at http://www.om-mp.be/omzendbrief/4016820/omzendbrief_col_8_d_d__15_06_2005.html

Bockstaele, Marc and others (eds.), *De Zoeking onderzocht* (An analysis of the search), Antwerp-Apeldoorn, Maklu, 2009, 403 pp.

* All URLs were last accessed in 10/2016.

Boulet, Gertjan, "Regulating Surveillance: The Belgian case," Deliverable 2.3 (The Legal Perspective) for the EU-funded project Increasing Resilience in Surveillance Studies (IRISS), pp. 49–52, 31 January 2013, available at http://irissproject.eu/wp-content/uploads/2013/04/Legal-perspectives-of-surveillance-and-democracy-report-D2.3-IRISS.pdf

Bourlet, Christina, "La lutte contre la fraude de mass: développements récents" (The fight against mass fraud: recent developments); in Dominique Grisay (ed.), *De la lutte contre la fraude à l'argent du crime: État des lieux,* Brussels, Groupe De Boeck, 2013, pp. 83–98.

Criminal Policy Service of the Ministry of Justice, reports in implementation of article 90*decies* CCP, available at http://www.dsb-spc.be/web/index.php?option=com_content&task=view&lang=nl&id=55

Cybersquad, presentation on the functions of Cybersquad, September 2012, available at https://www.b-ccentre.be/wp-content/uploads/2012/04/Cybersqu@d-28maart2012-v005.pdf

De Hert, Paul and Boulet, Gertjan, "The cooperation between Internet service/access providers and law enforcement authorities," country report for the Cybercrime Research Centre at Nicolaus Copernicus University (Poland), February 2015, 29 pp., available at http://www.cybercrime.umk.pl/files/files/Report%20Belgium_De%20Hert%20Boulet.docx

De Hert, Paul and Gutwirth, Serge, *Anthologie privacy/Anthologie de la vie privée* (Anthology of privacy), Academic and Scientific Publishers, 2013, 64 pp., available at http://www.anthologieprivacy.be/sites/anthology/files/documents/anthologie-privacy-asp_0.pdf

De Hert, Paul and Boulet, Gertjan, "Cybercrime report for Belgium," *International Review of Penal Law (RIDP / IRPL)*, 2013, issue 84, no. 1–2, pp. 12–59, available at http://www.penal.org/IMG/pdf/RIDP_2013_1_2_CD_Annexe.pdf, and *Electronic Review of the International Association of Penal* Law, 2013, http://www.penal.org/sites/default/files/files/RV-2.pdf

De Hert, Paul and Vermeulen, Mathias, "Toegang tot sociale media en controle door politie. Een eerste juridische verkenning vanuit mensenrechtelijk perspectief" (Access to social media and control by the police: a first legal exploration from the human rights perspective), *Panopticon*, 2012, vol. 33(2), pp. 258–272.

De Hert, Paul, "C.A.O. no. 81 en advies no. 10/2000 over controle van Internet en e-mail" (Labour law: Soft law on e-mail and Internet practices), *Rechtskundig weekblad*, 2002-2003, vol. 66/33, 19 April 2003, pp. 1281–1294.

De Hert, Paul and Van Leeuw, Frédéric, "Cybercrime Legislation in Belgium," in Eric Dirix and Yves-Henri Leleu (eds.), *The Belgian reports at the Congress of Washington of the International Academy of Comparative Law*, Brussels, Bruylant, 2011, pp. 867–956, available at http://www.vub.ac.be/LSTS/pub/Dehert/389.pdf

Delbrouck, Luk, "De proactieve recherche: een nieuw middel in de strijd tegen de georganiseerde criminaliteit?" (The proactive investigation: a new method in the fight against organized crime), *Jura Falconis*, 1999-2000, no. 1, 37 pp., available at https://www.law.kuleuven.be/jura/art/36n1/delbrouck.htm#N_136_

De Smet, Bart, "Voeging van strafdossiers op verzoek van de verdediging" (Adding a file at the request of the defense), *Rechtskundig Weekblad*, 2002–2003, p. 1022, annotation under Court of Appeal of Antwerp, 13 March 2002.

De Valkeneer, Christian, *Manuel de l'enquête pénale* (Manual on criminal investigation), Brussels, Larcier, 2006, 498 pp.

De Wolf, Daniel, "Rapport Belge" (Belgian report on criminal procedure), *Electronic Review of the International Association of Penal Law*, 2014, 52 pp., available at http://www.penal.org/sites/default/files/files/RA%20-%203.pdf

Dewandeleer, Dirk, "De kennisname van e-mails 'tijdens de overbrenging ervan', een verduidelijking van het telecommunicatiegeheim" (Taking knowledge of e-mails during the transmission phase. A clarification of the secrecy of telecommunications), annotation to the judgment of the Correctional Court of Leuven, 4 December 2007, *Tijdschrift voor Strafrecht*, 2008, vol. 3, pp. 226–231.

Dupont, Lieven, *Beginselen van strafrecht Deel 1* (Principles of criminal law vol. 1), Leuven, Acco, 2004, 229 pp.

Eubelius: "Legal Embedment of the Antigoon case law", December 2013, available at http://www.eubelius.be/en/spotlight/legal-embedment-antigoon-case-law

European Telecommunications Standards Institute, "TS 101-331 Lawful Interception (LI); Requirements of Law Enforcement Agencies," V1.1.1 (2001-08), 4.7.g, available at http://www.etsi.org/deliver/etsi_TS/101300_101399/101331/01.01.01_60/ts_101331v01 0101p.pdf

Facebook, "Government requests reports," available via https://govtrequests.facebook .com/

Federal Prosecutor's Office, Annual Report of the Public Prosecutor's Office to the Board of Prosecutors General for the period of 1 January 2012 till 23 December 2012, 2012, p. 124, available (in Dutch) at http://www.om-mp.be/images/upload_dir/jaarverslag 2012.pdf

Federal Science Policy Office (BELSPO), "Stated goals van autonome afhandeling door de politie (APA): zijn ze opportuun en worden ze bereikt?" (Stated goals of the Autonomic Police Treatment: are they opportune and have they been achieved?), dissemination activities of a government-funded research project on the opportunity of APT and evaluation of its effectiveness, from 1 December 2000 till 28 February 2003, SO/02/016, available via http://www.belspo.be/belspo/fedra/proj.asp?l=nl&COD=SO%2F02%2F016

Freyne, Thierry, "De bewaking van privécommunicatie en -telecommunicatie in strafonderzoeken: een stand van zaken" (The monitoring of private communications and telecommunications in criminal proceedings: a state of affairs), *Tijdschrift voor Strafrecht*, 2008, vol. 3, pp. 165–182.

Google, "Transparency Reports", available via http://www.google.com/transparencyreport/ ?hl=en_US

Goossens, Franky, *Politiebevoegdheden en mensenrechten in België. Rechtsvergelijkend en internationaal onderzoek* (Police powers and human rights in Belgium. Comparative and international research), doctoral thesis, Leuven, 2006, 778 pp., available at https://lirias.kuleuven.be/bitstream/1979/420/2/frankydoctoraat.pdf

Kennes, Laurent, *Manuel de la preuve en matière pénale* (Manual on evidence in criminal matters), Mechelen, Kluwer, 2009, 443 pp.

Kerkhofs, Jan and Van Linthout, Philippe, *Cybercrime*, Politeia, Brussels, 2013, 639 pp.

Konings, Charlotte and Oerlemans, Jaap-Jan, "Van een netwerkzoeking naar online doorzoeking: grenzeloos of grensverleggend" (From a network search to an online search: borderless or groundbreaking?), *Computerrecht*, 2013, vol. 5, pp. 23–32, available at https://www.b-ccentre.be/download/b-ccentre_legal/B-CCENTRE%20Van%20een%20netwerkzoeking%20naar%20online%20doorzoeking.pdf

Microsoft, "Law Enforcement Requests Reports", available at https://www.microsoft.com/about/corporatecitizenship/en-us/reporting/transparency/

National Labour Council, "National collective agreement no. 81 of 26 April 2002 on the protection of the private lives of employees with respect to controls on electronic on-line communications data", 26 April 2002, available via www.cnt-nar.be

Parliamentary preparatory works, Chamber of Representatives, regarding international mutual assistance in criminal matters, 2003–2003, no. 51 1278/001, 53 pp., available at http://www.dekamer.be/FLWB/pdf/51/1278/51K1278001.pdf

Parliamentary preparatory works, Belgian Chamber of Representatives, regarding special investigation methods and any other methods of investigation, 2001–2002, no. 50 1688/001, 193 pp., available via http://www.senate.be/www/?MIval=dossier&LEG=2&NR=1260&LANG=nl

Parliamentary preparatory works, modifying the Act of 30 June 1994 protecting privacy against the interception of communication and telecommunication, Belgian Chamber of Parliaments, 1996-1997, 29 May 1998, no. 49K1075/017, p. 10, available at http://www.dekamer.be/FLWB/PDF/49/1075/49K1075017.pdf

Parliamentary preparatory works, regarding the legislative proposal protecting privacy against the interception of communication and telecommunication, Belgian Senate, 1993-1994, 18 May 1994, no. 843-2, 346 pp., available at http://www.senate.be/lexdocs/S0539/S05390364.pdf

Parliamentary preparatory works, regarding the legislative proposal protecting privacy against the interception of communication and telecommunication, Belgian Senate, 1992–1993, 1 September 1993, no. 843-1, 67 pp., available at http://www.senate.be/lexdocs/S0539/S05390297.pdf

Pesquié, Brigitte (revised by Yves Cartuyvels), "The Belgian system", in Mireille Delmas-Marty and J.R. Spencer, *European Criminal Procedures*, Cambridge Studies in International and Comparative Law, Cambridge University Press, 2002, pp. 81–141.

Silva, Karine and Roex, Ruben, "Zombie alert: Assessing legitimacy of P2P botnet mitigation techniques", 2014, conference paper, 25th European Regional Conference of the International Telecommunications Society (ITS), Brussels, Belgium, 22–25 June 2014, 13 pp., available at http://econstor.eu/bitstream/10419/101402/1/795035411.pdf

Traest, Philip, "Judicial control on the gathering and reliability of technical evidence in a continental criminal justice system", conference paper for the 16th International Conference of the International Society for the Reform of Criminal Law, 2002, 13 pp., available at http://www.isrcl.org/Papers/Traest.pdf

Traest, Philip, "Rechts(on)zekerheid in materieel en formeel strafrecht en strafrechtelijk legaliteitsbeginsel" (Legal (un)certainty in material and formal criminal law, and the principle of legality in criminal law), *Rechtskundig Weekblad*, 1993–1994, pp. 1190–1207.

Twitter, "Transparency reports", available via https://transparency.twitter.com/

Voet, Stefaan, "Belgium's new specialized judiciary," *Russian Law Journal*, 2014, vol. II, Issue 4, pp. 129–145, available at http://www.russianlawjournal.org/index.php/jour/article/view/14/10

Van den Wyngaert, Chris, *Strafrecht, Strafprocesrecht & Internationaal Strafrecht in hoofdlijnen* (An Outline of Criminal Law, Criminal Procedural Law & International Criminal Law), Antwerp-Apeldoorn, Maklu, 2006, 1314 pp.

Verizon, "Transparency Reports", available via http://transparency.verizon.com/

Vermeulen, Gert, *Wederzijdse rechtshulp in strafzaken in de Europese Unie* (Mutual legal assistance in criminal matters in the European Union), Antwerp-Apeldoorn, Maklu, 1999, 632 pp.

Vermeulen, Gert, Vander Beken, Tom, De Busser, Els, Van den Wyngaert, Chris, Stessens, Guy, Masset, Adrien, and Meunier, Christophe, *Een nieuwe Belgisch wetgeving inzake internationale rechtshulp in strafzaken* (New Belgian legislation regarding international legal assistance in criminal matters), Antwerp-Apeldoorn, Maklu, 2002, 421 pp.

Verstraeten, Raf, *Handboek strafvordering* (Manual on criminal procedure), Antwerp, Maklu, 2007, 1193 pp.

Verstraeten, Raf and Verbruggen, Frank, *Straf- en strafprocesrecht voor bachelors* (Criminal law and criminal procedural law for bachelors), Antwerp-Apeldoorn, Maklu, 2007.

Vodafone, "Law Enforcement Disclosure Report," 2014, available at http://www.vodafone.com/content/sustainabilityreport/2014/index/operating_responsibly/privacy_and_security/law_enforcement.html

The Washington Post, "Do France and Belgium have direct wiretap access to telecom switches?," 7 June 2014, available at http://www.washingtonpost.com/news/volokh-conspiracy/wp/2014/06/07/do-france-and-belgium-have-direct-wiretap-access-to-telecom-switches/

List of Abbreviations

ADIV	Algemene Dienst Inlichtingen en Veiligheid (General Intelligence and Security Service of the Armed Forces)
APA	Autonome Politionele Afhandeling (Traitement Policier Autonome/Autonomic Police Treatment)
APO	Ambtshalve Politioneel Onderzoek (Enquête Policière d'Office/Autonomic Police Treatment)
APT	Autonomic Police Treatment

BBI	Bijzondere belastinginspectie (Special Tax Inspectorate)
BIPT	Belgian Institute for Postal Services and Telecommunications
BELSPO	Federal Science Policy Office
BISC	Belgian Internet Service Center
CC	Criminal Code
CCP	Code of Criminal Procedure
CETS	Convention on Cybercrime
CFI	Cel voor Financiële Informatieverwerking (Belgian Financial Intelligence Processing Unit)
Comité P	Vast Comité van toezicht op de politiediensten (Comité permanent de contrôle des services de police/ Standing Police Monitoring Committee)
CTIF	Cellule de Traitement des Informations Financières (Financial Intelligence Processing Unit)
DNS	Domain Name Service
EC	European Commission
ECHR	European Convention on Human Rights
ECtHR	European Court of Human Rights
FOD	Federale Overheidsdienst (Federal Public Service)
ISI	Inspection spéciale des impôts (Special Tax Inspectorate
ISP	Internet Service Provider
GISS	General Intelligence and Security Service of the Armed Forces
IMEI	International Mobile Station Equipment Identity
IMSI	International Mobile Subscriber Identity
LEMF	Law Enforcement Monitoring Facility
NTSU-CTIF	National Technical & Tactical Support Unit – Central Technical Interception Facility
SIM-commission	Administrative Commission responsible for monitoring the specific and exceptional intelligence collection methods used by the intelligence and security services
SGRS	Service général du Renseignement et de la Sécurité (General Intelligence and Security Service of the Armed Forces)
SPF	Service Public Fédéral (Federal Public Service)
Standing Committee I	Belgian Standing Intelligence Agencies Review Committee
VSSE	Veiligheid van de Staat / La Sûreté de l'Etat

Czech Republic
Slovakia*

National Rapporteur:
Radim Polčák

Subordinate Rapporteurs:
Jakub Harašta,
Pavel Loutocký
Jakub Míšek
Václav Stupka

Subordinate Rapporteur – Slovakia:
Tomáš Abelovský

* This report reflects legislation and case law as of September 2016.

Contents

I. Security Architecture and the Interception of Telecommunication

A. Law Enforcement Institutions and Security Services with Powers of Telecommunication Interception

1. National security architecture

One of the most important forming principles of the distribution of public powers in the Czech Republic is its totalitarian history. There is a strong distrust of official institutions in the general public. Probably due to this fact, it can be seen that the procedures and powers of public bodies and agencies are set very rigidly. The principle of legality is set in Art. 2 para. 3 of the Czech Constitution (Act No. 1/1993 Sb., Constitution of the Czech Republic), which states that "State authority is to serve all citizens and may be asserted only in cases, within the bounds, and in the manner provided for by law"[1] and in Art. 2 para. 2 of the Charter of Fundamental Rights and Freedoms (Resolution of the Presidium of the Czech National Council of 16 December 1992 on the declaration of the Charter of Fundamental Rights and Freedoms as a part of the constitutional order of the Czech Republic No. 2/1993 Sb.), which states that "State authority may be asserted only in cases and within the bounds provided for by law and only in the manner prescribed by law."[2] Since all the public authorities authorized to conduct the interception of telecommunication fall within the scope of these articles, they are permitted to act only within the framework of what is expressly allowed to them by law.

In the Czech Republic, there are two regimes under which electronic communications can be intercepted. The first is the regime of criminal procedure conducted by police forces, including a special regime of customs service, and the second is a regime of civil and military intelligence services.

Act No. 141/1961 Sb. Code of Criminal Procedure, which sets the rules for the interception of communications in criminal proceedings, defines police authorities for its purpose in Section 12 para. 2 quite broadly (informal translation):[3]

2) Police authorities mean

a) Bodies of the Police of the Czech Republic,

---

[1] English translation taken from the webpage of the Czech Constitutional Court. Online: http://www.usoud.cz/en/constitution-of-the-czech-republic/

[2] English translation taken from the webpage of the Czech Constitutional Court. Online: http://www.usoud.cz/en/charter-of-fundamental-rights-and-freedoms/

[3] English translation taken from the information system beck-online.

b) General Inspection of Security Forces in proceedings on criminal offences committed by members of the Police of the Czech Republic, members of the Prison Service of the Czech Republic, customs officers or employees of the Czech Republic classified to work in the Police of the Czech Republic, or on criminal offences by employees of the Czech Republic classified to work in the Prison Service of the Czech Republic or in the Customs Administration of the Czech Republic which were committed in connection with fulfilment of their employment duties,
c) appointed bodies of the Prison Service of the Czech Republic in proceedings on criminal offences of persons serving detention, a prison sentence or security detention that were committed in a custodial prison, prison or institute for the execution of security detention,
d) appointed customs authorities in proceedings on criminal offences committed by a breach of customs regulations or regulations on the import, export or transit of goods, even in cases of criminal offences by members of the armed forces or security forces, and by a breach of laws in the placement and purchase of goods in Member States of the European Communities if such goods are transported across the national borders of the Czech Republic, and in cases of tax infringements, where the customs authorities manage tax under special legal regulations,
e) appointed bodies of the Military Police in proceedings on criminal offences of members of the armed forces and persons who commit a criminal activity against members of the armed forces in military facilities, against military facilities, military material or other property of the State that is to be managed by the Ministry of Defence,
f) appointed authorities of the Security Information Service in proceedings on criminal offences committed by members of the Security Information Service,
g) appointed authorities of the Office for Foreign Relations and Information in proceedings on criminal offences committed by members of the Office for Foreign Relations and Information,
h) appointed authorities of Military Intelligence in proceedings on criminal offences committed by members of Military Intelligence,
i) appointed authorities of the General Inspection of Security Forces in proceedings on criminal offences committed by members of the General Inspection of Security Forces or on the criminal offences of employees of the Czech Republic classified to work in the General Inspection of Security Forces.

The police of the Czech Republic was established by Act No. 273/2008 Sb. on the police of the Czech Republic. Among its other duties, it is the main public authority for criminal investigation. It is organized on a geographical basis, as it is divided into divisions according to administrative regions. There are also several divisions with countrywide authority.[4] Of those, the most relevant Czech police divisions for this report are the National Antidrug Center,[5] Division for Uncovering

[4] In Czech: http://www.policie.cz/clanek/utvary-s-pusobnosti-na-celem-uzemi-cr-312510.aspx

[5] In Czech: www.policie.cz/narodni-protidrogova-centrala-skpv.aspx

of Corruption and Financial Criminality,[6] Division for Uncovering of Organised Crime,[7] and the Unit for Special Activities of Criminal Police and Investigation.[8]

The Czech police cannot use electronic communication interception as a preventive measure, since the law does not expressly allow it. This is due to the fact that Czech constitutional law strongly protects the privacy of an individual, and interception of communication is understood as a serious breach of such protection.[9] The law therefore quite rigidly formulates exceptions from this protection. Czech criminal procedure is governed by Act No. 141/1961 Sb. Code of Criminal Procedure. The interception of communication within the regime of the Code of Criminal Procedure can be undertaken only after the criminal proceedings have started. The preliminary hearing is the starting part of criminal proceedings in the Czech Republic and, as is stated in Section 158 of the Code of Criminal Procedure, it is commenced either by a criminal report submitted by a citizen or by the police authority itself as an *ex officio* act. It reads as follows (informal translation):

§ 158

(1) The Police Authority is obliged, based on their own findings, criminal reports, and instigations by other persons and authorities on the basis of which conclusions may be made on the suspicion of a criminal offence, to take all necessary investigations and measures to reveal the facts indicating that the criminal offence was committed and directed towards identifying the offender; they are obligated to take the necessary measures to prevent the criminal activity. The appointed authorities of the Prison Service of the Czech Republic shall inform the General Inspection of Security Forces without undue delay after they initiate such investigation.

(2) The public prosecutor and the police authority are required to accept reports of facts suggesting that the criminal offence was committed. At the same time, they are obligated to instruct the reporting person about the liability for knowingly false statements and if the reporting person requests it, to inform them on the effective measures taken within one month of the notification.[10]

Once the criminal proceedings have started and the legal prerequisites are met the police can commence with the interception.

A specific example of interception in accordance with the Code of Criminal Procedure is a regime of communication interception, which is grounded in Act

---

6 In Czech: http://www.policie.cz/clanek/uokfk-skpv-utvar-odhalovani-korupce-a-financni-kriminality-skpv.aspx

7 In Czech: http://www.policie.cz/clanek/vitam-vas-na-strankach-utvaru-pro-odhalovani-organizovaneho-zlocinu-570688.aspx

8 In Czech: http://www.policie.cz/clanek/utvar-zvlastnich-cinnosti-sluzby-kriminalni-policie-a-vysetrovani-716842.aspx

9 For example, the Czech Constitutional Court formulates the importance of this protection in Decision II. ÚS 502/2000 of 22 January 2001, which it followed up with Decision No. II. ÚS 615/06-1 of 23 May 2007, in which necessary conditions for allowing interception of communication were interpreted.

10 Section 158, Act. No. 141/1961 Sb. Code of Criminal Procedure. In: ASPI [legal information system].

No. 17/2012 Sb. on customs service of the Czech Republic. Customs can, in certain cases, be considered a police force[11] and can act in accordance with rules for the criminal proceedings for obtaining authorisation to conduct the interception. Section 63 of Act No. 17/2012 specifies the cases over which the customs service has jurisdiction. The section states:

§ 63 Basic Condition of Use

(1) Bodies of customs service may use operative search means, interception and recording of communication (thereinafter "operative search means") as set in the Code of Criminal Procedure, when fulfilling duties arising from international treaties during conducting of control of persons, about whom there exist serious reasons to suspect that they are breaching or have breached law of the second party to the treaty.

(2) Rights and duties of bodies of customs service arising from the statutes regulating criminal procedure are not affected by conduct of control in the meaning of paragraph 1.

(3) Operative search means may be used only in situation, when the breach of law of the second party to the treaty, would be considered in accordance with the Criminal Code[12] as an intentional crime, should it happen in the territory of the Czech Republic.[13]

As can be seen from the text, this can be understood as a preventive measure. The use of this provision is, however, strictly limited by the purpose of the interception, which is set out in paragraph 1 of the article:

§ 64

(1) Usage of operative search means must not follow any other purpose than the one, which is specified in the concerned international treaty. Rights and freedoms of intercepted persons can be restrained on in the necessary manner.[14]

The Czech Republic has three intelligence services: The Office for Foreign Relations and Information (foreign intelligence service), Security Information Service (interior counter-intelligence service) and Military Intelligence. They are strictly separated from each other. This separation can again be interpreted as a result of Czech totalitarian history and general distrust of public institutions, especially those with executive power of this kind. *Lex generalis* covering these services is Act No. 153/1994 Sb. on intelligence services of the Czech Republic; the special acts are Act No. 154/1994 Sb. on the Security Information Service and Act No. 289/2005 on Military Intelligence. The rules for communication interception when conducted by intelligence services are included in these acts.

A specific case connected with intelligence services is the National Security Authority,[15] a body responsible for personnel and facility security clearance proce-

[11] See *supra* note 1.

[12] Act No. 40/2009 Sb., Criminal Code.

[13] Section 63 of Act No. 17/2012 Sb. on customs service of the Czech Republic. In: beck-online [legal information system].

[14] Section 64 of Act No. 17/2012 Sb. on customs service of the Czech Republic. In: beck-online [legal information system].

[15] http://www.nbu.cz/en/

dures. It has overall competences in the area of the protection of classified information and, among other things, it issues personnel security clearance certificates. It is governed by Act No. 412/2005 Sb. on protection of secret information and security. Section 107 para. 3 of this act, which covers personal security clearance procedures, empowers the National Security Authority to ask an intelligence service to carry out an examination of possible security risks in the environment of the candidate for clearance purposes:

§ 107 Acts in the proceeding on issuance of personnel security clearance certificates

(3) In the proceedings on issuance of personnel security clearance certificates for the Top Secret degree the Office[16] shall conduct all the acts according to the paragraph 2 and furthermore it requests competent intelligence service to conduct an examination of possible security risks in the environment, in which the subject operates.[17]

This issue can be summed up as follows: There are two different and separate regimes of communication interception in the Czech Republic. Each of them has a different purpose and a different approval procedure (as can be seen in next question) and thus, generally speaking, information gained from one regime cannot be easily used in another.

Comparative note – Slovakia

It can be said that same situation applies in the Slovak Republic. The Slovak Constitution (Act No. 460/1992 Coll., Constitution of the Slovak Republic) states in Art. 2 para. 3 that state bodies can act only on the basis of the Constitution, within its limits, and to the extent and in a manner defined by law. Pursuant to Art. 19, everyone has the right to protection against unjustified interference with his or her private and family life and against the unjustified collection, publication, or other misuse of personal data. Art. 22 guarantees the secrecy of correspondence, other communications, and written messages delivered by post, and that of personal information. The privacy of letters, other communications, and written messages kept privately or delivered by post or otherwise, including communications made by telephone, telegraph, and other means, cannot be violated by anyone except in cases specified by law.[18] Therefore, all the public authorities authorized to conduct the interception of telecommunication fall within the scope of these articles. They are permitted to act only within what is expressly allowed them by law.

Also, there are two regimes under which electronic communications can be intercepted. The first is the regime of criminal procedure pursuant to Act No. 141/1961 in the code on the criminal trial (Code of Criminal Procedure). It is conducted

16 The National Security Authority.

17 Section 107 para. 3 of Act No. 412/2005 Sb. on protection of secret information and security. In: beck-online [legal information system].

18 English translation taken from the webpage of the Public Defender of rights. Online: http://www.vop.gov.sk/constitution-of-the-slovak-republic

by police forces or the court (comparable to the Czech procedure), under which a special regime of customs service can be included. According to the Code of Criminal Procedure, the order to intercept and record telecommunication can be issued by the presiding judge of a panel prior to the commencement of criminal prosecution or by a judge for pre-trial proceedings on a motion from a prosecutor. If the matter bears no delay and a prior order from a judge for pre-trial proceedings cannot be obtained, the order may be issued by a prosecutor before the commencement of criminal prosecution or in pre-trial proceedings, unless the interception and recording of telecommunication involves entry into the dwelling of a person; such order has to be confirmed by a judge for pre-trial proceedings within 24 hours of its issuance; failing that, the order becomes null and void and the information obtained on its basis may not be used for the purpose of criminal proceedings and must be immediately destroyed in a prescribed manner.[19]

The second regime is for civil and military intelligence services (Act No. 46/1993 Coll. on the Slovak Information Service and Act No. 198/1994 Coll. on Military Intelligence) and other entitled authorities (police corps, prison and court guards, and customs officers).

The difference between Slovak and Czech legislation is reflected in Act No. 166/2003 Coll. on the protection of privacy against unauthorized use of information-technical means amending and supplementing certain acts (Act on the Protection against Interception). This law stipulates the conditions required for the use of technical-intelligence measures without prior consent of the person whose privacy is infringed upon by the state body, which uses the intelligence-technical measures (ITM). This law does not apply to the use of ITM in the criminal proceedings in accordance with a specific law (Code of Criminal Procedure).[20] But there are notable exceptions. The ITM can be used by the Police Corps, Slovak Information Service, Military Intelligence, Railway Police, Corps of Prison and Judiciary Guards, and Customs Board in the extent pursuant to specific regulations. The execution of ITM for all authorities is technically provided by the Police Corps following the submission of a written approval of the legitimate authority. Generally, ITM can be used only if it is "inevitable in a democratic society to safeguard the security and defence of the country, to prevent and reveal criminal activities, or to protect the rights and freedoms of other persons."[21] Another general principle is that, by using ITM, these essential rights or freedoms can be infringed upon only to the necessary

---

[19] Section 115 para. 1 of No. 141/1961 in the Code on the Criminal Trial (Code of Criminal Procedure). Unofficial translation. Online: https://e-justice.europa.eu/fileDownload.do?id=11f9da19-253e-4f02-9a26-2e2285184e7a

[20] Section 1 of Act No. 166/2003 Zb. on the protection of privacy against unauthorised use of information-technical means amending and supplementing certain acts (Act on the Protection against Interception). Online: http://www.sis.gov.sk/files/zakony/act_166_2003.pdf

[21] Section 20 of the Act on the Protection against Interception.

extent and for a period of time not longer than necessary to attain the legal goal that it serves.

The Slovak Information Service is authorized to use these means in order to carry out its legal tasks. These measures can be utilized to infringe upon the privacy of persons without their prior approval in accordance with the conditions stated in the law. Also, they can be utilized upon prior approval of the judge. It is possible to utilize ITM for a period of no longer than 6 months. This period starts upon the day the approval is granted. If it is necessary to utilize several types of ITM at once or consecutively, each ITM can only be utilized within the scope approved. If ITM are to be utilized in places not accessible to the general public, the judge granting the approval decides whether the approval is also given to enter such places.[22]

Moreover, the Act on the Protection against Interception brings about a distributive option of intertwining the two regimes (intelligence and criminal procedure). In an exceptional case, if there is reasonable suspicion of a crime being committed and ITP might be used, the Police Corps may use it even without prior approval of the authorized judge. The case must be dealt with immediately and the approval of the authorized judge cannot be obtained in advance. Even the Police Corps are required to notify the authorized judge of the use of the ITP within one hour of the beginning of the use of this measure, they are exceeding their power based upon the Code of Criminal Procedure. The legal guarantee is such that, if the Police Corps does not obtain subsequent written approval from the authorized judge within twelve hours of the beginning of the use of the ITP or if the authorized judge does not grant subsequent approval, the use of this measure shall be immediately terminated. Information obtained in this way shall not be used and it is to be immediately destroyed. The state body, which has destroyed this information, must immediately notify the authorized judge of the destruction.[23] What is important, the Act on the Protection against Interception serves not only as the base for legal intelligence interception but it opens doors to using the obtained evidence in criminal proceedings.[24]

Ultimately, a practice comparable with that of the Czech Republic can be identified in the Slovak Republic. But the separation of the regimes is not very clear here, and intelligence legislation is interrelated with criminal procedure. Furthermore, it even passes specific power to police authorities, which are formally entitled under intelligence legislation and certain circumstances to intercept without court approval.

---

22 Slovak Information Service: Annual Report 2013. Online: http://www.sis.gov.sk/for-you/sis-annual-report-2013.html

23 Section 5 of the Act on the Protection against Interception.

24 Section 7 para. 2 of the Act on the Protection against Interception.

2. Powers for the interception of telecommunication

a) Law of criminal procedure

Communication interception in the criminal procedure is established in Section 88 of the Code of Criminal Procedure. The relevant paragraphs on the procedure of authorisation of the interception are as follows:

§ 88 Interception and recording of telecommunications

(1) If criminal proceedings are conducted for a crime for which the law stipulates a prison sentence with the upper penalty limit of at least eight years, for a criminal offence of machinations in insolvency proceedings under Section 226 of the Penal Code, violation of regulations on rules of competition under Section 248 Subsection 1 Paragraph e) and Subsection 2 through 4 of the Penal Code, negotiating advantages during public procurement, tender and auction under Section 256 of the Penal Code, machinations during public procurement and tenders under Section 257 of the Penal Code, machinations at a public auction under Section 258 of the Penal Code, misuse of powers of an official person under Section 329 of the Penal Code or for any other intentional criminal offence for which prosecution is stipulated in a declared international treaty, an order for the interception and recording of telecommunications may be issued if it may be reasonably assumed that facts relevant to the criminal proceedings will be obtained in this way and if there is no other way to achieve such purpose or if its achievement would be otherwise significantly reduced. The Police of the Czech Republic perform the interception and recording of telecommunications for the needs of all law enforcement authorities. The interception and recording of telecommunications between the defence counsel and the accused is inadmissible. If the police authority finds during the interception and recording of telecommunications that the accused has communicated with their defence counsel, they are obliged to immediately destroy the interception recording and not to use the information learned in this context in any way. The report on the destruction of the record shall be placed in the file.

(2) The presiding judge and, in preliminary proceedings upon the petition of the public prosecutor, the judge, is entitled to warrant the interception and recording of telecommunications. If there is a criminal proceeding for an intentional criminal offence, the prosecution of which is governed by the applicable international treaty, the order for the interception and recording of telecommunications must be issued in writing and must be justified, including a specific reference to the applicable international treaty. The order for the interception and recording of the telecommunications service shall include a determined user address or a user device and the user if their identity is known, and the period during which the interception and recording of telecommunications traffic is conducted cannot be longer than four months; the justification must include the specific facts that justify the issue of such order as well as its period. The order for the interception and recording of telecommunications shall immediately be forwarded to the police authority. In the preliminary hearing, the judge shall send a copy of the order for the interception and recording of telecommunications to the public prosecutor without undue delay.

(5) The law enforcement authority may, without the order for the interception and recording of telecommunications, order the interception and recording of telecommunications or conduct it themselves if there is a criminal proceeding for the criminal offence of human trafficking (Section 168 of the Penal Code), the delegation of custody of a child to someone else (Section 169 of the Penal Code), restriction of personal freedoms (Section 171 of the Penal Code), extortion (Section 175 of the Penal Code), kidnapping of a child and persons suffering from a mental disorder (Section 200 of the Penal Code),

violence against a group of people or an individual (Section 352 of the Penal Code), dangerous threats (Section 353 of the Penal Code) or dangerous persecution (Section 354 of the Penal Code), if the user of the intercepted unit agrees to such measure.[25]

The communication interception can be used for the sake of criminal proceedings only when the criminal proceedings are conducted for crimes specifically enumerated by the law. The general rule is that the interception must be initially authorized by a judge but, in certain cases, which are laid down in paragraph 5, prior consent of the person using the intercepted unit is sufficient.

The strict nature of this authorisation process was confirmed by the Czech Constitutional Court in Decision No. II. ÚS 615/06-1 of 23 May 2007. The court wrote the following in its decision:

> The right to protection of the secrecy of messages arising from Art. 13 of the Charter of Fundamental Rights and Freedoms, together with personal freedom and other constitutionally guaranteed fundamental rights, completes the personal sphere of an individual, whose individual integrity, as completely an essential condition for dignified existence and development of human life generally, must be respected and thoroughly protected as a token of respect for the rights and freedoms of man and citizen.[26]
>
> If the constitutional order permits a breach of this protection, it does so solely and exclusively in the interests of a democratic society, or in the interest of the constitutionally guaranteed fundamental rights and freedoms of others. […] It is therefore permissible only such infringement of the fundamental rights and freedoms by the state power, which is necessary in this sense.[27]
>
> It should be emphasized that an effective judicial review of the use of any operative means, with an overlap into the area of fundamental rights and freedoms, is absolutely crucial to a fair trial in criminal proceedings.[28]
>
> In terms of the constitutional order is a violation of the secrecy of messages possible only in cases and manner prescribed by law. Statutory regulation interfering with this right must be formulated so that it does not deny this fundamental human right and thus it must also be interpreted. […] A court order for interception and recording of telecommunication operations must be written and reasoned. It must therefore be issued in respect to a person against whom criminal proceeding is conducted. If the proceedings is conducted on the basis of reasonable suspicion it must be explained in a recital what evidence support such conclusion. The mere criminal complaint itself, if it does not include explanation, is not sufficient for court order. […] The order may therefore be issued only in duly commenced criminal proceedings for legally qualified crime, and must be supported by relevant clues from which we can derive reasonable suspicion of committing such a crime. The order must be individualized in a relation to the specific person that is the user of intercepted telephone device. […] Finally, the order must at least at a minimal level specifically indicate what facts relevant for the proceeding are to be thus identified, and what is inferred from that.[29]

---

25 Section 88 of Act No. 141/1961 Sb. on criminal procedure. In: ASPI [legal information system].

26 Paragraph 13 of the decision of the Czech Constitutional Court No. II. ÚS 615/06-1 from 23 May 2007. In: Codexis [legal information system].

27 *Ibid.*, paragraph 14.

28 *Ibid.*, paragraph 15.

29 *Ibid.*, paragraph 16.

This strict approach was also acknowledged in Art. 67 Internal Order of the Police President No. 30/2009 of 21 April 2009 on the fulfilment of operations in criminal proceedings,[30] which was repealed by the Order of the Police President No. 103/2013 on the fulfilment of certain operations of the bodies of police of the Czech Republic in criminal proceedings.

Outside the regime of criminal procedure, the police can conduct communication interception when supervising a person who is protected in the special regime of witness protection. This is done in accordance with Section 10a of Act No. 137/2001 Sb. on special protection of a witness and other persons in connection with criminal proceedings. This interception can be commenced only after prior judicial authorisation:

§ 10a Permission to check on a protected person

(1) If there is given suspicion that the protected person fails to comply with the obligations specified in § 6, and is unable to verify this suspicion in another way, the Police is authorised, to the strictly necessary extent, to gain knowledge in a classified manner using technical or other means. The Police is authorised to make sound, visual or other records, conduct interception of communication and require on the person performing telecommunications services data on telecommunications traffic, which are the subject of telecommunications secrecy and subject to the protection of personal and agency data.

(2) Acquisition of audio, video or other recordings, interception and recording of telecommunications traffic and requesting data on telecommunications traffic is possible only with the prior consent of the presiding judge of the High Court into whose jurisdiction belongs the seat of the police department or the prison service, which provides special protection and assistance. Against a decision to authorize or reject the application is not subject to appeal.[31]

The collection of traffic and location data by providers of electronic communications (data retention) and the possibility to access such data during the criminal proceedings by the police is laid down in Section 88a of Act No. 141/1961 Sb. Code of Criminal Procedure:

§ 88a

(1) If, for the purposes of criminal proceedings conducted for an intentional criminal offence for which the law sets out a prison sentence with an upper penalty limit of at least three years, for the criminal offence of violating the confidentiality of messages (Section 182 of the Penal Code), for the criminal offence of fraud (Section 209 of the Penal Code), for the criminal offence of unauthorised access to computer systems and information media (Section 230 of the Penal Code), for the criminal offence of procuring and possessing access devices and computer system passwords and other such data (Section 231 of the Penal Code), for the criminal offence of dangerous threats (Section 353 of the Penal Code), for the criminal offence of dangerous persecution (Section 354 of the Penal Code), for the criminal offence of spreading alarming news (Section 357 of the Penal Code), for the criminal offence of encouraging a criminal offence (Section 364

[30] Available in Czech online: http://www.pecina.cz/files/pokyn2.pdf

[31] Section 10a of Act No. 137/2001 Sb. on special protection of a witness and other persons in connection with criminal proceedings and on change of Act No. 99/1963 Sb., Civil Procedure Code.

of the Penal Code), for the criminal offence of approving a criminal offence (Section 365 of the Penal Code) or for an intentional criminal offence for which prosecution is stipulated in a proclaimed international treaty binding on the Czech Republic, it is necessary to ascertain data on the telecommunications service that are the subject of a telecommunications secret or that are subject to the protection of personal and intermediation data, and there is no other way to achieve the pursued purpose or if its achievement would be otherwise significantly harder, their release to the public prosecutor or to the police authority shall be ordered by the presiding judge in proceedings before the court and by the judge upon the petition of the public prosecutor in a preliminary hearing. If there are criminal proceedings for a criminal offence the prosecution of which is stipulated in such international treaty, the order for ascertaining data on the telecommunications service must be issued in writing and must be justified, including a specific reference to the proclaimed international treaty. If the request applies to a particular user, their identity must be stated in the order, if known.

(2) The public prosecutor or the police authority by whose decision the matter was finally concluded, and in proceedings before the court the presiding judge of the court of first instance after the final conclusion of the matter, shall inform the user referred to in Subsection 1, if known, of the ordered ascertainment of data on the telecommunications service. The information shall identify the court which issued the order for the ascertainment of data on the telecommunications service, and detail the period to which such order applied. Such information shall include instructions on the right to submit to the Supreme Court, within six months of receipt of this information, a petition to review the legality of the order for the ascertainment of data on the telecommunications service. The presiding judge of the court of first instance shall submit the information without undue delay after the final conclusion of the matter, the public prosecutor by whose decision the matter was finally concluded shall submit the information without undue delay after expiration of the period for the review of their decision by the Attorney General under Section 174a, and the police authority by whose decision the matter was finally concluded shall submit the information without undue delay after expiration of the period for the review of their decision by the public prosecutor under Section 174 Subsection 2 Paragraph e).

(3) The presiding judge, the public prosecutor or the police authority shall not submit the information under Subsection 2 in proceedings on a crime committed by an organised group for which the law stipulates a prison sentence with an upper penalty limit of at least eight years, in proceedings on a criminal offence committed for the benefit of an organised criminal group, in proceedings on the criminal offence of participation in an organised criminal group (Section 361 of the Penal Code), or if the commission of the criminal offence involved several persons and in relation to at least one of them criminal proceedings have not yet been finally concluded or if criminal proceedings are conducted against the person to whom the information is to be submitted, or if providing such information could defeat the purpose of the particular or some other criminal proceedings, or if it could threaten national security, life, health, or the rights or freedoms of individuals.

(4) An order under Subsection 1 is not required if the user of the telecommunications equipment to whom the data on the performed telecommunications service relates gives their approval for the provision of the information.[32]

[32] Section 88a of Act No. 141/1961 Sb. on criminal procedure. In: ASPI [legal information system].

In those cases, enumerated in paragraph 1, police can gain access to traffic and location data after preliminary judicial authorisation.

General authorisation for the Czech police to access location and traffic data is laid down in Section 66 para. 3 of Act No. 273/2008 on the Police of the Czech Republic:

§ 66 Obtaining of information from records

(3) Police may, in cases prescribed by law and to the extent necessary to fulfill a specific task, request the legal or natural person providing a public communications network or publicly available electronic communications the traffic and location data in a manner, which enables remote and continuous access, unless another law provides otherwise. These persons are obliged to grant the request without undue delay, as and to the extent determined by other legislation.[33]

In three situtations, however, the Czech police can access location and traffic data even outside the regime of criminal procedure.

The first situation concerns the search for persons and things. This authorisation to access traffic and location data is established in the second paragraph of Section 68 of the Police Act.

§ 68 Search for persons and things

(2) Police can request legal or natural person providing a public communications network or publicly available electronic communications service traffic and location data in a manner enabling remote and continuous access, for a purpose of ongoing search for wanted or missing persons and for the purpose of identifying a person of unknown identity or the identity of the found corpse, unless another law provides otherwise. The information is provided in the form and to the extent determined by other legislation.[34]

Interestingly, location and traffic data can be accessed without prior judicial authorisation in this regime. This statement is also valid for the second situation, which is access to location and traffic data for the purpose of the fight against terrorism and preventing specific terroristic threats as laid down in Section 71 of the Police Act.

§ 71

A police division, *competent in fight* against *terrorism, may for the purpose of preventing and detecting specific threats of terrorism to the extent necessary to request the*

a) legal or natural person providing a public communications network or publicly available electronic communications to provide traffic and location data in a manner enabling remote and continuous access, unless *another law provides otherwise*; *Information will be provided in the form and to the extent determined by other legislation.*[35]

---

[33] Act No. 273/2008 on the Police of the Czech Republic. In: beck-online [legal information system].

[34] Act No. 273/2008 on the Police of the Czech Republic. In: beck-online [legal information system].

[35] *Ibid.*

The fact that location and traffic data can be accessed without prior judicial authorisation and the lack of other checks and balances[36] puts a strong tool in the hands of the police, which could be easily abused by the collection of a disproportional amount of data. This could lead to a serious threat to personal data and privacy.

The last situation, in which the police can access traffic and location data outside the regime of criminal proceedings involves supervision over a person who is protected by the special regime of witness protection. Similar to communication interception, this permission is regulated by Section 10a of Act No. 137/2001 Sb. on special protection of a witness and other persons in connection with criminal proceedings.[37] In this case, prior judicial authorisation is necessary to access traffic and location data.

b) Preventive law

The Czech police cannot use electronic communication interception as a preventive measure, since the law does not expressly allow it.

c) Law of intelligence agencies

Generally speaking, the conditions which need to be met in order to legally carry out communication interception within the regime of intelligence agencies are less strict than those for interception in the criminal proceedings.

The wording of statutory authorisation to conduct communication interception in Acts No. 154/1994 Sb. on the Security Information Service and No. 289/2005 on Military Intelligence is practically identical. In both acts, the interception is grounded in Sections 8 and 9:

---

36 Section 11 of the Police Act sets a general principle of proportionality; however, it is the opinion of the reporteur that this general provision is not sufficient reinsurance that the legal authorisation to collect such data will not be abused.

"Section 11 Adequacy of the procedure

A policeman and police employee are required to

ensure that no person suffered unwarranted injury due to their actions,

ensure that their decision not to act did not resulted in unsubstantiated harm to persons whose security is endangered,

proceed in a way that any possible interference with the rights and freedoms of persons to whom the act is directed, or any others, did not exceed what is necessary to achieve the objective pursued by the act."

Act No. 273/2008 on the Police of the Czech Republic. In: beck-online [legal information system].

37 See *supra* note no. 24.

§ 8 – Intelligence technology

(1) Intelligence technology for the purposes of this Act means the technical facilities and equipment, especially electronic, photo-technical, chemical, physic-chemical, radio-optical, mechanical, or their files used in classified manner, if it causes interference with the fundamental rights and freedoms in

a) searching, opening, examining or evaluating transported consignments,
b) interception or recording of telecommunications, radio communication or other similar operation, or surveying data about this operation,
c) making video, audio or other records,
d) Search using technical means that could prevent or impede the fulfilment of operations within the scope of Military Intelligence/ Security Information Service,
e) identification of persons or objects, or to identify their movements using surveillance techniques and baits.

(2) Using intelligence technology, if it is not interfering with fundamental rights and freedoms, is not

a) capturing, listening, monitoring and evaluating information, which are distributed in a way that allows to access them by previously undefined group of persons
b) making video or audio recordings,
c) use security techniques and baits,
d) monitoring of telecommunications, radio communication or other similar operations without tapping its content, or collecting data on the traffic.

§ 9 – Application of intelligence technology

(1) Intelligence technology can be used by The Military Intelligence/the Security Information Service only when initially authorised by a written permission of the presiding judge of the High Court in whose jurisdiction falls the Ministry of Defence/the Security Information Service (hereinafter referred to as "judge"), under assumption that detecting and documenting of the activities for which is the technology to be used, would be ineffective or substantially more difficult or impossible, should it be done in a different way.

(2) Use of intelligence technology must not exceed the scope of the authorization of a judge under paragraph 1 and must not interfere with the rights and freedoms beyond what is strictly necessary.

(3) The Military Intelligence/the Security Information Service can technically secure the use of intelligence technology for the needs of other competent authorities, if they so request and submit appropriate authorization for the use of intelligence technology issued by a special legal regulation.

(4) The Military Intelligence/the Security Information Service is entitled to demand from the other for such activity authorized bodies the use of technical security intelligence technology for its own use. In this case, it is obliged to demonstrate that the use of intelligence technology has been authorised under provision this Act.

(5) Military Intelligence/the Security Information Service is entitled to the extent required for the performance of a specific operation, request a legal or natural person providing a public communications network or publicly available electronic communications service

a) the establishment or security interface for connecting the terminal telecommunications equipment for the interception or recording messages at specified points of their network, and

b) the provision of operational and localization data, in the form and to the extent determined by special legislation.[38]

The Office for Foreign Relations and Information is not expressly authorized by law to conduct communication interception. It is out of the scope of its competence, since the information collected by means of interception would be from within the borders of the Czech Republic. However, should the Office need to conduct such an interception, it can request it to be carried out by other intelligence services, most likely the Security Intelligence Service. This can be done on the basis of Section 9 of Act No. 153/1994 Sb. on intelligence services of the Czech Republic, which allows cooperation between services based on an agreement between them:

§ 9

Intelligence services cooperate with each other on the basis of agreements, which are concluded with the consent of the Government.[39]

Such interception would be completely within the legal regime of Act No. 154/1994 Sb. on the Security Information Service.

Even though the intelligence service needs judicial approval for the communication interception, just as it is needed in criminal proceedings, it is not limited to specific situations like the investigation of a crime enumerated in the statue. It is therefore legally easier to obtain such approval. This difference was elaborated by the Czech Constitutional Court in Decision No. I. ÚS 3038/07-1 from 29 February 2008 in which the Court stated that information obtained from the regime of intelligence service communication interception cannot be freely used in criminal proceedings.[40] Following a reminder of the Constitutional Court in this case, there is a difference in the purposes of the two regimes of communication interception. In the case of the criminal proceedings regime, the entire process is only within the judiciary branch of the state power, the purpose being solely the solving of crime; the evidence is obtained by the police based on the rules of the Code of Criminal Procedure and subject to a closer judicial review. In the case of the intelligence regime, it is rooted in the executive branch of state power, the purpose being national security; the judicial review is much less extensive than in the case of criminal proceed-

38 The provision marked here as paragraph 5 is marked as Section 8a in Act 154/1994 Sb. on security information service. Act No. 154/1994 Sb. on security information service and No. 289/2005 on military intelligence. In: beck-online [legal information system].

39 Act No. 153/1994 Sb. on intelligence services of the Czech Republic. In: beck-online [legal information system].

40 In this case, the criminal proceedings against the defendant were commenced after the police obtained the military intelligence recording from the interception of the communication to which the defendant was a party. She was, however, not the legitimate subject of the interception. She issued a complaint against the commencing of the criminal proceedings, which was denied by the public prosecutor. After a series of appeals, the Constitutional Court ruled in her favour.

ings. The court writes in paragraph 29: "Intelligence service interceptions do not reach the guarantee quality, which is required by the Code of Criminal Procedure and therefore they cannot be used in the criminal proceedings, because they were not obtained in the legal manner."[41]

d) Financial and customs investigation service

As discussed above in I.A.1., the legal regime for communication interception specifically for the customs investigation service is stipulated in Section 63 of Act No. 17/2012 Sb. on customs service of the Czech Republic. This section, however, does not establish a new unique regime for message interception. It is only a specification of the criminal procedure regime, since the customs service may serve as a police force only in the first phase of the criminal proceedings, the preliminary hearing, and only in a situation described in the above-mentioned Section 63.

Aside from the police and intelligence services, access to traffic and location data can be requested by the Czech National Bank. This can be done as a part of its responsibility to supervise the capital market, and prior judicial authorisation is required. However, the Czech National Bank is entitled to request the data from providers of electronic communications services directly, that means without use of police services:

§ 8

(1) The Czech National Bank is entitled for the purpose of performance of supervision over capital market to

a) request, after prior written authorisation by the presiding judge of the High Court under whose jurisdiction belongs the seat of the Czech National Bank, from a legal or natural person providing a public communications network or publicly available electronic communications traffic and location data in accordance to special legislation, if it can be reasonably assumed that data provided may contribute to the clarification of facts important for the detection of an administrative offense in the area of business or commerce in the capital market under the act governing capital market undertakings, including the offender, and if the pursued objective cannot be achieved differently, or if can be achieved only by exerting a disproportionate effort.[42]

---

[41] Paragraph 29 of the decision of the Czech Constitutional Court No. I. ÚS 3038/07-1 from 29 February 2008. In: Codexis [legal information system].

[42] Act No. 15/1998 Sb. on the supervision in the area of capital market and change and supplementation of some acts. In: beck-online [legal information system].

Comparative note – Slovakia

A similar approach is applied in Slovak Republic. Communication interception in the criminal procedure is regulated in Section 115 of the Code of Criminal Procedure:[43]

§ 115

(1) Where criminal proceedings are conducted in respect of a felony, corruption, criminal offence of the abuse of power of public official, criminal offence of laundering the proceeds of crime, or in respect of an intentional criminal offence where so provided by a promulgated international treaty, it shall be possible to issue an order to intercept and record telecommunications if there are reasonable grounds to believe that it will reveal the facts that are materially relevant for criminal proceedings. Where, in the course of intercepting and recording telecommunications, the accused is found to be in communication with his defence counsel, no information thus obtained may be used for the purposes of criminal proceedings, and any such information must be forthwith destroyed in a prescribed manner; this shall not apply to information relating to a case in which a lawyer does not represent the accused as his defence counsel.

(2) The order to intercept and record telecommunications shall be issued by the presiding judge of a panel prior to the commencement of criminal prosecution, or by a judge for pre-trial proceedings on a motion from a prosecutor. If the matter bears no delay and a prior order from a judge for pre-trial proceedings cannot be obtained, the order may be issued by a prosecutor before the commencement of criminal prosecution or in pre-trial proceedings, unless the interception and recording of telecommunications involves the entry into the dwelling of a person; such order shall have to be confirmed by a judge for pre-trial proceedings within 24 hours of its issuance; failing that, the order shall become null and void and the information obtained on its basis may not be used for the purposes of criminal proceedings and shall have to be immediately destroyed in a prescribed manner.

(3) The order to intercept and record telecommunications shall have to be in writing and based on circumstantial reasons, separately for each telephone subscriber or technical equipment. The order shall have to specify the telephone subscriber or technical equipment and, if known, the person whose telecommunications are intercepted and recorded, and the length of time during which the interception and recording of telecommunications are to be performed. Interception and recording may not exceed six months. This period may by extended by another two months, also repeatedly, on a motion from a prosecutor or a judge for pre-trial proceedings. Interception and recording of telecommunications operations shall be performed by the competent department of the Police Corps.

(4) Police officers or the competent department of the Police Corps shall be obliged to continuously review the grounds for the order to intercept and record telecommunications. Where such grounds cease to exist, interception and recording of telecommunications shall have to be discontinued, even before the expiry of the time limit referred to in paragraph 3. This fact shall be immediately notified in writing to the entity that issued the order to intercept and record telecommunications; in pre-trial proceedings, it shall also be notified to the prosecutor.

---

[43] Section 115 of No. 141/1961 in the code on criminal trials (Code of Criminal Procedure). Unofficial translation. Online: https://e-justice.europa.eu/fileDownload.do?id=11f9da19-253e-4f02-9a26-2e2285184e7a

(5) In criminal proceedings conducted in respect of an intentional criminal offence which is different from the one referred to in paragraph 1, the order to intercept and record telecommunications may be issued by the presiding judge of a panel or, prior to the commencement of prosecution or in pre- trial proceedings, by a judge for pre-trial proceedings acting on a motion from a prosecutor, but only with the consent of the subscriber to the telecommunication equipment subjected to interception or recording.

(6) If the record of telecommunications is to be used as evidence, a verbatim transcript made by the officer of the Police Corps carrying out the interception of telecommunications shall have to be attached, wherever the recording makes it possible, containing information about the place, time and legal grounds for interception. A verbatim transcript of the record of telecommunications, which is not secret, signed by the Police Corps officer who drew it up, shall be inserted in the file; if the verbatim transcript of telecommunication records contains a classified fact, it shall be classified according to separate legal provisions. The transcript of telecommunications shall be used as evidence after the interception of telecommunications has been discontinued. In pre-trial proceedings, where the circumstances of the case warrant it, the recording of telecommunications may be submitted to the court even without a transcript of the recording, if the accompanying report gives the data concerning the time, place and legality of interception, and concerning the persons subject to the recording of telecommunications, provided that the recording of telecommunications is intelligible.

(7) The recording may be used as evidence in a different criminal matter from the one that is subject to interception and recording of telecommunications only if such other matter is also heard in simultaneous proceedings concerning a criminal offence referred to in paragraph 1.

(8) If the interception and recording did not produce any facts relevant for criminal proceedings, the criminal procedure authority or the relevant department of the Police Corps shall have to destroy the obtained records forthwith in a prescribed manner. The protocol on the destruction of the recordings shall be inserted in the file. The destruction of the recordings shall be notified to persons referred to in paragraph 3 who do not have the right to view the file; the notification shall be made by the body whose decision has finally settled the matter, or, in the proceedings before the court, by the presiding judge of a panel of a first-instance court within three years from the date on which criminal prosecution in the case was finally concluded; this shall not apply to the proceedings concerning particularly serious felonies or the felonies committed by organised groups, criminal groups or terrorist groups, or criminal offences committed by more than one person if at least one of the perpetrators is still under prosecution, or if the provision of such information could obstruct the purpose of criminal proceedings.

(9) The provisions of paragraphs 1 to 8 shall apply, as appropriate, to the content data or operational data transmitted in real time via computer systems.

The intercepted communication and recordings can be used for the sake of criminal proceedings only if the proceedings are being conducted for crimes specifically enumerated by the law. The general rule is that the interception must be initially authorized by a judge. A comparable provision is that on creating visual, audio, or audio-visual recordings pursuant to Section 114 of the Code of Criminal Procedure. This particular provision is concentrated more on local area monitoring and wiretapping than telecommunication interception. It is used for intentional crimes (higher value of the penalty range exceeds 3 years), corruption, abuse of the power by a public officer, money laundering, or another crime recognized by MLA.

The data retention (traffic and location data) by providers of electronic communications and possibilities to access such data in the criminal proceedings by the Police Corps are laid down in Section 116 of the Code of Criminal Procedure. The Slovak Constitutional Court recently held this provision to be unconstitutional:[44]

§ 116

(1) In criminal proceedings held in respect of an intentional criminal offence, it will be possible to issue an order for the disclosure and provision of telecommunications data that are subject to telecommunications secrecy or enjoy personal data protection, if such data are necessary to clarify the facts relevant for criminal proceedings.

(2) The order to disclose and provide telecommunications data shall be issued in writing by the presiding judge of a panel prior to the commencement of criminal prosecution, or by a judge for pre- trial proceedings on a motion from a prosecutor in pre-trial proceedings, which must be based on circumstantial reasons; the order shall be served on the persons referred to in paragraph 3.

(3) Legal entities or natural persons carrying out telecommunications activities shall notify the presiding judge of a panel, or, in pre-trial proceedings, a prosecutor or a police officer about effected telecommunications.

(4) The provisions of paragraphs 1 to 3 shall apply, as appropriate, to the content data or operational data transmitted in real time via computer systems.

Regarding this obligation, the providers of electronic communications were obliged to store traffic data, location data, and data about the communicating parties for a period of six months (in the case of Internet, e-mail, or VoIP communications) or for a period of 12 months (in case of other communications). It was held that the legal framework regulating access to data retention data was completely arbitrary and considerably less stringent than comparable provisions on wiretapping.[45]

Also, strong powers arise from Act No. 171/1993 Coll. on the Police Corps. The Police Corps can use ITM and conclude operative-investigative activities to perform tasks in the fight against terrorism, money laundering, narcotics, nuclear materials, and forgery. Also, ITM are used to assist exposed witnesses and in the witness protection program according to a special regulation. Another option is protection of an undercover agent when detecting tax evasion and illicit financial activities. The scope of the Police Corps' competence regarding interception is quite broad. According to European case law, and also domestic case law, the police cannot use ITM in to intercept a communication between client and attorney. The attorney-client privilege is recognized in criminal matters only.

---

[44] Press release by the Slovak Constitutional Court from April 29, 2015. sp. zn. PL. ÚS 32/2015. Online: https://e-justice.europa.eu/fileDownload.do?id=11f9da19-253e-4f02-9a26-2e2285184e7a

[45] The decision was issued almost a year after the CJEU had proclaimed the Data Retention Directive invalid in the spring of 2014. See Slovakia: GERA, M. Mass surveillance of citizens is unconstitutional. EDRi. May 4, 2015. Online: https://edri.org/slovakia-mass-surveillance-of-citizens-is-unconstitutional/

According to the Act on the Protection against Interception, ITM refers primarily to electro-technical, radio-technical, photo-technical, optical, mechanical, chemical, and other technical measures and equipment or their sets, used in a covert manner to: search for, open, examine, and assess mail and other transported packages, monitor and record telecommunication activities, and make and use the visual, audio, and other recordings.[46] The most important provision for the Slovak Intelligence Service and other authorities empowered to employ interception activities arises from the following provision of the Act on the Protection against Interception:[47]

Article 4

(1) Technical-intelligence measures shall be used only on the basis of a prior written approval of the legitimate judge[48] (hereinafter "approval") and only for a set period of time, not exceeding six months. The term shall go into effect on the day the approval is granted. If it is inevitable to use simultaneously or subsequently several kinds of technical-intelligence measures, each of them shall be used only to the extent of the expressly granted approval. If the technical-intelligence measure is to be used in places, which are not accessible to the public, the legitimate judge shall also decide whether his approval applies also to the entry into such places.

(2) The legitimate judge who has granted the approval to use the technical-intelligence measures can, on the basis of a new request, extend the duration of the time period, but in each case for no longer than other six months. This term shall go into effect on the day the further approval is granted (hereinafter "further approval"). Further approval shall be granted in writing not later than on the last day of the term in accordance with paragraph 1. If the term cited in paragraph 1 expires and the further approval is not granted, the use of the technical-intelligence measure shall be ceased on the last day of the term set in the approval.

(3) The request to grant approval to use a technical-intelligence measure (hereinafter "the request") shall be submitted in writing to the competent court. The request shall contain the following data:

a) Specification of the type of the technical-intelligence measure to be used and of the location of its use, the proposed time of duration of its use, data on the person against whom the use of this technical-intelligence measure is directed,
b) Information on the previous ineffectual or considerably difficult revelation and documentation of activities, which constitute the reason of submitting the request,
c) The rationale for using the technical-intelligence measure. The court must not make a decision on the request, which does not contain the data required by the law. It shall return the request to the applicant.

(4) The request is submitted by the state body, which intends to use a technical-intelligence measure to implement its legitimate activities (Section 2, paragraph 2).

(5) It is not possible to lodge a legal remedy against the decision on approval.

(6) The legitimate judge who has granted the approval to use the technical-intelligence measures shall be required to review systematically the existing rationale of their use. If

---

46 Article 2 of the Act on the Protection against Interception.

47 Article 4 of the Act on the Protection against Interception.

48 Article 13, Sections 2 and 3, and Article 20, Section 2 of the Law of the Slovak National Council No. 335/1991 in the Code on the Courts and Judges, as stated in Article III of the Law No. 185/2002 in the Code on the Judicial Council of the Slovak Republic and on the Amendment and Supplementation of Some Laws.

the rationale no longer applies, he shall be required to issue a decree immediately that the use of these measures cease.

As mentioned above, the Slovak regulation for intelligence services, which is also broadly used by police authorities, has lower prerequisites than those of the Code of Criminal Procedure. Approval by a judge as a guarantee of lawful process is sometimes omitted due to the need for faster and more flexible investigative reactions to dangerous forms of criminality. However, these powers are to be controlled and supervised by means of judicial power, because they can harbour misbalance or a potential risk of abuse.

3. Responsibility for the technical performance of interception measures

In the Czech Republic, the technical implementation of communication interception is done by the state agencies, with the cooperation of legaly bound subjects in accordance with Act No. 127/2005 Sb. on electronic communication. Section 97 para. 1 of the Act on Electronic Communications establishes a duty for the legal or natural person providing a public communications network[49] or publicly available electronic communications service[50] to provide and secure interfaces at specified points of the network for connection of terminal equipment for message tapping and recording. This is done at the requesting party's expense. This section authorizes the police of the Czech Republic, Security Information Service, and Military Intelligence to do so.

Access to traffic and location data is laid down in Section 97 para. 3 in a similar fashion. This provision authorises public authorities involved in the criminal proceedings, the police (for the sake of search for missing persons and things and prevention of terrorist activities), the intelligence services, and the Czech National Bank to request the legal or natural person providing a public communications network or publicly available electronic communications service to provide traffic and location data:

§ 97 Interface for communication interception and message recording

(1) Legal or natural person providing a public communications network or publicly available electronic communications service is required at the expense of the applicant to establish and ensure designated points on its network interface for connecting the terminal telecommunication equipment for wiretapping and recording information for

---

[49] § 2 letter j) defines the public communication network as "an electronic communications network which is used wholly or mainly for the provision of publicly available electronic communications services and which supports transmission of information between end nodes of the network or an electronic communications network via which is provided service of television or radio broadcasting."

[50] § 2 letter o) defines the publicly available electronic communications service as "electronic communications service from the use of which no person is excluded beforehand."

a) Police of the Czech Republic for the purposes established by special legislation,
b) Security Information Service for the purposes established by special legislation,
c) Military Intelligence for the purposes established by special legislation

(2) A legal entities or natural person providing public communications network or providing publicly accessible services of electronic communications is obliged to retain traffic and location data generated or processed within the provision of public telecommunications networks and provision of publicly available services of electronic communications […]. Legal entities and natural persons providing public communications networks or providing publicly available services of electronic communications are obliged to retain traffic and location data regarding unsuccessful call attempts solely under the circumstances when such data is generated and processed and simultaneously retained or recorded. Legal entities and natural persons retaining traffic and location data pursuant the first and the second sentences are obliged to immediately upon request provide such data to the bodies authorised to request such data as set forth by special regulations. Simultaneously such a person is obliged to ensure that the content of the messages and communications is not retained with the data described pursuant to the first and the second sentence. The period for which the data are retained must not be shorter than 6 months and longer than 12 months. Upon expiration of the above period the person retaining the data pursuant to the first and the second sentences is obliged to destroy the data should they have not been provided to the bodies authorised to request such data pursuant to special regulation or unless set forth otherwise by this Act. (Section 90).

(3) The extent of traffic and location data retained pursuant to para. 3, the period for which the data are retained pursuant to paragraph 3 and the form and manner in which they are to be submitted to the bodies authorised to use such data upon request pursuant to special regulation is to be set forth by a statutory instrument.[51]

When it comes to the criminal procedure regime of communication interception, the Unit for Special Activities[52] (a division with a countrywide authority) is the only division of the Czech police authorized to conduct the interception operations. A detailed procedure for this process is set out by the Order of the Police President No. 186/2011 upon request for tapping and recording of telecommunication traffic and upon request for traffic and location data, which was amended by the Order of the Police President No. 139/2012. This order is unfortunately not publicly accessible. However, the technical and request process is quite well described in the document "Analysis of tapping and recording of telecommunication traffic," which was published by the Police Presidium of the Czech Republic on 6 June 2014.[53]

When the conditions of Section 88 para. 1 are met, the authorized person, who is the policeman working on the criminal case, can request the interception. This request must contain a brief summary of the factual situation of the case and the reasoning for the request. It must especially contain anticipated facts, which are important for the case, and which should be uncovered during the interception.

---

[51] Act No. 127/2005 Sb. on electronic communications and on amendment to some related laws (Act on Electronic Communications).

[52] Webpage of the division in Czech: http://www.policie.cz/clanek/utvar-zvlastnich-cinnosti-sluzby-kriminalni-policie-a-vysetrovani-716842.aspx

[53] In Czech online: www.mvcr.cz/soubor/ppr-102-31-cj-2014-990390-analyza-odposlechu-a-sledovani-za-rok-2013-pdf.aspx

Furthermore, the request must include identification of the user unit that is to be intercepted (number, address, and name of its user, if known) and the period of time for which the interception should be conducted. This period may be no longer than four months. Before approval of the request, the designated officer of the Unit for Special Activities must be consulted; he/she will evaluate the request from a technical and operative point of view and decide whether the interception is possible and doable.[54]

If the criminal proceedings are in the preliminary hearing phase, the request is send to the Public Prosecutor, who then requests the interception from the court. In later phases of the proceedings, the court can be contacted directly. The court then issues a decision, namely a court order, which is delivered back to the Public Prosecutor (preliminary hearing) or directly back to the authorized person, who then delivers it to the Unit for Special Activities. When the conditions of Section 88 para. 1 are met, the authorized officer must obtain consent from the person using the intercepted unit. Once again, a properly filled out request is delivered to the Unit for Special Activities. In both situations, the division conducts the requested communication interception and the result of it, which is a sound recording recorded on a non-rewritable medium, is delivered back to the authorized person, who issued the request in the first place.

The court order must be specific and justified, including for example a reference to the specific international treaty, should the interception be conducted in the context of an intentional criminal offense for which prosecution is stipulated in a declared international treaty. The order must contain specific identification of the intercepted unit (address and identity of its user, if known) and the time period for which the interception is authorized.

After the end of the interception, the police body must in a short time evaluate the recordings and insert statistical data into the specialized system MU II. If the recordings are not to be used in the criminal proceedings, they must be destroyed three years after the proceeding has legally ended.

If the recording of the telecommunication service is to be used as evidence, it is necessary to accompany it with a transcript, giving the place, time, manner, and contents of the record as well as the authority that issued the record. The police authority is obliged to label other records, securely store them so as to protect them against unauthorized misuse, and indicate the place of storage in the transcript. In another criminal case other than that for which the interception and recording of the telecommunication service was performed, the recording may be used as evidence

[54] Analysis of tapping and recording of telecommunication traffic, p. 16.

if there is a criminal prosecution in this matter for a criminal offense referred to in para. 1 of Section 88 or with the consent of the user of the intercepted station or device:

§ 88

(6) If the record of the telecommunications service is to be used as evidence, it is necessary to accompany it with the transcript, giving the place, time, manner and contents of the record, as well as the authority which issued the record. The police authority is obliged to label other records, securely store them so as to protect them against unauthorised misuse, and indicate the place of storage in the transcript. In another criminal case other than the one in which the interception and recording of telecommunications service was performed, the recording may be used as evidence if there is a criminal prosecution in this matter for a criminal offence referred to in Subsection 1, or with the consent of the user by the intercepted station.

(7) If the interception and recording of the telecommunications service did not find any facts relevant to the criminal proceedings, the police authority, after approval by a court and in preliminary hearings, the public prosecutor, must immediately destroy all records after three years from the final conclusion of the matter. If the police authority was informed of an extraordinary appeal within the set deadline, they shall destroy the records of the interception after the decision on the extraordinary appeal or after a final conclusion on the matter. The police authority shall send a transcript on the destruction of the record of the interception to the public prosecutor, whose decision finally concluded the matter and in proceedings before the court, to the presiding judge in the first instance, for the record on file. [55]

The following diagram shows the request procedure for authorisation of communication interception.[56]

Section 19 of Act No. 273/2008 on the Police of the Czech Republic authorizes the police forces to provide technical support and conduct communication interception for another public authority following a request and if that body is authorized to perform such action. The other public authority must declare this fact in its request:

§ 19 – Technical support

(1) The police can technically provide the use of intelligence technology or bait and security technology or a surveillance of persons and goods at the request of a public authority, which is authorised for such use.

(2) The public authority in the request demonstrates that the use of intelligence technology or surveillance of people and goods is authorised under special legal act.[57]

---

[55] Section 88 of Act. No. 141/1961 Sb. on criminal procedure. In: ASPI [legal information system].

[56] Analysis of tapping and recording of telecommunication traffic, p. 15.

[57] Section 19 of Act No. 273/2008 on the Police of the Czech Republic. In: beck-online [legal information system].

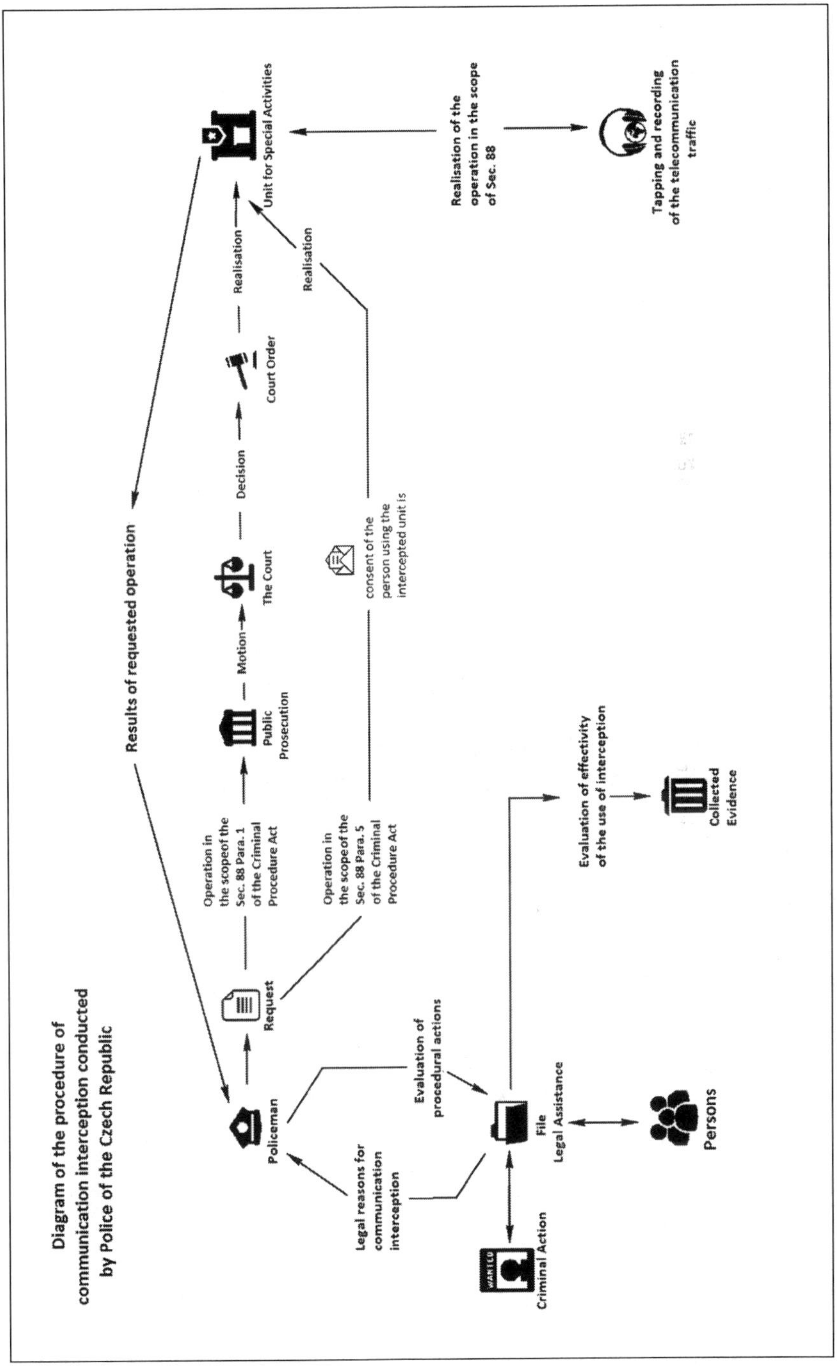
Diagram of the procedure of communication interception conducted by Police of the Czech Republic
Results of requested operation
Policeman
Request
Operation in the scopeof the Sec. 88 Para. 1 of the Criminal Procedure Act
Public Prosecution
Motion
The Court
Decision
Court Order
Realisation
Unit for Special Activities
Operation in the scopeof the Sec. 88 Para. 5 of the Criminal Procedure Act
consent of the person using the intercepted unit is
Realisation
Realisation of the operation in the scope of Sec. 88
Tapping and recording of the telecommunication traffic
Evaluation of procedural actions
Legal reasons for communication interception
File
Legal Assistance
Persons
Criminal Action
Evaluation of effectivity of the use of interception
Collected Evidence

This is the case for customs service since even though it is authorized by Section 63 of the Act on Customs Service of the Czech Republic to use communication interception, Act No. 127/2005 on electronic communications does not set a duty for electronic communications providers to allow customs service access to the networks. Customs therefore use services of the police (and therefore the Unit for Special Activities). However, the general directorate of customs is authorized to technically secure for other public authorities the application of intelligence techniques, including communication interception (Section 4 para. 5 letter c) of the Act on Customs Service). Similar to the above-mentioned Section 19 of Act No. 273/2005, this can be done upon request when the other public authority is authorized to perform such action:

§ 4 Jurisdiction

(5) The General directorate of customs

c) in cooperation with public authorities secures, especially technically, the use of intelligence and security equipment or surveillance of persons and things, if the relevant public authority proves that the it is authorized by law to conduct the interception.[58]

Interception of communication can be conducted by intelligence services within their specific legal regime. The rules for communication interception carried out by the Security Information Service and Military Intelligence are, as could be seen in above, almost identical. Both services can request the interception from the provider of public electronic communications and both can serve as technical support for other public bodies having authorisation to conduct communication interception (Section 9 paras. 4 and 5 of Act No. 289/2005 on Military Intelligence and Section 8a and Section 9 para. 4 of Act No. 154/1994 Sb. on the Security Information Service).[59]

The judicial authorisation procedure is the same for both intelligence agencies, and it is laid down in Section 10 of their respective acts (Act No. 289/2005 on Military Intelligence and Act No. 154/1994 Sb. on the Security Information Service):

Section 10 Authorisation to the use of intelligence technology

(1) The judge will issue the authorisation to the use of intelligence technology on the basis of written request, which includes

a) kind of intelligence technology, which is going to be used, period of time during which it is going to be used, basic identification data about the person (if known), against which the technology is going to be used, number of telephone or other similar station, should it be used for the communication interception, as well as the place of use of intelligence technology. Should the intelligence technology be used against member of government, member of Parliament or judge of the Constitutional court, or should the right to untouchability of household be breached, this information must be included in the request;

---

[58] Section 19 of Act No. 273/2005 on customs service of the Czech Republic. In: beck-online [legal information system].

[59] See *supra*, question No. 2.

b) reasons for the use of intelligence technology;
c) information about any prior use of information technology against person indicated in the letter a) including the information, how was decided about that request.

(2) The judge will decide about the request without delay.

(3) The use of intelligence technology can be authorised only for the necessary period of time, at longest for 3 months. This period of time can be prolonged after a new request, but maximally only for 3 more months.

(4) The decision about authorisation to use of intelligence service includes kind of intelligence technology, which is going to be used, period of time during which it is going to be used, basic identification data about the person (if known), against which the technology is going to be used, number of telephone or other similar station, should it be used for the communication interception, as well as the place of use of intelligence technology.

(5) The judge issues along with the decision about authorisation to use of intelligence service also an abstract made from this decision, which includes the necessary identification data and statement, whether by use of intelligence service is breached the right to untouchability of household. The abstract does not include reasoning.

(6) Should the judge deny the request for authorisation to the use of intelligence technology, the decision must contain reasoning for such decision.

(7) Appellation against the decision is not allowed.[60]

An example of a public authority that can request the use of communication interception from the police and intelligence services is the General Inspection of Security Forces. According to Section 9 para. 2 a) of Act No. 341/2011 Sb. on the General Inspection of Security Forces, this authority can request communication interception of Security Forces and other public bodies to be conducted for the purpose of fulfilling its inspection duties. This interception is carried out within the legal regime of criminal procedure, since the request must include authorisation issued in the process governed by the Code of Criminal Procedure:

§ 9

(3) General Inspection may require from Security Forces and other public authorities, if it is necessary for the performance of a specific task of the Inspection

a) technical and personal resources for interception and recording of telecommunication operations or for operative intelligence means. In the request the Inspection demonstrates that the use of interception and recording of telecommunication operations or monitoring people and things have been permitted under the Code of Criminal Procedure.[61]

The Chamber of Deputies of the Czech Parliament is the control body in regard to the communication interception for the police of the Czech Republic (Section 98 of Act No. 273/2008 Sb. on the Police of the Czech Republic) and the customs service (Section 65 of Act No. 17/2012 on the customs service of the Czech Republic). The Chamber of Deputies is also a control body for intelligence services in

---

[60] Act No. 154/1994 Sb. on security information service and Act No. 289/2005 on military intelligence. In: beck-online [legal information system].

[61] Section 9 of Act No. 341/2011 Sb. on general inspection of security force. In: beck-online [legal information system].

general (Section 21 of the Military Intelligence Act and Section 18 of the Security Information Service Act); however, supervision of specific communication interceptions is done by courts (Section 11 of the Military Intelligence Act as well as of the Security Information Service Act).

General authorisation to request from electronic communications providers access to traffic and location data by the police of the Czech Republic is found in Section 66 para. 3 of Act No. 273/2008 on the Police of the Czech Republic. General authorisation to access such data by the intelligence services is found in Section 8a of Act No. 154/1994 Sb. on the Security Information Service and in Section 8 para. 5 of Act No. 289/2005 on Military Intelligence. Authorisation to access such data by the Czech National Bank is found in Section 8 of Act No. 15/1998 Sb. on supervision in the area of capital market and change and supplementation of some acts.

Comparative note – Slovakia

In the Slovak Republic, the technical implementation of communication interception is done by the state authorities (police corps or intelligence services) with the cooperation of legally bound subjects pursuant to Act No. 351/2011 Coll. on electronic communication. Section 63 para. 7 of the Act on Electronic Communications establishes a duty for the provider of a public communications network or publicly available electronic communications service to provide and secure interfaces at specified points of the network for the connection of terminal equipment for message tapping and recording.

4. Legitimacy of data transfers between different security services

Generally speaking, the situation in the Czech Republic is similar to the situation in Germany because the regimes and functions are separate from one another. There are several reasons for this. The first one is the above-mentioned strong principle of legality. If the possibility of data transfer and sharing of information is not expressly written in the law, the agency cannot use the information collected by another agency. If the possibility of information transfer is written in the law it can be done only within the scope of the legal permission. The second reason for the separation is that different agencies intercept communications for different purposes and thus the process of obtaining permission for such interception also differs. Should the information be used in another regime than that for which they were collected, especially if interception conducted by the intelligence service is to be used in the criminal proceedings, it would be considered unlawful evidence and, as such, would not be admissible by the court. In paragraph 25 of the above-mentioned Decision No. I. ÚS 3038/07-1 from 29 February 2008,[62] the Czech Constitu-

---

[62] Paragraph 25 of the decision of the Czech Constitutional Court No. I. ÚS 3038/07-1 from 29 February 2008. In: Codexis [legal information system].

tional Court states that silence of the Code of Criminal Procedure about the possibility of using a communication interception obtained by a body other than the police, or not obtained in compliance with the Code of Criminal Procedure, as evidence in criminal proceedings needs to be interpreted in the light of the principle of legality, and therefore such interception cannot be used as an evidence.

a) Exchange of data between law enforcement authorities and preventive police authorities

Due to the fact that police authorities do not possess the legitimisation to conduct communication interception for preventive purposes, and the interceptions for criminal proceedings are case-specific, this question is irrelevant for the Czech Republic.

b) Passing on of data by intelligence agencies

A general authorisation for the intelligence services to pass on data is given in Section 8 para. 3 of Act No. 153/1994 Sb. on intelligence services of the Czech Republic:

§ 8 Reporting by Intelligence Services and tasking Intelligence Services

(3) Intelligence services report to public and police authorities information about findings, which fall within their jurisdiction. *This does not apply if providing* of the information *threatens important interest pursued by the relevant intelligence service.*[63]

The intelligence service must provide information to other public bodies and police forces, findings which fall within their jurisdiction. It is not, however, permitted to pass on too much specific information, for that would be a violation of the principle of legality, as stated by the Czech Constitutional Court in paragraph 28 of the above-mentioned Decision No. I. ÚS 3038/07-1 from 29 February 2008.[64]

Passing on information within different intelligence services is not expressly covered by the law; therefore, it can only be carried out within the scope of the general provision.

c) Passing on of data to intelligence agencies

There are no specific provisions that expressly allow data to be passed from communication interception to intelligence services. However, there are authorisations for passing on information in general. This authorisation is not so specific and

---

63 Section 8 of Act No. 153/1994 Sb. on intelligence services of the Czech Republic. In: beck-online [legal information system].

64 *Ibid.*, paragraph 28.

strong, so the principle of legality could be breached should it be used disproportionally.

For the police, the authorisation is laid down in Section 78 of Act No. 273/2008 Sb. on the Police of the Czech Republic. This section allows the police to hand over information, which was acquired during the fulfilling of their duties, to the national member of Eurojust, National Security Office, intelligence services of the Czech Republic, Military Police, Ministry of the Interior and other public bodies, should it be necessary for services in their jurisdiction:

§ 78 Handover of information

(1) Police hands over information including the information processed in the police registers, which are gained during carrying out its tasks, to the national member of Eurojust, the National Security Office, the intelligence services of the Czech Republic, Military Police, the Ministry, the Prison Service of the Czech Republic, the Customs Administration of the Czech Republic and other public authorities, if it is necessary to perform the tasks within their scope.

(2) The Police does not pass the information if it would jeopardize the accomplishment of police tasks.[65]

Section 57 of Act on Customs Service of the Czech Republic (Act No. 17/2012 Sb.) contains very similar authorisation. This section authorizes customs services to pass on information to the same degree as does the above-mentioned Section 78 for the police:

§ 57 Handover of information

(1) Customs authorities shall hand over information to

a) police,

b) intelligence services of the Czech Republic,

c) Military Police,

d) Ministry of Interior,

e) Prison Service of the Czech Republic,

f) the National Security Office, and

g) other public authorities, which in the area of competence of the customs administration are responsible for supervision or which conduct the proceedings on an administrative offense.

(2) Customs authorities hand over the information referred to in paragraph 1 only if the information is necessary for the performance of the legal tasks of these bodies.

(3) Customs authorities shall not transmit information when it would significantly jeopardize the performance of its duties.[66]

---

[65] Section 78 of Act No. 273/2008 Sb. on the Police of the Czech Republic. In: beck-online [legal information system].

[66] Section 57 of Act No. 17/2012 Sb. on customs service of the Czech Republic. In: beck-online [legal information system].

The same scope also covers Section 37 of the Act on the General Inspection of Security Forces (Act No. 341/2011 Sb.), which authorizes General Inspection to pass on information to other public bodies:

§ 37 Handover of information

(1) Inspection hands over information, including personal data and information processed in the records of inspection, which are gained in carrying out its tasks to the Czech Republic Police, Prison Service of the Czech Republic, the Customs Administration of the Czech Republic, the Czech Republic's intelligence services, military police and other public authorities, if it is necessary to perform the tasks within their jurisdiction.

(2) The Inspection shall without undue delay hand over information which were collected during carrying out its tasks and which can be used in course of exempting a member of security forces from a service to the Director of the security forces; If this member is the director of a national security force, the inspection passes the information to his superior, Staff officers.

(3) Inspection of the information referred to in paragraphs 1 and 2 are not handed over, if it would undermine tasks of the Inspection.[67]

Comparative note – Slovakia

The legitimacy of data transfers between different security services in the Slovak Republic is the subject of current discussion. Even the authorities do not have the legitimization to intercept for preventive purposes; there is no clear separating line between criminal procedure and intelligence procedure. The above-mentioned Act on the Protection against Interception empowers both bodies to legally intercept. The general rule is that a copy of the intercepted data (electronic evidence), which has been made by using ITP, can be released only to the case-related and locally authorized state body if the copy can serve as evidence in a procedure led before the authorized state body within the limits of its authority as established by law. The case-related and locally authorized state body, to which the recording has been released, is allowed neither to make a copy of the recording, nor to release its transcription for inspection or copying to another person, to another state body, or to a body of the local government or of any other self-administration. The regulation is lacking a definition of what a "case-related and locally authorized state body" is. This question must be decided by future case law.[68]

---

[67] Section 37 of Act No. 341/2011 Sb. on general inspection of security force. In: beck-online [legal information system].

[68] Exemplary case of unclear evidence transfer: The Antimonopoly Office of the Slovak Republic in the Dawn Raid had been forbidden by the Supreme Court to proceed with further browsing of electronically stored information of those under investigation (known as the prohibition of illegal intervention act). However, the Office issued the data obtained according to Section 89 of the Code of Criminal Procedure to the police corps (i.e., National Criminal Agency). The police, after disclosing the data (subsequently!), issued the order pursuant to Section 90 Code of Criminal Procedure on issuing of computer data. The Constitutional Court held in the matter of illegal evidence that "the complainants' argu-

B. Statistics on Telecommunication Interception

1. Obligation to collect statistics

There is no such obligation present in Czech law. However, the police compile statistics based on the order of the Police President No. 31/2012 on the analytical and statistical information system MU II. This order is, unfortunately, not publicly available.

Comparative note – Slovakia

The obligation to collect statistics in Slovak law can be found in the Act on the Protection against Interception. According to Section 6 para. 3, the state body maintains an overview of the number of issued approvals and dismissed requests (for ITP) and is responsible for its completeness. Therefore, each state body (Police Corps, Slovak Information Service, Military Intelligence, Railway Police, Corps of Prison and Judiciary Guards, and Customs Board) has the obligation to collect these statistics. Separate statistics are also created by the courts, Ministry of Justice, Ministry of Interior Affairs, and the public prosecutor's office regarding criminal procedure.

2. Current data

The Czech police annually publish statistical reports on the use of electronic interceptions and the interception of people and things. The most recent one is a report from the year 2013, which was published on 6 June 2014.[69] These statistics include only communication interception, which is conducted within the regime of criminal proceedings under the provision of Section 88 of Act No. 141/1961 Sb. Code of Criminal Procedure. Communication interception by intelligence services and customs in accordance with their special legal regimes is therefore not included in these statistics. Statistics on these kinds of communication interceptions are not publicly accessible.

The following information is taken from police statistics, which present, e.g., the absolute number of interceptions, the number of intercepted stations and people,

ment is invalid about that the authority has produced the evidence from the poisonous tree. The Antimonopoly Office was obliged to comply with the obligation imposed on it by the judgment of the Supreme Court, and to stop viewing the data. On other hand, this decision had no influence on obligation to issue the data to the police [according the Code of Criminal Procedure]." Decision of the The Constitutional Court of the Slovak Republic, spis. zn. III. ÚS 24/2012-53, January 17,012. Online: http://www.concourt.sk/SearchRozhodnutiav01/rozhod.do?urlpage=dokument&id_spisu=422752

69 In Czech online: www.mvcr.cz/soubor/ppr-102-31-cj-2014-990390-analyza-odposlechu-a-sledovani-za-rok-2013-pdf.aspx

	Total	Regional Police Directorates	The Office of Criminal Service and Investigation	Division for the Uncovering of Organised Crime	National Antidrug Center	Division for the Uncovering of Corruption and Financial Crime
Processed Criminal Files	135 731	134 923	N/A	184	147	477
No. of criminal files where communication interception could have been used	47 944	47 513	N/A	93	91	247
No. of criminal files where communication interception was used	1175	949	21	93	47	65
Percentage of criminal files where interception was realized to criminal files where it was legally possible to conduct it	2,5%	2,0 %	N/A	100 %	51,6 %	26,3 %
No. of intercepted telecommunication units	6 689	4 095	51	990	964	589
No. of intercepted persons	4 258	2 581	36	518	628	495
Average no. of units per Person	1,6	1,6	1,4	1,9	1,5	1,2
Average no. of units per Criminal file	5,7	4,3	2,4	10,6	20,5	9,1
No. of units intercepted after authorisation by a judge (section 88, para. 1 of the Code of Criminal Procedure)	6540	3947	51	989	964	589
No. of units intercepted after consent of intercepted person (section 88, para. 5 of the Code of Criminal Procedure)	149	148	0	1	0	0

and the differentiation of interceptions according to type of crime and overall effectivity of interceptions. The statistics do not, however, distinguish interceptions based on their nature, namely whether they are electronic in the meaning of, e.g., the detection of keystrokes, data tracking, etc. or whether they are telephonic interceptions.

The table on page 285 is a summary of data taken from the above-mentioned analysis.

The analysis also offers a chart with data concerning the effectivity of the perfomed interceptions. There are several categories that are used for this evaluation.

1) Active / Inactive interception

"Active" refers to interception that was commenced by the Unit for Special Activities of Criminal Police and Investigation and the information collected. Further categories (Nos. 2, 3, and 4) are subdivisions of this category.

There are two kinds of an "inactive" interception.

a) The Unit for Special Activities of Criminal Police obtained an authorized request for the interception, the interception was commenced and realized, but no recordings for the criminal procedure were obtained. An example of this situation is that the mobile telephone was inactive or the person of interest was not present in the Czech Republic.
b) The Unit for Special Activities of Criminal Police obtained an authorized request for the interception; however, the interception was not realized. For personal, technical, or other reasons no actions were taken by the Unit for Special Activities of Criminal Police for the entire time of validity of court authorisation, and therefore no recordings were collected.

2) Direct influence on the criminal procedure

The collected information was, or will be, used:

a) As evidence in ongoing criminal proceedings;
b) For tactical reasons and further investigation;
c) To prevent another crime;
d) To capture a criminal offender.

3) Indirect influence on the criminal procedure

Collected information was, or will be, used for a discovery of:

a) A new criminal activity on the part of the criminal offender who was subjected to the interception;

b) A new criminal activity on the part of third persons who were not initially subjected to the ongoing interception.

4) Information obtained via the interception was not used

This category covers ineffective interception, because it did not lead to any information that could be used in the criminal procedure.

	Total	Regional Police Directorates	The Office of Criminal Service and Investigation	Division for the Uncovering of Organised Crime	National Antidrug Center	Division for the Uncovering of Corruption and Financial Crime
No. of intercepted telecommunication units	6 689	4 095	51	990	964	589
Inactive interception	578	386	0	27	126	39
Direct influence on the criminal procedure only	4123	2176	47	759	736	406
Indirect influence on the criminal procedure only	15	15	0	0	0	0
Combination of direct and indirect influence on the criminal procedure	1081	898	0	110	36	37
Information obtained via the interception not used	891	620	4	94	66	107

In 2013, the average length of interception was 97.26 days.[70]

When compared with previous years, an increasing tendency in the number of communication interceptions can be seen starting in the year 2009.

	2006	2007	2008	2009	2010	2011	2012	2013
No. of intercepted units	7 599	5 491	4 973	4 571	5 006	5 766	6 241	6 689

[70] Police analysis, p. 80.

Comparative note – Slovakia

– *Slovak Intelligence Service (2013 – recent data)*[71]

In 2013, the Slovak Intelligence Service (SIS) submitted 235 requests to use ITM; the court issued 230 approvals; 5 requests were rejected. Of 230 uses of information-technical means, all cases were evaluated in terms of aims and purposes as stated by law. The aims and purposes as defined by law were fulfilled in 217 uses of information-technical means; in 13 cases they were not. In 2013, upon requests of the SIS, 187 court rulings on providing the subject of telecommunication secrecy were issued that included lists of data of communicating parties (billing), locations, and additional operational data relating to users of telecommunication services.

	Section 2(1(a))	Section 2(1(b))	Section 2(1(c))	Total
Number of ITM requests – Section 4 (1)	0	206	29	235
Court approvals	0	202	28	230
Rejected	0	4	1	5
Number of ITM renewal requests to prolong the period of ITM use for the same case – Section 4 (2)	0	0	0	0
Court approvals	0	0	0	0
Rejected	0	0	0	0
Number of ITM uses that fulfilled the aims and purposes as stated by law	0	191	26	217
Number of ITM uses that did not fulfill the aims and purposes as stated by law	0	11	2	13
Number of ITM uses where information was used as evidence in criminal proceedings	–	–	–	–
Number of illegitimate ITM uses	0	0	0	0

[71] Slovak Intelligence Service. Annual Report. Online: http://www.sis.gov.sk/for-you/sis-annual-report.html

– *General Prosecution in the Slovak Republic (2013 – recent data)*[72]

		2013	2012	2011
Producing video, audio, or audio-visual recordings (Section 114 of the Code of Criminal Procedure)	Number of requests	70	103	96
	Court approvals	62	99	95
The interception and data retention (Sections 115 and 116 of the Code of Criminal Procedure)	Number of requests	4395	3459	2576
	Court approvals	3700	2826	2327

– *Police Corps (2014 – recent data)*[73]

	Section 2(1(a))	Section 2(1(b))	Section 2(1(c))	Total
Number of ITM requests – Section 4 (1)	–	1165	61	1226
Court Approvals	–	1089	57	1146
Rejected	–	76	4	80
Number of ITM renewal requests to prolong the period of ITM use for the same case – Section 4 (2)	–	148	10	158
Court approvals	–	134	10	144
Rejected	–	14	–	14
Number of ITM uses that fulfilled the aims and purposes as stated by law	–	1058	62	1120
Number of ITM uses that did not fulfill the aims and purposes as stated by law	–	165	5	170
Number of ITM uses where information was used as evidence in criminal proceedings	–	110	9	119
Number of illegitimate ITM uses	–	–	–	–

– *Military Intelligence (2014 – recent data)*[74]

	Section 2(1(a))	Section 2(1(b))	Section 2(1(c))	Total
Number of ITM requests – Section 4 (1)	0	25	1	26

72 General Prosecution of Slovak Republic. Annual Report 2013. Online: http://www.genpro.gov.sk/spravy-o-cinnosti-12b7.html

73 Parliamentary Committee for Defense and Security. Annual Report 2013. Online: http://www.nrsr.sk/dl/Browser/Committee?committeeExternalId=125

74 Parliamentary Committee for Defense and Security. Annual Report 2013. Online: http://www.nrsr.sk/dl/Browser/Committee?committeeExternalId=125

Court approvals	0	23	1	24
Rejected	0	2	0	2
Number of ITM renewal requests to prolong the period of ITM use for the same case – Section 4 (2)	0	17	0	17
Court approvals	0	17	0	17
Rejected	0	0	0	0
Number of ITM uses that fulfilled the aims and purposes as stated by law	0	40	1	41
Number of ITM uses that did not fulfill the aims and purposes as stated by law	0	2	0	2
Number of ITM uses where information was used as evidence in criminal proceedings	0	0	0	0
Number of illegitimate ITM uses	–	–	–	–

– *Customs Board (2014 – recent data)*[75]

	Section 2(1(a))	Section 2(1(b))	Section 2(1(c))	Total
Number of ITM requests – Section 4 (1)	0	155	0	155
Court approvals	0	141	0	141
Rejected	0	14	0	14
Number of ITM renewal requests to prolong the period of ITM use for the same case – Section 4 (2)	0	14	0	14
Court approvals	0	13	0	13
Rejected	0	1	0	1
Number of ITM uses that fulfilled the aims and purposes as stated by law	0	150	1	150
Number of ITM uses that did not fulfill the aims and purposes as stated by law	0	2	0	2
Number of ITM uses where information was used as evidence in criminal proceedings	0	5	0	5
Number of illegitimate ITM uses	–	–	–	–

75 Parliamentary Committee for Defense and Security. Annual Report 2013. Online: http://www.nrsr.sk/dl/Browser/Committee?committeeExternalId=125

The relevant provisions of the Act on the Protection against Interception read as follows:

Article 2

(1) For the purposes of this Law, the technical-intelligence measures are primarily electro-technical, radio- technical, photo-technical, optical, mechanical, chemical, and other technical measures and equipment or their sets, used in a covert manner in:

a) Searching for, opening, examination, and assessment of mail and other transported packages,
b) Monitoring and recording of telecommunication activities,
c) Making and using the visual, audio, and other recordings.

Article 4

(1) Technical-intelligence measures shall be used only on the basis of a prior written approval of the legitimate judge (hereinafter "approval") and only for a set period of time, not exceeding six months. The term shall go into effect on the day the approval is granted. If it is inevitable to use simultaneously or subsequently several kinds of technical-intelligence measures, each of them shall be used only to the extent of the expressly granted approval. If the technical-intelligence measure is to be used in places, which are not accessible to the public, the legitimate judge shall also decide whether his approval applies also to the entry into such places.

(2) The legitimate judge who has granted the approval to use the technical-intelligence measures can, on the basis of a new request, extend the duration of the time period, but in each case for no longer than other six months. This term shall go into effect on the day the further approval is granted (hereinafter "further approval"). Further approval shall be granted in writing not later than on the last day of the term in accordance with para. 1. If the term cited in para. 1 expires and the further approval is not granted, the use of the technical-intelligence measure shall be ceased on the last day of the term set in the approval.

Article 5

(1) In an exceptional case, if there is a reasonable suspicion of a crime being committed and a technical- intelligence measure might be used by the Police Corps to fulfil its tasks, if the case is to be dealt with immediately and the approval of the legitimate judge cannot be obtained in advance, the Police Corps may use a technical-intelligence measure even without a prior approval. The Police Corps shall be required to notify the legitimate judge of the use of the technical-intelligence measure within one hour from the beginning of the use of this measure, and to submit the request, in accordance with Section 4, para. 3, to the legitimate judge within six hours from the beginning of the use of the technical-intelligence measure. The request shall contain also the time datum on the beginning of the use of the technical-intelligence measure.

(2) If the Police Corps does not obtain a subsequent written approval of the legitimate judge within twelve hours from the beginning of the use of the technical-intelligence measure or if the legitimate judge does not grant the subsequent approval, the use of this measure shall be immediately ceased. Information obtained in this way shall not be used and it shall be immediately destroyed. The state body, which has destroyed this information, shall immediately notify the legitimate judge of the destruction.

II. Principles of Telecommunication Interception in Constitutional Law and Criminal Procedure

A. Constitutional Safeguards of Telecommunication

1. Areas of constitutional protection

The Czech Republic also has, apart from the constitution itself, other documents that together form the Czech constitutional black-letter law – these are the constitutional laws and the Charter of Fundamental Rights and Freedoms. Together, these documents form the Czech Consitutional Order *(Ustavni poradek)*. Basic safeguards for the protection of fundamental rights are laid down in the Charter of Fundamental Rights and Freedoms that provides for their listing as well as brief explanations.

Recently applicable Czech constitutional law (valid since 1993) already acknowledges privacy as a distinct distributive (individual) right. Apart from being mentioned in Art. 7(1) of the Charter of Fundamental Rights and Freedoms, it is also laid down specifically with regard to personal life in Art. 10(2), with regards to personal data in Art. 10(3), and with respect to communications and records in Art. 13.

Article 7(1) reads as follows (informal translation[76]):

> Inviolability of the person and of privacy is guaranteed. It may be limited only in cases specified by law.

Article 10(2) reads as follows (informal translation):

> Everybody is entitled to protection against unauthorized interference in his or her personal and family life.

Article 10(3) reads as follows (informal translation):

> Everybody is entitled to protection against unauthorized gathering, publication or other misuse of his or her personal data.

Article 13 reads as follows (informal translation):

> Nobody may violate secrecy of letters and other papers and records whether privately kept or sent by post or in another manner, except in cases and in a manner specified by law. Similar protection is extended to messages communicated by telephone, telegraph or other such facilities.

Privacy is laid down in the aforementioned provisions as a right *per se* (it does not form a subsequent right) that can be claimed individually. This means that privacy as a regulatory phenomenon consists of individualized protective rights that

---

[76] Resolution of the Praesidium of the Czech National Council No. 2/1993 Sb., English translation available at http://www.psp.cz/cgi-bin/eng/docs/laws/1993/2.html. For further citations, see *ibid.*

are all subject to judicial protection. This also means that whenever privacy is at stake, it should always be possible to individually seek direct judicial protection or at least a judicial review of administrative decisions or other regulatory actions.

a) Secrecy of telecommunication

The secrecy of telecommunication is specifically recognized as a fundamental right in Art. 13 of the Charter of Fundamental Rights and Freedoms (see above). Legislation thereof is analogous to the traditional secrecy of letters, whereas any limitation of this protection has to be based on statutory law. This implies that telecommunication secrecy cannot be limited by bylaws or administrative decisions *per se* – any such limitation has to be grounded in the statutory law.

The fact that the secrecy of telecommunication is recognized by the Charter of Fundamental Rights and Freedoms as a distributive right implies that any infringement has to be reviewable by an independent judiciary. Together with the fact that telecommunication secrecy is a highly sensitive issue in the Czech Republic, this principle correspondingly led to currently applicable strict statutory safeguards for wiretapping.

b) Confidentiality and integrity of information systems

There are no specific constitutional provisions regarding the confidentiality and integrity of information systems. Such protection, however, can be derived from more general fundamental rights. In this respect, it is to be noted that there is a reason to distinguish between the confidentiality and integrity of information systems as such and the confidentiality and integrity of data that are stored or communicated therein.

In the first case, specific protective tools are correspondingly based on the general protection of property laid down in Art. 11(1) that reads as follows: "Everybody has the right to own property. The ownership right of all owners has the same statutory content and enjoys the same protection, inheritance is guaranteed."

The latter case, i.e., the protection of data stored in information systems, is based on fundamental rights protecting specific types of information. Apart from the protection of privacy and personal data, these might include, e.g., the protection of trade secrets, protection of health records, protection of speech, etc.

The issue of confidentiality and the integrity of information systems is also closely linked to the active component of the concept of informational self-determination (see below). Recently, the protection of informational self-determination served as a constitutional basis for the adoption of the Cybersecurity

Act,[77] which is primarily aimed at the establishment of security measures for protection of the confidentiality, security, and availability of critical information infrastructure.

c) Core area of privacy

The term "privacy" is used in Czech law to mean two things. One meaning is that it serves as a general constitutional principle, described above in II.A.1. Another meaning of the term "privacy" *(soukromi)* is primarily found in the Civil Code, and it establishes civil remedies for cases of infringement.

In Czech civil law, privacy protection is systematically put under the more general category of personality protection (apart from privacy, personality protection also includes the protection of dignity, esteem, etc.). The more general term "right to respect for private life" is regularly used when privacy is used as a regulatory principle that should limit powers or rights that lead to access to or processing of information originating in the private sphere of an individual (typically in personal data protection law, law on electronic communications, criminal procedure, etc.

d) Right to informational self-determination

The German judicial concept of informational self-determination was adopted into Czech law through decisions of the Czech Constitutional Court. It has recently been used in Czech constitutional practice as a common denominator for various individual information rights.

The Czech Constitutional Court distinguishes between active and passive components of informational self-determination, whereas the passive component concerns various individual information rights that consist of the protection of information related to an individual from an unlawful interference. The active component of informational self-determination is based on the assumption that one cannot live a regular personal life without the ability to actively communicate (i.e., without the possibility to have an access to the means of communication that became established as a standard in the conventional interpersonal exchange of information).

The Constitutional Court used the active component of informational self-determination in a case in which a woman was sentenced for an economic crime, including subsequent damages.[78] In the trial, her petition for *pro bono* legal representation was refused based upon the fact that she regularly paid a relatively high

---

77 Act No. 181/2014 Sb., English translation available at https://www.govcert.cz/download/nodeid-1143/

78 Decision No. I. ÚS 22/10, English translation available online at http://www.usoud.cz/en/decisions/?tx_ttnews%5Btt_news%5D=372&cHash=1c2ede3ef55d98e9b6f7c2ebd4dc416b

fee for her cable TV and Internet connection at home (which was interpreted as a demonstration of the fact that she has sufficient funds to pay for her legal representation). The Constitutional Court held that requiring her to give up her Internet connection would mean a disproportionate limitation of her right to informational self-determination, one of the components of such right being the right to actively communicate. This decision of the Constitutional Court was partly criticized for its reasoning because the court did not acknowledge the fact that the Internet connection might be obtained at significantly lower rates and that the active component of informational self-determination does not include a right to have an access to cable TV. However, the inclusion of the active component of informational self-determination had been accepted in Czech doctrine as one of possible forms of the interpretation of the right to personal life:

> The court held (official translation): The Constitutional Court also ascribed to this concept of the right to a private life, when it stated in its judgment file no. II. ÚS 517/99 that: "[T]he right to protection of personal privacy is the right of a natural person to decide according to his own deliberation whether, or to what extent and in what manner, the facts of his own personal privacy are to be made accessible to other subjects, and at the same time to defend oneself against (resist) unjustified interference in that sphere by other persons. Excessive emphasis on the positive component of the right to protection of one's private life leads to inappropriately narrowing of protection to merely seeing to it that the facts of a person's private life not be [disclosed] without his consent or without reasons recognized by the law, and thus the integrity of the internal sphere, which is essential for positive personal development, not be violated. The Constitutional Court does not share this narrowed understanding, because respect for private life must, to a certain degree, include the right to form and develop relationships with other human beings. Respect for private life, thus understood, includes the commitment of the state to act in a manner that permits the normal development of these relationships" [see judgment file no. II. ÚS 517/99 of 1 March 2000 (N 32/17 SbNU 229)].
>
> […]
>
> Therefore, it is the duty of the courts to review the unique aspects of each case so that, apart from observing the guarantees of a fair trial, the individual's other fundamental rights are also preserved, in this case the right to a private life [G. Dürig (G. D., Der Grundrechtssatz von der Menschenwürde, Archiv des öffentlichen Rechts 81, 1956, p. 127) formulated the well-known theory of the object, which was adopted in the case law of the German Constitutional Court, connected to questions of human dignity. According to this theory human dignity is violated when state authority places a particular individual into the role of an object, where he becomes a mere means, and is reduced to the form of a fungible value. One can conclude that a person not only the object of social "relationships," but also becomes the object of the law, if he is forced to subject to it completely in its interpretation and application, i.e. without taking into account his individual interests, or fundamental rights]. In addition to the subjective factors on the part of the individual, when evaluating whether expenses are "usual or justified" it is also necessary to take into account objective factors, which include, among other things, technological developments (e.g. mobile telephones, the internet) and related changes in methods of communication, obtaining information, contacts with government offices, association, etc., or the development of technologies, through which the individual's right to personal development, relationship with other people and the outside world, i.e. the right to a private life, is realized (point 17).

The active component of informational self-determination is to be distinguished from freedom of speech. Freedom of speech covers rights to actively communicate information to the public, i.e., the right to bring one's speech to the public space. In contrast, the active component of the right to informational self-determination (i.e., the right to communicate) includes only those forms of active communication that are common for individual private (personal) life, including private interpersonal communication, an individual requesting information (e.g., by browsing on a website), etc.

Comparative note – Slovakia

Constitutional protection in the Slovak Republic has some of the same principles, background, and roots as those in the Czech legal system. The written constitution along with other documents forms Slovak constitutional law. The Charter of Fundamental Rights and Freedoms (Act No. 23/1991 Coll.) is identical with the Czech charter. Therefore, basic safeguards for the protection of fundamental rights are laid down in an identical document and they are also reflected in the text of the Constitution (Act No.460/1992 Coll.).

Selected articles of the Slovak Constitution (covered also by The Charter of Fundamental Rights and Freedoms) are:[79]

Article 16

(1) The inviolability of the person and its privacy is guaranteed. It may be limited only in cases laid down by law.

(2) No one may be tortured, or subjected to cruel, inhuman, or humiliating treatment or punishment.

Article 20

(1) Everyone has the right to own property. The ownership right of all owners has the same legal content and protection. Inheritance is guaranteed.

(2) The law shall lay down which property, other than property specified in Article 4 of this Constitution, necessary to ensure the needs of society, the development of the national economy and public interest, may be owned only by the state, municipality, or designated legal persons. The law may also lay down that certain things may be owned only by citizens or legal persons resident in the Slovak Republic.

(3) Ownership is binding. It may not be misused to the detriment of the rights of others, or in contravention with general interests protected by law. The exercising of the ownership right may not harm human health, nature, cultural monuments and the environment beyond limits laid down by law.

(4) Expropriation or enforced restriction of the ownership right is possible only to the necessary extent and in the public interest, on the basis of law and for adequate compensation.

---

[79] *Ibid.* The Constitution of the Slovak Republic.

Article 22

(1) Secrecy of letters, other communications and written messages delivered by post and personal information shall be guaranteed.

(2) No one may violate the privacy of letters and the secrecy of other written documents and records, whether they are kept in privacy, or sent by mail or in any other way, with the exception of cases which shall be laid down by law. Equally guaranteed is the secrecy of messages conveyed by telephone, telegraph, or other similar means.

(3) No one may violate the privacy of letters and the secrecy of other written documents and records, whether they are kept in privacy, or sent by mail or in any other way, with the exception of cases which shall be laid down by law. Equally guaranteed is the secrecy of messages conveyed by telephone, telegraph, or other similar means.

The secrecy of telecommunication is recognized as a fundamental right in Art. 22 of the Constitution and in Art. 13 of the Charter of Fundamental Rights and Freedoms. The written constitution or charter does not recognize the confidentiality and integrity of information systems. However, it can be interpreted from a more general fundamental right, e.g., the general protection of property contained in Art. 20 of the Constitution or in Art. 11 para. 1 of the Charter. Theoretically, the protection of informational self-determination could serve as a constitutional basis for the protection of cybersecurity. A cybersecurity law for Slovakia is currently in progress, unfortunately still with an unknown outcome. But it is highly probable that this legislative document will be inspired by Czech law.[80] Also, the same situation could be determined for the term "privacy." The term "privacy" in Slovak law has two main meanings. One of them denotes a general constitutional principle; another meaning of the term "privacy" (súkromie) emerges from the Civil Code (Act No. 40/1964 Coll.) and establishes civil remedies for cases of infringement:[81]

Protection of personhood

Section 11

An individual shall have the right to protection of his or her personhood, in particular of his or her life and health, civic honour and human dignity as well as of its privacy, name and expressions of personal nature.

Ultimately, the constitution or charter does not explicitly define the right to informational self-determination. In addition, the Slovak Constitutional Court has not yet answered this question. Only legal scholars and academic literature are currently arguing about the interpretation of this concept. [82]

---

[80] The Concept of Cybersecurity in Slovak Republic. Government materials. Online: https://lt.justice.gov.sk/Attachment/Vlastný%20materiál_docx.pdf?instEID=-1&attEID=75645&docEID=413095&matEID=7996&langEID=1&tStamp=20150218154455240

[81] Act No. 40/1964 Zb. – The Civil Code. Unofficial translation. Online: http://ceflonline.net/wp-content/uploads/Slovakia-Property-Relations.pdf

[82] Čičkánová, D.: Procesnoprávne aspekty práva na informačné sebaurčenie a práva byť zabudnutý. Bratislavské právnické fórum 2013. Bratislava: Univerzita Komenského, Právnická fakulta, 2013.

2. Proportionality of access to data

The doctrine of proportionality has constitutional origins, but it can now be seen as being applied by regular courts and even by administrative authorities. The methodological grounds for the proportionality of rights were established in a Decision of the Constitutional Court No. P. ÚS 4/94. In this case, the Court assessed the constitutional compliance of the institution of anonymous witness and had to find a proportional balance between witness protection and the fair trial rights of the accused.

With respect to a proportionate balancing of rights, the Court ruled that (official translation[83]):

> When considering the possibilities of restricting a basic right or freedom for the benefit of another basic right or freedom the following conditions can be stipulated governing the priority of one basic right or freedom:
>
> The first condition is their mutual comparison, the other is the requirement to examine the substance and the sense of the fundamental right or freedom being restricted (Art. 4 para. 4 of the Charter of Fundamental Rights and Freedoms[1]).
>
> The mutual comparison of colliding fundamental rights and freedoms is based upon the following criteria:
>
> The first is the criterion of applicability, i.e. a reply to the question whether the institute restricting a certain basic right allows the achievement of the desirable aim (the protection of another basic right). In the given case the legislator can be affirmed in that the institute of anonymous witness allows to achieve the aim, i.e. to guarantee the inviolability of his person.
>
> The second criterion for measuring basic rights and freedoms is the criterion of necessity residing in the comparison of the legislative means restricting some basic right or freedom with other provisions allowing to achieve the same objective, however, without impinging upon fundamental rights and freedoms. The reply to the fulfilment of the criterion of necessity in the second case is not unambiguous: in addition to the legislative construction allowing the anonymity of the witness the government can use also other means for his protection (such as the utilization of anonymous testimony as a criminalistic means for further examination, offering protection to the witness, etc.).
>
> The third criterion is the comparison of the importance of both conflicting basic rights. In the case under consideration one of them is the right of fair trial ensuring the right for personal freedom, the other is the right of personal inviolability. These basic rights are prima facie equal.
>
> The comparison of the importance of colliding basic rights (after having fulfilled the condition of appropriateness and necessity) resides in weighting empirical, systemic, contextual and value oriented arguments. As an empirical argument the factual seriousness of a phenomenon can be understood that is connected with the protection of certain fundamental right (in the case under consideration this is the increasing number of cases of threatening and terrorising of witnesses by organized crime). A systemic argument means considering the sense and the classification of the respective fundamental right or freedom within the system of basic rights and freedoms (the right to fair trial in this

---

[83] Decision No. Pl. ÚS 4/94, English translation available at http://www.usoud.cz/en/decisions/?tx_ttnews%5Btt_news%5D=611&cHash=f69da5fcba1a2e433d74385371b3a196

connection is part of the general institutional protection of basic rights and freedoms). As contextual argument also further adverse impacts of the restriction of one fundamental right due to the favouring another right can be understood (in the given case the possibility of misusing the institute of anonymous witness in the criminal procedure). The value argument represents considering the positive aspects of the conflicting fundamental rights as regards the accepted hierarchy of values.

Part of comparing the relative weight of the conflicting basic rights is also considering the utilization of legal institutes minimizing the intervention into one of them, supported by arguments.

As a result, the Court established a three-step test that consists of the following parts:

- Suitability – whether the respective limitation of fundamental right(s) is able to serve the desired purpose.
- Necessity – whether there might not be some other alternative ways to achieve the desired effect without the need to limit respective fundamental right(s).
- Proportionality *stricto sensu* – whether there is a reason to prefer *ad hoc* one fundamental right over another.

If some limitation of a fundamental right is able to pass the above test, the additional need arises to assess whether the respective fundamental right will be limited only to a necessary extent. This assessment, also known as the limited proportionality test, is in many cases crucial. In the above cited case of anonymous witness as well as in the case of data retention, the respective instruments went through all three tests. This means that the court stated that these measures were fit for the purpose, there we no reasonable alternatives, and there was a reason to prefer certain fundamental rights over others. However, the court held that the way in which these instruments were legislated into statutory law leads to a greater than necessary impact on respective fundamental rights. In other words, the Constitutional Court regularly holds that an instrument is proportionate *per se*, but it needs to be legislated using less intrusive measures or implementing more safeguards/balances.

The Czech doctrine of proportionality is to large extent inspired by German constitutional practice as well as by the teachings of German legal scholars. Consequently, fundamental rights are all methodologically treated as legal principles, which means that none of them is *per se* superior to the other (their mutual relations have to be always resolved *ad hoc* in case of their collision). Thus, it is impossible to state, e.g., that privacy is generally more relevant than freedom of speech – on the contrary, every conflict of fundamental rights (or, in general, constitutional principles) has to be assessed on a case-by-case basis.

a) Implications for invasions of the secrecy of telecommunication

The doctrine of proportionality has been used in a number of cases, namely with regard to wiretapping. In most cases, the courts (the Supreme Court and the Constitutional Court) did not assess the mere question of *whether* wiretapping is compliant with a proportionate understanding of constitutional rights, but it also reviewed only *how* wiretapping was used in a particular case, including its procedural aspects. This means that in the Czech judicial practice wiretapping is not normally subject to review as to its mere existence but rather as to the form in which it is used in specific cases.

One specific issue in a number of cases also considered by the Constitutional Court was in the transferability of wiretapped records. In this respect, the Court had to deal with subjective and substantive transfers. Substantive transfers are those that occur when, e.g., the police receive a court order for wiretapping based on a specific suspicion of a crime and it later turns out that it might be used as an evidence in a different criminal matter (e.g., the court order is obtained for the suspicion of fraud and it turns out later that wiretapped data can be used as crucial evidence in a case of blackmail). In these cases, the Constitutional Court has regularly ruled in favour of such use of wiretapped data.

In contrast, subjective transfers are those that take place not just based upon different causes but between different institutions. For instance, the domestic intelligence agency receives a court order for intelligence purposes and it turns out that the data can be used by the police in the investigation of a crime. In these cases, the Constitutional Court has regularly ruled against the admissibility of such evidence in criminal trials. However, it did rule that once the eventuality of possible use of wiretapped data by different institution arises, such institution is obliged to request a new order.

b) Implications for access to traffic data

In terms of protection of fundamental rights against state intrusions, the Czech Republic is substantially different from countries that did not suffer from the Nazi or Communist rule. Even 25 years after political changes in 1989, the general social assumption about the normal functioning of the state and its security institutions is *a priori* negative. Even the Supreme Administrative Court and the Constitutional Court present themselves as judicial bodies whose main purpose is to protect an individual against intrusions committed by the state. Consequently, there is significant level of suspicion about any new forms of state activity that intrude on individual constitutional rights.

Unlike some other EU Member States, the Czech Republic had data retention legislated prior to the adoption of the Directive. Upon its adoption, the provisions laid down in the Telecommunications Act were broadened as was also the range of state institutions entitled to ask for this data.

The recently applicable version of data retention legislation is valid after the Constitutional Court had ruled against its first implementation. Using the doctrine of proportionality, the Constitutional Court stated that the retention as such might be suitable to fulfil all three steps of the proportionality test, but that it does not meet the requirement of minimum possible intrusion (see *supra* II.A.2.).

The Court ruled that (official translation):[84]

> The primary function of the right of respecting private life is to provide space for development and self-realization of the individual personality. Apart from the traditional definition of privacy in its space dimension (protection of the home in a broader sense) and, in connection with the autonomous existence and public authority, undisturbed creation of social relationships (in a marriage, family or society), the right to respecting private life also includes the guarantee of self-determination in the sense of primary decision-making of an individual about themselves. In other words, the right to privacy also guarantees the right of an individual to decide, at their own discretion, whether and to what extent, how and under what circumstances the facts and information concerning their personal privacy should be made accessible to other entities. This aspect of the right to privacy takes the form of the right to informational self-determination, expressly guaranteed in Article 10, para. 3 of the Charter.
>
> The right to informational self-determination is thus a necessary condition not only for free development and self-realization of an individual, but also for establishing free and democratic communication rules. Put it simply, under the circumstances of an omniscient and omnipresent state and public authority, the freedom of expression, the right of privacy and the right of the free choice of behaviour and acting become virtually non-existent and illusionary.
>
> Although the prescribed obligation to retain traffic and location data does not apply to the content of individual messages [see Article 1, para. 2 of the Directive 2006/24/EC of the European Parliament and Council of 15 March on the retention of data generated or processed in connection with the provision of publicly available electronic communications services or of public communications networks and amending Directive 2002/58/EC (hereafter only as the Data Retention Directive) and the contested provisions of Section 97, para. 3, sentence 4) of Law No. 127/2005 Coll. on Electronic Communications and Amendment of Some related Acts (Act on Electronic Communications) in their latest wording] the data on the users, addresses, precise time, dates, places, and forms of telecommunications connection, provided that monitoring takes place over an extended period of time and when combined together, allows compiling detailed information on social or political membership, as well as personal interests, inclinations or weaknesses of individual persons.
>
> On condition that the criminal law allows for exercising the public interest to prosecute criminal activity by means of robust tools the use of which results in serious limitations of the personal integrity and fundamental rights and freedoms of an individual, then when applied, constitutional law limits have to be respected.
>
> Restrictions imposed on personal integrity and individual privacy (i.e. breaching the respect towards them) may only be applied as an absolute exception, provided it is deemed necessary in a democratic society, unless it is possible to meet the purpose pursued by the public interest in any other way and if it is acceptable from the perspective of the legal existence and respecting effective and specific guarantees against arbitrariness. Essential presumptions of a due process require that the individual be provided with sufficient guarantees against the potential abuse of power by the public authorities.

---

[84] Decision No. Pl. ÚS 24/10, English translation available at http://www.usoud.cz/en/decisions/?tx_ttnews%5Btt_news%5D=40&cHash=c574142df486769e0b435954fead08c3

> With respect to the seriousness and extent of the infringement of the right to privacy in the form of the right to informational self-determination (in the sense of Article 10, para. 3 and Article 13 of the Charter), represented by the use of the retained data, the legislature limited the possibility to use the retained data only for the purposes of criminal proceedings prosecuting serious crime and only in the case that such an objective cannot be achieved using any other means. In fact, this is anticipated not only by the Data Retention Directive, referred to above, but also by the provisions of Section 88, para. 1 of the Code of Criminal Procedure, defining the conditions for enacting interception and records of telecommunications operation ("on condition that criminal proceedings related to serious crime have been initiated"), from which the afore-mentioned legal regulation included in the provisions of Section 88a of the Code of Criminal Procedure as a whole deviates without any due reason, providing for the legal regulation in obvious contradiction to the opinions of the Constitutional Court.
>
> As for the examined case of global and preventive collection and retention of data on electronic communications, the need to have such guarantees available is becoming even more important to the individual owing to the current enormous and fast-moving development and occurrence of new and more complex information technologies, systems and communication tools, which unavoidably results in the borders between private and public space being blurred to the benefit of the public sphere, since in the virtual environment of information technologies and electronic communications (in the so-called cyberspace), every single minute, especially owing to the development of the Internet and mobile communications, thousands or even millions of items of data and information are recorded, collected and virtually made accessible, interfering with the private (personality) sphere of the individual, yet if asked, they would probably be reluctant to knowingly let someone else in.

We could speculate that the original draft of the reasoning of this decision might have contained even stronger statements about the actual constitutional disproportionality of the instrument of data retention as such. The final version of the reasoning, however, includes these formulations only in the form of rhetoric questions and only as a part of its *obiter dictum*. The very strong standing of the Court against the form in which data retention had been previously legislated can be in any case seen in the fact that respective provisions of Czech statutory law were repealed with immediate effect (this caused significant problems for law enforcement and security authorities in the interval between publication of the decision and adoption of new legislation).

In addition to above cited decision, the Constitutional Court also ruled against a provision that originally provided the opportunity to request traffic data for the purpose of criminal procedure. In this case, the Court basically stated that procedural safeguards when requesting of traffic data should analogically be as strong as those in the case of wiretapping. The Court ruled (official translation):[85]

> It may be summarised that although Section 88a of the Code of Criminal Procedure contains the complete legal regulation of the access of the bodies active in criminal proceedings to the telecommunication traffic data, this access is expressly conditioned only by stipulating that the relevant data may be identified exclusively for the purposes of clarification of the circumstances significant for the criminal proceedings. Although the as-

[85] Decision No. Pl. ÚS 24/11, English translation available at http://www.usoud.cz/fileadmin/user_upload/ustavni_soud_www/decisions/pdf/Pl_US_24-11.pdf

> sessment as to whether this condition has been met is granted to the presiding judge or the judge within the preliminary proceedings who decides on ordering such data, its very general and vague definition cannot be deemed sufficient, taking into account the absence of any further regulation concerning the subsequent disposal of the data, as well as in view of the fact that disclosing the data in question represents, in relation to the affected users of electronic communications services, an interference with their fundamental right to privacy in the form of the right to informational self-determination pursuant to Art. 10, para. 3 and Art. 13 of the Charter and Art. 8 of the Convention. Above all, the legislature failed to reflect at all in the contested provision the requirement of the proportionality of interference with fundamental rights with respect to the pursued goal, since the access to the data in question is provided for, in essence, as a common means of collecting evidence for the purposes of criminal proceedings, conducted even for any criminal offence. In view of the seriousness of the relevant interference with the private sphere of the individual, this limitation will only stand the test provided that it meets the conditions arising from the proportionality principle. This means that the access of the bodies active in criminal proceedings to the telecommunications traffic data may only come into question on condition that the purpose of the criminal proceedings cannot be achieved in any other way, that the legal regulation contains sufficient guarantees preventing the use of such data for any other purposes than those assumed by law, and that the restriction of the individual's right to informational self-determination does not amount to an excessive interference with respect to the importance of specific societal relationships, interests or values that are subject to the criminal offence for which the corresponding criminal proceedings are conducted. The contested provision does not respect these limitations, while this deficiency may not be eliminated even by means of the stipulated judicial review. In their decision making on ordering disclosure of the relevant data, courts may grant protection to the right to informational self-determination with respect to the facts of a particular case, yet their case law cannot replace the absence of a sufficiently definite and legitimate legal regulation, which is, pursuant to Art. 4, para. 2 of the Charter, a condition for placing limitations upon fundamental rights and freedoms in general.

In comparison with the case of substantive statutory provisions laying down mere data retention obligations, the procedural constitutional disproportionalities were not considered as equally problematic by the Constitutional Court, despite having been found unconstitutional. We could also speculate that the Court might have noted serious problems caused by the immediate effect of its prior decision on data retention. Consequently, Section 88a of the Code of Criminal Procedure was repealed with enough delay to enable the adoption of a constitutionally compliant alternative.

The Court also expressly stated that, although the statutory procedure was unconstitutional as such, it does not imply *per se* a lack of constitutional compliance (and subsequent inadmissibility of retained data as evidence) in individual criminal cases. Despite later attempts by several accused or sentenced individuals to challenge the admissibility of such evidence in their trials, the results were mostly in favour of actual admissibility. In this respect, we might state that the lack of proportionality of substantive and procedural statutory rules for data retention were, in practice, often remedied by the constitutionally compliant actions of respective police forces, state prosecutors, etc. In other words, the police or Public Prosecutor acted at a higher standard of protection of individual rights in certain cases compared to what was expressly demanded by the applicable law.

c) Implications for intrusion into information systems

For a relatively long time, Czech law did not include any instrument making it *per se* illegal to intrude on an information system. Criminal law as well as civil law or administrative law included specific provisions that made it possible to sanction destructive intrusions (e.g., those that led to the damage of these systems or revelations of data) or intrusions against certain types of systems (e.g., systems containing classified data). Yet, mere intrusion was not *per se* subject to any kind of legal sanctions.

From the beginning of 2010, the Czech criminal law contains different provisions providing for criminal liability in cases of simple intrusions. Consequently, it is possible to prosecute an offender upon proving the mere fact of intrusion (i.e., without the need to prove actual damage). The respective provisions of the Act No. 40/2009 Sb. the Criminal Code read as follows:

§ 182 Violating confidentiality of messages

(1) Whoever intentionally violates the confidentiality

a) of a closed letter or other document during the provision of postal services or transported by other transport services or transport facilities,

b) of data, text, voice, audio or video messages sent via electronic communications networks and attributable to an identified subscriber or user who receives the message, or

c) of non-public transmission of computer data into a computer system, from or within which, including electromagnetic radiation from a computer system, transferring such computer data, shall be punished by a prison sentence of up to two years or punishment by disqualification.

(2) Whoever with the intention to cause damage to another person or to procure an unauthorised benefit for themselves or another person

a) reveals the secret of which they learned from the document, telegram, telephone call or electronic transmission through a communications network, which was not intended for them, or

b) takes advantage of such secrets, shall be similarly punished.

(3) An offender shall be punished by a prison sentence of six months to three years or punishment by disqualification, if

a) they committed an act referred to in Subsection 1 or 2 as a member of an organised group,

b) they committed such an act out of reprehensible motives,

c) they caused substantial damage by committing such an act, or

d) they committed such an act with the intention of gaining a substantial benefit for themselves or someone else.

(4) An offender shall be punished by a prison sentence of one to five years or a monetary penalty, if

a) they committed an act referred to in Subsection 1 or 2 as an official person,
b) they caused large-scale damage by committing such an act, or
c) they committed such an act with the intention to procure another large-scale benefit for themselves or someone else.

(5) An employee of postal services, telecommunications services or computer system or anyone else engaged in communication activities who
a) commits an act referred to in Subsection 1 or 2,
b) intentionally allows another person to commit such an act, or
c) amends or suppresses the document contained in a postal consignment or transported by transport facilities or a report filed by non-public transmission of computer data, telephone, telegram, or in another similar manner, shall be punished by a prison sentence of one to five years, a monetary penalty or punishment by disqualification.

(6) An offender shall be punished by a prison sentence of three to ten years, if
a) they caused large-scale damage by committing an act referred to in Subsection 5, or
b) they committed such an act with the intention to procure another large-scale benefit for themselves or someone else.

§ 183 Breach of confidentiality of documents and other privately kept documents

(1) Whoever violates the confidentiality of documents or other documents, photographs, film or other recordings, computer data, or other documents kept privately by another person without authorisation, by publishing, making them available to third parties, or otherwise uses them, shall be punished by a prison sentence of up to one year, a punishment by disqualification, or forfeiture of items or other assets.

(2) An offender shall be punished by a prison sentence of up to two years, a punishment by disqualification, or forfeiture of items or other assets, if they committed an act referred to in Subsection 1 with the intention to procure material or other benefits for themselves or someone else, to cause damage to another person or other serious damage, or to jeopardise their social esteem.

(3) An offender shall be punished by a prison sentence of six months to five years or a monetary penalty, if
a) they committed an act referred to in Subsection 1 as a member of an organised group,
b) they committed such an act against another person for their actual or perceived race, ethnicity, nationality, political belief, religion, or because they are actually or allegedly non-religious,
c) they caused substantial damage by committing such an act, or
d) they committed such an act with the intention of gaining a substantial benefit for themselves or someone else.

(4) An offender shall be punished by a prison sentence of two to eight years, if
a) they caused large-scale damage by committing an act referred to in Subsection 1, or
b) they committed such an act with the intention to procure another large-scale benefit for themselves or someone else.

[…]

§ 230 Unauthorised access to computer systems and information media

(1) Whoever overcomes security measures and thus gains access to a computer system or part thereof without authorisation shall be punished by a prison sentence of up to one year, punishment by disqualification, or forfeiture of items or other assets.

(2) Any person who gains access to a computer system or information medium and

a) uses data stored in a computer system or information media without authorisation,

b) erases or otherwise destroys, damages, amends, suppresses, or corrupts the quality of data stored in a computer system or information media, or renders them unusable without authorisation,

c) forges or alters data stored in a computer system or information media so as to be considered authentic and according to them it was treated as if it was authentic data, notwithstanding the fact whether the data is directly readable and understandable, or

d) inserts data into a computer system or information media or performs any other intervention into the software or hardware of the computer or other technical data processing equipment without authorisation,

shall be punished by a prison sentence of up to two years, punishment by disqualification, or forfeiture of items or other assets.

(3) An offender shall be punished by a prison sentence of six months to three years, punishment by disqualification, or forfeiture of items or other assets, if they committed an act referred to in Subsection 1 or 2

a) with the intention to cause damage to another person or to obtain an unauthorised benefit for themselves or another person, or

b) with the intention to restrict the functionality of a computer system or other technical equipment for data processing without authorisation.

(4) An offender shall be punished by a prison sentence of one to five years or a monetary penalty, if

a) they committed an act referred to in Subsection 1 or 2 as a member of an organised group,

b) they caused substantial damage by committing such an act,

c) they caused substantial interference in the activities of the State Administration body, local government, court, or another public authority by committing such an act,

d) they procured a substantial benefit by committing such act for themselves or another person, or

e) they caused serious interference in the activity of a legal entity or natural person who is an entrepreneur by committing such an act.

(5) An offender shall be punished by a prison sentence of three to eight years, if ,

a) they caused large-scale damage by committing an act referred to in Subsection 1 or 2, or

b) they procured another large-scale benefit by committing such act for themselves or another person.

§ 231 Measures and possession of access devices and computer system passwords and other such data

(1) A person who intends to commit a criminal offence of violating confidentiality of messages under Section 182 Subsection 1 Paragraph b), c) or a criminal offence of unauthorised access to computer systems and information media under Section 230 Subsection 1, 2 produces, puts into circulation, imports, exports, transports, offers, provides,

sells, or otherwise makes available, procures for themselves or another person or possesses

a) a device or its component, process, instrument or any other means, including a computer programme, designed or adapted for unauthorised access to electronic communications networks, a computer system or part thereof, or

b) a computer password, access code, data, process or any other similar means with which they are able to gain access to a computer system or part thereof,

shall be punished by a prison sentence of up to one year, forfeiture of items or other assets, or punishment by disqualification.

(2) An offender shall be punished by a prison sentence of up to three years, punishment by disqualification, or forfeiture of items or other assets, if

a) they committed an act referred to in Subsection 1 as a member of an organised group, or

b) they procured a substantial benefit by committing such act for themselves or another person.

(3) An offender shall be punished by a prison sentence of six months to five years if they procured another large-scale benefit for themselves or another person by committing an act referred to in Subsection 1.

§ 232 Damage to computer systems and information medium records and intervention into the computer equipment out of negligence

(1) A person who violates, out of gross negligence, an obligation arising from their employment, occupation, position or function or one imposed by law, or one that is contractually assumed, and

a) destroys, damages, alters or renders unusable the data stored in a computer system or information media, or

b) makes an intervention into the hardware or software of the computer or other technical data processing equipment,

and thus causes substantial damage to the stranger's property, shall be punished by a prison sentence of up to six months, punishment by disqualification, or forfeiture of items or other assets.

(2) An offender shall be punished by a prison sentence of up to two years, punishment by disqualification, or forfeiture of items or other assets if they caused large-scale damage by committing an act referred to in Subsection 1.

The last article cited above provides for criminal sanctions only in cases in which damage to data is proven. It is analogous to the aforementioned provision in the repealed Criminal Code that originally served the purpose of protecting information systems against intrusions.

The inclusion of criminal sanctions for mere intrusion of information systems triggered a negative response mainly from computer scientists. There was even a popular petition against the adoption of new types of criminal conduct into the Criminal Code motivated by fears that the freedom of scientific research would be jeapordized (as with security assignments, research and development in computer sciences namely includes possession and use of intrusive tools that hypothetically fall under the above cited provisions). The Criminal Code, however, includes an escape clause (termed "material corrective" in Czech criminal law doctrine) that makes it possible to prosecute only conduct that is socially harmful. This requirement is laid down together with the *ultima ratio* principle in § 12 para. 2 that reads as follows (informal translation): "The criminal liability of an offender and the criminal consequences associated with it may only be applied in socially harmful cases where application of liability under another legal regulation is insufficient."

Comparative note – Slovakia

The doctrine of proportionality also has constitutional origins in the Slovak Republic. It is applied by Slovak Constitutional Court, very irregularly by regular courts, and even sometimes by administrative authorities. The methodological grounds of the concept of proportionality were explained in the Decision of the Constitutional Court No. II. ÚS 152/08 (unofficial translation): [86]

> "The proportionality test is typically based on the following three steps. The first step (A) is sufficiently important objective test (test of Legitimate aim / effect), accordingly the test of the suitability (Geeignetheit) or if action aims toward the goal which is enough important to justify intervention; the test of rational links between intrusion and intervention (authority order) and said methods (restricting the freedom of expression), if it is possible to achieve an acceptable target (the preservation of the personal honour).
>
> The second step (B) is the necessity test. It is the test of the necessity of used methods for the intrusion (Erforderlichkeit, necessity of the test, a test of subsidiarity), if there couldn't be used more moderate actions.
>
> Finally, the third step (C) is the proportionality test in stricto sensu (Angemessenheit test of proportionality in the strict sense, proporcionate effect), which includes both (C1) practical concordance (practical conformity), i.e. the test of preserving a maximum of both fundamental rights and second (C2) called as Alexy's weighing formula. An example of practical conformity could be a situation where the community instead of banning a meeting because in that place is at the same time held another meeting, involves police to conduct both meetings. [...] Weighing formula works with a three-level scale of values: 'low', 'medium' and 'substantial'. The intensity of intrusion to one of the fundamental right competes with the degree of the satisfaction rate of the second law in a collision. The intensity of intrusion and the degree of satisfaction have one of values-such as 'low', 'medium' and 'substantial.'"

The test has not been used regarding traffic data or intrusions into information systems in any notable case yet (it is usually used in conjuction with the preservation of personal honour, general publishing law, real estate law[87] or in cases regarding health insurance and profit[88]). One interesting case before the Constitutional

---

[86] Decision of the Slovak Constitutional Court No. II. ÚS 152/08. Online: http://portal.concourt.sk/

[87] Decision of the Slovak Constitutional Court No. PL. ÚS 3/00. Online: http://portal.concourt.sk/.

[88] Decision of the Slovak Constitutional Court No. Pl. ÚS 3/09. Online: http://portal.concourt.sk/.

Court on wiretapping has brought with it a minor explanation as regards the doctrine of proportionality, as the Court noted:[89]

> "Finally, the proportionality of the intrusion means that the intrusion can be executed only when it is necessary (the aim can not be achieved by moderate methods) and only in the spirit of the requirements placed on the democratic society of pluralism, tolerance and free spirit. […] The issuance of the order for the interception requires specific relevant explanatory argument, by which facts would fulfill the conditions laid down by law for the infringement of the right to privacy. The order or an approval can not be subject to review without such a reasoning relying on the specific facts.

Lawyers are anticipating the reasons for the recent decision of the Constitutional Court of Slovakia about mass surveillance of citizens, which has been held to be unconstitutional. So far, only the final outcome of the decision is known. The reasoning of the Court is expected to be available within three months, so perhaps the test of proportionality will be explained within the implications for access to traffic data.

3. Consequences for the interception of telecommunication

Historically, intrusive measures as well as protective instruments were primarily focused on real-time communication and specifically on telecommunication (nowadays indicated as "electronic communications"). Consequently, apart from the above cited Charter of Fundamental Rights and Freedoms, there is a set of more or less traditional black-letter rules that lay down in detail procedures for wiretapping and subsequent use of acquired data.

In contrast, Czech law does not have experience with stored communications, i.e., with data that, for some reason, are stored somewhere and could be also used as evidence or as security intelligence. The only examples of relatively detailed rules that are related to stored communications are those implemented for the retention of traffic data. In any case, there is still a lack of more detailed provisions for communications (data) stored on personal devices and those stored by providers of information society services apart from electronic communications service providers.

For example, acquisition and forensic analysis of mobile communication devices are subject to the same rules as the acquisition of any other tangible assets. Similarly, there are no specific rules for the police or other forces with investigative powers to request data that are stored, mostly with the consent of users, by providers of hosting services[90] that fall outside the licensing regulations for providers of ser-

---

[89] Decision of the Slovak Constitutional Court No. I. ÚS 114/2012 (informal translation). Online: http://portal.concourt.sk/Zbierka/2012/29_12s.pdf

[90] Art. 14 of Directive 2000/31/EC of the European Parliament and of the Council of 8 June 2000 on certain legal aspects of information society services, in particular electronic commerce, in the Internal Market ("Directive on electronic commerce").

vices of electronic communication. This, of course, does not mean that the police or the Prosecution Service would be entirely disqualified from working with stored e-mails or files in clouds – in these cases, they just have to apply general rules originally made with an entirely different teleology. Apart from the lack of efficiency, redundant formalities, or sometimes even the lack of logical sense (in some areas, the police uses the terms related to stored tangible assets in order to obtain stored data), this situation might also lead to a higher risk of *ad hoc* disproportionate infringement of constitutional rights. In the view of the national rapporteur, it is just a matter of time when the courts will start ruling against the admissibility of evidence obtained from stored communications if the general procedural tools used to acquire it did not *de facto* provide for enough safeguards as to informational self-determination or other individual (distributive) information rights.

a) Protection of the secrecy of telecommunication

Apart from the Charter of Fundamental Rights and Freedoms (cited *supra* II.2.1.), the secrecy of telecommunication is protected by a number of statutory provisions. In particular, the Act on Electronic Communications contains the following specific provisions (informal translation[91]):

§ 87

(1) The rights and obligations relating to personal data protection, not regulated in this Volume, shall be governed by a special legal regulation.

(2) For the purposes of this Volume, consent based on a special legal regulation shall also be understood to mean consent granted by electronic means, including, but not limited to, the completion of an electronic form on the Internet.

(3) Supervision over compliance with obligations while processing personal data according to this Act shall be provided by the Office for Personal Data Protection in accordance with a special legal regulation.

§ 88 Securing the protection of personal, traffic and location data and the confidentiality of communications

(1) An undertaking providing a publicly available electronic communications service is obliged to:

a) take technical and organisational measures to safeguard the security of the service in respect of the protection of natural persons' personal information in accordance with a special legal regulation, protection of traffic and location data, and confidentiality of the communications of natural persons and legal entities in providing the service; if necessary, the provider concerned shall, upon written agreement, also cooperate with the undertaking providing the communications network to provide protection,

b) prepare internal technical and organisational regulations to provide data protection and communications confidentiality in accordance with Clause (a) above; secure data protection and communications confidentiality with respect to the existing tech-

---

[91] Act No. 127/2005 Sb., English translation available online at http://www.mpo.cz/dokument156553.html.

nical capabilities and the costs needed to provide protection at a level adequate to the risks of compromising the protection,

c) inform the subscribers concerned about the specific risk of the disturbance of network security in relation to data protection in accordance with Clause (a) above, and if the risk is beyond the scope of the measures taken by the undertaking, it shall also inform the subscribers about all the possible ways of remedying the situation, including the costs associated therewith,

d) establish internal procedures for handling requests for access to users' personal data; at the request of the Office for Personal Data Protection, undertakings providing a publicly available electronic communications service shall provide it with information about these procedures, the number of applications received, the legal justification of such requests and their responses.

(2) An undertaking providing a publicly available electronic communications service shall submit to the Office, if the Office so requests, the regulations referred to in Subsection 1 (c). If the Office finds that those regulations are in contradiction with this Act, the Office shall immediately notify the undertaking to that effect and shall grant the undertaking a reasonable period of time to remove any deficiencies.

(3) The Office is entitled, having requested the submission of the regulations referred to in Subsection 1 (b), to inspect how the undertakings providing a publicly available electronic communications service comply with those regulations, with the exception of inspections of compliance with obligations relating to the protection of personal data.

(4) In the event of a breach of protection of the personal data of a natural person, the undertaking providing a publicly available electronic communications service shall notify this fact to the Office for Personal Data Protection without undue delay. Such a notification shall contain a description of the consequences of the breach of protection and the technical protection measures the undertaking has adopted, or proposes adopting.

(5) In the event of a breach of protection of the personal data of a user pursuant to Subsection 4 might have a particularly serious impact on the privacy of a natural person, or if an undertaking providing a publicly available electronic communications service failed to take measures to remedy this situation and which would have been sufficient to protect the personal data at risk, in accordance with an assessment by the Office for Personal Data Protection, it shall also notify this fact to the individual concerned and to the Office for Personal Data Protection. In this notification, the undertaking shall indicate the nature of the breach of personal data protection, recommendations for the implementation of interventions to mitigate the impact of the breach of personal data protection and the contact information location.

(6) The Office for Personal Data Protection is entitled, after investigating the situation resulting from the breach of protection pursuant to Subsection 4 above, to impose an obligation on an undertaking providing a publicly available electronic communications service to inform the individual concerned of the breach of personal data protection, if it has not already done so.

(7) An undertaking providing a publicly available electronic communications service shall maintain, only for the purposes of reviewing compliance with obligations pursuant to Subsections 4 and 5, a list of breaches of personal data protection, including information on the circumstances of the breach, its impacts and measures adopted to remedy the situation. An implementing legal regulation may lay down more detailed conditions under which the undertaking providing a publicly available electronic communications service is required to notify any breach of personal data protection, the format of such a notification and the manner in which the notification is to be made.

§ 88a

(1) A legal entity or a natural person providing a public communications network or a publicly available electronic communications service shall ensure that the traffic and location data stored in accordance with Section 97 Subsection 3 are of the same quality and subject to the same security and protection against unauthorised access, alteration, destruction, loss or theft or other unauthorised processing or use, as the information referred to in Section 88; this does not affect the obligations set out in a special legal regulation[34]).

(2) A legal entity or a natural person providing a public communications network or a publicly available electronic communications service shall draft internal technical and organisational rules to ensure data protection in accordance with Subsection 1; it shall provide data protection with regard to the existing technical possibilities and to the costs required to provide protection at a level appropriate to the risk of breach of protection. The provisions of Section 88 Subsections 2 to 7 shall apply mutatis mutandis to data protection under this provision.

§ 89 Confidentiality of communication

(1) Undertakings providing a public communications network or a publicly available electronic communications service shall implement technical and organisational measures to safeguard the confidentiality of the messages and the related traffic and location data, which are transmitted via their public communications network and the publicly available electronic communications services. In particular, such undertakings shall not admit any tapping, message storage, or any other types of interception or monitoring of messages, including the data contained therein and related thereto, by any persons other than the users, without the consent of the users concerned, unless otherwise provided in an Act[36]). This shall not be to the prejudice of the technical storage of data as needed for message transmission without affecting the confidentiality principle.

(2) A message means any information being exchanged or transmitted between a finite number of subscribers or users via the publicly available electronic communications service, except for the information transmitted as part of the public radio or television broadcasting service via the electronic communications network, unless it can be allocated to an identifiable subscriber or user receiving that information.

(3) Anybody wishing to use, or using, the electronic communications network for the storage of data or for gaining access to the data stored in the subscribers' or users' terminal equipment shall inform those subscribers or users beforehand in a provable manner about the extent and purpose of processing such data and shall offer them the option to refuse such processing. This obligation does not apply to activities relating to technical storage or access and serving exclusively for the purposes of performing or facilitating message transmission via the electronic communications network, nor does it apply to cases where such technical storage or access activities are needed for the provision of an information society service explicitly requested by the subscriber or user.

§ 90 Traffic data

(1) Traffic data mean any data processed for the purposes of the transmission of a message via the electronic communications network or for the billing thereof.

(2) An undertaking providing a public communications network or a publicly available electronic communications service who processes and stores traffic data, including the appropriate location data relating to a user or subscriber, shall erase such data, or render them anonymous, once they are no longer needed for message transmission, except as provided in Subsections 3 to 6. The obligation of the legal entity or natural person providing a public communications network or a publicly available electronic communi-

cations service to maintain traffic and location data in accordance with Section 97 shall remain unaffected.

(3) An undertaking providing a public communications network or publicly available electronic communications service shall store traffic data for services provided to a subscriber or user until such time as a dispute pursuant to Section 129 Subsection 3 has been resolved, or until the end of the period during which the prices may be billed or the provision of an electronic communications service may be legally challenged or settlement recovered.

(4) An undertaking providing a public communications network or a publicly available electronic communications service may process the traffic data essential for the billing of the service provided to a subscriber or user for access, to the end of the period during which payment may be recovered.

(5) Undertakings providing a public communications network or a publicly available electronic communications service may provide each other with data related to the provision of the service, including, but not limited to, data about the subscribers being connected, in order to ensure interconnection and access to the network, mutual billing, and identification of any abuse of the electronic communications network and services. Abuse of electronic communications networks and services means consistent late payment of bills in accordance with Section 64, or the making of malicious or annoying calls.

(6) For the purposes of marketing the electronic communications services, or for the provision of value-added services, the undertaking providing a publicly available electronic communications service may only process the data referred to in Subsection 1 above to the extend and for the period needed for such services or such marketing, provided the subscriber or user to whom the data relate have given their consent thereto. The subscriber or user may withdraw their consent to the processing of traffic data at any time.

(7) A value-added service means any service for which it is necessary to process traffic data – or location data other than traffic – beyond what is needed for the transmission of a message or for the billing thereof.

(8) The undertaking providing a publicly available communications service shall inform the concerned subscriber or user about the traffic data being processed and about the time for which such data may be processed for the purposes referred to in Subsections 3 to 5. For the purposes referred to in Subsection 6, the undertaking shall so inform the subscriber or user to whom the data apply before obtaining the consent of such a subscriber or user.

(9) An undertaking providing a public communications network and an undertaking providing a publicly available electronic communications service shall ensure that the traffic data processing, in accordance with Subsections 2 to 6 is restricted to:

a) the persons who were authorised to that effect by the undertaking and who are responsible for the billing or operations management, customer inquiries, fraud identification, electronic communications services marketing, or who provide value-added services, and
b) the extent essential for the activities referred to in Clause (a) above.

§ 91 Location data

(1) Location data means any data that are processed within the electronic communications network and that define the geographical location of the terminal equipment of a user of a publicly available electronic communications service.

(2) If an undertaking providing a public communications network or publicly available electronic communications service performs the processing of location data other than

traffic data, which have a bearing on a user or subscriber, such an undertaking shall render this data anonymous or obtain the user's or subscriber's consent to the processing of such data to the extent and for the period as needed for the provision of value-added services. Before gaining such consent, the undertaking shall inform the user or subscriber concerned about the type of location data to be processed other than traffic data, about the purpose and length of the processing and of whether the data are to be made available to a third party for the provision of value-added services. The user and subscriber may withdraw his/her consent to the data processing at any time.

(3) If the user or subscriber gave his/her consent to the processing of location data other than traffic data, the undertaking providing a public communications network or a publicly available electronic communications service shall offer the user or subscriber the operation of temporarily refusing the processing of the data in accordance with Subsection 2 above for every connection to the network of for every message transfer. Such an option shall be provided free of charge and only entail simple processes.

(4) An undertaking providing a public communications network, an undertaking providing a publicly available electronic communications service and an undertaking providing value-added services shall ensure that the data referred to in Subsections 2 and 3 are only processed by persons duly authorised and entitled to that effect by internal technical and organisational regulations within the meaning of Section 88 Subsection 1 (b); the processing must be restricted to the extent essential for the needs of such activities.

§ 92 Display of incoming call number

(1) An undertaking providing a publicly available telephone service is obliged, in the event that the opportunity is offered, to display the subscriber number:

a) of the calling subscriber, to offer the calling subscriber the possibility free of charge to prevent the display of his/her subscriber number for each individual call, using simple means. The calling subscriber shall have this option for each subscriber number,
b) of the calling subscriber, to offer the called subscriber the possibility of preventing the display of the calling subscriber number for incoming calls, using simple means and providing this function free of charge in justified cases, such justified cases being, without limitation, workstations from which personal crisis situations are solved (for example hot line services),
c) of the calling subscriber, and displaying this number before the call is actually connected, to offer the called subscriber the possibility of refusing the incoming calls, for which the calling subscriber restricted the display of his/her subscriber number, using simple means,
d) of the called subscriber, to offer the called subscriber the possibility of preventing the display of his/her subscriber number for the calling subscriber, using simple means and providing the service free of charge.

(2) The provisions of Subsection 1 (a) shall also apply to calls from the Member States of the European Union routed to third states. The provisions of Subsection 1 (b), (c) and (d) also apply to incoming calls from third states.

(3) Where display of the calling or called number is offered, the undertaking providing a publicly available electronic communications service shall inform the public of the possibilities referred to in Subsection 1 above.

(4) An undertaking providing a public communications network or a publicly available electronic communications service is entitled to cancel the barring of the display of the calling subscriber number:

a) temporarily, at the request of a subscriber, who has requested that a malicious or annoying call be traced; in such a case, the undertaking shall store and make accessible to the aggrieved subscriber information containing the calling subscriber identification, and
b) and continue to process the location data during the transmission of calls to every emergency call number operated by the relevant facility for the reception of such calls, even despite a temporary ban or the lack of consent from the subscriber concerned.

(5) An undertaking providing a public communications network or a publicly available electronic communications service shall make public in its commercial facilities, and in a manner allowing remote access, the mandatory procedures to be followed in order to impose the two options referred to in Subsection 4 above, and shall inform its subscribers to that effect.

§ 93 Abuse of electronic mail addresses of the sender

It is prohibited to use any electronic mail address to send a message or messages to third parties without the consent of the holder of that electronic mail address.

§ 94 Call forwarding

(1) Any undertaking providing a public communications network or a publicly available electronic communications service shall ensure, using simple means, that every subscriber can enjoy, free of charge, the possibility of preventing automatic forwarding of calls by a third party to the subscriber's terminal equipment.

(2) In the event that, during the provision of the publicly available electronic communications service, calls are forwarded automatically or in a concealed manner to another service or to a service provided by another undertaking, or a new connection is established, thereby increasing the price to be charged, the person providing the publicly available electronic communications service shall notify the user of this fact free of charge and allow him/her to stop the call before it is forwarded or a new call is established. If calls are forwarded or a new connection is established and, as a result, the price to be charged is increased without notification of the user to that effect by the person providing a publicly available electronic communications service at the increased price, the Office shall decide to stop the provision of such service.

§ 95 Subscriber directories

(1) Anybody gathering subscribers' personal data in order to issue a subscriber directory, whose purpose is to search for detailed contact information about persons on the basis of their names and, if applicable, other identifying elements, to the minimum extent necessary, shall:

a) inform the subscribers concerned, free of charge and before the inclusion of their data in the directory, of the purpose of the printed of electronic directory of subscribers, which is to be made available to the public either directly or through the subscriber directory inquiry services, as well as of other possibilities for its use, based on the search functions contained in the electronic versions of the directory,
b) obtain the prior consent of the subscribers to the publication of their personal data in accordance with Section 41 Subsection 5 and ensure that the subscribers have an opportunity to determine which of their personal data, from the range of information relevant for the purposes of the directory, as defined by the directory publisher, are to be included in the public directory; further, it must be ensured that the subscribers are able to verify such information and to request the amendment or removal of such information. At the same time, the person gathering such information must ensure

that the subscribers can indicate, with their personal information, that they do not wish to be contacted for marketing purposes. Non-inclusion in the public directory of subscribers, the verifications, corrections and removal of information from the directory and the information concerning the subscriber's wish not to be contacted for marketing purposes shall be free of charge.

(2) If the purpose of the public directory is other than to search for detailed contact information about a person on the basis of his/her name, and, if applicable, other identifying elements, to the minimum extent necessary, anybody intending to issue such a subscriber directory must first ask for the additional consent of the subscribers concerned.

§ 96

(1) It is prohibited to use electronic communications networks or services to offer any marketing advertising or any other method of offering goods or services to those subscribers who indicated in the public directory of subscribers in accordance with Section 95 Subsection 1 (b) or Section 95 Subsection 2 that they do not wish to be contacted for marketing purposes.

(2) It is prohibited to use electronic communications networks or services for the purposes of direct marketing by means of automated calling systems without human intervention (automatic calling equipment), facsimile machines or electronic mail, without the prior consent of the subscriber or user concerned.

(3) No undertaking providing subscriber directory enquiry services with information about subscriber numbers or other details may disclose any subscriber data not contained in the public directory.

(4) The provisions of Sections 95 and 96 shall apply mutatis mutandis to the data of subscribers who are legal entities.

(5) A provider of a publicly available electronic communications service, whose business interests are harmed by violations of the obligations set out in Subsections 1 to 4 above, is entitled to seek judicial protection on behalf of subscribers whose rights have been harmed by such behaviour. This does not affect the right of a party to pursue their claims in court in their own right.

The aforementioned provisions lay down in relatively detailed manner the duties of electronic communications service providers to protect substantive data (content), traffic data, and related metadata (e.g., directories) from unlawful interference. In any case, the aforementioned provisions, whenever they apply to personal data, act as *lex specialis* in relation to the Personal Data Protection Act.[92] Any subsequent forms of processing of personal data, including the rights of data subjects, limitations as to transfers of data to other jurisdictions, etc. are regulated by the Personal Data Protection Act. The subsequent applicability of the Act became apparent in a case in which a user requested traffic data from the operator of his mobile phone – his request was based on a general provision of the Personal Data Protection Act that lays down a duty on the part of a controller to inform the data subject, upon request, about any personal data thereof that are being processed. The respective provision reads as follows (informal translation):

---

[92] Act No. 101/2000 Sb., English translation available at https://www.uoou.cz/en/vismo/zobraz_dok.asp?id_org=200156&id_ktg=1107

§ 12 Data subject's access to information

(1) If the data subject requests information on the processing of his personal data, the controller shall be obliged to provide him with this information without undue delay.

(2) The contents of the information shall always report on:

(a) the purpose of personal data processing;

(b) the personal data or categories of personal data that are subject of processing including all available information on their source;

(c) the character of the automated processing in relation to its use for decision-making, if acts or decisions are taken on the basis of this processing the content of which is an interference with the data subject's rights and legitimate interests;

(d) the recipients or categories of recipients.

(3) For provision of this information the controller shall be entitled to require a reasonable reimbursement not exceeding the costs necessary for provision of information.

(4) The controller's obligation to provide the data subject with information pursuant to Article 12 may be met by a processor on behalf of the controller.

Apart from providers of services of electronic communication, it should be noted that general provisions of data protection law also apply to other information society providers (e.g., online messengers, hosting providers, etc.) However, these providers are not recognized by Czech law as telecommunication providers, so their obligations will not be dealt with here.

b) Protection of the confidentiality and integrity of information systems

The issues of confidentiality and integrity of information systems (and eventually of the third aspect of IT security, i.e., availability) do not constitute a specifically recognized constitutional principle. As noted above, they are constitutionally protected mainly through the protection of the respective systems as such (namely by the general protection of property) or by the protection of data that are stored therein (i.e., by the protection of informational self-determination, freedom of speech, freedom of scientific research, right to work, etc.).

Confidentiality and integrity, however, shape a specific part of Czech law on electronic communications. The respective provisions of the Act on Electronic Communications read as follows (informal translation):[93]

§ 98 The security and integrity of public electronic communications networks and services

(1) An undertaking providing a public communications network or a publicly available electronic communications service shall ensure the security and integrity of its network and the security of the services it provides. For this purpose, the undertaking is, in particular, entitles to adopt technical and organisational rules created in accordance with network plans pursuant to Subsection 2. With regard to the technical capabilities of these rules to ensure a level of security that corresponds to the existing level of risk,

---

93 Act No. 127/2005 Sb., English translation available online at http://www.mpo.cz/dokument156553.html

with the aim of preventing or minimising the impact of incidents on users and of the interconnection of networks. Security of networks and services means their ability to resist random incidents or unlawful or malicious actions that seriously compromise the availability or interoperability of services and network integrity.

(2) To ensure the integrity of public communications networks, the Office shall issue network plans (Section 62), in which it defines the basic characteristics of those networks and their interfaces which are essential for the interconnection of public communications networks, for access thereto, for the connection of non-public communications networks and to ensure the continuity of provision of those services which are provided through public communications services.

(3) An undertaking providing a public electronic communications network or a publicly available electronic communications service may adopt a measure to suspend provision of the service or to deny access to the service in cases where there is a threat or occurrence of a serious breach of the security and integrity or its network as a result of damage or destruction of electronic communications facilities, mainly due to major industrial accidents or natural disasters. Such suspension or denial of service must be restricted to the time strictly necessary and, if it is technically possible, access to emergency numbers must be maintained.

(4) An undertaking providing a public electronic communications network or a publicly available electronic communications service shall immediately inform the Office, the entities operating facilities for reception of emergency calls – and, using suitable means, also the users – about the serious breach to security and the loss of network integrity, the extent and reasons for the suspension of the services provided or the denial of access thereto, the measures adopted and of the expected time of removal of the causes pursuant to Subsection 3. The scope and form of the information to be provided shall be stipulated by the Office in an implementing legal regulation. In the event that this information is published in the public interest, the Office may inform the general public thereof in a suitable manner.

(5) Each year the Office shall submit to the Commission and the European Network and Information Security Agency (ENISA) a summary report for the previous calendar year, informing of the notifications and actions taken pursuant to Subsections 3 and 4, in the scope and format specified by the Commission.

(6) The Office may impose an obligation to carry out a safety audit on an undertaking providing a public communications network or a publicly available electronic communications service. This audit must be conducted by a qualified independent entity and the costs shall be borne by the undertaking. An undertaking providing a public communications network or a publicly available electronic communications service is also required, at the request of the Office, to submit to it the information needed to assess network security and integrity and service security, the safety audit and the results thereof.

§ 99 Security, integrity and service provision in crisis situations

(1) In a crisis situation, an undertaking providing a public communications network or a publicly available electronic communications service is required, following its own technical and organisational rules, to ensure the security and integrity of its network and the interoperability of the services provided. The particulars to be included in the technical and organisational rules are stipulated by the Office in an implementing legal regulation.

(2) An undertaking referred to in Subsection 1 above shall submit to the Office at its request documents specifying the technical and organisational rules referred to in Subsection 1 above and shall allow the Office to monitor compliance with these rules. In the event any discrepancy is found between these documents and the legal regulations, the

Office is entitled to inform the undertaking concerned of this fact and to set it a reasonable period within which such discrepancies are to be removed.

(3) An undertaking providing a public communications network or a publicly available telephone service is entitled, when a crisis situation is threatened or during a crisis situation39), at the request of the Ministry of Interior, to provide priority connections to the public communications network and access to the publicly available telephone service to crisis communications subscribers, in accordance with a special legal regulation. For that purpose, it is entitled, to the extent to which it is absolutely necessary, to restrict or suspend the provision of a publicly available telephone service. It shall immediately inform the Office of any restriction or suspension of a publicly available telephone service, including the scope thereof. This restriction may only be imposed for the period for which it is absolutely necessary, and access to emergency numbers must be maintained.

(4) In a crisis situation, an undertaking referred to in Subsection 1 above shall immediately inform the Office of any threat to or breaches of the security and integrity of its network and the security of services, including measures adopted or envisaged to remedy this situation and the date by which the causes are expected to be removed.

The above cited provisions of the Act on Electronic Communications cover providers of services of electronic communication. Apart from that, the confidentiality and integrity of information systems and information networks is also subject to the Cybersecurity Act[94] that defines its main aim, i.e., the security of information, in §2 c) as follows (informal translation): "Security of information means ensuring confidentiality, integrity and availability of information."

Under normal circumstances, the Cybersecurity Act applies to administrators of information and communication systems belonging to a specifically listed critical information infrastructure, to administrators of important information systems (specifically listed public information systems), and to administrators of important networks (i.e., networks with direct cross-border connectivity). Regardless of their nature (i.e., private or public entities), these entities are namely obliged to implement standard security measures and to report in real-time the occurrence of cybersecurity incidents to national or governmental CERT. They also have to obey administrative orders issued by the National Security Authority *(Narodni bezpecnostni urad)*. Similar to the case of the Act on Electronic Communications, lack of compliance is considered an administrative offense.

c) Protection of the core area of privacy

The only part of Czech law where privacy *stricto sensu* is explicitly tackled is private law. However, the Civil Code, despite being adopted only in 2012, reflects neither the recently problematic nature of the concept of privacy nor its current technological determination. As a result, the Civil Code includes only very general provisions whose meanings for everyday life in today's information society is highly uncertain.

---

[94] Act No. 181/2014 Sb., English translation available at https://www.govcert.cz/download/nodeid-1143/

Moreover, the Civil Code introduces an extremely broad concept of an asset *(vec)* – assets are considered anything (including rights) "distinguished from an individual and useful to humans." This traditional Austro-German concept was implemented into Czech law entirely recently and thus there is a substantial lack of case law that would clarify even basic interpretative questions. In particular, it is questionable whether personal data or other data that originate in the private information sphere of an individual might be considered as "assets." On the one hand, they can be distinguished from individuals (they can exist independently), on the other, they are still strictly related to individuals. This is similar to the situation with profiles on user-generated-content services processing personal data (e.g., social networks).

The relative uncertainty of the meaning of privacy *stricto sensu* in private law leads to problematic situations in practice because even very basic disputes have to be handled as serious cases. In such cases, even standard courts have to apply the doctrine of proportionality described in II.A.2. above. For example, the Regional Court of Brno had to decide a case in which the owner of an apartment building installed cameras into the entrance hall and justified their presence with the purpose of preventing theft from mailboxes. The court applied the full proportionality test and held that such an installation is not proportionate, as there are less privacy-intrusive alternatives available to achieve the same purpose (i.e., to preventively protect mailboxes).

The relatively vague nature of the meaning of the term "privacy" in Czech law (let it be constitutional or private law) causes the concept of privacy not to be used in administrative or criminal law. In particular, liability for administrative offenses and crimes is constructed upon more formally defined terms like "personal data," "traffic data," "correspondence," etc.

Comparative note – Slovakia

The same applies in the Slovak Republic. Intrusive measures as well as protective instruments were primarily focused on real-time communications and specifically on telecommunication. However, Slovak criminal law already has experience with stored data (communication). A new provision in the Code of Criminal Procedure states:[95]

§ 90 Safeguarding and surrendering computer data

(1) If the clarification of facts relevant for criminal proceedings requires to safeguard stored computer data, including operational data saved through the computer system, the presiding judge of a panel or a prosecutor prior to the commencement of criminal prosecution or in pre-trial proceedings, respectively, may issue an order based on circumstantial reasons to the person who has possession of or control over such data, or to the provider of such services, requesting them to

[95] *Ibid.* Code of Criminal Procedure.

a) safeguard and maintain integrity of such data,
b) enable making and keeping copies of such data,
c) prevent access to such data,
d) remove such data from the computer system,
e) surrender such data for the purposes of criminal proceedings.

(2) The order referred to in paragraph 1 shall have to specify the period during which the data are to be safeguarded, not exceeding 90 days; a new order shall have to be issued for any extension of that period.

(3) Where there is no longer a need to safeguard computer data, including operational data for the purposes of criminal proceedings, the presiding judge of a panel or a prosecutor prior to the commencement of criminal prosecution or in pre-trial proceedings, respectively, shall issue an order reversing the obligation to safeguard the data.

(4) The order referred to in paragraphs 1 to 3 shall be served on the person who has possession of or control over such data, or on the provider of such services, who may be also imposed the duty to treat the measures set out in the order as confidential.

(5) The person who has possession of or control over computer data shall surrender these data, or the provider of services shall surrender the information that is in his possession or under his control in connection therewith to the authority that issued the order pursuant to paragraph 1.

Another example is the provision implemented for the retention of traffic data in Act No. 361/2011 Coll. The Slovak Constitutional Court has repealed these provisions (Section 58 paras. 5, 6, 7 and 8) as unlawful in view of the European trends in mass surveillance issues:[96]

Section 58

(1) User identification means a unique identification code, login name, or other unique mark assigned to a subscriber at the conclusion of the contract of the provision of public services or to a user during a registration of the Internet access services or communications services via Internet.

(2) Cell identification (cell ID) means the identity of the radio mobile network cell from which a call via a mobile terminal equipment originated or terminated.

(3) For the purposes of retaining data under Subsections 5 to 8, telephone service means the ca lls inc lud ing te lep ho ne ca lls, vo ic e ma il, co nfere nce ca lls a nd da ta t ra ns mis s io n, supplementary services including call forwarding and call transfer and messaging and multimedia services including SMS, enhanced media services (EMS) and MMS.

(4) For the purposes of retaining data under Subsections 6 and 7, unsuccessful call attempt means the call which has been successfully connected to the calling party terminal equipment but such a call has not been answered by the called user or his terminal equipment or there has been a network management intervention.

(5) For the purposes under Subsection 7, the undertaking shall be obliged to retain traffic data, location data and data of the parties who communicated from the date of making the communication during:

a) Six months in case of Internet access, Internet electronic mail and telephoning through Internet, and
b) Twelve months in case of other types of communication.

96 *Ibid.* Code of Criminal Procedure.

(6) The undertaking shall retain data under Subsection 5 in the scope in which it produces or processes while provisioning a service or network. The undertaking shall retain the data under Subsection 5 related to the unsuccessful call attempts which the undertaking produces or processes and retain in terms of the telephone numbers, or records in case of the Internet data. The data related to unconnected calls shall not be retained. The list of data which the undertaking shall be obliged to retain under this Subsection and Subsection 5 is referred to in Annex2.

(7) On the basis of a written request and without delay, the undertaking shall be obliged to provide data retained under Subsections 5 and 6 including the subscriber's data in the scope under Section 63, Subsection 1, Letter b) under conditions set in Section 63, Subsection 6 to the bodies acting in the criminal proceedings, court and other state body for the purposes of investigation, detection and prosecution of criminal offences related to terrorism, illegal trading, organized criminal activity, leakage and threatening of the concealed facts and to criminal offences committed by dangerous grouping; the data and information shall be retained only in an electronic form.

(8) The undertaking shall be obliged to administer a yearly statistics on the retained data which shall contain:

a) A number of cases in which the required data was provided to other state bodies under Section 55, Subsection 6,
b) The time elapsed between the date on which the data were retained and the date on which an authority acting in a criminal proceedings, court or other state body requested the provision of the data, and
c) The number of cases where the requests for data could not be met.

(9) Statistics under Subsection 8 shall not contain personal data. The undertaking shall provide statistics under Subsection 8 to the Ministry within January, 31 of the next year. The Ministry shall subsequently submit statistics to the European commission.

(10) Where retaining the data under Subsection 6, the undertaking shall ensure that:

a) The retained data shall be of the same quality and subject to the same security and protection as the data which the undertaking processes or retains when providing networks or services,
b) The data shall be subject to the relevant technical and organisational measures to protect the data against accidental or unlawful destruction, accidental loss or alteration, unauthorised or unlawful storage, processing, access or publishing,
c) The data shall be subject to the relevant technical and organisational measures to ensure that the data can be accessed by the authorised persons only acting under the authority or power of attorney of the undertaking and authorities acting in a criminal proceedings, court or other state bodies and their entrusted or otherwise authorised members or staff,
d) The data, except those that have been provided and secured, shall be destroyed at the end of the period of retention.

Protection of the confidentiality and integrity of information systems is also a specific part of the Slovak law on electronic communications. The respective provisions of the Act on Electronic Communications read as follows (informal translation):[97]

---

[97] Act No.351/2011 Zb. on electronic communication. Unofficial translation. Online: http://www.teleoff.gov.sk/data/files/22211.pdf

Section 64 Security and integrity of public networks and services section

(1) The undertaking that provides public networks or public services shall be obliged to take appropriate technical and organisational measures to protect security of its networks and services, which with regard to the technology state shall ensure such a level of security that is adequate to the risk posed. Measures shall be taken in particular to prevent and minimise impact of security incidents on users and interconnected networks.

(2) The undertaking that provides public networks shall be obliged to maintain integrity of its networks in order to ensure the continuity of provisioning services over those networks.

(3) The undertaking that provides public networks or services shall be obliged, without delay, to inform the Office about a breach of security or integrity that has had a significant impact on the operation of networks or services.

(4) If it is in the public interest, the Office shall publish information under Subsection 3 or, on the basis of a request of the Office, the undertaking shall publish such information.

(5) In case of a particular risk of a breach of the network security, the provider of public services shall be obliged to inform subscribers concerned about such a risk and any possible remedies, including likely costs necessary to avert the threat.

(6) The undertaking that provides public networks or services shall be obliged:

a) Upon the request of the Office, to provide the relevant information necessary to assess security and integrity of its services and networks, including the documented security policies,
b) To enable a security audit carried out by a qualified independent person selected by the Office or the Office itself, while the cost of the audit shall be covered by the undertaking.
c) To provide the results of the audit to the Office and, upon the request, the Office for protection of personal data,
d) To cooperate with the Office in investigation of cases of non-compliance with regulations and their impact on network security and integrity and, upon the request, to provide the Office with relating relevant information.

(7) The details on maintaining the network integrity and parameters thereof and the notification obligation of the undertaking under Subsections 3 to 5 and 6, Letter a) shall be regulated by a generally binding legal regulation issued by the Office.

(8) The undertaking providing public networks and associated facilities shall be obliged to ensure that its network and associated facilities comply with technical standards and technical specifications for networks or services under Section 14, Subsection 2, Letter q) in terms of:

a) Network traffic security,
b) Network integrity maintaining,
c) Service interoperability,
d) Terminal equipment connection.

(9) Where appropriate, the Office shall provide information under Subsection 3 to regulatory authorities in the Member States and agency ENISA[47]. The Office shall annually submit the European Commission and ENISA a summary report on the notifications under Subsection 3 and any related measures taken.

Furthermore, the protection of the confidentiality and integrity of information systems and information networks is the main subject of cybersecurity law, which is currently in the making. Protection of the core area of privacy is also defined *stricto sensu* by the 1964 Civil Code. This outdated legislation does not reflect the currently problematic nature of the concept of privacy or its current technological determination. As in the new Czech Civil Code, it includes only very general provisions whose meanings for the everyday life of our information society are highly impractical.

4. Statutory protection of personal data

a) Criminal liability for the unlawful infringement of telecommunication

The Criminal Code offers a number of options that cover different possibilities of unlawful interference with communication networks. The Czech Republic is a party to the Budapest Treaty, so these provisions reflect standard types of crimes laid down therein. In particular, unlawful interference can be typically subsumed under the following crimes (full texts of respective provisions are cited *supra* II.A.2.c):

- § 182 Violating Confidentiality of Messages
- § 230 Unauthorised Access to Computer Systems and Information Media

It is worth noting that specific provisions of the Act on Electronic Communications and the Cybersecurity Act lay down technical requirements for providers of various telecommunication services. As a result, there is a reason to expect that such services are properly technically secured and that any unlawful interference would require overcoming certain security measures. Thus, it is also possible to sanction the unlawful interference through the possession crime aimed at devices and tools (including passwords), the aim of which is to access protected systems or networks – in particular, the Criminal Code provides for § 231 Measures and Possession of Access Devices and Computer System Passwords and other such Data (full text is cited *supra* II.A.2.c).

It can also be noted that Czech criminal law also sanctions preparatory activities as well as attempted crimes. The respective provisions read as follows (informal translations[98]):

§ 20 Premeditation

(1) Conduct that is based in an intentional creation of conditions for the commission of a particularly serious crime (Section 14 Subsection 3), especially in its organisation, the acquisition or adaptation of the means or instruments for its commission, in conspiracy, unlawful assembly, in the instigation or aiding of such a crime, shall be deemed a premeditation only if the criminal law applicable for a specific criminal offence expressly stipulates for it and an attempt or completion of a particularly serious crime did not occur.

[98] Act No. 40/2009 Sb., citation of the English translation taken from the legal information system ASPI.

(2) Premeditation is punishable pursuant to the criminal penalty set out for a particularly serious crime to which it leads, unless the criminal law stipulates otherwise.

(3) Criminal liability for the premeditation to commit a particularly serious crime shall expire if an offender voluntarily waived further conduct towards the commission of a particularly serious crime and

a) removed the risk to an interest protected by criminal law which occurred due to the attempted premeditation, or

b) reported the premeditation to commit a particularly serious crime at a time when the risk to an interest protected by criminal law which occurred due to the attempted premeditation could still be removed; reporting must be performed to the public prosecutor or the police authority. A soldier may report it to their commander.

(4) If there are several persons involved in an act, the criminal liability for the premeditation is not void in the case of an offender who acted in such manner, despite their timely reporting or earlier participation in such act, if it is completed by other offenders.

(5) The provisions of Subsection 3 and 4 shall have no effect on the criminal liability of an offender for any other committed criminal offence which they have already committed by their conduct pursuant to Subsection 1.

§ 21 Attempt

(1) Any conduct that leads directly to the completion of a criminal offence and which the offender committed with the intention of the commission of a criminal offence, if the completion of the criminal offence did not occur is defined as an attempt to commit a criminal offence.

(2) An attempted criminal offence shall be punishable under the criminal penalty set for a completed criminal offence.

(3) Criminal liability for an attempted criminal offence shall expire if an offender voluntarily waived further conduct leading to the completion of a criminal offence and

a) removed the risk to an interest protected by criminal law which occurred due to the attempted criminal offence, or

b) reported the attempted criminal offence at a time when the risk to an interest protected by criminal law which occurred due to an attempted criminal offence could still be removed; reporting must be performed to the public prosecutor or the police authority. A soldier may report it to their commander.

(4) If there are several persons involved in an act, the criminal liability for an attempt is not void in the case of an offender who acted in such manner, despite their timely reporting or earlier participation in such act, if it is completed by other offenders.

(5) The provisions of Subsection 3 and 4 shall have no effect on the criminal liability of an offender for any other completed criminal offence which they have already committed by their conduct pursuant to Subsection 1.

Stored communications are protected by the criminal law namely through the crime defined in § 183 as Breach of Confidentiality of Documents and other Privately Kept Documents (full text is cited *supra* II.A.2.c). Subsequently, it is also possible to use § 230 Unauthorised Access to Computer Systems and Information Media and § 231 Measures and Possession of Access Devices and Computer System Passwords and other such Data.

In any case, it is relatively complicated to formulate doctrinal opinions about specific elements of the aforementioned protective provisions, as relevant case law is still lacking. For example, there have been no cases so far that would provide answers as to the applicability of § 230 or § 231 in relation to decryption keys or other tools making it possible to work with encrypted data.

b) *Protection of professional secrets in criminal procedure*

Czech law does not have a common denominator for professional secrets. However, certain types of data are specifically protected in criminal procedural law through the general protection of confidentiality and protection of classified information. Duties of secrecy are contained in different parts of Czech statutory law. The most important examples for the scope of this study include duties of attorney-client privilege laid down in the Advocacy Act,[99] those defined in medical law (confidentiality of health records), banking law (confidentiality of bank account data), those defined in the Act on Electronic Communications, and those laid down in the Cybersecurity Act (secrecy of records on cybersecurity incidents). Some secrecy duties are very specific. For example, with regard to security files, i.e., personal files assembled by the National Security Authority in the course of evaluation of applicants for security clearance (i.e., for permission to handle classified information), there are only extremely exceptional cases in which, together with client data held by solicitors, these data might be used in criminal proceedings. For other types of data covered by secrecy duties, respective statutory provisions always contain relatively easily applicable procedures for the exclusion of secrecy duties.

The main provision covering the use of data where secrecy duties apply is contained in Section 8 of the Code of Criminal Procedure that reads as follows (informal translation):

§ 8

(1) Public authorities, legal entities and natural persons are required to comply with letters of request from law enforcement authorities for the performance of their actions without undue delay and unless a special regulation stipulates otherwise, to comply without payment. Furthermore, public authorities are also obliged to immediately notify the public prosecutor or the police authorities of facts indicating that a criminal offence has been committed.

(2) If the criminal proceedings require a proper investigation of the circumstances suggesting that a criminal offence has been committed or to assess the circumstances of the accused during court proceedings or for the enforcement of a decision, the public prosecutor and, after the indictment or a punishment petition, the presiding judge may request information that is subject to banking secrecy and data from the security register. Pursuant to Section 180 of the Penal Code, the law enforcement authority may request individual data obtained under a special Act for statistical purposes during the criminal proceedings. The conditions under which the law enforcement authority may require the data obtained in the administration of taxes are stipulated under a special Act. Data ob-

[99] Act No. 85/1996 Sb., English translation available at http://www.cak.cz/assets/act-on-legal-profession_219_2009.pdf

tained under this provision may not be used for a purpose other than the criminal proceedings for which such data was requested.

(3) For the reasons as stated in Subsection 2, the presiding judge may, and upon the proposal of the public prosecutor during a preliminary hearing, order the surveillance of the bank accounts or accounts of persons entitled to the records of investment instruments under a special Act for a maximum period of six months. If the reason for which the surveillance of an account was ordered exceeds this time, it may be extended upon the order of a judge from a court of higher instance and, during preliminary hearing, upon the proposal of the public prosecutor of the County Court judge for a further six months, and such prolongation can be performed repeatedly. Information obtained under this provision may not be used for a purpose other than the criminal proceedings for which it was obtained.

(4) The performance of obligations under Subsection 1 may be rejected with reference to the obligation to maintain the secrecy of classified information protected by a special Act or imposed by the State or the recognised duty of confidentiality; this does not apply,

a) if the person who has the obligation would otherwise risk criminal prosecution for the failure to notify or prevent a criminal offence, or

b) in executing the request of a law enforcement authority with regards to a criminal offence, where the requested person is also the reporter of the criminal offence.

The State recognised obligation of confidentiality under this Act does not consider such obligation the scope of which is not defined by law but instead arises from a legal action taken under the law.

(5) Unless a special Act stipulates the conditions under which information may be disclosed for the purpose of criminal proceedings that are deemed classified pursuant to such Act or which is subject to an obligation of secrecy, such information may be requested for criminal proceedings upon the prior consent of the judge. This does not affect the obligation of confidentiality of an attorney under the Advocacy Act.

(6) The provisions of Subsection 1 and 5 shall not affect the obligation of confidentiality imposed on the basis of a declared international treaty to which the Czech Republic is bound.

It is to be noted that recognised by criminal procedural law are only those secrecy duties that are laid down by statutory law (not those that are e.g. established between parties by a non-disclosure agreements).

The provision cited above might imply that the most sensitive type of data covered by secrecy duties are those of a client that are processed by his/her solicitor. Their higher level of statutory protection is based on the right to a fair trial, which also includes the right to professional representation before the court. Such representation involves the client being able to openly provide his/her solicitor with complete data about his/her case (including information that might not be favourable to her court standing). Consequently, such data have to be excluded from being available to the prosecutors or the police. Therefore, when data processed by solicitors are to be gathered and used in criminal proceedings, a special procedure involving the bar association and a court decision is required.

The so-called "advocate confidentiality," namely its range and possibilities for abuse, is permanently under debate in the Czech Republic. On the one hand, solicitors tend to abuse this statutory limitation when dealing with corruption, money laundering, operations prohibited by antitrust laws, etc.[100] On the other hand, the Public Prosecution Service is constantly testing the boundaries of this statutory protection and hence raids on stored solicitor communications are not uncommon.

Recently, a highly debated case was decided in which the Public Prosecution Service requested permission to search a cloud storage facility that contained solicitor communications.[101] The respective law firm refused to provide the requested data with reference to the aforementioned "advocate confidentiality." The Public Prosecution Service requested a court warrant. The court held, however, that data stored in a cloud, i.e., off the premises of the solicitor, should not be regarded as client-solicitor communication – solicitors are obliged to keep such data under their physical control. The court considered their storage on a cloud service as a proof of the fact that these data are not to be regarded solicitor-client communication.

This decision triggered strong reactions from the Bar Association and its members, because it can be technically interpreted in a sense that data protected under "advocate confidentiality" are only those that are physically stored within the premises of respective solicitors. This would technically disable solicitors from using cloud services (even those based on specifically rented secure servers). However, the reasoning of the decision was not very specific as to the technical details under which seizure of solicitor data in the cloud is possible, so there is reason to expect further development in the Czech case law on this matter.

c) Principle of "purpose limitation of personal data"

The principle of purpose limitation of personal data is incorporated in the Personal Data Protection Act. The most important provisions laying down purpose limitation read as follows (informal translation):[102]

§ 5

(1) The controller shall be obliged to:

(a) specify the purpose for which personal data are to be processed;

[…]

(d) collect personal data corresponding exclusively to the specified purpose and in an extent that is necessary for fulfilment of the specified purpose;

(e) preserve personal data only for a period of time that is necessary for the purpose of their processing. After expiry of this period, personal data may be preserved only for purposes of the state statistical service, and for scientific and archival purposes.

---

[100] This was noted even in a decision of the Constitutional Court No. III ÚS 3988/13, available in Czech (no known English translations are available to date) at http://nalus.usoud.cz/Search/ResultDetail.aspx?id=83083&pos=1&cnt=1&typ=result

[101] Interim decision (usneseni) No. Nt 615/2014, available in Czech (no known English translations are available to date) at http://www.scribd.com/doc/235322741/Nt-615-2014

[102] Act No. 101/2000 Sb., English translation available at https://www.uoou.cz/en/vismo/zobraz_dok.asp?id_org=200156&id_ktg=1107

When using personal data for these purposes, it is necessary to respect the right to protection of private and personal life of the data subject from unauthorised interference and to make personal data anonymous as soon as possible;

(f) process personal data only in accordance with the purpose for which the data were collected. Personal data may be processed for some other purpose only within the limits of the provisions of Article 3(6) or if the data subject granted his consent herewith in advance;

[…]

(h) ensure that personal data that were obtained for different purposes are not grouped.

(2) The controller may process personal data only with the consent of data subject. Without such consent, the controller may process the data:

(a) if he is carrying out processing which is essential to comply with legal obligation of the controller;

(b) if the processing is essential for fulfilment of a contract to which the data subject is a contracting party or for negotiations on conclusion or alteration of a contract negotiated on the proposal of the data subject;

(c) if it is essential for the protection of vitally important interests of the data subject. In this case, the consent of data subject must be obtained without undue delay. If the consent is not granted, the controller must terminate the processing and liquidate the data;

(d) in relation to personal data that were lawfully published in accordance with special legislation. However, this shall not prejudice the right to the protection of private and personal life of the data subject, or

(e) if it is essential for the protection of rights and legitimate interests of the controller, recipient or other person concerned. However, such personal data processing may not be in contradiction with the right of the data subject to protection of his private and personal life;

(f) if he provides personal data on a publicly active person, official or employee of public administration that reveals information on their public or administrative activity, their functional or working position, or

(g) if the processing relates exclusively to archival purposes pursuant to a special Act.

(3) If the controller processes personal data on the basis of a special Act, he shall be obliged to respect the right to protection of private and personal life of the data subject.

[…]

The above cited provisions are general and apply to all sorts of personal data, including data processed by providers of electronic communications services, information society services, etc. General purpose limitation, however, does not apply to security, defence, and law enforcement bodies, as these are exempted by § 3 para. 6, which reads as follows (informal translation):

The provisions of Article 5(1) and Articles 11 and 12 of this Act shall not apply to processing of personal data necessary to fulfil obligations of the controller provided by special Acts to ensure:

(a) security of the Czech Republic,

(b) defence of the Czech Republic,

(c) public order and internal security,

(d) prevention, investigation, detection and prosecution of criminal offences,

(e) important economic interest of the Czech Republic or of the European Union,

(f) important financial interest of the Czech Republic or of the European Union, in particular the stability of financial market and currency, functioning of currency circulation and system of payments as well as budgetary and taxation measures, or
(g) exercise of control, supervision, surveillance and regulation related to exercise of public authority in the cases under (c), (d), (e) and (f), or
(h) activities related to disclosure of files of the former State Security.

The exemption of the aforementioned authorities and public bodies from general purpose limitation does not mean that the purpose limitation would not apply at all. Such processing is also limited by its purpose, because the Act expressly states that processing powers are to ensure (i.e., the purpose of) security, defence, etc. Respective state authorities and other bodies are then limited as to the scope and methods of processing of personal data by statutes that specifically define their powers. All such authorities are then internally and externally supervised, so the purpose limitation applies not directly through the Personal Data Protection Act but through regular limitations and supervisory powers over their activities. It is also to be noted that a general constitutional principle applies about the possibility of state institutions to engage only in operations that are expressly ordered or permitted by the law – this principle is laid down in Art. 2(3) of the Constitution that reads as follows (official translation):[103] "State power shall serve all citizens and may be applied only in cases, within limits and by methods defined by law."

Comparative note – Slovakia

The Slovak Penal Code (Act No. 300/2005 Coll.) covers criminal liability for the unlawful infringement of telecommunication. Likewise, the Slovak Republic is a member of the Budapest Treaty,[104] so these provisions reflect standard types of crimes. Typical crimes are breach of mailing secrets; harm done to and abuse of an information carrier; and breach of confidentiality of spoken utterance and other personal expression. The Slovak Penal Code reads as follows: [105]

Section 196 Breach of mailing secrets

(1) Any person who intentionally breaches

a) the secrecy of letter through spying or opening a sealed letter or other written communication delivered by postal service or in other habitual manner,
b) the secrecy of information transferred via electronic communication service, or

[103] Constitutional Act No. 1/1993 Sb., English translation available at http://www.psp.cz/cgi-bin/eng/docs/laws/1993/1.html

[104] Budapest Convention on Cybercrime. Online: http://conventions.coe.int/Treaty/Commun/QueVoulezVous.asp?NT=185&CM=8&DF=02/06/2010&CL=ENG

[105] Act. No. 300/2005 Zb. Penal Code. Unofficial translation: Ďurčová, M. Online: www.legislationline.org/documents/id/16895

c) the secrecy of private transfer of computerized data to the computer system, out of it or within it, including electromagnetic radiation from computer system transferring such computerized data,

shall be liable to a term of imprisonment of up to three years.

(2) Any employee of the provider of postal service or electronic communication service who commits the offence referred to in paragraph 1, or wilfully enables another to commit such offence, or who alters or withholds a written communication delivered by postal service or in other habitual manner or communication transferred via electronic communication service shall be liable to a term of imprisonment of one to five years.

(3) The offender shall be liable to a term of imprisonment of four to ten years if he commits the offence referred to in paragraphs 1 or 2,

a) and causes substantial damage through its commission,

b) by reason of specific motivation, c) acting in a more serious manner.

Section 247 Harm done to and abuse of an information carrier

(1) Any person who, with the intention to cause damage or other prejudice to another, or to obtain unjust benefit for himself or other, gains access without lawful authority to a computer system, an information carrier or the part thereof and

a) makes unauthorised use of his information,

b) unlawfully destroys, damages, deletes, alters such information or reduces their quality,

c) makes an unauthorised intervention into the computer hardware or software, or

d) obstructs the operation of computer system by inserting, transferring, damaging, deleting,

reducing the quality, modifying or suppressing the computer data, or creates non-authentic data with the intention to be deemed or handled as authentic ones for legal use,

shall be liable to a term of imprisonment of between six months and three years.

(2) The same sentence as referred to in paragraph 1 shall be imposed on the offender who, with the intention to commit the offence referred to paragraph 1,

a) using technical means, makes an unauthorised monitoring of the closed transfer of computer data into the computer system, out of or within it, or

b) procures or makes accessible a computer programme and other equipments or computer password, access code or similar data enabling the access to the computer system in its entirety or to the part thereof.

(3) The offender shall be liable to a term of imprisonment of one to five years if he commits the offence referred to in paragraphs 1 or 2, and causes substantial damage through its commission.

(4) The offender shall be liable to a term of imprisonment of three to eight years if he commits the offence referred to in paragraph 1, a) and causes large-scale damage through its commission, or b) as a member of a dangerous grouping.

Section 377 Breach of confidentiality of spoken utterance and other personal expression

(1) Any person who breaches the confidentiality of private spoken utterance or other personal expression by its unlawful recording, and makes such recording accessible to a third person or uses it otherwise, and thus causes serious prejudice to the rights of another, shall be liable to a term of imprisonment of up to two years.

(2) The offender shall be liable to a term of imprisonment of between six months and three years if he commits the offence referred to in paragraph 1

a) as a member of an organised group,
b) and causes substantial damage through the commission of such offence, or
c) with the intention of obtaining substantial benefit for himself or another.

(3) The offender shall be liable to a term of imprisonment of between six months and five years if he

a) commits the offence referred to in paragraph 1 as a public official,
b) and causes large-scale damage through the commission of such offence, or
c) commits such offence with the intention of obtaining large-scale benefit for himself or another.

Protection of professional secrets in criminal procedural law is guaranteed by a dual concept: the obligation to maintain confidentiality (known as attorney-client privilege in Anglo-American law) and the ban on witness examination. For example, Act No. 586/2003 Coll. on the Legal Profession,[106] which regulates the attorney profession in Section 23 of this act, defines the scope of the obligation to maintain confidentiality:

Section 23

(1) The lawyer is obliged not to reveal any information learnt in connection with the practice of law and shall treat such information as strictly confidential.

(2) The lawyer may be released from the duty of confidentiality by the client, and after his client´s death or dissolution only by the client´s legal successor. If the client has several legal successors, release from the duty of confidentiality shall take effect subject to the prior written consent of all legal successors.

(3) The lawyer shall not disclose confidential information despite his having been released from this duty by the client or all his legal successors, if the lawyer comes to a conclusion that any such release and disclosure would be detrimental to the client and might cause harm to the client.

(4) The lawyer may reveal information to a person, to whom he wishes to issue a derivative power of attorney in respect of individual legal acts, provided that such a person himself is bound by confidentiality under separate legal rules.

(5) The lawyer may disclose any confidential information to the court of law or any other authority, if the matter handled by such authorities concerns a dispute between the lawyer and his client, or the client's legal successor.

(6) The lawyer may not claim confidentiality in a disciplinary proceeding under this Act. Details shall be laid down in the Bar's Disciplinary Rules.

(7) The duty of confidentiality shall be observed during temporary suspension from the practice and shall even survive the lawyer's disbarment.

(8) The duty of confidentiality shall apply mutatis mutandis to:

a) employees of the lawyer, of the general non-commercial partnership, of the limited liability partnership, or of a limited liability company,

[106] Act No. 586/2003 Zb. on the legal profession and on amending Act No. 455/1991 Zb. on business and self-employment services (Business Licensing Act) as amended. Unofficial translation. Online: http://www.ccbe.org/fileadmin/user_upload/NTCdocument/en_slovak_rep_parlia1_1188889665.pdf

b) other persons, who are in connection therewith engaged in the provision of legal services,

c) members of the Bar's governing bodies and its employees [Sec. 66(4)].

(9) The duty of confidentiality shall not apply to any cases of lawful disclosure that would prevent a crime.

(10) The duty of confidentiality under a separate legal rule1 shall not be affected or prejudiced hereby.

However, the Code of Criminal Procedure contains a ban on witness examination in the case of an attorney admitted to the bar:

§ 129

(1) Witnesses shall not be asked to testify on the matters that involve secret data, the data they are obliged to keep secret, except when the competent body waives the confidentiality obligation. The waiver can be denied only if it could endanger the defence or security of the State, or could cause other equally serious damage; the denial of waiver shall always have to be justified.

(2) Neither shall a witness be asked to testify if his testimony would constitute the breach of confidentiality obligation prescribed or recognised by law or by an international treaty, unless that obligation is waived by the competent body or the body in whose interest such obligation was imposed.

(3) The ban on interrogation pursuant to paragraph 2 shall not apply to the testimony given in respect of an offence that the witness has the obligation to report under the Criminal Code.

Also, the principle of purpose limitation of personal data has been incorporated into the Personal Data Protection Act (Act No. 122/2013 Coll.). In a similar way to the Czech Republic, the most important provisions lay down the purpose of limitation:[107]

Section 6 Controller

(1) Personal data may be processed on its own behalf only by the controller. The controller processes personal data pursuant to Section 9, in the manner which is pursuant to morality and only pursuant to specified or determined purpose.

(2) The controller shall be obliged to

a) determine the purpose of personal data processing before commencement of the processing of personal data; the purpose of personal data processing has to be determined unambiguously and concretely and has to be in accordance with the Constitution of the Slovak Republic, constitutional Acts, Acts and international treaties which the Slovak Republic is bounded by,

b) determine the conditions of the processing of personal data so that no harm comes to the data subject's rights pursuant to Law,

c) obtain personal data solely for a defined or determined purpose; obtaining of personal data under the pretext of a different purpose or activity shall be inadmissible,

---

[107] Act No. 122/2013 Zb. on protection of personal data and on changing and amending of other acts, resulting from amendments and additions executed by Act. No. 84/2014 Zb. (Unofficial translation) Online: http://www.dataprotection.gov.sk/uoou/sites/default/files/kcfinder/files/Act_122-2013_84-2014_en.pdf

d) ensure that only such personal data are processed, the extent and contents of which correspond with the purpose of their processing and are necessary for its achieving,

e) ensure that personal data are processed and used solely in the manner adequate to the purpose for which they were collected; combining of personal data obtained for various purposes shall be inadmissible,

f) process only accurate, complete and, where necessary, updated personal data in respect of the purpose of their processing; the controller shall be obliged to block inaccurate and incomplete personal data and rectify or complete them without undue delay; inaccurate or incomplete personal data that cannot be rectified or completed in order to make them accurate and complete shall be clearly marked by the controller and destroyed without undue delay,

g) ensure that collected personal data are processed in the manner enabling identification of the data subjects only during a time period necessary for achieving the purpose of processing,

h) destroy personal data whose purpose of processing terminated; personal data may be further processed also after the termination of the purpose of the processing only under conditions stipulated in Paragraph 5,

i) process personal data in accordance with morality and act in a manner not contrary to Law.

(3) The controller shall be exempted from the obligation under Paragraph 2 Point a)

only if the purpose of the processing of personal data is stipulated by a special Act in accordance with conditions referred under Paragraph 2 Point a). The controller shall be exempted from the obligation to determine the conditions and manner of the processing of personal data under Paragraph 2 Point b) only if they are stipulated by a generally binding legal regulation. The controller shall be obliged to fulfil the rest of the obligations under Paragraph 2 Points c) to i) also in the course of the processing of personal data pursuant to a special Act; this shall not affect the provision under Section 10 Paragraph 4 the first sentence.

(4) The controller cannot process collected personal data pursuant to a different purpose that is incompatible with the original purpose of the processing.

(5) Processing of collected personal data in the course of previously determined purpose and after its termination is admissible in the necessary extent for the historical research, scientific research or statistical purposes which shall not be deemed incompatible with the original purpose of processing. The controller shall not use the processed personal data to support measures or actions taken against the data subject and against interests of data subject and as restriction of data subject's rights and freedoms. In the course of personal data processing for the purposes pursuant to the first sentence, the controller shall mark, anonymise them if it allows achieving the purpose of processing and destroy them immediately as they become obsolete.

These provisions are general and also apply to all sorts of personal data including the data processed by providers of electronic communications services, information society services, etc. The provisions of Section 6 paras. 2 to 5 do not apply to the processing of personal data necessary for safeguarding the public interest, provided that the controller fulfils the obligations expressly stipulated by a special act determined for safeguarding of

– security of the Slovak Republic (e.g., Act of the National Council of the Slovak Republic No. 46/1993 Coll. on Slovak Intelligence Service, as amended; Consti-

tutional Act No. 227/2002 Coll. on National Security in Times of War, State of War, Exceptional State and State of Emergency);
- defence of the Slovak Republic;
- public policy and security;
- prevention, preclusion, detection, and documentation of criminal offenses, identification of their perpetrators, investigation and prosecution of perpetrators of criminal offenses;
- detection of violations of ethical codices in regulated professions and regulated specialized activities;
- important economic or financial interests of the Slovak Republic or the European Union, including monetary, budgetary, and tax matters;
- inspection, surveillance, supervision, or regulatory functions connected with the exercise of official authority in cases referred to in points c) to f);
- protection of the data subject or of the rights and freedoms of others.

On top of this, the Act on the Protection of Personal Data shall not apply to personal data, which are:
- processed by the natural person for his own needs within the framework of purely personal or household activities, mainly the keeping of a personal address book or correspondence;
- obtained accidentally without prior determination of the purpose and means of processing, without the intent of their further processing in an organized system according to special criteria, and which are not further systematically processed.

B. Powers in the Code of Criminal Procedure

1. Requirement of (reasonable) clarity for powers in the law of criminal procedure

As noted above, the Czech Republic has relatively long experience with situations in which the purpose of state authorities, including those involved in criminal proceedings, did not consist of much more than oppressing citizens with an incompliant political persuasion. Consequently, recently applicable limitations of powers of institutions involved in criminal proceedings are strict, and there is a general tendency to strictly and precisely outline these powers as such. A basic summary of the principles that govern Czech criminal procedure is provided in Section 2 of the Code of Criminal Procedure that reads as follows (informal translation[108]):

---

[108] Act No. 141/1961 Sb., English citations taken from the information system ASPI.

§ 2 Basic principles of criminal procedure

(1) No person shall be prosecuted other than for legitimate reasons and in a manner as stipulated by this Act.

(2) A person against whom a criminal procedure is carried out may not be perceived as guilty until the final convicting judgment of the court pronounces them as guilty.

(3) The public prosecutor is obliged to prosecute all criminal offences of which they learn, unless the law or a promulgated international treaty to which the Czech Republic is bound stipulates otherwise.

(4) Unless this Act stipulates otherwise, the law enforcement authorities act *ex officio*. Criminal cases must be dealt with expeditiously without undue delays; the most expeditious procedure shall be taken in particular for custody matters and the matters in which property was impounded if this is required with regard to the value and nature of the impounded property. Criminal cases shall be dealt with with a full investigation of rights and freedoms guaranteed by the Charter of Fundamental Rights and Freedoms and by international treaties on human rights and fundamental freedoms that the Czech Republic is bound by; when conducting acts of criminal proceedings, the rights of persons that such acts affect may be intervened only when justified by law and to the extent necessary to ensure the purpose of criminal proceedings. The law enforcement authorities shall not take the content of petitions affecting the performance of such obligations into account.

(5) Law enforcement authorities act in accordance with their rights and obligations under this Act and with the assistance of the parties so as to duly establish the facts of the case of which no reasonable doubt exists and to the extent that is necessary for their decisions. A confession of the accused shall not relieve the law enforcement authorities from the obligation to examine all the relevant circumstances of the case. During the preliminary hearings, the law enforcement authorities shall ascertain all the circumstances for and against the person against whom the proceeding is pending with the same care and in the manner provided by this Act even without petitions of the parties to an action. In proceedings before the court the public prosecutor and the accused may support their position with the proposal and submission of evidence. The public prosecutor must prove the guilt of the defendant. However, this does not relieve the court of the obligation to provide additional evidence to the extent required for their decision.

(6) Law enforcement authorities shall review the evidence according to their conviction based on careful consideration of all the circumstances of the case separately and as a whole.

(7) All law enforcement authorities shall cooperate with public interest groups and utilise their educational activities.

(8) A criminal prosecution before the courts is only possible on the basis of an indictment, a petition for punishment or a petition for approval of an agreement on the declaration of guilt and acceptance of punishment (hereinafter referred to as an "agreement on guilt and punishment") served by the public prosecutor. A bill of indictment in proceedings before the court is represented by the public prosecutor.

(9) In criminal proceedings before the court, decisions are made by the court or a single judge; the presiding judge or a single judge decides alone only if so expressly stipulated by the law. Should the decision during a preliminary hearing be made by a court in the first instance, then such decisions shall be made by a judge.

(10) Criminal cases are heard in public before the court so that citizens may observe and participate in hearing. At the main trial and public hearing, the public may be excluded only in cases expressly stipulated for in this Act or in a special Act.

(11) Proceedings before the courts are oral; the testimony of witnesses, experts and the accused are normally undertaken through an interrogation.

(12) When deciding during a main trial, as well as during public, custody and closed hearings, the court may only take into account evidence that was given during such proceedings.

(13) The person against whom criminal proceedings have been initiated must be instructed in every stage of the proceedings in an appropriate and comprehensible manner as to their rights granting them the full use of defence and that they may choose their defence counsel; all law enforcement authorities are required to enable them to exercise their rights.

(14) Law enforcement authorities conduct the proceedings and produce decisions in the Czech language. Any person who declares that they do not speak Czech is entitled to speak their mother tongue or a language that they indicate they can speak to the law enforcement authorities.

(15) At every stage of the proceedings the law enforcement authorities are obliged to make it possible for the victim to fully exercise their rights and are also obliged to instruct the victim of the victim's rights in an appropriate and comprehensible manner under the law so that the victim can achieve satisfaction of their claims; the proceedings must be conducted with the required consideration for the victim and while being duly regardful of their person.

The need for strict clarity of powers was also one of main reasons why the Constitutional Court quashed the former implementation of data retention obligations, as it contained only general formulations instead of an explicit list of institutions entitled to ask for retained traffic data and the precise establishment of respective procedures, explicitly including the possibility of judicial review. The Court ruled (official translation[109]):

37. In its judgments, the conditions outlined above have been specified by the Constitutional Court when assessing the admissibility of the intervention of the public authority to individual privacy taking the form of telecommunication operation interception [cf. e.g. the quoted Judgments file reference II. ÚS 502/2000, file reference IV. ÚS 78/01, file reference I. ÚS 191/05, or file reference I. ÚS 3038/07 issued on 29 February 2008 (N 46/48 SbNU 549)]. The infringement of the individual's fundamental right to privacy in the form of the right to informational self-determination in the sense of Article 10, para. 3 and Article 13 of the Charter, due to the prevention of and protection against criminal activity is thus possible only by means of imperative legal regulations which have to conform to, above all, the rights arising from the principle of the legal state (rule of law state) and which meet the requirements arising from the proportionality test when, in the case of a conflict between the fundamental rights and freedoms with the public interest or any other fundamental rights and freedoms, the purpose (objective) of such infringement must be assessed in relation to the means applied, whereas it is the proportionality principle (in a broader sense) that provides the standard for such assessment. The wording of such legal regulations must be precise and unambiguous, while also being sufficiently predictable so that it provides potentially affected individuals with sufficient information on the circumstances and conditions under which the public authority is entitled to interfere with their privacy and so that they can act accordingly in order to avoid conflict with the restricting norm. Moreover, the powers granted to the relevant authorities, as well as the manner and the rules of application, must be strictly defined so that individuals are provided with protection against arbitrary infringements. From the perspective of the proportionality principle (in a broader sense), assessing the admissi-

---

[109] Decision No. Pl. ÚS 24/10, English translation available at http://www.usoud.cz/en/decisions/?tx_ttnews%5Btt_news%5D=40&cHash=c574142df486769e0b435954fead08c3

bility of the infringement in question includes three criteria. The first one lies in assessing the eligibility of fulfilling the purpose (or appropriateness as well), where it is determined whether the specific measure itself is capable of achieving the intended purpose, being the protection of another fundamental right or public interest. The second criterion consists in assessing the necessity, i.e. examining whether, upon selecting the appropriate means, the one being most considerate of the fundamental right has been opted for. And finally, it is necessary to assess the adequacy (in a narrower sense), i.e. whether the prejudice to the fundamental right is not disproportionate in relation to the intended purpose, which means that the measures imposing a restriction on fundamental rights and freedoms must not, in case of a collision of the fundamental right or freedom with public interest, exceed (through their negative consequences) the positive aspects represented by the public interest in these measures [cf. the Judgment file reference Pl. ÚS 3/02 issued on 13 August 2002 (N 105/27 SbNU 177; 405/2002 Sb.)].

[…]

51. Under no circumstances may the stipulation of the duty imposed on legal entities or natural persons to secure that "the content of message should not be retained together with the defined data" (Section 97, para. 3, sentence four) or the duty to "eliminate them upon the expiration of the period unless they have been provided to the competent authorities in compliance with a special legal regulation or unless stated otherwise within the Act (Section 90)" (Section 97, para. 3, sentence six) be deemed by the Constitutional Court as providing sufficient, unambiguous, detailed and appropriated guarantees. The retention period itself, "no shorter than 6 months and longer than 12 months", the expiration of which determines the obligation to remove the data, can also be deemed as ambiguous and totally insufficient with respect to the extent and sensitivity of the retained data. None of these obligations is provided, in more detail, with the rules and specific procedures for how to meet them; the requirements concerning the security of the retained data have not been defined in a stringent manner; it is not sufficiently clear how the data are handled, either by legal entities or natural persons collecting and retaining the location and traffic data, or by the competent public authorities when requested; and the manner in which the data are removed has not been specifically determined either. Similarly, the liability or possible sanctions for failure to comply with such duties, including the absence of the possibility for the individuals affected to seek efficient protection against potential misuse, arbitrariness or failure to comply with the relevant duties have not been defined either. Supervision provided by the Office for Personal Data Protection, as anticipated in the Act on Electronic Communications (Section 87 and further), "over observing the duties and obligations when processing personal data" or the corresponding instruments of its activities and monitoring cannot be considered as an adequate and effective means of protecting the fundamental rights of the individuals affected, since they do not control the instrument by themselves [see the Judgment file reference Pl. ÚS 15/01 issued on 31 October 2001 (N 164/24 SbNU 201; 424/2001 Coll.) where appropriate]. As a consequence, the actions referred to above, constituting an obvious infringement of the fundamental right to privacy in the form of the right to informational self-determination (in the sense of Article 10, para. 3 and Article 13 of the Charter) and due to the legal regulation being considered as insufficient and failing to meet the afore-mentioned constitutional requirements, occur beyond the scope or reach of any immediate (yet subsequent) review, particularly a judicial one, the necessity of which has also been expressed by the ECHR in the Decision concerning the case of Camenzind v. Switzerland, referred to above.

It should be noted that the Public Prosecution Service and the police had internally implemented relatively strict procedures that provided for case-by-case precise documentation of each request and that also included court orders (despite that this procedure is not prescribed by the law). Consequently, retained data that had been used in certain prior cases did not have to be declared inadmissible evidence.

Lack of clarity was also the main reason for the above cited Constitutional Court decision repealing former provisions of the Code of Criminal Procedure that provided for a competence on the part of the Public Prosecutor to request retained data. In that case, the Court ruled:[110]

> 24. The wording of the contested provision implies that the order for disclosure of the telecommunication traffic data is only expressly conditioned by the fact that such measures must pursue the goal of "clarification of the circumstances significant for criminal proceedings". The Constitutional Court believes that the limits of the fundamental right to informational self determination regulated in this manner are formulated too widely and vaguely, and in essence, they allow the relevant data to be requested and used by the bodies active in criminal proceedings each time a certain connection with the on-going criminal proceedings may be associated with them. At the same time, the Court is aware of the obligation of public authorities to apply sub-constitutional legal regulations in compliance with the constitutional order, which in this case implies their duty to examine, in every specific matter, whether apart from identifying the telecommunication traffic data of a specific person there is not, in respect to the seriousness of the criminal offence, any other possibility to achieve the goal of the criminal proceedings otherwise or whether it does not amount to an inadequate interference with the individual's fundamental right. It also considers important that the protection of fundamental rights and freedoms is subject to, in every individual case, review of an independent and impartial court, since decision making on issuing the relevant order is granted by the contested provision to the presiding judge or the judge within the preliminary proceedings, whereas such orders must be issued in writing and accompanied with reasoning. Nevertheless, these are guarantees that allow protection to be provided against an inadequate interference with the right to informational self-determination with respect to the facts of a particular case, yet they cannot eliminate the deficiencies consisting in indefiniteness and too general a character of the contested legal regulation in such a way that they would replace, on their own and in general terms, the consideration of the legislature on the intensity of a certain public interest in restricting a fundamental right or freedom in the case of individual criminal offences and the manner (i.e. specific form) of such restriction, including the afore-mentioned subsequent guarantees when disposing of the relevant data, which represent a political decision adopted within the limits defined by the constitutional order, with their own detailed abstract consideration. If adopted by courts, this approach would also be inconsistent with Art. 4, para. 2 of the Charter, pursuant to which limitations of the fundamental rights and freedoms may be placed upon them only by law, since only the legislature is provided with the constitutional capacity, upon imposing a certain duty, to give preference, at its own discretion and while respecting the proportionality principle, of the public interest approved by the constitutional order to the fundamental right in a type-defined legal relation. Furthermore, leaving the determination of the constitutionally constituent limits only on the decision-making practice of courts would not be consistent with the requirement of legal certainty, since any potential interference with the right to informational self-determination is not, as a consequence of the indefiniteness of the current legal regulation, predictable for the individual to such an extent that would correspond to the seriousness of any possible negative effects onto their privacy. It may thus be stated that it

[110] Decision No. Pl. ÚS 24/11, English translation available at http://www.usoud.cz/fileadmin/user_upload/ustavni_soud_www/decisions/pdf/Pl_US_24-11.pdf

is this indefiniteness that represents the primary deficiency of the contested legal regulation, as far as its constitutional review is concerned.

Comparative note – Slovakia

The situation about requirements of (reasonable) clarity for powers in the law of criminal procedure is very close to Czech law. The fundamental rules that govern Slovak criminal procedure are provided in Section 2 of the Code of Criminal Procedure, which reads as follows:[111]

§ 2 Fundamental rules of criminal procedure

(1) No person may be prosecuted as accused on other than the legal grounds and in other manner than that provided for under the present Act.

(2) Fundamental rights and freedoms of persons may be, in cases permitted by law, interfered with to the extent necessary to achieve the purpose of criminal proceedings with due respect to the dignity of persons and their privacy.

(3) Unless this Act provides otherwise, any interference with fundamental rights and freedoms under this Act before the commencement of the criminal prosecution or in pre-trial proceedings shall be decided by a judge for pre-trial proceedings; the judge for pre-trial proceedings shall also decide on other matters as provided for by this Act.

(4) Any person subject to criminal prosecution shall be presumed innocent until proven guilty by a final sentencing judgment.

(5) A prosecutor represents the State in criminal proceedings. Unless this Act, an international treaty promulgated in a manner prescribed by law (hereinafter referred to as "international treaty") or the decision of an international organisation which is binding on the Slovak Republic provides otherwise, the prosecutor shall have the duty to prosecute all criminal offences that came to his knowledge.

(6) Unless this Act provides otherwise, the bodies involved in criminal proceedings and the courts shall act *ex officio*. They shall have the duty to deal with the cases involving detention as a matter of priority and without undue delay. The bodies involved in criminal proceedings or the courts shall not take account of the petitions whose content infringes on the fulfilment of this duty.

(7) Every person shall have the right to a fair hearing of his criminal case by an independent and impartial tribunal in reasonable time and in his presence, and to have an opportunity to comment on any adduced evidence, unless this Act provides otherwise.

(8) No person may be prosecuted in respect of an act for which he had already been finally convicted or from which he had been acquitted. This principle shall not exclude the use of extraordinary remedies as prescribed by law.

(9) Every person subject to criminal prosecution shall have the right to defence.

(10) The bodies involved in criminal proceedings shall proceed so as to properly establish the facts of the case that do not give rise to reasonable doubts, to the extent necessary for making the decision. They shall procure the evidence as part of their official duties. The parties shall also be granted the right to procure the evidence. The bodies involved in criminal proceedings shall thoroughly clarify the circumstances regardless of whether they prejudice or benefit the accused, and they shall take the evidence in either direction so as to enable the court to arrive at a fair decision.

[111] *Ibid.* Code of Criminal Procedure.

(11) The court may also take other evidence than those proposed by the parties. The parties shall have the right to supply the evidence proposed by them.

(12) The bodies involved in criminal proceedings and the court shall evaluate the legally obtained evidence in accordance with their deep conviction based on the careful examination of all the facts of the case, separately and jointly, irrespective of whether they were supplied by the court, the bodies involved in criminal proceedings or by one of the parties to the proceedings.

(13) All the bodies involved in criminal proceedings shall co-operate with associations of citizens and shall make use of the educational impact thereof.

(14) All parties shall have equal status before the court.

(15) Criminal prosecution before the court shall only be initiated on the basis of a motion or an indictment filed by a prosecutor who shall represent the prosecution or the motion in the proceedings before the court.

(16) In criminal proceedings before the court, the decision shall be made by a panel of judges, a single judge or by a judge for pre-trial proceedings. A presiding judge of a panel, a single judge or a judge for pre-trial proceedings shall have the sole authority to decide the case only when the law expressly provides for it.

(17) Criminal cases shall be heard in open court. Public attendance may be excluded from the main hearing or open court hearing only in cases explicitly provided for under the present Act. The judgment shall always be announced in open court.

(18) Proceedings before the court shall be oral; exceptions are provided for under this Act. The examination of evidence shall be carried out by the court, which, however, leaves the examination of the accused, witnesses and expert witnesses to the parties, starting with the one that proposed or procured the evidence.

(19) When deciding at the main trial, open or closed court hearing, the court may only take account of the evidence taken during the hearing, unless otherwise provided by law.

(20) If the accused, his legal guardian, the injured party, a participating person or witness declares that he does not speak the language of the proceedings, he shall have the right to be assigned an interpreter or a translator.

Also, in many criminal cases, the Supreme Court of the Slovak Republic or the Slovak Constitutional Court has interpreted these fundamental rules defining reasonable clarity for powers in the law of criminal procedure.

2. Differentiation and classification of powers in the law of criminal procedure

Coercive powers related to telecommunication data are relatively precisely defined in criminal procedure. In this respect, Czech law is relatively specific with its bilateral regulation of wiretapping and retention of traffic data. This means that duties and procedures which apply to providers of electronic communications services are defined in Act on Electronic Communications, while procedures that apply to the police or Prosecution Service are laid down in the Code of Criminal Procedure. The reason for this dichotomy is that wiretapping and data retention also serve other purposes than just criminal procedure. Consequently, provisions laid down in the Act on Electronic Communications cover the obligations of providers of services of electronic communications in general and specify only purposes for which respective data might be requested. Procedures for requesting these data are then laid down in specific acts (incl. the Code of Criminal Procedure).

The respective provisions of the Act on Electronic Communications read as follows (informal translation[112]):

§ 97

(1) A legal entity or natural person providing a public communications network or a publicly available electronic communications service shall, at the expense of the requesting party, provide and secure interfaces at specified points of the network to connect terminal equipment for message tapping and recording:

a) for the Police of the Czech Republic for the purposes specified in a special legal regulation,

b) for the Security Information Service for the purposes specified in a special legal regulation,

c) for the Military Intelligence service for the purposes specified in a special legal regulation.

(2) The bodies listed in Subsection 1 above shall prove their authorisation for message tapping and recording by submitting a written application, which contains a reference number under which the court ruling is filed by this body, and which is signed by the person responsible from the body listed in Subsection 1 above for the performance of the message tapping and recording. In the event of message tapping and recording by the Police of the Czech Republic in accordance with special legal regulations36) the written application shall contain a reference number under which the consent of the user of the station monitored is filed by the Police of the Czech Republic.

(3) A legal entity or a natural person providing a public communications network or a publicly available electronic communications service shall for a period of 6 months traffic and location data which are created or processed during the operation of their public communications networks and during the provision of their publicly available electronic communications services. A legal entity or a natural person providing a public communications network or a publicly available electronic communications service is only required to store data relating to unsuccessful call attempts only when these data are created or processed and at the same time stored or recorded. At the same time, such a legal entity or natural person is required to ensure that, during the performance of the obligation referred to in the first and second sentences, no message content has been stored, and that no content thus stored has been further distributed. A legal entity or a natural person who stores traffic and location data is required, on request, immediately to provide them to:

a) criminal law enforcement authorities for the purposes of and under the conditions laid down in a special legal regulation,

b) the Police of the Czech Republic for the purposes of initiating a search for a specific wanted or missing person, for the identification of persons of unknown identity or the identity of a corpse that has been discovered, for the prevention or detection of specific terrorist threats or for the verification of a protected person, while complying with the conditions set out in a special legal regulation,

c) the Security Information Service, for the purposes of and under the conditions laid down in a special legal regulation,

---

[112] Act No. 127/2005 Sb., English translation available online at http://www.mpo.cz/dokument156553.html

d) the Military Intelligence service for the purposes of and under the conditions laid down in a special legal regulation,

e) the Czech National Bank for the purposes of and under the conditions laid down in a special legal regulation.

After expiry of the period referred to in the first sentence above, the legal entity or natural person who stores the traffic and location data is required to destroy them, unless they were provided to the bodies authorised to use them under a special legal regulation, or unless otherwise provided in this Act (Section 90).

(4) The traffic and location data pursuant to Subsection 3 above are primarily data leading to the tracing and identification of the source and address of the communication, and also data leading to the identification of the date, time, method and duration of the communication. The scope of the traffic and location data stored in accordance with Subsection 3 above, the form and method of their transmission to the bodies authorised to use them under a special legal regulation, and the method of their disposal is stipulated in an implementing legal regulation.

(5) A legal entity or natural person providing a publicly available telephone service is required, on request, to provide information from the database of all its subscribers to the publicly available telephone service to a body authorised to request them in accordance with a special legal regulation, at their own expense. The form and scope of the information provided is stipulated in an implementing legal regulation.

(6) Where a legal entity or natural person providing a public communications network or a publicly available electronic communications service introduces into its activities any coding, compression, encryption or any other method of transmission that makes the messages being transmitted incomprehensible, such a person shall ensure that the messages requested and the traffic and location data related thereto are provided in a comprehensible manner at the termination points for connection of the terminal equipment referred to in Subsection 1 above.

(7) For fulfilling the obligations specified in Subsections 1, 3 and 5 above, the legal entity or natural person is entitled to reimbursement for effectively incurred costs from the authorised body which requested or ordered such an action. The amount and method of reimbursement for the effectively incurred costs is set out in an implementing legal regulation.

(8) A person referred to in Subsection 1 above and its employees are required to maintain the confidentiality of any tapping or recording of messages requested or implemented in accordance with Subsections 1 and 2 and data requested or provided in accordance with Subsections 3 and 5 and matters related thereto.

(9) The technical and operational conditions and points for the connection of terminal telecommunications equipment for the tapping or recording of messages is set out in an implementing legal regulation.

(10) A legal entity or natural person providing a public communications network or a publicly available electronic communications service shall keep records on:

a) the number of cases where, on requested, it provided traffic and location data to the bodies authorised to request them,

b) the period that elapsed, in each case, from the date on which the storage of the traffic and location data began to the date on which the authorised body requested such data, and

c) the number of cases when it was not able to comply with a request to provide traffic and location data.

(11) A legal entity or a natural person providing a public communications network or a publicly available electronic communications service is required to provide to the Office

the collective records referred to in Subsection 10 above, for the previous calendar, in electronic form, at the latest by 31 January of the following calendar year. The records provided may not contain personal and identification data. The Office shall immediately send the collective records received to the Commission.

(12) The form of the records provided under Subsection 11 and the method of their submission to the Office is stipulated in an implementing legal regulation.

The respective provisions of the Code of Criminal Procedure read as follows (informal translation[113]):

§ 88

(1) If criminal proceedings are conducted for a crime for which the law stipulates a prison sentence with the upper penalty limit of at least eight years, for a criminal offence of machinations in insolvency proceedings under Section 226 of the Penal Code, violation of regulations on rules of competition under Section 248 Subsection 1 Paragraph e) and Subsection 2 through 4 of the Penal Code, negotiating advantages during public procurement, tender and auction under Section 256 of the Penal Code, machinations during public procurement and tenders under Section 257 of the Penal Code, machinations at a public auction under Section 258 of the Penal Code, misuse of powers of an official person under Section 329 of the Penal Code or for any other intentional criminal offence for which prosecution is stipulated in a declared international treaty, an order for the interception and recording of telecommunications may be issued if it may be reasonably assumed that facts relevant to the criminal proceedings will be obtained in this way and if there is no other way to achieve such purpose or if its achievement would be otherwise significantly reduced. The Police of the Czech Republic perform the interception and recording of telecommunications for the needs of all law enforcement authorities. The interception and recording of telecommunications between the defence counsel and the accused is inadmissible. If the police authority finds during the interception and recording of telecommunications that the accused has communicated with their defence counsel, they are obliged to immediately destroy the interception recording and not to use the information learned in this context in any way. The report on the destruction of the record shall be placed in the file.

(2) The presiding judge and, in preliminary proceedings upon the petition of the public prosecutor, the judge, is entitled to warrant the interception and recording of telecommunications. If there is a criminal proceeding for an intentional criminal offence, the prosecution of which is governed by the applicable international treaty, the order for the interception and recording of telecommunications must be issued in writing and must be justified, including a specific reference to the applicable international treaty. The order for the interception and recording of the telecommunications service shall include a determined user address or a user device and the user if their identity is known, and the period during which the interception and recording of telecommunications traffic is conducted cannot be longer than four months; the justification must include the specific facts that justify the issue of such order as well as its period. The order for the interception and recording of telecommunications shall immediately be forwarded to the police authority. In the preliminary hearing, the judge shall send a copy of the order for the interception and recording of telecommunications to the public prosecutor without undue delay.

(3) The police authority is obliged to continuously assess whether the reasons which led to an order for the interception and recording of telecommunications are still valid. If the reasons have expired, they are obligated to immediately terminate the interception and

[113] Act No. 141/1961 Sb., English citations taken from the information system ASPI.

recording of telecommunications even before the end of the period referred to in Subsection 2. They will immediately notify the presiding judge in writing, who issued the order for the interception and recording of telecommunications, and in the preliminary hearing, the public prosecutor and the judge.

(4) Based on the assessment of the current course of the interception and, recording of telecommunications, the judge of a superior court and, in the preliminary hearing upon the petition of the public prosecutor, deputy county court judge may extend the duration of the interception and recording of telecommunications traffic even repeatedly, however, always only for a maximum period of four months.

(5) The law enforcement authority may, without the order for the interception and recording of telecommunications, order the interception and recording of telecommunications or conduct it themselves if there is a criminal proceeding for the criminal offence of human trafficking (Section 168 of the Penal Code), the delegation of custody of a child to someone else (Section 169 of the Penal Code), restriction of personal freedoms (Section 171 of the Penal Code), extortion (Section 175 of the Penal Code), kidnapping of a child and persons suffering from a mental disorder (Section 200 of the Penal Code), violence against a group of people or an individual (Section 352 of the Penal Code), dangerous threats (Section 353 of the Penal Code) or dangerous persecution (Section 354 of the Penal Code), if the user of the intercepted unit agrees to such measure.

(6) If the record of the telecommunications service is to be used as evidence, it is necessary to accompany it with the transcript, giving the place, time, manner and contents of the record, as well as the authority which issued the record. The police authority is obliged to label other records, securely store them so as to protect them against unauthorised misuse, and indicate the place of storage in the transcript. In another criminal case other than the one in which the interception and recording of telecommunications service was performed, the recording may be used as evidence if there is a criminal prosecution in this matter for a criminal offence referred to in Subsection 1, or with the consent of the user by the intercepted station.

(7) If the interception and recording of the telecommunications service did not find any facts relevant to the criminal proceedings, the police authority, after approval by a court and in preliminary hearings, the public prosecutor, must immediately destroy all records after three years from the final conclusion of the matter. If the police authority was informed of an extraordinary appeal within the set deadline, they shall destroy the records of the interception after the decision on the extraordinary appeal or after a final conclusion on the matter. The police authority shall send a transcript on the destruction of the record of the interception to the public prosecutor, whose decision finally concluded the matter and in proceedings before the court, to the presiding judge in the first instance, for the record on file.

(8) The public prosecutor or the police authority, by whose decision the case was finally concluded, and in proceedings before the court the presiding judge in the first instance after the final conclusion of the matter, shall inform the person referred to in Subsection 2, if known, on the ordered interception and recording of telecommunications service. The information includes the designation of the court that issued an order for the interception and recording of telecommunications service, the duration of the interception and the date of the conclusion. Part of the information includes the instructions on the right to submit, within six months of receipt of this information, a petition to review the legality of the order for the interception and recording of telecommunications service to the Supreme Court. The presiding judge of the court in the first instance shall submit the information without undue delay after the final conclusion of the matter, the public prosecutor by whose decision the matter was finally concluded shall submit the information without undue delay after expiration of the period for the review of their decision by the Attorney General under Section 174a and the police authority by whose decision

the matter was finally concluded shall submit the information without undue delay after expiration of the period for the review of their decision by the public prosecutor under Section 174 Subsection 2 Paragraph e).

(9) The presiding judge, the public prosecutor or the police authority does not submit the information under Subsection 8 in proceedings on a crime committed by an organised group for which the law stipulates a prison sentence with the upper penalty limit of at least eight years, in proceedings on criminal offences committed for the benefit of an organised criminal group, in proceedings for criminal participation in an organised criminal group (Section 361 of the Penal Code), or if the criminal offence involved more people and in relation to at least one of them the criminal proceedings have not yet been finally concluded or if it is against the person to whom the information was submitted, is the subject of criminal proceedings, or if providing such information could defeat the purpose of the criminal proceedings, including those referred to in Subsection 6, or if it could lead to threats to national security, life, health, or the rights and freedoms of individuals.

§ 88a

(1) If, for the purposes of criminal proceedings conducted for an intentional criminal offence for which the law sets out a prison sentence with an upper penalty limit of at least three years, for the criminal offence of violating the confidentiality of messages (Section 182 of the Penal Code), for the criminal offence of fraud (Section 209 of the Penal Code), for the criminal offence of unauthorised access to computer systems and information media (Section 230 of the Penal Code), for the criminal offence of procuring and possessing access devices and computer system passwords and other such data (Section 231 of the Penal Code), for the criminal offence of dangerous threats (Section 353 of the Penal Code), for the criminal offence of dangerous persecution (Section 354 of the Penal Code), for the criminal offence of spreading alarming news (Section 357 of the Penal Code), for the criminal offence of encouraging a criminal offence (Section 364 of the Penal Code), for the criminal offence of approving a criminal offence (Section 365 of the Penal Code) or for an intentional criminal offence for which prosecution is stipulated in a proclaimed international treaty binding on the Czech Republic, it is necessary to ascertain data on the telecommunications service that are the subject of a telecommunications secret or that are subject to the protection of personal and intermediation data, and there is no other way to achieve the pursued purpose or if its achievement would be otherwise significantly harder, their release to the public prosecutor or to the police authority shall be ordered by the presiding judge in proceedings before the court and by the judge upon the petition of the public prosecutor in a preliminary hearing. If there are criminal proceedings for a criminal offence the prosecution of which is stipulated in such international treaty, the order for ascertaining data on the telecommunications service must be issued in writing and must be justified, including a specific reference to the proclaimed international treaty. If the request applies to a particular user, their identity must be stated in the order, if known.

(2) The public prosecutor or the police authority by whose decision the matter was finally concluded, and in proceedings before the court the presiding judge of the court of first instance after the final conclusion of the matter, shall inform the user referred to in Subsection 1, if known, of the ordered ascertainment of data on the telecommunications service. The information shall identify the court which issued the order for the ascertainment of data on the telecommunications service, and detail the period to which such order applied. Such information shall include instructions on the right to submit to the Supreme Court, within six months of receipt of this information, a petition to review the legality of the order for the ascertainment of data on the telecommunications service. The presiding judge of the court of first instance shall submit the information without undue delay after the final conclusion of the matter, the public prosecutor by whose de-

cision the matter was finally concluded shall submit the information without undue delay after expiration of the period for the review of their decision by the Attorney General under Section 174a, and the police authority by whose decision the matter was finally concluded shall submit the information without undue delay after expiration of the period for the review of their decision by the public prosecutor under Section 174 Subsection 2 Paragraph e).

(3) The presiding judge, the public prosecutor or the police authority shall not submit the information under Subsection 2 in proceedings on a crime committed by an organised group for which the law stipulates a prison sentence with an upper penalty limit of at least eight years, in proceedings on a criminal offence committed for the benefit of an organised criminal group, in proceedings on the criminal offence of participation in an organised criminal group (Section 361 of the Penal Code), or if the commission of the criminal offence involved several persons and in relation to at least one of them criminal proceedings have not yet been finally concluded or if criminal proceedings are conducted against the person to whom the information is to be submitted, or if providing such information could defeat the purpose of the particular or some other criminal proceedings, or if it could threaten national security, life, health, or the rights or freedoms of individuals.

(4) An order under Subsection 1 is not required if the user of the telecommunications equipment to whom the data on the performed telecommunications service relates gives their approval for the provision of the information.

It is to be noted that, despite formally having the opportunity to request wiretapping or retained traffic data, the police has *de facto* extremely limited options to use this coercive power in criminal proceedings. As a result, no situations occur in practice in which the police would directly request wiretapping or traffic data for the purpose of criminal procedure – if the respective data are needed in criminal procedings, such requests are always made through the Public Prosecution Office.

As noted above in II.A.3., there are, apart from traffic data, no distinct procedural rules for specific coercive powers to obtain stored communications. Consequently, stored communications are gathered and forensically exploited based upon general rules enabling the police or the Public Prosecution to secure assets, request information, conduct surveillance, etc. The use of these powers is discussed in detail in III. below.

Comparative note – Slovakia

Coercive powers related to telecommunication data are defined in Slovak criminal procedure by criminal law legislation, which regulates wiretapping on one side and retention of traffic data on the other. Duties and procedures that apply on the side of providers of electronic communications services are defined in the Act on Electronic Communications, while procedures that apply on that of the police or Prosecution Service are laid down in the Code of Criminal Procedure or the Act on the Protection against Interception (see Chapter I.A.1.). The reason for this separation is that wiretapping and data retention also serve other purposes than just criminal procedure. Consequently, provisions laid down in the Act on Electronic Communications cover the obligations of providers of services of electronic communications in general. Also, they specify only purposes for which respective data might be requested. Ultimately, it is important to note that the situation here is currently unclear due to the Constitutional Court decision about the invalidity of relevant provisions in the Act on Electronic Communications.

III. Powers for Accessing Telecommunication Data in the Law of Criminal Procedure

A. Overview

The most important regulation for interception of electronic communications and for otherwise accessing electronic communications data for the purpose of criminal investigations is contained in the Code of Criminal Procedure.[114]

There are two specific provisions of the Code of Criminal Procedure, which allow law enforcement authorities to intercept electronic communications and to access electronic communications data for the purpose of criminal investigations – Sections 88 and 88a.

The first of these lays down rules for the interception and recording of telecommunication and the second one for the accessing of data on telecommunication services, which are subject to telecommunication secrecy or subject to the protection of personal and intermediation data. Section 88 basically allows law enforcement authorities to intercept and record the content of data transmission in real time under specified conditions in criminal proceedings, whereas Section 88a allows them to access traffic and location data under specified conditions, which must be retained by entities providing a public communications network[115] or publicly available electronic communications service[116] (ISPs) in accordance with the Act on Electronic Communications.[117]

Since there are no other specific rules for specific coercive powers to obtain stored data, communication stored by the user or the ISP is being accessed and processed under more general provisions, which allow law enforcement authorities to

---

114 Act No. 141/1961 Sb. Code of Criminal Procedure.

115 Electronic communications network used wholly or mainly for the provision of publicly available electronic communications services, which support the transfer of information between end nodes of the network. See Section 2 of the Act on Electronic Communications.

116 Publicly available service normally provided for remuneration, which consists wholly or mainly in the transfer of signals via electronic communications networks. See Section 2 of the Act on Electronic Communications.

117 Act No. 127/2005 Sb. on electronic communications and amending certain related laws (the Act on Electronic Communications).

obtain (either voluntarily or upon request, according to Section 78 of the Code of Criminal Procedure) or seize (Section 79 of the Code of Criminal Procedure) devices and storage mediums in which the data are stored; to conduct surveillance (Section 158d of the Code of Criminal Procedure) of persons and things, during which the data may be gathered; or to request respective information or data using a production order (Section 8 of the Code of Criminal Procedure).

Czech statutory law also includes other laws that deal with interception or are somehow important for it, primarily Act No. 127/2005 Sb. on electronic communications and its implementing regulations, Act No. 273/2008 Sb. on the Police of the Czech Republic, and Act No. 85/1996 Sb. on advocacy. These acts will be described in more detail below.

Comparative note – Slovakia

The Code of Criminal Procedure in the Slovak Republic is the central point for law enforcement authorities to intercept electronic communications and to otherwise access electronic communications data for the purpose of criminal investigation. As was mentioned before, among the most important provisions are those regulating: General duty to surrender a thing (Section 89), safeguarding and surrendering computer data (Section 90), interception (Section 115), and access to traffic and location data (Section 116), the latter provision having been recently repealed.

Strong powers for the law enforcement authorities accessing telecommunication data can be found in the Act on the Protection against Interception, which stipulates the conditions required for the use of ITM (intelligence technical measures) without the prior consent of the person whose privacy is to be infringed upon by the state body using the ITM.

B. Interception of Content Data

1. Statutory provision

As in most countries, the Czech Republic has one main provision in the law of criminal procedure, which deals with the interception of the content of communication in transmission – Section 88 of the Code of Criminal Procedure. Below is the wording of the entire provision (informal English translation[118]):

---

118 Act No. 141/1961 Sb., English citations were taken from the information system ASPI.

§ 88 – Interception and recording of telecommunications

(1) If criminal proceedings are conducted for a crime for which the law stipulates a prison sentence with the upper penalty limit of at least eight years, for a criminal offence of machinations in insolvency proceedings under Section 226 of the Penal Code, violation of regulations on rules of competition under Section 248 Subsection 1 Paragraph e) and Subsection 2 through 4 of the Penal Code, negotiating advantages during public procurement, tender and auction under Section 256 of the Penal Code, machinations during public procurement and tenders under Section 257 of the Penal Code, machinations at a public auction under Section 258 of the Penal Code, misuse of powers of an official person under Section 329 of the Penal Code or for any other intentional criminal offence for which prosecution is stipulated in a declared international treaty, an order for the interception and recording of telecommunications may be issued if it may be reasonably assumed that facts relevant to the criminal proceedings will be obtained in this way and if there is no other way to achieve such purpose or if its achievement would be otherwise significantly reduced. The Police of the Czech Republic perform the interception and recording of telecommunications for the needs of all law enforcement authorities. The interception and recording of telecommunications between the defence counsel and the accused is inadmissible. If the police authority finds during the interception and recording of telecommunications that the accused has communicated with their defence counsel, they are obliged to immediately destroy the interception recording and not to use the information learned in this context in any way. The report on the destruction of the record shall be placed in the file.

(2) The presiding judge and, in preliminary proceedings upon the petition of the public prosecutor, the judge, is entitled to warrant the interception and recording of telecommunications. If there is a criminal proceeding for an intentional criminal offence, the prosecution of which is governed by the applicable international treaty, the order for the interception and recording of telecommunications must be issued in writing and must be justified, including a specific reference to the applicable international treaty. The order for the interception and recording of the telecommunications service shall include a determined user address or a user device and the user if their identity is known, and the period during which the interception and recording of telecommunications traffic is conducted cannot be longer than four months; the justification must include the specific facts that justify the issue of such order as well as its period. The order for the interception and recording of telecommunications shall immediately be forwarded to the police authority. In the preliminary hearing, the judge shall send a copy of the order for the interception and recording of telecommunications to the public prosecutor without undue delay.

(3) The police authority is obliged to continuously assess whether the reasons, which led to an order for the interception and recording of telecommunications are still valid. If the reasons have expired, they are obligated to immediately terminate the interception and recording of telecommunications even before the end of the period referred to in Subsection 2. They will immediately notify the presiding judge in writing, who issued the order for the interception and recording of telecommunications, and in the preliminary hearing, the public prosecutor and the judge.

(4) Based on the assessment of the current course of the interception and, recording of telecommunications, the judge of a superior court and, in the preliminary hearing upon the petition of the public prosecutor, deputy county court judge may extend the duration of the interception and recording of telecommunications traffic even repeatedly, however, always only for a maximum period of four months.

(5) The law enforcement authority may, without the order for the interception and recording of telecommunications, order the interception and recording of telecommunications or conduct it themselves if there is a criminal proceeding for the criminal offence

of human trafficking (Section 168 of the Penal Code), the delegation of custody of a child to someone else (Section 169 of the Penal Code), restriction of personal freedoms (Section 171 of the Penal Code), extortion (Section 175 of the Penal Code), kidnapping of a child and persons suffering from a mental disorder (Section 200 of the Penal Code), violence against a group of people or an individual (Section 352 of the Penal Code), dangerous threats (Section 353 of the Penal Code) or dangerous persecution (Section 354 of the Penal Code), if the user of the intercepted unit agrees to such measure.

(6) If the record of the telecommunications service is to be used as evidence, it is necessary to accompany it with the transcript, giving the place, time, manner and contents of the record, as well as the authority, which issued the record. The police authority is obliged to label other records, securely store them so as to protect them against unauthorised misuse, and indicate the place of storage in the transcript. In another criminal case other than the one in which the interception and recording of telecommunications service was performed, the recording may be used as evidence if there is a criminal prosecution in this matter for a criminal offence referred to in Subsection 1, or with the consent of the user by the intercepted station.

(7) If the interception and recording of the telecommunications service did not find any facts relevant to the criminal proceedings, the police authority, after approval by a court and in preliminary hearings, the public prosecutor, must immediately destroy all records after three years from the final conclusion of the matter. If the police authority was informed of an extraordinary appeal within the set deadline, they shall destroy the records of the interception after the decision on the extraordinary appeal or after a final conclusion on the matter. The police authority shall send a transcript on the destruction of the record of the interception to the public prosecutor, whose decision finally concluded the matter and in proceedings before the court, to the presiding judge in the first instance, for the record on file.

(8) The public prosecutor or the police authority, by whose decision the case was finally concluded, and in proceedings before the court the presiding judge in the first instance after the final conclusion of the matter, shall inform the person referred to in Subsection 2, if known, on the ordered interception and recording of telecommunications service. The information includes the designation of the court that issued an order for the interception and recording of telecommunications service, the duration of the interception and the date of the conclusion. Part of the information includes the instructions on the right to submit, within six months of receipt of this information, a petition to review the legality of the order for the interception and recording of telecommunications service to the Supreme Court. The presiding judge of the court in the first instance shall submit the information without undue delay after the final conclusion of the matter, the public prosecutor by whose decision the matter was finally concluded shall submit the information without undue delay after expiration of the period for the review of their decision by the Attorney General under Section 174a and the police authority by whose decision the matter was finally concluded shall submit the information without undue delay after expiration of the period for the review of their decision by the public prosecutor under Section 174 Subsection 2 Paragraph e).

(9) The presiding judge, the public prosecutor or the police authority does not submit the information under Subsection 8 in proceedings on a crime committed by an organised group for which the law stipulates a prison sentence with the upper penalty limit of at least eight years, in proceedings on criminal offences committed for the benefit of an organised criminal group, in proceedings for criminal participation in an organised criminal group (Section 361 of the Penal Code), or if the criminal offence involved more people and in relation to at least one of them the criminal proceedings have not yet been finally concluded or if it is against the person to whom the information was submitted, is the subject of criminal proceedings, or if providing such information could defeat the purpose of the criminal proceedings, including those referred to in Subsection 6, or if it

could lead to threats to national security, life, health, or the rights and freedoms of individuals.

Comparative note – Slovakia

The relevant provisions of the Slovak Penal Code read as follows:[119]

Section 115 – Interception and recording of telecommunications

(1) Where criminal proceedings are conducted in respect of a felony, corruption, criminal offence of the abuse of power of public official, criminal offence of laundering the proceeds of crime, or in respect of an intentional criminal offence where so provided by a promulgated international treaty, it shall be possible to issue an order to intercept and record telecommunications if there are reasonable grounds to believe that it will reveal the facts that are materially relevant for criminal proceedings. Where, in the course of intercepting and recording telecommunications, the accused is found to be in communication with his defence counsel, no information thus obtained may be used for the purposes of criminal proceedings, and any such information must be forthwith destroyed in a prescribed manner; this shall not apply to information relating to a case in which a lawyer does not represent the accused as his defence counsel.

(2) The order to intercept and record telecommunications shall be issued by the presiding judge of a panel prior to the commencement of criminal prosecution, or by a judge for pre-trial proceedings on a motion from a prosecutor. If the matter bears no delay and a prior order from a judge for pre-trial proceedings cannot be obtained, the order may be issued by a prosecutor before the commencement of criminal prosecution or in pre-trial proceedings, unless the interception and recording of telecommunications involves the entry into the dwelling of a person; such order shall have to be confirmed by a judge for pre-trial proceedings within 24 hours of its issuance; failing that, the order shall become null and void and the information obtained on its basis may not be used for the purposes of criminal proceedings and shall have to be immediately destroyed in a prescribed manner.

(3) The order to intercept and record telecommunications shall have to be in writing and based on circumstantial reasons, separately for each telephone subscriber or technical equipment. The order shall have to specify the telephone subscriber or technical equipment and, if known, the person whose telecommunications are intercepted and recorded, and the length of time during which the interception and recording of telecommunications are to be performed. Interception and recording may not exceed six months. This period may by extended by another two months, also repeatedly, on a motion from a prosecutor or a judge for pre-trial proceedings. Interception and recording of telecommunications operations shall be performed by the competent department of the Police Corps.

(4) Police officers or the competent department of the Police Corps shall be obliged to continuously review the grounds for the order to intercept and record telecommunications. Where such grounds cease to exist, interception and recording of telecommunications shall have to be discontinued, even before the expiry of the time limit referred to in paragraph 3. This fact shall be immediately notified in writing to the entity that issued the order to intercept and record telecommunications; in pre-trial proceedings, it shall also be notified to the prosecutor.

(5) In criminal proceedings conducted in respect of an intentional criminal offence which is different from the one referred to in paragraph 1, the order to intercept and rec-

---

119 *Ibid.* Penal Code.

ord telecommunications may be issued by the presiding judge of a panel or, prior to the commencement of prosecution or in pre- trial proceedings, by a judge for pre-trial proceedings acting on a motion from a prosecutor, but only with the consent of the subscriber to the telecommunication equipment subjected to interception or recording.

(6) If the record of telecommunications is to be used as evidence, a verbatim transcript made by the officer of the Police Corps carrying out the interception of telecommunications shall have to be attached, wherever the recording makes it possible, containing information about the place, time and legal grounds for interception. A verbatim transcript of the record of telecommunications, which is not secret, signed by the Police Corps officer who drew it up, shall be inserted in the file; if the verbatim transcript of telecommunication records contains a classified fact, it shall be classified according to separate legal provisions. The transcript of telecommunications shall be used as evidence after the interception of telecommunications has been discontinued. In pre-trial proceedings, where the circumstances of the case warrant it, the recording of telecommunications may be submitted to the court even without a transcript of the recording, if the accompanying report gives the data concerning the time, place and legality of interception, and concerning the persons subject to the recording of telecommunications, provided that the recording of telecommunications is intelligible.

(7) The recording may be used as evidence in a different criminal matter from the one that is subject to interception and recording of telecommunications only if such other matter is also heard in simultaneous proceedings concerning a criminal offence referred to in paragraph 1.

(8) If the interception and recording did not produce any facts relevant for criminal proceedings, the criminal procedure authority or the relevant department of the Police Corps shall have to destroy the obtained records forthwith in a prescribed manner. The protocol on the destruction of the recordings shall be inserted in the file. The destruction of the recordings shall be notified to persons referred to in paragraph 3 who do not have the right to view the file; the notification shall be made by the body whose decision has finally settled the matter, or, in the proceedings before the court, by the presiding judge of a panel of a first-instance court within three years from the date on which criminal prosecution in the case was finally concluded; this shall not apply to the proceedings concerning particularly serious felonies or the felonies committed by organised groups, criminal groups or terrorist groups, or criminal offences committed by more than one person if at least one of the perpetrators is still under prosecution, or if the provision of such information could obstruct the purpose of criminal proceedings.

(9) The provisions of paragraphs 1 to 8 shall apply, as appropriate, to the content data or operational data transmitted in real time via computer systems.

The relevant provisions of the Act on the Protection against Interception read as follows:[120]

Article 1

(2) This Law does not apply to the use of technical-intelligence measures in the criminal proceeding in accordance with a specific law.

Article 2

(1) For the purposes of this Law, the technical-intelligence measures are primarily electro-technical, radio-technical, photo-technical, optical, mechanical, chemical, and other technical measures and equipment or their sets, used in a covert manner in:

120 *Ibid.* Act on the Protection against Interception.

a) Searching for, opening, examination, and assessment of mail and other transported packages,

b) Monitoring and recording of telecommunication activities,

c) Making and using the visual, audio, and other recordings.

(2) Technical-intelligence measures can be used by the Police Corps, Slovak Information Service, Military Intelligence, Railway Police, Corps of Prison and Judiciary Guards, and Customs Board (hereinafter "the state body") to the extent pursuant to specific regulations.

(3) The use of technical-intelligence measures for the Railway Police, Corps of Prison and Judiciary Guards, and Customs Board is technically provided by the Police Corps following the submission of a written approval of the legitimate judge granted to the state body, for which the use of the technical-intelligence measure is provided.

(4) For monitoring and recording the telecommunication transmissions, only such a technical-intelligence measure shall be used, which enables immediately to identify the final telecommunication equipment having been used for monitoring and recording the telecommunication transmissions, which will not enable to delete the data identifying this equipment, and which will not enable to delete the time of monitoring and recording the telecommunication transmissions.

(5) The member or employee of the state body, who fulfils the tasks connected with the technical provision of the use of technical-intelligence measures, shall be required to undergo the psycho-physiological examination of veracity in terms set by the head of the state body.

(6) The local administration authorities, the private security services, and any other legal entity or natural person shall not use any technical-intelligence measure.

Article 3

(1) A technical-intelligence measure shall be used only if it is inevitable in a democratic society to safeguard the security and defence of the country, to prevent and reveal criminal activities, or to protect the rights and freedoms of other persons. By using a technical-intelligence measure, the essential right or freedom can be infringed upon only to the inevitable extent and for a period of time not longer than inevitable to attain the legal goal, to which it serves.

(2) The data obtained by technical-intelligence measures shall be used exclusively for achieving the objective when fulfilling the tasks of the state, which meet the requirements in accordance with Paragraph 1.

Article 4

(1) Technical-intelligence measures shall be used only on the basis of a prior written approval of the legitimate judge (hereinafter "approval") and only for a set period of time, not exceeding six months. The term shall go into effect on the day the approval is granted. If it is inevitable to use simultaneously or subsequently several kinds of technical-intelligence measures, each of them shall be used only to the extent of the expressly granted approval. If the technical-intelligence measure is to be used in places, which are not accessible to the public, the legitimate judge shall also decide whether his approval applies also to the entry into such places.

(2) The legitimate judge who has granted the approval to use the technical-intelligence measures can, on the basis of a new request, extend the duration of the time period, but in each case for no longer than other six months. This term shall go into effect on the day the further approval is granted (hereinafter "further approval"). Further approval shall be granted in writing not later than on the last day of the term in accordance with Paragraph 1. If the term cited in Paragraph 1 expires and the further approval is not

granted, the use of the technical-intelligence measure shall be ceased on the last day of the term set in the approval.

(3) The request to grant approval to use a technical-intelligence measure (hereinafter "the request") shall be submitted in writing to the competent court. The request shall contain the following data:

a) Specification of the type of the technical-intelligence measure to be used and of the location of its use, the proposed time of duration of its use, data on the person against whom the use of this technical-intelligence measure is directed,
b) Information on the previous ineffectual or considerably difficult revelation and documentation of activities, which constitute the reason of submitting the request,
c) The rationale for using the technical-intelligence measure.

The court must not make a decision on the request, which does not contain the data required by the law. It shall return the request to the applicant.

(4) The request is submitted by the state body, which intends to use a technical-intelligence measure to implement its legitimate activities (Section 2 para. 2).

(5) It is not possible to lodge a legal remedy against the decision on approval.

(6) The legitimate judge who has granted the approval to use the technical-intelligence measures shall be required to review systematically the existing rationale of their use. If the rationale no longer applies, he shall be required to issue a decree immediately that the use of these measures cease.

2. Scope of application

a) Object of interception

The object of interception is broadly specified as "telecommunication traffic." Neither the legislature nor case law deals with a definition of this term. Traditionally, this term means communication between persons via landlines, mobile phones, fax, radio, or similar devices. However, due technological developments, the interpretation of this term is changing. Nowadays, it would probably cover all sorts of communication transferred via telecommunication and electronic communications networks, including communication between computers or other communication devices as well as any kind of IP traffic, regardless of whether it was generated by persons or computers. Even content data transferred while surfing the web using electronic communications networks may be the object of interception.

When defining the term "telecommunication traffic," the literature usually refers to the Act on Electronic Communications.[121] The act itself does not contain a definition of the term, but we may understand it as meaning content transferred via electronic communications networks, which are defined by the act as transmission systems and, where applicable, switching or routing equipment and other facilities,

---

[121] For example, Šámal, Pavel. Trestní řád: komentář. 7., extended release. In Prague: C.H. Beck, 2013, Velké komentáře.

including network elements that are inactive and that permit the transmission of signals.[122]

Another implication may be found elsewhere in the Act on Electronic Communications, specifically in Section 89, which deals with the confidentiality of communication (informal translation[123]):

Section 89 Confidentiality of communication

(1) Undertakings providing a public communications network or a publicly available electronic communications service shall implement technical and organisational measures to safeguard the confidentiality of the messages and the related traffic and location data, which are transmitted via their public communications network and the publicly available electronic communications services. In particular, such undertakings shall not admit any tapping, message storage, or any other types of interception or monitoring of messages, including the data contained therein and related thereto, by any persons other than the users, without the consent of the users concerned, unless otherwise provided in an Act. This shall not be to the prejudice of the technical storage of data as needed for message transmission without affecting the confidentiality principle.

(2) A message means any information being exchanged or transmitted between a finite number of subscribers or users via the publicly available electronic communications service, except for the information transmitted as part of the public radio or television broadcasting service via the electronic communications network, unless it can be allocated to an identifiable subscriber or user receiving that information.

[…]

Thus, according to the provision cited above and other references, we may conclude that telecommunication traffic may be defined as any data transferred via public electronic communications networks between a finite number of subscribers or users. Since it is impossible to tell in advance whether intercepted electronic communications will or will not contain such data, any interception should take place only after the interception order has been issued.

b) Temporal limits of telecommunication

aa) Access to ongoing telecommunication

Access to ongoing electronic communications is definitely covered by the above-mentioned provision. The police may, upon receiving the interception order, intercept any data that are "in traffic" – from the moment they are sent from the source device to the moment they are received by the destination device. Therefore, it also covers the interception of electronic communications data that are temporarily stored during the process of transmission.

---

[122] Section 2 letter h) of Act No. 127/2005 Sb. on electronic communications.

[123] Act No. 127/2005 Sb., English translation available online at http://www.mpo.cz/dokument156553.html

The electronic communications data, which are stored before or after the process of transmission (e.g., e-mail drafts or sent e-mails, e-mails stored by the provider, received e-mails stored by the recipient, or completely web-based communication such as in social networks), are not protected by telecommunication secrecy but are recognized as documents stored in private, which means that access to such data is covered by different provisions of the Code of Criminal Procedure (see below).

bb) Access after the end of telecommunication transmission

Since the Code of Criminal Procedure is rather old, it does not deal with access to data or stored electronic communications in detail. The only detailed rules are related to access to the traffic data retained by electronic communications service providers.[124] Apart from that, there are no specific provisions providing clear rules for accessing the communication data. Therefore, if there is a need to access communication data, the law enforcement authorities are forced to apply more general rules, which were originally made for different purposes.

Methods usually used to access electronic communications data stored before the beginning or after the end of telecommunication transmission (message drafts, sent messages, stored received messages, etc.) vary, depending on the source of such data.

The communication data may be stored in a device (hard drives, flash drives, mobile phones, computers, etc.), which may be acquired following provisions on the obligation to release property,[125] or the seizure of property,[126] seized during house or personal searches,[127] or examined.[128] Such communication data can be accessed without further consent from the judge or Public Prosecutor. There is also discussion on which data are considered to be stored in the seized computer system. For example, according to some interpretations, even communication data that are stored in connected[129] cloud storage may be accessed from the seized device without further consent, because it is considered a part of such computer system. There is, however, no official opinion or judicial decision that would clarify this matter.

If the data is stored elsewhere (by the provider, in the cloud, in someone else's device, etc.), then it is protected as records stored in private and may be accessed

[124] Section 88a of Act No. 141/1961 Sb., Code of Criminal Procedure.

[125] Section 78 of Act No. 141/1961 Sb., Code of Criminal Procedure.

[126] Section 79 of Act No. 141/1961 Sb., Code of Criminal Procedure.

[127] Section 82 of Act No. 141/1961 Sb., Code of Criminal Procedure.

[128] Section 113 of Act No. 141/1961 Sb., Code of Criminal Procedure.

[129] Connected cloud storage means a situation when the seized device is actively using a cloud storage service, which still synchronizes with the device files stored in the cloud after the device is seized.

only with prior consent of a judge (surveillance of persons or items[130]) or prior consent of the respective user. This approach is also supported by Opinion No. 1/2015 of the Supreme Public Prosecutor's Office, which states (informal translation[131]):

> "The current content of the e-mail inbox is determined by the will of the user and can be accessed following the rules stipulated in section 158d para. 3. of the Code of Criminal Procedure, which can be considered a legal license to overcome the constitutional right to privacy of records located in e-mail inbox [...]."

However, this applies only to the data stored in the device or on the server at the moment of seizure or first access. Should the seized device or obtained access be further used for interception of transmission received in the future, an order for the interception and recording of telecommunication is necessary. This is also supported by the above cited opinion, which in para. 3 states (informal translation):

> "Access to the e-mail communication in real time is possible only following the rules specified in section 88 para. 1 of the Code of Criminal Procedure, because, like the telecommunications traffic, it also takes place in an electronic communications network."

The Czech government is aware of the obsolescence of the Code of Criminal Procedure and is therefore preparing its complete recodification. As far as the national rapporteur knows, during the preparation of the recodification, the possibility of introducing specific provisions for access to electronic data, including communication data, is also being discussed. However, the entire process of recodification is in its infancy, and so we cannot expect any substantial changes in the legislation in the near future.

Comparative note – Slovakia

Slovak law broadly defines the object of an interception (order or approval to intercept and record telecommunication). A similar situation applies here; neither legislature nor case law deals with the definition of this term. Another important term is ITM (intelligence-technical measures). These measures are defined as electro-technical, radio-technical, photo-technical, optical, mechanical, chemical, and other technical measures and equipment or their sets, used in a covert manner to: a) search for, open, examine, and assess mail and other transported packages; b) monitor and record telecommunication activities; c) make and use the visual, audio, and other recordings.

Regarding access to ongoing telecommunication, the above-mentioned provisions cover this type of the interception. The investigator may intercept any data

---

[130] Section 158d of Act No. 141/1961 Sb., Code of Criminal Procedure.

[131] Opinion No. 1/2015 of the Supreme Public Prosecutors Office on the harmonization of interpretation of laws dealing with access to mobile devices and other storage media, including the content of e-mail inboxes. This document is not available in English, translation by the national rapporteur.

that are "in traffic" – from the moment they are sent from the source device to the moment they are received by the destination device. The provisions on safeguarding and surrendering computer data pursuant to Section 90 of the Code of Criminal Procedure regulate access after the end of telecommunication transmission.

3. Special protection of confidential communication content

The main provision provides protection only for the communication between the defence counsel and the accused. Such a communication is inadmissible in criminal proceedings and, if the police authorities find during the interception that the accused has communicated with his/her defence counsel, they are obliged to immediately destroy the interception recording and not use the information learned in this context in any way.[132] These rules are deemed rather problematic by some sources. The reason is that most interceptions are conducted before the commencement of the criminal prosecution and, in this stage, the person against whom the criminal proceedings are being conducted is not referred to as the accused. Therefore, *stricto sensu* interpretation of the provision would mean that, before the commencement of criminal prosecution, the police would be able access and use even the communication between the person against whom the criminal proceedings are being conducted and his/her attorney. Some sources see this as an intrusion into the right to a fair trial.[133]

However, the protection of the communication between the defence counsel and the accused is not absolute. Particularly when the communication relates to a crime, which is committed by the defence counsel in cooperation with the accused, then the protection does not apply. This approach is even supported in the Decision of Constitutional Court No. I.ÚS 1638/14, which states (informal translation[134]):

> [...] However, as is clear from the case law of the European Court of Human Rights and of the Supreme Court, the protection of communication between solicitor and his client is not absolute, inviolable and under certain circumstances may be limited. Possible criminal activity of the solicitor, both to the detriment of the client or to the detriment of others in complicity with the client, can't be considered as the provision of legal services, and in such a case it is impossible to provide any protection of such activity. [...]

Comparative note – Slovakia

Pursuant to Section 115 of the Code of Criminal Procedure, if the accused is found to be in communication with his defence counsel, no information thus ob-

---

132 Section 88 para. 1 of Act No. 141/1961 Sb., Code of Criminal Procedure.

133 For example, in Czech, see Vantuch, P. Nová úprava odposlechu v trestním řádu od 1.7.2008. Bulletin advokacie, 2008, no. 10, p. 29.

134 Decision No. I. ÚS 1638/14. Available online in Czech at http://nalus.usoud.cz/Search/GetText.aspx?sz=1-1638-14_1. Provided excerpt translated by the national rapporteur.

tained may be used for the purpose of criminal proceedings, and any such information must be destroyed forthwith in a prescribed manner. This regulation does not apply to information relating to a case in which a lawyer does not represent the accused as his defence counsel. A similar regulation applies for the duty to surrender a thing pursuant to Section 89 para. 2, for safeguarding and surrendering computer data, respectively, pursuant to Section 90 of the Code of Criminal Procedure.

4. Execution of telecommunication interception

The criminal law does not specify which modes of interception law enforcement authorities should use. According to Act No. 237/2008 Sb. on the Police of the Czech Republic, these activities are conducted by the Czech police (informal translation[135]):

§ 19

The police can technically provide the use of intelligence technologies or bait and security techniques or surveillance of persons and items at the request of the national authority, which is authorised for such use.

State authority shall demonstrate in the request, that the use of intelligence technologies or surveillance of persons and items is allowed according to other legislation.

A special police unit called Unit for Special Activities is responsible for the interception. The Unit for Special Activities is a specialized unit, which, in accordance with the Code of Criminal Procedure, the Act on the Police of the Czech Republic, and other relevant legislation, carries out interception and recording of telecommunication traffic and surveillance of persons and items for authorized security bodies. It is the only unit authorized to carry out these operations and this position is reflected in its organizational structure – its headquarters are located in Prague and it also has subsidiaries in each region of the Czech Republic. Every interception order is forwarded to this unit, which subsequently carries out the interception. The recordings of intercepted traffic are then provided to the investigator who is responsible for the respective criminal prosecution.

The specific methods they use are classified, but, as far as the national rapporteur knows, the police usually intercept the communication using dedicated access points, which ISPs are obliged to install into their infrastructures.[136] They can probably also intercept the communication without any recourse to third parties (ISPs) using special equipment and tools, even though it is not very common. Also, if practical, the police may also order the ISP to extract and surrender specific stored communication data.

---

135 Act No. 237/2008 Sb. on the Police of the Czech Republic. This act is not available in English, translation provided by the national rapporteur.

136 See Section 97 of Act No. 127/2005 Sb. on electronic communications.

There are no accompanying investigative measures mentioned in the main provision itself. Law enforcement authorities may, however, follow different provisions in order to access houses or other places[137] or to be able to use specific technical measures to gain access to the communication.[138]

Comparative note – Slovakia

The Code of Criminal Procedure does not stipulate which modes of interception law enforcement authorities should use. Minor regulations regarding ITM are embodied in the Act on the Protection against Interception (see above). Also, these activities are conducted by the Slovak Police Corps pursuant to Section 36 of Act No. 171/1993 Coll. on the Police Corps.

5. Duties of telecommunication service providers to cooperate

a) Possible addressees of duties of cooperation

There is no specific provision requiring ISPs to execute interception orders themselves. However, any natural or legal person is required to comply with letters of request from law enforcement authorities for the performance of their actions according to Section 8 of the Code of Criminal Procedure (informal translation[139]):

§ 8

(1) Public authorities, legal entities and natural persons are required to comply with letters of request from law enforcement authorities for the performance of their actions without undue delay and unless a special regulation stipulates otherwise, to comply without payment. Furthermore, public authorities are also obliged to immediately notify the public prosecutor or the police authorities of facts indicating that a criminal offence has been committed.

Hence, if the interception can only be done by ISPs in specific cases, then they are required to execute the order.

As far as the national rapporteur knows, classified agreements between the Unit for Special Activities and some ISPs exist (especially on the IP-application level – social networks, cloud providers, etc.), which simplify such cooperation.

Additionally, the Act on Electronic Communications obliges entities providing a public communications network or publicly available electronic communications service to install specific equipment for interception in their infrastructures and to

137 See Section 82 of Act No. 141/1961 Sb. on criminal procedure.

138 See Section 158d of Act No. 141/1961 Sb. on Code of Criminal Procedure.

139 See Section 8 of Act No. 141/1961 Sb. on Code of Criminal Procedure, cited below.

cooperate during an interception (see below). These entities are defined in the following provisions (informal translation[140]):

Section 2 Definitions

For the Purposes of this Act

[…]

f) "provision of an electronic communications network" means the establishment, operation or supervision of such a network, or making it accessible,

[…]

h) "electronic communications network" means transmission systems and, where applicable, switching or routing equipment and other facilities, including network elements which are inactive and which permit the conveyance of signals by wire, by radio, by optical or by other electromagnetic means, including satellite networks, fixed circuit-switched or packet-switched networks and mobile terrestrial networks, electricity cable systems, to the extent that they are used for the purpose of transmitting signals, networks used for radio and television broadcasting and cable television networks, irrespective of the type of information conveyed,

[…]

j) "public communications network" means an electronic communications network used wholly or mainly for the provision of publicly available electronic communications services, and which supports the transfer of information between network termination points, or an electronic communications network through which a service distributing radio and television broadcasts is provided,

[…]

n) "electronic communications services" means a service normally provided for remuneration which consists wholly or mainly in the conveyance of signals on electronic communications networks, including telecommunications services and transmission services in networks used for broadcasting, and on cable television networks, but excluding services that offer content by means of electronic communications networks and services, or exercise editorial control over the offered content transmitted using electronic communications networks and services; it does not include information society services, which do not consist wholly or mainly in the conveyance of signals on electronic communications networks,

o) "publicly available electronic communications service" means an electronic communications service from the use of which no person is excluded beforehand,

[…]

It is important to note that these obligations apply only to the aforementioned providers of a network infrastructure or electronic communications service, which are licensed by the Czech Telecommunications Office. However, providers of services of information society services[141] (IP-application level – Internet applications, cloud, e-mail services, social networks, etc.) are not specifically obliged to provide such cooperation.

---

[140] Act No. 127/2005 Sb., English translation available online at http://www.mpo.cz/dokument156553.html

[141] According to Act No. 480/2004 Sb. on some services of the information society.

b) Content of duties to cooperate

According to Section 97 of Act No. 127/2005 Sb. on electronic communications, the entity providing a public communications network (infrastructure providers working at the IP-transport level) or publicly available electronic communications service (access providers at the IP-transport level) is required to allow interception and recording of transferred communication at the expense of the police. Relevant parts of the above-mentioned provision are cited below (informal translation[142]).

§ 97

(1) A legal entity or natural person providing a public communications network or a publicly available electronic communications service shall, at the expense of the requesting party, provide and secure interfaces at specified points of the network to connect terminal equipment for message tapping and recording:

for the Police of the Czech Republic for the purposes specified in a special legal regulation 36),

[...]

(2) The bodies listed in Subsection 1 above shall prove their authorisation for message tapping and recording by submitting a written application, which contains a reference number under which the court ruling is filed by this body, and which is signed by the person responsible from the body listed in Subsection 1 above for the performance of the message tapping and recording. In the event of message tapping and recording by the Police of the Czech Republic in accordance with special legal regulations36) the written application shall contain a reference number under which the consent of the user of the station monitored is filed by the Police of the Czech Republic.

[...]

(3) A legal entity or natural person providing a publicly available telephone service is required, on request, to provide information from the database of all its subscribers to the publicly available telephone service to a body authorised to request them in accordance with a special legal regulation, at their own expense. The form and scope of the information provided is stipulated in an implementing legal regulation.

(4) Where a legal entity or natural person providing a public communications network or a publicly available electronic communications service introduces into its activities any coding, compression, encryption or any other method of transmission that makes the messages being transmitted incomprehensible, such a person shall ensure that the messages requested and the traffic and location data related thereto are provided in a comprehensible manner at the termination points for connection of the terminal equipment referred to in Subsection 1 above.

(5) For fulfilling the obligations specified in Subsections 1, 3 and 5 above, the legal entity or natural person is entitled to reimbursement for effectively incurred costs from the authorised body which requested or ordered such an action. The amount and method of reimbursement for the effectively incurred costs is set out in an implementing legal regulation.

(6) A person referred to in Subsection 1 above and its employees are required to maintain the confidentiality of any tapping or recording of messages requested or implemented in accordance with Subsections 1 and 2 and data requested or provided in accordance with Subsections 3 and 5 and matters related thereto.

---

[142] Act No. 127/2005 Sb., English translation available online at http://www.mpo.cz/dokument156553.html

(7) The technical and operational conditions and points for the connection of terminal telecommunications equipment for the tapping or recording of messages is set out in an implementing legal regulation.

(8) A legal entity or natural person providing a public communications network or a publicly available electronic communications service shall keep records on:

a) the number of cases where, on requested, it provided traffic and location data to the bodies authorised to request them,
b) the period that elapsed, in each case, from the date on which the storage of the traffic and location data began to the date on which the authorised body requested such data, and
c) the number of cases when it was not able to comply with a request to provide traffic and location data.

(9) A legal entity or a natural person providing a public communications network or a publicly available electronic communications service is required to provide to the Office the collective records referred to in Subsection 10 above, for the previous calendar, in electronic form, at the latest by 31 January of the following calendar year. The records provided may not contain personal and identification data. The Office shall immediately send the collective records received to the Commission.

(10) The form of the records provided under Subsection 11 and the method of their submission to the Office is stipulated in an implementing legal regulation.

According to this provision, these providers are required to install a dedicated interface in their infrastructures, which the Unit for Special Activities can use to connect its devices to access ongoing traffic.

c) Duties to provide technical infrastructure

Communication providers are required to follow rules on interception capabilities in their networks, specified in Decree No. 336/2005 Sb. In accordance with this decree, providers and the police shall agree on the technical parameters of the equipment, which the provider will purchase and install into the network or service in order to provide an interface to connect devices for wiretapping (informal translation[143]):

§ 7

(1) A legal entity or natural person providing a public communications network or a publicly available electronic communications service shall (hereinafter "operator") shall equip its network or service with interface for connecting devices for interception on the basis of the request from competent authority.

(2) If the operator is developing a new network or service, expanding or changing significantly existing network or service, he shall prompt competent authority to issue a request for equipping the network or service with interface for connecting interception devices. The competent authority shall issue the request within 15 days from prompting.

---

[143] Decree No. 336/2005 Sb. on technical and operational conditions and points of connection of the telecommunications equipment for interception and recording of telecommunications traffic. This decree is not available in English to date. Cited provision translated by the national rapporteur.

(3) On the basis of request issued according to the paragraph 1 or 2, the operator in co-operation with the competent authority shall propose possible technical solutions, including the reasons for their implementation and calculation of cost of each solution.

(4) Chosen solution and its parameters shall be specified in a record jointly elaborated by the competent authority and the operator. The record shall also include calculation of financial cost and method and schedule of the payment.

d) Security requirements for data transfers by communication service providers

According to Section 13 of Decree No. 336/2005 Sb., the intercepted communication is transferred to the police via hard data link or via secure virtual channel on the Internet (using the standardized communication protocol SFTP – the provider accesses the police server). The data provided should be equipped with a specific identifier and a time-stamp. The integrity of the data is to be ensured by creating a fingerprint using the SHA-1 hash function. Intercepted e-mails may also be sent to the police via dedicated SMTP server. There are no specific rules for the transfer of the intercepted data to authorities in a foreign country. The respective provision states the following (informal translation[144]):

Packet Networks Outputs

§ 13

(1) The output of the network or service is provided via

a) hard data link, or

b) secure virtual channel on the Internet using standardized communication protocol FTP, server shall be provided by competent authority and operator should connect as a client.

(2) Sent data unit shall be equipped with identifier of user address and serial number or time stamp. Data integrity of the data unit shall be ensured by creation of file stamp using hash function SHA-1.

(3) During the interception of e-mails, may the operator, with consent from the competent authority, send copies of messages using protocol for transferring e-mail to the SMTP server provided by the competent authority.

e) Checks, filtering, and decryption obligations of communication service providers

As far as the national rapporteur is aware, no checks and filtering obligations for Internet providers are mentioned in the statutory law. ISPs (providers of a public communications network or a publicly available electronic communications service) are, however, according to Section 97 of the Act on Electronic Communica-

---

144 Section 13 of Decree No. 336/2005 Sb. on technical and operational conditions and points of connection of the telecommunications equipment for interception and recording of telecommunications traffic. This decree is not available in English to date. Cited provision translated by the national rapporteur.

tions, obliged to provide access to decrypted traffic if they are using any form of encryption (informal translation[145]):

§ 97 Tapping and recording messages

[…]

(4) Where a legal entity or natural person providing a public communications network or a publicly available electronic communications service introduces into its activities any coding, compression, encryption or any other method of transmission that makes the messages being transmitted incomprehensible, such a person shall ensure that the messages requested and the traffic and location data related thereto are provided in a comprehensible manner at the termination points for connection of the terminal equipment referred to in Subsection 1 above.

If the communication is encrypted by the user or by the provider of IP-application level services, then the ISP is not obliged to assist the competent authorities in decrypting such encryption in any way. Also, these rules do not apply in case of providers of information society services (IP-application level); however, they may be required by the police authority performing surveillance in order to provide access to decrypted communication data, if it is necessary for successful surveillance of persons and items, according to Section 158d para. 9 of the Code of Criminal Procedure (informal translation[146]):

§ 158d Surveillance of persons and items

[…]

9) Operators of telecommunications activity, their employees, and other persons who participate in the operation of telecommunications activity, as well as the post office or the person performing the transport of the consignments are obligated to provide the police authority performing the surveillance with the necessary assistance free of charge and in accordance with their instructions. At the same time, they may not claim the obligation of professional confidentiality imposed by special Acts.

Comparative note – Slovakia

Possible addressees of duties of cooperation are any subjects able to assist in criminal procedure. Therefore, any natural or legal person is required to comply with the letters of request from law enforcement authorities for the performance of their actions without undue delay. The related provision in the Code of Criminal Procedure, reads as follows:[147]

§ 3 Assistance provided by public authorities, legal entities and natural persons

(1) Public authorities, self-governing higher territorial units, municipalities and other legal entities and natural persons shall have the duty to provide assistance to the bodies involved in criminal proceedings and the courts in the fulfilment of their tasks having re-

---

145 Act No. 127/2005 Sb., English translation available online at http://www.mpo.cz/dokument156553.html.

146 Act No. 141/1961 Sb. on criminal procedure. Translation taken from the legal information system ASPI.

147 *Ibid.* Code of Criminal Procedure.

lation to criminal proceedings. The State shall reimburse related substantiated material costs incurred by other legal entities and natural persons, unless otherwise provided by a separate regulation. The motions filed to this effect shall be heard and decided pursuant to the provisions of Section 553 paragraphs 4 and 5; they may only be filed by persons who incurred such material costs.

The content of duties to cooperate arises from the essence of criminal procedure. According to the Act on Electronic Communications, the subject of telecommunication secrecy shall cooperate with public authorities. This is also valid for provision of the technical infrastructure; security requirements for data transfers by communications service providers; checks, filtering, and decryption obligations of communications service providers. The relevant provision reads as follows:[148]

Section 63 Telecommunications secrecy

(1) The subject of telecommunications secrecy shall be:

a) The content of conveyed messages,

b) The related data of the communicating parties which are the telephone number, business name and the place of business of a legal person, or business name and the place of business of a natural person – undertaker or the personal data of a natural person which are the name, surname, title and permanent residence address; the data published in the telephone directory shall not be subject to telecommunications secrecy.

c) Traffic data, and

d) Location data.

(2) Everybody who becomes familiar with the subject of telecommunications secrecy when providing networks and services, using the services, accidentally or otherwise shall be obliged to keep telecommunications secrecy.

(3) Telecommunications secrecy may be disclosed to the Office, the subscriber and user concerned, his authorized representatives or legal successors if hereinafter not provided otherwise.

(4) For the purposes of working in conjunction with other state bodies under Section 55, Subsection 6, the undertaking that provides public services may collect and process the subscribers' data in the scope defined in Section 56, Subsection 3.

(5) On the basis of a written request, the undertaking providing public networks or public services shall be obliged under Section 55, Subsection 6 to permit online, direct and continuous access to the subscribers' data of its own network or services in the scope of data under Subsection 4 and the user allocated identification and Internet protocol address; it shall be obliged, upon a request, to provide such data together with the data on the base stations of the public telephone network and database of International Mobile Subscriber Identity (IMSI) in an electronic form and intelligible manner without delay also on a physical information carrier. The state body to which such access has been enabled shall cover the cost for ensuring the online access up to the interface of the undertaking and the physical information carrier.

(6) The undertaking shall be obliged to provide other state body under Section 55, Subsection 6 for the purposes of fulfilling its tasks under special regulations, on the basis of a written request and with the court's consent or on court's order under special regula-

148 *Ibid.* Act on Electronic Communications.

tions 45 with the data which are subject to telecommunications secrecy under Subsection 1, Letter b) to d); in case of the data necessary for searching for missing persons and stolen motor vehicles shall be acted under a special regulation46. The undertaking shall be obliged to provide those data to other state body under Section 55, Subsection 6, in a written form or encrypted electronic form and in an intelligible manner. The state body to which such data have been provided shall cover the cost for physical carriers.

(7) The undertaking providing public networks or public services shall be also obliged:

a) To operate public networks or provide public services by means of such technology, including its individual parts and software, which makes it possible to connect and operate the equipment for listening and tapping of traffic in a network owned by the state and the online access under Subsections 5 and 6,

b) On the basis of other state body under Section 55, Subsection 6, to permit the connection of the equipment for listening and tapping of traffic under the technical specification of such equipment to be connected; the state body which has requested the connection of the equipment for listening and tapping of traffic in the network shall cover the cost for the procurement of the equipment for listening and tapping of traffic in the network, including its software and the provision of maintenance support of such equipment,

c) to cooperate with the Police Corps and authorities acting in a criminal proceedings when disclosing malicious calls and scaremongering,

d) On the basis of a justified summons, to restrict, without delay, the traffic of a public network or the provision of a public service for the time and in the scope necessary, if it is necessary to protect the constitutional establishment or internal order or state security or state defence and there is an imminent danger to the detriment of life and health; the minister of interior of the Slovak Republic and in case of his absence the minister of defence of the Slovak Republic shall issue the summons. The state body on which request the network traffic was restricted shall be responsible for any detriments incurred by restricting the network traffic,

e) On the basis of a written request in justified cases related to fulfilling the tasks of state security and defence to provide other state body under Section 55, Subsection 5 with the service presentation of calling line identification, and this even in case that the calling line has restricted presentation of its identification; the state body shall be held responsible for any detriment caused by the misuse of the information provided about personal data since the moment it was provided with the requested data,

f) To act in subsequent conjunction with the court, the authority acting in a criminal proceedings and other state body under Section 55, Subsection 6 which is necessary to fulfil their tasks and execute their powers under this Act and special regulations.

(8) The undertaking providing public networks or public services which uses coding, compression, encryption or other manner of concealing of signal conveyance, shall be obliged, at its own expense, to provide, in a comprehensible manner, the information collected while listening and tapping traffic in networks to other state body or authority acting in a criminal proceedings. On the basis of a proposal of the National Security Office, the Slovak Intelligence Service, the Military Intelligence or Police Corps, the Office shall issue a list of equipment using coding, compression, encryption or similar equipment which shall be prohibited to connect to the network.

(9) The undertaking's staff shall be obliged to keep secrecy about provisioning information and data or other conjunction under this Act. Only the state body to which information and data or other conjunction were provided may lift the obligation to keep secrecy. This is without prejudice to the provisions of a special regulation.

6. Formal prerequisites of interception orders

a) Competent authorities

The interception of electronic communications may be conducted only after the interception order is issued. The interception order is a decision *sui generis*.

Only the Public Prosecutor can apply for the interception order in preliminary proceedings, usually after consultation with the police investigator. Prior to submitting the application, the Public Prosecutor usually verifies whether the criminal proceedings are being conducted for a crime for which the interception can be ordered. He particularly assesses whether the offense described in the record of the commencement of the criminal proceedings or in the resolution to initiate the criminal prosecution corresponds with legal classification used. He also assesses whether it may be reasonably assumed that facts relevant to the criminal proceedings will be obtained during the interception if there is no other way to achieve such purpose or if its achievement would otherwise be significantly reduced.

Justified application is then presented to the judge, who can authorize the interception by issuing the order according to Section 88 para. 2 of the Code of Criminal Procedure (informal translation):

§ 88 Interception and recording of telecommunications

[…]

(2) The presiding judge and, in preliminary proceedings upon the petition of the public prosecutor, the judge, is entitled to warrant the interception and recording of telecommunications. […] The order for the interception and recording of telecommunications shall immediately be forwarded to the police authority. In the preliminary hearing, the judge shall send a copy of the order for the interception and recording of telecommunications to the public prosecutor without undue delay.

[…]

This procedure is described in detail in Section 32 of the instruction of the Ministry of Justice Ref. No. 505/2001-Org, which issues the internal and office directives for courts (informal translation[149]):

Section 32 Interception and recording of telecommunications

(1) The judge shall, at the time of reachability, apply procedure described in section 27 para. 1.

(2) The judge shall decide on the application of the public prosecutor for interception and recording of telecommunications traffic in accordance with section 88 para. 2 of the Code of Criminal Procedure (hereinafter "interception") without delay or within the period agreed with the public prosecutor; on the proposal of the public prosecutor to extend duration of the interception (section 88 para. 4 of the Code of Criminal Procedure) will the judge decide no later than the last working day before the expiry of the previ-

149 Instruction of the Ministry of Justice Ref. No. 505/2001-Org, which issues the internal and office directives for courts. Provision translated by the national rapporteur.

ously issued interception order, if the public prosecutor filed the proposal at least 3 working days before expiry of the interception order.

The order is then forwarded to the investigator and to the Unit for Special Activities, which carries out the interception.

These rules apply even in the case of any type of emergency.

b) Formal requirements for applications

There are no specific requirements for applications but, according to Art. 67 of the binding Guideline of the Police President No. 30/2009 Sb. on the tasks in criminal proceedings,[150] an application usually contains the following information:

- the identifier of the device or the user, if his identity is known;
- specific facts about the case, which justify the need to issue the interception order and its duration;
- if the criminal proceedings are being conducted for an intentional criminal offense for which prosecution is stipulated in a declared international treaty, a reference to this treaty;
- a description of the offense and its legal classification;
- a list of interception orders already issued for the same identifier;
- the application for an interception order itself.

The complexity of justification and description of the case in individual applications varies, depending on the complexity of each case. The application may also be submitted with investigative files or other additional materials. Applications are submitted to the court in written form.

c) Formal requirements for orders

Basic formal requirements for interception orders are defined in Section 88 para. 2 of the Code of Criminal Procedure as follows (informal translation):

> [...] The order for the interception and recording of the telecommunications service shall include a determined user address or a user device and the user if their identity is known, and the justification of the order must include the specific facts that justify the issue of such order as well as its period. [...]

The Constitutional Court in its Decision No. II. ÚS 615/06[151] also dealt with formal requirements of interception orders. According to the Decision, the interception order must be supported by relevant evidence from which we can derive reasonable suspicion of committing a crime. The mere existence of criminal complaint

---

[150] Binding Guideline of the Police President No. 30/2009 Sb. on the tasks in criminal proceedings. Available online in Czech at http://www.pecina.cz/files/pokyn2.pdf

[151] Decision No. II. ÚS 615/06. Available online in Czech at http://nalus.usoud.cz/Search/GetText.aspx?sz=2-615-06_1

is not sufficient justification for issuing the interception order. In addition, the court stated that the interception order must be individualized in relation to a specific person or device. It must also specifically state which facts relevant to the criminal proceedings will probably be obtained. The court criticized the practice of issuing some interception orders even though the material conditions of the case had not been sufficiently assessed. Hence, the interception order also must contain an assessment of these conditions.

Based on these findings, the interception order should contain at least the following:

- the interception order;
- identifier of the user or the device;
- the name of the user, if known (name, address, etc.);
- the identification of the crime for which the criminal proceedings are being conducted (reference to international treaty if applicable);
- the duration of the interception (no longer than 4 months).

Additionally, the justification of the order should contain:

- specific facts about the case, which justify issuance of the interception order and its duration;
- the purpose of the interception;
- an explanation of the reasons why there is no other way to achieve such purpose or why its achievement would otherwise be significantly reduced.

Comparative note – Slovakia

The competent authority to warrant the interception and recording in a criminal procedure is always a legitimate body (judge or prosecutor). Usually, the order to intercept and record telecommunication is issued by the presiding judge of a panel prior to the commencement of criminal prosecution or by a judge for pre-trial proceedings on a motion from a prosecutor. If the matter bears no delay and a prior order from a judge for pre-trial proceedings cannot be obtained, the order may be issued by a prosecutor before the commencement of criminal prosecution or for pre-trial proceedings, unless the interception and recording of telecommunication involves entry into the dwelling of a person. A judge for pre-trial proceedings must confirm this type of the order within 24 hours of its issuance. Failing that, the order becomes null and void and the information obtained on its basis may not be used for the purpose of criminal proceedings and have to be immediately destroyed in a prescribed manner.

The order to intercept and record telecommunication must be issued in writing and based on circumstantial reasons, separate for each telephone subscriber or item of technical equipment. The order has to specify the telephone subscriber or technical equipment and, if known, the person whose telecommunication is to be intercepted and recorded, as well as the length of time for which the interception and recording of telecommunication are to be performed.

However, the request to grant approval to use an ITM according to the Act on the Protection against Interception must also be submitted in writing and contain the following data:

a) specification of the type of the ITM to be used and the location of its use, the proposed duration of its use, data on the person against whom the use of this technical-intelligence measure is directed;
b) information on previous ineffectual or considerably difficult revelation and documentation of activities, which constitute the reason for submitting the request;
c) the rationale for using the ITM.

7. Substantive prerequisites of interception orders

a) Degree of suspicion

Required degree of suspicion is not specified in the positive law, but it usually is evaluated on the case by case basis by the judge. In some interception orders judges did not assess the degree of suspicion enough, so the Constitutional Court stated in the above cited decision, that the order should contain at least relevant clues from which we can derive reasonable suspicion of committing required crime.

b) Predicate offences

According to Section 88 para. 1 of the Code of Criminal Procedure, the interception order can be justified by following crimes:

- machinations in insolvency proceedings;
- violation of regulations on rules of competition;
- negotiating advantages during public procurement, tenders, and auctions;
- machinations during public procurement and tenders;
- machinations at a public auction;
- misuse of powers by an official person;
- other intentional criminal offenses for which prosecution is stipulated in a declared international treaty.

Additionally, the interception order can be justified in case of crimes for which the law stipulates the upper value of the prison sentence range as at least eight years.

c) *Persons and connections under surveillance*

As far as the national rapporteur is aware, anyone and any device that fall within the scope of Act on Electronic Communications may be subject to an interception order if the required criteria are met and if the judge considers the reasoning of the application sufficient. According to Section 2 of the Act on Electronic Communications, the user is defined as "anyone who uses or requests a publicly available electronic communications service;" thus it includes users of IP-transport level services as well as users of IP-application level services.

Since the interception order has to include a determined user address or user device, it cannot target specific communication content but only a particular person.

There is also debate over whether the interception order also covers transmission outside of the network. In a recent decision, it was mentioned that the interception record also contained conversation which took place near the phone, at the moment connection was being established to another phone.[152] According to technicians, the phone transmits surrounding sounds even before the other party to the call picks up the phone and, according to the above-mentioned decision, even these sounds are part of the interception record. Use of such a record as evidence is rather problematic, because nobody can reasonably expect that the phone transmits surrounding sounds to the provider even before the call itself begins. There is, however, no case law at the moment that would clarify this matter.

d) *Principle of subsidiarity*

The order for the interception and recording of telecommunication may be issued if it can be reasonably assumed that facts relevant to the criminal proceedings will be obtained in this way and if there is no other way to achieve said purpose or if its achievement would otherwise be significantly reduced.[153] The investigator, the Public Prosecutor and, most importantly, the judge should therefore consider whether the specific facts relevant for criminal proceedings could be secured by other less intrusive means of investigation referred to in the Code of Criminal Procedure.

This approach is based upon basic principles of criminal proceedings defined in Section 2 of the Code of Criminal Procedure, especially the principle of proportionality and the principle of moderation formulated in Section 2 para. 4 as follows (informal translation):

> [...] Criminal cases shall be dealt with with a full investigation of rights and freedoms guaranteed by the Charter of Fundamental Rights and Freedoms and by international

---

152 Page 50 of the decision of the city court in Prague of 30 April 2014 no. 42 T 8/2013. Available in Czech at http://www.pecina.cz/files/Rozsudek_MS-P_30.4.2014.pdf

153 Section 88 para. 1 of Act No. 141/1961 Sb., Code of Criminal Procedure.

treaties on human rights and fundamental freedoms that the Czech Republic is bound by; when conducting acts of criminal proceedings, the rights of persons that such acts affect may be intervened only when justified by law and to the extent necessary to ensure the purpose of criminal proceedings.[…]

e) Proportionality of interception in individual cases

There is no additional obligation for the authorizing authority to verify that the interception is proportionate to the seriousness of the offense in an individual case. The proportionality is, however, always assessed in the interception order. For example, if the police authority were to apply for too many interception orders in one case, the judge would probably refuse to issue it, because he would find it disproportionate and against the principle of moderation formulated in the above cited Section 2 para. 4 of the Code of Criminal Procedure.

f) Consent of a communication participant to the measure

If the user of the intercepted unit agrees to such a measure, the law enforcement authority may order the provider to intercept and record telecommunication or conduct it himself, even without the order for the interception and recording of telecommunication, but only if there is a criminal proceeding for following criminal offenses:

- human trafficking;
- the delegation of custody of a child to someone else;
- restriction of personal freedoms;
- extortion;
- kidnapping of a child and persons suffering from a mental disorder;
- violence against a group of people or an individual;
- dangerous threats;
- dangerous persecution.[154]

This provision is criticized by some, because it infringes the telecommunication secrecy of intercepted user who did not provide the consent. Normally, such infringement is justified on the basis of a proper court order, in which the judge assesses whether there is a reasonable reason for interception; in this case, however, the protection is somewhat weaker. Yet, some kind of protection is provided according to the General Instruction of the Supreme Public Prosecutor No. 8/2009 on criminal proceedings, which states in Section 45 (informal translation[155]):

---

[154] Section 88 para. 5 of Act No. 141/1961 Sb., Code of Criminal Procedure.

[155] General Instruction of the Supreme Public Prosecutor No. 8/2009 on criminal proceedings. Cited provision translated by the national rapporteur.

Section 45 Interception without court order

Public prosecutor shall make sure, that if police authority order interception and recording of telecommunication without court order, it shall inform him immediately. The public prosecutor then assesses whether the interception was ordered in the criminal proceedings for the offence for which it is possible to use this measure, and that throughout the period of interception such qualification is justified. If the public prosecutor considers, that the interception could not lead to obtaining of facts important for the criminal proceedings, or that the consent is invalid or was waived, he orders the police authority to immediately discontinue the interception and destroy obtained records. Obtained information can't be in this case further used. If the interception is ordered by the public prosecutor, the provisions on the interception ordered by the judge shall adequately apply.

Comparative note – Slovakia

Substantive prerequisites for interception orders according to the Code of Criminal Procedure are very similar to those of the Czech regulation.

It is only possible to issue an order to intercept and record telecommunication where criminal proceedings are conducted in respect of the following:

- felony;
- corruption;
- a criminal offense regarding the abuse of power by a public official;
- the criminal offense of laundering the proceeds of crime;
- an intentional criminal offense where so provided for by a promulgated international treaty.

In additon, there must be always reasonable grounds to believe that interception will reveal the facts that are substantially relevant for criminal proceedings.

In criminal proceedings conducted in respect of an intentional criminal offense not contained in the above-mentioned list, the order to intercept and record telecommunication may be issued by the presiding judge of a panel or, prior to the commencement of prosecution or during pre-trial proceedings, by a judge for pre-trial proceedings acting on a motion from a prosecutor, but only with the consent of the subscriber to the telecommunication equipment subjected to interception or recording.

However, substantive prerequisites for interception orders according to the Act on the Protection against Interception are quite vague. Even though this law does not apply in the criminal proceedings, it is very often used by investigators. Basically, this law entitles the Police Corps, Slovak Information Service, Military Intelligence, Railway Police, Corps of Prison and Judiciary Guards, and Customs Board to shift obtained evidence from the intelligence regime to the criminal procedure. It is stated that ITM shall be used in a democratic society only to safeguard the security and defence of the country, to prevent and reveal criminal activities, or to protect the rights and freedoms of other persons. When using ITM, an essential right or freedom can be infringed upon only to the inevitable extent and for such period of time necessary to attain the legal goal it serves. The data obtained by ITM shall be used exclusively to achieve the objective of fulfilling the tasks of the state. Ultimately, ITM can be used only on the basis of prior written approval by the responsible judge. In an exceptional case, if there is reasonable suspicion of a crime being committed and an ITM might be used by the Police Corps to fulfil its tasks, the Police Corps may use an ITM even without a prior approval if the case is to be dealt with immediately and approval of the legitimate judge cannot be obtained in advance.

8. Validity of interception order

a) Maximum length of interception order

The maximum length of an interception order is four months.

b) Prolongation of authorization

Based on the assessment of the ongoing course of the interception, the judge of a superior court and, in a preliminary hearing upon petition of the Public Prosecutor, a deputy county court judge may even extend the duration of the interception and recording of telecommunication traffic repeatedly, however always only for a maximum period of four months.

c) Revocation of authorization

There is no positive provision that would deal with possibility of revocation of the interception order. In the opinion of the national rapporteur, however, the issuing judge may decide to revoke the order when a lack of substantive prerequisites for the interception becomes apparent. The Constitutional Court may also revoke the interception order.

According to Section 88 para. 8 of the Code of Criminal Procedure, the Supreme Court may subsequently review the legality of the interception order, following the procedure described in Sections 314l–314n of the Code of Criminal Procedure (informal translation):

§ 314l

(1) Upon the petition of the person referred to in Section 88 Subsection 8, the Supreme Court, in closed hearing, shall examine the legality of the warrant for the interception and recording of the telecommunications service.

(2) Upon the petition of the person referred to in Section 88a Subsection 2, the Supreme Court, in closed hearing, shall examine the legality of the order for the ascertainment of data on the telecommunications service.

§ 314m

(1) If the Supreme Court finds that the warrant for the interception and recording of the telecommunications service or the order for the ascertainment of data on the telecommunications service was issued or its performance was contrary to law, they shall pronounce the violation of the law by a resolution.

(2) An appeal against such decision is not permissible.

§ 314n

(1) If the Supreme Court finds that the warrant for the interception and recording of the telecommunications service was issued and its performance was in compliance with the conditions set out in Section 88 Subsection 1 or the order for the ascertainment of data on the telecommunications service was issued and its performance was in compliance with the conditions set out in Section 88a Subsection 1, they shall pronounce in a resolution that the law was not violated.

(2) An appeal against such decision is not permissible.

The police authority is also obliged to continuously assess whether the reasons that led to an order for the interception and recording of telecommunication are still valid. If the reasons are no longer valied, the police are obligated to immediately terminate the interception and recording of telecommunication, even before the end of the period for which the interception order was issued. The judge who issued the order for the interception and recording of telecommunication must also be immediately informed in writing.[156]

Comparative note – Slovakia

According to the Code of Criminal Procedure, interception and recording may not exceed six months. This period may by extended by another two months, also repeatedly, on motion of a prosecutor or a judge for pre-trial proceedings.

According to the Act on the Protection against Interception, interception and recording may not exceed six months. This period may by extended by another six months, also repeatedly, on motion of the Police Corps or other entitled authority.

According to the Code of Criminal Procedure, police officers or the competent department of the Police Corps are obliged to continuously review the grounds for the order to intercept and record telecommunication. Where such grounds exist, interception and recording of telecommunication have to be discontinued, even before expiry of the time limit. The entity that issued the order to intercept and record telecommunication shall immediately be informed in writing; in pre-trial proceedings, the prosecutor shall also be notified.

The authorized judge who granted the approval to use the ITM is required to systematically review the existing rationale of their use pursuant to the Act on the Protection against Interception. If the rationale no longer applies, he is obliged to im-

---

156 Section 88 para. 3 of Act No. 141/1961 Sb., Code of Criminal Procedure.

mediately issue a decree that the use of these measures are to stop. However, in the opinion of the national rapporteur, the practice of the authorities is very unclear in this matter and no relevant statistics have been published yet.

9. Duties to record, report, and destroy

a) Duty to record and report

Intercepted data and communication are securely stored by the Unit for Special Activities and provided to the police investigator. He then assesses the content of the data and prepares the interception record – a document that usually contains transcripts of parts of the communication relevant to the criminal proceedings. If the record is to be used as evidence in the criminal proceedings, it needs to be accompanied by a protocol. According to Section 88 para. 6 of the Code of Criminal Procedure, the protocol must contain information on the place where the interception was conducted, time of interception, manner of interception, authority who issued the recording, and general information on contents of the record. The protocol must also contain general information required by Section 55 of the Code of Criminal Procedure as follows (informal translation):

§ 55 General provisions for transcript recording

(1) Unless the law stipulates otherwise, at any action of criminal proceedings a transcript is recorded, usually during an action or immediately after, which must include

a) the name of the court, public prosecutor or other law enforcement authority,

b) the place, time and subject of an action,

c) name and surname of officials and their functions, name and surname of the parties present, the name, surname and address of the legal representatives, legal counsel and agents who participated in the action, and in the case of the victim and the accused also the address that is specified for the purpose of delivery, and other data necessary to establish or verify identities, including date of birth or birth certificate numbers,

d) brief and concise statements of the course of an action which would be seen as preserving the statutory provisions governing the conduct of an action, essential contents of the decisions announced during an action, and if a copy of the decision was delivered immediately after reaching the decision, and the confirmation of this service; if there is a literal transcript of the person's statement, it is necessary to indicate such in the transcript accordingly so that it is possible to safely identify the beginning and end of the literal transcript,

e) petitions of the parties, issued instructions, and/or an expression of the instructed persons,

f) objections of the parties or the persons interviewed during the execution of an action or the content of the transcript.

(2) Should the identified condition indicate that the witness or persons close to them appear to be under threat of bodily harm or any other serious risk of violation of their fundamental rights in relation to their testimony and witness protection can not be safely ensured by some other means, the law enforcement authorities shall take steps to conceal the identity of the witness; the name and surname and other personal information is not recorded in the transcript but are kept separate from the criminal file and only law

enforcement authorities may gain access to such details for the purpose of the case. A witness shall be instructed on the right to request confidentiality of their identity and must sign the transcript under an assumed name and surname under which they are further recorded. If the protection of such persons is required, law enforcement authorities must take all necessary steps without undue delay. A special manner to protect witnesses and persons close to them is stipulated by a special Act. If the reasons for the confidentiality of identity and a separate record of personal data of witnesses has expired, the authority responsible for the legal proceedings at the time shall revoke the level of classification of information, attach the information to the criminal file, and the identity and details of the witnesses cease to be classified; this does not apply to the classified identity of persons listed in Section 102a.

(3) The transcript drawn up on the conflict shall include literal testimonies of the confronted persons, as well as the wording of questions and answers; and the circumstances that are important in terms of the purpose and implementation of the confrontation. The transcript is drawn up about the recognition and it must include detailed circumstances under which the recognition was performed, in particular the order in which the persons or items are shown to the suspect, accused or witness, the time and conditions of their observations and their opinions; the recognition conducted in the preliminary hearing is usually video recorded. The transcript drawn up about the investigative attempt, the reconstruction and on-site review is necessary to describe all the circumstances under which these actions were carried out in detail, including their contents and results; if the circumstances of the case do not exclude it, video recordings, sketches, and other appropriate tools shall, if possible, be included in the transcript. Similarly, it is necessary to proceed even if an event when the implementation of other evidence is not explicitly provided by law.

(4) The transcript in the Czech language is drawn up on the testimony of a person even if the questioned person speaks another language; depending on the literal testimony, the reporter or an interpreter shall record the relevant part of the testimonies in the language spoken by the person who testifies.

(5) The correct transcript is guaranteed by the person who performs the operation.

The police authority is not obliged to provide any reports on the progress of the interception or any other final report to the judge. The record is, however, available to the Public Prosecutor, who should regularly assess its content and the legality of the interception.

b) Duty to destroy

If the interception did not uncover any facts relevant to the criminal proceedings, the police authority, after approval by a court and, in preliminary hearings, the Public Prosecutor, must immediately destroy all records three years after the matter has been concluded.[157]

If the police authority was informed of an extraordinary appeal within the set deadline, the records of the interception shall be destroyed after the decision on the extraordinary appeal has been taken or after the matter has been concluded.

157 Section 88 para. 7 of Act No. 141/1961 Sb., Code of Criminal Procedure.

The police authority is responsible for the destruction of the record and a transcript of the destruction of the record of the interception must also be sent to the Public Prosecutor, whose final decision concluded the matter. In proceedings before the court, the destruction transcript must be sent to the presiding judge in the first instance, for the record on file. The police authority also orders the Unit for Special Activities to destroy their respective records.

Also, if the police authority finds that the accused has communicated with his/her defence counsel during the interception and recording of telecommunication, the respective part of the interception recording must be destroyed immediately. In this case, the report on the destruction of the record is to be placed in the file.[158]

Comparative note – Slovakia

According to the Code of Criminal Procedure, if the record of telecommunication is to be used as evidence, a verbatim transcript made by the officer of the Police Corps carrying out the interception of telecommunication has to be attached, wherever the recording makes it possible, containing information about the place, time, and legal grounds for interception. A verbatim transcript of the record of telecommunication that is not secret, signed by the Police Corps officer who drew it up, must be inserted in the file. In a situation in which the verbatim transcript of telecommunication records contains a classified fact, it is classified according to separate legal provisions. Also, the transcript of telecommunication can be used as evidence after the interception of telecommunication has been discontinued. In pretrial proceedings, if the circumstances of the case warrant it, the recording of telecommunication may be submitted to the court even without a transcript of the recording – the accompanying report gives the data concerning the time, place, and legality of interception as well as the persons subject to the recording of telecommunication, provided that the recording of telecommunication is intelligible.

If the interception and recording did not produce any facts relevant for criminal proceedings, the criminal procedure authority or the relevant department of the Police Corps must destroy the obtained records forthwith in a prescribed manner. The protocol on the destruction of the recordings must be inserted in the file.

According to the Act on the Protection against Interception, if the information obtained using ITM is to be used as evidence in a criminal proceeding, the state body must produce a written record with the data on the location, time, and legitimacy of using the ITM. The recording and its verbatim transcription to the written record must also be enclosed. Information obtained by using ITM, which does not

158 Section 88 para. 1 of Act No. 141/1961 Sb., Code of Criminal Procedure.

apply to the rationale of the use cited in the request, can be used in the criminal proceedings only if it concerns a criminal activity in connection with which an ITM can be used.

If the ITM has been used in contravention with the law, no state body or other body of public power is allowed to use the recording, or any other result of the illegal use of ITM obtained in such manner, as evidence or to recognize it as evidence, except for a criminal or disciplinary procedure against the person who has made the recording illegally or has ordered its generation. The recording or another result obtained illegally must be destroyed in the presence of the authorized judge, authorized to grant the approval, within twenty-four hours of the illegal use of the ITM.

A written statement shall be produced on the destruction of the recording or of any other result, including the reason for destroying this recording or result, the personal data of the person who has ordered or approved the use of the ITM (title, name, surname, and position), the personal data of the person who has ordered or approved the destruction of the recording or of any other result (title, name, surname, and position), and the personal data of the legitimate judge present during the destruction (title, name, surname, position, and the identification of the competent court). Before being destroyed, the recording or any other result of the use of ITM may not be copied or transcribed in written or any other form.

10. Notification duties and remedies

a) Duty to notify persons affected by the measure

The Public Prosecutor or the police authority, upon whose decision the case was finally concluded, and, in proceedings before the court, the presiding judge in the first instance after the final conclusion of the matter, shall inform the affected person, if known, about the ordered interception and recording of telecommunication service.[159] The information should include the designation of the court that issued an order for the interception and recording of telecommunication service, the duration of the interception, and the date of the conclusion.

The information about the interception is not provided to the affected person in the following cases:

- when criminal proceedings are conducted for specific crimes;
- when the criminal offense has involved several people and the criminal proceedings have not yet been concluded in relation to at least one of them;

[159] Section 88 para. 8 of Act No. 141/1961 Sb., Code of Criminal Procedure.

– when it could lead to threats to national security, life, health, or the rights and freedoms of individuals, etc.[160]

b) Remedies

The affected person may file a petition to review the legality of the order for the interception and recording of telecommunication services with the Supreme Court.[161] The procedure of judicial review is described in provisions 314l–314n of the Code of Criminal Procedure (cited *supra* in II.B.8.a)

c) Criminal consequences of unlawful interception measures

The officials conducting interceptions illegally may be held liable for the criminal offense of violating the confidentiality of messages according to Section 182 of the Penal Code (informal translation[162]):

Section 182 Violating confidentiality of messages

(1) Whoever intentionally violates the confidentiality

a) of a closed letter or other document during the provision of postal services or transported by other transport services or transport facilities,

b) of data, text, voice, audio or video messages sent via electronic communications networks and attributable to an identified subscriber or user who receives the message, or

c) of non-public transmission of computer data into a computer system, from or within which, including electromagnetic radiation from a computer system, transferring such computer data,

shall be punished by a prison sentence of up to two years or punishment by disqualification.

(2) Whoever with the intention to cause damage to another person or to procure an unauthorised benefit for themselves or another person

a) reveals the secret of which they learned from the document, telegram, telephone call or electronic transmission through a communications network, which was not intended for them , or

b) takes advantage of such secrets, shall be similarly punished.

(3) An offender shall be punished by a prison sentence of six months to three years or punishment by disqualification, if

a) they committed an act referred to in Subsection 1 or 2 as a member of an organised group,

b) they committed such an act out of reprehensible motives,

---

160 See Section 88 para. 9 of Act No. 141/1961 Sb., Code of Criminal Procedure.

161 Section 88 para. 8 of Act No. 141/1961 Sb., Code of Criminal Procedure.

162 Act No. 40/2009 Sb., Penal Code. Translation taken from the legal information system ASPI.

c) they caused substantial damage by committing such an ac, or
d) they committed such an act with the intention of gaining a substantial benefit for themselves or someone else.

(4) An offender shall be punished by a prison sentence of one to five years or a monetary penalty, if
a) they committed an act referred to in Subsection 1 or 2 as an official person,
b) they caused large-scale damage by committing such an act, or
c) they committed such an act with the intention to procure another large-scale benefit for themselves or someone else.

They and also the judge who issues illegal interception order may be held liable for the criminal offense of abuse of powers by an official according to Section 329 of the Penal Code (informal translation):

Section 329 Abuse of powers of an official person

(1) An official person who, with the intention to cause damage or other serious harm to another person or to procure an unauthorised benefit for themselves or another person
a) performs their powers in a manner contrary to another legal regulation,
b) exceeds their powers, or
c) fails to meet an obligation under their powers,
shall be punished by a prison sentence of one to five years or punishment by disqualification.

(2) An offender shall be punished by a prison sentence of three to ten years, if
a) they procured a substantial benefit for themselves or another person by committing an act referred to in Subsection 1 ,
b) they committed such an act on another person for their actual or perceived race, ethnicity, nationality, political belief, religion, or because they are actually or allegedly non-religious,
c) they caused substantial disruption to the activities of a public administration body, local government, court or another public authority by committing such an act,
d) they caused serious disruption to the activities of a legal entity or natural person who is an entrepreneur by committing such an act,
e) they committed such an act while abusing the vulnerability, addiction, anxiety, cognitive weakness, or inexperience of another person, or
f) they caused substantial damage by committing such an act.

(3) An offender shall be punished by a prison sentence of five to twelve years or forfeiture of property, if
a) they procured another large-scale benefit for themselves or another person by committing an act referred to in Subsection 1, or
b) they caused large-scale damage by committing such an act.

(4) Premeditation is punishable.

A Parliamentary Commission to monitor the use of interception and recording of telecommunication traffic controls the interception of communication according to

Section 98 of the Act on the Police of the Czech Republic as follows (informal translation[163]):

Section 98

Supervision of the use of interception and recording of telecommunications, use of surevillance of persons and items and interference with the operation of electronic communications

(1) Supervision of the use of interception and recording of telecommunications, use of surevillance of persons and items under other legislation, and interference with the operation of electronic communications is performed by the Chamber of Deputies, which for this purpose establishes a supervisory body. The supervisory body shall consist of MPs designated by the Chamber of Deputies.

(2) Supervision pursuant to paragraph 1 is performed by the supervisory body in the relevant police departments, after notification to the Minister. The Minister presents to the supervisory body at least twice a year a report on the use of these measures. This does not affect the right of the supervisory body to require information and participation in meetings from others.

(3) Minister shall submit to the Government, to the relevant committee of the Chamber of Deputies and to supervisory body once a year analysis of the use of measures listed in paragraph 1.

(4) The procedure in this provision is not affected by the directive on controlling.

Comparative note – Slovakia

Persons who do not have the right to view the criminal file shall be notified of the destruction of the recordings. The notification is made by the body whose decision has finally settled the matter, or, in proceedings before the court, by the judge presiding over the panel of a first-instance court within three years of the date on which criminal prosecution in the case was concluded. This does not, however, apply to proceedings concerning particularly serious felonies or felonies committed by organized groups, criminal groups, or terrorist groups. It also does not apply to criminal offenses committed by more than one person if at least one of the perpetrators is still under prosecution or if the provision of such information could obstruct the purpose of the criminal proceedings.

11. Confidentiality requirements

Information about specific measures implemented to allow communication interception is classified (reserved) according to Act No. 412/2005 Sb. on the Protection of Classified Information.[164] If anyone discloses classified information to an unau-

---

[163] Act No. 273/2008 Sb. on the Police of the Czech Republic. This act is not available in English. Provided provision translated by the national rapporteur.

[164] Act No. 412/2005 Sb. on the protection of classified information. This act is not available in English.

thorized person, he/she may, according to Section 140 of the Act on the Protection of Classified Information, be fined for administrative offense in the amount up to 5,000,000 Czech crowns, and also prosecuted for criminal offense of endangering classified information according to Sections 317 or 318 of the Code of Criminal Procedure (informal translation):

§ 317 Endangering classified information

(1) Whoever pries information classified under another legal regulation with the aim to disclose it to an unauthorised person, whoever with such an aim collects data containing classified information, or whoever discloses such classified information intentionally to any unauthorised person, shall be punished by a prison sentence of up to three years or punishment by disqualification.

(2) An offender shall be punished by a prison sentence of two to eight years, if

a) they intentionally disclosed classified information to any unauthorised person under another legal regulation classed as "Top Secret" or "Secret",

b) they committed an act referred to in Subsection 1, though the obligation to protect the classified information was specifically imposed upon them, or

c) they procured a substantial benefit for themselves or another person, or they caused substantial damage or a particularly serious consequence by committing such act.

(3) An offender shall be punished by a prison sentence of five to twelve years, if

a) the act referred to in Subsection 1 relates to classified information from the area of security of the defensibility of the Czech Republic classed in another legal regulation as "Top Secret", or

b) they committed such act during a state of national emergency or war.

(4) Premeditation is punishable.

§ 318 Endangering classified information out of negligence

Whoever, out of negligence, causes the disclosure of classified information under another legal regulation classed as "Top Secret" or "Secret" shall be punished by a prison sentence of up to three years or punishment by disqualification.

According to Section 97 para. 8 of the Act on Electronic Communications, ISPs and their employees are also required to maintain the confidentiality as regards any tapping or recording of messages requested or implemented and data requested or provided. The ISP may be fined up to 20.000.000 Czech crowns for violating this duty of confidentiality (Section 118 of the Act on Electronic Communications).

Comparative note – Slovakia

The same applies in the Slovak Republic regarding Act No. 215/2014 Coll. on the Protection of Classified Information and Act No. 351/2011 Zb. on electronic communications.

C. Collection and Use of Traffic Data and Subscriber Data

1. Collection of traffic data and subscriber data

a) Collection of traffic data

aa) Relevant provision

The relevant provision is Section 88a of the Code of Criminal Procedure. It reads as follows (informal translation):

§ 88a

(1) If, for the purposes of criminal proceedings conducted for an intentional criminal offence for which the law sets out a prison sentence with an upper penalty limit of at least three years, for the criminal offence of violating the confidentiality of messages (Section 182 of the Penal Code), for the criminal offence of fraud (Section 209 of the Penal Code), for the criminal offence of unauthorised access to computer systems and information media (Section 230 of the Penal Code), for the criminal offence of procuring and possessing access devices and computer system passwords and other such data (Section 231 of the Penal Code), for the criminal offence of dangerous threats (Section 353 of the Penal Code), for the criminal offence of dangerous persecution (Section 354 of the Penal Code), for the criminal offence of spreading alarming news (Section 357 of the Penal Code), for the criminal offence of encouraging a criminal offence (Section 364 of the Penal Code), for the criminal offence of approving a criminal offence (Section 365 of the Penal Code) or for an intentional criminal offence for which prosecution is stipulated in a proclaimed international treaty binding on the Czech Republic, it is necessary to ascertain data on the telecommunications service that are the subject of a telecommunications secret or that are subject to the protection of personal and intermediation data, and there is no other way to achieve the pursued purpose or if its achievement would be otherwise significantly harder, their release to the public prosecutor or to the police authority shall be ordered by the presiding judge in proceedings before the court and by the judge upon the petition of the public prosecutor in a preliminary hearing. If there are criminal proceedings for a criminal offence the prosecution of which is stipulated in such international treaty, the order for ascertaining data on the telecommunications service must be issued in writing and must be justified, including a specific reference to the proclaimed international treaty. If the request applies to a particular user, their identity must be stated in the order, if known.

(2) The public prosecutor or the police authority by whose decision the matter was finally concluded, and in proceedings before the court the presiding judge of the court of first instance after the final conclusion of the matter, shall inform the user referred to in Subsection 1, if known, of the ordered ascertainment of data on the telecommunications service. The information shall identify the court which issued the order for the ascertainment of data on the telecommunications service, and detail the period to which such order applied. Such information shall include instructions on the right to submit to the Supreme Court, within six months of receipt of this information, a petition to review the legality of the order for the ascertainment of data on the telecommunications service. The presiding judge of the court of first instance shall submit the information without undue delay after the final conclusion of the matter, the public prosecutor by whose decision the matter was finally concluded shall submit the information without undue delay after expiration of the period for the review of their decision by the Attorney General under Section 174a, and the police authority by whose decision the matter was finally concluded shall submit the information without undue delay after expiration of the peri-

od for the review of their decision by the public prosecutor under Section 174 Subsection 2 Paragraph e).

(3) The presiding judge, the public prosecutor or the police authority shall not submit the information under Subsection 2 in proceedings on a crime committed by an organised group for which the law stipulates a prison sentence with an upper penalty limit of at least eight years, in proceedings on a criminal offence committed for the benefit of an organised criminal group, in proceedings on the criminal offence of participation in an organised criminal group (Section 361 of the Penal Code), or if the commission of the criminal offence involved several persons and in relation to at least one of them criminal proceedings have not yet been finally concluded or if criminal proceedings are conducted against the person to whom the information is to be submitted, or if providing such information could defeat the purpose of the particular or some other criminal proceedings, or if it could threaten national security, life, health, or the rights or freedoms of individuals.

(4) An order under Subsection 1 is not required if the user of the telecommunications equipment to whom the data on the performed telecommunications service relates gives their approval for the provision of the information.

Additionally, traffic data which is not subject of a telecommunication secret or that are subject to the protection of personal and intermediation data may be requested following the procedure stipulated in Section 66 para. 3 of Act No. 273/2008 Sb. on the Police of the Czech Republic (informal translation[165]):

Section 66 Requesting information from records

(3) The police may, in cases prescribed by the law and to extent necessary to fulfill a specific task, request from the provider of public communications network or publicly available electronic communications service traffic and location data in a manner enabling remote and continous access, unless other legal provision doesn't states otherwise. These providers are obliged to grant the access without undue delay, and in form and extent determined by other legislation.

bb) Substantive prerequisites of collection

Section 88a of the Code of Criminal Procedure specifies the types of crime for which the retained traffic data could be requested. A general requirement is that the crime being prosecuted should be intentional, i.e., one for which the law provides for imprisonment with a maximum penalty of at least three years. This, however, does not apply to the exhaustive list of crimes, which cannot be prosecuted in practice without traffic and location data, i.e., crimes committed by means of electronic communication.[166] As the Explanatory Memorandum[167] explains: "should the po-

165 Act No. 273/2008 Sb. on the Police of the Czech Republic. The act is not available in English to date. Cited provision translated by national rapporteur.

166 The full list with the relevant sections of Penal Code No. 40/2009 Sb. includes the following crimes: violating the secrecy of conveyed messages (Sec. 182), fraud (Sec. 209) unlawfully gained access to a computer system or data carrier (Sec. 230), acquisition and receipt of access equipment or codes for computer systems or other similar data (Sec. 231), criminal threat (Sec. 353), stalking (Sec. 354), spreading of false news (Sec. 357), incitement (Sec. 364) and criminal connivance (Sec. 365).

lice during investigation of these crimes have had no chance to get traffic and location data, one could consider the decriminalization of such conduct, as these crime would be virtually inexplicable." Ultimately, the data could be also requested for the purpose of criminal proceedings against an intentional crime, which the Czech Republic is required to prosecute pursuant to an international treaty and which is binding for the Czech Republic.

The provision cited above also states that the order for the ascertainment of data on the telecommunication service can be issued only if there is no other way to achieve the pursued purpose or if its achievement would be otherwise significantly more difficult.

cc) Formal prerequisites of collection

The Public Prosecutor prepares the application for a court order to request traffic data in preliminary proceedings, usually on the basis of a written and reasoned proposal from the police authority. Before he submits the application, he must assess whether the order is necessary in order to obtain facts relevant to the criminal proceedings, whether there is no other way to achieve the pursued purpose, whether the criminal proceedings are being conducted for an adequate criminal offense, and whether he has enough information about the case to properly determine which data are to be obtained. He should mention these facts in the application, in which he also indicates the scope of the required data and formulates a proper justification.[168] The completed application is then forwarded to the judge, who evaluates the information provided and, if satisfied, issues the order to request traffic data. The order usually contains basically the same information as the application. The order is then forwarded to the Public Prosecutor.

dd) Duty of addressees to disclose information

The duty of addressees to retain and subsequently disclose traffic data is specifically mentioned in Section 97 para. 3 of the Act on Electronic Communications, which states (informal translation):

Section 97 Tapping and recording messages

(3) A legal entity or a natural person providing a public communications network or a publicly available electronic communications service shall for a period of 6 months traffic and location data which are created or processed during the operation of their public

---

[167] Explanatory Memorandum to Act No. 127/2005 Sb. on electronic communications and on amendment to some related laws (Act on Electronic Communications), as amended, and certain other laws. Available online in Czech: http://www.psp.cz/sqw/text/orig2.sqw?idd=84557.

[168] According to the General Instruction of the Supreme Public Prosecutor No. 8/2009, on criminal proceedings.

communications networks and during the provision of their publicly available electronic communications services[37b]). A legal entity or a natural person providing a public communications network or a publicly available electronic communications service is only required to store data relating to unsuccessful call attempts only when these data are created or processed and at the same time stored or recorded. At the same time, such a legal entity or natural person is required to ensure that, during the performance of the obligation referred to in the first and second sentences, no message content has been stored, and that no content thus stored has been further distributed. A legal entity or a natural person who stores traffic and location data is required, on request, immediately to provide them to:

criminal law enforcement authorities for the purposes of and under the conditions laid down in a special legal regulation[59]),

the Police of the Czech Republic for the purposes of initiating a search for a specific wanted or missing person, for the identification of persons of unknown identity or the identity of a corpse that has been discovered, for the prevention or detection of specific terrorist threats or for the verification of a protected person, while complying with the conditions set out in a special legal regulation[60]),

the Security Information Service, for the purposes of and under the conditions laid down in a special legal regulation[37]),

the Military Intelligence service for the purposes of and under the conditions laid down in a special legal regulation[37a]),

the Czech National Bank for the purposes of and under the conditions laid down in a special legal regulation[61]).

After expiry of the period referred to in the first sentence above, the legal entity or natural person who stores the traffic and location data is required to destroy them, unless they were provided to the bodies authorised to use them under a special legal regulation, or unless otherwise provided in this Act (Section 90).

(4) The traffic and location data pursuant to Subsection 3 above are primarily data leading to the tracing and identification of the source and address of the communication, and also data leading to the identification of the date, time, method and duration of the communication. The scope of the traffic and location data stored in accordance with Subsection 3 above, the form and method of their transmission to the bodies authorised to use them under a special legal regulation, and the method of their disposal is stipulated in an implementing legal regulation.

According to this provision, ISPs (of services at the IP-transport level) are required to retain specific traffic data for a period of six months. General categories of data that are subject to data retention are mentioned in para. 4 of the respective provision; a more detailed list of these data is specified in Section 3 of Decree No. 357/2012 Sb. on storing, handing over and liquidation of traffic and location data, which is not available in English. The data to be retained can be divided into two general groups:

- data used to identify the source and recipient of the data communication (telephone numbers, IMEIs, IP addresses, MAC addresses, port number, IMSI identifier, account identifier – e-mail, username, etc.);
- data used to identify the date, time, manner, and duration of a communication (communication protocol details, type of communication, time and date of communication, duration, length, etc.).

Providers of information society services (IP-application level) are not specifically required to retain any traffic data; however, they can do so with the consent of users. The extent of the data that are retained in this way varies, depending on the type of service.[169]

In practice, orders to request traffic data are usually carefully evaluated by ISPs themselves. If the order is not specific enough or does not contain all the information required by the law, they usually refuse to release the data.

ee) Automated procedure of disclosure

As far as the national rapporteur knows, as of now it is not possible to access traffic data by way of an automated online procedure. The only authority that could request traffic data from ISPs is the Unit for Special Activities. They usually send the request to the ISP via e-mail, which, after receiving the request, releases the requested data in a prescribed format. The Unit for Special Activities then forwards the data to the police authority.

b) Collection of subscriber data

aa) Relevant provision

Subscriber data can be requested from providers of a public communications network or a publicly available electronic communications service (IP-transport level services) following the same procedure as in the case of traffic data – Section 88a of the Code of Criminal Procedure.

A different procedure applies if subscriber data is reqested from ISPs providing services on the IP-application level according to the Act on Information Society Services. In this case, the data may be requested according to Section 8 of the Code of Criminal Procedure (informal translation):

> **§ 8**
>
> (1) Public authorities, legal entities and natural persons are required to comply with letters of request from law enforcement authorities for the performance of their actions without undue delay and unless a special regulation stipulates otherwise, to comply without payment. Furthermore, public authorities are also obliged to immediately notify the public prosecutor or the police authorities of facts indicating that a criminal offence has been committed.
>
> […]
>
> (5) Unless a special Act stipulates the conditions under which information may be disclosed for the purpose of criminal proceedings that are deemed classified pursuant to such Act or which is subject to an obligation of secrecy, such information may be re-

---

[169] For example, social media services usually retain a lot of traffic and location data, whereas hosting providers retain just a few.

quested for criminal proceedings upon the prior consent of the judge. This does not affect the obligation of confidentiality of an attorney under the Advocacy Act.

(6) The provisions of Subsection 1 and 5 shall not affect the obligation of confidentiality imposed on the basis of a declared international treaty to which the Czech Republic is bound.

bb) Prerequisites of data collection

The subscriber data may be requested from the provider of IP-application level services by means of a production order issued by the police or Public Prosecutor according to the above cited Section 8 of the Code of Criminal Procedure. If the respective subscriber data are subject to an obligation of secrecy, then they can only be requested for criminal proceedings upon the prior consent of the judge (Section 8 para. 5). This, of course, does not affect the obligation of confidentiality an attorney has under the Advocacy Act.

The communication data from ISPs of IP-transport level services may be requested in cases specifically stipulated[170] in Section 88a of the Code of Criminal Procedure upon an order issued by a judge upon application by the Public Prosecutor. The formal requirements are the same as for the order to release traffic data.

cc) Duty of addressees to disclose information in manual and automated procedures

As far as the national rapporteur is aware, it is not possible to access traffic data by way of an automated online procedure. If the subscriber data are requested from providers of IP-transport level services (under the Act on Electronic Communications) according to Section 88a of the Code of Criminal Procedure, then the manual procedure is the same as in the case of the order to release traffic data. Here, the duty to disclose information comes from the provision stipulated in Section 97 para. 3 of the Act on Electronic Communications.

However, if the data are requested from providers of IP-application level services (under the Act on Information Society Services), then the police authority can request the data directly from the provider (the Unit for Special Activities is not involved). And, only if the data are subject to an obligation of secrecy, may such information be requested for criminal proceedings – only upon the prior consent of a judge. The duty to disclose the data comes from the general duty to comply with letters of request from law enforcement authorities stipulated in the above cited Section 8 para. 1 of the Code of Criminal Procedure.

---

170 If the criminal procedure is conducted for listed crimes and if there is no other way to achieve the pursued purpose or if its achievement would be otherwise significantly more difficult.

c) *"Data retention"*

The "full-scale" data retention regime was first introduced on 1 May 2005 by the Act on Electronic Communications. The act contained quite a vague formulation, which linked substantially to the implementing Decree No. 485/2005 Coll. on the extent of traffic and location data, the period of time for which such data are retained, and the manner in which they are submitted to bodies authorized to use the data that laid out the technical details. This entire data retention regulation was rather unclear and loose.

After the adoption of the directive in 2006, the act was amended by Act No. 247/2008; however, as regards the extent of the data to be retained, the Czech implementation went far beyond what was requested by the directive: the amount of transferred data, IMEI and SIM card relationships, and the type of encryption of the communication had to be retained.

After harsh criticism of the data retention regime, a group of 51 MPs and senators submitted a petition to the Constitutional Court requesting review of the constitutionality of the regime and annulment of its relevant provisions The Constitutional Court ruled on this matter in Decision No. Pl. ÚS 24/10,[171] described above in II.B.

The new version of data retention was introduced in 2012 by Act No. 273/2012 Sb., amending Act No. 127/2005 Sb. on electronic communications and on amendment to some related laws (Act on Electronic Communications) and certain other laws. The technical details were prescribed by Decree No. 357/2012 on storing, handing over and liquidation of traffic and location data. The new wording of Section 97 entails a taxative enumeration of the subjects empowered to request the data. Also, the new Section 88a of the Act on Electronic Communications was added, which requires ISPs to ensure the security and confidentiality of the retained data as well as their destruction in an irreversible manner. According to the new wording of Section 97 of the Act on Electronic Communications, ISPs are required to retain specific traffic data for a period of six months.

The following categories of data are subject to the data retention:

- data used to identify the source and recipient of the data communication (telephone numbers, IMEIs, IP addresses, MAC addresses, port numbers, IMSI identifiers, account identifiers – e-mails, usernames, etc.);
- data used to identify the date, time, manner, and duration of a communication (communications protocol details, type of communication, time and date of the communication, duration, length, etc.).

[171] Decision No. PL. ÚS 24/10. English translation available at http://www.usoud.cz/en/decisions/?tx_ttnews%5Btt_news%5D=40&cHash=c574142df486769e0b435954fead08c3

§ 97 Tapping and recording messages

[…]

(1) A legal entity or a natural person providing a public communications network or a publicly available electronic communications service shall for a period of 6 months traffic and location data which are created or processed during the operation of their public communications networks and during the provision of their publicly available electronic communications services[37b]). A legal entity or a natural person providing a public communications network or a publicly available electronic communications service is only required to store data relating to unsuccessful call attempts only when these data are created or processed and at the same time stored or recorded. At the same time, such a legal entity or natural person is required to ensure that, during the performance of the obligation referred to in the first and second sentences, no message content has been stored, and that no content thus stored has been further distributed. A legal entity or a natural person who stores traffic and location data is required, on request, immediately to provide them to:

a) criminal law enforcement authorities for the purposes of and under the conditions laid down in a special legal regulation[59]),
b) the Police of the Czech Republic for the purposes of initiating a search for a specific wanted or missing person, for the identification of persons of unknown identity or the identity of a corpse that has been discovered, for the prevention or detection of specific terrorist threats or for the verification of a protected person, while complying with the conditions set out in a special legal regulation[60]),
c) the Security Information Service, for the purposes of and under the conditions laid down in a special legal regulation[37]),
d) the Military Intelligence service for the purposes of and under the conditions laid down in a special legal regulation[37a]),
e) the Czech National Bank for the purposes of and under the conditions laid down in a special legal regulation[61]).

After expiry of the period referred to in the first sentence above, the legal entity or natural person who stores the traffic and location data is required to destroy them, unless they were provided to the bodies authorised to use them under a special legal regulation, or unless otherwise provided in this Act (Section 90).

(2) The traffic and location data pursuant to Subsection 3 above are primarily data leading to the tracing and identification of the source and address of the communication, and also data leading to the identification of the date, time, method and duration of the communication. The scope of the traffic and location data stored in accordance with Subsection 3 above, the form and method of their transmission to the bodies authorised to use them under a special legal regulation, and the method of their disposal is stipulated in an implementing legal regulation.

Comparative note – Slovakia

The collection and use of traffic data and subscriber data can be acquired by means of a warrant pursuant to Section 115 (with sctricter requirements) of the Code of Criminal Procedure. Recently, the Slovak Constitutional Court repealed the warrant according to Section 116 (with more lenient formal requirements) on disclosure and provision of telecommunication data. It ruled that the mass surveillance of citizens (easy access to data retention) is unconstitutional. The decision was made in the context of proceedings initiated by Members of Parliament in co-operation with the European Information Society Institute,[172] a Slovakian-based think tank. The Grand Chamber of the Constitutional Court ruled in matter No. PL. ÚS 10/2014 that provisions of the Act on Electronic Communications (which until now required providers to retain the communication of their users), provisions of the Penal Code, and provisions of the Police Force Act, which allowed access to this data, were in contradiction to the constitutionally guaranteed rights of citizens to privacy and personal data.[173] As a result, these provisions have been repealed. The current situation is unclear at the moment, and it is expected that the Constitutional Court will provide the reasoning for this decision soon. Meanwhile, the authorities can undertake the procedure with higher requirements according to Section 115 of the Code of Criminal Procedure or resort to the blanket procedure in the Act on the Protection against Interception.

2. Identification of device ID (IMEI), card number (IMSI), and location of mobile terminal devices

In the Czech Republic, the identification and location of devices easy, because such information is retained by the internet service providers ("ISPs") according to the above cited Section 97 of the Act on Electronic Communications and Decree No. 357/2012 Sb. on storing, handing over and liquidation of traffic and location data. These data could also be requested from the ISP following the standard procedure described in Section 88a of the Code of Criminal Procedure or in Section 66 of the Act on the Police of the Czech Republic, which are also cited above.

Therefore, the police is not forced to use any special measures to identify or locate devices like silent SMS or IMEI-IMSI catchers.

Comparative note – Slovakia

Same applies in the Slovak Republic regarding Act No. 351/2011 Coll. on electronic communications. In case of a call from a mobile telephone network, where the calling party number is not available, providers usually track the international mobile equipment identification – unique identification of a piece of mobile terminal equipment functioning as a controlling technical measure to identify the goods (IMEI).

---

172 http://www.eisionline.org/index.php/sk/

173 Gera, M.: Slovakia: Mass surveillance of citizens is unconstitutional. Online: https://edri.org/slovakia-mass-surveillance-of-citizens-is-unconstitutional/

D. Access to (Temporarily) Stored Communication Data

There is no specific provision that would allow law enforcement authorities to access stored communication data, which is why they follow procedures defined in more general provisions. The fact that regional police units work rather independently has, in the past, led to the situation that different regions were following different general provisions for accessing communication data. For example, in the South Moravian Region, the law enforcement authorities accessed remotely stored e-mails using an order to request traffic data according to Section 88a of the Code of Criminal Procedure, whereas, in the Pilsen Region, the same data were accessed following provision Section 158d para. 3 of the Code of Criminal Procedure on surveillance of persons and items.

Since this situation led to many problems, the Supreme Public Prosecutor's Office decided to harmonize procedures applied by law enforcement authorities in different regions of the Czech Republic. Opinion No. 1/2015 of the Supreme Public Prosecutor's Office on harmonization of the interpretation of laws dealing with access to mobile devices and other storage media, including the content of e-mail inboxes, states that, in order to access the stored communication data, the procedure mentioned in Section 158d of the Code of Criminal Procedure, the Surveillance of Persons and Items, shall be followed.

A further description of the differences between access to the data in traffic and stored data is provided above in III.B.2.a).

§ 158d Surveillance of persons and items

(1) The surveillance of persons and items (hereinafter referred to as "surveillance") means acquiring knowledge about persons and items performed in a classified manner by technical or other means. If the police authority finds during the surveillance that the accused communicates with their defence counsel, they are required to immediately destroy the records with the content of the communication, and the information that they learned in this context they are not allowed to use in any way.

(2) Surveillance during which audio, video or other records are to be obtained may be performed only upon the written authorisation of the public prosecutor.

(3) If the surveillance is to interfere with in the inviolability of residence, the confidentiality of correspondence, or finding the contents of other documents and records kept in private with the use of technology, then it may be performed only with the prior authorisation of a judge. When entering a residence, no actions other than those that lead to the planting of technical equipment can be performed.

(4) The authorisation referred to in Subsection 2 and 3 can only be issued upon written request. The request must be justified by a suspicion of specific criminal activity and, if known, with the information about the persons or items that are to be surveilled. The authorisation must state the period during which the surveillance will be carried out and this must not be longer than six months. This period may be extended by those who authorised it on the basis of a new written request, but still not exceeding six months.

(5) If the matter cannot be delayed and it is not a case referred to in Subsection 3, the surveillance may be initiated even without prior authorisation. However, the police authority is obliged to additionally request the authorisation without undue delay and if it

is not received within 48 hours they are required to cease the surveillance, destroy any records, and not to use any information found in this context.

(6) Without compliance with the conditions referred to in Subsection 2 and 3, the surveillance may performed only if the person whose rights and freedoms are to be interfered with by surveillance gives their express consent. If such consent is subsequently withdrawn, surveillance shall immediately terminate.

(7) If the record of the surveillance is to be used as evidence, it is required that the transcript is attached with the particulars referred to in Section 55 and 55a.

(8) If no facts important to the criminal proceedings were found, it is necessary to destroy the records in the prescribed manner.

(9) Operators of telecommunications activity, their employees, and other persons who participate in the operation of telecommunications activity, as well as the post office or the person performing the transport of the consignments are obligated to provide the police authority performing the surveillance with the necessary assistance free of charge and in accordance with their instructions. At the same time, they may not claim the obligation of professional confidentiality imposed by special Acts.

(10) In a criminal matter other than that which the surveillance was performed for under the conditions referred to in Subsection 2, the records obtained through surveillance and the attached transcript may be used as evidence only if there is, in this case, a pending criminal proceeding on an intentional criminal offence or if the person whose rights and freedoms the surveillance interfered with, gives their consent.

Comparative note – Slovakia

To permanently or temporarily access stored data, the law enforcement authorities in the Slovak Republic usually resort to a measure called safeguarding and surrendering computer data pursuant to Section 90 of the Code of Criminal Procedure (see above). If the clarification of facts relevant for criminal proceedings requires the safeguarding of stored computer data, including operational data saved through the computer system, the presiding judge of a panel or a prosecutor, prior to the commencement of criminal prosecution or in pre-trial proceedings, respectively, may issue an order based on circumstantial reasons. It is issued to the person who has possession of or control over such data or to the provider of such services, requesting them to do as follows:

- safeguard and maintain the integrity of such data;
- enable the making and keeping of copies of such data;
- prevent access to such data;
- remove such data from the computer system;
- surrender such data for the purpose of criminal proceedings.

1. Online searches with the help of remote forensic software

Online searches are not regulated by any specific provision. Also, there is not much experience with use of specialized remote forensic tools. However, the police probably use them even for online searches, as an investigative measure. Various forensic tools could probably be used for online searches during the general surveillance of persons and items according to Section 158d of the Code of Criminal Procedure. If the use of these technologies interferes with the inviolability of residence, the confidentiality of correspondence, or protection of the contents of other documents and records kept in private with the use of technology, then the search may be performed only with prior authorisation of a judge. However, because there is a lack of relevant case law, it is impossible to predict whether the use of such measures would be considered proportionate. In the opinion of the national rapporteur, use of these measures would at least interfere with the principle of proportionality and the principle of moderation formulated in the above cited Section 2 para. 4 of the Code of Criminal Procedure. Evidence obtained this way would also be probably considered inadmissible, the reason being that rules on surveillance of persons and items do not provide enough safeguards. Therefore, the introduction of a specific provision will be probably necessary in the future.

There are also known cases in which such a measure was conducted by the victim in a state of self defence or extreme emergency according to Sections 28 and 29 of the Penal Code (informal translation[174]):

Section 28 Extreme emergency

(1) An act, which is otherwise criminal, whereby a person tries to avert a risk imminently threatening an interest protected by criminal law, is not a criminal offence.

(2) Extreme emergency shall not apply if such risk could be otherwise averted under the given circumstances, or if the consequences caused are evidently equally serious or even more serious than those imminent, or if the person at risk was obliged to endure them.

Section 29 Self defence

(1) An act, which is otherwise criminal, whereby a person tries to avert an imminently threatening or continuous assault on an interest protected by criminal law, is not a criminal offence.

(2) Self defence shall not apply if the defence was clearly disproportionate to the method of the assault.

Evidence gathered during use of these measures was then provided to the police authority for the purpose of criminal proceedings. There is an ongoing discussion in the Czech Republic as to whether this is legal and proportionate and whether such evidence would be admissible.

Comparative note – Slovakia

The same applies in the Slovak Republic.

---

[174] Act No. 40/2009 Sb., Penal Code. Translation taken from the legal information system ASPI.

2. Search and seizure of stored communication data

a) Special provisions

There are no special provisions dealing with seizure of stored communication data in Czech criminal procedure.

b) Applicability of seizure provisions to electronic data

As far as the national rapporteur knows, the data itself cannot be seized; however, a police authority could seize a device or storage media in which the data has been stored (hard drives, flash drives, mobile phones, computers, etc.), following provisions on the seizure of property (Section 79 of the Code of Criminal Procedure) or during house or personal searches (Section 82 of the Code of Criminal Procedure) (informal translation[175]):

§ 79 Seizure of property

(1) If the property important to the criminal proceedings is not released when those who have it in their possession are prompted, it may be removed from their possession on the warrant of the presiding judge, and in preliminary hearing, the public prosecutor or police authority. The police authority needs to have the prior approval of the public prosecutor for the issue of such warrant.

(2) If the authority that issued the warrant for the seizure of the property does not seize such property themselves, the police authority shall do so on the basis of the warrant.

(3) Without the prior consent referred to in Subsection 1 the warrant may be issued by the police authority only if prior approval cannot be achieved and the matter cannot be delayed.

(4) A person who is not involved in the matter shall take part in seizing the property.

(5) The transcript of the release and seizure of the property must also contain a sufficiently accurate description of the released or seized property that would make it possible to determine its identity.

(6) The authority that performed the action shall immediately issue a written confirmation of the receipt of the property, or a copy of the transcript to the person who released the property, or from whom it was removed.

§ 82 Reasons for house and personal searches and search of other premises and land

(1) A house search can be conducted if there is a reasonable suspicion that a person or property important for criminal proceedings is present in the residence or other premises used for housing or on premises associated with them (residence).

(2) Due to the grounds provided for in Subsection 1 a search of non-residential premises (other premises) and land, if not publicly accessible, may be performed.

---

[175] Act No. 141/1961 Sb., Code of Criminal Procedure. Translations taken from the legal information system ASPI.

(3) Personal searches may be performed if there is a reasonable suspicion that someone is carrying property important to criminal proceedings.

(4) A detained person and a person who was arrested or taken into custody may even be inspected if there is a suspicion that they are in possession of a weapon or other property that could endanger their own or someone else's life or health.

Such data can be accessed and used without further consent from the judge or Public Prosecutor.

There is also debate over which data are considered to be stored in the seized computer system. For example, according to some interpretations, even communication data stored in connected cloud storage may be accessed from the seized device without further consent of the judge or Public Prosecutor, because it is considered part of a computer system. There is, however, no official opinion or case law that could clarify this matter.

c) Different standards of protection for stored and for transmitted data

Safeguards and requirements for the interception of communication differ from interception and access to stored data.

The interception of communication may, according to Section 88 of the Code of Criminal Procedure, be carried out only if respective criminal proceedings are conducted for specific crimes, if it may be reasonably assumed that facts relevant to the criminal proceedings will be obtained, and if there is no other way to achieve such purpose or if its achievement would be otherwise significantly diminished. In the case of access to the stored data during surveillance of persons and items (Section 158d of the Code of Criminal Procedure), however, there are no such conditions.

Additionally, if the police authority wished to conduct an interception, it always requires an order issued by a judge; in the case of access to the stored data, the consent of the judge is necessary only if the interception interferes with in the inviolability of residence, the confidentiality of correspondence, or finding the contents of other documents and records kept in private with the use of technology.

Therefore, the legal protection of data in traffic is far better than the protection of stored data.

d) Open and clandestine access to stored data

Law enforcement authorities can, according to Section 158d of the Code of Criminal Procedure, access stored communication in a clandestine way during the surveillance of persons and items (informal translation):

§ 158d Surveillance of persons and items

(1) The surveillance of persons and items (hereinafter referred to as "surveillance") means acquiring knowledge about persons and items performed in a classified manner by technical or other means. […]

It is not necessary to inform the suspect and/or the provider. However, since assistance from the provider is usually necessary, the authorities have to inform at least him.

Comparative note – Slovakia

As mentioned above, in order access permanently or temporarily stored data, the law enforcement authorities in the Slovak Republic usually resort to a measure called safeguarding and surrendering computer data pursuant to Section 90 of the Code of Criminal Procedure (see above).

The order must specify the period in which the data are to be safeguarded, not exceeding 90 days. A new order must be issued for any extension of that period. When there is no longer a need to safeguard computer data, including operational data for the purpose of criminal proceedings, the presiding judge of a panel or a prosecutor, prior to the commencement of criminal prosecution or in pre-trial proceedings, respectively, shall issue an order reversing the obligation to safeguard the data. The order is served to the person in possession of or with control over such data, or to the provider of such services, who may be also imposed with the duty to treat the measures set out in the order as confidential. The person in possession of or with control over computer data must surrender these data, or the provider of services must surrender the information in his possession or under his control in connection therewith to the authority that issued the order.

Ultimately, with these measures, investigators usually inititate the procedure to issue a warrant for a house search pursuant to Section 100 or for a warrant to search other premises or landed property pursuant to Section 101 of the Code of Criminal Procedure.

3. Duties to cooperate: production and decryption orders

In the Czech Republic, there is no special regulation providing cooperation duties for decoding encrypted data or handing over the necessary passwords.

However, one is required to comply with letters of request from law enforcement authorities for the performance of their actions without undue delay.[176] Such a request may even include the order to decrypt data or to provide passwords. If the

[176] Section 8 para. 1 of Act No. 141/1961 Sb., Code of Criminal Procedure.

decrypted data or passwords are subject to an obligation of secrecy, they may be requested for criminal proceedings upon prior consent of the judge.

Requested parties may, however, argue that disclosure of requested information interferes with their rights in connection with the principle of the prohibition on self-incrimination, in which case they are not obliged to comply.

Since there is no specific provision and a lack of specific case law on this matter, it is difficult to guess what would happen if the police authority were to request provision of decrypted data or passwords. The national rapporteur tried to ask police investigators and public prosecutors whether they have had any experience with such cases but did not receive any information.

Comparative note – Slovakia

The same applies in the Slovak Republic.

IV. Use of Electronic Communication Data in Judicial Proceedings

A. Use of Electronic Communication Data in the Law of Criminal Procedure

The Code of Criminal Procedure does not specifically regulate the regime of intercepted electronic communications data in criminal proceedings; thus it is necessary to follow general rules on the interception and recording of telecommunication under Section 88 of the Code of Criminal Procedure. This section does not make any difference between various forms of intercepted communication.

The basic requirement to order the recording of telecommunication for the criminal proceedings is the drawing up of a protocol on such order, which must fulfil statutory requirements under Section 88 para. 6 of the Code of Criminal Procedure; it has to fulfil certain formal conditions. Lack of fulfilment (particularly regarding information about the place, time, method of performing the recording, authority that issued the recording) can be overcome, even at the stage of criminal proceedings, in the same manner as any other formal defects of the protocol, e.g., hearing of the person who participated in the performance of the act as the witness. This cannot be considered an inadmissible manipulation in the recording of telecommunication.

The content of the recording is also an essential requirement of the protocol related to the recording of telecommunication. The transcript of each part of the communication in such recording is, however, not the essential requirement of the protocol; it is sufficient to provide information about each part of the communication concerning the time, telephone numbers (or other identification related to other types of exchange of information), and identification of the participants in the exchange of information. The procedure stated above was also confirmed by the High Court in Prague.[177] It is, however, quite customary and also recommended to present the intercepted material in transcribed form to the court.

Another important aspect when introducing the recording as evidence in the criminal proceedings is its unaltered form. Assuming that, in the specific case, there is no apparent devaluation or any other reduction in the information value of the evidence, the applicability of the evidence in the criminal proceedings is not affected in any way. Technical measures to compress the content of intercepted communication cannot therefore be considered as unauthorized interference with the evidence in accordance with Section 88 of the Code of Criminal Procedure (such as the compression of the communication on a data carrier). The use of only a part of the communication related to the criminal case is also considered admissible.[178]

Comparative note – Slovakia

The same applies in the Slovak Republic. The Code of Criminal Procedure does not specifically regulate the regime of electronically intercepted communication data in criminal proceedings. Authorities must follow the regulations in Section 115 of the Code of Criminal Procedure or sections of the Act on the Protection against Interception. The most important part of any interception is the transcript, which has to fulfil all formal requirements. Usually, a verbatim transcript made by the officer of the Police Corps is attached to the criminal file, which must contain information about the place, time, and legal grounds for the interception. According to recent opinions, any elimination of the deficits of the protocol by the police can be challenged as a manipulation of the consistency of the lawful evidence. The content of the recording is also an essential requirement of the protocol. The recording may be used as evidence in a different criminal matter from the one that is subject to interception and recording of telecommunication only if such other matter is also being heard in simultaneous proceedings concerning a criminal offense referred to in Section 115 para. 1 of the Code of Criminal Procedure (felony, corruption, criminal offense of the abuse of power by a public official, criminal offense of laundering the proceeds of crime, or an intentional criminal offense where so provided for by a promulgated international treaty).

---

[177] The decision of the High Court in Prague dated 18 January 2001, file number 4 To 3/01. In: beck-online [legal information system].

[178] This opinion was confirmed by the Supreme Court. The decision of the Supreme Court dated 24 June 2009, file number 5 Tdo 572/2009. In: beck-online [legal information system].

B. Inadmissibility of Evidence as a Consequence of Inappropriate Collection

It is not permissible to exclude any type of evidence except in cases in which the Code of Criminal Procedure indicates the inadmissibility of certain means of evidence, procedure, or act.[179] The Code of Criminal Procedure, however, does not contain any further statement, which would require explicit enumeration of all the cases of inadmissible evidence. This is why it is necessary to follow general requirements on the admissibility of evidence under the Code of Criminal Procedure and with respect to the proceedings.[180] The inadmissibility of evidence is therefore deduced mainly from the interpretation of the provisions. There are two main approaches of the Constitutional Court to the inadmissibility of evidence as to whether there was any misconduct in obtaining the evidence. The first concept is based on the fact that the evidence is inadmissible because of the prohibition of arbitrariness, which sets out the obligation of the courts and other criminal proceedings authorities not to deviate in any way from the rules of procedure.[181] The second approach is based on infringement of the right to a fair trial through a breach of right of another person, e.g., privacy rights.

---

179 Section 89 para. 2. Code of Criminal Procedure. In: ASPI [legal information system].

"Evidence may be anything that may help to clarify matters, in particular the testimonies of the accused and witnesses, expert opinions, items and documents relevant to the criminal proceedings, and examinations. Each party may seek, submit, or propose the implementation of evidence. The fact that the law enforcement authority did not seek or request it is not grounds for the rejection of such evidence."

Section 89 para. 3. Code of Criminal Procedure. In: ASPI [legal information system].

"Evidence obtained by unlawful coercion or threat of coercion may not be used in the proceedings except when used as evidence against the person that used coercion or threatened coercion."

180 It is also necessary to keep Section 8c and Section 30 para. 4 of the Code of Criminal Procedure in mind.

§ 8c Code of Criminal Procedure. In: ASPI [legal information system].

"Pursuant to Section 88 no person shall disclose information on the court order or interception performance and recording of telecommunications traffic without the consent of persons whom such information concerns or information derived thereof, data on telecommunications traffic detected on the basis of an order under Section 88a, or information obtained by the surveillance of people and items under Section 158d Subsection 2 and 3, if such information allows the identification of the person and if such were not used as evidence in proceedings before the court."

§ 30 para. 4 Code of Criminal Procedure. In: ASPI [legal information system].

"The judge who took part in the decision making process of the earlier proceedings is excluded from the proceedings on the review of the order for the interception and recording of telecommunications traffic. The judge who participated in the decision making process on the review of the order for the interception and recording of telecommunications traffic is further excluded from the decision making process of the subsequent proceedings."

181 The decision of the Constitutional Court dated 3 March 2005, file number III. ÚS 501/04. In: beck-online [legal information system].

Specific questions connected with the inadmissibility of the interception (Section 88) are described subsequently. Generally, the records of communication of a person that were acquired against the law (especially if the conditions under Section 88 were not fulfilled) are taken as absolutely inadmissible evidence. Transcripts of such recordings cannot be filed in the criminal file. If this happens, the transcript, as well as the records themselves, cannot be used in criminal proceedings as evidence.[182]

On the basis of Section 88 para. 1 sentence 3, the interception and recording of telecommunication between the defence counsel and the accused only is inadmissible and it has to be destroyed. Such prohibition does not apply, however, to the communication of the accused person with his/her family members.[183] It is also necessary to fully follow the conditions stipulated under Section 88 para. 6[184] to attach the protocol containing the information specified above[185] in order to be able to use the evidence in the criminal proceedings. Only the recordings of telecommunication, relevant for the case may be included in the criminal case file. Other communication in the meaning of Section 88 para. 6 must protected against unauthorized use and kept outside the criminal case file. It is especially necessary to protect personal data and third person data contained in the records, which has no connection to the criminal proceedings.[186]

The interception and recording of telecommunication for the purpose of criminal proceedings is governed by the provisions of Section 88 of the Code of Criminal Procedure. This allows taking such action, also before the commencement of the prosecution, but only in the case of emergency and urgent operations. The interception can be used in criminal proceedings only if it was conducted on the basis of Section 88 of the Code of Criminal Procedure. Interception carried out under amy other legal act, e.g., under Act No. 283/1991 Sb. on the Police of the Czech Repub-

---

[182] The decision of the Regional Court in České Budějovice dated 29 September 1994, file number 4 To 354/94. In: beck-online [legal information system].

[183] The decision of the Supreme Court dated 15 June 2011, file number 4 Pzo 3/2011-37. In: beck-online [legal information system].

[184] § 88 para. 6. Code of Criminal Procedure. In: ASPI [legal information system].

"If the record of the telecommunications service is to be used as evidence, it is necessary to accompany it with the transcript, giving the place, time, manner and contents of the record, as well as the authority which issued the record. The police authority is obliged to label other records, securely store them so as to protect them against unauthorised misuse, and indicate the place of storage in the transcript. In another criminal case other than the one in which the interception and recording of telecommunications service was performed, the recording may be used as evidence if there is a criminal prosecution in this matter for a criminal offence referred to in Subsection 1, or with the consent of the user by the intercepted station."

[185] The decision of the High Court in Prague dated 18 January 2001, file number 4 To 3/01. In: beck-online [legal information system].

[186] The decision of the Constitutional Court dated 16 September 2010, file number III. ÚS 3221/09. In: beck-online [legal information system].

lic or under Act No. 13/1993 Sb., Customs Act, can be used only for the purposes defined by these acts (the means of operative techniques). This must be respected even if the evidence was collected under the same conditions that would otherwise be sufficient to carry out urgent interception according to the Code of Criminal Procedure. Records of such interception (and the interception itself) as well as any other operative technique materials cannot be used as evidence.[187] It was decided previously by the European Court of Human Rights in the case of *A. v. France* that interference with privacy with the attendance of police authorities was found to breach Art. 8 of the Convention for the Protection of Human Rights and Fundamental Freedoms (in this case, a detained suspected hitman, in cooperation with the police, recorded a phone call in which suspected persons revealed the details of the murder).[188]

Despite the fact that the evidence was obtained in violation of the law, such evidence may still be used in criminal proceedings. The Constitutional Court stated that in order for an audio recording recorded by a private person without the consent of the person whose voice was recorded to be used as evidence, it is necessary to consider firstly whether the evidence in the form of, e.g., an audio recording on a cell phone of the witness stands alone in a concrete situation when evaluating the guilt of the offender or whether the court also has other evidence at its disposal, which significantly supports the merits of the accusation and which is also supported by such recording of the conversation.[189] The information contained in the recording can serve as evidence in criminal proceedings only if the invasion of privacy is justified by the overriding interests of the person who provided the information in the manner described and then used. According to the opinion of the courts, illegally taken recording can be used only as supportive evidence to verify the facts stated in both interception and witness testimony.[190] Given the fact that there are rules on interception of the recording of telecommunication by the authorities that allow (among other data) acquiring the content of telephone messages, it is also possible to follow these rules when acquiring these "other" data, i.e., during the process of recording the telecommunication.[191]

---

187 The Act on the Police of the Czech Republic and the Customs Act have been amended; however, the decision of the High Court serves as an example of narrow interpretation of the possibility to use the intercepted evidence in criminal proceedings. The decision of the High Court in Prague dated 8 June 2000, file number 2 To 73/2000. In: beck-online [legal information system].

188 *A. v. France*, decision of 23 November 1993, Application No. 14838/89. In: HUDOC [legal information system].

189 The decision of the Constitutional Court dated 20 October 2011, file number II. ÚS 143/06. In: beck-online [legal information system].

190 This was confirmed by the decision of the Supreme Court of 3 May 2007, file number 5 Tdo 459/2007 or by the decision of the Supreme Court of 25 September 2013, file number 8 Tdo 908/2013. In: beck-online [legal information system].

191 The decision of the Constitutional Court dated 22 January 2001, file number II. ÚS 502/2000. In: beck-online [legal information system].

It is necessary to state since when the intercepted communication can be used as evidence in criminal proceedings, e.g., the example of cell phones. In criminal proceedings, cell phones are perceived as any other tangible things. The data stored on cell phones are evaluated in a similar way. The authorities in criminal proceedings can therefore extract all the data stored on the phone and such evidence can be used in criminal proceedings. But it is necessary to distinguish the specific moment at which the communication was taking place and to distinguish the use of various procedural instruments.[192] This was confirmed by the Explanatory Opinion of the Supreme Public Prosecutor's Office No. 4/2005.[193] Following this opinion, the police authorities do not need an interception order from the judge (issued on the basis of Section 88 of the Code of Criminal Procedure) if the data had already been delivered and present on the cell phone even before the moment at which the police authority took the cell phone into its possession.[194] This means that all the data stored on the cell phone at moment of securing it may be used as evidence.

In the case of uncollected voicemail, it is necessary to issue an interception order according to Section 88 of the Code of Criminal Procedure. Voicemail (unlike unread SMS message) is not stored directly on the mobile phone. Voicemail can only be collected from the data storage of a service provider through the cell phone. Such data cannot be used as evidence in the criminal proceedings only on the basis of seizure of property proceedings. It was stated in the Explanatory Opinion of the Supreme Public Prosecutor's Office No. 1/2015 that it is necessary to issue an interception order prior to the commencement of the communication itself if the voicemail is planned to be used as the evidence.[195]

The communication, which is not statically stored via secured remote service or storage but is still the subject of electronic communications (e-mail or other messenger communication services), has a special position. The Explanatory Opinion states that the provider of electronic communications is not entitled to store and to

---

[192] Such interpretation was confirmed by the decision of the Supreme Court dated 15 December 2000, file number 7 Tz 9/2000. In: beck-online [legal information system].

[193] The Supreme Public Prosecutor's Office, SL 788/2004, The Collection of the Explanatory Opinions of the Supreme Public Prosecutor's Office, No. 4/2005, in Brno 6 June 2005, accessible at: http://www.nsz.cz/images/stories/PDF/Stanoviska_Proces/2005/stanovisko%204-2005.pdf. This opinion also stated that the data stored in the SIM card inserted in the cell phone have the same status as the data stored directly in the cell phone.

[194] It is necessary to state that securing of the cell phone was issued under different provisions than the provision concerning interception. In this case, the proceedings are stated in Section 78 (obligation to release property) and Section 79 (seizure of property). Code of Criminal Procedure. In: ASPI [legal information system].

[195] The Supreme Public Prosecutor's Office, 1 SL 760/2014, The Collection of the Explanatory Opinions of the Supreme Public Prosecutor's Office, No. 1/2015, in Brno 26 January 2015, accessible at: http://www.nsz.cz/images/stories/PDF/Stanoviska_Proces/2015/1_SL_760-2014.pdf

transfer message content.[196] The Supreme Public Prosecutor's Office then concludes on the basis of such statement that Section 88 of the Code of Criminal Procedure can be only used for realtime communication. The communication (in the past or in the present) provided through information society services is, however, recorded and stored. Such communication (e-mail, online messengers) could not be provided in the meaning of its general purpose without the possibility to store the information. Thus, if the communication was stored on any device, there should be no limitation to using such data (despite the facts stated by the Explanatory Opinion) after the moment the interception order is properly issued. If the device was already seized as the communication was still ongoing (e.g., unread e-mail), it will still be necessary to issue an interception order on the basis of Section 88 of the Code of Criminal Procedure.

If the evidence (interception) was acquired legally, it cannot be excluded by the court only because of the fact that the legal regulation on evidence proceedings has changed. The legality of such proceedings is decided on the basis of the legal regulation that was in the force at the time the measures to acquire such evidence were taken.[197]

When disclosing the commission of serious crimes, the police can interfere in a lawful manner with different developmental stages of a criminal offense. It cannot provoke (initiate) the criminal activity that would not be committed without such provocation. The opinion that the duty of the police is always to prevent the commission of the criminal offense in its initial stage would prevent the use of operative and investigative methods (interception). This would make such methods useless and would lead to paralysis on the part of the police to carry out its tasks in the process of detection of serious criminal offenses and to reveal the identity of the offender. It is also necessary to address the question of culpability in relation to the application of a higher criminal sentence when deciding whether the requirement of Section 88 para. 1[198] is fulfilled or not.[199]

From the point of view of constitutionally protected fundamental rights, it is highly inadmissible that, for clarification and verification of the facts indicating that the crime was committed (commencement of operations), it cannot be allowed

---

196 The Supreme Public Prosecutor's Office, 1 SL 760/2014, The Collection of the Explanatory Opinions of the Supreme Public Prosecutor's Office, No. 1/2015, in Brno 26 January 2015, accessible at: http://www.nsz.cz/images/stories/PDF/Stanoviska_Proces/2015/1_SL_760-2014.pdf. p. 8.

197 The decision of the Constitutional Court dated 7 May 2014, file number Pl. ÚS 47/13. In: beck-online [legal information system].

198 The interception can be used only in the case of serious crimes, thus it is necessary to consider whether such crime described in Section 88 para. 1 had really been committed.

199 The decision of the High Court in Prague of 19 January 2006, file number 2 To 139/2005. In: beck-online [legal information system].

to use interception to subsequently justify that a serious crime (under Section 88 para. 1) has been committed.[200]

In its decision, the Constitutional Court strongly stressed that, if there are any specific facts supporting the suspicion for committing a serious crime, then, with regard to the constitutional limits of regulation of interception, such facts have to be clearly apparent in the rationale of the interception order. The specific rationale, however, contained only very vague argumentation to support the suspicion that a person was in attendance during a particular criminal action. The interception order did not include specific facts from which it was clear that a particular person was suspected of committing the criminal offense. It is necessary to use proper and persuasive argumentation in the interception order on why it was decided to use such a strong procedural instrument as interception.[201] Without proper rationale in the interception order, the information gained on this basis cannot be used in the criminal proceedings.

The facts stated above serve as the general concept on how the limitation and consideration of the admissibility of interception as evidence works in the criminal proceedings. It relied especially on the rulings of the higher courts. If the above indicated limits are exceeded, the use of interception as evidence cannot be found to be legitimate; thus, the communication data contained in the interception will be regarded as illegally obtained.

Comparative note – Slovakia

The same applies in the Slovak Republic. In criminal proceedings, the examination of evidence is carried out by the court, which, however, leaves the examination of the accused, witnesses, and expert witnesses to the parties involved, starting with the one that proposed or procured the evidence.

Anything that may contribute to proper clarification of the matter and what was obtained as evidence under the Code of Criminal Procedure or under a special law (Act on the Protection against Interception or Act on the Police Corps) may serve as evidence. This is an important aspect of "legality of evidence."

Evidence is categorized as: testimony of witnesses, experts; reports and expert opinions; review of testimony on the location of the crime; recognition of suspect; reconstruction; investigative experiments; survey of objects and documents relevant for criminal proceedings; and any notification/information obtained through use of ITM or operative activities.

---

[200] The decision of the Constitutional Court dated 27 September 2014, file number II. ÚS 789/06. In: beck-online [legal information system].

[201] The decision of the Constitutional Court dated 27 January 2010, file number II. ÚS 2806/08. In: beck-online [legal information system].

The bodies involved in criminal proceedings must proceed so as to properly establish the facts of the case that do not give rise to reasonable doubt, to the extent necessary for making the decision. They procure the evidence as part of their official duties. Also, the parties are granted the right to procure the evidence. The bodies involved in criminal proceedings thoroughly clarify the circumstances, regardless of whether they prejudice or benefit the accused. They also take the evidence in either direction, so as to enable the court to arrive at a fair decision. The crucial principle for the evaluation of evidence is that authorities evaluate the evidence in accordance with their firm conviction – based on careful examination of all the facts of the case, separately and jointly, irrespective of whether they were supplied by the court, the bodies involved in criminal proceedings, or by one of the parties to the proceedings.

It is very important that the bodies involved in criminal proceedings and the court evaluate only legally obtained evidence. This legal aspect emphasizes the admissibility of the evidence, which is embodied in Section 2 para. 12 of the Code of Criminal Procedure. Therefore, we can also conclude that the inadmissibility of the evidence is deduced mainly by the interpretation of the above-mentioned principles of the evidence-producing process.

Any interceptions that were acquired against the law are commonly evaluated as absolutely inadmissible evidence. Transcripts of such recordings cannot be filed in the criminal file or read before the court. According to the opinion of some scholars, "the evidence obtained against the law is passing its inadmissibility and procedural invalidity on the further evidence, which is arising from the content of the first inadmissible evidence."[202]

Emphasis is also put on the interception of a communication between the attorney (defence counsel) and client. Pursuant to Section 115 para. 1 of the Code of Criminal Procedure, no information thus obtained may be used for the purpose of criminal proceedings, and any such information must be immediately destroyed in a prescribed manner. However, this does not apply to information relating to a case in which a lawyer does not represent the accused as his defense counsel (criminal attorney).

The challenge is the "dual" legal regime of interception. The interception should be used in criminal proceedings only if it was conducted on the basis of Section 115 of the Code of Criminal Procedure. Interception carried out under any other legal act, e.g., under the Act on the Protection against Interception, should be used only for the purposes defined only by this act. The problem comes with the legal definition, which is not limited to operative techniques only. According to this act, ITM can be used exclusively to achieve the security and defense of the

202 Minarik, Š. Trestný poriadok. Komentár. Iura edition, spol. s r.o. 2010, Bratislava. p. 389.

country, to prevent and reveal criminal activities, or to protect the rights and freedoms of other persons. This is quite a broad definition, which covers criminal proceedings and pre-trial matters as well. To finish this ambiguous definition, it is further required that when using ITM, essential rights or freedoms can be infringed upon only to the necessary extent and for a period of time no longer than necessary to attain the legal goal it serves.

In one notable case, in which the interception carried out under the Act on the Protection against Interception was used in criminal proceedings, the Slovak Constitutional Court declared that "there can not be any doubt that the approval or order [to intercept] must be justified in each case, whether issued under the Criminal Code or under the law on protection against interception. This is because it is a serious intrusion to the fundamental right of persons. Also, they have no possibility to appeal [...] Therefore they are entitled to review the validity of issued order subsequently. Such review requires specific arguments explaining facts needed to interfere the right to privacy. Without such a justification relying on the specific facts there is no review. At first glance, it might be seemed that regarding the secret nature of interception would be intolerable and counterproductive to state in the reasoning specific facts justifying the granting of an order, as these could disturb their purposes. In fact, the opposite is true. Precisely because of the secret nature of the interception, nothing prevents the court to mention the reasons which led him to issue the order."[203]

C. Use of Data Outside the Main Proceedings

1. Data from other criminal investigations

The interception and recording of telecommunication can be used in another criminal case as evidence under the condition that:

- In such another criminal case, there is a criminal prosecution for criminal offense referred in Section 88 para. 1 of the Code of Criminal Procedure. These are crimes for which the law stipulates a prison sentence with the maximum limit of at least eight years (machinations in insolvency proceedings, violation of regulations on rules of competition, negotiating advantages during public procurement/tender and auction, misuse of powers of an official person or for any other intentional criminal offense for which prosecution is stipulated in a declared international treaty), or

---

[203] Decision of the Slovak Constitutional Court No. I. ÚS 274/05-73. Online: http://portal.concourt.sk/

– with the consent of the user of the intercepted station (anyone who uses or requests a publicly available electronic communications service).[204]

It should be stated that, if there was an interception order issued on the basis of commission of a serious criminal offense (as stated in Section 88 para. 1 of the Code of Criminal Procedure), in the first case of criminal prosecution, then the fact that the criminal prosecution against the same person for another criminal offense (which was however not serious criminal offense mentioned in Section 88 para. 1) was initiated after that, does not mean that the interception would be illegal against that person. The interception cannot, however, be used as evidence for a second and less serious offense; it can be used to support the facts only in the first case of criminal prosecution.[205]

The requirements that have to be contained in the interception order are listed in Section 88 para. 2 of the Code of Criminal Procedure:

> The interception order and recording of the telecommunications service shall include a determined user address or a user device and the user if their identity is known, and the period during which the interception and recording of telecommunications traffic is conducted cannot be longer than four months; the justification must include the specific facts that justify the issue of such order as well as its period.

In the case of possible use of the intercepted data for the prosecution of individuals who were not the subject of the interception order, it has to be concluded that, if there was already ongoing interception, evidence on the basis of such interception can also be used for the criminal offense that was discovered during the interception. This evidence can, however, be used if the discovered criminal offence fulfils the conditions of serious crime listed in Section 88 para. 1. If these conditions are fulfilled, then it is not relevant whether the interception was allowed and the recording acquired regarding the suspect, accused, or any other person.[206]

2. Data from preventive investigations

The case law of the European Court of Human Rights, in limiting the fundamental right to privacy for security reasons, strictly restricts the conditions for the applicability of evidence obtained by limiting privacy. It approves only such practices, which can offer adequate safeguards to protect fundamental rights, e.g., against abuse or arbitrariness because, in the opposite case (and also because of present

---

204 Section 88 para. 6 sentence 3 Code of Criminal Procedure. In: ASPI [legal information system]. The wording of Section 88 para. 6 was enacted in 1 July 2008, but the use of evidence in other criminal offence proceedings under certain conditions had already been expressed in the decision of the Constitutional Court of 27 April 1994, file number II. ÚS 6/93. In: beck-online [legal information system].

205 The decision of the Supreme Court dated 13 April 2011, file number 4 Pzo 2/2010. In: beck-online [legal information system].

206 The decision of the Supreme Court dated 9 October 2003, file number 2 To 144/03. In: beck-online [legal information system].

technological possibilities), democracy itself is at stake. This principle was also highlighted in the case of *Klass and others v. Germany* (especially in paragraphs 42, 48, 49, 50).[207]

Based on the above-mentioned arguments, the Constitutional Court considered the possibility of using interception outside the criminal proceedings (intelligence service) in criminal proceedings. Interception of communication by public authorities (as well as any other type of secret surveillance) represents a serious limitation of fundamental rights. It is implied from the interception order that the limitation of personal integrity and privacy may very rarely be made by public authorities, only when necessary and if the aim of pursuing public interest cannot otherwise be achieved. Failure to comply with certain conditions means that such action is unconstitutional.

Intelligence law incorporates less limiting rules on the breach of privacy; these milder conditions are only tolerated when limited by strict intent of the use of the gathered information and also by the seriousness of possible danger.

Using intelligence interception in criminal proceedings as evidence of guilt is foreseen neither in the Code of Criminal Procedure nor in the law on intelligence services. In concrete cases, interceptions were acquired pursuant to the act relating to the intelligence services. The intelligence service crossed the boundaries of the law when it provided a highly concretized, extensive set of information to the authorities prosecuting a criminal offence. Intelligence services in relation to criminal proceedings law are only entitled to provide basic and general information (Section 8 para. 3 of Act No. 153/1994 Sb. on intelligence services of the Czech Republic). Any use of interception outside the sphere of application of the law on intelligence services was and is an ongoing violation of fundamental human rights. It was explicitly stated that the potential threat of terrorist attack also cannot breach the barrier of constitutional mechanisms.[208]

3. Data from foreign jurisdictions

The questions on acquiring, using, and admitting evidence of intercepted data abroad are regulated mainly by Act No. 104/2013 Sb. on international judicial cooperation in criminal matters. This law deals with issues of interception in Section 47, where the possibility to provide legal assistance to another state based on the principle of reciprocity is established. This section, however, states that it is unconditionally necessary to respect the rules incorporated in the Code of Criminal Procedure.

---

[207] *Klass and others v. Germany*, decision of 6 September 1978, Application No. 5029/71. In: HUDOC [legal information system].

[208] The decision of the Constitutional Court dated 29 February 2008, file number I. ÚS 3038/07. In: beck-online [legal information system].

If an international treaty stipulates that the interception can be carried out by a foreign country on the territory of the Czech Republic without the technical assistance of the Czech Republic, the Regional Court in Prague is responsible for deciding on the consent to interception or its continuation; if a preliminary procedure is conducted in the foreign state, which will perform the interception, the Public Prosecutor from the Regional Prosecutor's Office in Prague decides on the admissibility of such interception. Consent to interception or its continuation can be granted only if the conditions set out in Section 88 of the Code of Criminal Procedure are fulfilled.[209]

If an international treaty stipulates that it is possible to carry out the interception of telecommunication from the Czech Republic on the territory of a foreign state without its technical assistance, the prosecutor and – after filing the indictment – the court informs the foreign state about the anticipated interception in the manner provided by that international treaty.[210]

The general rule to respect the requirements under Section 88 of the Code of Criminal Procedure has also been highlighted by the Supreme Court in the past and before Act No. 104/2013 Sb. on international judicial cooperation in criminal matters was in force. It was also stressed that it is necessary to rationalize intervention into privacy in this decision.[211]

Comparative note – Slovakia

Use of data outside the main proceedings in Slovak criminal procedure are based on the following assumptions:

- Criminal proceedings are conducted in respect of a felony, corruption, criminal offence of the abuse of power by a public official, laundering the proceeds of crime, or in respect of an intentional criminal offence where so provided by a promulgated international treaty, and if there are reasonable grounds to believe that it will reveal facts that are materially relevant for criminal proceedings;
- another matter is also being heard in simultaneous proceedings.

In practice, it is questionable what "simultaneous proceedings" means.

One line of thought involves the interpretation that two proceedings must be taking place at the same time as the moment of the obtaining of the evidence (record-

[209] Section 64 para. 1. Act No. 104/2013 Sb. on international judicial cooperation in criminal matters. In: beck-online [legal information system].

[210] Section 64 para. 2. Act No. 104/2013 Sb. on international judicial cooperation in criminal matters. In: beck-online [legal information system].

[211] The decision of the Supreme Court dated 13 April 2007, file number 11 Tz 129/2006. In: beck-online [legal information system].

ing). The second scholarly opinion (Šámal[212]) argues that two proceedings have to be taking place at the same time at the moment of the executing of the evidence (the moment of the producing the evidence).

Ultimately, there is always a possibility to use the evidence in another proceeding if the user of the intercepted station or concerned person consents.

Regarding data from preventive investigations, kindly refer to the previous chapter on the inadmissibility of evidence as a consequence of inappropriate collection, where the case is mentioned in which the interception carried out under the Act on the Protection against Interception was used in criminal proceedings. Under certain circumstances, this type of evidence could be used in criminal proceedings. But it has to fulfil formal criteria laid down in the Code of Criminal Procedure.

Data from foreign jurisdictions are obtained in accordance with the Code of Criminal Procedure or valid MLA.

Under Section 533 of the Code of Criminal Procedure, the general rule is that any request for legal assistance shall, in addition to a precise description of the required act of assistance, contain a description of the facts of the offence that is the basis of the request, legal denomination of the offence together with a verbatim wording of the pertinent legal provisions, the personal data of the accused or, as the case may be, of the victim or the witnesses if their examination is requested, as well as further details required for the proper execution of the requested legal assistance. The request shall contain the exact specification of the requesting authority, its file number, the date of the request, and it shall bear the signature of the responsible officer and the round seal of the requesting authority. The request and the supporting documents shall be accompanied by translation into a foreign language by an official translator, if required.

Under Section 532 of the Code of Criminal Procedure, requests for legal assistance emanating from the Slovak pre-trial authorities shall be transmitted abroad through the General Prosecutor's Office. Requests for legal assistance emanating from the Slovak courts shall be transmitted abroad through the Ministry of Justice. Diplomatic channels are another option to cooperate.

D. Challenging the Probity of Intercepted Data

According to Section 88 para. 8 of the Code on Criminal Proceedings, after the criminal case becomes final, the prosecutor or the presiding judge of the court of first instance informs the person who is the user of the device about the interception order and the recording of telecommunication, unless exceptions under Sec-

212 Šámal, P. Odposlech a záznam telekomunikačního provozu ve světle judikatúry. Soudní rozhledy, C.H. Beck. 2000. č.3. pp. 68-69.

tion 88 para. 9 are fulfilled.[213] Such person may submit a proposal to review the legality of the interception to the Supreme Court within six months; the Supreme Court, in proceedings under Section 314l–314n[214] of the Code of Criminal Proceedings, by resolution, either rules that the law was violated or declares that the law was not violated. This decision is not subject to appeal.

The prerequisite for filing a petition before the Supreme Court for review of the legality of interception in accordance with Section 314l is Section 88 para. 8, accordingly that the case was ended. It is also necessary that the presiding judge of the court of first instance or the prosecutor subsequently inform the person authorized to file such petition about the ordered interception. A proposal to review the legality of interception cannot therefore be submitted to the Supreme Court before the relevant case is final and without subsequent sending of the information to the

[213] Section 88 para. 9. Code of Criminal Procedure. In: ASPI [legal information system].

"The presiding judge, the public prosecutor or the police authority does not submit the information under Subsection 8 in proceedings on a crime committed by an organised group for which the law stipulates a prison sentence with the upper penalty limit of at least eight years, in proceedings on criminal offences committed for the benefit of an organised criminal group, in proceedings for criminal participation in an organised criminal group (Section 361 of the Penal Code), or if the criminal offence involved more people and in relation to at least one of them the criminal proceedings have not yet been finally concluded or if it is against the person to whom the information was submitted, is the subject of criminal proceedings, or if providing such information could defeat the purpose of the criminal proceedings, including those referred to in Subsection 6, or if it could lead to threats to national security, life, health, or the rights and freedoms of individuals."

[214] § 314l Code of Criminal Procedure. In: ASPI [legal information system].

"(1) Upon the petition of the person referred to in Section 88 Subsection 8, the Supreme Court, in closed hearing, shall examine the legality of the warrant for the interception and recording of the telecommunications service.

(2) Upon the petition of the person referred to in Section 88a Subsection 2, the Supreme Court, in closed hearing, shall examine the legality of the order for the ascertainment of data on the telecommunications service."

§ 314m Code of Criminal Procedure. In: ASPI [legal information system].

"(1) If the Supreme Court finds that the warrant for the interception and recording of the telecommunications service or the order for the ascertainment of data on the telecommunications service was issued or its performance was contrary to law, they shall pronounce the violation of the law by a resolution.

(2) An appeal against such decision is not permissible."

§ 314n Code of Criminal Procedure. In: ASPI [legal information system].

"(1) If the Supreme Court finds that the warrant for the interception and recording of the telecommunications service was issued and its performance was in compliance with the conditions set out in Section 88 Subsection 1 or the order for the ascertainment of data on the telecommunications service was issued and its performance was in compliance with the conditions set out in Section 88a Subsection 1, they shall pronounce in a resolution that the law was not violated.

(2) An appeal against such decision is not permissible."

authorized person. If such petition is filed, even if the above stated conditions were not fulfilled, the Supreme Court rejects it as inadmissible.[215]

In accordance with Sections 314l et seq. of the Code of Criminal Procedure, in the procedure for review of an interception order, review by the Supreme Court is limited to only the assessment of legality of the issued interception order and the recording of telecommunication. Therefore, in these proceedings, the Supreme Court cannot deal with, e.g., any objection related to the performance of duties of the police authority in accordance with Section 88 para. 3 or objections against the evaluation of the results of the interception directed against the rationale of the court, which decided such interception.[216]

Under the conditions of Section 88 paras. 1, 2, it is also exceptionally possible to also order the interception during the phase of enforcement proceedings in connection with the search of a convicted person who is meant to be imprisoned for the offence listed in Section 88 para. 1. It is, however, permitted to use the interception only when any other procedures on how to locate such person have failed. The legality of such interception can also be examined by means of the procedure described under Sections 314l–314n.[217]

Comparative note – Slovakia

Challenging the probity of intercepted data in Slovak law is different from the Czech possibility to review the interception decision by the Supreme Court. The Code of Criminal Procedure does not recognize such a process.

If the interception did not produce any facts relevant for criminal proceedings, the criminal procedure authority or the relevant department of the Police Corps must destroy the obtained records immediately in a prescribed manner. There should be a protocol on the destruction, which becomes part of the criminal file. According to Section 115 para. 8 of the Code of Criminal Procedure, persons who do not have the right to view the criminal file shall be notified of the destruction of the recordings. Furthermore, the notification shall be made by the body whose decision ultimately settled the matter, or, in proceedings before the court, by the presiding judge of a panel of a first-instance court within three years of the date on which criminal prosecution in the case was concluded. It is important to note that this will not apply to proceedings concerning particularly serious felonies or the felonies committed by organized groups, criminal groups, or terrorist groups or to

[215] The decision of the Supreme Court dated 14 October 2010, file number 4 Pzo 1/2010. In: beck-online [legal information system].

[216] The decision of the Supreme Court dated 13 April 2011, file number 4 Pzo 2/2010. In: beck-online [legal information system].

[217] The decision of the Supreme Court dated 5 June 2013, file number Tpjn 304/2012. In: beck-online [legal information system].

criminal offences committed by more than one person if at least one of the perpetrators is still under prosecution or if the provision of such information could obstruct the purpose of the criminal proceedings.

Currently, there is an ongoing discussion about possible options to challenge such interception decisions. In one related decision, the Slovak Constitutional Court established that:[218] "the appeal against the consent, nor command [to interception] is not permitted. The concerned person is not able to seek protection at the general court in connection with the fact that his conversation has been intercepted. The general court could not review the eligibility of the issuance of a final consent or order, and it is precisely because the consent or order are valid and enforceable decisions, by which is the court bound. [...] The concerned person whose conversation has been intercepted can challenge the illegality of the interception and the consequent uselessness of listened conversation as the evidence in criminal court proceedings. He can do so only by the simultaneous fulfilment of two conditions. A criminal case has to reach the trial stage and the concerned person shall be a party to the criminal proceedings, either as a charged person or as a person claiming damages. Also, it means the protection by the criminal court will not come up to the case, which not even comes before the criminal court, nor to the case, in which the concerned persons are not parties to criminal proceedings." The Constitutional Court stated that, unless the complainant argues that the records were obtained illegally, he can still put forward this argument in the context of criminal proceedings, particularly in his defence before the competent court. He could request to review illegally obtained evidence and therefore it should not be taken into the court's consideration. It would be a matter for the court or other law enforcement agencies to consider such an argument and draw conclusions from it. But it would also mean that the person whose telephone conversation was intercepted must be able to defend himself/herself against the very fact of interception. The Slovak Constitutional Court has divided this procedural right into two parts: claiming privacy rights and claiming the use of interception of communications as evidence in criminal proceedings. In this context, the Slovak Constitutional Court declared that the illegal interceptions intruded upon the claimant's rights and his freedoms (they were invalid due to lack of reasoning). He repealed the orders to intercept and also settled the claim, which has to be paid by the state, to his financial satisfaction.

Therefore, the conclusion for the options to challenge the probity of intercepted data in the Slovak Republic can be found in hardly accessible procedural tools:

- Constitutional complaint (Act. No. 38/1993 Coll. on the organization of the Constitutional Court of the Slovak Republic, proceedings, and the status of its judges);
- Private action for the protection of personality (Act No. 40/1964 Coll. Civil Code).

---

218 Decision of the Slovak Constitutional Court No. I. ÚS 274/05. Unofficial translation. Online: http://portal.concourt.sk/

V. Exchange of Intercepted Electronic Communication Data between Foreign Countries

A. Legal Basis for Mutual Legal Assistance

International conventions on MLA have priority of application in Czech Law according to the Art. 10 of Act No. 1/1993 Sb., Constitution of the Czech Republic. Specifically, for MLA this is also listed in Art. 3 para. 2 of Act No. 104/2013 Sb. on International Judicial Cooperation in Criminal Matters.

Art. 10 [informal translation]

Promulgated international agreements ratified by the Parliament and binding the Czech Republic are part of law; if the agreement differs from the Act, international agreement shall be used.

Art. 3 para. 2 [informal translation]

This Act governs the procedure, unless the international conventions stipulates otherwise.

Therefore, the application of national legislation is directly related to the absence of international agreement regulating the same topic. Application of national legislation is also possible when an international convention does not regulate the topic in sufficient detail. This is the case for both multilateral and bilateral agreements.

1. International conventions

The Czech Republic has signed and ratified the following conventions:

- European Convention on Mutual Assistance in Criminal Matters, 1959, promulgated as no. 550/1992 Sb.
- Additional Protocol to the European Convention on Information on Foreign Law, 1978, promulgated as no. 31/1997 Sb.
- Second Additional Protocol to the European Convention on Mutual Assistance in Criminal Matters, 2001, promulgated as no. 48/2006 Sb. m. s.
- Convention on Mutual Assistance in Criminal Matters between the Member States of the European Union, 2000, promulgated as no. 55/2006 Sb. m. s.
- Additional Protocol to the Convention on Mutual Assistance in Criminal Matters between the Member States of the European Union, 2001, promulgated as no. 56/2006 Sb. m. s.
- European Convention on Extradition, 1957, promulgated as no. 549/1997 Sb.
- Additional Protocol to the European Convention on Extradition, 1975, promulgated as no. 29/1997 Sb.
- Second Additional Protocol to the European Convention on Extradition, 1978, promulgated as no. 30/1997 Sb.

- Third Additional Protocol to the European Convention on Extradition, 2010, promulgated as no. 34/2013 Sb. m. s.
- Convention on Cybercrime, 2001, promulgated as no. 104/2013 Sb. m. s.
- United Nations Transnational Organized Crime Convention, 2000, promulgated as 75/2013 Sb.

The Czech Republic has signed and ratified many other international agreements shaping its penal policy and firmly placing it within the international framework.[219] However, the above-mentioned agreements currently have the biggest influence on MLA in the Czech Republic.

2. Bilateral treaties

The Czech Republic has signed and ratified the following bilateral treaties involving Germany:

- Agreement between the Czech Republic and the Federal Republic of Germany on amendments to the European Convention on Mutual Assistance in Criminal Matters, promulgated as no. 68/2002 Sb. m. s.
- Note of the Ministry of Foreign Affairs of the Czech Republic of June 19, 2002 on change of designation and jurisdiction of organs listed in Art. 19 para. 1 and Art. 20 para. 4 of the Agreement between the Czech Republic and the Federal Republic of Germany on amendments to the European Convention on Mutual Assistance in Criminal Matters, promulgated as no. 126/2002 Sb. m. s.
- Note of the Ministry of Foreign Affairs of the Czech Republic of September 8, 2005 on change of designation and jurisdiction of organs listed in Art. 19 para. 1 and Art. 20 para. 4 of the Agreement between the Czech Republic and the Federal Republic of Germany on amendments to the European Convention on Mutual Assistance in Criminal Matters, promulgated as no. 124/2005 Sb. m. s.
- Note of the Embassy of the Federal Republic of Germany of January 5, 2006 on change on change of designation and jurisdiction of organs listed in Art. 23 para. 3 no. 2 b) of the Agreement between the Czech Republic and the Federal Republic of Germany on amendments to the European Convention on Mutual Assistance in Criminal Matters, promulgated as no. 30/2006 Sb. m. s.

The first above-mentioned bilateral agreement stipulates in Art. 17 special methods of investigation and cooperation, which are relevant for the purpose of electronic communication interception. The incoming request can be taken further only if it is submitted by the court or accompanied by the statement of the court from which it is clear that all the conditions for interception would be met if the interception were to take place within the territory of the state issuing the request. The pur-

---

[219] Agreements on prohibition and punishment of white slave trade, trade in women of full age, genocide, etc.

pose of this provision is to ensure that the issuing state is not able to deliberately lower the standard of procedural checks. The second condition that has to be met is that the interception warrant could be issued by the state receiving the request. The purpose of this provision is to ensure that the receiving state does not warrant interception that would have otherwise been unlawful. Also, the interception can proceed further only if the person or device subjected to interception is located within the territory of the state receiving the request; or located within the state issuing the request but the interception cannot be carried out without the cooperation of the state receiving the request; or within the territory of the third state but the state issuing the request needs the technical assistance of the state receiving the request.

The second, third, and fourth of the above-mentioned bilateral agreements reflected organizational changes within both Czech and German law enforcement. Therefore, they did not bring about any substantial change to the matter of electronic communication interception itself.

It is also possible to seek legal assistance without multilateral or bilateral agreements. In this case, the Ministry of Justice needs to issue a confirmation of reciprocity.[220] This is even preferable, according to some experts, because the absence of international conventions allows them to follow less formal procedures.[221]

3. National regulation

Act No. 104/2013 Sb. on Mutual Judicial Assistance in Criminal Matters [Zákon o vzájemné justiční spolupráci ve věcech trestních] (hereinafter referred to as ZMJS) is the main legal instrument governing judicial MLA at the national level.

ZMJS was adopted only recently and has been in effect since the 1 January 2014.[222] However, this creates only mild interpretational problems, since most of the provisions were previously contained in Act No. 141/1961 Code of Criminal Procedure [Trestní řád]. Nonetheless, warranting an interception in the case of MLA is extremely rare (see statistics below). Usually, MLA does not seek to obtain the warrant but merely seeks to receive the evidence already obtained for the purpose of criminal proceedings abroad.

Overall, for the purpose of electronic communication interception in another state, the law does not foresee any special procedure. Standard requests in accordance with international conventions, possible bilateral treaties, or general provisions of ZMJS can be submitted.

---

220 In case the confirmation has already been issued, notice can be found on the Intranet of prosecutors.

221 Comp. Novotná, J.: Právní pomoc v cizím státu v přípravném řízení trestním. 3. vydání. Praha : C.H. Beck, 2015, p. 212.

222 Previous national regulation was contained in Act No. 141/1961 on criminal procedure [Trestní řád].

However, the special case of cross-border interception is contained in the law and is governed by Art. 64 of ZMJS. The Czech national regulation requires explicit permission by multilateral or bilateral agreement in order to use cross-border interception without the technical assistance of the other state.

B. Requirements and Procedure (Including the Handling of Privileged Information)

1. Incoming requests

The procedure is fairly straightforward and follows the conditions set out in Art. 18 para. 3 of the Convention on Mutual Assistance in Criminal Matters between the Member States of the European Union.

Art. 18 para. 3 [official translation]

By way of derogation from Article 14 of the European Mutual Assistance Convention and Article 37 of the Benelux Treaty, requests under this Article shall include the following:

(a) an indication of the authority making the request;

(b) confirmation that a lawful interception order or warrant has been issued in connection with a criminal investigation;

(c) information for the purpose of identifying the subject of this interception;

(d) an indication of the criminal conduct under investigation;

(e) the desired duration of the interception; and

(f) if possible, the provision of sufficient technical data, in particular the relevant network connection number, to ensure that the request can be met.

However, certain problem might appear concerning the admissibility of the evidence obtained in this way. According to Art. 42 para. 2 ZMJS, the interception can be used for the purpose of Czech criminal procedure if it was obtained in accordance with either foreign or Czech provisions. The Supreme Court ruled on this in its Decision on Case 11 Tz 129/2006 of 13 April, 2007, in which it was concluded that, once the requirements prescribed by Czech law are met, nothing prevents the evidence obtained by interception of communication from being used in Czech criminal procedure, even if obtained abroad.

Two organs handle the incoming requests. At the pre-trial stage, the responsible organ is the Department of International Affairs of the Supreme Public Prosecutor's Office. The responsible organ at the trial stage is the International Department for Criminal Matters of the Ministry of Justice of the Czech Republic. The request is then passed to the organ responsible for issuing a warrant for the purpose of pre-trial or trial proceedings. The national law does not prescribe any special procedure, save for the above-mentioned responsible organs. There is no duty to filter or delete the privileged information from the intercepted communication.

Art. 42 para. 2 [informal translation]

Evidence obtained at the request of the judicial authority of the foreign authority may be used in criminal proceedings in the Czech Republic only if they were acquired in accordance with the laws of the foreign country, or in accordance with Czech law.

2. Outgoing requests

Any procedures needed to intercept electronic communications are followed in the foreign state and by its organs; therefore, the Czech Republic and its organs do not have to issue a warrant. The foreign body is generally satisfied with the content of the request for legal assistance provided by the Public Prosecutor – the prosecutor, however, must assure the foreign organ that all the conditions laid down by Czech law have been met. Then, the foreign organ issues the warrant normally prescribed by its own national law. However, if the foreign organ refuses to issue its own warrant with the argument that it cannot be done without a Czech warrant, the prosecutor requests the warrant and it is then transferred to the foreign organ according to Art. 45 ZMJS.

The special situation of cross-border interception that was already mentioned above is not, *stricto sensu* a request for a warrant. It serves mainly to inform the foreign state that the Czech Republic will be performing the interception itself within the foreign jurisdiction without the need for technical assistance. Therefore, the principle *locus regit actum* is violated, because Czech law governs the interception. Also, the criminal jurisdiction of the foreign state is violated, because the Czech organs will perform the interception. This is the main reason why this is possible only if permitted *expressis verbis* by the international agreement.

3. Technical regulation

The technical regulation of every interception of communication data involves the following measures:

- File material exists in four places – ÚZČ (Útvar zvláštních činností, "the Unit for Special Activities of Criminal Police and Investigation", specialized department within the Czech police responsible for deployment of interception of communication), authorized body (department requesting the interception of communication), Public Prosecutor, and the court;
- Request can be edited only by the department possessing the files for the specific interception;
- System can be accessed only by the authorized person, based on individual authentication information;
- Log of every access is archived and accessible centrally within the ÚZČ;
- Interception is activated by the ÚZČ – Center of information systems. The center cannot edit the request and does not have access to the intercepted records.

The Czech Republic is experimenting with the electronic criminal file in order to make the criminal procedure more efficient. The whole system is governed by the general law governing criminal procedure and also by the special bylaws governing the filing system – mainly the Instruction of the Ministry of Justice No. 505/2001-Org on Interior and Office Regulation for district, regional, and higher courts. Theoretically, once the electronic filing system is fully implemented, the criminal procedure can be conducted electronically as a whole and, at that point, a real-time transfer mechanism can be implemented. At this time, the electronic filing system of the Czech police is accessible to the prosecution by guaranteed and secured connection through the centralized communication infrastructure. This partial cooperation was made possible by the Order of the Police President No. 125/2008, but full-scale electronization is still to be achieved.

Additional technical regulation is provided by the Czech Act No. 412/2005 Sb. on the Protection of Classified Information.[223] The Czech police constantly argues that, according to Section 65 of Act No. 141/1961 Sb., the obtained communication data are classified, possessing the "confidential" secrecy level.

Section 65

(1) The accused, victim and party to an action, their defence counsel and their agents have the right to inspect files, with the exception of the voting record and the personal data of the witnesses in accordance with Section 55 Subsection 2, to make extracts from them and notes, and make copies of files and their parts at own expense. The same right applies to the legal representatives of the accused, victim or the party to an action if they are denied legal capacity or if their legal capacity is restricted. Other people may then do so with the consent of the presiding judge and in criminal proceedings with the consent of the public prosecutor or the police authority only if it is necessary to exercise their rights.

(2) The public prosecutor or the police authority are entitled to inspect the files, along with the other rights referred to in Subsection 1, and they may deny them based on important reasons in the preliminary hearing. The public prosecutor is obligated to urgently review the severity of the grounds on which those rights are denied by the police authority and the request of the person to whom the refusal concerns. These rights can not be denied to the accused and the defence counsel once they have been advised of the possibility to study the files, and when concluding an agreement on guilt and punishment.

(3) Those who had the right to be present to an action can not be denied access to the transcript of such an action. The accused and their legal counsel could not be denied access to the resolution to initiate criminal prosecution (Section 160 Subsection 1).

(4) The rights of public authorities to access the files under other legal regulations are not established with prejudice to the provisions of the preceding Subsections.

(5) When authorising access to the files, it is necessary to take such steps to preserve the secrecy of the classified information protected by a special Act which is related to the state ordered or recognised confidentiality obligation.

According to the Czech police, the request to maintain secrecy also covers the intercepted communication data, because of its protection by law. This interpretation

223 Available in English at http://www.nbu.cz/en/legislation/

is criticized by some police officers and public prosecutors; however, the current practice is most likely not going to change within the foreseeable future due to lack of political will at police headquarters.

4. Real-time transfer of communication data

As mentioned above, intercepted communication can be transferred in real-time or subsequently according to Art. 18 of the Convention on Mutual Assistance in Criminal Matters between the Member States of the European Union, which has application priority over national law. However, based on individual consultations, it appears that the Czech Republic is poorly prepared for such a real-time solution and subsequent transfers are generally used.

Art. 19 of the Convention regarding access to communication providers also takes priority in application, but intercepted communication cannot be transferred without the involvement of a domestic authority.

C. European Investigation Order

Based on individual interviews with police officers and public prosecutors, only minor adjustments are expected. Moreover, the Czech government has not issued any official statement regarding the European Investigation Order so far.

D. Statistics

Complete statistics regarding the number of warrants for electronic communication interceptions are, unfortunately, unavailable. For the sake of secrecy and the confidentiality of investigation, the available statistics do not contain the absolute number of interceptions but only the number of police files in which electronic communication interception was enacted. In the last several years, the number of police files containing interception for mutual legal assistance has been consistently low.

In 2011,[224] there was one police file containing an interception at the the regional police headquarters level[225] and five police files containing interceptions in nation-

---

[224] Analýza odposlechů a záznamů telekomunikačního provozu a sledování osob a věcí dle trestního řádu a rušení provozu elektronických komunikací Policií ČR za rok 2011. Praha, 2012. 176 p. Available at http://www.mvcr.cz/soubor/ppr-2261-13-cj-2012-0099ta-analyza-2012-final-ver-pdf.aspx. p. 58.

[225] Region of Ústí na Labem.

wide units.[226] The total number of files with electronic communication interceptions was 731 at the regional level and 206 at the national level.

In 2012,[227] the number of police files with electronic communication interceptions rose to 1120 at the national level, but none of them contained interception warrants based on mutual legal assistance. Within the nationwide units, there were 240 files with interception but only six stemming from mutual legal assistance.[228]

In 2013,[229] only three[230] of 1175 files at the regional level contained electronic communication interceptions based on mutual legal assistance. On a nationwide scale, there were three[231] of 226 files.

Comparative note – Slovakia

The same applies in the Slovak Republic. International conventions on MLA have priority of application over Slovak Law according to Art. 7 of the Slovak Constitution (Act. No. 460/1992 Coll.):[232]

Art. 7

(1) The Slovak Republic may enter into a state union with other states upon its free decision. The decision on entering into a state union with other states, or on withdrawal from this union, shall be made by a constitutional law which must be confirmed by a referendum.

(2) The Slovak Republic may, by an international treaty ratified and promulgated in a manner laid down by law, or on the basis of such treaty, transfer the exercise of a part of its rights to the European Communities and European Union. Legally binding acts of the European Communities and European Union shall have primacy over the laws of the

---

226 2 for Útvar pro odhalování organizovaného zločinu [Organised Crime Unit], 1 for Národní protidrogová central [National Anti-drug Unit], 1 for Úřad služby kriminální policie a vyšetřování [Criminal and Investigation Unit] and 1 for Útvar pro odhalování korupce a finanční criminality [Corruption and Financial Crimes Unit].

227 Analýza odposlechů a záznamů telekomunikačního provozu a sledování osob a věcí dle trestního řádu a rušení provozu elektronických komunikací Policií ČR za rok 2012. Praha, 2013. 151 s. http://www.mvcr.cz/soubor/analyza-odposlechu-a-zaznamu-pdf.aspx. p. 54.

228 3 for Úřad služby kriminální policie a vyšetřování [Criminal and Investigation Unit], 2 for Útvar pro odhalování organizovaného zločinu [Organised Crime Unit], 1 for Národní protidrogová central [National Anti-Drug Unit].

229 Analýza odposlechů a záznamů telekomunikačního provozu a sledování osob a věcí dle trestního řádu a rušení provozu elektronických komunikací Policií ČR za rok 2013. Praha, 2014. 140 p. Available at http://www.mvcr.cz/soubor/ppr-102-31-cj-2014-990390-analyza-odposlechu-a-sledovani-za-rok-2013-pdf.aspx. p. 48.

230 2 for region Ústí nad Labem and 1 for the capital of Prague.

231 2 for Útvar pro odhalování organizovaného zločinu [Organised Crime Unit], 1 for Národní protidrogová central [National Anti-drug Unit].

232 Slovak Constitution. Act No. 460/1992 Zb. Official translation. Slovak Parliament. Online: http://www.nrsr.sk/web/Static/en-US/NRSR/Dokumenty/constitution.doc

Slovak Republic. Undertaking of legally binding acts that require implementation shall be executed by law or a government ordinance pursuant to Article 120, paragraph 2.

(3) The Slovak Republic may, with the aim of maintaining peace, security and democratic order, under the terms laid down by an international treaty, join an organization of mutual collective security.

(4) In order for any international treaties on human rights and fundamental freedoms, international political treaties, international treaties of military nature, international treaties establishing the membership of the Slovak Republic in international organizations, international economic treaties of general nature, international treaties whose execution requires a law and international treaties which directly constitute rights or obligations of natural persons or legal persons to be valid, an approval of the National Council of the Slovak Republic is required prior to their ratification.

(5) International treaties on human rights and fundamental freedoms, international treaties whose executions does not require a law and international treaties which directly establish rights or obligations of natural persons or legal persons and which were ratified and promulgated in a manner laid down by law shall have primacy over the laws.

The Slovak Republic has signed and ratified the following conventions:

- European Convention on Mutual Assistance in Criminal Matters, 1959
- Additional Protocol to the European Convention on Information on Foreign Law, 1978
- Second Additional Protocol to the European Convention on Mutual Assistance in Criminal Matters, 2001
- Convention on Mutual Assistance in Criminal Matters between the Member States of the European Union, 2000
- Additional Protocol to the Convention on Mutual Assistance in Criminal Matters between the Member States of the European Union, 2001
- European Convention on Extradition, 1957
- Additional Protocol to the European Convention on Extradition, 1975
- Second Additional Protocol to the European Convention on Extradition, 1978
- Third Additional Protocol to the European Convention on Extradition, 2010
- Convention on Cybercrime, 2001, promulgated as United Nations Transnational Organized Crime Convention, 2000

The Slovak Republic has signed and ratified the following bilateral treaties involving Germany:

- Agreement between the Government of the Czech and Slovak Federal Republic and the Federal Republic of Germany on cooperation in combating organized crime, 1991, promulgated as Act. No. 631/1992 Coll.

The national regulation for international cooperation (international legal assistance) is based on Section 531 and, further, on the Code of Criminal Procedure. The basic principle says that the provisions shall be applied unless an international treaty (MLA) provides otherwise.

Requests by Slovak authorities are regulated as follows:[233]

§ 532 Form of transmission of requests

(1) Requests for legal assistance emanating from the Slovak pre-trial authorities shall be transmitted abroad through the General Prosecutor's Office. Requests for legal assistance emanating from the Slovak courts shall be transmitted abroad through the Ministry of Justice. Diplomatic channels shall not be excluded.

(2) If an international treaty provides so, the Slovak authorities may transmit their requests abroad through other channels than the ones provided for in paragraph 1. The policeman may transmit the requests abroad solely through the good offices of a prosecutor.

Section 533 Contents and form of request

(1) A request for legal assistance shall, in addition to a precise description of the required act of assistance, contain a description of the facts of the offence which is the basis of the request, the legal denomination of the offence together with a verbatim wording of the pertinent legal provisions, the personal data of the accused or, as the case may be, of the victim or the witnesses if their examination is requested, as well as further details required for the proper execution of the requested legal assistance.

(2) The request shall contain the exact specification of the requesting authority, its file number, the date of the request and it shall bear the signature of the responsible officer and the round seal of the requesting authority.

(3) The request and the supporting documents shall be accompanied by a translation into a foreign language done by an official translator if in relation to the requested State such translation is required.

Section 534 Postal service

Service of documents on a person abroad by post shall be admissible only if so permitted by an international treaty.

Section 535 Validity of procedural acts

Service effected by a foreign authority upon a request by the Slovak authority as well as evidence taken by such authorities shall be valid if they were carried out in accordance with the law of the requested State or if they comply with the law of the Slovak Republic.

Section 536 Summoning persons from abroad

(1) If the personal appearance of a person who stays abroad is required at a procedural act, he must be served the summons by a request for legal assistance. His appearance must not be compelled by the threat of the use of coercive measures.

(2) The person who appears in the territory of the Slovak Republic on the basis of a summons must not be subjected to criminal prosecution, convicted or restricted in his personal liberty in respect of a criminal offence committed prior to his entering the territory of the Slovak Republic.

(3) Criminal prosecution, conviction or restriction of personal liberty of the summoned person shall, however, be admissible:

a) in respect of the criminal offence for which the person was summoned as accused,

---

[233] *Ibid.* Code of Criminal Procedure.

b) if, after giving evidence, the summoned person remains in the territory of the Slovak Republic for a period of more than 15 days, having had an opportunity to leave,

c) if the summoned person leaves the territory of the Slovak Republic and returns voluntarily or is lawfully returned to the Slovak Republic from another State.

Requests by foreign authorities are regulated as follows: [234]

Section 537 Manner and form of execution of request

(1) Slovak authorities shall carry out the legal assistance requested by foreign authorities in the manner provided for in this Code or in an international treaty. If the legal assistance shall be provided on the basis of an international treaty by a procedure not provided for in this Code, the responsible prosecutor shall decide how such assistance shall be carried out.

(2) At a request by the foreign authority the assistance may be provided on the basis of the legal provisions of another State, unless the requested procedure is contrary to the interests protected by Article 481.

(3) In order to execute the letter rogatory under section 539 para. 1 it is required that the act which the letter rogatory concerns is a criminal offence not only under the legal system of the requesting State but also under the legal system of the Slovak Republic.

Section 538 Responsibility for execution of requests

(1) Requests of a foreign authority for legal assistance shall be sent to the Ministry of Justice.

(2) The district prosecutor's office in whose district the requested assistance shall be carried out shall have the responsibility for the execution of the request for legal assistance made by a foreign authority. If more prosecutors` offices have territorial jurisdiction, the ministry of justice shall send the request to the General Prosecution for the decision on which prosecution office shall provide for its execution.

(3) If the foreign authority requests that the examination of a person or another act of legal assistance shall be executed by the court by the reason of applicability of the act in the criminal proceedings in requesting State, the prosecutor shall submit the request in that part for execution to the District Court in whose district the requested assistance shall be carried out. If the exclusive subject of the request is the act, which has to be executed by a court, the request shall be sent to the court directly by the Ministry of Justice.

Section 539 Authorisation of assistance by court

(1) If under this Code the taking of evidence requested by the foreign authority requires an authorisation by the court, such authorisation shall be given by a judge upon a motion by the prosecutor responsible for the execution of the request.

(2) If the assistance shall be provided on the basis of foreign legal provisions, the judge shall decide upon a motion by the prosecutor whether the foreign procedure does not conflict with the interests protected by the provisions of Article 481. If he does not find such a conflict he shall authorise the provision of the assistance and shall at the same time decide how the evidence shall be taken. An appeal by the prosecutor, with a postponing effect, shall be admissible against the court's decision.

The decision of the court on contradiction of procedure under foreign provision is not required if it concerns delivery of a document or instruction of a person under foreign provision.

[234] *Ibid.* Code of Criminal Procedure.

(3) The District Court in whose district the assistance shall be carried out shall have jurisdiction to decide under the paragraphs 1 and 2.

Section 540 Acts by foreign authorities

(1) Foreign authorities may not execute any acts of legal assistance in the territory Slovak Republic by themselves.

(2) A foreign consular office having jurisdiction for the territory of the Slovak Republic may carry out, if so mandated by the authorities of the State it represents and on their behalf, procedural acts for criminal proceedings only with the prior consent given by the Ministry of Justice. Service of documents on the national of the represented State or the examination of a person who appears voluntarily shall not require any prior consent by the Ministry of Justice.

(3) The presence of representatives of the foreign authorities as well as other persons at the execution of legal assistance by the Slovak authority shall only be possible with the prior consent by the responsible prosecutor; if the request shall be executed by the court, the consent shall be given by this court.

Section 541 Service of documents

(1) If the document to be served on an addressee in the Slovak Republic is written in the Slovak language or in a language which, taking into account all circumstances of the case, is deemed to be understood by the addressee, or if a translation into such language is attached to the document and no personal service is requested, the document shall be served on the addressee in accordance with the provisions of this Code governing the service in proper hands. Service by deposit shall be admissible only after a repeated attempt to serve.

(2) If the document is not in the language specified in paragraph 1 and no translation into such language is attached to the document, and the requesting authority was not required under an international treaty to provide such translation, the authority executing the assistance shall arrange for the Slovak translation and subsequently serve the document as provided for in paragraph 1. Otherwise it shall serve the document on the addressee only should he accept it voluntarily after being advised of the possibility to refuse the service.

(3) If the requesting authority requests personal service of the documents, the documents shall be served on the addressee in person. In such an event, the service under paragraph 1 shall not be admissible and should even the repeated attempt to serve the document in person fail, the authority effecting the service shall return the request non-executed and in the cover letter it shall specify the reasons for the failure of service. The addressee shall confirm the effected service by signing the receipt provided by the requesting authority or in the protocol of the authority effecting the service. If the addressee refuses to accept the documents for reasons specified in paragraph 2, the authority effecting the service shall record this fact in the receipt provided by the requesting authority or in the cover letter by which it returns the request to the requesting authority.

Section 542 Examination under oath

(1) If requested by the foreign authority, witnesses, experts and parties may also be examined under oath; prior to the oath they must be advised of importance of the statement and of the consequences of perjury.

(2) The wording of the oath for the witnesses and parties shall be the following: "I swear on my honour that I shall say the truth and nothing but the truth and withhold nothing intentionally."

(3) The wording of the oath for the expert witness shall be the following: "I swear on my honour that I shall give my expert opinion according to my best knowledge and conscience. I declare that I am aware of criminal consequences of false expert opinion."

Division Four

Some special forms of legal assistance

Section 543 Transit

(1) The Minister of Justice shall have the authority to grant the transit of a person through the territory of the Slovak Republic for the purposes of criminal prosecution or execution of a prison sentence upon a request by a foreign authority. During the transfer the personal liberty of the transferred person will be restricted in order to prevent his escape; in order to restrict the personal liberty of the transferred person the coercive measures under special law shall be used.

(2) The decision granting the transfer for purposes which imply the return transfer through the territory of the Slovak Republic shall be deemed as a decision granting such return transfer as well.

Section 544 Cross-border observation and pursuit

(1) In accordance with the terms of an international treaty the police authority may, in observing a person, enter the territory of another State and continue the observation of the person even on the territory of that State.

(2) The authorisation to proceed under paragraph 1 shall be issued by the presiding judge or in the pre-trial by the prosecutor.

(3) In the case of urgency, the procedure under paragraph 1 shall be possible also without an authorisation solely on the basis of consent by the Chief of Police or by the person entitled by the the Chief of Police. The authority having jurisdiction to authorise under paragraph 2 shall be informed without delay.

(4) Foreign authorities may carry out the observation in the territory of the Slovak Republic in accordance with the terms of an international treaty. If the international treaty does not specify which Slovak authority has jurisdiction to grant the permission to carry out the cross-border observation in the territory of the Slovak Republic, the permission shall be given by the prosecutor or in urgent cases by the Chief of Police or the person entitled by him/her. The Chief of Police or the person entitled by him/her shall inform about the given permission the competent prosecutor who shall decide on continue the observation.

Section 545 Temporary surrender of detained person abroad

(1) At the request of a foreign authority a person in custody or serving a prison sentence in the Slovak Republic may be temporarily surrendered abroad for the purposes of giving evidence.

(2) The person specified in paragraph 1 may be temporarily surrendered only if:

a) he is not the accused in the proceedings abroad and he consents with the temporary surrender,

b) his absence does not alter the purpose of the custody or the enforcement of the sentence carried out in the Slovak Republic

c) the temporary surrender does not inadequately extend the length of custody in the Slovak Republic, or the temporary surrender does not extend the length of the prison sentence served in the Slovak Republic.

Section 546

(1) The Minister of Justice shall have the authority to grant the temporary surrender abroad. In his decision he shall set out an appropriate deadline for the return of the person to the territory of the Slovak Republic.

(2) After the temporary surrender was granted, the decision to transfer the person abroad shall be made by the district court in whose district the person is in custody or serving the prison sentence.

Section 547

(1) The time the person spent in custody abroad shall not be counted against the deadlines under Article 76. The decision to this effect shall be taken by the court, and in the pre-trial by the judge upon the motion of the prosecutor.

(2) The time specified in paragraph 1 shall be counted against the length of the sentence served in the Slovak Republic.

(3) An appeal against the decisions under the paragraphs 1 and 2 shall be admissible.

Section 548

Articles 545 to 547 shall be applied mutatis mutandis to the transfer of a person abroad to participate in an act of legal assistance carried out in the territory of another State upon a request by the Slovak authorities.

Section 549 Temporary surrender of detained person from abroad for execution of procedural acts

(1) If in the criminal proceedings in the Slovak Republic the personal appearance of a person other than the accused is necessary for evidentiary purposes and such person is in custody or serving a prison sentence abroad, the prosecutor or the judge may request the Ministry of Justice to arrange the temporary surrender of the person to the territory of the Slovak Republic. The motion submitted to the Ministry of Justice shall specify the procedural acts for which the presence of the person is necessary as well as the date or the period of time for which the personal appearance shall be arranged.

(2) If the requested State authorised the temporary surrender to the territory of the Slovak Republic, the presiding judge of a panel, or in the pre-trial upon the motion by the prosecutor judge for pre-trial proceedings, shall decide that during the period of the temporary surrender in the Slovak Republic such person shall be held in custody. In this resolution shall be specified that the custody shall commence on the day of the surrender of the person to the territory of the Slovak Republic.

(3) The provisions of the paragraphs 1 and 2 shall be applied mutatis mutandis to the surrender of a person from abroad to participate in an act of legal assistance carried out in the territory of the Slovak Republic upon a request by the foreign authorities.

Section 550 Surrender of things

(1) Upon a request by a foreign authority the seizure of a thing and its subsequent surrender abroad can be effected.

(2) The requested authority may postpone the surrender of the seized thing if the Slovak authorities need it in their criminal proceedings.

(3) When surrendering the seized thing the requested authority shall request its return from the foreign authority. It may, however, expressly waive this right or may agree that the thing shall be returned directly to its rightful owner.

(4) These provisions shall be applicable mutatis mutandis to the surrender of a thing seized with the person whose extradition is sought. Such thing shall be surrendered to the foreign authorities, whenever possible, together with the extradited person.

Section 551 Seizure of property

(1) Under the conditions specified in an international treaty the court may, on the basis of a request by the foreign authority, and upon a motion by the prosecutor, order the provisional seizure of the movables, immovables, financial assets at the bank account, in a branch of a foreign bank, securities or another property located in the territory of the Slovak Republic, that is intented to be used to commit a criminal offence, was used to commit a criminal offence or is a proceed of crime, and its forfeiture or seizure is expected. Provisions of Section 95 paragraphs 3, 4 and 6, and Section 96 paragraphs 3 and 5 shall be applied mutatis mutandis.

(2) The District Court in whose district the property to be seized is located shall have jurisdiction to decide on the motion under paragraph 1.

(3) If the case is urgent, the prosecutor may deliver an order pursuant to the paragraph 1, which has to be approved in 48 hours by the judge competent under paragraph 2, otherwise it shall expire.

(4) The District Court shall revoke the provisional seizure on the basis of a motion of the foreign authority which asked for the provisional seizure, or on the basis of conditions set out in an international treaty. The District Court may also revoke the provisional seizure if the foreign state in proper time does not ask for execution of foreign property decision concerning the seized property.

Section 552 Information from criminal records

Any request by a foreign authority for information from the criminal records shall be submitted to the Prosecutor General's Office.

The direct extraction and transfer of intercepted electronic communications data among foreign police and judicial authorities are currently under development. Unfortunately, there is no public information on the technical regulation or the real-time transfer of communication data. From a legal perspective, the Slovak Republic as a member of the EU has all the necessary tools to cooperate with other Member States. Correspondingly, new information technologies are forcing local authorities to find new channels of cooperation overseas (MLA, diplomatic channels, etc.). In addition, the European Investigation Order is not very well communicated by EU politicians or legal scholars. This topic is still very marginal for many legal practitioners. Lastly, there are no public statistics from the Slovak Ministry of Justice or from the General Prosecution on the extent of MLA requests.

Bibliography*

Analýza odposlechů a záznamů telekomunikačního provozu a sle-dování osob a věcí dle trestního řádu a rušení provozu elektro-nických komunikací Policií ČR za rok 2013. Praha, 2014. Available at http://www.mvcr.cz/soubor/ppr-102-31-cj-2014-990390-analyza-odposlechu-a-sledovani-za-rok-2013-pdf.aspx

Analýza odposlechů a záznamů telekomunikačního provozu a sledování osob a věcí dle trestního řádu a rušení provozu elektronických komunikací Policií ČR za rok 2011. Praha, 2012. Available at http://www.mvcr.cz/soubor/ppr-2261-13-cj-2012-0099ta-analyza-2012-final-ver-pdf.aspx

Analýza odposlechů a záznamů telekomunikačního provozu a sledování osob a věcí dle trestního řádu a rušení provozu elektronických komunikací Policií ČR za rok 2012. Praha, 2013. Available at http://www.mvcr.cz/soubor/analyza-odposlechu-a-zaznamu-pdf.aspx

Čičkánová, D., Procesnoprávne aspekty práva na informačné sebaurčenie a práva byť zabudnutý. Bratislavské právnické fórum 2013. Bratislava: Univerzita Komenského, Právnická fakulta, 2013.

Minarik, Š., Trestný poriadok. Komentár. Iura edition, spol. s r.o. 2010, Bratislava

Novotná, J., Právní pomoc v cizím státu v přípravném řízení trestním. 3. vydání. Praha: C.H. Beck, 2015.

Šámal, P., Trestní řád: komentář. 7., extended release. In Prague: C.H. Beck, 2013, Velké komentáře.

Šámal, P., Odposlech a záznam telekomunikačního provozu ve světle judikatúry. Soudní rozhledy, C.H. Beck. 2000.

Vantuch, P., Nová úprava odposlechu v trestním řádu od 1. 7. 2008. Bulletin advokacie, 2008

List of Abbreviations

ASPI	Automated legal information system
Cell ID	Cell Identification
CERT	Computer Emergency Response Team
EMS	Enhanced media service

* All URLs were last accessed in 10/2016.

ENISA	European Network and Information Security Agency
IMEI	International Mobile Station Equipment Identity
IMSI	International Mobile Subscriber Identity
IP	Internet protocol
ISP	Internet service provider
ITM	Information and Technical Mean
ITP	Information and Technical Procedure
MAC adress	Media access control address
MLA	Mutual Legal Assistance
MMS	Multimedia Messaging Service
Sb.	Sbírka zákonů (Collection of Law)
Sb. m. s.	Sbírka mezinárodních smluv (Collection of international treaties)
SFTP	Secure File Transfer Protocol
SHA-1	Secure Hash Algorithm 1
SIM	Subscriber identity module
SMPT	Simple Mail Transfer Protocol
SMS	Short Message Service
spis. zn.	Spisová značka (case number)
ÚZČ	Útvar zvláštních činností (Unit for Special Activities of Criminal Police and Investigation)
VoIP	Voice over IP
ZMJS	Zákon o vzájemné justiční spolupráci ve věcech trestníc (Act No. 104/2013 Sb. on Mutual Judicial Assistance in Criminal Matters)

France*

National Rapporteur:
Estelle De Marco

* This report reflects legislation and case law as of April 2016.

Contents

I. Security Architecture and the Interception of Telecommunication

A. Law Enforcement Institutions and Public Authorities with Powers of Electronic Communications Interception

Several legal regimes organise the interception and the collection of electronic communications under French law. However, comprehensive and updated statistics are not consistently available in all cases.

1. Legal regimes organising the interception and the collection of electronic communications

Under French law, electronic communications are defined as "emissions, transmissions or reception of signs, signals, writings, images or sounds, by electromagnetic means."[1]

The formula "electronic communications" has replaced the term "telecommunications" according to a law of 9 July 2004.[2] Therefore, where French law still mentions the term of "telecommunications," this notion has to be understood as "electronic communications."

The interception of electronic communications is not provided for as such. French law distinguishes between several types of communications, which may be intercepted or accessed by judicial institutions and/or administrative services following different kinds of procedures, mainly within the framework of the application of either (repressive) penal law, or State security law (which includes the prevention of terrorism, of organised crime, and of organised delinquency). Additionally, some traffic data may be accessed for the purpose of the prevention of attacks on automated data processing systems.

These types of communications and the legal regimes governing their interception or collection are the following:

- Electronic correspondence. These communications receive strong legal protection and may only be intercepted under strict conditions. Electronic correspondence interceptions are organised by repressive penal law and state security law.

---

[1] Art. L. 32-1 of the Post and Electronic Communications Code (PECC).

[2] Law n°2004-669 of 9 July 2004; see also Court of cassation, criminal chamber, 8 July 2015, available at http://www.legalis.net/spip.php?page=jurisprudence-decision&id_article=4696

- Traffic and connection data. Several procedures allow the access to or the interception of a limited list of this kind of data under particular conditions:
  - Access to traffic and connection data retained by certain service providers is organised by repressive penal law and state security law. Additionally, access to these data may take place for the purposes of the prevention of terrorist acts and of the prevention of attacks on automated data processing systems.
  - Real time collection of these data on service providers' networks is organised for the prevention of terrorist acts only, by State security law n° 2015-912 of 24 July 2015 (entered into force October 2015[3]).
  - Direct collection of some of these data (including location data) by means of an intrusion into the computer system is organised by the above-mentioned State security law n° 2015-912 of 24 July 2015.
  - Geolocation of a person, a vehicle or an object, is organised by repressive penal law and the above-mentioned State security law n° 2015-912 of 24 July 2015.
- Other forms of private communications, as well as public communications, are not subject to specific intercept or access procedures. They may be collected within the framework of the application of the three following more general procedures:
  - The ordinary legal system governing search and seizure of information held by a third party, organised by repressive penal law;
  - A procedure that permits requiring from electronic communications operators the preservation of the content of the information accessed by their users, organised by repressive penal law;
  - A procedure allowing remote computer data capture, organised by repressive penal law and the above-mentioned State security law n° 2015-912 of 24 July 2015.
- Finally, all communications may be monitored at the service provider level for the purposes of real-time detection of "connections that may reveal a terrorist threat," as permitted by the above-mentioned State security law n° 2015-912, for the prevention of terrorism only.

[3] Law n° 2015-912 of 24 July 2015 relating to intelligence, JORF n°0171 of 26 July 2015, p. 12735, text n°2; legislative dossier available at http://www.senat.fr/dossier-legislatif/pjl14-424.html. Its entry into force was scheduled the day after the publication of a decree nominating the President of a new established "National Commission for intelligence techniques control," which replaces the current "National Commission for security intercepts control." This Decree was published on 2 Oct. 2015 (Decree of 1 October 2015 on the composition of the National Commission for intelligence techniques control/*Décret du 1er octobre 2015 relatif à la composition de la Commission nationale de contrôle des techniques de renseignement*), JORF n°0228 of 2 Oct. 2015 p. 17882, text n°26.

2. Powers for the interception of electronic communications

Powers for the interception of electronic communications are different depending on the legal regime.

a) Law of penal procedure

Electronic correspondence may be intercepted in limited situations, following the procedure described in articles 100 to 100-7[4] and article 706-95 of the Penal Procedure Code.

Traffic and connection data retained by service providers[5] can be requisitioned according to articles 77-1-1 (preliminary investigation), 60-1 (flagrancy investigation) and 99-3 (investigation procedure conducted by an investigative judge) of the Penal Procedure Code.

Real-time geolocation of a person, a vehicle or an object, without the consent of this person or the owner of this vehicle or object, can be done in limited situations according to articles 230-32 to 230-44 of the Penal Procedure Code.

The ordinary legal system governing search and seizure of information held by a third party is set out in articles 76 to 76-3 (preliminary investigation), 56 to 59 (flagrancy investigation), 92 to 99-4 (investigation procedure conducted by an investigative judge), and 706-89 (in relation with a limited list of crime or misdemeanours) of the Penal Procedure Code.

The procedure that permits requiring the preservation of the content of the information accessed by their users by electronic communications operators is described in articles 77-1-2 (preliminary investigation), 60-2 (flagrancy investigation) and 99-4 (investigation procedure conducted by an investigative judge) of the Penal Procedure Code.

The procedure that allows remote computer data capture (in relation with a limited list of crime or misdemeanours) is described in articles 706-102-1 to 706-102-9 of the Penal Procedure Code.

---

4 These and the following articles are available in French language at https://www.legifrance.gouv.fr/

5 On the basis of art. L. 34-1 PECC and of art. 6 of the Law n°2004-575 of 21 June 2004 regarding confidence in the digital economy (called "LCEN").

b) *Law of intelligence agencies*

aa) Areas in question

The following provisions may be used within the framework of the search for information by intelligence services and agents of several ministries listed by law and their implementing administrative acts, in the pursuit of a limited number of objectives.

Until October 2015 these objectives were:[6] national security; safeguard of essentials elements of the French scientific and economic potential; prevention of terrorism; prevention of organised crime and organised delinquency; prevention of the reconstitution or of the preservation of disbanded groups.[7]

These objectives have been replaced by the search for information relating to the defence and promotion of the following "fundamental interests of the nation":[8]

- National independence, territorial integrity, and national defence;
- Major interests of foreign policy, implementation of France's European and International commitments, and prevention of any form of foreign interference;
- Major economic, industrial, and scientific interests of France;
- Prevention of terrorism;
- Prevention of:
  - attacks against the republican form of French institutions,
  - actions pursuing the reconstitution or the preservation of disbanded groups,[9]
  - collective violence likely to cause serious harm to public peace;
- Prevention of organised crime and delinquency;
- Prevention of proliferation of weapons for mass destruction.

It must also be noted that, despite the fact that the aforementioned objectives are theoretically the only ones that can justify the exercise of the exceptional measures described in the next subsection, French law requires that any (other) crime or misdemeanour discovered upon exercising these special powers is brought to the atten-

---

[6] Former art. L. 241-2 Internal Security Code (ISC).

[7] Art. L. 212-1 ISC lists exhaustively the categories of groups that must be disbanded by decree issued by the Council of Ministers (such as groups provoking armed events in the streets).

[8] According to the new art. L. 811-3 ISC, created by Law n° 2015-912 of 24 July 2015 relating to intelligence, JORF n°0171 of 26 July 2015, p. 12735, text n°2; legislative dossier available at http://www.senat.fr/dossier-legislatif/pjl14-424.html. This article entered into force on 3 Oct. 2015 (see footnote n°3).

[9] Art. L. 212-1 ISC. See footnote n°7 above.

tion of the public prosecutor (who has the discretion to take action on it), accompanied by related information.[10]

bb) Legal provisions

Electronic correspondence could be intercepted, until October 2015, following the procedure described in former articles L. 241-1 *et seq.* of the Internal Security Code. This procedure has been replaced by a new one that results from the law of 24 July 2015 (entered into force on 3 October 2015[11]). This procedure is now described in articles L. 852-1 and L. 821-1 *et seq.* of the Internal Security Code.

Traffic and connection data[12] retained by service providers[13] can be accessed according to articles L. 851-1 and L. 851-4 of the new Internal Security Code 5 (including access by "network solicitation" and "real-time transmission by operators"), corresponding to former articles L. 246-1 to L. 246-4 of the Internal Security Code.

---

10 Former art. L. 242-8 ISC (relating to correspondence intercepts) and current (from the 3 Oct. 2015) art. L. 811-2 of the latter Code (relating to all the measures described in the next subsection). These articles refer to art. 40 of the Penal Procedure Code (PPC), which in turn lays down this obligation.

11 Law n° 2015-912 of 24 July 2015 relating to intelligence, *op. cit.*

12 More precisely, data that may be accessed are more widely identified by law (in art. L. 851-1, former art. L. 246-1) as being "*information or documents processed or stored* by (ISP's) networks or electronic communications services, including technical information relating to the identification of subscription or connection numbers to electronic communications services, to the census of all subscription numbers and connection numbers of a specified person, to the geolocation of terminal equipment used, and to a user's communications regarding the list of called and calling numbers, the duration and date of communications." The decree of application of the original provision (art. L. 246-1, created by Law n°2013-1168 of 18 Dec. 2013, art. 20), specified that these data are the ones, which are of a technical nature only and cannot relate to the content of communications that can be accessed by the judiciary for the repression of crimes (Decree n°2014-1576 of 24 Dec. 2014 – http://www.legifrance.gouv.fr/eli/decret/2014/12/24/PRMD1422750D/jo). The decree of application of the new law (Decree n° 2016-67 of 29 Jan. 2016) refers to the same data. It provides for an additional list of data that may be accessed by intelligence services or other Ministries, but only within the framework of administrative correspondence intercepts. It should be noted that the French Constitutional Council has recalled that traffic data that can be accessed for intelligence purposes cannot be related to the content of correspondence or to consulted information (Decision n°2015-713 DC, recital n° 55, http://www.conseil-constitutionnel.fr/conseil-constitutionnel/root/bank/download/cc2015713dc.pdf – press release: http://www.conseil-constitutionnel.fr/conseil-constitutionnel/francais/les-decisions/acces-par-date/decisions-depuis-1959/2015/2015-713-dc/communique-de-presse.144139.html).

13 These data are retained on the basis of art. L. 34-1 PECC (relating to electronic communications operators and access providers) and of art. 6 of the Law n°2004-575 of 21 June 2004 regarding confidence in the digital economy, so-called LCEN (relating to access and hosting providers).

Direct collection of some of these data (connection data of a technical nature enabling the identification of terminal equipment or the identification of the subscription number of its user, as well as location data of terminal equipment) by means of an intrusion into the computer system is organised by the new article L. 851-6 of the Internal Security Code.

Real-time geolocation of a person, a vehicle or an object, without the consent of this person or the owner of this vehicle or object, is organised by the new article L. 851-5 of the Internal Security Code.

The procedure that allows remote computer data capture is organised by the new article L. 853-2 of the Internal Security Code.

Globally, the situations in which access to the types of data discussed above may take place are wider, persons who may access them are more numerous, accessed data are potentially more numerous, and safeguards in place are lower than those that govern the implementation of access to traffic and connection data by the judiciary for the purpose of the repression of penal infringements.

c) Prevention of attacks on automated data processing systems

Some limited traffic data, namely the identity, the postal address and the electronic address of users or owners of vulnerable, threatened or attacked information systems, retained by electronic communications operators,[14] can be requisitioned according to article L. 2321-3 of the Defence Code, by authorised and sworn agents from the national authority for information systems, in order to alert these persons to the vulnerability or the compromise of their system.

d) Prevention of terrorist acts

All the measures described in the subsection relating to the law of intelligence agencies are applicable for the prevention of terrorist acts.

In addition, for the purpose of terrorism prevention only, there exists

- The possibility to implement on service providers' networks an automated processing aimed at detecting "connections that may reveal a terrorist threat," under new article L. 851-3 of the Internal Security Code.
- The possibility to request real time collection of traffic and connection data (relating to a person previously identified as presenting a threat) on service providers' networks , under new article L. 851-2 of the Internal Security Code.

[14] On the basis of art. L. 34-1 PECC.

e) Customs Investigation Service

According to article 28-1 of the Penal Procedure Code, some specially nominated customs agents may be authorised to conduct judicial investigations in order to look for and report a limited list of infringements, including infringements to the customs Code. Within that framework, judicial procedures described in subsection a. above may be applicable.

In addition, the Decree n° 2015-1185 of 28 September 2015,[15] adopted in order to apply Law n° 2015-912 includes the National Directorate for Custom Intelligence and Investigations *(Direction nationale du renseignement et des enquêtes douanières)* in the list of specialised intelligence services that are entitled to exercise the powers described in subsection b. above. This Directorate is an agency with national authority, within the General Directorate for customs and indirect rights, which itself rests with the Ministry of Finance.[16]

Moreover, according to the new article L. 811-4 of the Internal Security Code, a decree issued by the Council of State designates services other than intelligence services that may be authorised to exercise the powers granted to intelligence services as they have been detailed in subsection b. above, and these services may belong to customs services. The Decree n°2015-1639 of 11 December 2015[17] did not designate services other than some services that belong to the Ministry of Defence and the Ministry of Interior. However, subsequent decrees might follow.[18]

3. Responsibility for the technical performance of interception measures

Under French law, the technical enforcement of interception and data collection measures follows certain rules:

- Regarding correspondence interceptions performed by the judiciary for the purpose of the repression of crimes and misdemeanours, the investigating judge or

---

15 Décret n° 2015-1185 du 28 septembre 2015 portant désignation des services spécialisés de renseignement, JORF n°0225 du 29 septembre 2015 p. 17344, texte n°1.

16 http://www.douane.gouv.fr/articles/a12574-la-direction-nationale-du-renseignement-et-des-enquetes-douanieres.

17 Décret n° 2015-1639 du 11 décembre 2015 relatif à la désignation des services autres que les services spécialisés de renseignement, autorisés à recourir aux techniques mentionnées au titre V du livre VIII du code de la sécurité intérieure, pris en application de l'art. L. 811-4 du Code de la sécurité intérieure, JORF n°0288 du 12 décembre 2015 p. 22978, texte n° 28.

18 Before the entry into force of Law n° 2015-912 of 24 July 2015 – therefore before the 3 Oct. 2015 – agents of the Ministry for economy, therefore possibly customs agents, could access traffic and connection data if individually appointed and duly authorised, for limited purposes listed in former art. 241-2 ISC (former art. 246-1 ISC created by art. 20 of Law n° 2013-1168 of 18 Dec. 2013). Correspondence intercept could also be authorised on the proposal of the Ministry in charge of customs (former art. L. 242-1 ISC).

the police officer appointed by this judge can require any qualified agent belonging to a service or organisation placed under the authority of the Ministry in charge of electronic communications, or any qualified agent belonging to an authorised electronic communications service provider, to perform the installation of an interception system.[19]

- Regarding remote computer data capture performed by the judiciary for the purpose of the repression of certain crimes and misdemeanours, the investigating judge or the police officer appointed by this judge can require any qualified agent belonging to a service, a unit or a body placed under the authority of the Ministry of Interior or the Ministry of Defence, and which list is established by decree, to perform the installation of the technical devices that enable data captures authorised by law.[20]
- Regarding geolocation of a person, a vehicle or an object performed by the judiciary in certain situations, the investigating judge or the police officer appointed by this judge can require any qualified agent belonging to a service, a unit or a body placed under the authority of the Ministry of Interior (the list of which is established by decree), to perform the installation and of the removal of the technical device that enables geolocation as authorised by law.[21]
- Regarding search and seizures performed by the judiciary for the purpose of the repression of crimes and misdemeanours, where it is necessary to perform technical or scientific examinations, the public prosecutor or police officer (depending on the nature of the procedure – flagrancy or preliminary investigation) may call upon any qualified person.[22] When the procedure is directed by an investigating judge, search and seizures are performed by this judge or the police officer appointed by this judge.[23]
- Regarding intelligence gathering techniques (including the prevention of terrorism, organised crime and organised delinquency), Law n° 2015-912 states that the Prime Minister organises traceability of the execution of authorised techniques.[24]

This law also states that all these techniques can only be implemented by agents individually appointed and authorised for the purpose.[25] This is repeated in the provision relating to the possibility of directly collecting some traffic and connection

[19] Art. 100-3 PPC.

[20] Art. 706-102-6 PPC.

[21] Art. 230-36 PPC.

[22] Arts. 60 (flagrancy investigation), 77-1 (preliminary investigation) PPC.

[23] Art. 97 PPC.

[24] Art. L. 822-1 ISC.

[25] Art. L. 821 ISC.

data[26] by means of an intrusion into the computer system.[27] In addition, in that case, technical devices that are used for the purpose are recorded in a special register made available to the National Commission for the control of intelligence techniques.[28]

The technical performance of the other intelligence gathering techniques is subject to two different procedures:

- Electronic correspondence intercepts,[29] administrative access to traffic and connection data,[30] administrative direct access to traffic and connection data using "network solicitation" and "real-time transmission by operators,"[31] and concerning the prevention of terrorism only, real time collection of traffic and connection data[32] and monitoring of service providers' networks in order to detect "connections that may reveal a terrorist threat,"[33] can only be technically performed following the procedure described in article L. 871-6 of the Internal Security Code,[34] which takes over the provisions of the former article L. 242-9 of the Internal Security Code, which was relating to correspondences intercept only.[35] According to article L. 871-6, the above-mentioned measures can only be technically performed by qualified agents belonging to the organisation or the service provider in whose premises and installations the measure must be implemented. Regarding qualifications, only the technically competent agents who (1) have been employed for at least two years at the same electronic communications operator, and (2) have not been convicted or found guilty of any criminal offence recorded in bulletin n° 2 of their criminal records[36] are able to perform these tasks.
- Real-time geolocation of a person, a vehicle or an object, without the consent of this person or the owner of this vehicle or object,[37] and remote computer data

---

26 Namely technical connection data enabling the identification of terminal equipment or the identification of the subscription number of its user, as well as location data of terminal equipment.

27 Art. L. 851-6, II ISC.

28 Art. L. 851-6, II ISC.

29 Art. L. 852-1 ISC.

30 Art. L. 851-1 ISC.

31 Art. L. 851-4 ISC.

32 Relating to a person previously identified as presenting a threat on service providers' networks, art. L. 851-2 ISC.

33 Art. L. 851-3 ISC.

34 Created by art. 11 of Law n° 2015-912 of 24 July 2015.

35 The only element that changes, beyond the fact that the procedure is extended to more numerous measures, is that the technical performance of these measures can only be performed by order of the Prime Minister, whereas such an order was the duty of the Ministry for electronic communications in former art. L. 242-9.

36 Art. R 242-4 ISC; see also art. R. 242-6.

37 Art. L. 851-5 ISC.

capture[38] can only be technically performed following the procedure described in the new article L. 853-3 of the Internal Security Code.[39] According to this article, entrance to a vehicle or to a private location can only be performed by agents individually appointed and authorised for the purpose, who belong to one of the services that may be authorised to use intelligence gathering techniques, the list of which is established by decree issued by the Council of State.[40]

4. Legitimacy of data transfers between security and law enforcement agencies

Services in charge of the repression of criminal offences and services in charge of the prevention of terrorism and organised crime and delinquency are separated, and exchanges of data between these services constitute an exception.

a) Separation of functions

The repressive function and the intelligence function are separated, though some services exercising the first one and some services exercising the second one come under the control of the same ministry (Ministry of Interior). Moreover, most communications intercepts as defined above are performed under the control of an independent judge within the framework of crime repression, whereas they are performed under the control of an independent administrative authority within the framework of intelligence gathering.

b) Exchange of data between law enforcement authorities and intelligence agencies

No accessible general rule provides for the possibility of exchanging information between law enforcement authorities and intelligence agencies, except where a crime or a misdemeanours is discovered during the gathering of intelligence information.

aa) Passing on of data by law enforcement authorities to intelligence agencies

Law n° 2015-912 provides intelligence agencies with the same – and even wider – intercept capabilities as the judiciary, which renders global information exchange unnecessary (in addition, constraints on judges for the purpose of preserving fundamental rights are stronger).

---

38 Art. L. 853-2 ISC.

39 Created by art. 6 of Law n° 2015-912 of 24 July 2015.

40 Art. L. 853-3, § 2 ISC.

bb) Passing on of data by intelligence agencies to law enforcement authorities

According to article 40 of the Penal Procedure Code, when an established authority, a public officer or a public servant learns, during the performance of their duties, of a crime or of a misdemeanour, they must give notice of it to the public prosecutor, and must provide this magistrate with any information, official records and other investigative acts relating to this crime or misdemeanour. The public prosecutor evaluates what further action should be taken in accordance with article 40-1 of the Penal Procedure Code.

B. Statistics on Electronic Communications Interception

Before the entry into force of law n° 2015-912, communication intercepts performed under intelligence law were subject to an annual report of the National Commission for the Control of Security Interceptions (*Commission nationale de contrôle des interceptions de sécurité*, CNCIS), which has been replaced in the new law by the National Commission for the Control of Intelligence Techniques (*Commission nationale de contrôle des techniques de renseignement*, CNCTR).

According to the CNCIS in its report for the years 2013-2014,[41] 6,182 correspondence intercepts were requested in 2013 (4,213 initial requests and 1,969 renewals), and 6,145 correspondence intercepts were requested in 2012 (4,022 initial requests and 2,123 renewals).[42]

Moreover, in 2013, 321,243 requests of access to traffic data were issued for national security (71%), delinquency and organised crime prevention (22%), terrorism prevention (3%), protection of the economic and scientific potential (3%), and reconstitution of disbanded groups (1%). 315,792 of these requests were for identification, or requests regarding the history of an identifier or the identification of a cell. 5,451 measures consisting of traffic details (which are more intrusive) were also reviewed. 7% of the measures were refused and 10% were subject to referral for additional information prior to their validation. The number of requests that were met increased by 61% in comparison with 2012. This increase relates exclusively to identification measures.[43]

Moreover, 36,712 additional requests (compared with 29,322 in 2012) were related to combatting terrorism. 34,366 were validated (compared with 26,563 in 2012). A percentage close to 65% was composed of requests for subscriber identification, and a percentage close to 35% was composed of requests for traffic de-

---

41 This report is available at http://www.ladocumentationfrancaise.fr/var/storage/rapports-publics/154000101.pdf

42 See p. 80 of the report.

43 See pp. 96 *et seq.* of the report.

tails. In 2013, 20% of these requests related to fixed telephony, 67% to mobile telephony, and 13% to Internet.[44]

Regarding communications intercepts performed by the judiciary for the repression of crime and delinquency, less exact figures are known. In 2012, 35,000 telephone communications intercepts, 650,000 judicial requisitions of traffic data and 12,000 geolocations took place.[45]

II. Principles of Electronic Communications Interception in Constitutional and Criminal Procedural Law

Constitutional principles frame the powers for interception and collection of electronic communications that are set out in the Penal Procedure Code.

A. Constitutional Safeguards of Electronic Communication

Constitutional safeguards of electronic communications have consequences for the description of the powers for intercepting or collecting electronic communications in the Penal Procedure Code, and are reflected in other legal texts.

1. Areas of constitutional protection

French constitutional safeguards do exist but do not refer explicitly to the protection of electronic communications.

The right to respect for private and family life is protected by the French Constitutional Council under "articles 2 and 4[46] of the French Human and Citizens Rights

---

44 See p. 99 of the report.

45 Club DJS, "Les écoutes judiciaires – Contributions au débat," 1 April 2014, http://www.droits-justice-et-securites.fr/2014/04/les-ecoutes-judiciaires/; *Franck Johannès*, "Les écoutes judiciaires ont explosé depuis 2006," 18 March 2014, Le Monde, http://www.lemonde.fr/societe/article/2014/03/18/les-ecoutes-judiciaires-ont-explose-depuis-2006_4384910_3224.html. Some publications evoke the number of 20,000 instead of 35,000 communication intercepts, see http://www.senat.fr/leg/ppr13-422.html. Some media evokes in addition 5,500,000 "additional services" such as access to detailed invoicing: see *Franck Johannès*, above [last accessed on 19 Sept. 2015].

46 Art. 2: "The aim of every political association is the preservation of the natural and imprescriptible rights of Man. These rights are Liberty, Property, Safety and Resistance to Oppression"; Art. 4: "Liberty consists in being able to do anything that does not harm others: thus, the exercise of the natural rights of every man has no bounds other than those that ensure to the other members of society the enjoyment of these same rights. These bounds may be determined only by Law." The Declaration is available in English on the

Declaration of 1789,"[47] the latter Declaration being included in the so-called French "constitutionality bloc" (which has a constitutional value). The French Constitutional Council also protects some aspects of the right to respect for private life under the principle of personal freedom,[48] the guarantor of which is the Parliament, in accordance with article 34 of the Constitution.[49]

a) Secrecy of telecommunication

The respect for private and family life includes the secrecy of correspondence[50] transmitted by means of electronic communications, and information consulted using an electronic communications network.[51] It also includes the protection of connection and traffic technical data.[52]

Constitutional Council website: http://www.conseil-constitutionnel.fr/conseil-constitutionnel/root/bank_mm/anglais/cst2.pdf

47 See, e.g., French Constitutional Council, Decision n° 2004-492 DC of 2 March 2004, J.O. 10 March 2004, p. 4637, recital n° 4; Decision n° 2005-532 DC of 19 Jan. 2006, recital n° 9.

48 Other elements of personal freedom are, under French law, the freedom of movement, the right to not being arbitrarily arrested or sequestered, the right to be judged with all legal guarantees and the principle of inviolability of the home. See Jacques Robert et Jean Duffar, *Droits de l'homme et libertés fondamentales*, éd. Montchrestien, 7ème éd., 1999, p. 27; art. 136 PPC; Estelle De Marco, "Analyse du nouveau mécanisme de prévention de la contrefaçon à la lumière des droits et libertés fondamentaux," 4 June 2009, Juriscom.net, p. 3, available at http://www.juriscom.net/uni/visu.php?ID=1133

49 The Constitutional Council considers that the refusal to take into consideration the right to respect of private life can be liable to hurt personal freedom: Decision n° 94-352 DC, 18 Jan. 1995, J.O. 21 Jan. 1995, p. 1154 and JCP 1995, II, 22 525, note *Frédérique Lafay*. The Council also analysed the implementation of technical mechanisms allowing picking-up, fixing or registering words or images without the consent of interested people, in the light of personal freedom: Decision n° 2004-492 DC, 2 March 2004, JORF 10 March 2004, p. 4637. The Council also extends the notion to some personal data filing systems: Decision n° 2004-492 DC, 2 March 2004, JORF 10 March 2004, p. 4637, § n° 64. On all these elements, see Estelle De Marco, "Analyse du nouveau mécanisme de prévention de la contrefaçon à la lumière des droits et libertés fondamentaux", *op. cit.* and Estelle De Marco, *L'anonymat sur Internet et le droit*, thesis, Montpellier 1, 2005, ANRT, n° 20. The French Constitution is available in English on the Constitutional Council website: http://www.conseil-constitutionnel.fr/conseil-constitutionnel/root/bank_mm/anglais/constiution_anglais_juillet2008.pdf

50 It also includes the "freedom" to correspond: see, e.g., Estelle De Marco, *L'anonymat sur Internet et le droit*, thesis, Montpellier 1, 2005, ANRT, n° 132 *et seq.*; Virginie Peltier, *Le secret des correspondances*, PU d'Aix-Marseille, 1999, p. 99 *et seq., n°119 et seq.*; Pierre Kayser, *La protection de la vie privée par le droit*, PU d'Aix-Marseille/Economica, 3rd ed., 1995, especially pp. 11–12, p. 60.

51 See, e.g., French Constitutional Council, Decision n°2015-478 QPC of 24 July 2015, recital n° 10 *et seq.*

52 French Constitutional Council, Decision n°2005-532 DC of 19 Jan. 2006, recitals n° 9 to n° 21.

b) *Personal data protection*

In addition, the respect for private and family life includes the right to the protection of personal data, and more precisely "collection, recording, retention, consultation and communication of personal data."[53]

2. Proportionality of access to data

According to the French Constitutional Council, limitations to the right to private and family life, which include, as already analysed, the protection of electronic communications and personal data, "must be justified by a reason in the public interest and implemented properly and in a manner proportionate to this end."[54] In other decisions, in relation to the preservation of the freedom of expression, the Council used a slightly different test that any limitation to this right must be necessary, adequate and proportionate to the aim pursued.[55]

Overall, the meaning of these formulas is close to the notions of "necessity" and "proportionality" used by the European Court of Human Rights.[56] Indeed, in the words of a legal author, the French Constitutional Council seems to have "aligned its jurisprudence with the one of the E. Court H. R., since it performs a similar proportionality test, between general interests on the one hand and the limitation

---

[53] French Constitutional Council, Decision n° 2012-652 DC of 22 March 2012, recital n° 8; Decision n° 2013-681 DC of 5 Dec. 2013, recital n° 27; see also French Constitutional Council, Commentary on the Decision n° 2014-690 DC of 13 March 2014, p. 20.

[54] French Constitutional Council, Decision n° 2012-652 DC of 22 March 2012, recital n° 8; Decision n° 2013-681 DC of 5 Dec. 2013, recital n° 27; see also French Constitutional Council, Commentary on the Decision n°2014-690 DC of 13 March 2014, p. 20, available at http://www.conseil-constitutionnel.fr/conseil-constitutionnel/root/bank/download/2014690DCccc_690dc.pdf [last accessed on 18 Sept. 2015].

[55] See, e.g., French Constitutional Council, Decision 2009-580 DC of 10 June 2009, recital n° 15; Decision 2012-647 DC of 28 Feb. 2012, recital n° 5; Decision n°2010-3 QPC of 28 May 2010, recital n° 6.

[56] The European Convention on Human Rights (ECHR) is in France of infra-constitutional but supra-legal force, even though the national law is subsequent to the Convention. Indeed, the Convention is directly integrated into the local system by the Constitution, as its art. 55 states that "Treaties or agreements duly ratified or approved shall, upon publication, prevail over Acts of Parliament, subject, with respect to each agreement or treaty, to its application by the other party" (the second part of the text does not receive application because the principle of reciprocity does not apply as regards the ECHR.). See Frédéric Sudre, "La dimension internationale et européenne des libertés et droits fondamentaux," in *Libertés et droits fondamentaux*, under the direction of Rémy Cabrillac, Marie-Anne Frison-Roche, Thierry Revet, ed. Dalloz, 11th ed., 2005, p. 39, n° 68; Estelle De Marco and Cormac Callanan, in C. Callanan, M. Gercke, E. De Marco and H. Dries-Ziekenheiner, *Internet blocking – balancing cybercrime responses in democratic societies*, October 2009, n° 6.5.2.2, available at http://www.aconite.com/blocking/study (French version available at http://juriscom.net/2010/05/rapport-filtrage-dinternet-equilibrer-les-reponses-a-la-cybercriminalite-dans-une-societe-democratique-2/) [last accessed on 18 Sept. 2015].

brought to a freedom on the other hand, based on the principle of separation of powers."[57]

The Constitutional Council may verify the adequacy of the measure in relation with its aim,[58] the appropriateness of the resources allocated in pursuit of this aim (even though the Council considers that it is not its duty to verify if the aim could have been achieved using other means),[59] and the necessity to combat the issue that justifies the measure[60] (which are the three elements that compose the notion of "necessity" according to the European Court of Human Rights[61]).

Regarding proportionality in the strictest sense, and particularly in the area of the protection of the right to private life, the French Constitutional Council considers that it is the mission of the Parliament, on the basis of article 34 of the Constitution, to lay down the rules relating to fundamental safeguards that must be granted to individuals for the exercise of their public freedoms.[62] In addition, the Constitutional Council generally verifies whether legal guarantees are adequate and sufficient.[63]

---

57 Olivier Dutheillet de Lamothe, "L'influence de la Cour européenne des droits de l'Homme sur le Conseil constitutionnel," 13 Feb. 2009, Conseil constitutionnel, visite du Président et d'une délégation de la Cour européenne des droits de l'homme au Conseil constitutionnel, http://www.conseil-constitutionnel.fr/conseil-constitutionnel/root/bank_mm/pdf/Conseil/cedh_130209_odutheillet.pdf, p. 9. See also Estelle De Marco, *Analyse du nouveau mécanisme de prevention de la contrefaçon à la lumière des droits et libertés fondamentaux*, 4 June 2009, p. 16, Juriscom.net, http://juriscom.net/2009/06/hadopi-analyse-du-nouveau-mecanisme-de-prevention-de-la-contrefacon-a-la-lumiere-des-droits-et-libertes-fondamentaux/

58 See, e.g., French Constitutional Council, Decision n° 2009-599 DC of 29 Dec. 2009, recital n° 81; see also Valérie Goesel-Le Bihan, "Le contrôle de proportionalité exercé par le Conseil constitutionnel, technique de protection des libertés publiques?" http://juspoliticum.com/Le-controle-de-proportionnalite.html [last accessed on 22 Sept. 2015].

59 See, e.g., French Constitutional Council, Decision n°2000-433 DC of 27 July 2000, recital n° 41; see also Valérie Goesel-Le Bihan, "Le contrôle de proportionalité exercé par le Conseil constitutionnel, technique de protection des libertés publiques?", *op. cit.*

60 See, e.g., French Constitutional Council, Decision 2009-580 DC of 10 June 2009, recital n° 13.

61 See, e.g., Estelle De Marco et al., *D3.3 – Legal recommendations*, Deliverable, ePOOLICE project (early Pursuit against Organized Crime Using Environmental Scanning, the Law and Intelligence Systems), project n° FP7-SEC-2012-312651, version 1.2 of 29 Aug. 2014 and version 1.3 of 10 Dec. 2014.

62 See, e.g., French Constitutional Council, Decision 2009-580 DC of 10 June 2009, recital n° 23, *op. cit.*

63 See, e.g., French Constitutional Council, Decision n° 2013-681 DC of 5 Dec. 2013, recital n° 28; French Constitutional Council, Decision n° 2012-652 DC of 22 March 2012, recital n° 8; see also *La proportionnalité dans la jurisprudence constitutionnelle*, 5ème conférence des Chefs d'institution de l'Association des Cours constitutionnelles ayant en partage l'usage du français, 8–13 July 2008, p. 7, available at http://www.conseil-constitutionnel.fr/conseil-constitutionnel/root/bank_mm/Bilan_2008/confV_accpuf_libreville_juillet2008.pdf

Among these legal guarantees or safeguards, lies the respect of the principle that offences and penalties must be defined by law. Other safeguards are the respect of the rights of the defence;[64] the limitation of the duration of the measure;[65] the limitation of the number of people who may suffer from the limitation;[66] the limitation and the definition of the purposes[67] and of the situations[68] in which the measure can be exercised; and the existence of an independent control of the implementation of the measure.[69] During these controls, the nature and sensitivity of data that may be collected are naturally also taken into account.[70]

3. Consequences for the interception of telecommunication

The consequences of the Constitutional Council jurisprudence is that the law authorising the limitation of the right to private life must be necessary and proportionate, which implies that it provides for adequate safeguards. Otherwise, the Constitutional Council may declare the law unconstitutional, if the law is referred to it before it is enacted. The request must in this case be submitted by the President of the Republic, the Prime Minister, the President of one of the two Parliament's chambers, or by 60 members of the National Assembly or 60 members of the Senate.[71]

In addition, after the law is enacted, citizens can challenge the compliance of a law with the Constitution on the occasion of a trial. The judge must in this case, if the request is considered admissible and if criteria established by law are met,[72] transmit the request to the Court of Cassation or to the Council of State (depending on the nature of the trial), which may transfer in turn the request to the Constitutional Council.[73]

---

[64] See, e.g., French Constitutional Council, Decision 2009-580 DC of 10 June 2009, recital n° 14, *op. cit.*

[65] See, e.g., French Constitutional Council, Decision 2004-492 DC of 2 March 2004, recital n° 59; Decision n° 2013-681 DC of 5 Dec. 2013, recital n° 28.

[66] See, e.g., French Constitutional Council, Decision 2004-492 DC of 2 March 2004, recital n° 59, *op. cit.*; Decision n° 2012-652 of 22 March 2012, recital n° 10.

[67] See, e.g., French Constitutional Council, Decision n° 2012-652 of 22 March 2012, recital n° 10 *op. cit.*

[68] See, e.g., French Constitutional Council, Decision 2004-492 DC of 2 March 2004, recital n° 59, *op. cit.*; Decision n° 2013-681 DC of 5 Dec. 2013, recital n° 28.

[69] See, e.g., French Constitutional Council, Decision 2004-492 DC of 2 March 2004, recital n° 59, *op. cit.*

[70] See, e.g., French Constitutional Council, Decision n° 2012-652 of 22 March 2012, recitals n° 10 and n° 11, *op. cit.*

[71] Art. 61 French Constitution.

[72] These criteria are set out in the organic law n° 2009-1523 of 10 Dec. 2009.

[73] Art. 61-1 French Constitution. See also "Comment saisir le Conseil constitutionel?," http://www.conseil-constitutionnel.fr/conseil-constitutionnel/francais/le-conseil-

4. Statutory protection of personal data

In addition to the constitutional protection, all private life aspects are protected by the French civil judge on the basis of article 9 of the civil Code and of article 8 of the European Convention on Human Rights (ECHR).[74] Moreover, some other legal provisions protect specific private life aspects or more generally personal or confidential data, such as the following:

- Correspondence (including electronic correspondence) is protected during transmission by articles 226-15 and 432-9 of the French Penal Code.[75]
- The protection of personal data is organised by Law n° 78-17 of 6 January 1978 (last modified in 2015). Some of its provisions are subject to penal charges according to articles 226-16 to 226-24 of the French Penal Code. The principle of specified, explicit and legitimate purpose is declared in Article 6 of Law n° 78-17.
- Attacks on automated data processing systems are punished by articles 323-1 to 323-8 of the French Penal Code, last modified in 2015.[76]

---

constitutionnel/la-saisine/comment-saisir-le-conseil-constitutionnel-/comment-saisir-le-conseil-constitutionnel.17421.html

74 See, e.g., a case of annulment of a criminal procedural act consisting of the geolocation of the accused, because French law did not provide for a clear legal basis authorising such a procedural act and providing for adequate safeguards: Cass. crim., 22 October 2013, n°13-81945.

75 Art. 226-15 French Penal Code (PC): "Maliciously opening, destroying, delaying or diverting of correspondence sent to a third party, whether or not it arrives at its destination, or fraudulently gaining knowledge of it, is punished by one year's imprisonment and a fine of € 45,000.""The same penalty applies to the malicious interception, diversion, use or disclosure of correspondence sent, transmitted or received by electronic means, or the setting up of a device designed to produce such interceptions." Art. 432-9: "Except where provided for by law, the ordering, committing or facilitation of the misappropriation, suppression or opening of correspondence, and the disclosure of the contents of such correspondence, by a person holding public authority or discharging a public service mission acting in the course of or on the occasion of his office or duty, is punished by three years' imprisonment and a fine of € 45,000.

The same penalties apply to the persons referred to under the previous paragraph, or to employees of electronic communication networks open to the public, or to employees of a supplier of telecommunication services, who, acting in the performing of their office, order, commit or facilitate, except where provided for by law, any interception or misappropriation of correspondence sent, transmitted or received by a means of telecommunication, or the use or the disclosure of its contents."

76 An English version of these provisions that does not take into account the most recent legal modifications is available at http://www.legifrance.gouv.fr/content/download/1957/13715/version/4/file/Code_33.pdf. Most modifications are relating to penalties, which have been increased.

B. Powers in the Penal Procedure Code

As a result of constitutional principles, powers in the law of criminal procedure must be clearly defined by specific provisions.

1. Requirement of (reasonable) clarity for powers in the law of criminal procedure

As has been described in A above, the definition of coercive powers in criminal procedural law must be described by the law itself, and the principle "no crime without legal definition" is applicable under French law, meaning *inter alia* that criminal statutes must be defined precisely by the legislator before the commission of a criminal act can be assumed.

2. Differentiation and classification of powers in the law of criminal procedure

As a consequence, coercive powers in French criminal procedural law must be based on differentiated, precise, and specific provisions.

III. Powers for Accessing Electronic Communication Data in the Law of Criminal Procedure

Powers of accessing electronic communications, understood in a broad sense, cover powers relating to the interception of content data, including sounds and visual images, and to the collection and retention of technical connection and traffic data.

A. Overview

As explained in subsections I.A.1. and 2., the above-mentioned powers are subject to several procedures precisely described in the Penal Procedure Code.

B. Interception of Content Data

It has already been noted that the French Penal Procedure Code distinguishes between correspondence and other kinds of electronic data and communications. Correspondence can be intercepted following a specific procedure, whereas other procedures enable the interception of other type of communications (beyond the search and seizure procedure, which will be analysed later in this report).

These other procedures are the following: a procedure allowing remote data capture, and a procedure that requires electronic communications operators to preserve the content of the information accessed by their users.

1. Statutory provision

a) Correspondence interceptions

The interception of the content of electronic correspondence is set out in articles 100 to 100-7[77] and article 706-95 of the Penal Procedure Code:[78]

Article 100:

For the investigation of felonies and misdemeanours, if the penalty incurred is equal to or in excess of two years' imprisonment, the investigating judge may order the interception, recording and transcription of correspondence transmitted by means of telecommunications where the requirements of the investigation call for it. Such operations are made under his authority and supervision.

The interception decision is made in writing. It is not a jurisdictional decision and cannot be appealed.

Article 100-1:

The order made pursuant to article 100 must include all the details identifying the link to be intercepted, the offence which justifies resorting to an interception, and the duration of this interception.

Article 100-2:

This decision can last for a maximum duration of four months. It may be extended only by following the same conditions as to form and duration.

Article 100-3:

The investigating judge or the judicial police officer appointed by him may require any qualified agent of a service or institution placed under the authority or supervision of the Minister in charge of telecommunications, or any qualified agent of a network operator or authorised purveyor of telecommunication services to set up an interception device.

Article 100-4:

The investigating judge or the judicial police officer appointed by him drafts an official record of both the interception and recording operations. This official record mentions the date and time when the operation started and ended.

The recordings are placed under closed official seals.

---

77 An English translation of these articles taking into account modifications of the law up to 2005 is found at http://www.legifrance.gouv.fr/content/download/1958/13719/version/3/file/Code_34.pdf (Art. 100-5 was modified in 2010).

78 An English translation of these articles taking into account modifications of the law up to 2005 is found at http://www.legifrance.gouv.fr/content/download/1958/13719/version/3/file/Code_34.pdf (Art. 706-95 was modified by a law of 2015).

Article 100-5:

The investigating judge or the judicial police officer appointed by him transcribes any correspondence which is useful for the discovery of the truth. An official record is made of these transcriptions. The transcription is attached to the case file.

Correspondence in a foreign language is transcribed into French with the assistance of an interpreter appointed for this purpose.

On penalty of nullity, no transcription may be made of any correspondence with an advocate relating to the exercise of the defendant's rights.

On penalty of nullity, no transcription may be made of any correspondence with a journalist allowing identifying a source in breach of Article 2 of the Law of 29 July 1881 on Freedom of the Press.

Article 100-6:

The recordings are destroyed on the request of the district prosecutor or of the public prosecutor upon the expiry of the limitation period for prosecution.

An official record is made of the destruction.

Article 100-7:

No interception may be made on the telephone line of a member of Parliament or senator unless the president of the assembly he belongs to is informed of the interception by the investigating judge.

No interception may be made on a telephone line connecting the chambers or domicile of an advocate unless the president of the bar association is informed of this by the investigating judge.

No interception may be made on a telephone line connecting the chambers or domicile of a judge or prosecutor unless the president or the prosecutor general of the court with jurisdiction over the area in question is informed of this by the investigating judge.

The formalities set out by the present article are prescribed under penalty of nullity.

Article 706-95:

If the needs of a flagrancy inquiry or a preliminary inquiry into one of the offences within the scope of articles 706-73[79] and 706-73-1[80] justify this, the liberty and custody

---

[79] Art. 706-73 lists the following crimes and misdemeanours under the Penal Code unless otherwise stated: (1°) murder committed by an organised gang under 8° of article 221-4; (2°) torture and acts of barbarity committed by an organised gang contrary to article 222-4; (3°) felonies and misdemeanours relating to drug trafficking contrary to articles 222-34 to 222-40; (4°) felonies and misdemeanours relating to kidnapping and false imprisonment committed by an organised gang contrary to article 224-5-2; (5°) felonies and aggravated misdemeanours relating to human trafficking contrary to articles 225-4-2 to 225-4; (6°) felonies and aggravated misdemeanours relating to procuring contrary to articles 225-7 to 225-12; (7°) theft committed by an organised gang contrary to article 311-9; (9°) the felony of destroying, defacing or damaging property committed by an organised gang, contrary to article 322-8; (10°) felonies relating to counterfeiting contrary to articles 442-1 and 442-2; (11°) felonies and misdemeanours which constitute acts of terrorism contrary to articles 421-1 to 421-6; (12°) misdemeanours relating to weapons committed by an organised gang contrary to articles L. 2339-2, L. 2339-3, L. 2339-10, L. 2341-4, L. 2353-4 and L. 2353-5 of the Code of defence, or contrary to articles L. 317-2, L. 317-4, L. 317-7 of the internal security Code; (13°) misdemeanours in relation to the illegal entry, movement and residence of a foreigner in France committed by an organised gang, contrary to article L. 622-1 of the Code on the entry and residence for foreigners and on the right to asylum; (14°) money laundering misdemeanours contrary to articles 324-1 and 324-2, or

judge of the district court may, at the request of the district prosecutor, authorise the interception, recording or transcription of correspondence by telecommunication, under the provisions of paragraph two of article 100, article 100-1 and articles 100-3 to 100-7, for a maximum period of one month, renewable once under the same conditions of form and duration. These operations are carried out under the supervision of the liberty and custody judge.

For the application of the provisions of articles 100-3 to 100-5, the powers conferred on the investigating judge or the judicial police officer nominated by him are exercised by the district prosecutor or the judicial police officer appointed by him.

The liberty and custody judge who has authorised this interception is immediately informed by the district prosecutor of any actions carried out in accordance with the previous paragraph, including official records drafted pursuant to his authorisation, by way of the application of articles 100-4 and 100-5.

b) Remote data capture

Remote data capture is set out in articles 706-102-1 to 706-102-9 of the Penal Procedure Code:[81]

---

receiving stolen property contrary to articles 321-1 and 321-2, of the products, income and items resulting from the offences mentioned in 1° to 13°; (15°) membership of a conspiracy misdemeanours contrary to article 450-1, where the action aims to prepare one of the penal infringements mentioned in 1° to 14° and 17°; (16°) failure to justify resources corresponding to lifestyle misdemeanour contrary to article 321-6-1, when this misdemeanour is connected to one of the penal infringements listed in 1° to 15° and 17°; (17°) crime of hijacking of aircraft, ships or any other means of transport committed by an organised gang under article 224-6-1; (18°) crimes and misdemeanours sentenced to ten years of imprisonment contributing to proliferation of weapons of mass destruction and the means of delivering them under article 706-167; (19°) misdemeanours of mining or licensable substance holding without an authorisation or exploitation permit, accompanied by damage to the environment, committed by an organised gang, under article L. 512-2 of the mining Code, where it is related to one of the penal infringements mentioned in 1° to 17° of the current article; (20°) activities or employees concealment misdemeanour, misdemeanour of using the services of a person performing undeclared work, illegal subcontracting, illicit supply of workers, employment of foreign nationals without a work permit contrary to 1° and 3° of article L. 8221-1 and to articles L. 8221-3, L. 8221-5, L. 8224-1, L. 8224-2, L. 8231-1, L. 8234-1, L. 8234-2, L. 8241-1, L. 8243-1, L. 8243-2, L. 8251-1 et L. 8256-2 of the Labour Code. In addition, paragraph (8°) mentions aggravated felonies of extortion contrary to articles 312-6 and 312-7, but this paragraph has been declared unconstitutional and was removed from the penal procedure Code on 1st September 2015 (see Decision n° 2014-420/421 QPC of the Constitutional Council of 9 Oct. 2014, recital n° 25).

[80] Art. 706-73-1 lists the following crimes and misdemeanours under the Penal Code: (1°) offence of fraud committed by an organised gang under the last paragraph of article 313-2; (2°) misdemeanours listed in paragraph (20°) of article 706-73; (3°) money laundering misdemeanours contrary to articles 324-1 and 324-2, or receiving stolen property contrary to articles 321-1 and 321-2, of the products, income and items resulting from the offences mentioned in 1° and 2° of the current article; (4°) membership of a conspiracy misdemeanours contrary to article 450-1, where the action aims to prepare one of the penal infringements mentioned in 1° to 3° of the current article; (5°) failure to justify resources corresponding to lifestyle misdemeanour contrary to article 321-6-1, when this misdemeanour is in link with one of the penal infringements listed in 1° to 4° of the current article.

[81] See note on English translation of these articles above.

Article 706-102-1:

For the investigation of crimes or offences coming within the scope of articles 706-73[82] and 706-73-1,[83] and where the requirements of the investigation call for it, the investigating judge may, after having requested the opinion of the district prosecutor, authorise, by way of reasoned order, judicial police officers and agents that have been appointed by rogatory commission, to implement a technical device aiming to access computer data, in all places and without the consent of the concerned people, and to register, store and transmit those data, as they are displayed on the screen of the user of the computer system, or as they are typed by the user of the system, or as they are transmitted or received by audio-visual devices. These operations are carried out under the supervision of the investigating judge.

Article 706-102-2:

The decisions of the investigating judge, taken according to article 706-102-1, mention the penal infringement that justifies the operation, the exact location or the comprehensive description of the computer systems concerned and the duration of operations. The formalities set out by the present article are prescribed under penalty of nullity.

Article 706-102-3:

These decisions are valid for a maximum duration of four months. They may be extended, exceptionally and under the same conditions as to form and duration, where the investigation so requires.

The investigating judge may, at all times, require the interruption of operations.

Article 706-102-4:

Under penalty of nullity, these operations shall be limited to the investigation and identification of penal infringements mentioned in the authorisation of the investigating judge.

The fact that these operations reveal other penal infringements not mentioned in the investigating judge's decision is not a cause for nullity of incidental proceedings.

Article 706-102-5:

In order to implement the technical device mentioned in article 706-102-1, the investigating judge may authorise the introduction to a vehicle or to a private place, including outside the times mentioned in article 59 of the Penal Procedure Code,[84] without the knowledge or without the consent of the owner or of the possessor of the vehicle or of the occupier or of any person having a right to this vehicle or place. If the device must be introduced in a home before 6 am or after 9 pm, the authorisation must be delivered by the liberty and custody judge, on the special request of the investigating judge. These operations cannot pursue any other aim than implementing the technical device and are performed under the authority and supervision of the investigating judge. The current paragraph is also applicable to operations aimed at uninstalling the technical device that has been implemented according to article 706-102-1.

In order to implement this device, the investigating judge may also authorise the transmission of this device by means of an electronic communications network. These operations are performed under the authority and supervision of the investigating judge. The

---

[82] See footnote n°79.

[83] See footnote n°80.

[84] Art. 59 states that, except where they are requested from within a building or in the exceptional cases provided for by law, searches and house visits may not be undertaken before 6 am or after 9 pm.

current paragraph is also applicable to operations aiming at uninstalling the technical device that has already been implemented.

The technical device mentioned in article 706-102-1 can neither be implemented in a computer system located in places covered by articles 56-1,[85] 56-2[86] and 56-3,[87] nor in the vehicle, the business premises or the home of people mentioned in article 100-7.

Article 706-102-6:

The investigating judge or the judicial police officer appointed by him may require any qualified agent of a service or unit or body placed under the authority or supervision of the Ministry of Interior or of the Ministry of Defence, a list of which is determined by means of a Decree, in order to install the device mentioned in article 706-102-1.

Article 706-102-7:

The investigating judge or the judicial police officer appointed by him drafts an official record of both the installation of the device mentioned in article 706-102-1 and the data capture operations. This official record mentions the date and time when the operation started and ended.

The recordings are placed under closed official seals.

Article 706-102-8:

The investigating judge or the judicial police officer appointed by him describes or transcribes, in an official record filed in the criminal case file, the data that are needed to ascertain the truth. No sequence relating to private life but that has no relation with penal infringements mentioned in the authorisation can be kept in the criminal case file.

Data in a foreign language are transcribed into French with the assistance of an interpreter appointed for this purpose.

Article 706-102-9:

The recordings of computer data are destroyed on the request of the district prosecutor or of the public prosecutor upon the expiry of the limitation period for prosecution.

An official record is made of the destruction.

c) Interception of the content of the information accessed by users of electronic communications operators' services

The interception of the content of the information accessed by users of electronic communications operators' services is set out in articles 60-2 (flagrancy investigation), 77-1-2 (preliminary investigation), and 99-4 (investigation procedure conducted by an investigating judge) of the Penal Procedure Code.

Article 60-2, §2 *et seq.*:

A judicial police officer, intervening on the orders of a district prosecutor authorised in advance by a decree from the liberty and custody judge, may require telecommunications operators, particularly those mentioned in 1 of I of article 6 of Law no. 2004-575

---

85 This article refers to business premises or the home of advocates.

86 This article refers to business premises of media companies, audio-visual communication companies, online public communication companies, press agencies, to the professional vehicles of these companies and to journalists' home where the investigation is relating to this journalist's professional activities.

87 This article refers to professional premises of doctors, notaries, or bailiffs.

of 21 June 2004 relating to confidence in the digital economy,[88] to take without delay all appropriate measures to ensure the preservation, for a period that may not exceed one year, of the text of the information consulted by persons using the services provided by the operators.

The organisations or persons to which this article applies must make the required information available as quickly as possible by means of telecommunication or computers.

Refusal to respond to such a request without a legitimate reason is punished by a fine of €3,750.

[…]

Article 77-1-2, §2 *et seq.*:

On the authorisation of the custody judge, given jurisdiction, to this end, by the district prosecutor, a police officer may carry out the measures provided for by the second paragraph of article 60-2.

The organisations or persons concerned make the required information available as quickly as possible, by means of telecommunication or computers.

Refusal to respond to such a request without a legitimate reason is punished subject to the provisions of the fourth paragraph of article 60-2.

Article 99-4, §2 *et seq.*:

With the express permission of the investigating judge, a judicial police officer may issue the demands provided for by the second paragraph of article 60-2.

The organisations or persons concerned must put the requisite information at their disposal by telecommunication or by use of computers as quickly as possible.

Refusal to respond to these demands without legitimate grounds is punished in accordance with the provisions of the fourth paragraph of article 60-2.

2. Scope of application

The object of interception and the temporal limits of electronic communications are subject to some matters of dispute.

a) Object of interception and temporal limits of electronic communication

The subject-matter of the interception and the temporal limits of the protection of electronic communications are different, depending on the procedure that is followed.

aa) Correspondence interception

In the above-mentioned provisions relating to correspondence interception, the subject-matter of the interception is correspondence transmitted by means of electronic communications.

---

[88] These persons are Internet access service providers.

The notion of "electronic correspondence," as well as the notion of "correspondence" more widely does not have any comprehensive legal definition.[89] Correspondence has been defined by the legal literature only, as being "personal and temporal communication, which allow interactivity, and which are addressed to determined and individualised persons."[90] This definition may be considered as applying to correspondence that is protected under the French Penal Code during the time of their transmission,[91] and which may be subject to interceptions in compliance with the French Penal Procedure Code. Before and after transmission, correspondence may further receive the protection, as already mentioned in this report, of the French Civil Code, and it is in this case commonly referred to as "private correspondence." Since the definition of correspondence, according to the legal literature, applies to both the information medium and the information that is communicated,[92] the notion of electronic correspondence is restricted to correspondence emitted, transmitted or received electromagnetically, in the form of signs, signals, writing, images or sounds.[93]

As a consequence of this definition, the provisions that define electronic communications and the provisions of the French Penal Procedure Code relating to correspondence intercept, data that can be captured under the interception procedure is analogous to communication (voice and data) via landlines, and IP traffic of a person-to-person-communication.

Regarding the interception of other types of private communications, such as IP traffic between a person and an automated information system,[94] IP-traffic between a person's computer and their data storage in a cloud or other remote storage of data processing systems, and IP traffic between two independent computer systems (e.g., between an automated machine and its computer-based automated control centre), other procedures included in the Penal Procedure Code are more suitable,

---

89 French law only evokes "private correspondence" in a negative way, within the provisions dedicated to public communications (Art. 1, IV, subparas. 3 and 4 of Law n°2004-575 of 21 June 2004 regarding confidence in the digital economy (called "LCEN"): "Public communication using electronic means shall mean any sign, signal, writing, image, sound or messages of all kinds, which are made available to the public by electronic means, and which have not the character of a private correspondence"; "Online public communication shall mean any transmission, on individual request, of digital data that have not the character of a private correspondence [...]."

90 Estelle De Marco, *L'anonymat sur Internet et le droit*, thesis, Montpellier 1, 2005, ANRT, n° 637. See also Virginie Peltier, Le secret des correspondances, PU d'Aix-Marseille 1999.

91 Estelle De Marco , not. n° 641; Virginie Peltier.

92 Estelle De Marco; Virginie Peltier.

93 As a consequence of the French legal definition of "electronic communications" which are "emissions, transmissions or reception of signs, signals, writings, images or sounds, by electro-magnetic means:" Art. L. 32-1 PECC.

94 Such as communication with a webserver while downloading a website.

such as the search and seizure procedure, the procedure enabling remote computer data capture and the special procedure that requires electronic communications operators to preserve the content of the information accessed by their users.

bb) Remote data capture

In the above-mentioned provisions relating to remote data capture, the subject-matter of the interception is any computer data exactly as it is displayed on the screen of the user of the computer system, or as it is typed by the user of the system, or as it is transmitted or received by audio-visual devices. As a consequence, the interception concerns all type of electronic and audio-visual communications, of a private and public nature.

cc) Interception of the content of the information accessed by users of electronic communications operators' services

In the above-mentioned provisions relating to this kind of interception, the subject-matter of the interception is the content of the information accessed by users. Therefore the interception covers public and private communications such as the information accessed during internet surfing.

b) Current matters of dispute

aa) Rules protecting correspondence before their reception by the recipient

One question is whether correspondence stored by a hosting provider, in a traditional mail box or on a social network, should be intercepted using the correspondence interception procedure or if they may be accessed via the search and seizure procedure.

A legal analysis performed in accordance with the doctrinal definition of correspondence and the principles enshrined in the decisions of both the French Constitutional Council and the European Court of Human Rights leads to the conclusion that no correspondence should be accessed outside the procedure set-up for correspondence interception, whatever its medium of transmission and its medium of storage, after they have been sent by the sender and before they have been received by the recipient.

Indeed, the penal protection of a correspondence (which imposes the use of the interception procedure if its content must be accessed for the purpose of criminal repression) begins when the message is sent, and ends "when the last piece of information has been received."[95] Such a reception must be understood as a reception

[95] Virginie Peltier, *op. cit.*, p. 471.

by the recipient, and not as reception in the medium of storage only, a medium which may be used to visualise the correspondence online, or to store the message until the recipient downloads it. The message stays therefore protected until the recipient opens it and decides to leave it stored on the server, or downloads it. This analysis, which is implied by the definition of correspondence, is also confirmed by Article 226-15 of the French Penal Code, which states that correspondence is protected whether or not it has "arrived at their destination." Such an analysis is also compatible with Recital n° 27 of Directive 2002/58/EC[96], transposed under French law, according to which "the exact moment of the completion of the transmission of a communication […] may depend on the type of electronic communications service that is provided. […] For electronic mail the transmission is completed as soon as the addressee collects the message, typically from the server of his service provider."[97]

However, the Court of Cassation stated in a case of 8 July 2015[98] that emails may be seized in the mailbox hosted by the service provider, on the basis of a judicial search, without making a distinction between emails actually received by the recipient (and therefore opened by this recipient), and emails technically received by the hosting provider but not opened by the recipient. Indeed, the Court states that "collection, registration and transcription of correspondence sent or received by telecommunication means before the date of the written decision of correspondence interception taken by the investigating judge […] must be performed in compliance with provisions regulating seizure."[99]

This decision could be called into question in the future.

bb) Direct access to mailboxes using their password

As we will analyse later, the law concerning the retention of connection data (see III.C. below) imposes the retention of certain information provided at the time of the contract subscription or of the creation of the users' account, including – only where the provider usually collects such information – the password and the data that enable the modification or verification of this password, in its latest and updated form. Even if the interception procedure must in theory be used to access elec-

---

[96] Directive 2002/58/EC of 12 juillet 2002, J.O.C.E. n° L. 201 of 31 July 2002, p. 37.

[97] On the discussion see Estelle De Marco, *L'anonymat sur Internet et le droit*, *op. cit.*, n°641.

[98] Court of cassation, criminal chamber, 8 July 2015, available at http://www.legalis.net/spip.php?page=jurisprudence-decision&id_article=4696

[99] Translated from French: "l'appréhension, l'enregistrement et la transcription de correspondances émises ou reçues par la voie des télécommunications antérieurement à la date de la décision écrite d'interception prise par le juge d'instruction […] doivent être réalisés conformément aux dispositions légales relatives aux perquisitions."

tronic correspondence, access to passwords enables the access of these messages in practice.

3. Special protection of confidential communication content

Firstly, as has been mentioned above (III.B.1.), correspondence can only be intercepted under strict conditions when its sender or recipient practices certain occupations. Some types of correspondences are also protected against transcription. Secondly, remote data capture is not possible in certain places. Finally, the interception of the information accessed online may concern any person since no special protection is in place.

a) Privileged correspondence

Article 100-7 of the Penal Procedure Code provides special protection for the Parliament's members, advocates, judges and prosecutors. This article states that, under penalty of nullity,

- No interception may be made on the telephone line of a member of Parliament or senator unless the president of the assembly he belongs to is informed of the interception by the investigating judge;
- No interception may be made on a telephone line connecting the chambers or domicile of an advocate unless the president of the bar association is informed of this by the investigating judge; and
- No interception may be made on a telephone line connecting the chambers or domicile of a judge or prosecutor unless the president or the prosecutor general of the court with jurisdiction over the area in question is informed of this by the investigating judge.

b) Prohibition of transcription of certain types of correspondence

In addition to the rules described above, article 100-5 of the Penal Procedure Code states that, on penalty of nullity:

- No transcription may be made of any correspondence with an advocate relating to the exercise of the defendant's rights, and
- No transcription may be made of any correspondence with a journalist allowing identifying a source in breach of Article 2 of the Law of 29 July 1881 on freedom of the press.

c) Privileged computer data within the framework of remote data capture

Remote data capture cannot be performed:

- In the vehicle, the business premises or the home of members of Parliament, advocates, judges and prosecutors;
- In the business premises of media companies, audio-visual communication companies, online public communication companies, press agencies, in the professional vehicles of these companies;
- In a journalist's home;
- In the professional premises of doctors, notaries, or bailiffs.

4. Execution of electronic communications interception

As explained previously, according to Article 100-3 of the Penal Procedure Code, correspondence interception may be performed by any qualified agent belonging to a service or body placed under the authority of the Ministry in charge of electronic communications, or any qualified agent belonging to an authorised electronic communications service, if required by the investigating judge or the police officer appointed by this judge. The execution mode is determined by the investigative judge.

Regarding remote data capture, according to Article 706-102-6 of the Penal Procedure Code, the installation of the device that is necessary to perform data capture may be performed by any qualified agent belonging to a service or unit or body placed under the authority or supervision of the Ministry of Interior or of the Ministry of Defence and of which a list is determined by means of a decree.[100]

Regarding finally the interception of the content of the information accessed by users of electronic communications operators' services, such an interception is required from electronic communication operators and internet access service providers, who must make the required information available as quickly as possible by means of telecommunication or computers.

5. Duties of electronic communication service providers to cooperate

French law includes some general provisions that recall the duty of electronic communications service providers[101] – and more widely the duty of any citizen[102] – to provide support to justice for the manifestation of the truth.

---

100 This list is available in art. D15-1-6 PPC.

101 Art. L. 33-1, I, §§ 5, 6° and 7° PECC that "the setting up and the exploitation of electronic communications networks are subject to the respect for rules relating to […]" public order, national defence and public security requirements, including rules that are necessary to the setting up of communications intercepts required for public security purposes. Art. L. 32-1, II, § 7° also considers as a general objective (to be enforced by the Ministry for Electronic Communications and the regulatory authority) the respect by operators of the public order and of obligations of defence and public security.

More particularly, electronic communications operators[103] and internet access providers[104] must take without delay all appropriate measures to ensure the preservation of the text of the information consulted by persons using the services they provide, when they are required to do so according to article 60-2 of the Penal Procedure Code, and refusal to respond to such a request without a legitimate reason is punishable by a fine of €3,750.

Electronic communications operators have a general obligation, sometimes recalled by additional specific provisions relating to specific questions, to respect the rules relating to the protection of personal data,[105] the secrecy of correspondence,[106] and the confidentiality and neutrality of content transmitted using their networks.[107] These stakeholders are also obliged to ensure the integrity and the security of their networks.[108] French law does not provide for particular requirements for the transfer of content data following a judicial request, but these general principles do apply.

In addition, a decree plans the creation of a "judicial interceptions platform," placed under the responsibility of the Ministry for Justice,[109] the purpose of which is to receive and store:

- The content of electronic communications intercepted on the basis of articles 74-2, 80-4, 100 to 100-7 and 706-95 of the Penal Procedure Code;

102 Art. 10 French Civil Code states: "Everyone is required to lend his aid to the court so that the truth may be revealed. He who, without legitimate reason, evades that obligation when it is legally required of him, may be compelled to comply with it, if need be on pain of a periodic penalty payment or of a civil fine, without prejudice to the right to recover damages". See the English translation of the French Civil Code on Legifrance (the French public service for the dissemination of law) at https://www.legifrance.gouv.fr/affichCode.do?cidTexte=LEGITEXT000006070721&dateTexte=20160929

103 Electronic communications operators are defined in art. L. 32, § 15°PECC as "natural or legal persons who exploit an electronic communications network opened to the public or who provide the public with an electronic communications service" (the notion of "provision" being understood here as the transmission of electronic communications on a network).

104 Internet access providers are defined in art. 6, I, § 1 of Law 2004-575 of 21 June 2004 as "persons whose activity is to provide an access to online public communication services."

105 General rules are included in art. L. 32-1, II, § 6°PECC and in Law n°78-17 of 6 Jan. 1978. Specific obligations are, e.g., included in provisions relating to the retention of traffic data.

106 The general rule is included in art. L. 32-1, II, § 6° PECC and in art. 226-15 Penal Code. Specific obligations are for example included in art. L. 32-3 PECC, in addition to art. 432-9 Penal Code which specifically sanctions correspondence violation where committed by electronic communications operators.

107 General rules are included in art. L. 32-1, II, § 6° and L. 33-1, b) PECC. Specific obligations are, e.g., included in art. L. 32-3-3 of the same code.

108 See, e.g., art. L. 33-1, a) PECC.

109 Decree n°2014-1162 of 9 Oct. 2014, creating arts. R. 40-42 to R. 40-55 PPC.

– Data and information communicated by service providers within the framework of three procedures: the procedure for the interception of the content of the information accessed by users of electronic communications operators' services (articles 60-2 §2 *et seq.*; 77-1-2 §2 *et seq.* and 99-4 §2 *et seq.* of the Penal Procedure Code), the procedure for requesting traffic and connection data (articles 60-1; 77-1-1 and 99-3 of the Penal Procedure Code), and the procedure for accessing, including remotely, information stored in computer and data processing systems (60-2,§1 and 5; 77-1-2 §1 and 99-4 §1 of the same Code).

This platform was not yet operational at the time of writing.[110]

6. Formal prerequisites of interception orders

As can be noted by reading statutory provisions relating to correspondence interceptions, remote data capture and interception of the content of the information accessed by the users of electronic communications networks, each of these procedures obeys different rules.

a) Competent authorities

aa) Correspondence interception

The principle is that correspondence interception must be ordered by the investigating judge, and the interception is made under his authority and supervision.

This order is issued by the initiative of the investigating judge, where the requirements of the investigation call for it, for the investigation of felonies and misdemeanours where the penalty incurred is equal to or in excess of two years imprisonment,[111] or if a person has disappeared.[112]

Moreover, the judge responsible for enforcing sentences can order such correspondence interception, for the same kinds of felonies and misdemeanours indicated above, where one or several reasonable grounds enable the belief that a person, having served his sentence, does not respect the prohibition written in the initial sentence, to contact certain persons or to be in certain areas.[113] The judge responsible for enforcing sentences issues the order on his own initiative or, in some specific situations described by the penal Code, on the request of the district prosecutor.

---

110 See, e.g., Xavier Berne, "Ecoutes: la mise en place de la PNIJ avance doucement," 14 Aug. 2015, available at http://www.nextinpact.com/news/96181-ecoutes-mise-en-place-pnij-avance-doucement.htm

111 Art. 100 PPC.

112 Art. 80-4 PPC.

113 Art. 709-1-3 PPC.

Additionally, the liberty and custody judge of the district Court may, where the requirements of the investigation call for it, on the request of the district prosecutor, order a correspondence intercept in the search for an escaping person. Correspondence interceptions are performed under the authority and supervision of this liberty and custody judge.[114]

The liberty and custody judge of the district Court may also order a correspondence interception, on the request of the district prosecutor, where the requirements of a flagrancy or preliminary investigation in relation with limited penal infringements[115] call for it.[116]

bb) Remote data capture

The principle is that remote data capture must be ordered by the investigating judge for the investigation of specific crimes and misdemeanour exhaustively listed,[117] after having requested the opinion of the district prosecutor. The measure is implemented and performed under his authority and supervision.

cc) Interception by service providers of the content of the information accessed by their users

During a flagrancy investigation, the preservation of the text of the information consulted by persons using their services may be requested by a judicial police officer, intervening on the orders of a district prosecutor authorised in advance by a decision from the liberty and custody judge.[118]

During a preliminary investigation, the preservation of this information may be requested by a judicial police officer, if authorised to do so by the liberty and custody judge. This authorisation is issued on the request of the district prosecutor.[119]

Where the investigation is conducted by an investigating judge, the preservation of this information may be requested by a judicial police officer, with the express permission of the investigating judge.[120]

---

114 Art. 74-2 PPC.

115 See footnotes n°79 and n°80.

116 Art. 706-95 PPC.

117 See footnotes n°79 and n°80.

118 Art. 60-2 PPC.

119 Art. 77-1-2 PPC.

120 Art. 99-4 PPC.

b) Formal and substantive requirements for applications and orders

Requirements for applications and orders differ depending on the procedure that is followed.

aa) Correspondence interceptions

Provisions that are specific to correspondence interceptions do not particularly regulate the form of the requests made by the district prosecutor to the competent judge.

Correspondence interception orders must be made in writing, must specify all the details identifying the link to be intercepted, the offence which justifies resorting to an interception and the duration of this interception, and must be justified according to the provisions recalled in subsection a. above, such as the situation where the requirements of the investigation call for it, or where there is grounds to believe that a person does not respect a prohibition on contacting certain persons (provisions which are supposed to ensure proportionality of the measure to the seriousness of the offence). They can only be issued in relation with the penal infringements listed in the texts that authorise the interception measure, also recalled above in subsection a. Within those limits, the Penal Procedure Code does not specify the persons (such as suspects, intermediaries or communication partners) who can be placed under surveillance. Nor does it require that less intrusive means must be first considered or tried.

bb) Remote data capture

Provisions that are specific to remote data capture do not particularly regulate the form of the opinion transmitted by the district prosecutor to the investigating judge.

The investigating judge may issue remote data capture orders only where the requirements of the investigation call for it, after having requested the opinion of the district prosecutor. Under penalty of nullity, remote data capture orders must be made in writing, must mention the penal infringement that justifies the operation, the exact location or the comprehensive description of concerned computer systems and the duration of operations. The penal infringement that justifies the operation must belong to the list set-up by articles 706-73 and 706-73-1 of the Penal Procedure Code.[121] All these details are supposed to ensure proportionality of the measure to the seriousness of the offence. Within these limits, the Penal Procedure Code does not specify the persons who can be placed under surveillance,or require that less intrusive means must be first considered or tried.

---

[121] See footnotes n°79 and n°80.

cc) Interception by service providers of the content of the information accessed by their users

Provisions that are specific to the interception of the content of the information accessed by users of electronic communications services do not regulate either the form of the requests made by the district prosecutor to the competent judge, or the order of this judge, or the requests made to internet service providers.

Content interception orders must be made in writing and must specify all the details identifying the link to be intercepted, the offence which justifies resorting to an interception as well as the duration of this interception. In addition, they must be justified according to the provisions recalled in subsection a. above, such as the situation where the requirements of the investigation call for it, or where there is one ground to believe that a person does not respect a prohibition to contact certain persons (provisions which are supposed to ensure proportionality of the measure to the seriousness of the offence). They can only be issued for the penal infringements listed in the texts that authorise the interception measure, also recalled above in subsection a.

Again, the Penal Procedure Code does not specify the persons (such as suspects, intermediaries or communication partners) who can be placed under surveillance or require that less intrusive means are considered or tried. The measure may be ordered in case of any penal infringement that justifies one of the three forms of judicial investigation set out under French law (flagrancy investigation, preliminary investigation or investigation procedure conducted by an investigating judge).

7. Validity of interception orders

Conditions for the validity of interception orders differ depending on the procedure that is followed.

a) Correspondence interception

aa) Maximum length of interception order

Correspondence interceptions ordered by the investigating judge, and by the judge responsible for enforcing sentences, must have a maximum duration of four months. The measure may be extended by following the same conditions as to form and duration. The Penal Procedure Code does not provide for a maximum of possible renewals.

Correspondence interceptions ordered by the liberty and custody judge of the district Court must have:

– A maximum duration of two months in the case of a search for an escaping person. In this situation, the measure may be extended by following the same conditions as to form and duration, with a maximum duration of six months regarding misdemeanour (and with no limits regarding crimes).

- A maximum duration of one month in case of a flagrancy investigation or a preliminary investigation in relation with a restricted list of penal infringements.[122] In this situation, the measure may be extended only once by following the same conditions as to form and duration.

bb) Revocation of authorisations

In all situations, any correspondence which is useful for the discovery of the truth is transcribed. The Penal Procedure Code does not require that the interception must be halted if it reveals information pointing to the commission of offences not anticipated or mentioned in the interception order. On the contrary, such information could be subject to the opening of a new investigation on the basis of article 40 of the Penal Procedure Code.[123]

For the rest, the Penal Procedure Code is silent on the possibility for the competent judge to revoke his interception authorisation.

b) Remote data capture

aa) Maximum length of interception order

Remote data capture orders must have a maximum duration of four months. They may be extended, exceptionally and under the same conditions as to form and duration, where the investigation so requires.[124]

bb) Revocation of authorisations

Only the data that are needed to ascertain the truth are described or transcribed, in an official record filed in the criminal case file, and no sequence relating to private life and that has no relation with penal infringements mentioned in the authorisation can be kept in the criminal case file.[125]

Under penalty of nullity, operations shall be limited to the investigation and identification of penal infringements mentioned in the authorisation of the investi-

---

122 See footnotes n°79 and n°80.

123 According to art. 40 PPC, "every constituted authority, every public officer or civil servant who, in the performance of his duties, has gained knowledge of the existence of a felony or of a misdemeanour is obliged to notify forthwith the district prosecutor of the offence and to transmit to this prosecutor any relevant information, official reports or documents". See the English translation of the French Penal Procedure Code noted above.

124 Art. 706-102-3 PPC.

125 Art. 706-102-8 PPC.

gating judge, but the fact that these operations reveal other penal infringements not mentioned in the investigating judge's decision is not a cause for nullity of incidental proceedings, as explicitly mentioned in article 706-102-4 of the Penal Procedure Code.

In addition, such information could be subject to the opening of a new investigation on the basis of article 40 of the Penal Procedure Code.[126]

Finally, the investigating judge may, at all times, require the interruption of operations.[127]

c) Interception by service providers of the content of the information accessed by their users

aa) Maximum length of interception order

The preservation of the text of the information consulted by persons using the services provided by the operators must not exceed one year.

bb) Revocation of authorisations

The Penal Procedure Code does not set out particular conditions regarding the specification, in the preservation authorisation and request, of the offence that justifies the request for information preservation. The Penal Procedure Code is also silent on the possibility for the competent judge to revoke his authorisation.

8. Duties to record, report, and destroy

Duties to record, report and destroy differ depending on the procedure that is followed.

a) Correspondence interception

Each interception and recording operation must be the object of the drafting of an official record, which must mention the date and time when the operation started and ended. Recordings are placed under closed official seals.[128] An official record is also made of any correspondence transcription, and attached to the case file.[129]

---

[126] See footnote n°123.

[127] Art. 706-102-3 PPC.

[128] Art. 100-4 PPC.

[129] Art. 100-5 PPC.

Recordings are destroyed on the request of the district prosecutor or of the public prosecutor upon the expiry of the limitation period for prosecution. An official record is made of the destruction.[130]

Reports of operations are addressed to the judge who authorised them.[131]

b) Remote data capture

The same procedure is followed as for correspondence interceptions, with similar rules on official seals,[132] official records,[133] and destruction.[134] Reports of operations are addressed to the investigating judge.[135]

c) Interception by service providers of the content of the information accessed by their users

The articles of the Penal Procedure Code that are specific to these kinds of interceptions do not regulate either the recording and reporting of operations, or the destruction of recordings.

9. Notification duties, remedies and consequences

Procedural efficiency implies the secrecy of interception measures.[136] Therefore, the accused can only have knowledge of their existence and results at the moment he is granted access to the entire procedural case file, this moment being determined by the Penal Procedure Code, depending on the nature of the procedure.[137]

Procedural acts resulting from these measures can be annulled, especially where a substantive requirement laid down in the Penal Procedure Code has not been respected which has affected the interests of the concerned party, or where it is provided in the provision of the Penal Procedure Code related to the concerned measure.[138]

---

130 Art. 100-6 PPC.

131 Arts. 100, 74-2 and 706-95 PPC.

132 Art. 706-102-7 PPC.

133 Art. 706-102-8 PPC.

134 Art. 706-102-9 PPC.

135 Arts. 706-102-1 and 706-102-5 PPC.

136 See, e.g., Jacques Beaume, *Rapport sur la procédure* pénale, July 2014, p. 43 available at http://www.justice.gouv.fr/publication/rap-beaume-2014.pdf

137 See mainly arts. 393, 278, and 279 PPC.

138 See mainly arts. 170, 171 and 385 PPC.

For example, as we analysed it, the penalty of nullity is the consequence of a correspondence interception that takes place without respecting the requirements surrounding the implementation of such a measure on the line of a protected person (such as advocates or journalists) mentioned in articles 100-5 and 100-7 of the Penal Procedure Code.

10. Confidentiality requirements

Any person who provides support to the investigation must keep his or her support measure confidential, including internet service providers. Any violation of this obligation of professional secrecy may incur a penal sanction under articles 226-13 and 226-14 of the Penal Procedure Code.[139]

C. Collection and Retention of Traffic Data and Subscriber Data

Several provisions regulate the collection of traffic and subscriber data, data retention and the location of mobile terminal devices.

1. Collection of traffic data and subscribers data

a) Relevant information and prerequisite of collection

aa) Requisition of traffic and connection data

Traffic and connection data retained by service providers can be requisitioned according to articles 77-1-1 (preliminary investigation), 60-1 (flagrancy investigation) and 99-3 (investigation procedure, conducted by an investigative judge) of the Penal Procedure Code.

Article 60-1:

The district prosecutor or a judicial police officer may, by any means, order any person, establishment or organisation, whether public or private, or any public services likely to possess any documents relevant to the inquiry in progress, including those produced from a computer system or a personal data processing system, to provide them with these documents, including in digital format. Without legitimate grounds, the duty of professional secrecy may not be given as a reason for non-compliance. […]

[…], failure to respond to such an order as quickly as possible is punished by a fine of €3,570. […]

Article 77-1-1:

The district prosecutor or on his authorisation a judicial police officer, may, by any means, order any person, establishment or organisation, whether public or private, or

139 Art. 11 PPC.

any public services liable to possess any documents relevant to the inquiry in progress, including those produced from a computer system or a personal data processing system, to provide them with these documents, including in digital format. Without legitimate grounds, the duty of professional secrecy cannot be given as a reason for non-compliance with this order. […]

Where there is no response to these orders, the provisions of the second paragraph of article 60-1 are applicable. […]

Article 99-3:

An investigating judge or judicial police officer delegated by him may, by any means, order any person, establishment or organisation, whether public or private, or any public services liable to possess any documents relevant to the investigation, including those produced from a computer system or a personal data processing system, to provide them with these documents, including in digital format. Without legitimate grounds, the duty of professional secrecy may not be given as a reason for non-compliance with such an order. […]

Where the person does not respond to this order, the provisions of the second paragraph of article 60-1 are applicable.

[…]

bb) Remote access to stored data

In addition, the first paragraphs of articles 60-2, 77-1-2 and 99-4 of the same Code organise the possibility to access, including remotely, information stored in computer and data processing systems:

Article 60-2, §1:

At the request of a judicial police officer, who can intervene by means of telecommunications or computers, public organisations or private legal persons, with the exception of those set out in the second paragraph of article 8, II, 3° and in article 67, 2° of Law no. 78-17 of 6 January 1978 relating to computers, databases and liberties,[140] must make available information helpful for the discovery of the truth, with the exception of information the secrecy of which is protected by statute, where it is stored in one or more computer or data processing systems that they administer.

Article 60-2, §5:

A Decree of the Council of State made on the advice of the National Commission for Data Protection determines the categories of organisation covered by the first paragraph, and also the methods for examining, transmitting and processing the required information.[141]

Article 77-1-2, §1:

On the authorisation of the district prosecutor, a judicial police officer may carry out the measures provided for by the first paragraph of article 60-2.

---

140 These persons are the members of a non-profit association or entity of a philosophical, political, religious or trade-union character, the persons who have regular contacts with such association or entity within the framework of its activities (art. 8, II, 3°, § 2 of Law n°78-17), and professional journalists (art. 67, 2° of Law n° 78-17).

141 Decree n°2008-150 of 19 Feb. 2008, creating arts. R. 15-33-67 to R. 15-33-75 PPC.

Article 99-4, §1:

Where necessary to carry out a rogatory commission, a judicial police officer may issue the demands provided for by the first paragraph of article 60-2.

cc) Access to subscribers lists

Finally, article L. 33-1, V of the Post and Electronic Communications Code requires electronic communications operators to enable access by the judiciary, the national police, the national gendarmerie, fire and rescue services, and emergency services, when these services act within the framework of their respective judicial or rescue missions, to the comprehensive, unredacted and updated list of their users and subscribers.

b) Duty of addressees to disclose information

Internet access service providers and hosting providers who do not retain connection data according to article 6 of the Law n° 2004-275, or answer a communication request form the judiciary, may be punished by one year imprisonment and a fine of €75,000.[142]

Electronic communications operators and internet access service providers who do not retain traffic data within the conditions laid down by law (including not anonymising these data when required by law) may be punished by one year imprisonment and a fine of €75,000.[143] Non-disclosure is punished by article 60-1 of the Penal Procedure Code.

Article 60-1 is also applicable to the non-disclosure of users and subscribers lists.

c) Automated procedure of disclosure

The procedure to be followed to access information remotely, on the basis of article 60-2, §1 of the Penal Procedure Code, is described in articles R. 15-33-67 to R. 15-33-75 of the Penal Procedure Code. Article R. 15-33-72 notably provides that technical arrangements for requesting and transmitting the data are defined in an agreement between the Ministry for Justice and, depending on the situation, the Ministry of interior or the Ministry of Budget, with each organisation or legal person liable for communicating data under article 60-1 of the Penal Procedure Code.[144]

---

142 Art. 6, VI of Law n°2004-575 of 21 June 2004 regarding confidence in the digital economy (called "LCEN").

143 Art. L. 39-3 PECC.

144 The comprehensive list of the categories of concerned legal persons is included in art. R. 15-33-68 PPC.

2. Data retention

The obligations of internet services providers to retain traffic and connection data are laid down in article L. 34-1 of the post and electronic communications Code (retention of traffic data by operators and internet access providers) and article 6, II of the Law n° 2004-575 (retention of connection data by internet access providers and hosting providers)[145].

Data to be retained are specified in two decrees:

- Decree 2006-358 of 24 March 2004, which creates articles R. 10-12 *et seq.* of the post and electronic communications Code, issued under article L. 34-1 of the same Code;
- Decree 2011-219 of 25 February 2011, issued under article 6 of Law n° 2004-575.

Traffic data to be retained (for a duration of one year) under article L. 34-1 of the Post and Electronic Communications Code, in order to identify and prosecute penal infringements, according to article R. 10-13 of the same Code, are the following technical data:

- Information enabling the identification of the user;
- Data relating to terminal communication equipment used;
- Technical specifications and date, time and duration of each communication;
- Data relating to complementary services requested or used and their providers;
- Data enabling the identification the recipients of the communication.

In addition to these data, for telephony activities, the operator must retain data that enable the identification of the origin and the location of the communication.

Connection data to be retained (for a duration of one year) under article 6 of Law n° 2004-575 according to Decree n° 2011-219, are once again only technical data, excluding other types of information (such as names, passwords, etc.) if such data are not usually collected. These data include – notably – the following:

- The identifier of the connection;
- The identifier attributed to the subscriber;
- The identifier of the terminal used for the purpose of the connection, when providers access such information;
- The dates and times at which the connection begins and ends;
- The specifications of the line of the subscriber;
- Certain information provided at the time of the contract subscription or of the creation of the users' account, including – only where the provider usually col-

145 Law n°2004-575 of 21 June 2004 regarding confidence in the digital economy (called "LCEN").

lects such information – the password and the data that enables the modification or verification of this password, in their latest and updated form.

3. Location of mobile terminal device

Real-time geolocation of a person, a vehicle or an object, without the consent of this person or the owner of this vehicle or object, can be done in limited situations according to articles 230-32 to 230-44 of the Penal Procedure Code.

To reach this aim, according to article 230-32, any technical means may be used.

D. Access to Stored Communication Data

In addition to the procedures already studied that enable the access of certain kinds of stored communication data, French law authorises search and seizure, accompanied by a duty to cooperate.

1. Search and seizure of stored electronic communication data

Search and seizure of information held by a third party is set out in articles 76 to 76-3 (preliminary investigation), 56 to 59 (flagrancy investigation), 92 to 99-4 (investigation procedure conducted by an investigative judge), and 706-89 (in relation with a limited list of crime or misdemeanours) of the Penal Procedure Code.

This general procedure is applicable to stored electronic communication data. As already explained previously in this report, it is supposed to apply to the content of private correspondence – where such correspondence is involved – only before it is sent or after it has been received, which should be understood as receipt by the recipient himself and not the services of the hosting provider only.

Safeguards and requirements are different from those surrounding the interception of correspondence and remote access to data, since the privacy limitation is in this case considered lower. For example, the procedure of search and seizure can be used within the framework of any investigation, and is not limited to the investigation of certain kinds of penal infringements only. Safeguards include the drafting of an official report of the search, the initiation of steps that are necessary to ensure the observance of professional secrecy and the defendant's rights, the inventory and placement under official seals of any document or article seized, a restriction of access to consulted documents and information to the police officer who carries out the search and potential qualified persons requisitioned to help him, and the presence, during search and seizure, of the person in whose domicile the search is made or of two witnesses. In addition, certain categories of persons are more particularly protected.

2. Duties to cooperate: production and decryption orders

A duty to cooperate is set out in relation with the search and seizure procedure, and non-cooperation is punished by the Penal Code. However, these provisions do not apply to the defendant, who only risks an increase of the sentence in case he or she is found guilty.

a) Duties to cooperate

During search and seizure, judicial police officers may, by any means, request any person who may be aware of the security measures applied in order to protect the data that can be accessed during the search, or who may supply them with the information that is necessary to access to these data. Failure to respond to this request at the earliest opportunity is punishable by a fine of €3,750, except for some particularly protected people to whom such a sanction does not apply (advocates, media companies, audio-visual communication companies, online public communication companies, press agencies, journalists, doctors, notaries, bailiffs).[146] This provision is applicable to requests for the decryption of seized documents.

In addition, the Penal Code punishes some refusals to cooperate.

Article 432-15-2 (as last modified by law n° 2001-1062) states:

> A penalty of three years' imprisonment and a fine of €45,000 are incurred by anyone who, having the key to decipher an encrypted message which may have been used to prepare, facilitate or commit a felony or a misdemeanour, refuses to disclose that key to the judicial authorities or to operate it following instructions issued by the judicial authorities under of title II and III of Book I of the Code of penal procedure.
>
> Where the refusal was made where the disclosure of the key or its operation would have prevented the commission of a felony or a misdemeanour or would have limited its consequences, the penalty is increased to five years' imprisonment and a fine of €75,000.

b) Non application to the defendant

These provisions are not applicable to the defendant, in accordance with the principle of prohibition of self-incrimination. Doctrine and practitioners agree on that issue, even if no court decision seems to have been issued on that particular question.[147]

However, a defendant who refused to cooperate could be punished more severely if found guilty, on the basis of article 132-79 of the Penal Code.

---

[146] Art. 57-1 PPC.

[147] See, e.g., Camille Polloni, "Si la police le demande, est-on obligé de donner son mot de passe?," 5 Feb. 2015, Rue 89, available at http://rue89.nouvelobs.com/2015/02/05/si-police-demande-est-oblige-donner-mot-passe-257509. This press article includes the interview of advocates and National Gendarmerie representatives.

Article 132-79 (inserted and last modified by Law n° 2004-575):

Where a means of encryption, in the sense of article 29 of act no. 2004-575 of 21 June 2004 used to ensure confidentiality in the digital economy has been used to prepare or commit a felony or a misdemeanour, or to facilitate the preparation of commission of a felony or a misdemeanour, the maximum prison sentence incurred is raised as follows:

1° where the offence is punished by thirty years' imprisonment, this is increased to life imprisonment;

2° where the offence is punished by twenty years' imprisonment, this is increased to thirty;

3° where the offence is punished by fifteen years' imprisonment, this is increased to twenty;

4° where the offence is punished by ten years' imprisonment, this is increased to fifteen;

5° where the offence is punished by seven years' imprisonment, this is increased to ten;

6° where the offence is punished by five years' imprisonment, this is increased to seven;

7° where the offence is punished by a maximum of three years' imprisonment, this is doubled.

The provisions of the present article are, however, not applicable to the perpetrator of or the accomplice to an offence who, at the request of the judicial or administrative authorities, has provided them with an unencrypted version of the coded messages and the secret keys necessary to decipher them.

3. Power of judicial authorities to decrypt encrypted data that are necessary to ascertain the truth

Articles 230-1 to 230-5 of the Penal Procedure Code provide for the possibility for judicial authorities to decrypt encrypted data that are necessary to ascertain the truth.[148]

Article 230-1 (inserted by Law no. 2001-1062 of 15 November 2001 art. 30 Official Journal of 16 November 2001); (Act no. 2004-575 of 21 June 2004 art. 38 Official Journal of 22 June 2004) (Modified by Law n°2014-1353 of 13 November 2014):

Without prejudice to the provisions of articles 60, 77-1 and 156, where it appears that data seized or obtained during the course of the inquiry or investigation has been altered, preventing access to or understanding of the information in clear that it contains, or where it appears that these data are protected by an authentication mechanism, the district prosecutor, the investigating jurisdiction, the judicial police officer authorised by the district prosecutor or by the investigating judge, or the trial court seized of the case may appoint any qualified legal or natural person to carry out the technical operations necessary to obtain access to this information, to obtain a readable version of this information, and also, where a method of encryption has been used, the secret key for decoding it, if this appears necessary.

---

[148] The following articles correspond to the translation proposed by Legifrance, and modified by the author of the current report in order to take into account most recent modifications made to these articles by Law n° 2014-1353 of 13 Nov. 2014.

If the person thus appointed is a legal person, his legal representative submits for the approval of the district prosecutor, the judicial police officer or the court seized of the case the name of the natural person or persons who, within this legal person and under its name, will carry out the technical operations mentioned in the first paragraph. Unless these persons are registered on a list provided for by article 157, the persons thus nominated swears the oath provided for by the second paragraph of article 60 and by article 160, in writing.

If the penalty applicable to the offence is of at least two years' imprisonment and the needs of the inquiry or investigation justify this, the district prosecutor, the investigating jurisdiction, the judicial police officer authorised by the district prosecutor or by the investigating judge, or the trial court seized of the case may order the use of means protected by National Defence secrecy, following procedures laid down by the present chapter.

Article 230-2 (inserted by Law no. 2001-1062 of 15 November 2001 article 30 Official Journal of 16 November 2001) (Modified by Law n°2014-1353 of 13 November 2014):

Where the district prosecutor, the investigating court, the judicial police officer authorised by the district prosecutor or by the investigating judge, or the trial court in charge of the case decide to use, for the procedures mentioned in article 230-1, means protected by official State secrecy, the written submission must be sent to a technical organisation subject to the obligations of National Defence secrecy and designated for this purpose by Decree, along with the medium containing the data to be deciphered or a copy of it. This submission fixes the time limit in which these deciphering procedures must be carried out. The time limit may be extended under the same conditions or form. At any time, the district prosecutor, the investigating court, the judicial police officer authorised by the district prosecutor or by the investigating judge, or the trial court which is in charge of the case or which has requisitioned the technical organisation, may order the interruption of these prescribed procedures.

Data protected in the interests of national security may only be passed on under the conditions provided for by law n 98-567 of 8th July 1998 establishing the Advisory Commission for National Defence Secrecy.

Article 230-3 (inserted by Law no. 2001-1062 of 15 November 2001 art. 30 Official Journal of 16 November 2001) (Modified by Law n°2014-1353 of 13 November 2014):

As soon as the procedures have been completed, or as soon as it becomes clear that the procedures are technically impossible, or at the expiry of the time limit prescribed, or when an interruption order is received from the district prosecutor, the investigating court, the judicial police officer authorised by the district prosecutor or by the investigating judge, or the trial court in charge of the case, the results obtained and the documents received are returned by the head of the technical organisation to the author of the request. Subject to the obligations of National Defence secrecy, the results are accompanied by technical instructions enabling them to be understood and used, as well as by a statement drawn up by the head of the technical organisation, which attests to the genuineness of the results.

The facts thus obtained are recorded in an official record marking their receipt and are added to the case file of the proceedings.

Article 230-4 (inserted by Law no. 2001-1062 of 15 November 2001 art. 30 Official Journal of 16 November 2001) (Modified by Law n°2014-1353 of 13 November 2014):

Judicial decisions taken pursuant to the present chapter do not have judicial status and are not subject to appeal.

Article 230-5 (inserted by Law no. 2001-1062 of 15 November 2001 art. 30 Official Journal of 16 November 2001) (Modified by Law n°2014-1353 of 13 November 2014)

Without prejudice to any obligations relating to National Defence secrecy, officials to whom requests are made under the provisions of the present chapter are obliged to bring their support to justice.

E. Taking of Audio Recordings and Visual Images

In addition to the above-mentioned procedures, article 706-96 of the Penal Procedure Code authorises, in certain situations, the installation a technical device designed to hear, preserve, transmit or record words spoken by any person or persons in a private or confidential context, in private or public places or vehicles, or the images of any person or persons in a private place, without the consent of the persons concerned. These procedures are carried out under the authority and supervision of the investigating judge.[149]

This procedure is not properly speaking a procedure that enables the interception of electronic communications, but may have such an interception as a result, notably through the recording of private images.

IV. Use of Electronic Communication Data in Judicial Proceedings

France applies the rule of evidence by all means,[150] subject to lawfulness and fairness, as long as this evidence can be discussed among the parties following the principle that both sides must be heard, in such a way that the right to a fair hearing is upheld).

---

[149] This paragraph is available in English at http://www.legifrance.gouv.fr/content/download/1957/13715/version/4/file/Code_33.pdf. However, the entire provision translated in the above-mentioned document has not been updated (the provision was last amended by Law n°2015-993).

[150] See notably art. 427 PPC. Production of evidence is regulated in arts. 427 to 457 PPC (in relation to misdemeanours) and in arts. 306 *et seq.* and 323 to 346 PPC (in relation to crimes).

A. Use of Electronic Communication Data in the Law of Criminal Procedure

Since evidence can be established by any means, electronic communication data are admissible in Justice in the same way as other proof, to the extent that their collection and the way they are presented before the court comply with legal rules and a principle of fairness.

Indeed, evidence must be collected in compliance with law,[151] since rules of procedure are established in order to preserve the rights of the defence.[152] A police record has probative value only if its form complies with requirements and if its author acted in the performance of their duties, on an issue falling within the scope of their responsibilities, and if they have reported what they have seen, heard, or noticed personally.[153]

Moreover, the principle of fairness of evidence was established by the *Cour de cassation* (the French Supreme Court), as a condition for the exercise of the rights of the defence, and, more generally, as condition for a fair trial.[154]

However, these requirements of lawfulness and of fairness are more strictly enforced in relation to evidence produced by the public authority (or by a private party on the instructions of the public authority), in comparison with evidence produced by a private party.

1. Evidence produced by public authorities

Evidence produced by public authorities may be the result of certain positive acts, but it must not be the result of acts that conduced the author to commit a penal infringement, in other worlds these acts must not have provoked or incited the commission of the penal infringement that is being proven.[155] More widely, the

151 Art. 427 PPC.

152 Pascal Lemoine, "La loyauté de la preuve (à travers quelques arrêts récents de la chambre criminelle)," Cour de cassation annual report 2004, available at https://www.courdecassation.fr/publications_26/rapport_annuel_36/rapport_2004_173/deuxie me_partie_tudes_documents_176/tudes_diverses_179/travers_quelques_6401.html#n_20_

153 Art. 429 PPC.

154 Pascal Lemoine, "La loyauté de la preuve (à travers quelques arrêts récents de la chambre criminelle)," *op. cit.*

155 Cass. crim., 27 Feb. 1996, "Schuller" court case, bull. crim. 1996, n° 93; JCP 96, ed. G, II-22629, note M.-L. Rassat; D. 96, p. 346, note Ch. Guéry; Cass. crim., 11 May 2006, pourvoi n°05-84.837, bull. crim. 2006, n°132; see Pascal Lemoine, *op. cit.* See also Cour de cassation, rapport annuel 2012, *La preuve*, Livre 3, partie 4, Titre 2, Chapitre 2 – Admissibilité des modes de preuve, available at https://www.courdecassation.fr/publi cations_26/rapport_annuel_36/rapport_2012_4571/livre_3_etude_preuve_4578/partie_4_ administration_preuve_4589/principes_gouvernant_4591/admissibilite_modes_26241.html

Cour de cassation rejects evidence obtained by fraudulent means.[156] Evidence thus obtained will be declared inadmissible,[157] and may even result in the nullity of proceedings.[158]

However, the *Cour de cassation* does accept provocations that are not at the origin of the penal infringement, but which enable the infringement to be proven.[159]

2. Evidence produced by private parties

The criminal chamber of the *Cour de cassation* considers that the judge does not have the power, based on articles 427 *et seq.* of the Penal Procedure Code, to reject evidence obtained by a party for the sole reason that this evidence has been unlawfully obtained.[160] Therefore, illegal and unfair means of proof are accepted by French courts, where the evidence is provided by a private party, especially where the way the evidence has been collected was justified by the necessity of proving a fact and the impossibility of proving it otherwise.[161]

The judge must in such a case appreciate the probative value of the evidence.[162]

However, lawfulness and fairness is required where the private party who produces the evidence has acted in collaboration with public authority agents (under their instructions or with their assistance).[163]

---

[156] Cass. crim., 28 Oct. 1991, bull. crim., n° 381; JCP, 1991.II.21704, note J. Pannier.

[157] Cass. crim., 9 Aug. 2006, n° 06-83.219, bull. crim. 2006, n° 202; Cass. crim., 7 Feb. 2007, pourvoi n° 06-87.753, bull. crim. 2007, n° 37; Cass. crim., 4 June 2008, pourvoi n° 08-81.045, bull. crim. 2008, n° 141; see Cour de cassation, rapport annuel 2012, *La preuve, op. cit.*

[158] Cass. crim., 27 Feb. 1996, bull. crim. 1996, n° 93.

[159] Cass. crim., 30 April 1998, pourvoi n° 97-85.747, bull. crim. 1998, n° 147; Cass. crim., 8 June 2005, pourvoi n° 05-82.012, bull. crim. 2005, n° 173; Cass. crim., 16 Jan. 2008, pourvoi n° 07-87.633, bull. crim. 2008, n° 14; see Cour de cassation, rapport annuel 2012, *La preuve, op. cit.*

[160] Cass. crim. 15 June 1993: bull. crim., n° 210 6 April 1993, JCP 1993, II, 22144, note M.-L. Rassat; see Pascal Lemoine, "La loyauté de la preuve (à travers quelques arrêts récents de la chambre criminelle)," *op. cit.*

[161] Cass. crim., 31 Jan. 2007, pourvoi n° 06-82.383, bull. crim. 2007, n° 27. See Cour de cassation, rapport annuel 2012, *La preuve, op. cit.*

[162] Cass crim., 15 June 1993, pourvoi n° 92-82.509, bull. crim. 1993, n° 210; Cass. crim., 6 April 1994, pourvoi n° 93-82.717, bull. crim. 1994, n°136; see Cour de cassation, rapport annuel 2012, *La preuve, op. cit.*

[163] Ex. Cass. crim., 11 May 2006, pourvoi n° 05-84.837, bull. crim. 2006, n°132. See Cour de cassation, rapport annuel 2012, *La preuve, op. cit.*

B. The Right for the Accused to Challenge the Probity of Intercepted Data

The *Cour de cassation* does accept the admissibility of some proof obtained by illicit or unfair means under the strict condition that such proof does not entail a breach of the rights of defence. As a consequence, the Court verifies that the produced evidence has been submitted to a debate between the parties.[164]

Indeed, the principle that both parties must be heard is set out in the Penal Procedure Code,[165] which implies that each of the parties can access the evidence produced by the other parties and has the time and the right to challenge this evidence. Therefore, the accused is entitled to challenge the means used and the procedure that has been followed in order to intercept electronic communications.

Proof to the contrary can in principle be established by any means, unless the law states otherwise, which is the case in very few matters. For example, where police records have been established by police officers or agents who received from a special legal provision the power of recording misdemeanours through police records, evidence to the contrary can only be produced in writing or by testimony.[166] Moreover, some special laws set out that some particular official records are considered to be valid proof until specific proceedings are launched to challenge the authenticity of facts.[167] Finally, written proof cannot result from correspondence between the accused and their attorney-at-law,[168] and the court can always order a forensic examination, if deemed necessary.[169]

V. Exchange of Intercepted Electronic Communication Data between Foreign Countries

A. Legal Basis for Mutual Legal Assistance

International judicial cooperation is regulated by articles 694 *et seq.* of the Penal Procedure Code. These provisions apply in the absence of any international convention or bilateral treaty stipulating otherwise.

164 See Cour de cassation, rapport annuel 2012, *La preuve, op. cit.*

165 See, e.g., art. 427 PPC.

166 Art. 431 PPC.

167 Art. 432 PPC.

168 Art. 433 PPC.

169 Arts. 434, 310 PPC.

Within the limits of the provisions of these articles, which are detailed below, and within the limits of the powers for accessing electronic communications set out in the French Penal Procedure Code, mutual legal assistance may enable real-time access to electronic communication data.

1. General provisions

Article 694:[170]

In the absence of any international conventions stipulating otherwise:

1° Requests for mutual assistance coming from French judicial authorities and addressed to foreign judicial authorities are sent through the intermediary of the Minister of Justice. The enforcement documents are sent to the authorities of the requesting State through the same channels.

2° Requests for judicial assistance coming from foreign judicial authorities are sent through diplomatic channels. The enforcement documents are sent to the authorities of the requesting State through the same channels.

In urgent cases, requests for mutual assistance sought by the French or foreign authorities may be directly sent to the authorities of the State who are competent to enforce them. The transmission of the enforcement documents to the authorities of the requested State is carried out in the same way and under the same conditions. However, unless there is an international convention stipulating otherwise, requests for judicial assistance coming from foreign judicial authorities and addressed to the French judicial authorities must be the subject of an opinion sent through diplomatic channels by the foreign government concerned.

Article 694-1:

In urgent cases, requests for judicial assistance coming from foreign judicial authorities are sent, according to the distinctions set out in article 694-2, to the district prosecutor or the investigating judge of the territorially competent district court. They may also be sent to these judges through the intermediary of the prosecutor general.

If the district prosecutor receives a request for judicial assistance directly from a foreign authority which may only be executed by the investigating judge, he sends it to the latter to be carried out, or seizes the prosecutor general in the case provided for by article 694-4.

Before executing a request for judicial assistance of which he has directly be seized, the investigating judge immediately sends this to the district prosecutor for his opinion.

Article 694-2:

Requests for judicial assistance coming from foreign judicial authorities are executed by the district prosecutor or by judicial police officers or agents nominated for this purpose by this prosecutor.

They are executed by the investigating judge or judicial police officers acting in the context of a rogatory letter where they require particular procedural acts which may not be ordered or executed in the course of a preparatory investigation.

---

170 See the English translation of the French Penal Procedure Code proposed by Legifrance at http://www.legifrance.gouv.fr/content/download/1958/13719/version/3/file/Code_34.pdf (arts. 694 to 694-4 in this document correspond to their current version. Further articles have mostly been modified since the translation has been done).

Article 694-3:

Requests for judicial assistance coming from foreign judicial authorities are executed according to the procedural rules provided for by the present Code.

However, if the request for judicial assistance specifies this, it is executed in accordance with the procedural rules indicated by the competent authorities of the requesting State, on the condition, under penalty of nullity, that these rules do not reduce the rights of the parties or the procedural guarantees provided for by the present Code. Where the request for judicial assistance may not be executed in accordance with the stipulations of the requesting State, the competent French authorities immediately inform the authorities of the requesting State and indicate under which conditions the request may be executed. The competent French authorities and those of the requesting State may agree on the outcome of this request later on, where appropriate by subjecting it to the aforesaid conditions.

The irregularity of the sending of the request for judicial assistance may not constitute grounds for nullity of the acts executed in enforcing this request.

Article 694-4:

If the enforcement of a request for judicial assistance coming from a foreign judicial authority is liable to threaten public order or the fundamental interests of the nation, the district prosecutor seized of this request in accordance with the third paragraph of article 694-1 sends this to the prosecutor general who decides, if appropriate, to seize the Minister of Justice and gives, where applicable, notice of this reference to the investigating judge.

If he is seized, the Minister of Justice informs the authority which made the request, if appropriate, that no action, total or partial, may be taken in relation to the request. This information is communicated to the judicial authority concerned and blocks the enforcement of the request for judicial assistance or the return of the enforcement documents.

2. Provisions specific to cooperation between France and other EU Member States

Article 695-1:

Unless a foreign convention stipulates otherwise, and subject to the provisions of article 694-4, requests for judicial assistance are sent and enforcement documents returned directly between the judicial authorities territorially competent to issue and enforce them, in accordance with the provisions of articles 694-1 to 694-3.

Article 695-2:

Where there is need to carry out, in the context of a French prosecution, either complex inquiries involving the mobilisation of extensive resources and which concern other member states or where several member states are carrying out inquiries into offences which call for coordinated and concerted action between the member states concerned, with the prior agreement of the Minister of Justice and the consent of the member state or states concerned, the competent judicial authority may create a joint investigation team.

Foreign agents seconded by another member state to a joint investigation team may, within the limits of the powers conferred on them by their role, and under the supervision of the competent judicial authorities, have as their mission, as appropriate, over the whole of the national territory:

1° the establishment of any felonies, misdemeanours or petty offences, and to record these in an official record, if necessary in the forms provided for by the law of their state;

2° the reception of the official reports of any statements made to them by any person liable to provide information on the facts in question, if necessary in the forms provided for by the law of their state;

3° the secondment of French judicial police officers in the exercise of their duties;

4° the carrying out of any surveillance and, if they are authorised for this purpose, infiltration, under the conditions provided for by articles 706-81 onwards, and which is necessary for the application of articles 694-7 and 694-8.

Foreign officers attached to a joint investigation team may carry out these missions subject to the consent of the member state which has implemented their secondment.

These officers may only carry out the operations for which they have been designated. None of the powers which are the preserve of the French judicial police officer who is in charge of the team may be delegated to them.

The original copy of the official records which they prepare, and which must be drafted or translated into French, is attached to the case file.

Article 695-3:

In the context of a joint investigation team, French judicial police officers and agents attached to a joint investigation team may carry out operations ordered by the head of the team, over the whole of the territory of the State in which they are operating, within the limit of the powers conferred on them by the present Code.

Their tasks are defined by the authorities of the Member State competent to direct the joint investigation team in the territory where the team is working.

They may receive statements and record offences in the forms provided for by the present Code, subject to the consent of the State in whose territory they are operating.

B. Requirements and Procedure

1. Simplified exchange of information, implementing Decision 2006/960/JAI of 18 December 2006

The simplified exchange of information, implementing Decision 2006/960/JAI of 18 December 2006, is regulated in articles 695-9-31 to 695-9-49.

a) General provisions

Article 695-9-31 authorises National police and gendarmerie services and certain custom services to exchange, with competent services of another Member State, information that is at their disposal, in the aim of preventing a penal infringement, of collecting evidence in relation with a penal infringement or of searching for perpetrators of a penal infringement, either they detain it or they can access it, especially through the consultation of a data processing system, without making it necessary to take or ask for a requisition measure or another coercive measure.

Article 695-9-32 sets out that exchanged information is confidential, which must be guaranteed by its means of transmission and of storage.

b) Requests for information issued by French services

Articles 695-9-33 to 695-9-36:

When reasons exist to assume that a Member state holds information described in article 695-9-31 that is useful in order to prevent a penal infringement, or that is useful to investigations aiming at establishing evidence of a penal infringement or to search for its perpetrators, services and units mentioned in article 695-9-31 may request the transmission of this information from the relevant services of this State. The request for transmission must provide the reasons on which they base their assumption that this information is in the possession of these services, and must mention the purposes of the request for information, and, when this information is related to an identified individual, it must mention the link between this person and the purposes of the request (article 695-9-33).

Obtained information cannot be used as evidence without the agreement of the Member State that has transmitted it (article 695-9-34). This information cannot be used for other purposes (purposes other than those mentioned in the request) without the agreement of the Member State that has transmitted it, unless they may prevent a clear and immediate danger for public security (article 695-9-35). These provisions do not prevent the possibility for relevant authorities to control the modalities of processing and storage of transmitted information (article 695-9-35). If the transmitting State asks for it, the service or unit that obtained the information informs the relevant service of this State about the use that has been made of this information (article 695-9-36).

c) Requests for information received by French services

Articles 695-9-37 to 695-9-47:

Services and units mentioned in article 695-9-31 transmit, when requested so by relevant services of an EU member State, the information mentioned in the same article and that is useful in order to prevent a penal infringement, or that is useful to investigations aiming at establishing evidence of a penal infringement or to search for its perpetrators (article 695-9-37).

If the information mentioned in article 695-9-31 may be useful to another Member State to prevent one of the penal infringements mentioned in article 695-23[171] and punished by at least three years of imprisonment, or if this information may be useful to this other member State in order to conduct investigations aiming at establishing evidence of such a penal infringement or to search for its perpetrators, the service or unit that holds this information transmits it to this other Member State without the need of having received a corresponding request (article 695-9-38).

When this information is initially transmitted by another Member State on the basis of the framework decision 2006/960/JAI, it may only be transmitted to another Member State following the conditions imposed by the first transmitting Member State. When this information is initially transmitted by another Member State on a basis other than

---

[171] Art. 695-23 lists several penal infringements including (non-exhaustively) participation in a criminal organisation, terrorism, human trafficking, child pornography and sexual exploitation of children, cybercrime.

the framework decision 2006/960/JAI, or by a non-EU Member State, it may only be transmitted to another Member State with the agreement of the first transmitting State and under the conditions imposed by this State, in all the situations where France must respect these principles according to an International agreement (article 695-9-39).

Information can only be transmitted, to the relevant services of the Member State that requested it, with the authorisation of a judge, each time such an authorisation is mandatory under French law in order to access this same information or to transmit this same information to a judicial police service or unit. The request for authorisation is addressed to the relevant judge by the service or unit to which the information is requested. Elements of an ongoing penal procedure can only be transmitted with the authorisation of the investigating court in charge of the case, or with the authorisation of the public prosecutor when the trial court has been seized (article 695-9-40).

Services or units mentioned in article 695-9-31 cannot refuse to communicate information requested by a Member State, unless reasons exist to think that such communication:

- could be prejudicial to the fundamental interests of the State in terms of National security;
- could be prejudicial to ongoing investigations in penal matters or would jeopardise people's security;
- or would be clearly disproportionate or pointless in relation to the purposes for which the information has been requested (article 695-9-41).

Services or units mentioned in article 695-9-31 may refuse to transmit requested information when it relates to a penal infringement punished in France by a year or less of imprisonment and when they consider that the information is not of sufficient interest to justify the constraints attached to its transmission (article 695-9-42).

On the occasion of the transmission of the information, the service or unit mentioned in article 695-9-31 indicates to the receiving service the conditions of use of the information. Each time it deems it is necessary, it may ask the receiving service to provide information about the use that has been made of the transmitted information (article 695-9-43).

Where information has been transmitted by a service or unit mentioned in article 695-9-31 to the relevant service of a Member State and where the latter considers transmitting it to another State or using it for another purpose than the one for which the transmission was permitted, the service or unit that made the original transmission is competent to consider whether the new transmission or the new use should be authorised, on the request of the receiving State, and, if needed, to determine the conditions of it (article 695-9-44).

Information transmitted by the service or unit mentioned in article 695-9-31 may be used by the receiving service as evidence, unless it was otherwise stipulated on the occasion of its transmission (article 695-9-45).

Information transmitted by the service or unit mentioned in article 695-9-31 to the relevant service of a Member State is also transmitted to the Eurojust and Europol units, to the extent it relates to a penal infringement falling within their mandate (article 695-9-46).

Contact points to whose requests for transmission of information can be addressed by relevant services of Member States are nominated by order of the Ministry for Justice, of the Ministry of interiors and of the Ministry responsible for the budget (article 695-9-47).

Application of previous provisions to certain States that are not members of the European Union (articles 695-9-48 and 695-9-49)

Articles 695-9-31 to 695-9-47 are applicable to the exchange of information mentioned in article 695-9-31 between services and units mentioned in the latter article and relevant services from States which are not members of the EU but which are associated with the implementation, the application and the development of the Schengen *acquis* (article 695-9-48).

Modalities of application of articles 695-9-31 to 695-9-48 are determined by a Decree issued by the Council of State (article 695-9-49).

2. Other provisions

Other provisions, not detailed or reproduced in this report, are related to Eurojust (articles 695-4 to 695-7), to the national members of Eurojust (articles 695-8 to 695-9), and to the issue and execution of orders freezing property or evidence under the European Union framework decision of 22 July 2003 (articles 695-9-1 to 695-9-30).[172]

172 Arts. 695-9-1 to 695-9-9 and arts. 695-9-14, 695-9-18, and 695-9-26 can be read in their current version in the Legifrance translation available at http://www.legifrance.gouv.fr/content/download/1958/13719/version/3/file/Code_34.pdf. The other articles have been modified since 2005 (i.e., since this translation has been performed).

Bibliography*

Beaume, Jacques, Rapport sur la procédure pénale, July 2014, p. 43, available at http://www.justice.gouv.fr/publication/rap-beaume-2014.pdf

Chefs d'institution de l'Association des Cours constitutionnelles ayant en partage l'usage du français, "La proportionnalité dans la jurisprudence constitutionnelle," 5ème conférence, 8–13 July 2008, p. 7, available at http://www.conseil-constitutionnel.fr/conseil-constitutionnel/root/bank_mm/Bilan_2008/confV_accpuf_libreville_juillet2008.pdf

Commission nationale de contrôle des interceptions de sécurité, CNCIS, report for the years 2013–2014, http://www.ladocumentationfrancaise.fr/var/storage/rapports-publics/154000101.pdf

Cour de cassation, rapport annuel 2012, *La preuve*, Livre 3, partie 4, Titre 2, Chapitre 2 – Admissibilité des modes de preuve, available at https://www.courdecassation.fr/publications_26/rapport_annuel_36/rapport_2012_4571/livre_3_etude_preuve_4578/partie_4_administration_preuve_4589/principes_gouvernant_4591/admissibilite_modes_26241.html

De Marco, Estelle, "Analyse du nouveau mécanisme de prévention de la contrefaçon à la lumière des droits et libertés fondamentaux," 4 June 2009, Juriscom.net, http://www.juriscom.net/uni/visu.php?ID=1133

– *L'anonymat sur Internet et le droit.* Thesis, Montpellier 1, 2005, ANRT.

De Marco, Estelle et al., *D3.3 – Legal recommendations*, Deliverable, ePOOLICE project (early Pursuit against Organized Crime Using Environmental Scanning, the Law and Intelligence Systems), project n° FP7-SEC-2012-312651, version 1.2 of 29 August 2014 and version 1.3 of 10 December 2014.

De Marco, Estelle/Callanan, Cormac, in: C. Callanan/M. Gercke/E. De Marco/H. Dries-Ziekenheiner, *Internet blocking – balancing cybercrime responses in democratic societies*, October 2009, n° 6.5.2.2, available at http://www.aconite.com/blocking/study (French version available at http://juriscom.net/2010/05/rapport-filtrage-dinternet-equilibrer-les-reponses-a-la-cybercriminalite-dans-une-societe-democratique-2/)

Dutheillet de Lamothe, Olivier, "L'influence de la Cour européenne des droits de l'Homme sur le Conseil constitutionnel, 13 février 2009, Conseil constitutionnel, visite du Président et d'une délégation de la Cour européenne des droits de l'homme au Conseil constitutionnel, http://www.conseil-constitutionnel.fr/conseil-constitutionnel/root/bank_mm/pdf/Conseil/cedh_130209_odutheillet.pdf

Goesel-Le Bihan, Valérie, "Le contrôle de proportionalité exercé par le Conseil constitutionnel, technique de protection des libertés publiques?", http://juspoliticum.com/Le-controle-de-proportionnalite.html

* All URLs were last accessed in 10/2016.

Kayser, Pierre, *La protection de la vie privée par le droit.* 3rd ed. PU d'Aix-Marseille/Economica 1995.

Lafay, Frédérique, note under Decision of the Constitutional Council n° 94-352 DC, 18 January 1995, J.O. 21 January 1995, p. 1154 and JCP 1995, II, 22525.

Lemoine, Pascal, "La loyauté de la preuve (à travers quelques arrêts récents de la chambre criminelle)," Cour de cassation annual report 2004, available at https://www.courdecassation.fr/publications_26/rapport_annuel_36/rapport_2004_173/deuxieme_partie_tudes_documents_176/tudes_diverses_179/travers_quelques_6401.html

Peltier, Virginie, *Le secret des correspondances.* PU d'Aix-Marseille 1999.

Rassat, Michèle-Laure, note under Cass. crim., 15 June 1993: bull. crim., n° 210. 6 April 1993, JCP 1993, II, 22144.

– note under Cass. crim., 27 February 1996, "Schuller" court case, bull. crim. 1996, n° 93; JCP 1996, ed. G, II, 22629.

Robert, Jacques/Duffar, Jean, *Droits de l'homme et libertés fondamentales.* 7th ed. Montchrestien 1999, p. 27.

Sudre, Frédéric, "La dimension internationale et européenne des libertés et droits fondamentaux." In: Rémy Cabrillac/Marie-Anne Frison-Roche/Thierry Revet (dir.), *Libertés et droits fondamentaux.* 11th ed. Dalloz 2005.

List of Abbreviations

bull. crim.	Bulletin de la Cour de Cassation, chambre criminelle (reports of the Court of Cassation's decisions, criminal chamber)
Cass. crim.	Cour de Cassation, chambre criminelle (Criminal Chamber of the Court of Cassation)
CNCIS	Commission nationale de contrôle des interceptions de sécurité (National Commission for the Control of Security Interceptions)
CNCTR	Commission nationale de contrôle des techniques de renseignement (National Commission for the Control of Intelligence Techniques)
D.	Recueil Dalloz (law journal)
dir.	sous la direction (edited by)
DJS	Droits, Justice et Sécurités (laws, justice and securities)
E. Court H. R.	European Court of Human Rights
ECHR	European Convention on Human Rights
IP	Internet Protocol

ISC	Internal Security Code
JCP	La semaine juridique (law journal)
JCP. ed. G	La semaine juridique édition génerale (law journal, general edition)
J.O.	Journal Officiel (official gazette of the French Republic)
JORF	Journal officiel de la République française (official gazette of the French Republic)
PC	Penal Code
PECC	Post and Electronic Communications Code
PPC	Penal Procedure Code

Germany*

National Rapporteurs:
Benjamin Vogel (Sections I.–III.B.)
Patrick Köppen (Sections III.C.–IV.)
Thomas Wahl (Section V.)
Sections I.–IV. translated by *Daniel Burke*

* This report reflects legislation and case law as of September 2016.

Contents

I. Security Architecture and the Interception of Telecommunication

A. Law Enforcement Institutions and Security Services with Powers of Telecommunication Interception

1. National security architecture

In Germany, the prevention and prosecution of crime is handled by various authorities. The focus lies upon the repressive tasks of public prosecutors, who are declared competent for criminal prosecution by the Code of Criminal Procedure (*Strafprozessordnung*, StPO), and the police authorities supporting them.

Additionally, police authorities are charged with the preventive task of averting danger, as stipulated in the Federal Criminal Police Office Act (*Bundeskriminalamtgesetz*, BKAG), the Federal Police Act *(Bundespolizeigesetz)* and the Police Acts of the *Länder* (the *Länder* being the 16 states of the Federal Republic of Germany) *(Landespolizeigesetze)*. The Federal Criminal Police Office *(Bundeskriminalamt)* supports public prosecutors in law enforcement activities involving certain forms of serious crime and is responsible for the aversion of dangers connected with international terrorism. The Federal Police *(Bundespolizei)* is competent for averting danger particularly in the fields of border protection, the safety of railway facilities, and aviation security. It is also responsible for the prosecution of certain offences connected with its preventive duties. For all other areas, the police authorities of the *Länder* are charged with averting danger and assisting public prosecutors in their law enforcement activities.

The tasks of intelligence agencies also belong to the field of prevention. Concerning state security (and in some *Länder*, also concerning organised crime) the Federal (*Bundesamt für Verfassungsschutz*, BfV) and State Offices for the Protection of the Constitution *(Verfassungsschutzämter der Länder)* are entrusted with collecting and analysing information. Pursuant to the Act on the Federal Intelligence Service (*Gesetz über den Bundesnachrichtendienst*, BNDG), the Federal Intelligence Service (*Bundesnachrichtendienst*, BND) gathers information of relevance to foreign and security policy, thus functioning as a foreign intelligence service. In individual cases, the Federal Intelligence Service may also take action to protect the health or life of a person in a foreign country. In the Federal Ministry of Defence's area of responsibility, the collection and analysis of information critical to state security is carried out by the Military Counterintelligence Service (*Militärischer Abschirmdienst*, MAD).

The Customs Criminal Office *(Zollkriminalamt)* and the Customs Investigation Offices *(Zollfahndungsämter)* are charged with monitoring foreign trade and the cross-border movement of goods. According to the Customs Investigation Act *(Gesetz über das Zollkriminalamt und die Zollfahndungsämter)*, their activities in this field include tasks of both preventive and repressive nature – the latter involves giving support to public prosecutors in criminal prosecution. In order to detect the commission of customs-related offences, the Customs Criminal Office continually monitors the internal and transnational movement of goods, capital, and services.

2. Powers for the interception of telecommunication

a) Law of criminal procedure

Pursuant to Section 100a StPO, the prosecution authorities are authorised to intercept telecommunication. This requires in particular the suspicion – based on specific facts – that certain serious offences have already been committed. The order must be given or confirmed by a judge.

b) Preventive law

Moreover, the interception of the content of telecommunication is permitted for preventive purposes according to Section 20l BKAG and the police laws of most *Länder*. As a prerequisite, this generally requires a – future – danger threatening the existence or security of the state, the life, health, or liberty of a person, or property of substantial value.[1] Suspicion of preparing particularly serious crimes, such as terrorist offences or violations of the War Weapons Control Act *(Kriegswaffenkontrollgesetz)*, also grants some police authorities the power to intercept telecommunication.[2] Such suspicion must be based on the existence of facts. Finally, the preventive interception of telecommunication is not exempt from the requirement of a judicial order or confirmation. Likewise, telecommunication providers' duties of information disclosure concerning traffic and subscriber data are stipulated explicitly in Section 20m BKAG and the police laws of most *Länder*.[3] Furthermore, the Federal Criminal Police Office is authorised to perform clandestine intrusions

---

1 Section 20l Subsection 1 BKAG and, e.g., Article 34a Subsection 1 BayPAG; Section 10b Subsection 1 HamDVPolG; Section 15a HSOG; Section 34a SOG M-V; Section 33a Subsection 1 NdsSOG; Section 31 POG RP; Section 28b SaarPolG; Section 17b SOG LSA; Section 185a LVwG SchlH; Section 34a ThürPAG; cp. *Schenke*, Polizei- und Ordnungsrecht, 2013, pp. 122 et seq.

2 See Section 20l Subsection 1 Sentence 1 No. 2 in connection with Section 4a Subsection 1 Sentence 2 BKAG; Section 33b Subsection 1 BbgPolG.

3 Section 20m BKAG and, e.g., Section 23a BWPolG; Article 34a Subsection 2 No. 2 BayPAG; Section 15a Subsection 3 HessSOG; Section 33a Subsection 2 No. 3, 33b Subsection 1 NdsSOG; see *Schenke*, Polizei- und Ordnungsrecht, pp. 125 et seq.

into information systems pursuant to Section 20k BKAG, as well as to employ IMSI-catchers for determining the location of active mobile terminal devices or for determining device or card numbers pursuant to Section 20n BKAG.

c) Law of intelligence agencies

As laid down in Section 1 Subsection 1 No. 1 in connection with Section 3 Subsection 1 of the Act Restricting the Secrecy of the Post, of Letters, and of Telecommunication (*Gesetz zur Beschränkung des Post-, Brief- und Fernmeldegeheimnisses*, G 10), the Federal and State Offices for the Protection of the Constitution, the Military Counterintelligence Service, and the Federal Intelligence Service are authorised to monitor the communication of individual connections for the purpose of averting danger threatening the free democratic basic order or the existence or security of Germany or its *Länder*. This requires that someone is under suspicion of planning, committing, or having committed offences pertaining to state security (so-called telecommunication interception in the individual case). In this case, the order to execute the measure is not given by a judge but by the Federal Ministry of the Interior or the competent state ministry, as the case may be. Furthermore – and in contrast to the powers of criminal procedure – establishing suspicion requires only mere factual indications. According to Section 8 G 10, the Federal Intelligence Service may, in individual cases, also intercept international telecommunication in order to protect a person in a foreign country from imminent danger to life or health.

Section 1 Subsection 1 No. 2 in connection with Section 5 G 10 allows the Federal Intelligence Service to monitor international telecommunication by utilising search terms in order to collect information relating to certain forms of serious transnational crime; it may do this without existing suspicion[4] (so-called strategic telecommunication interception). However, the measure may not lead to the deliberate surveillance of a domestic telecommunication connection.

With the Counter-Terrorism Act of 2002 *(Terrorismusbekämpfungsgesetz)*, the Federal Office for the Protection of the Constitution, the Federal Intelligence Service, and the Military Counterintelligence Service were granted the power to gather customer and user-related information from telecommunication and teleservice companies in individual cases, and to use IMSI-catchers for determining the location of an active mobile terminal device or for determining the device or card number (Section 8a Subsection 2 Sentence 1 No. 4, 5 of the Federal Constitutional Protection Act, *Bundesverfassungsschutzgesetz*, BVerfSchG); Section 2a Sentence 1 BNDG; Section 4a Sentence 1 of the Military Counterintelligence Service Act (*Gesetz über den militärischen Abschirmdienst*, MADG). The requests for information must be applied for in writing at the Federal Ministry of the Interior (for the Federal

---

[4] *Bergemann*, in: Denninger/Rachor, Handbuch des Polizeirechts, p. 942.

Office for the Protection of the Constitution), the Federal Chancellery (for the Federal Intelligence Service), or the Federal Ministry of Defence (for the Military Counterintelligence Service). The corresponding orders may only concern persons against whom there are factual indications of vigorously promoting the severe threats meant to be cleared up with the information request (Section 8a Subsection 3 No. 1 BVerfSchG), or concerning whom such indications do not exist, but where specific facts give rise to the assumption that they are using services for the benefit of such persons (Section 8a Subsection 3 No. 2a BVerfSchG). Originally, the Counter-Terrorism Act's period of validity was set to end in 2007. This period was first extended until 2016 and recently again until 2021.[5]

d) Customs Investigation Service

Finally, Section 23a Subsection 1 of the Customs Investigation Act grants the Customs Investigation Office power to intercept telecommunication when and if facts support the assumption that persons are preparing certain offences specified in the War Weapons Control Act. According to Section 23a Subsection 3 of the Customs Investigation Act, such authorisation is also granted when facts support the assumption that persons are preparing the unlawful export of nuclear goods or certain goods designated for military deployment. The interception must be ordered by a judge.

3. Responsibility for the technical implementation of interception measures

The interception is carried out by the competent authority itself. The telecommunication service providers are only required to enable the authorities to perform their measure; compare, for instance, Section 100b Subsection 3 StPO, Section 2 Subsection 1 G 10. To this end, they are required to provide the authority with a copy of the extracted telecommunication, see Section 7 Subsection 1 of the Telecommunication Interception Regulation (*Telekommunikationsüberwachungsverordnung*, TKÜV). Knowledge of the communication's content is gained and recorded solely by the authority's employees, not by the telecommunication service provider's personnel. From a technical point of view, the surveillance is implemented by the respective *Länders'* Criminal Police Offices *(Landeskriminalämter)*, the Federal Criminal Police Office, the Customs Investigation Service, the Federal and State Offices for the Protection of the Constitution, the Military Counterintelligence Service, or the Federal Intelligence Service.

---

[5] Gesetz zur Verlängerung der Befristung von Vorschriften nach den Terrorismusbekämpfungsgesetzen; BGBl. 2015 I S. 2161.

4. Legitimacy of data transfers between security agencies

The activities of prosecution authorities, of preventive police authorities, and of intelligence agencies are in principle segregated. Organisational overlaps occur only insofar as investigative measures of criminal procedure are regularly executed by the police authorities (which also perform preventive tasks). Under certain statutorily defined conditions, the disclosure to other authorities of data collected during such telecommunication interception measures is admissible. However, such a rededication requires a statutory authorisation, as personal data may in principle only be used for the (exact) purpose that justified their collection. Through this principle of purpose limitation, a proportionate balance is ensured between the investigative measure leading to the collection of the data on the one hand, and the purpose of the collected data's use on the other hand.[6]

a) Exchange of data between prosecution authorities and preventive police authorities

Rededicating data that was collected within the criminal procedure framework by way of telecommunication interception for the purpose of averting danger is possible in principle, see Section 481 Subsection 1 StPO and, for example, Article 38 Subsection 2 BayPAG. Sometimes, however, state law permits such a rededication only for the purpose of averting a danger to life, health, or liberty of a person or for fighting certain serious crimes, see, for example, Section 38 Subsection 1 Sentence 3 BWPolG.

In contrast, the possibilities for rededicating data collected during a preventively based measure of telecommunication interception for the purpose of criminal prosecution are much more limited. Such data may only be used as evidence for the prosecution of crimes to the extent that the interception measure could also have been ordered pursuant to the Code of Criminal Procedure, see Section 161 Subsection 2 Sentence 1.

b) Disclosure of data by intelligence agencies

Under certain restrictive conditions, data gathered through the interception of telecommunication may be exchanged between intelligence agencies on the one hand, and police and prosecution authorities on the other hand. The disclosure of data collected by the intelligence authorities by way of telecommunication interception to police and prosecution authorities is only admissible if this is necessary for the prevention or prosecution of certain crimes related to state security, as well

---

6 See BVerfG NJW 1984, 419; *Ambs*, in: Erbs/Kohlhaas, Strafrechtliche Nebengesetze, Section 13 BDSG, para. 2; *Petri*, in: Denninger/Rachor, Handbuch des Polizeirechts, p. 839.

as certain other serious crimes, see Section 4 Subsection 4 in connection with Section 3 Subsection 1, 1a or Section 7 Subsection 4 G 10 for the telecommunication interception in individual cases, and Section 7 Subsection 4, Section 8 Subsection 6 G 10 for the strategical interception of telecommunication.

c) Disclosure of data to intelligence agencies

The disclosure of data collected by prosecution authorities during telecommunication interception measures to intelligence agencies is also only permissible to a limited extent. The disclosure to the Federal Office for the Protection of the Constitution, the Federal Intelligence Service, or the Military Counterintelligence Service is admissible only if there exists suspicion of the commission of certain offences pertaining to state security, see Section 18 Subsection 6, Section 22 BVerfSchG, and Section 8 Subsection 4 BNDG. Similarly, the disclosure of data gathered during preventive telecommunication interception by the *Länder's* police authorities is restricted in the *Länder's* police laws, and usually does not permit a disclosure to intelligence agencies.[7]

B. Statistics on Telecommunication Interception

1. Obligation to collect statistics

In the field of criminal prosecution, a legal obligation to compile detailed statistics concerning the number of telecommunication interception measures exists with regard to measures carried out under Sections 100a StPO and 100g StPO. As stipulated in Section 100b Subsection 5 StPO, the *Länder* and the Attorney General report annually to the Federal Office of Justice *(Bundesamt für Justiz)* on the telecommunication interception measures ordered within their respective area of competence. The Federal Office of Justice then prepares a summary of the measures ordered nationwide during the reporting year and publishes it on the internet.

In this respect, Section 100b Subsection 6 StPO requires the disclosure of the number of proceedings in which telecommunication interception was ordered, the number of interception orders issued (differentiating between initial and extension orders, as well as landline, mobile, and internet communication), and the underlying offences prompting the respective measures. Section 100g Subsection 4 StPO declares Section 100b Subsection 5 StPO to be also applicable for traffic data.

---

[7] See Article 34c Subsection 4 BayPAG; Section 34a Subsection 8 SOG M-V; Section 39 Subsection 2 Sentence 2 NdsSOG; Section 31 Subsection 7 in connection with Section 29 Subsection 5 POG RP; Section 36 Subsection 1 ThürPAG; see also *Petri*, in: Denninger/Rachor, Handbuch des Polizeirechts, pp. 867 et seq.

Pursuant to Section 1 Subsection 1 of the Act on the Parliamentary Control of Federal Intelligence Activities (*Gesetz über die parlamentarische Kontrolle nachrichtendienstlicher Tätigkeit des Bundes*, PKGrG), the measures executed within the framework of the Counter-Terrorism Act are subject to the control of the Parliamentary Control Panel. The Panel annually provides the *Bundestag* with a report on the implementation, type, scope, and the grounds for ordering such measures, stipulated in Section 8b Subsection 3 Sentence 2 and Subsection 10 Sentence 1, Section 9 Subsection 4 Sentence 7 BVerfSchG, Section 2a Sentence 4, Section 3 Sentence 2 BNDG and Section 4a Sentence 1, Section 5 MADG.

2. Current data

a) Law enforcement authorities

aa) Measures pursuant to Section 100a StPO

The Federal Office of Justice's statistics on the number of measures ordered by the *Länder* and the Attorney General pursuant to Section 100a StPO hardly changed between 2011 and 2014.[8] However, the number of orders for the interception of internet communication increased between 2011 and 2012.

Orders pursuant to § 100a StPO (Germany as a whole)						
Year	Procedures	Number of interception orders issued		Type of communication intercepted		
		Initial orders	Extension orders	Landline	Mobile	Internet
2011	5516	18029	3089	3621	17568	1345
2012	5678	19616	3445	3902	19666	4476
2013	5669	19398	3519	3271	19670	5033
2014	5625	19795	3587	3303	20499	5485
2015	5945	18640	3950	3332	21905	7431

bb) Measures pursuant to Section 100g StPO

Over recent years, the Federal Office of Justice's statistics on the measures ordered pursuant to Section 100g StPO have shown a marked rise both in the total number of proceedings as well as in the number of initial orders issued.

---

[8] Find the annual statistics at: https://www.bundesjustizamt.de/DE/Themen/Buergerdienste/Justizstatistik/Telekommunikation/Telekommunikationsueberwachung.html

Orders pursuant to § 100g StPO (Germany as a whole)					
Year	Procedures	Number of interception orders issued		Predicate offences	
		Initial orders	Extension orders	pursuant to Section 100g Subsection 1 Sentence 1 No. 1 StPO	pursuant to Section 100g Subsection 1 Sentence 1 No. 2 StPO
2011	7986	13743	410	13236	921
2012	9901	17137	462	16590	1014
2013	12572	20242	681	19310	1634
2014	13979	21926	775	21170	1534
2015	16117	26265	899	25552	1613

b) *Intelligence agencies*

Since there are no general statistics on the intelligence agencies' activities in the area of telecommunication interception, only measures taken under the Counter-Terrorism Act can be statistically described.[9]

aa) Request for information from telecommunication and teleservice companies

The following statistics cover requests for information under Section 8a Subsection 2 Nos. 4 and 5 BVerfSchG, Section 2a BNDG and Section 4a MADG concerning traffic data pursuant to Section 96 Subsection 1 Nos. 1 to 4 of the Telecommunication Act (*Telekommunikationsgesetz*, TKG), as well as corresponding data collected by teleservices. The majority of requests for information served the purpose of investigating Islamist activities.[10]

Requests for information from telecommunication and teleservice companies				
Year	BfV	BND	MAD	Total
2010	42	0	1	43
2011	34	0	0	34
2012	34	0	0	34
2013	54	0	0	54
2014	37	0	2	39

[9] The Parliamentary Control Panel's latest report was published on 29 January 2016 in BT-Drs. 18/7424.

[10] *Ibid.*, pp. 7 et seq.

bb) IMSI-Catcher

The same holds true for the use of IMSI-catchers pursuant to Section 9 Subsection 4 Sentence 1 BVerfSchG, Section 3 Sentence 2 BNDG and Section 5 MADG: Their employment, executed exclusively by the Federal Office for the Protection of the Constitution, also primarily targeted Islamist activities.[11]

Year	IMSI-catcher-deployment by the BfV
2010	16
2011	14
2012	17
2013	26
2014	16

II. Principles of Telecommunication Interception in Constitutional and Criminal Procedural Law

A. Constitutional Safeguards of Telecommunication

1. Areas of constitutional protection

a) Secrecy of telecommunication

Article 10 of the German Basic Law (*Grundgesetz*, GG) represents the central constitutional norm safeguarding the secrecy of telecommunication. It protects the confidentiality of the incorporeal transmission of information to an individual recipient using telecommunication devices. The secrecy of telecommunication covers both the content of telecommunication as well as the circumstances of the communication process. Thus, telecommunications traffic data are protected from state knowledge and from being processed.[12] Data subsequently stored in the communication service provider's sphere continue to be protected by the secrecy of telecommunication even when the communication's content has already reached its recipient.[13]

---

11 *Ibid.*, pp. 8 et seq.

12 BVerfG NJW 2006, 976 (978); NJW 2008, 822 (825); NJW 2010, 833 (835); NJOZ 2010, 1492 (1493).

13 BVerfG NJW 2009, 2431.

b) *Confidentiality and integrity of information systems*

Data stored on a computer are afforded protection by the fundamental right to confidentiality and integrity of information systems, a construction by the Federal Constitutional Court *(Bundesverfassungsgericht)*. It primarily offers protection against secret access to an information system, by way of which the system's use could be monitored and its storage media surreptitiously read.[14]

c) *Core area of privacy*

Furthermore, the interception of telecommunication must respect an inviolable area of privacy, the protection of which follows from the constitutional primacy of human dignity. Each individual must have the opportunity to express him- or herself without fear of being monitored by government institutions: this includes things such as sentiments and feelings, reflections, opinions, and experiences of a strictly personal nature. This core area of privacy is deemed absolutely inviolable. Even substantial public interests cannot justify an infringement.[15] However, only such investigative measures are precluded that render likely the capture of unconditionally protected information. The obtainment of such communication content in other ways merely leads to the prohibition of its utilisation.[16] Thus, communication is protected when it takes place between persons sharing a special relationship of trust within the scope of this core area. This may concern family members or other very close friends. However, this protection is afforded only as long as there are no concrete indications that the conversation's expected content will exhibit an immediate connection to a criminal offence.[17]

d) *Right to informational self-determination*

Personal data are also protected by the constitutionally guaranteed right to informational self-determination. It gives individuals the right to decide in principle on the disclosure and use of their personal data. In particular, this protects the placement of reasonable faith in the identity of one's communication partner. Communication content stored in the recipient's sphere after conclusion of the communication process is covered solely by this fundamental right; it is no longer covered by the constitutional protection of the secrecy of telecommunication.[18] Furthermore, the right to informational self-determination provides protection

---

[14] BVerfG NJW 2008, 822.

[15] BVerfG NJW 2004, 999 (1002); NJW 2012, 907 (908); NJW 2016, 1781, 1787.

[16] See BVerfG NJW 2012, 907 (908).

[17] BVerfG NJW 2004, 999 (1003), NJW 2008, 822 (833); NJW 2016, 1781, 1787.

[18] BVerfG NJW 2006, 976 (978); BVerfG NJW 2008, 822 (825); NJW 2009, 2431 (2432).

against government bodies purposefully compiling, storing, and possibly analysing together with other data such information as was acquired by screening publicly available content in the absence of a statutory basis.[19] Due to their constituting an encroachment on the right to informational self-determination, such measures require a proportionate statutory basis justified by a prevailing general interest.[20] When assessing the gravity of the encroachment connected with an investigation measure, the processed data's relevance to personality is of special significance.[21] A measure is considered highly invasive in particular when the relevant data allow conclusions about the nature and intensity of interpersonal relationships, personal interests, habits and tendencies, or the content of communication.[22]

2. Proportionality of access to data

The Constitution demands that all forms of government intervention in an individual's rights be proportionate. The principle of proportionality requires that every encroachment on fundamental rights serve a legitimate purpose, be suitable for achieving its objective, and be necessary and proportionate to the objective pursued.[23]

a) Implications for encroachments on the secrecy of telecommunication

The invasion of privacy, coupled with the secrecy employed in the process, give the interception of telecommunication a high degree of invasiveness.[24] With respect to the principle of proportionality, telecommunication interception thus belongs to the most demanding procedural investigative measures, as far as prerequisites are concerned.

b) Implications for access to traffic data

The principle of proportionality is also of relevance for the access to telecommunication traffic data. In line with decisions by the Federal Constitutional Court, the invasiveness of such measures is rising due to the continuing digitalisation of telecommunication. The quantity and the substance of accruing traffic data serve to paint an ever clearer picture of communication participants. Increasingly, commu-

---

19 BVerfG NJW 2008, 822 (836). For more on so-called internet investigations, see *Böckenförde*, JZ 2008, 925 (935).

20 See BVerfG NJW 1984, 419; *Di Fabio*, in: Maunz/Dürig, Grundgesetz-Kommentar, Article 2, paras. 179 et seq.

21 BVerfG NJW 2007, 2464 (2470).

22 See BVerfG NJW 2006, 976 (980).

23 BVerfG NJW 2007, 2464 (2468); NJW 2008, 822 (828).

24 See BVerfG NJW 2008, 822 (830).

nication data allow conclusions to be drawn about their personality, and even the generation of a personality profile becomes a real possibility.[25] Considering this, the access to mere traffic data (without even targeting communication content) is in and of itself viewed as a significant encroachment on the secrecy of telecommunication.

c) *Implications for intrusion into information systems*

Finally, the principle of proportionality is also of particular importance for secret intrusions into information systems. Privately or commercially used computers or comparable terminal devices (such as mobile phones) may contain such vast and varied amounts of personal data that access to these systems can provide insight into a significant part of a person's private life. It may also enable a meaningful analysis of one's personality.[26] Clandestine access to an information system thus gives the acting government body access to a stock of data that easily surpasses what traditional sources of information can offer with respect to scope and variety.[27]

3. Consequences for the interception of telecommunication

a) *Protection of the secrecy of telecommunication*

In accordance with Article 10 Subsection 2 GG, an encroachment on the secrecy of telecommunication (encompassing both the access to communication content and traffic data) requires statutory authorisation. Considering, with a view to the principle of proportionality, the highly invasive character of accessing the content of ongoing telecommunication, considerable requirements must be met. In particular, the interception of telecommunication is admissible only for the prosecution of *serious* criminal offences.

b) *Protection of the confidentiality and integrity of information systems*

The prosecution authorities' possibilities for secretly accessing terminal devices for interception purposes are limited by the fundamental right to confidentiality and integrity of information systems. Secret access to information systems (espionage of stored data or surveillance of system utilisation) is considerably more invasive than the interception of ongoing telecommunication. If a measure of telecommunication interception is not to be evaluated as an encroachment of this nature (but merely as an encroachment on the secrecy of telecommunication), then it must be

---

25 BVerfG NJW 2006, 976 (980).

26 BVerfG NJW 2008, 822 (827).

27 BVerfG NJW 2008, 822 (829).

technically ensured that data on the terminal device unrelated to the ongoing telecommunication are not accessed simultaneously.[28] While at least the secret extraction of data not stemming from ongoing communication by clandestine access to a person's terminal device is – within narrow limits – constitutionally admissible, it is currently not provided for in the StPO.[29]

c) Protection of the core area of privacy

Further constitutional requirements for the interception of telecommunication also result from the constitutional protection of the core area of privacy. A communication's relevance to this core area must be considered both before ordering an interception measure and during its performance. Depending on the conclusions of this consideration, the measure must be refrained from or collected data must be deleted, where necessary (see also below III.B.3.a.bb.).[30]

4. Statutory protection of personal data

a) Criminal liability for the unlawful infringement of telecommunication

The unlawful overhearing or recording of non-publicly spoken words is punishable in accordance with Section 201 of the German Criminal Code (*Strafgesetzbuch*, StGB). The violation of the secrecy of telecommunication by an employee of a telecommunication service provider can also entail a criminal sentence pursuant to Section 206 StGB. The unlawful obtaining of data especially protected against unauthorised access is punishable under Section 202a StGB when accomplished by circumventing such protection. Finally, the unauthorised obtaining of data by technical means from a non-public transfer of data is declared a criminal offence in Section 202b StGB. Section 89 TKG in connection with Section 148 Subsection 1 No. 1 TKG prohibit, under threat of criminal prosecution, the overhearing of messages of a radio facility as well as the subsequent disclosure of the content received.

b) Protection of professional secrets in criminal procedural law

Certain information worthy of protection is safeguarded by Section 160a in connection with Sections 53, 53a StPO against investigative measures of criminal procedure. This includes, in particular, communication within certain relationships of trust, such as with clergy, attorneys-at-law, and medical practitioners. Some of

---

[28] BVerfG NJW 2008, 822 (825 et seq.); NJW 2016, 1781, 1786.

[29] *Graf*, Beck-OK StPO, Section 100a, para. 108.

[30] BVerfG NJW 2008, 822 (834); NJW 2016, 1781, 1787.

these statutory regulations protect the constitutional core area of privacy. Their scope of protection, however, goes beyond what is constitutionally required.

c) Principle of "purpose limitation of personal data"

The powers of criminal procedure are also shaped by the principle of purpose limitation of personal data. This principle declares that data may generally be used only in accordance with the purpose they were collected for. Subsequently, personal data obtained through investigative measures must be deleted when and to the extent that they are no longer required for the purpose they had been collected for. Among other things, Section 101 Subsection 8 StPO thus prescribes the mandatory deletion of data acquired through telecommunication interception once they are no longer necessary for criminal prosecution. As a consequence of the principle of purpose limitation, any amendment to the initial purpose of the collection requires a statutory basis. Section 477 Subsection 2 Sentence 2 StPO constitutes such a basis. According to this provision, if a measure is only admissible where specified criminal offences are suspected, then any personal data obtained on the basis of such a measure may be used for evidentiary purposes in other criminal proceedings only if they concern a criminal offence, for the prosecution of which such a measure could have been ordered.

B. Powers in the Code of Criminal Procedure

1. Requirement of (reasonable) clarity for powers in the law of criminal procedure

Powers in the law of criminal procedure must satisfy the constitutional requirements of clarity and specificity. They are to ensure that the democratically legitimised parliamentary legislature itself must make all substantial decisions on the infringement of fundamental rights and the scope of the encroachments. Clarity and specificity of a provision are also meant to enable citizens to inform themselves about the legal situation in advance and show them which encroaching measures they might have to expect. The legislature must therefore, in a sector-specific way, determine occasion, purpose, and limits of invasive actions with sufficient precision and legal clarity.[31] Infringements of lower intensity, however, may be justified on the basis of statutory general clauses.[32]

---

31 BVerfG NJW 2004, 2213 (2215); NJW 2008, 822 (827 et seq.).

32 See BGH NJW 1991, 2651; *Pfeiffer*, Strafprozessordnung, Section 161, para. 1.

2. Differentiation and classification of powers in the law of criminal procedure

The Code of Criminal Procedure furnishes law enforcement authorities with a differentiated arsenal of coercive powers. As a rule, the more invasive a measure, the more precisely defined are the possible predicate offences, the necessary degree of suspicion, and the manner of a measure's implementation.

III. Authority to Access Telecommunication Data in the Law of Criminal Procedure

A. Overview

The secret interception of ongoing telecommunication is authorised by Section 100a StPO. Communication data saved on storage media can additionally be obtained by way of open seizure of the storage medium pursuant to Section 94 StPO and its surrender can be demanded in accordance with Section 95 StPO. As stipulated by Section 110 Subsection 3 StPO, during a search pursuant to Sections 102 et seqq. StPO, the examination of an electronic storage medium may be extended to cover physically separate storage media (such as a server accessible online), insofar as they are accessible from the storage medium. Finally, Section 100g StPO grants access to traffic data and Section 100j StPO grants access to subscriber data stored with the telecommunication service provider.

B. Interception of Content Data

1. Statutory empowerment

The main provision in the law of criminal procedure dealing with the interception of telecommunication is Section 100a Subsection 1 StPO. It reads as follows (excerpt only):

(1) Telecommunication may be intercepted and recorded even without the knowledge of the persons concerned if

1. certain facts give rise to the suspicion that a person, either as perpetrator or participant, has committed a serious criminal offence referred to in Subsection 2 or, in cases where there is criminal liability for attempt, has attempted to commit such an offence or has prepared such an offence by committing a criminal offence; and
2. the offence is one of particular gravity in the individual case as well; and
3. other means of establishing the facts or determining the accused's whereabouts would be much more difficult or offer no prospect of success.

Section 100a Subsection 2 StPO lists the serious criminal offences that Subsection 1 makes reference to. An overview over these offences can be found in the annex to this report.

Section 100b StPO deals with the procedure concerning an order for intercepting telecommunication. It reads:

> (1) Measures pursuant to Section 100a may be ordered by the court only upon application by the public prosecution office. In exigent circumstances, the public prosecution office may also issue an order. An order issued by the public prosecution office shall become ineffective if it is not confirmed by the court within three working days. The order shall be limited to a maximum duration of three months. An extension by not more than three months at a time shall be admissible if the prerequisites for the order continue to exist, taking into account the information obtained during the investigation.
>
> (2) The order shall be given in writing. The operative part of the order shall indicate
>
> 1. where known, the name and address of the person against whom the measure is directed;
> 2. the telephone number or other code of the telephone connection or terminal device to be intercepted, insofar as there are no particular facts indicating that they are not simultaneously assigned to another terminal device;
> 3. the type, extent and duration of the measure specifying the time of its conclusion.
>
> (3) On the basis of this order all persons providing, or contributing to the provision of, telecommunication services on a commercial basis shall enable the court, the public prosecution office and officials working in the police force to assist it (Section 152 of the Courts Constitution Act), to implement measures pursuant to Section 100a and shall provide the required information without delay. Whether and to what extent measures are to be taken in this respect shall follow from the Telecommunication Act and from the Telecommunication Interception Regulation issued thereunder. Section 95 Subsection 2 shall apply accordingly.
>
> (4) If the prerequisites for making the order no longer prevail, the measures implemented on the basis of the order shall be terminated without delay. Upon termination of the measure, the court which issued the order shall be notified of its results.
>
> (5) The *Länder* and the Attorney General shall submit a report to the Federal Office of Justice every calendar year by 30 June of the year following the reporting year, concerning measures ordered pursuant to Section 100a within their area of competence. The Federal Office of Justice shall produce a summary of the measures ordered nationwide during the reporting year and shall publish it on the internet.
>
> (6) The reports pursuant to Subsection 5 shall indicate:
>
> 1. the number of proceedings in which measures were ordered pursuant to Section 100a Subsection 1;
> 2. the number of orders to intercept telecommunication pursuant to Section 100a Subsection 1, distinguishing between
>   a) initial and extension orders, as well as
>   b) landline, mobile and internet telecommunication;
> 3. in each case the predicate offence by reference to the categories listed in Section 100a Subsection 2.

2. Scope of application

a) Object of interception

Section 100a StPO authorises prosecution authorities to intercept "telecommunication." This term, however, is not defined in the Code of Criminal Procedure. According to present case-law, the term "telecommunication" describes the incorporeal transmission of information through electromagnetic or optical signals, similar to the interpretation in the Telecommunication Act.[33] But aside from that, a multitude of questions concerning the provision's scope of application remain due to the lack of an explicit statutory clarification. These questions have yet to be answered fully by the courts.

aa) Content of communication

Apart from analogous communication between persons, Section 100a StPO also covers the internet-based and other electronic transmission of voice, symbols, pictures, and sound. Not only are telephone and email captured, but also chats, messaging, online fora, and other confidential communication.[34] The specific mode of transmission used (cable-bound or wireless, analogous or digital) is irrelevant.[35] The term "telecommunication" also covers data which do not form the actual content of the message: in particular, this applies to the transmission of traffic data between a communication service provider and the terminal devices of the communication participant.[36]

bb) Communication between persons

A prerequisite for the interception of telecommunication pursuant to Section 100a StPO is that a person uses telecommunication equipment, meaning he or she communicates by means of such equipment.[37] The automated, and consequently non-deliberate, reception of messages on an answering machine, or the arrival of

---

[33] BGH NStZ 2003, 668 (669); KK/*Bruns*, Section 100a, para. 4; Meyer-Goßner/*Schmitt*, Section 100a, para. 6. However, the Federal Constitutional Court favours a more generous interpretation of "telecommunication" as used in Article 10 Subsection 1 GG: It does not support the "purely technical understanding of telecommunication found in the TKG," but chooses to focus instead "on the holder of the fundamental right and his need for protection due to the involvement of third parties in the process of communication," BVerfG NJW 2009, 2431 (2433).

[34] KK/*Bruns*, Section 100a, para. 14; Meyer-Goßner/*Schmitt*, Section 100a, para. 7; *Singelnstein*, NStZ 2012, 593 (595).

[35] BVerfG NJW 2007, 351 (353); NJW 2009, 2431 (2432).

[36] BGH NStZ 2003, 668 (669).

[37] BGH NStZ 2003, 668 (669).

email in a mailbox, and even the unsuccessful attempt at establishing a communication connection also all constitute telecommunication.[38]

According to the (controversial) opinion of the first chamber of the second senate of the Federal Constitutional Court, when data transfer takes place exclusively between technical devices, it only constitutes telecommunication if these data (concerning, for example, the data exchange between a mobile device and the mobile provider during a conversation) accrue in connection with a specific telecommunication process or while establishing a telecommunication connection. Telecommunication thus requires an individualised exchange of information induced by a human being.[39] Consequently, such data that a mobile device transmits to the network in standby mode in order to show its operative readiness would not constitute telecommunication.[40]

cc) Surfing as telecommunication

In line with this broad construction of "telecommunication," Section 100a StPO in principle covers all traffic of data with the internet by means of a telecommunication device. Thus, the upload and download of data to or from third party servers is also captured.[41] Practitioners apparently assume that the surveillance of such data flows is unconditionally permissible.[42] Some academic literature is of the opinion that at least the surveillance of surfing behaviour during the capture of IP-based data transfers is not covered by the term "telecommunication" as used in the Code of Criminal Procedure.[43] An explicit clarification of this issue by the higher courts has, however, not yet been provided (see also below III.B.c.cc.).

b) Temporal limits of telecommunication

aa) Access to ongoing telecommunication

According to the courts, the interception of telecommunication covers the technological process of sending, transmitting, and receiving messages.[44] The drafting of a message for later transmission and the connected storage of this draft therefore

---

38 BGH NStZ 2003, 668 (669).

39 BVerfG NJW 2007, 351 (353).

40 BVerfG NJW 2007, 351 (353).

41 Thus also *Kudlich*, GA 2011, 193 (199).

42 See LG Ellwangen, decision of 28 May 2013 – 1 Qs 130/12; critical of the decision *Albrecht/Braun*, HRRS 2013, 500 et seqq.

43 *Hiéramente*, StraFo 2013, 96 et seq.; *Albrecht/Braun*, HRRS 2013, 500 et seq.; Meyer-Goßner/*Schmitt*, Section 100a, para. 7d.

44 BGH NStZ 2003, 668 (669); KK/*Bruns*, Section 100a, para. 18.

does not represent a part of the communication process.[45] Despite much criticism in academic literature[46] accessing the content of messages during ongoing communication even while the data are still on the sender's system, that is, had not left it yet, with the aim of sidestepping encryption was, in the past, deemed permissible by some practitioners[47] (for more on the relevant issues as well as further aspects of so-called source telecommunication surveillance, see below III.B.2.c.aa.).[48]

bb) Access after the end of telecommunication transmission

Access to communication data already received and stored in the exclusive sphere of the recipient (on the hard drive or mobile phone, for instance) is not covered by telecommunication interception.[49] The same holds true for data stored in the exclusive sphere of the sender. However, emails stored with the recipient's mail provider can be classified as belonging to the transmission process even after they are retrieved by their recipient. In this respect, the courts allow accessing the data stored by the mail provider in accordance with the regulations on seizure: in contrast to telecommunication interception, this measure must be performed overtly.[50] Nonetheless, covertly accessing the emails stored by the mail provider still remains possible on the basis of Section 100a StPO, precisely because the communication process is deemed to be continuing in the form of email storage by the mail provider – even after their retrieval by the recipient (for more, see D.2.c.bb.(2)).[51]

Although the issue has not been explicitly addressed by the higher courts, this also means that Section 100a StPO is applicable when confidential communication (such as in social networks or private chatrooms) is exchanged on a communication platform simultaneously viewed by all communication participants and real time access to this communication ensues secretly.[52] For non-real time access on such

---

45 *Kudlich*, GA 2011, 193 (202).

46 *Becker/Meinecke*, StV 2011, 50 (52); *Braun*, jurisPR-ITR 3/2011; *Brodowski*, JR 2011, 533 (537); *Buermeyer/Bäcker*, HRRS 2009, 433 (439); *Kudlich*, GA 2011, 193 (206); *Sieber*, Gutachten 69. Deutscher Juristentag, C 104 et seq.; *Wolter*, in: SK-StPO, Section 100a, para. 27.

47 LG Landshut NStZ 2011, 479; LG Hamburg MMR 2011, 693; KK/*Bruns*, Section 100a, para. 28; Meyer-Goßner/*Schmitt*, Section 100a, para. 7b.

48 LG Landshut NStZ 2011, 479; LG Hamburg MMR 2011, 693; KK/*Bruns*, Section 100a, para. 28; Meyer-Goßner/*Schmitt*, Section 100a, para. 7a et seq.; in contrast, however, see LG Hamburg MMR 2008, 423.

49 BVerfG NJW 2006, 976 (978); NJW 2009, 2431 (2432); KK/*Bruns* Section 100a, para. 4.

50 BGH NStZ 2009, 397 (398); KK/*Bruns*, Section 100a, para. 19.

51 BVerfG NJW 2009, 2431 (2434); BGH NJW 2010, 1297 (1298).

52 KK/*Bruns*, Section 100a, para. 21; Meyer-Goßner/*Schmitt*, Section 100a, para. 6c; *Singelnstein*, NStZ 2012, 593 (597); of a different view *Meinicke*, StV 2012, 463 (464).

communication platforms, the deliberations concerning access to emails apply accordingly.[53]

c) Current matters of dispute

Some of the issues not yet conclusively resolved by the courts concerning Section 100a StPO's scope of application are particularly contentious.

aa) Source telecommunication surveillance

Some academic literature demands that – contrary to current practice or at least practice until now, as approved of by courts of lower instance[54] – source telecommunication surveillance should not be based on Section 100a StPO.[55] They claim that source telecommunication surveillance requires an independent statutory authorisation as it encroaches on the integrity of the targeted information system and this invasion of the communication partner's information system creates the possibility of accessing extensive amounts of data, above and beyond the individual communication. Even assuming such access were non-deliberate, the mere risk of data being obtained without authorisation leads to a significant increase in the measure's invasiveness. Source telecommunication surveillance thus impacts not only the constitutionally protected secrecy of telecommunication because of the connected secret invasion of information systems, but also concerns the constitutional right of personality in the form of a right to integrity and confidentiality of information systems. In consequence, its prerequisites are more rigorous than for the mere interception of telecommunication. The Federal Constitutional Court views source telecommunication surveillance as encroaching only upon the secrecy of telecommunication provided it is ensured that the surveillance is limited exclusively to data from ongoing telecommunication, in other words when no data outside of the ongoing telecommunication are obtained while accessing the communication participant's terminal device. This, however, must be ensured by technical means and legal standards.[56] Yet, according to academic literature, such legal standards are not contained in Section 100a StPO.[57] Furthermore, they claim, practical experience suggests that it is not technically feasible to comply with the Fed-

---

[53] KK/*Bruns*, Section 100a, para. 21; Meyer-Goßner/*Schmitt*, Section 94, para. 16b; Section 100a, para. 6c.

[54] LG Landshut NStZ 2011, 479; LG Hamburg MMR 2011, 693. Thus also KK/*Bruns*, Section 100a, para. 28; Meyer-Goßner/*Schmitt*, Section 100a, para. 7b.

[55] *Braun*, jurisPR-ITR 3/2011; *Brodowski*, JR 2011, 533 (537); *Buermeyer*/*Bäcker*, HRRS 2009, 433 (439); *Sieber*, Gutachten 69. Deutscher Juristentag, C 104 et seq.; *Wolter*, in: SK-StPO, Section 100a, para. 27.

[56] See BVerfG NJW 2008, 822 (826); NJW 2016, 1781, 1796.

[57] *Sieber*, Gutachten 69. Deutscher Juristentag, C 104.

eral Constitutional Court's demand for a limitation to data from the ongoing communication process.[58] As a result, a separate legal provision governing source telecommunication surveillance is called for.[59]

bb) Accessing external storage media as communication

Not yet decided by the superior courts is whether or not such data transfers are to be treated as telecommunication which are caused by someone accessing external storage media over the internet – as is the case with cloud computing – in order to retrieve their own data, thus not constituting communication from another person.[60] In light of the courts' interpretation of "telecommunication" outlined above, in principle it seems permissible to intercept the respective up- and downloads from or to the internet user's terminal device on the basis of Section 100a StPO.[61] Some academics, however, demand that the exchange of data between the internet user and their online-accessible external storage media not be treated as telecommunication.[62] Particularly when considering the outsourcing of data from a stationary hard drive to a cloud provider's server, they say it becomes clear that accessing such a transfer of data is – contrary to a formal view (data transfer between the operator of an external server and the internet user) – functionally not an equivalent to accessing communication between persons. Instead, it equates to a secret search of an internet user's internal store of data. Such an encroachment is therefore much more invasive than the interception of telecommunication with another person. It rather resembles an online search and thus, in the opinion of these academics, should not be treated as the interception of telecommunication.[63]

cc) Evaluation of surfing behaviour

The application of Section 100a StPO to the documentation and analysis of an internet user's surfing behaviour has not yet been conclusively addressed by the

---

58 *Buermeyer/Bäcker*, HRRS 2009, 433 (439); *Singelnstein*, NStZ 2012, 593 (598).

59 *Klesczewski*, ZStW 123 (2011), 737 (744); *Sieber*, Gutachten 69. Deutscher Juristentag, C 105; *Wolter*, in: SK-StPO, Section 100a, para. 30. The report of the expert commission appointed by the German Federal Ministry of Justice has, in the meantime, arrived at the same conclusion, p. 76, available online at https://www.bmjv.de/SharedDocs/Downloads/DE/pdfs/Abschlussbericht_Reform_StPO_Kommission.pdf

60 For it *Singelnstein*, NStZ 2012, 593 (595); against it *Sieber*, Gutachten 69. Deutscher Juristentag, C 107.

61 *Kudlich*, GA 2011, 193 (207).

62 *Braun*, jurisPR-ITR 18/2013.

63 *Sieber*, Gutachten 69. Deutscher Juristentag, C 107; *Singelnstein*, NStZ 2012, 593 (595).

courts either.[64] To be sure, publicly accessible websites do not represent confidential information.[65] To what extent accessing websites constitutes telecommunication within the meaning of Section 100a StPO is, however, not quite so clear. The analysis of surfing behaviour and particularly of queries on search engines often facilitates extensive conclusions about the user's personality and may even allow for the creation of a comprehensive character profile. Some therefore claim the invasiveness of surfing behaviour analysis to be much greater than that of intercepting interpersonal communication, leading some academics to oppose a corresponding application of Section 100a StPO under these circumstances.[66]

3. Special protection of confidential communication content

For certain kinds of communication content, the Code of Criminal Procedure provides special protection against investigative measures. Moreover, the courts have derived additional safeguards from the Constitution. The privileging of certain information affects the implementation of interception measures, and may also have an impact upon the obtained information's admissibility as evidence.

a) Privileged communication

aa) Professional secrets

(1) Unconditionally protected professional secrets

Section 160a Subsection 1 Sentence 1 in connection with Section 53 StPO affords unconditional protection against telecommunication interception to clergymen in their capacity as spiritual advisors, defence counsels of the suspect, attorneys, as well as members of the *Bundestag*, a *Landtag* (state parliament), or the European Parliament concerning information entrusted to them or that became known to them in this capacity. Also protected under Section 160a Subsection 3 in connection with Section 53a StPO are their assistants and persons involved in the professional activities as part of their training.

Interception measures which target persons entrusted with unconditionally protected professional secrets and which are likely to result in insights regarding the unconditionally protected information are prohibited pursuant to Section 160a Subsection 1 StPO. Information obtained in spite of this may not be used, not even as a

64 For an application LG Ellwangen jurisPR-ITR 18/2013; against it *Braun*, jurisPR-ITR 18/2013.

65 BVerfG NJW 2007, 351 (353); *Kudlich*, GA 2011, 193 (198).

66 *Braun*, jurisPR-ITR 18/2013; *Albrecht*/*Braun*, HRRS 2013, 500 (504 et seq.); *Hiéramente*, StraFo 2013, 96 (100); Meyer-Goßner/*Schmitt*, Section 160a, para. 7.

mere clue in investigative proceedings.[67] Records thereof are to be deleted without delay. The circumstances of their obtainment and deletion, however, are to be documented. The same applies when, in the course of an investigative measure targeting someone not covered by this unconditional protection, information is obtained from the person and the obtained information itself is unconditionally protected.

If it becomes clear that one of the interlocutors is a defence counsel of the suspect, the interception must be aborted; should this be technically unfeasible, there must at least be no analysis of the conversation.[68]

(2) Conditionally protected professional secrets

Section 160a Subsection 2 in connection with Section 53 StPO affords conditional protection against telecommunication interception to patent attorneys, notaries, certified public accountants, sworn auditors, tax consultants, doctors, psychologists, psychotherapists, pharmacists, midwives, members of a pregnancy counselling agency, and drug dependency counsellors in a counselling agency, concerning information entrusted to them or that became known to them in this capacity. Also protected under Section 160a Subsection 3 in connection with Section 53a StPO are their assistants and persons involved in the professional activities as part of their training.

Conditional protection is also granted to professional journalists as well as their assistants and persons involved in the professional activities as part of their training. Protected subject matter includes information pertaining to origin and content of contributions, documents, and messages, and to profession-related perceptions. However, this applies only to the extent to which the materials concern the editorial part of the medium.

For cases in which the interception measure concerns a conditionally protected person and is likely to yield conditionally protected information, Section 160a Subsection 2 StPO determines that this circumstance is to be given special consideration when assessing a measure's proportionality. In procedures not concerning a criminal offence of substantial significance, the interest in criminal prosecution does not usually prevail. The measure must then be refrained from or, if this is an option for the kind of measure in question, be limited. This special principle of proportionality accordingly applies to the use of findings for evidentiary purposes. A criminal offence of substantial significance can be assumed when the specific offence exhibits at least an intermediate level of criminality, significantly disturbs peace under the law, or may significantly compromise the population's sense of

---

67 Meyer-Goßner/*Schmitt*, Section 160a, para. 4.

68 BGH StraFo 2005, 296; Meyer-Goßner/*Schmitt*, Section 100a, para. 21.

legal security.[69] These prerequisites are usually not met when the offence is punishable by a maximum prison sentence of less than five years.[70] With criminal offences of substantial significance, the legitimacy of an interception measure or the exploitation of information gained through it depend upon a balancing of interests. Decisive factors include the interest in effective criminal prosecution and the reaching of a just decision on the one hand, and the public interest in the holder of the professional secret following his occupation as well as the individual's interest in not revealing the secret entrusted to him or her, on the other hand.[71]

(3) No protection in case of suspicion against the holder of professional secrets

In line with Section 160a Subsection 4 StPO, the provisions on unconditional and conditional protection of professional secrets are not applicable when factual indications give rise to the suspicion that the protected person is involved with the offence being investigated, or participated in giving aid to the offender after the crime, in obstructing justice, or in dealing with stolen goods. Concerning the suspect's defence counsel, however, the suspicion of having given aid, obstructed justice, or dealt with stolen goods for the benefit of the suspect is insufficient for precluding the proscription of interception.[72]

bb) Protection of the core area of privacy

Special protection against telecommunication interception is accorded by Section 100a Subsection 4 StPO to information pertaining to the core area of privacy.[73] This includes, for instance, the expression of innermost feelings or expressions of sexuality.[74] Protection of this core area can be assumed particularly when the person concerned communicates with people with whom he has a special relationship of trust connected with the core area. Such people may include close family members, priests, telephone pastors, criminal defence attorneys, or – in individual cases – doctors.[75] However, this does not apply when there are concrete indications that the content of the prospective conversation will have an immediate connection to the crime.[76]

---

[69] See BVerfG NJW 2004, 999 (1010); NJW 2005, 1338 (1339).

[70] See BVerfG NJW 2009 2431 (2435).

[71] KK/*Griesbaum*, Section 160a, para. 14; Meyer-Goßner/*Schmitt*, Section 160a, para. 9a.

[72] Meyer-Goßner/*Schmitt*, Section 100a, para. 21.

[73] BVerfG NJW 2005, 2603 (2611).

[74] BVerfG NJW 2004, 999 (1003); NJW 2012, 907 (908).

[75] BVerfG NJW 2012, 833 (837).

[76] BVerfG NJW 2004, 999 (1003).

When factual indications support the assumption that telecommunication interception would yield information exclusively from the core area of privacy, Section 100a Subsection 4 StPO declares the measure to be completely inadmissible. When such a relationship of trust becomes discernible, telecommunication interception may not be performed.[77] However, cases where measures can be expected to yield *exclusively* information from the core area will hardly ever occur in practice.[78] Thus, the Federal Constitutional Court considers it practically unavoidable in many cases that the investigative authorities will take notice of information during the telecommunication interception before they are able to recognise its connection to the core area; in these cases, the Constitution does not require refraining from the intrusion from the outset merely due to the risk of infringing the core area of privacy during the collection process.[79]

Apart from that, information from the core area of privacy obtained through the interception of telecommunication may not be utilised. Any recordings thereof are to be deleted without delay. The circumstance of their obtainment and deletion, however, are to be documented. The passing on or other use of content connected with the core area, even as investigative clues, is prohibited.[80]

b) Responsibility for ensuring protection

The protection of professional secrets and the core area of privacy must already be considered by the public prosecution office when filing an application, as well as subsequently by the court charged with deciding on the application.

If, in exceptional circumstances, the continuation of an ongoing interception measure is noticeably and unquestionably inadmissible (this instance will be rare as interception is mostly performed by way of automated recording and not listened to in real time) then the investigators charged with performing the measure are required to discontinue the interception.[81]

After examining the data, the deletion of non-exploitable information is generally performed by the investigator who carried out the measure. The public prosecution office can be consulted before making a decision, provided this does not lead

---

77 BVerfG NJW 2012, 833 (837).

78 This is reflected in the legislative reasons, which give communication with telephone counselling services offered by religious institutions as the sole example, see BR-Drs. 275/07, p. 98.

79 BVerfG NJW 2012, 833 (837).

80 BVerfG NJW 2012, 833 (838).

81 See BVerfG NJW 2012, 833 (838).

to an unwarranted delay to necessary deletion.[82] For other information, the public prosecution office decides on its usability in the course of the following proceedings.[83]

4. Performance of telecommunication interception

a) Performance by the authorities with or without the help of third parties

The interception of telecommunication can be performed by the telecommunication service provider extracting data and surrendering it to the prosecution authorities. This is the method generally used. Even when done in this way, only the prosecution authorities gain any knowledge of the communication's content.[84] Involving the telecommunication service provider is, however, not absolutely necessary. According to prevailing opinion, the prosecution authorities are also permitted to perform the interception by their own means,[85] for instance, by intercepting signals of a wireless network.[86]

b) Accompanying powers for the performance of interception

For telecommunication service providers, Section 100b Subsection 3 StPO stipulates a duty to cooperate in the technical execution of telecommunication interception. Furthermore, encroaching on the integrity of the targeted person's terminal device is currently considered legally permissible in practice.[87] Thereby, software is to be installed, which allows for circumventing the encryption of communication data by manipulating the processing of the data (so-called source telecommunication surveillance, see supra III.B.2.c.aa.). The legality of a physical intrusion into the concerned person's rooms as a preparatory measure based on Section 100a StPO is an issue of some controversy.[88] In any case, there is no legal provision explicitly authorising such a measure. Usually, however, the intrusion will be rendered unnecessary by the telecommunication provider's duties to cooperate and thus, at any rate, be deemed disproportionate.

---

82 Meyer-Goßner/*Schmitt*, Section 100a, para. 27.

83 BVerfG NJW 2012, 833 (838).

84 BeckTKG-Komm/*Eckhardt*, Section 110, para. 31.

85 *Bär*, MMR 2008, 215 (219); Meyer-Goßner/*Schmitt*, Section 100a, para. 8; *Singelnstein*, NStZ 2012, 593 (599); of a different opinion *Wolter*, Section 100b, para. 19.

86 KK/*Bruns*, Section 100a, para. 15.

87 KK/*Bruns*, Section 100a, para. 28; Meyer-Goßner/*Schmitt*, Section 100a, para. 7b.

88 BVerfG NJW 2008, 822 (826) apparently considers it legal; see also LG Hamburg MMR 2011, 693 (696).

5. Telecommunication service providers' duties to cooperate

In light of the regular necessity of having private communication service providers cooperate, their relevant duties have been extensively regulated.

a) Possible addressees of duties to cooperate

Pursuant to Section 100b Subsection 3 Sentence 1 StPO, all persons providing or contributing to telecommunication services are obliged to facilitate measures for the interception of telecommunication and to provide the required information without delay. The provision must be read in line with the terminology of the TKG: Pursuant to Section 3 No. 24 TKG, telecommunication services are services which consist completely or predominantly in the transmission of signals via telecommunication networks.[89] This includes access and network providers in particular, but also covers services that offer online communication as an internet application to the extent that the focus of their activities lies on the technical aspects of the telecommunication process.[90] Thus, email and VoIP services also fall under Section 3 No. 24 TKG, insofar as they provide an independent switching service.[91] Since Section 100b Subsection 3 Sentence 1 StPO also covers the contribution to the provision of telecommunications, the operators of the IT infrastructure are principally also required to cooperate with the prosecution authorities. Furthermore, such access providers that do not themselves provide the identification in question, yet still temporarily contribute to the provision of an internet connection for this identification through roaming are also required to participate in interception measures.[92] Moreover, duties to cooperate and provide information pursuant to Section 100b Subsection 3 Sentence 1 StPO also exist for the operators of closed communication systems such as intra-company communication networks (e.g., in-house extensions and intranets).[93] This holds true regardless of whether telecommunication services are provided free of charge or in return for payment.[94]

---

89 BeckTKG-Komm/*Eckhardt*, Section 110, para. 22; Meyer-Goßner/*Schmitt*, Section 100b, para. 8.

90 BeckTKG-Komm/*Eckhardt*, Section 110, para. 12; BerlKommTKG/*Säcker*, Section 3 paras. 72 et seq. Regarding the question of how application services on the higher internet protocol levels are covered by the TKG or the TMG (and regarding the proposal of a functional assessment for dealing with the issue), see *Brunst*, Anonymität im Internet, pp. 325 et seq., 380 et seq.

91 If the providers simultaneously provide information of their own, this specific activity is subject to the TMG, cp. BerlKommTKG/*Säcker*, Section 3, para. 71.

92 BGH ErmR, NStZ 2003, 272.

93 KK/*Bruns*, Section 100b, para. 12; Meyer-Goßner/*Schmitt*, Section 100b, para. 8.

94 Section 3 No. 24 TKG also views provision in exchange for payment as the norm, cp. BeckTKG-Komm/*Schütz*, Section 3, para. 78.

b) *Content of duties to cooperate*

The interception order issued either by a court upon application of the public prosecution office or, in exigent circumstances, in the form of an order by the public prosecution office itself, entails pursuant to Section 100b Subsection 3 StPO that all persons providing or contributing to telecommunication services must enable the court, the public prosecution office, and officials working in the police force to implement measures pursuant to Section 100a StPO and provide them with the required information without delay.

For operators of telecommunication facilities with which publicly available telecommunication services are rendered (for the entities this includes, see c.aa.), the technical and organisational implementation of the interception and the ensuing obligations are further specified in Section 110 TKG and in the TKÜV.[95] For telecommunication services not covered by the TKG and the TKÜV (i.e., in particular the operators of closed communication systems), these specific provisions do not apply.[96]

Pursuant to Section 5 Subsection 2 Sentence 1 TKÜV, the operator of a public telecommunication system must provide the authorised bodies (cp. Section 2 No. 3 TKÜV) at the handover point with a full copy of the telecommunication taking place via its telecommunication system under the identification to be intercepted. For every intercepted identification, the authorised body supplies the obligated party with the designation of the recording lines to which the intercept copy is to be transferred.

According to Section 6 Subsection 1 TKÜV, the obligated party must ensure that these orders can be implemented without delay; the same applies for a premature abortion of the interception measure, if so required by the authorised body. Pursuant to Section 9 Subsection 1 Sentence 1 TKÜV, the transmission principally is to take place via networks with switching functions. In the case of transmission lines that serve direct subscriber-related access to the internet, the copy of the intercept is to be transmitted using internet protocol, Section 9 Subsection 2 TKÜV.

Pursuant to Section 5 Subsection 1 No. 3 TKÜV, the duty to cooperate in the interception measure also covers telecommunication data contained in a storage facil-

---

[95] According to Section 110 Subsection 2 TKG, the Federal Government is empowered to make arrangements concerning the fundamental technical requirements and the key organisational aspects for the implementation of intercepts, and to determine the cases in which and the conditions under which compliance with certain technical requirements can be dispensed with on a temporary basis. The technical details are then stipulated by the Federal Network Agency pursuant to Section 110 Subsection 3 TKG. The permissibility of transmissions must, however, in all cases, still be determined based on the relevant specific regulation, i.e., Section 100a StPO in particular; regarding this, see BeckTKG-Komm/ *Eckhardt*, Section 110, paras. 71, 72.

[96] SK-StPO/*Wolter*, Section 100b, para. 24.

ity allocated to the identification to be intercepted (such as a mobile identification or an email address). To this end, the telecommunication service providers must also facilitate accessing communication content routed directly to storage facilities allocated to the identification to be intercepted.[97] This concerns, for example, voicemail stored in voicemail boxes, or messages stored on email servers. As part of the intercept copy, the telecommunication service provider must also provide the authorities with extensive traffic data concerning the intercepted telecommunication (such as the location of a mobile terminal device), see Section 7 Subsection 1 Sentence 1 TKÜV. This means that not only is the content of communication extracted, but also data regarding the specific circumstances of the communication.

c) Duties to provide technical and organisational infrastructure

aa) Obligated parties

Pursuant to Section 100b Subsection 3 Sentence 2 StPO in connection with Section 110 Subsection 1 Sentence 1 No. 1 TKG, the operators of telecommunication facilities that offer publicly available telecommunication services, must, at their own cost, maintain the technical means (hardware and software[98]) for the execution of telecommunication interception and make the organisational arrangements necessary for its prompt implementation. According to Section 110 Subsection 1 Sentence 1 No. 1a TKG, this maintenance duty also extends to forms of telecommunication that are based on the simultaneous utilisation of two or more telecommunication facilities (such as is particularly the case with VoIP telephony, where access providers and VoIP providers collaborate).[99] These provisions lead to telecommunication providers actively participating in the search for innovative solutions to ensure the ability to intercept VoIP telephony.[100] Pursuant to Section 110 Subsection 1 Sentence 2 TKG, persons that provide publicly available telecommunication services without operating the necessary telecommunication facility themselves must also assure that the operator of the facilities can implement telecommunication interception orders promptly. An obligation pursuant to Section 110 Subsection 1 TKG exists only when the services are offered within the TKG's scope of application. Thus, providers of publicly available telecommunica-

---

97 BMWi, reasoning behind the draft of a regulation on the technical and organisational implementation of telecommunication interception measures of 25 October 2001, p. 6 (available online at http://www.bfdi.bund.de/SharedDocs/VortraegeUndArbeitspapiere/20011025UllrichBegruendungTKUeV.pdf).

98 BeckTKG-Komm/*Eckhardt*, Section 110, para. 30; BerlKommTKG/*Klesczewski*, Section 110, para. 34.

99 BeckTKG-Komm/*Eckhardt*, Section 110, para. 32; BerlKommTKG/*Klesczewski*, Section 110, para. 2.

100 See BT-Drs. 16/2581, p. 28.

tion services using email servers located in a foreign country to provide email services in Germany are also covered.[101]

However, as per Section 3 Subsection 2 Sentence 1 TKÜV, these duties regularly do not apply to telecommunication services with less than 10,000 subscribers or other parties enjoying the right of use (No. 5), as well as network nodes for interconnection with the internet (No. 2). For the latter, there is an exception to the exception if they serve as switches between publicly available telephone services and international networks (so-called "Auslandsköpfe"; literally translated as "foreign heads"). Operators of closed communication systems are also not obliged to maintain a technical and organisational infrastructure, since they are not subject to Section 110 Subsection 1 Sentence 1 No. 1 TKG in the first place (see above).

bb) Individual technical obligations

The technical requirements for interception measures are defined in Section 6 to 11 TKÜV. In particular, Section 7 TKÜV stipulates exactly which data are to be provided. According to Section 110 Subsection 3 TKG in connection with Section 11 TKÜV, the technical particulars concerning the implementation of telecommunication interception shall be stipulated in a detailed Technical Directive (TR TKÜV) by the Federal Network Agency *(Bundesnetzagentur)* with the participation of the associations of the telecommunication service provider industry, as well as the authorised bodies.[102] International technical standards are to be taken into consideration; deviations from the standards need to be justified with an explanation. In this way, one hopes to avoid stand-alone solutions and keep the costs for the parties involved as low as possible.[103]

cc) Organisational obligations

The organisational and protective requirements are stipulated in Sections 12 to 17 TKÜV. Pursuant to Section 12 TKÜV, the telecommunication service provider must ensure that it has taken all necessary organisational steps for handling orders. In particular, it must also ensure that it can receive an order outside of its usual business hours without delay. Furthermore, it must ensure that it has competent personnel available at all times to answer enquiries from the authorised body.

Section 15 provides for confidentiality obligations concerning the way in which orders are implemented and requires that the protection of information related to interception measures be ensured. Pursuant to Section 16 Subsection 1 TKÜV, the telecommunication service provider must ensure that every application of its inter-

---

[101] BeckTKG-Komm/*Eckhardt*, Section 110, para. 94.

[102] See the Technical Directive TKÜV (TR TKÜV).

[103] BT-Drs. 15/2316, p. 94.

ception equipment is protocolled automatically and fully when the data necessary for the technical implementation are entered. According to Section 16 Subsection 2 TKÜV, the telecommunication service provider must ensure through technical configuration that personnel entrusted with the practical implementation of the interception have no access to the protocol data. Rules on the checking and deletion of protocol data, as well as on the destruction of documentation can be found in Section 17 TKÜV.

Furthermore, pursuant to Section 5 Subsection 5 TKÜV, the telecommunication service provider must inform the authorised body directly after the conclusion of the activities necessary for thc technical implementation of an order of the point in time of actual setting up and of the identification actually carried out. This applies correspondingly to the transmission of information regarding the point in time of the termination of an interception measure. These provisions are especially of interest with regard to calculating the duration stipulated in the order.[104]

Sections 19 and 20 TKÜV specify the demonstration duties of Section 100 Subsection 1 No. 3 TKG, according to which the telecommunication service provider must demonstrate that his technical equipment and organisational arrangements meet the requirements of the TKÜV and of the TR TKÜV.

d) Protection obligations for the transmission of data by communication service providers

In line with Section 14 Subsection 1 TKÜV, the obligated party must provide state-of-the-art protection against unauthorised use of the technical equipment used to control the interception functions and the handover point, including the transmission paths between these.

Pursuant to Section 14 Subsection 2 Sentence 1 TKÜV, the copy of the intercept is to be protected by appropriate procedures against cognisance by unauthorised third parties. Procedures guaranteeing appropriate protection against transmission to unauthorised parties are to be applied when transmitting the copy of the intercept to the authority's recording lines. The corresponding necessary procedures are stipulated in more detail in the TR TKÜV. According to Section 14 Subsection 2 Sentence 7 TKÜV, the protective requirement of Section 14 Subsection 2 Sentence 1 TKÜV is regarded as fulfilled where the copy of the intercept is transmitted to the recording lines via dedicated transmission paths or via telecommunication networks with line-switching technology in light of the configuration principles underlying these transmission media.

---

[104] BeckTKG-Komm/*Eckhardt*, Section 110, para. 73.

e) Control, filter, and decryption obligations of communication service providers

Pursuant to Section 5 Subsection 2 TKÜV, the telecommunication service provider must provide the prosecution authorities with a full copy of the telecommunication which is conducted under the identification to be intercepted. In doing so, the telecommunication service provider must ensure that the data provided contains only the telecommunication referred to by the order, meaning, for example, that only data from the timeframe specified in the interception order are provided.[105]

According to Part A, Annex G of the TR TKÜV, "broadcasting distribution services or similar services intended for the public (e.g., IPTV, Video on demand)" for which measures need not be taken pursuant to Section 3 Subsection 2 No. 4 TKÜV should as far as possible not be included in the intercept copy of an internet connection. Further filtering of content by the telecommunication service provider is, however, not envisaged. Instead, only the prosecution authorities are authorised to take note of the content of the intercepted communication;[106] Section 88 Subsection 3 Sentence 1 TKG prohibits service providers from obtaining knowledge of the content or circumstances of the telecommunication beyond the extent necessary for the commercial provision of their services.[107] Therefore all of the internet traffic routed through the intercepted line is extracted and forwarded to the prosecution authorities according to Section 5 Subsection 2 TKÜV.

Also, there exists no obligation to decrypt encrypted communication.[108] Section 5 Subsection 2 TKÜV merely obliges telecommunication service providers to provide the authorities with a copy of the telecommunication to be intercepted.

6. Formal prerequisites of interception orders

a) Competent authorities

Pursuant to Section 100b Subsection 1 StPO, the telecommunication interception order can in principle be issued only by a court and only upon application by the public prosecution office. In exigent circumstances – in other words when one could expect the delay caused by waiting for a judicial decision to lead to the failure of the interception measure – the order may also be issued by the public prosecution office.

---

[105] See BerlKommTKG/*Klesczewski*, Section 110, para. 43.

[106] BeckTKG-Komm/*Eckhardt*, Section 110, para. 31.

[107] Accordingly, a provider cannot be obliged to extract only specific IP data streams of a line for the authorised body's benefit. The precept of encroaching on the individual user's secrecy of telecommunication as little as possible does not constitute a violation of the ban on listening in on conversations pursuant to Section 88 TKG. See BGH, decision of 20 August 2015, Az. StB 7/15.

[108] BeckTKG-Komm/*Eckhardt*, Section 110, para. 72.

b) Requirements for applications

The law dictates no formal requirements for the public prosecution office's application. However, the competent judge must independently check whether the legal prerequisites for the requested measure are met. He is not bound by the investigative authorities' evaluation of the suspicious circumstances or of individual pieces of evidence while making his assessment. He must therefore be presented with all evidence relevant to the decision, and in complex cases with the investigation file as well. It is insufficient if the public prosecution office merely sums up and provides an evaluation of the main evidence in the application.[109]

c) Formal requirements for orders

According to Section 100b Subsection 2 StPO, the order is to be given in writing. This formal requirement is met when the order is issued by fax or email; however, in these cases, the original or a certified copy of the order must subsequently be provided within a week, Section 12 Subsection 2 TKÜV. The order has to indicate, where known, the name and address of the person against whom the measure is directed, the telephone number or other code of the telephone connection or terminal device to be intercepted, as well as the type, extent, and duration of the measure while specifying the time of its conclusion. While the grounds for the order are to be given pursuant to Section 34 StPO (e.g., whether its objective is to investigate a set of circumstances or to determine the location), the criminal charge is not included.[110]

7. Substantive prerequisites of interception orders

a) Degree of suspicion

Section 100a Subsection 1 No. 1 StPO requires merely an ordinary degree of suspicion of someone having committed or participated in the commission of a serious criminal offence, or in cases where there is criminal liability for attempt, having attempted to commit such an offence or having prepared such an offence by committing a criminal offence. This suspicion must be founded on a sufficient basis of fact. This requires circumstances suggesting that someone has committed an offence or participated in the commission of an offence. The suspicion must have reached a certain degree of concretisation and substantiation founded on a coherent basis of fact.[111]

---

109 BVerfG NJW 2016, 1781, 1786; BGH NJW 2010, 1297 (1298).

110 KK/*Bruns*, Section 100a, paras. 5 et seq.

111 BVerfG NJW 2007, 2749 (2751); BGH NJW 2010, 711.

b) Predicate offences

Telecommunication interception pursuant to Section 100a Subsection 1 No. 1 StPO is an option only regarding certain serious criminal offences within the meaning of Section 100a Subsection 2 StPO (as listed in the annex below). Additionally, the deed forming the object of the investigation must be of some gravity in the individual case. For assessing this gravity, focus lies not on the likely sentencing range, but rather on an evaluative contemplation of the particular crime, with factors including the infringed legal interest's worthiness of protection, or a perpetrator's collaboration with other offenders.[112]

c) Persons and connections under surveillance

According to Section 100a Subsection 3 StPO, the interception measure can be directed against the accused or against persons of whom it may be assumed, on the basis of certain facts, that they are receiving or transmitting messages intended for, or transmitted by, the accused, or that the accused is using their connection.

The order may only be directed against *specific* persons.[113] As Section 100b Subsection 2 Sentence 2 No. 1 StPO shows, their identity need not yet be known at the time the interception order is issued. Where a targeted person's identity is not known, Section 100b Subsection 2 Sentence 2 No. 2 StPO stipulates that the order can simply indicate a certain telephone number or other code of identification for the targeted telephone connection or terminal device, in particular to an email box, a certain IP address, an IMSI, or IMEI.[114] However, giving the device number is only admissible when it can be ruled out that the same number is simultaneously assigned to another terminal device.[115]

d) Principle of subsidiarity

Section 100a Subsection 1 No. 3 StPO stipulates that telecommunication interception is permissible only when other means of establishing the facts or determining the accused's whereabouts would be significantly more difficult or altogether futile. A significantly greater degree of difficulty can be assumed particularly when much more time would have to be expended in order to investigate the offence absent the interception measure, leading to a considerable delay of the proceedings.[116]

---

112 BVerfG NJW 2012, 833 (836); Meyer-Goßner/*Schmitt*, Section 100a, para. 11.

113 Meyer-Goßner/*Schmitt*, Section 100a, para. 16.

114 KK/*Bruns*, Section 100b, para. 8.

115 KK/*Bruns*, Section 100b, para. 8; Meyer-Goßner/*Schmitt*, Section 100b, para. 4.

116 Meyer-Goßner/*Schmitt*, Section 100a, para. 13.

e) Proportionality of interception in individual cases

Just as with any governmental encroachment on citizens' rights, a measure of telecommunication interception must also be proportionate in each individual case.[117] Proportionality can be negated particularly when a measure, while not expected to result *exclusively* in information related to the core area of privacy (in this case the measure would in any event be inadmissible pursuant to Section 100a Subsection 4 Sentence 1 StPO), is likely to yield some information related to the core area of privacy. The degree of likelihood that information pertinent to the investigation can be obtained by the interception measure may also have an impact on the assessment of proportionality.

f) Consent to the measure by a communication participant

An order under Section 100a StPO is only dispensable when all parties to the communication have consented to the interception.[118] The situation when one party to the communication allows law enforcement officials to read or listen to the communication is not covered by Section 100a StPO. This concerns cases in which law enforcement officials gain knowledge of the communication's content in the way technically intended. This does not affect the communication procedure's confidentiality; it is only the trust which one communication participant may have placed in the other that is disappointed.[119] Section 100a StPO safeguards the secrecy of telecommunication only against external third party access to remote communication. It does not cover the trust communication partners place in each other.[120]

8. Validity of interception order

a) Maximum duration of interception order

According to Section 100b Subsection 1 StPO, the court order of telecommunication interception shall be limited to a maximum duration of three months. An extension of up to three months at a time is admissible if the prerequisites for the order continue to exist, taking into account the information obtained during the investigation.

An order issued by the public prosecution office in exigent circumstances becomes ineffective if it is not confirmed by the court within three working days.

---

117 BerlKommTKG/*Klesczewski*, Section 110, para. 5; SK-StPO/*Rudolphi*, Section 100a, para. 13.

118 KK/*Bruns*, Section 100a, para. 3; Meyer-Goßner/*Schmitt*, Section 100b, para. 1.

119 BVerfG NJW 2002, 3619 (3620); NJW 2008, 822 (835).

120 BVerfG NJW 2008, 822 (835).

b) Prolongation of authorisation

An overall temporal limitation of the measure is not stipulated by the law, neither concerning the number of possible prolongations nor concerning the cumulative duration of interception. But if the measure produces no information supporting the underlying suspicion, then its necessity and thus its proportionality will appear increasingly questionable. There are no special formal requirements for the prolongation of authorisation.

c) Revocation of authorisation

When the prerequisites for issuing the order no longer prevail, Section 100b Subsection 4 StPO requires that measures implemented on the basis of the order be terminated without delay. The respective order can be revoked both by the public prosecution office and by the court.[121] A revocation is necessary particularly when the suspicion proves to be unfounded, the interception ceases to be indispensable for the investigation or it no longer promises to be successful.[122]

9. Duties to record, report, and destroy

a) Duty to record and report

Personal data acquired through a measure of telecommunication interception are to be labelled accordingly, see Section 101 Subsection 3 Sentence 1 StPO. After conclusion of the interception, the court which ordered the measure is to be notified of its results according to Section 100b Subsection 4 Sentence 2 StPO. Reports on the measure's progress during its performance are not obligatory.

b) Duty to destroy

When personal data obtained through the measure are no longer necessary for the purposes of criminal prosecution or a possible court review of the measure, they shall be deleted without delay according to Section 101 Subsection 8 StPO. The fact of their deletion is to be documented. Not subject to deletion are chance discoveries unrelated to the measure's underlying procedure, but which are required as evidence for another criminal procedure and can be used for this purpose.[123] The decision on deletion is in principle made by the public prosecution office. The

---

[121] Meyer-Goßner/*Schmitt*, Section 100b, para. 9.

[122] Meyer-Goßner/*Schmitt*, Section 100b, para. 9.

[123] Meyer-Goßner/*Schmitt*, Section 101, para. 27.

court decides once the case is pending.[124] Not only must the technical recordings of the interception be destroyed; the same applies to written records made.[125]

10. Notification duties and remedies

a) Duty to notify persons affected by the measure

The parties involved in the intercepted telecommunication are to be notified according to Section 101 Subsection 4 StPO. The notification is to be dispensed with where an affected person's protection-worthy overriding interests represent an obstacle thereto. This may be the case, for instance, when the measure has yielded no evidence incriminating the accused and the notification could prove damaging to his reputation with regard to his conversation partners.[126] The notification of a person not targeted by the measure can furthermore be dispensed with when this person was only insignificantly affected by the measure and where it can be assumed that he has no interest in being notified. This exception thus can only be applied to persons accidentally covered by the interception; it does not apply to the targeted persons.[127]

According to Section 101 Subsection 5 StPO, notification is to be made as soon as possible without endangering the purpose of the investigation, the life, physical integrity, and personal liberty of another person, or significant assets. Where a notification which had been deferred based on one of these reasons is not carried out within twelve months after completion of the measure, any further deferrals are subject to the court's approval according to Section 101 Subsection 6 StPO. The court may approve the permanent dispensation with notification where there is a probability bordering on certainty that the prerequisites for notification will not be fulfilled, even in future.

b) Remedies

As stipulated by Section 101 Subsection 7 StPO, the persons participating in intercepted communication may apply for a judicial review of the lawfulness of the measure, as well as of the manner and means of its implementation for up to two weeks following their notification. When an affected party gains knowledge of the measure, that person may file an application even before the measure's completion.

---

124 Meyer-Goßner/*Schmitt*, Section 101, para. 28.

125 Meyer-Goßner/*Schmitt*, Section 101, para. 28.

126 Meyer-Goßner/*Schmitt*, Section 101, para. 16.

127 Meyer-Goßner/*Schmitt*, Section 100b, para. 17.

c) Criminal law consequences of unlawful interception measures

The unlawful eavesdropping or recording of non-publicly spoken words is subject to criminal sanctions under Section 201 StGB. The provision is also applicable to oral statements transmitted via telecommunication. For public officials, the provision provides for a higher sentencing range. If the statutory prerequisites of telecommunication interception are not fulfilled, then the acting official lacks authorisation, and, in consequence, faces criminal sanctions given the necessary intent.

When the legal prerequisites for interception are not met and the individual acts with the necessary knowledge and intent, then public officials may also be held criminally liable concerning the transmission of non-spoken statements. According to Section 202a StGB, whosoever unlawfully obtains access to data for himself or another that are not intended for him and are protected against unauthorised access, is criminally liable if he does so by circumventing the protection. This primarily concerns the unauthorised access to information systems by way of hacking.[128] However, data during their transmission are only covered by the provision when they are especially protected, in particular when they are encrypted.[129] As an unauthorised official interception order to a telecommunication service provider does not constitute a circumvention of special protection, no liability pursuant to Section 202a StGB ensues. However, Section 202b StGB also declares criminally liable whosoever unlawfully obtains data not intended for him, for himself or another by technical means from a non-public data transmission. Whether the data are especially protected (such as through encryption), is irrelevant. All forms of non-public electronic data transmission, in particular email, fax, VoIP, and internet chats are covered by the provision.[130]

d) Control by supervisory bodies

Furthermore, a non-judicial, independent supervision of interception measures can be performed by the respective data protection commissioners of the *Länder*, whose competency in these cases follows either explicitly from state provisions or from their general allocation of duties.[131]

---

[128] Schönke/Schröder/*Eisele*/*Lenckner*, Section 202a, para. 18; NK/*Kargl*, Section 202a, para. 12.

[129] NK/*Kargl*, Section 202b, para. 2.

[130] Schönke/Schröder/*Eisele*, Section 202b, para. 4; NK/*Kargl*, Section 202b, para. 2.

[131] An explicit provision can be found, e.g., in Section 30 Subsection 4 Sentence 1 BayDSG; pursuant to Sentence 2, the control is possible only after the conclusion of the investigative procedure and only if the collection of data was not reviewed by a court.

11. Confidentiality requirements

a) *Obligations of telecommunication service providers to maintain secrecy*

According to Section 5 Subsection 4 Sentence 1 TKÜV, telecommunication service providers must ensure that the technical implementation of an interception order can be detected neither by the communication participants nor by third parties.

Pursuant to Section 15 TKÜV, the telecommunication service provider may not make available to unauthorised parties any information concerning the manner and means by which the interception orders are implemented by its telecommunication system (for instance concerning its interception concepts[132]). Furthermore, it has to ensure the protection of information relating to the interception measure. This applies particularly with respect to the unauthorised obtainment of information concerning the targeted IDs and the number of currently or previously targeted IDs.

b) *Sanctions against telecommunication service providers and their employees*

As obtaining knowledge of the content of intercepted telecommunication by the telecommunication service provider's employees is not permitted, they can also be held liable for eavesdropping on non-publicly spoken words according to Section 201 StGB. The unauthorised obtainment of knowledge concerning non-spoken statements may entail a criminal sanction for phishing under Section 202b StGB. Violating an obligation stipulated by Section 15 TKÜV (secrecy concerning the technical implementation of a measure) may be punished as a regulatory offence and can incur a fine of up to €500,000 pursuant to Section 149 Subsection 1 No. 22, Subsection 2 Sentence 1 TKG.

Moreover, when telecommunication is intercepted under Section 100a StPO, Section 17 Subsection 1 G 10 prohibits persons providing telecommunication services or contributing to the provision of such services from disclosing to other people the fact that telecommunication is being intercepted. Violating this obligation can be punished by up to two years in prison or a fine pursuant to Section 18 G 10.

---

132 BeckTKG-Komm/*Eckhardt*, Section 110, para. 79.

C. Collection and Use of Traffic Data and Subscriber Data

1. Collection of traffic data and subscriber data

a) Collection of traffic data

aa) Relevant information

Section 100g Subsection 1 StPO allows for the (long-term) collection of traffic data (Section 96, 3 No. 30 TKG) without knowledge of the person concerned for the purpose of establishing the facts or determining the suspect's whereabouts. Hence, information such as the number or ID of the telephone connection or terminal devices concerned, personalised authorisation codes, or – when mobile connections are targeted – location data can be obtained, in principle in real time (see Subsection 1 Sentence 3) and thus without (further) recourse to Section 100a StPO being necessary. In order to identify mobile devices that were connected to a certain radio cell at a certain point in time Section 100g Subsection 3 StPO allows for prosecution authorities to also request all traffic data accrued with regard to that radio cell ("radio cell inquiry"). In addition, Subsection 2 StPO empowers prosecutors to access traffic data retained without occasion by telecommunication providers. This will be discussed below (c.).

bb) Substantive prerequisites of collection

Collection of traffic data is only admissible when certain substantive prerequisites are met. Concerning the suspected crime, for instance, there must exist *certain* facts giving rise to the suspicion that the targeted person was involved in its commission (Subsection 1 Sentence 1) as perpetrator or participant (Sections 25 et seqq. StGB), and this criminal offence must furthermore be either of *substantial significance in the individual case*, Section 100g Subsection 1 Sentence 1 No. 1 StPO, or have been committed by means of telecommunication, Section 100g Subsection 1 Sentence 1 No. 2 StPO. Radio cell inquiries pursuant to Subsection 3 are only permitted under the conditions of Subsection 1 Sentence 1 No. 1.

The necessary certainty of the facts requires that the suspicion goes beyond vague clues or mere conjecture.[133] In settled case-law, the Federal Constitutional Court holds the element of "substantial significance" to be sufficiently clear for limiting the infringement of fundamental rights in criminal procedures.[134] Such offences are to be assumed when they exhibit at least an intermediate level of criminality, significantly disturb peace under the law, and could significantly compro-

[133] BVerfG NJW 2007, 2749 (2751); BGH NStZ 2010, 711; Meyer-Goßner/*Schmitt*, Section 100a, para. 9.

[134] See only BVerfG NJZ 2005, 1338, 1339.

mise the population's sense of legal security.[135] Decisive for the classification as a crime of intermediate nature is the abstract sentencing range.[136] According to a newer decision by the Federal Constitutional Court, crimes punishable by a maximum sentence of under five years of imprisonment do not necessarily constitute crimes of substantial significance.[137] In such cases, the circumstances of the individual case are decisive.[138] Misdemeanours punishable by not more than two years, however, should never constitute a criminal offence of substantial significance.[139]

When an offence of non-substantial significance is concerned but this offence has been committed via telecommunication (a case of Subsection 1 Sentence 1 No. 2), the subsidiarity clause in Subsection 1 Sentence 2 must be observed, meaning other means of establishing the facts or determining the whereabouts would offer no prospect of success and the collection of data is proportionate to the importance of the case.

cc) Formal prerequisites of collection

The formal prerequisites of measures according to Section 100g StPO are laid out in Section 101a StPO. Its Subsection 1 Sentence 1 refers to Section 100a Subsection 3 (see supra III.B.7.c.) and Section 100b Subsections 1–4 Sentence 1 StPO (see supra III.B.6.). In particular, this means that the judge is competent for issuing the order, Section 100b Subsection 1 Sentence 1 StPO. Its period of validity is to be limited to no more than three months, although this can be extended (Section 100b Subsection 1 Sentences 4, 5 StPO, cp. supra III.B.8.).

dd) Duty of addressees to disclose information

Telecommunication service providers are required to cooperate pursuant to Sections 101a Subsection 1 Sentence 1, 100b Subsection 3 StPO (see supra III.B.5.). Because of the reference to Section 100a Subsection 3 StPO, only traffic data may be requested that was accrued with regard to telecommunication devices registered in the suspect's name, or in the names of persons it may be assumed function as a messenger for the accused, or that the accused is using their connection (see supra III.B.7.c.).

---

135 BVerfG NJW 2009, 2431, 2435; BVerfG NJW 2005, 1338, 1339; BVerfG NJW 2004, 999, 1010.

136 BGH StV 2013, 1, 3, para. 31.

137 BVerfG NJW 2009, 2431, 2435.

138 BGH StV 2013, 1, 3, para. 31.

139 Meyer-Goßner/*Schmitt*, Section 98a, para. 5 with further references.

ee) Automated procedure of disclosure

An automated procedure of disclosure for traffic data does not exist.

b) Collection of subscriber data

aa) Relevant information

For purposes of establishing the facts or for determining the whereabouts of an accused person, subscriber data pursuant to the TKG, meaning data concerning the contractual relationship (Sections 95, 3 No. 3 TKG), and, pursuant to Section 111 TKG data to be collected by the telecommunication service providers at the beginning of a contractual relationship prior to the activation specifically for the benefit of information requests made by the authorities – such as telephone numbers, names connected to email addresses, dates of birth, the (international) mobile equipment identity number [IMEI], the (international) mobile subscriber identity number [IMSI] stored on the SIM-card, or *static* IP addresses)[140] – can be requested according to Section 100j StPO. *Dynamic* IP addresses are not covered by Section 111 TKG, as the "other connection codes" to be collected pursuant to Section 111 Subsection 1 Sentence 1 No. 1 TKG must be permanently assigned to a telephone subscriber.[141]

Section 100j Subsection 2 StPO, however, allows for a sort of reverse engineering by permitting prosecutors to request subscriber data correlating with a known IP address, therefore enabling them to "decrypt" dynamic IP addresses. The assignment of the (known) traffic datum "dynamic IP address" to an (unknown) subscriber is covered by the provision on subscriber data disclosure in Section 100j StPO and not by the provision on traffic data disclosure in Section 100g StPO, because during this procedure the dynamic IP address's traffic datum is relevant only indirectly and internally to the provider for determining the subscriber datum which is ultimately to be disclosed to the investigation authorities.

The provision on subscriber data disclosure in Section 100j Subsection 1 StPO also covers "data, by means of which the access to terminal devices or storage media installed in these terminal devices or physically separate therefrom, is protected" (Section 113 Subsection 1 Sentence 2 TKG). This includes, in particular, the PIN and PUK of a SIM-card, as well as passwords for online data storage systems (especially cloud services).

---

140 KK/*Bruns*, Section 100j, para. 2.

141 BeckTKG-Komm/*Eckhardt*, Section 111, para. 13.

bb) Prerequisites of data collection

In contrast to Section 100g StPO, there are no special prerequisites for information requests under Subsection 1 or 2 relating to the suspicion of crime or concerning the significance of the individual offence.

Regarding data that allow access to terminal or storage devices, Section 100j Subsection 1 Sentence 2 StPO additionally stipulates that information may only be requested if the statutory prerequisites for the use of the data are met. This is the case, for instance, when physically separate storage media are to be accessed during a court-ordered search pursuant to Section 110 Subsection 3 StPO, or when emails stored in an email account are to be accessed by way of an overt access measure pursuant to Section 94 et seqq. StPO.[142] Also, the requirement of a court decision in Subsection 3 Sentence 1 must be heeded in these cases. In exigent circumstances, the order may also be issued by the public prosecution office or its officials working in the police force, although a court decision must still be made afterwards without delay, Section 100j Subsection 3 Sentence 3 StPO.

Requests pursuant to Subsection 2 (personal information regarding dynamic IP addresses) are limited to isolated IP assignments at a specific point in time. Long-term assignments of (unknown) varying IP addresses to (known) subscribers (reverse situation of Section 100j Subsection 2 StPO), are possible only under Section 100g StPO.

cc) Duty of addressees to disclose information in manual and automated procedures

According to Section 100j Subsection 5 Sentence 1 StPO, any person providing or contributing to the provision of telecommunication services on a commercial basis can be an addressee of the aforementioned measures. Section 113 TKG authorises this person to transmit the aforementioned data to the investigation authorities in a manual procedure.

Alongside it, there exists an automated procedure of disclosure which is limited to data to be collected pursuant to Section 111 Subsection 1 Sentences 1, 3, 4 and Subsection 2 TKG. In this procedure, the prosecution authorities (cp. Section 112 Subsection 1 No. 1 TKG), among others, can instruct the Federal Network Agency to access the available data and to transmit them to the requesting authority, Section 112 Subsection 4 Sentence 1 TKG.

---

142 *Bär*, MMR 2013, 700, 703.

c) Telecommunication data retention

An obligation to retain traffic data for a certain period was introduced into the TKG (Section 113a) by the legislature in 2007 while implementing Directive 2006/24/EG. However, the provision was declared null and void by the Federal Constitutional Court in its decision from 2 March 2010 due to constitutional deficiencies.[143] Meanwhile, the directive which the provision was based on has also been declared invalid by the ECJ.[144] In October 2015, the *Bundestag* passed the "Law for the implementation of a retention obligation and a maximum retention period for traffic data," which has been in force since 18 December 2015, thereby once again providing for the unoccasioned retention of traffic data for a certain period.[145] However, the retention and other associated obligations need not be complied with before 1 July 2017.

aa) Retention obligations

Pursuant to Section 113b Subsection 2 TKG, providers of publicly available telecommunication services (see supra III.B.5.a.) are now required to retain, for a period of ten weeks, *inter alia*, the concerned telephone numbers or other IDs, the time, and the duration of all telephone calls (including the IP addresses involved as well as the assigned user ID in cases of VoIP). Furthermore, regarding mobile telecommunication, the retention obligation also covers the IMSI and IMEI, as well as the telephone numbers, and the time at which every SMS or MMS was sent or received.

Also to be retained for ten weeks according to Section 113b Subsection 3 TKG are a participant's assigned IP address, a definite connection ID, and an assigned user ID, as well as the time and duration of the respective internet use. Pursuant to Section 113b Subsection 4 TKG, the location data of users of mobile telephone or internet services must be retained for four weeks. Section 113 Subsection 5 TKG explicitly stipulates that the content of communication, data regarding the internet sites accessed, and data from electronic mail services may not be retained. Also, pursuant to Section 113 Subsection 6 TKG, the retention of traffic data may not cover connections to lines of telephone counselling services as per Section 90 Subsection 2 TKG.

Pursuant to Section 113c Subsection 2 TKG, data may not be transmitted for purposes other than the prosecution of particularly serious crimes, the prevention of

---

143 BVerfG NJW 2010, 833.

144 EuGH NJW 2014, 2169.

145 In academic literature, however, doubts are being voiced regarding the compatibility of the new provisions with EU law, see *Boehm/Andrees*, CR 2016, 146 et seqq.; *Roßnagel*, NJW 2016, 533 (539).

concrete dangers to life, limb, or liberty of a person or for the continued existence of the Federal Republic of Germany or one of its *Länder*, or for the purpose of subscriber data disclosure on the basis of Section 113 Subsection 1 Sentence 3 TKG, in which an IP address is used to determine the line assigned to it at a certain point in time. According to Section 113c Subsection 3 TKG, these data must be marked in such as fashion that it is distinctly recognisable that one is dealing with data retained pursuant to Section 113b TKG.

bb) Access to retained data

Accessing data retained pursuant to Section 113b TKG is subject to demanding substantive prerequisites, the level of which is comparable to that of the conditions for acoustic surveillance measures under Section 100c StPO. Pursuant to Section 100g Subsection 2 Sentence 1 StPO traffic data may be accessed when certain facts give rise to the suspicion that a person, either as perpetrator or participant, has committed a serious criminal offence as stipulated in Section 100g Subsection 2 Sentence 2 StPO (or has attempted to commit such an offence, as the case may be), the offence constitutes one of particular gravity in the individual case and other means of establishing the facts would be much more difficult or offer no prospect of success, and the collection of the data remains proportionate to the significance of the case. The list of offences in Section 100g Subsection 2 Sentence 2 StPO roughly resembles that of Section 100c Subsection 2 StPO. Section 100c Subsection 4 StPO prohibits accessing traffic data that concerns persons subject to professional secrecy according to Section 53 Subsection 1 Sentence 1 Nos. 1 to 5 that could be used to gain insights regarding which these persons could refuse to testify. By contrast, the prerequisites in Section 100j Subsection 2 StPO were not raised. It now stipulates that the traffic data retained pursuant to Section 113 Subsection 2 TKG may also be accessed within the framework of subscriber data disclosures regarding IP addresses.

Concerning formal prerequisites, Section 101a Subsection 1 StPO refers to Section 100a Subsection 3 StPO (see supra III.B.7.c.) and Section 100b Subsection 1 StPO (see supra III.B.6.), but without the possibility of the public prosecution office issuing an order in exigent circumstances. Such a possibility does, however, still exist for traffic data, which can be accessed pursuant to Section 100g Subsection 1 StPO – the provision thus does not cover data retained pursuant to Section 113b TKG: these may only be accessed under Section 100g Subsection 2 StPO. Pursuant to Section 101a Subsection 4 StPO, data accessed under Section 100g Subsection 2 StPO may be disclosed to other entities only to the extent that this is for purposes for which accessing the data would have been directly permissible as well. Concerning duties of notification and judicial review, Section 101a Subsection 6 StPO refers to Section 101 Subsection 4 to 7 StPO, but, *inter alia*, with the modification that the first deferral of a notification pursuant to Section 101 Subsection 5 Sentence 1 StPO requires a court order.

2. Determination of device ID (IMEI), card number (IMSI), and location of mobile terminal devices

a) Determination of device ID with the help of IMSI-catchers

Section 100i StPO regulates the collection of position and location reports sent by mobile terminal devices.[146] The provision is specifically designed for and limited to the use of so-called IMSI-catchers. By simulating a (fake) network cell for the mobile devices located within a certain radius, they can enable the capture of the IMSI and IMEI numbers of unidentified mobile phones (under Section 100i Subsection 1 No. 1 StPO).[147] Alternatively, the location of a mobile phone within the radius of a network cell can be determined (under Section 100i Subsection 1 No. 2 StPO).[148]

Concerning the substantive prerequisites of an order, see the remarks on Section 100g StPO; the same goes for the investigation objectives and the formal prerequisites (both supra III.C.1.cc.). In contrast to Section 100g (and Section 100a) StPO, however, the order is to be limited to a maximum duration of six months under Section 100i Subsection 3 Sentence 2 StPO. Where third party personal data is concerned, the subsidiarity clause in Section 100i Subsection 2 Sentence 1 StPO must be observed.

b) Location determination via "silent SMS"

Mobile phones regularly disclose their location in the mobile network in order to be accessible. To ensure this accessibility, the network requires knowledge only of the so-called location area, made up of a variable number of network cells which cover an equally variable geographic surface.[149] Such a rough determination of location, which can be obtained as a traffic datum according to Section 100g StPO, is frequently insufficient for investigation purposes.[150] The problem is that the exact network cell is not identified until an active connection is established.[151] To induce such an active connection, "silent SMS" are used. They remain hidden from

---

[146] Meyer-Goßner/*Schmitt*, Section 100i, para. 1.

[147] *Hegmann*, Beck-OK StPO, Section100i, para. 1.

[148] *Ibid.*, para. 5.

[149] Wikipedia, Location Area, accessible at: http://de.wikipedia.org/wiki/Location_Area [as of: 11 October 2014].

[150] *Graf*, Beck-OK StPO, Section 100a, para. 132.

[151] Wikipedia, Location Area, accessible at: http://de.wikipedia.org/wiki/Location_Area#Ortung_im_Mobilfunknetz

the mobile phone's user, but trigger the generation of the desired cell-specific traffic data again accessible on the basis of Section 100g StPO. "Silent SMS" play a significant role in (not only repressive) police (and intelligence) work. In the first half of 2014 alone, the Federal Office for the Protection of the Constitution, the Federal Criminal Police Office, and the Federal Police sent a combined 156,466 "silent SMS."[152]

It has not yet been conclusively settled whether there exists a statutory basis for this forced generation of traffic data, and if it does, which statutory basis this is. A key point in this discussion is the question to what extent Sections 100a et seqq. StPO, possibly in combination with the investigative general clause in Sections 163 Subsection 1, 161 Subsection 1 StPO, can be used beyond their respective wording for not only passively accessing data generated independent of investigation authorities, but also for actively inducing such a generation of data.[153]

D. Access to (Temporarily) Stored Communication Data

1. Online-searches by means of so-called remote forensic software

a) Lack of powers in the law of criminal procedure

Aside from the law of intelligence agencies, rules on access to information systems are found only in the preventive federal and some *Länder's* police laws for purposes of averting danger. The preventive police law provisions authorise general access to information systems ("online search" and "online surveillance"), and – as a special case – the surveillance and recording of telecommunication in such systems ("source telecommunication surveillance").[154] By contrast, the law of criminal procedure contains no such special powers. It is undisputed nowadays that the powers of intervention currently found in the Code of Criminal Procedure are insufficient to justify the infiltration of computer systems.[155]

---

152 BT-Drs. 18/2257, p. 9. The numbers concerning Customs were rated classified information.

153 For more, see *Eisenberg/Singelnstein*, NStZ 2005, 62–67.

154 Powers to perform online searches exist in Rhineland-Palatinate, Section 31c POG RP, Bavaria, Article 34d BayPAG, and for the Federal Criminal Police Office in Section 20k BKAG. Regarding source telecommunication surveillance, see above III.B.2.c.

155 Regarding the (non-)applicability of the general powers of intervention, see BGH MMR 2007, 237, with comment by *Bär*.

b) Use of data obtained during preventive police law-based measures in criminal proceedings

However, online searches are not completely irrelevant with regard to criminal procedure. While information obtained in the course of preventive police activities may not be exploited for *evidentiary purposes* due to the lack of corresponding powers in criminal procedure, under Section 161 Subsection 2 Sentence 1 StPO, such data may nevertheless be used as an investigative clue, according to prevailing opinion.[156]

2. Search and seizure of stored communication data

a) Overview

Thus far, the system of rules on search and seizure has hardly been adapted to the requirements of the digital age. Due to a lack of alternatives, the existing procedural instruments must be used. Regarding the search for electronic (communication) data, these are the rules on the search of private premises, persons, and objects for the purpose of discovering evidence, Sections 102 et seqq. StPO. But the basis upon this evidence may be permanently secured or seized has not been completely resolved for every type of case. The main provisions worth considering in this respect include, on the one hand, the general rules on seizure in Sections 94 et seqq. StPO, which are tailored to apply to tangible objects, as well as the corresponding special provisions on the seizure of postal items pursuant to Sections 99 et seq. StPO, and, on the other hand, the regulations authorising the surveillance of intangible telecommunication in Sections 100a et seq. StPO.

However, the differentiation between tangible and intangible plays no role when it comes to the question of which statutory powers of intervention apply to which cases. Rather, it is the mode of the intervention (isolated/long-term and open/clandestine) and whether an encroachment on ongoing telecommunication is to take place that are decisive, as Section 100a StPO functions as *lex specialis* in these cases (for more, see below c.).

b) Search for electronic data

aa) Examination of electronic data, Section 110 Subsection 1 StPO

Searches may be performed in respect of the suspect (Section 102 StPO) as well as in respect of other persons (Section 103 StPO). *Inter alia*, objects belonging to a person may be searched. This includes computers and other data storage devices.[157]

---

156 See Meyer-Goßner/*Schmitt*, Section 161, para. 18d.

157 *Hegmann*, Beck-OK StPO, Section 102, para. 13.

Usually, however, it won't be the computer or the data storage device itself that are of interest, but the data they contain. This makes it necessary to begin by sifting through the often vast amounts of data, first, in order to find out whether the sought-after data are on the computer or data storage device at all, and, second, in order to narrow down the available data to only the relevant files. A seizure of the entire computer and all of its data would usually be disproportionate (see below c.aa.).

For this reason, the public prosecution office and, if it so orders, the officials assisting it, may examine documents during the search with regard to their relevance, pursuant to Section 110 Subsection 1 StPO. The term "documents" here includes all written thought content, regardless of its physical form.[158] Thus, electronic data also constitutes "documents" under the provision.[159] For the purpose of examination, the documents may furthermore be provisionally secured and removed from the premise;[160] regarding electronic data, this means a digital copy may be created. Nevertheless, securing hardware is also permissible when this is necessary for the examination.[161]

Section 110 Subsection 1 StPO is meant to safeguard personality rights and preclude the excessive, long-term collection of data.[162] By limiting the right of examination and selection to certain persons (prosecution office and the officials assisting it), one hopes to prevent extensive exposure of thought content to the broad access of investigators before the seizure has been effected.[163] However, the protection of personality rights appears imperfectly implemented when it comes to provisionally securing data pursuant to Section 110 Subsection 1 StPO, as the legal provisions fail to provide for procedures ensuring that knowledge of the measure is obtained not merely by the document-holder directly affected by the search (thus allowing him to seek legal recourse), but that persons whose rights are impacted by the content of the documents, are – at least in special cases – also notified and thus enabled to seek legal review. The problem arises, for example, concerning the seizure of emails stored with the provider regarding the email account user or, more generally, regarding the sender and the recipient. The issue shall be dealt with in greater detail when discussing possibilities of open and clandestine collection of data (below e.).

---

158 BVerfG NStZ 2002, 377 (378); BGH CR 1999, 292 (293); KK/*Bruns*, Section 110, para. 2

159 *Ibid.*

160 BGH NStZ 2003, 670 (671); KK/*Bruns*, Section 110, para. 4.

161 BVerfG NStZ 2002, 377; *Park*, Handbuch Durchsuchung und Beschlagnahme, para. 223.

162 *Park*, Handbuch Durchsuchung und Beschlagnahme, para. 219.

163 *Ibid.* For comprehensive criticism of the provision, see *ibid.*, para. 220.

bb) Examination of physically separate data storage media, Section 110 Subsection 3 StPO

Section 110 Subsection 3 StPO contains the only special power of intervention regarding electronic data found in the rules on search and seizure. The provision's purpose is to prevent potential loss of evidence. It stipulates that the search may be extended to cover storage media physically separate from the location of the search – such as servers in the intranet or internet. However, this is only permitted under the condition that they are accessible from the storage medium found, for example, by means of passwords found on location.[164] Whether the person concerned by the search is entitled to do so is irrelevant.[165] There must be a concrete danger of losing evidence (Section 110 Subsection 3 Sentence 1 StPO) which is the case when the external storage medium cannot be seized in time.[166]

Measures pursuant to Section 110 Subsection 3 StPO often have bearing on third parties. In this respect, the question already posed in aa) becomes relevant: to what extent must the measure be made known and in what way can third parties seek legal recourse? In contrast to cases of examination under Section 110 Subsection 1 StPO, Section 110 Subsection 3 Sentence 2 Hs. 2 StPO refers to Section 98 Subsection 2 StPO, which grants every person concerned (regarding the provision's original scope of application: by the seizure) the possibility of applying for a court decision. This shall be discussed in more detail in d).

The access to external storage devices also poses problems with regard to such devices often not being located in Germany, but in foreign countries – without that fact being simple to determine.[167] Thus the question arises under which conditions other nations' sovereign rights are compromised by accessing storage media located abroad, thereby leading to the necessity of requesting mutual legal assistance. As far as can be seen, no relevant case-law yet exists. In the applicable commentaries, these open questions are frequently not discussed adequately; instead, a solution is often proposed with hardly any supporting reasoning.[168]

---

164 KK/*Bruns*, Section 110, para. 8; *Park*, Handbuch Durchsuchung und Beschlagnahme, para. 787.

165 Such a restriction was rejected during the legislative process with reference to Section 98 Subsection 2 StPO, see BT-Drs. 16/6979, p. 45. Also note, however, that according to Article 32 lit. b of the Council of Europe Convention on Cybercrime, storage media located in another country may be accessed only with the "lawful and voluntary consent of the person who has the lawful authority to disclose the data […] through that computer system".

166 *Hegmann*, Beck-OK StPO, Section 110, para. 13.

167 See *Sieber*, Gutachten 69. Deutscher Juristentag, C 36.

168 *Hegmann*, BeckOK StPO, Section 110, paras. 15 et seq.; Meyer-Goßner/*Schmitt*, Section 110 paras. 7a et seq.; KK/*Bruns*, Section 110, para. 8a; *Park*, Handbuch Durchsuchung und Beschlagnahme, para. 789. But see *Sieber*, Gutachten 69. Deutscher Juris-

c) *Applicability of seizure provisions to electronic data*

aa) Underlying principle

The traditional provisions on seizure in Sections 94 et seqq. StPO relate to (tangible) objects. However, constitutional and federal case law concurs that seizing storage media, including the data they contain, for use as evidence in criminal proceedings is also permissible on the basis of Sections 94 et seqq. StPO.[169] The principle of proportionality requires – *a maiore ad minus* – that the data storage media not be seized, but only the data they contain be secured to the extent this proves practically feasible.[170] Moreover, it must be ascertained that excessive data are not seized.[171]

bb) Collection of electronic data

The conditions under which stored electronic communication – such as emails on the provider's server – can be seized, has not been settled in every respect.

(1) Locally stored messages before, after, and during transmission

Cases, in which emails or messages to be transmitted by other means are still stored on the computer or mobile phone, for example, in form of a draft, as well as cases in which they have been retrieved and subsequently saved locally, are unproblematic. Due to the absence of the specific risks Article 10 Subsection 1 GG is meant to afford protection against, they are not covered by the secrecy of telecommunication.[172] Thus, the same rules apply as for any other type of data and they can be seized pursuant to Sections 94 et seqq. StPO (see aa.).[173]

Also unproblematic are situations in which emails are in the process of transmission. This applies during the following phases: first, after having been dispatched by the sender and prior to arriving at the sender's provider; second, after having been dispatched by the sender's provider and prior to arriving at the recipient's provider; and third, during retrieval by the recipient. Since it is necessary to inter-

---

tentag, C 139 et seq., regarding the problems connected with a nation conducting independent transnational investigations.

169 BVerfG NJW 2005, 1917 (1919); NJW 2006, 976; Meyer-Goßner/*Schmitt*, Section 94, para. 4.

170 BVerfG ZUM-RD 2005, 322 (330 et seq.).

171 BVerfG NJW 2005, 1917 (1920 et seq.); NJW 2009, 2431 (2436, para. 81); BGH NStZ 345 (346).

172 BVerfG NJW 2006, 976 (978 et seq.).

173 See *Graf*, Beck-OK StPO, Section 100a, para. 27.

vene in an ongoing telecommunication process in order to access the messages, only Section 100a StPO can serve as statutory basis for the intervention.[174]

(2) Communication data temporarily or permanently stored with third parties for the purpose of further transmission or safekeeping

Also settled is the question of isolated open access to emails stored with the recipient's provider. The Federal Constitutional Court declared such access permissible on the basis of Sections 94 et seqq. StPO. The issue had previously been disputed both regarding its constitutional and its criminal procedural dimensions.[175] Topics of this discussion included the intertwined questions of to what extent emails temporarily or permanently stored with the provider fall under the scope of the secrecy of telecommunication, and whether Sections 94 et seqq. StPO can even justify an encroachment on the secrecy of telecommunication. Many were of the opinion that the criminal procedural powers of intervention contained in the eighth chapter of the StPO related to specific encroachments on fundamental rights, and that these encroachments could be justified only on the basis of the corresponding provisions in the StPO. Thus, according to widespread opinion, encroachments on Article 10 Subsection 1 GG could only be based on Sections 99 and 100a StPO (as well as Section 100g StPO which is, however, not of relevance for the cases at hand).[176] They allow for clandestine access to ongoing communication, since the person concerned has no means of monitoring activities beyond his sphere of control. Pursuant to this view, on the one hand, these invasive measures constituted statutory realisations of the specific dangers that Article 10 Subsection 1 GG is to protect against. On the other hand, encroachments could only be justified under the conditions stipulated in these provisions, including adherence to the respective procedures.[177]

In its 2009 decision quoted above, the Federal Constitutional Court held that the specific dangers of spatially distanced communication, which Article 10 Subsection 1 GG is intended to provide protection against, only apply to data until such time as the party concerned gains exclusive control over the contents of his mail box.[178] Furthermore, it held that Sections 94 et seqq. StPO satisfied the constitu-

---

[174] *Ibid.*, para. 28.

[175] BVerfG NJW 2009, 2431 et seqq.

[176] Thus, specifically regarding the possibility of seizing emails at the provider based only on Section 100a StPO, e.g., LG Hamburg MMR 2008, 186 et seq.

[177] Regarding Section 100a StPO as a "conclusive regulation" cp. *Löwe/Rosenberg/Schäfer*, Section 100a (as of 1 April 1986), para. 5, according to which Section 100a StPO essentially differs from Section 99 StPO in that the former permits the interception of future, transient telecommunication, while Section 99 applies to earlier, fixed telecommunication, *ibid.*, Section 99, paras. 2 et seq.

[178] BVerfG NJW 2009, 2431 (2433, para. 46).

tional requirements for open and isolated encroachments on the secrecy of telecommunication.[179] It also declared that Sections 99, 100a and 100g StPO did not constitute *leges speciales* conclusively regulating such encroachments on the fundamental right.[180]

Yet even after this decision, uncertainties remain in cases in which communication is accessed without knowledge of the person concerned – possibly for an extended duration – by performing the interception at third parties employed by the person concerned for the further transmission or non-local storage of their messages.[181] This relates to cases, for example, in which emails are accessed which are temporarily or permanently stored with the recipient's provider or that are cached briefly with the sender's provider for onward transmission.[182] For encroachments of this kind, an application of Section 99 or Section 100a StPO can be considered. The two provisions differ markedly in their substantive prerequisites, as well as in their procedural requirements.[183] The question of which is applicable is of practical relevance, since it is not always possible to seize messages at the recipient's provider. If a suspect sends an email to a location beyond German jurisdiction where (timely) mutual legal assistance is not available, it can prove necessary to collect the data at the sender's provider during the brief phase of cache storage, that is, after arrival and prior to onward transmission. This would require a statutory power of intervention permitting not merely isolated access to data present at a certain time, but to first extract *all* emails for closer examination regarding their relevance and, when necessary, to seize them.

The issue has not yet been explicitly brought before the Federal Constitutional Court for clarification, and there is disagreement between the lower courts regard-

179 BVerfG NJW 2009, 2431 (2432 et seq.).

180 BVerfG NJW 2009, 2431 (2433 et seq., paras. 57 et seq.).

181 This sort of secret, possibly long-term collection from an information system of the person concerned is out of the question since it could be performed only by means of a – *de lege lata* inadmissible – online search or online surveillance (see above I.B.3.b.). At most, messages sent by the person concerned could in this way (permissibly) be intercepted within the framework of source telecommunication surveillance (see above III.B.2.c. aa.).

182 Regarding the mentioned seven phases, see *Graf*, Beck-OK StPO, Section 100a, para. 27.

183 Advocating an application of Section 99 StPO: AG Reutlingen, decision of 31 October 2011, Az.: 5 Ds 43 Js 18155/10 jug; apparently also LG Hildesheim, decision of 21 April 2010, Az.: 26 Qs 58/10; *Graf*, Beck-OK StPO, Section 100a, para. 30 ("for the interim"); *Bär*, MMR 2013, 700 (703). By contrast, proponents of Section 100a StPO: LG Landshut, decision of 21 May 2012, Az.: 6 Qs 82/12 (however, no general rejection of Section 99 StPO, see para. 16 of the decision); Meyer-Goßner/*Schmitt*, Section 100a, para. 6c; *Klein*, NJW 2009, 2396 (2399). The often quoted decision BGH NJW 2009, 1828 was made prior to the decision of the BVerfG. Thus it cannot readily be held to still apply unreservedly.

ing which solution is preferable.[184] However, in the Federal Constitutional Court's considerations underpinning its ruling on Sections 94 et seqq. StPO, the court formulated criteria by which the invasiveness of not only isolated and open, but also of long-term and secret seizures of communication data are to be assessed. Correspondingly, it also outlined the requirements for a statutory empowerment permitting these measures in such a way that one can at least identify provisions which clearly fail to meet these standards. In this respect, the decision continues along traditional lines in that it places stringent requirements on the justification of (possibly long-term) clandestine encroachments on the fundamental rights of data protection due to the ensuing limitation of the concerned party's ability to avail itself of a legal remedy.[185]

Regarding the level of invasiveness, the Federal Constitutional Court held:

> "The gravity of an encroachment is greater when it ensues secretly […]. The long-term encroachment on ongoing telecommunication is more intensive than a one-off and isolated collection of data, since the scope and variety of the obtained data is considerably greater […]. The possibility of the collected data being used for unspecified or not yet specified purposes also increases the gravity of the encroachment – even at the stage of collection […]. Finally, the degree of invasiveness is higher when the affected person has no influence on the data concerning him or her […]."[186]

Correspondingly, there exist certain thresholds for taking action in the law of criminal procedure:

> "[…] For clandestine encroachments on the secrecy of telecommunication as well as for access to comprehensive data stocks retained without suspicion […] and upon which the person concerned has no influence, particularly stringent standards for access apply regarding the gravity of the investigated crime and the degree of suspicion necessary […]. Whereas regarding an open measure ensuing from a search, one which does not encroach ongoing communication and is limited to the investigation's purpose, such as seizing emails stored on the provider's mail server, the prohibition of excessiveness – in face of the level of the state's interest in criminal prosecution – does not require that the seizure of emails stored on the provider's mail server be permitted only for the prosecution of particularly serious criminal offences (such as in Section 100c StPO), serious criminal offences (such as in Section 100a StPO), or criminal offences of substantial significance (as in Section 100g StPO). In line with the conditions regularly applicable for criminal investigations, the initial suspicion of a crime having been committed may suffice for allowing prosecution authorities to access communication content, if this ensues outside of ongoing telecommunication and with knowledge of the person concerned – such as in the case seizures."[187]

---

184 *Ibid.*

185 See, e.g., BVerfGE 120, 274 (323 et seqq., paras. 234 et seqq.) (online search); BVerfG NJW 2003, 1787 (1791) ("Prerequisite is a criminal offence of substantial significance, a concrete suspicion of commission"); BVerfG NJW 1973, 891–893. This is also pointed out by *Klein*, NJW 2009, 2996 (2998).

186 BVerfG NJW 2009, 2431 (2434, para. 68).

187 BVerfG NJW 2009, 2431 (2434 et seq., para. 69).

Thus, only regarding measures of open, isolated search and seizure did the Federal Constitutional Court hold that – due to their relatively minor level of invasiveness – neither a special degree of suspicion nor a limitation to certain criminal offences was necessary. However, Section 99 StPO, which allows for secret access according to Section 101 Subsection 5 StPO (a subsequent notification can even be dispensed with entirely pursuant to Section 101 Subsection 6 Sentence 3 StPO), places no substantive restrictions whatsoever on encroachments. Substantively, the initial suspicion of having committed (any) criminal offence is enough. In line with the court's reasoning, the fact that Section 100 StPO stipulates more stringent procedural requirements compared to those applicable for the normal seizure pursuant to Section 94 StPO cannot compensate for this deficiency, as procedural precautions only serve an ancillary function to the substantive balancing of interests.[188] In light of this case law, applying Section 99 StPO in the aforementioned scenarios seems a constitutionally questionable proposal. Yet the Federal Constitutional Court gave no conclusive indications as to whether or not it would be permissible – at least during an interim period – for lower courts to modify Section 99 StPO in line with constitutional requirements (in addition to the usual assessment of proportionality that has to be made in every case) and thus essentially to craft a suitable empowerment in each individual case themselves.[189]

d) Different standards of protection for stored and for transmitted data

With regard to the statutory law, the conditions for an encroachment seem to depend on whether stationary data or data in transmission is supposed to be accessed. A seizure pursuant to Sections 94 et seqq. StPO may be performed subject to much less stringent conditions than an encroachment on ongoing telecommunication, which Section 100a StPO is tailored to.

However, pursuant to the Federal Constitutional Court's outlined decision, the required level of protective preconditions is not determined by whether stationary data or data in transmission are concerned. Rather, what is decisive according to the criteria mentioned above is whether an encroachment ensues openly and only isolatedly or whether it ensues secretly and possibly extends over a long duration of

---

188 Regarding the procedural requirements, see BVerfG NJW 2009, 2431 (2437 et seqq., paras. 92 et seqq.).

189 Of this opinion, however, is *Bär*, who interprets the mention of Sections 99 and 100a StPO by the BVerfG NJW 2009, 2431 (2434, para. 58) not as a mere dismissal of a constitutionally relevant *lex-specialis*-relationship in favour of Sections 99 and 100a StPO (as the preceding para. 57 would suggest). *Graf*, Beck-OK StPO as of: 1 September 2015, Section 100a, para. 30 also assumes that Section 99 StPO continues to apply – albeit only for a short interim period until further action by the legislature –, although he substantiates this assumption with a reference to BGH NJW 2009, 1828 despite this decision having been made prior to that of the Federal Constitutional Court. See also the references above n. 183.

time, since in latter cases the court requires that higher standards be met regarding the gravity of the offence being prosecuted as well as regarding the degree of suspicion necessary. The legislature will have to use this as a guideline in an – urgently necessary – reform of the search and seizure provisions.

e) Open and clandestine access to stored data

Both searches pursuant to Sections 102 et seqq. StPO as well as seizures pursuant to Sections 94 et seqq. StPO principally constitute open measures. As a general rule, they both require a judicial order (Section 105 Subsection 1 Sentence 1 Hs. 1, Subsection 1 Sentence 2 Hs. 1 StPO, or Section 98 Subsection 1 Sentence 1 Hs. 1 StPO respectively), which entails a right to be heard pursuant to Article 103 Subsection 1 GG.[190] Entitled to this right is the person "whose (own) rights are infringed directly by the court order."[191] "Apart from those formally party to a procedure, this may also refer to the person substantively affected by the judicial decision."[192] Regarding content, this implies that a person thus formally or substantively concerned must be allowed to make a statement, and that his or her statements must be acknowledged and be taken into consideration.[193] So as not to undermine the right to be heard, the person concerned must be sufficiently heard prior to a decision.[194] Thus, the court must make sure that the procedure does not reach a stage in the decision-making process detrimental to the person concerned before that person has obtained knowledge of the procedure.[195]

This right, which is based on Article 103 Subsection 1 GG, has been implemented in statutory form, *inter alia* in Sections 33 and 35 StPO,[196] which also apply to judicial decisions on investigative measures. Thus, a person concerned must be given notice pursuant to Sections 33 Subsection 2, 35 Subsection 2 StPO of search and seizure orders, including the reasons given for the respective decision (see Section 34 StPO) by no later than the commencement of the measure.[197] The prior hearing demanded by Section 33 Subsections 3, 2 StPO can be dispensed with pursuant to Section 33 Subsection 4 StPO where it would endanger the success of the

---

190 Regarding seizure, cp. BVerfG NJW 1965, 1171 et seq.

191 BVerfG NJW 1988, 1963. Regarding the Code of Criminal Procedure, see KK/*Maul*, Section 35, para. 3.

192 BVerfG NJW 1988, 1963. Regarding the Code of Criminal Procedure, see *Larcher*, Beck-OK StPO, Section 35, para. 2.

193 Maunz/Dürig/*Schmidt-Aßmann*, GG, 74. suppl. 2015, Article 103 para. 69.

194 Maunz/Dürig/*Schmidt-Aßmann*, GG, 74. suppl. 2015, Article 103 para. 92.

195 BVerfGE 36, 85 (88).

196 KK/*Maul*, Section 35, para. 1.

197 Regarding search, BGH NStZ 2003, 273 et seq.; BVerfG NJW 2009, 2431 (2437, para. 95); *Ritzert*, Beck-OK StPO, Section 98, para. 5.

measure.[198] Moreover, it is currently common practice to withhold – based on an analogous application of Section 101 StPO, which regulates the procedure for the clandestine investigative measures exhaustively enumerated there – at least the reasons for the decision as long as their knowledge could endanger the investigation.[199] However, specifically in connection with a decision on an order to seize a whole email box, the Federal Court of Justice *(Bundesgerichtshof)* hinted in an *obiter dictum* at the unlawfulness of this practice by pointing out that – unlike Section 101 Subsection 5 StPO does with regard to the investigative measures listed in Section 101 Subsection 1 StPO – the Code of Criminal Procedure does not provide for deferring the notification based on an endangerment of the investigation's purpose regarding cases of seizure pursuant to Sections 94 et seqq. StPO.[200]

Thus, the openness of investigative measures depends first and foremost on the factual openness of their implementation, without all persons concerned needing necessarily to be informed of them in advance or at least without delay at their commencement.

By contrast, comprehensive statutory regulation on procedure exists in Section 101 StPO regarding planned clandestine measures. This includes, *inter alia*, Sections 99 and 100a StPO (see Section 101 Subsection 1 StPO). The provision contains a differentiated system concerning the handling of personal data as well as who is to be notified at what point in time of the encroaching measures performed, and which options for subsequent legal recourse are available. For example, regarding a measure pursuant to Section 99 StPO the sender and the addressee of a postal item, and regarding a measure pursuant to Section 100a the participants in the telecommunication under surveillance are to be notified as soon as this can be effected, *inter alia*, without endangering the purpose of the investigation (Section 101 Subsection 4 Sentence 1 Nos. 2, 3, Subsection 5 Sentence 1 StPO). However, notifications can be dispensed with when a non-targeted person was only tangentially affected by the measure and it may be assumed that the person has no interest in being notified (see Section 101 Subsection 4 Sentence 4 StPO).

When compared to these well thought-out and concise provisions, the state of the law appears insufficient with regard to formally open measures.[201] The latter also frequently have secretive elements but the respective statutory provisions are, in contrast to the rules on clandestine measures, deficient with respect to the protec-

198 This exception is constitutionally sound, see BVerfGE 100, 313 (361).

199 See BGH NStZ 2003, 273 (274) regarding the narrow limits of this possibility. See also BVerfG NJW 2009, 2431 (2437, para. 94), according to which it would be constitutionally unobjectionable even to withhold notice of the entire measure.

200 BGH NJW 2010, 1297 (1298). This development is pointed out by *Ritzert*, Beck-OK StPO, Section 98, para. 5. Yet at the same time she emphasises that seizures frequently only form part of a whole bundle of measures. The obligation to inform without delay could thus endanger ongoing measures, e.g., those pursuant to Section 100a StPO.

201 This discrepancy is also noted by *Brodowski*, JR 2009, 402 (407).

tive elements actually necessary with regard to the measures' frequent relevance to third parties' personality rights. Take the following example: the seizure of emails at the provider concerns not only the provider as custodian, but also the user of the mail box as well as all other participants in the communication. This situation principally seems comparable to that of a measure pursuant to Section 100a StPO – only in contrast to Section 100a StPO, there exists no procedural provision comparable to Section 101 Subsection 4 Sentence 1 No. 3 StPO. Third party rights are also affected when, during a search, (communication) data – possibly after first securing them – are comprehensively combed through for their relevance, Section 110 Subsections 1, 3 StPO. Communication relationships protected by Article 10 Subsection 1 GG or at least by the (constitutional) right to informational self-determination could thereby be subjected to the investigators' scrutiny, even if they later turn out to be irrelevant. Moreover, the examination pursuant to Section 110 Subsection 3 StPO, for instance, grants the power to access common shared drives which are not (solely) in the rightful power of disposition of the person concerned by the search, but are also used and furnished with data by third parties.

To the extent that the relevance to third parties is a consequence of a judicial decision, i.e. particularly in cases of seizure, the issue first comes up as one regarding the right to be heard. In accordance with the criteria mentioned at the beginning, one must thus determine when a third party is directly substantively affected. When this is the case, the third party must be notified of the decision pursuant to Section 35 StPO. This was held by the Federal Constitutional Court to necessarily apply to the user of a mail box seized at the provider.[202] However, the provisional securing and examination pursuant to Section 110 StPO is not based on a judicial decision, so that such a measure does not fall within the scope of protection of Article 103 Subsection 1 GG and Sections 33 and 35 StPO do not apply. Nevertheless, according to the Federal Constitutional Court, Section 98 Subsection 2 StPO can be applied by analogy for the benefit of the mail box user when emails are provisionally secured at the provider.[203] In consequence, the person concerned is able to apply for a court decision in cases in which the seizure was ordered by a non-judicial entity due to exigent circumstances. Furthermore, the person concerned is to be instructed as to his rights. To what extent the prosecution authorities need to take action regarding other persons affected, in particular whether these must also be

[202] BVerfG NJW 2009, 2431 (2437, para. 94). *Brodowski*, JR 2009, 402 (407) appears to have overlooked this requirement stipulated by the court. Nevertheless, a direct seizure at the provider will likely be the exception. First, a seizure of the entire mailbox usually proves disproportionate, BGH NJW 2010, 1297 (1298, para. 15 et seq.). Second, precisely specifying prior to an examination which data are to be seized will likely only be possible under exceptional circumstances.

[203] BVerfG NJW 2009, 2431 (2437, para. 94). Sentence 2 of Section 110 Subsection 3 StPO refers directly to Section 98 Subsection 2 StPO.

informed, remains open and is left for the responsible public prosecutor to decide in the individual case. This question is not answered by the StPO's general provisions granting a right to information (i.e., in particular Sections 475 and 491 StPO in connection with Section 19 of the Federal Data Protection Act (*Bundesdatenschutzgesetz*, BDSG).[204]

3. Duties to cooperate: production and decryption of data

The German StPO contains no special provisions on the basis of which the investigative authorities could demand the decryption of encrypted data or the surrender of the passwords necessary for decryption. The general rules concerning duties of witnesses and the obligation of the (non-accused) custodian to surrender objects in cases of seizure are of limited expedience and require – sometimes significant – restricting modifications to ensure proportionality.[205] Pursuant to Sections 48 Subsection 1 Sentence 2, 161a Subsection 1 StPO, non-suspect witnesses are required to testify truthfully regarding their own perceptions. This may include testifying about any access codes known to them.[206] By using this method, the prosecution authorities could potentially gain extensive access to personal data without the method being subject to substantive limitations. Until a statutory regulation is introduced, *Sieber* therefore advocates closely tying such access to the intended utilisation and the ensuing respective prerequisites.[207] The option of issuing a so-called production order, entailing the obligation to provide data in plain text form, does not exist on the basis of the current body of law, in particular not on the basis of Section 95 StPO. The obligation to surrender applies only to objects already in a person's custody.[208]

---

[204] It would therefore be advisable for the legislature to confront the issue and to standardise the manner in which the potentially affected third party fundamental rights (in particular the right to information following from the data protection rights, the right to a judicial review following from Article 19 Subsection 4 GG and Article 103 Subsection 1 GG) are to be accorded procedural protection. Regarding the relationship of Article 103 Subsection 1 GG to other provisions in the Constitution, see Maunz/Dürig/*Schmidt-Aßmann*, GG, 74. suppl. 2015, Article 103 paras. 6 et seqq. For the requirements concerning obligations to inform in the course of measures of criminal procedure, see esp. BVerfG NJW 2012, 833 (838 et seq.).

[205] Instructive: *Sieber*, Gutachten 69. Deutscher Juristentag, C 119–122.

[206] *Ibid.*, p. 120.

[207] *Ibid.*, p. 121.

[208] *Ibid.*, p. 121.

IV. Use of Communication Data in Judicial Proceedings

1. Use of communication data in the law of criminal procedure

The German StPO includes no special provisions regarding the introduction of electronic data. In principle, the court decides in what way electronic data are introduced into the main hearing and how they are used (Section 244 Subsection 2 StPO). Yet regarding strict evidentiary proceedings *(Strengbeweisverfahren)*[209] the StPO provides only for evidence in the form of witness testimony (Sections 48 et seqq. StPO), expert opinions (Sections 72 et seqq. StPO), documents (Section 249 StPO), and inspections (Section 86 StPO). All of these may be of relevance when it comes to introducing electronic data or their content. This applies both for seized data as well as for data intercepted in the course of ongoing telecommunication. During an inspection, the collected data are made directly audible or visible in the main hearing with the aid of a computer monitor or a loudspeaker.[210] In cases of documentary evidence, records or printouts of data are read out.[211] A supplementary hearing of the officer responsible for the data analysis as a witness can streamline the taking of evidence, particularly in cases where the amount of data concerned is vast.[212] Finally, experts can help the court assess the authenticity and integrity of data.

---

209 In the German law of criminal procedure, two different types of evidentiary proceedings may apply depending on which facts are to be ascertained and whether this is to ensue during the main hearing. In the main hearing, a strict evidentiary proceeding – with only certain forms of admissible evidence – applies when it comes to ascertaining the sequence of events fulfilling the elements of an offence, or regarding facts either relating to the defendant's guilt or which have an impact on the sentence. Outside the main hearing, or in the main hearing concerning facts other than those just mentioned, an open evidentiary proceeding applies. For more, see Meyer-Goßner/*Schmitt*, Section 244, paras. 6 et seqq.

210 BGH NStZ 2002, 493 regarding the introduction of conversation recordings into the main hearing.

211 *Graf*, Beck-OK StPO, Section 100a, para. 77.

212 *Ibid.* This does not violate the principle of immediacy of Section 250 StPO. For Sections 250 et seqq. StPO merely stipulate when *personal* evidence may be substituted or supplemented by *documentary* evidence. It does not prohibit substituting or supplementing documentary evidence by personal evidence. Hearing the officer responsible for the analysis must therefore (merely) be consistent with the court's general duty to accurately ascertain the facts of the case pursuant to Section 244 Subsection 2 StPO, see *Roxin/ Schünemann*, StPO, Section 46, para. 33. The lower evidentiary value of this testimony compared to the (direct) documentary evidence must, however, be taken into account when evaluating the evidence, *ibid.*, para. 34.

2. Inadmissibility of evidence as a consequence of inappropriate collection

a) Inadmissibility of evidence following the unlawful collection of evidence

Complicated legal issues arise when the prerequisites for collecting evidence are disregarded. It leads to the question of whether these unlawfully obtained pieces of evidence may still be admitted. On the one hand, this problem concerns the further utilisation during the investigative procedure, and on the other, it concerns their admissibility for evidentiary purposes during the main hearing. The correct way of handling these topics is subject to extremely contentious debate; the discussion of the issue is characterised by a myriad of academic papers and – sometimes contradictory – case law.[213] The following delineation shall – in line with the empirical nature of this study and the specific question posed – therefore confine itself to the basic principles of constitutional and federal court case law regarding the use of evidence in the main hearing.

Whether a conviction may be based on evidence obtained by way of procedurally unlawful coercive measures must be determined, for example, when rights to refuse to testify or to answer questions are disregarded while gathering evidence. This scenario concerns cases, for instance, where suspects' or their defence attorneys' laptops are seized, containing files relevant to their criminal defence. Regarding the accused person, the prohibition of seizure follows from an analogous application of Section 97 Subsection 1 StPO in connection with Article 2 Subsection 1, Article 20 Subsection 3 GG.[214] The defence attorney's files are protected pursuant to Sections 97 Subsection 1 Nos. 1, 2, 53 Subsection 1 Sentence 1 No. 2 StPO. The question whether unlawfully collected evidence may be admitted also arises, for example, when telecommunication interception under Sections 100a et seq. StPO is ordered without the necessary suspicion of a serious criminal offence pursuant to Section 100a Subsection 2 StPO having been committed, or when the order is issued by the public prosecution office despite the absence of exigent circumstances.

However, a ban on the admission does not automatically follow from such violations if the inadmissibility of evidence is not explicitly provided for by law – which it only exceptionally is (for instance, in Section 136a Subsection 3 Sentence 2 StPO). A ban on the admission of evidence "constitutes, from a constitutional point of view, an exception requiring grounds to be given" as it "impairs the ascertainment of a substantively correct and fair decision."[215] Thus, according to established case law of the Federal Court of Justice and the Federal Constitutional Court, a

213 For more, see *Roxin/Schünemann*, StPO, Section 24, paras. 13–67.

214 BGH NStZ 1998, 309 (310). Concerning the seizure of a laptop of which the suspect claims it contains files relevant to her defence, see BVerfG NStZ 2002, 377 et seqq.

215 BVerfG NJW 2012, 907 (910, para. 117).

weighing of interests in each individual case is required.[216] This can be summarised as follows in the words of the KG Berlin:[217]

> "In this respect, the seriousness of the breach of procedural law and the gravity of the alleged offence are of key significance. The seriousness of the breach of procedural law is determined particularly based on the degree of blame that can be placed on the person issuing the order or the person executing it, and based on the encroachment's impact on fundamental rights, as well as on whether the piece of evidence could have been obtained without a breach of law and whether the violated procedural rule primarily served to protect the suspect or other purposes. Regarding the alleged offence one must bear in mind that the interest in unrestricted investigation increases with the severity of the offence a person is suspected of."

Limits to the balancing of interests are not reached until "the defendant doesn't have adequate possibilities to exert an influence on the course and outcome of the proceedings, the minimum requirements as to reliable investigation of the truth are no longer met, or *admitting* [emphasis by the authors] the information as evidence would lead to a disproportionate encroachment" of the fundamental right concerned.[218]

> "Moreover, the admissibility of information obtained by violating legal provisions may not be affirmed where this would lead to encouraging the unlawful taking of evidence. A ban on the admission of evidence may hence be required particularly after serious, deliberate, or objectively arbitrary breaches of the law in which fundamental law-related safeguards have been intentionally or systematically disregarded."[219]

According to the established case law of the Federal Court of Justice concerning orders pursuant to Section 100a StPO, a ban on the admission of evidence exists at least when essential objective prerequisites for ordering the interception measure – such as the suspicion of an offence pursuant to Section 100a Subsection 2 StPO – are not fulfilled.[220]

The Federal Court of Justice has more precisely specified the necessary balancing of interests by means of a "maxim of proportionality."[221] According to this, criminal offences of substantial significance can justify the use of otherwise illegal investigative measures, if other investigative means would be considerably less likely to succeed or establishing the facts would be substantially more difficult.[222] Thus, the maxim of proportionality does not entail a shift in the standards applied

---

216 BGH NJW 1999, 959 (961).

217 KG Berlin, decision of 16 February 2005, Az. (5) 1 Ss 406/04 (63/04), para. 6.

218 BVerfG NJW 2012, 907 (910, para. 117).

219 BVerfG NJW 2012, 907 (910, para. 117). Also comparable BVerfG NJW 2009, 3225 et seq.

220 BGH NStZ 2006, 402 (403); NStZ 2003, 499.

221 *Roxin/Schünemann*, StPO, Section 24, paras. 30, 41.

222 See BGH GrS NJW 1996, 2940 (2941), for the use of a so-called "Hörfalle" (listening in on telephone conversations which the police induces a third party to lead with the suspect) on the basis of the investigative general clause of criminal procedure in Sections 161, 163 StPO.

when assessing the consequences of the unlawful collection of evidence. Rather, the assessment of the (performance of the) measure itself changes, depending on the significance of the offence and the availability of other investigative means.

Furthermore, for the ban on the admission of evidence to apply, the Federal Court of Justice requires in certain cases that the defendant – provided he is represented by a criminal defence attorney – explicitly object to the admission of unlawfully collected evidence.[223] Failing to do so precludes the right to raise the issue of admissibility on appeal.[224] This so-called objection solution applies, in particular, to a *violation of formalities of suspect interrogations* or in cases of secret investigative measures, such as the *interception of telecommunication.*[225]

In addition to the maxim of proportionality and the objection solution, an attempt to compensate procedural violations is made by applying special standards for the evaluation of evidence as well as by taking them into consideration when determining the sentence.[226] In detail, the relationship between the various instruments is unresolved.[227]

b) *Admissibility of evidence when conditions of collection remain unclear*

Problems also arise when the conditions of the collection of evidence and hence its lawfulness remains unknown because the prosecution authorities don't provide the relevant information. This may be the case when software solutions which were developed at great expense (e.g., for source telecommunication surveillance) would otherwise have to be revealed, thereby possibly compromising other investigations.[228] The prosecution authorities' interests in secrecy regarding their investigative methods can be guarded by excluding the public from the main hearing based on an endangerment of the public order pursuant to Section 172 No. 1 of the Courts Constitution Act (*Gerichtsverfassungsgesetz*, GVG).[229] To the extent this is deemed insufficient by the prosecution authorities', and particularly the police

---

223 For instructive commentary on the whole issue, see *Eschelbach*, Beck-OK StPO, Section 257, paras. 20 et seqq.

224 According to the courts, such a preclusion already applies if the objection is not made immediately following the introduction of the evidence into the main hearing pursuant to Section 257 Subsection 2 StPO, see BGH NJW 1992, 1463 as well as OLG Celle, NStZ 2014, 118 et seq.

225 *Eschelbach*, Beck-OK StPO, Section 257, para. 21.

226 *Roxin/Schünemann*, StPO, Section 24, para. 30; *Eschelbach*, Beck-OK StPO, Section 257, para. 21.

227 *Ibid.*

228 Regarding source telecommunication surveillance, see *Beuth*, Der neue Staatstrojaner des BKA ist fertig, Zeit Online from 15 August 2014, accessible at: http://www.zeit.de/digital/datenschutz/2014-08/staatstrojaner-bka-onlinedurchsuchung-fertig

229 *Allgayer*, Beck-OK StPO, Section 172 GVG; Section 133 Subsection 1 RiStBV.

force's point of view (which will likely be the case), there exists the possibility for the responsible minister of the interior – being the highest superior police authority – to issue a blocking order (so-called *Sperrerklärung*) pursuant to Section 96 Sentence 1 StPO.[230] This order must be based on the endangerment of the welfare of the Federal Republic or of one of the *Länder* (Section 96 Sentence 1 StPO). This also includes detriments regarding the state's obligation to avert danger and prosecute crimes.[231] In particular, blocking orders can apply to source code or records on program architecture and thus prevent a review.[232]

According to the Federal Court of Justice, the sentencing court may principally rely on the investigative procedure having been conducted in accordance with the law (although this most likely won't readily apply to evidence gathered in foreign countries, for instance, on the basis of a European Investigation Order).[233] If there is doubt regarding the investigation's lawfulness, then the existence of circumstances potentially leading to bans on the collection and admission of evidence must be examined in an open evidentiary proceeding *(Freibeweisverfahren)*.[234] When a (lawful) blocking order is issued, these efforts usually prove futile. In this case, the executive power's interests in maintaining secrecy work *in dubio pro reo* in criminal proceedings.[235] However, all this entails is that the court must resort to surrogates for the inaccessible primary pieces of evidence and take account of the finding's subsequent limitations by evaluating the evidence in a particularly cautious and critical manner.[236]

3. Use of data outside the original proceedings

The question to what extent data collected in criminal proceedings may be used for purposes other than those occasioning their collection requires a nuanced answer. One must differentiate between data collected in the framework of other re-

---

[230] Regarding the minister's competency, see BGH NJW 1981, 1052.

[231] Meyer-Goßner/*Schmitt*, Section 96, para. 7.

[232] In principle, Section 96 StPO does not apply to police authorities when they act in pursuit of repressive objectives (see *Wohlers*, in: SK-StPO, Section 96, para. 9). In this respect, they are subject to the instructional powers of the public prosecution office to whom they are obliged to transmit records of all developing investigations, see. Section 163 Subsection 2 StPO. However, Section 163 Subsection 2 StPO only applies to records accumulating in the course of the investigation, and not to documents pursuant to Section 96 StPO already generally available which also concern preventive police work.

[233] BGH NStZ 2006, 402 (403).

[234] BGH NJW 1961, 1979 (1980); BGH StV 2012, 3 (4).

[235] BVerfG NStZ 2007, 274 (275).

[236] BGH NJW 1985, 1789 (1790). Thus the dictum that interests in maintaining secrecy work "in dubio" really amounts to nothing more than a confirmation of the (supposedly) self-evident. See also above a) for the three other forms of dealing with procedural errors during the collection of evidence.

pressive investigative measures and data collected in the course of measures outside of criminal proceedings (for the latter, see above I.A.4., as well as below b.).

a) Data from other criminal investigations

If the data were collected on the basis of repressive measures, it is crucial to distinguish between data pertaining to different offences in a *substantive* sense but belonging to the same offence in a *procedural* sense, and data pertaining to offences lacking a direct connection to the original proceeding.[237]

Only in the latter case one can speak of a transfer in the first place and must this transfer be based on a legal provision governing the rededication.[238] Pursuant to Section 474 Subsection 1 StPO, information from proceedings other than the original proceeding may in principle be used. This use is, however, subject to certain restrictions when the relevant data were obtained on the basis of a measure only admissible where specified criminal offences are suspected, Section 477 Subsection 2 StPO. Pursuant to this provision, data from other criminal proceedings may in principle only be used "for evidentiary purposes" without the consent of the person concerned if the measure could also have been ordered for the prosecution of the criminal offence at hand – applied to Section 100a StPO this means only concerning an offence pursuant to Section 100a Subsection 2 StPO and provided the remaining prerequisites for an order are fulfilled. The restrictive wording "for evidentiary purposes" in Section 477 Subsection 2 Sentence 2 StPO leads to the question whether chance discoveries may be used at least as investigative clues in other criminal proceedings without consent and without the prerequisites for an order being fulfilled.[239] The matter appears not yet to have been explicitly addressed by existing case law. But with regard to the comparable provision of Section 161 Subsection 2 Sentence 1 StPO, prevailing opinion considers such use admissible (see above A.I.4.a.). However, Sections 100d Subsection 5,[240] 100i Subsection 2 Sentence 2,[241] 101a Subsections 4, 5[242] and 108 Subsections 2, 3 StPO[243] remain unaf-

---

237 Note: Regarding the facts and circumstances constituting "an offence" ("an" as in *one* instead of multiple different offences), German jurisprudence works with two different concepts of "offence" depending on whether the substantive assessment of the offence(s) is concerned (offence in a substantive sense) or the assessment is made with regard to procedural issues (offence in a procedural sense). With a few exceptions, the two concepts usually coincide in their conclusions. For more, see Meyer-Goßner/*Schmitt*, Section 264, para. 6.

238 *Wittig*, Beck-OK StPO, Section 474, paras. 1, 3.

239 See KK/*Grieg*, Section 477, para. 3.

240 Regulates the use of personal data gathered with the help of acoustic surveillance of private premises.

241 Prohibits further use of personal data from technical investigation measures concerning mobile terminal devices.

fected pursuant to Section 477 Subsection 2 Sentence 4 StPO. They take precedence as *leges speciales* regarding chance discoveries.

b) Data from preventive police law-based investigations

When personal data are collected on the basis of preventive (police) investigations, the principle of purpose limitation generally prohibits a subsequent rededication. However, Section 161 Subsection 2 StPO allows the public prosecution office to use such data for evidentiary purposes if an empowerment for a corresponding (not necessarily identical) measure principally exists in the StPO and if such a measure could have been ordered under the circumstances of the case in question ("hypothetical surrogate measure"). This also applies to cases in which the use of collected data for purposes of criminal prosecution is already envisaged.[244]

V. Exchange of Intercepted Electronic Communication Data between Foreign Countries

A. Legal Basis for Mutual Legal Assistance

The exchange of intercepted electronic communication data between Germany and foreign countries is part of the scheme on mutual legal assistance in criminal matters (in the following: MLA). In German law, it is also called "other legal assistance" *(sonstige Rechtshilfe)*. Sometimes – in a narrower sense – the term "evidence gathering abroad" is used, too. According to Section 1 Subsection 3 of the Act on International Cooperation in Criminal Matters of 23 December 1982

---

[242] Subsection 4: Regulates the use of traffic data collected in the course of criminal proceedings.

Subsection 5: Regulates the use of traffic data collected in the course of police law investigations.

[243] Subsection 2: Objects relating to the termination of a pregnancy which are found at the premise of a physician are inadmissible as evidence in respect of a criminal offence pursuant to Section 218 StPO.

Subsection 3: Limited admissibility of further use of objects covered by the right to refuse to testify accorded to certain bearers of professional secrets.

[244] Take, e.g., Section 34c Subsection 4 No. 2 BayPAG, which, among others, refers to the collection of telecommunication data permitted under Section 34a BayPAG. Whether Section 34a BayPAG permits source telecommunication surveillance is, however, disputed. The difference to other statutory powers of intervention which do not explicitly deal with the encroachment on information systems is that in connection with the adoption of Section 34d BayPAG the Bavarian *Landtag* explicitly decided to keep the provision based on the premise that it grants the power to perform source telecommunication surveillance, see the amendment proposal BayLT Drs. 15/10345, p. 7, adopted in the resolution proposal BayLT Drs. 15/10948.

(*Gesetz über die international Rechtshilfe in Strafsachen*, IRG – in the following: AICCM), provisions of international treaties shall take precedence before the provisions of this law to the extent that they have become directly applicable national law. In order to become directly applicable, the treaties must be enacted in the form of federal law (Article 59 Subsection 2 of the Basic Law). Furthermore, the relevant treaty provision must be self-executing, that is, it must be clear and sufficiently determined, and it must impose duties or rights for state organs or individuals without the need for further implementation by a national law.

Section 1 Subsection 4 AICCM stipulates that this Act shall govern the support in criminal proceedings involving a Member State of the European Union. This means that the German law implementing Union law on judicial cooperation, such as Framework Decisions or Directives, is embedded in the AICCM. The relationship between the implementing law and international treaties/conventions is regulated in the different parts of the AICCM relating to the specific form of international cooperation in criminal matters. Regarding "other legal assistance," Section 91 Subsection 2 AICCM stipulates that the German law implementing Union law that regulates mutual assistance matters, such as the Directive on the European Investigation Order, takes precedence over the international agreements mentioned in Section 1 Subsection 3 AICCM, insofar as it contains exhaustive regulations. This means that the rules of international MLA conventions or treaties may remain applicable if they facilitate legal cooperation in criminal matters. However, the stipulation cannot be interpreted as being a general rule that MLA can be provided on the most efficient and most favorable legal basis ("principle of the most favorable MLA rule" – *Grundsatz der Meistbegünstigung*). If a MLA request is declared inadmissible in accordance with the rules implementing the Union law, it cannot be circumvented by resorting to "more MLA-friendly" treaty provisions.[245] Since, however, the Union law and the national German implementation law already contain provisions that strengthen and facilitate MLA to the greatest possible extent in comparison to previous MLA agreements, the question as to the applicable law regarding the relationship between Union law and treaties on international cooperation in criminal matters is more or less theoretical.

Since Directive 2014/41/EU regarding the European Investigation Order in criminal matters has not yet been implemented and is therefore not yet applicable in Germany, the current legal basis for cooperation regarding the interception and recording of telecommunications is currently governed above all by international conventions and treaties applicable to Germany. These international agreements are presented first. The presentation starts with international multilateral conventions (cf. 1.); some remarks have already been made in this part concerning the future legal basis as provided for by Union law. Then, bilateral agreements are explained,

245 *Wörner*, in: Ambos/König/Rackow (eds.), Rechtshilferecht in Strafsachen, HT 4, mn. 477 with further references.

in particular those that contain specific provisions on the interception of telecommunications (cf. 2.). Lastly (under 3.), the question is answered as to whether the interception of telecommunications is also possible with countries that are not part of a MLA treaty (so-called non-treaty-based MLA).

1. International (multilateral) cooperation

As far as multilateral international agreements on mutual legal assistance applicable to the interception of electronic communications are concerned, the conventions/treaties that Germany ratified and applies are listed in the following section. A distinction should be made in this context between a first layer and a second layer. The first layer concerns whether the international MLA conventions or treaties are generally applicable to any criminal offense (a) or whether they regulate cooperation for a specific crime (b); the second layer concerns the various "legal areas" that must be distinguished, that is, whether cooperation relates to contracting parties of the conventions/treaties established by the Council of Europe (European level), to Member States of the European Union (EU level), or to third countries (global and UN level).

a) Non-crime specific international MLA conventions

aa) European level (cooperation within the Council of Europe)

Germany ratified and applies the *European Convention on Mutual Assistance in Criminal Matters of 20 April 1959.*[246] It entered into force for Germany on 1 January 1977. According to the German understanding, the general clause of this Convention (Article 1) includes the obligation to provide legal assistance in case of a request on the interception of electronic communications. The reasoning behind this is that the 1959 Convention does not contain an exclusive listing of possible MLA measures.

The following declarations and reservations of Germany with regard to the 1959 Convention should be considered in the context of the interception of telecommunications:

- Regarding Article 5: "Search and seizure of property is permitted only if the conditions of Article 5, paragraph 1.a and c of the European Convention on Mutual Assistance in Criminal Matters have been met."
- Regarding Article 16: "Where the request for mutual assistance and the annexed documents are not in the German language they must be accompanied by trans-

[246] Since the 1959 Convention is a so-called "open" Convention, non-European parties can also be part of it. Therefore, cooperation on the basis of this Convention between Germany and – e.g. – Chile, Israel, and South Korea is also possible.

lations of the request and the supporting documents into the German language or into one of the official languages of the Council of Europe."

Furthermore, Germany ratified the *Additional Protocol to the European Convention on Mutual Assistance in Criminal Matters of 17 March 1978*, which entered into force for Germany on 6 June 1991. Germany made the following reservations and declarations with respect to the 1978 Additional Protocol:

- "Regarding Article 2 of the Additional Protocol, the Federal Republic of Germany, in accordance with Article 8(2)(a), reserves the right to make the execution of letters rogatory of any kind in proceedings concerning contraventions of regulations governing international transfer of capital and payments, dependent on the condition that the offence motivating the letters rogatory is punishable under German law as well, or would be so punishable after analogous conversion of the facts."
- "Regarding Article 2 of the Additional Protocol, the Federal Republic of Germany, in accordance with Article 8(2)(a), reserves the right to make the execution of letters rogatory for search or seizure of property in respect of other fiscal offences dependent on the condition that the offence motivating the letters rogatory is punishable under German law as well, or would be so punishable after analogous conversion of the facts."
- "Regarding Article 8 of the Additional Protocol, the Federal Republic of Germany proceeds on the understanding that under the scope of application of the Convention, as extended by the Additional Protocol, there is no obligation to render assistance in the event that the effort and expenses to be expected in executing the letters rogatory are disproportionate to the subject-matter and execution could thus prejudice essential German interests."

Germany also ratified the *Second Additional Protocol to the European Convention on Mutual Assistance in Criminal Matters of 8 November 2001*, which entered into force on 1 June 2015. The following reservations and declarations are worth noting:

- "In accordance with Article 26 (5) of the Second Additional Protocol, the Federal Republic of Germany declares that, within the framework of procedures for which it could have refused or limited the transmission or the use of personal data in accordance with the provisions of the Convention or one of its Protocols, personal data transmitted to another Party may not be used by the other Party for the purposes of Article 26 (1) unless with the previous consent of the Federal Republic of Germany."
- "In addition to [the above], the Federal Republic of Germany declares the following concerning the whole of Article 26 of the Second Additional Protocol: In applying this Article, it is the understanding of the Federal Republic of Germany that the Parties remain free, in consideration of the data protection interests of the persons concerned, to apply provisions that rule out the transmission of data to

another Party or that allow transmission only subject to certain conditions. The Federal Republic of Germany therefore reserves the right, as necessary, to make the exchange of personal data dependent on compliance with the data protection requirements of the domestic law of the Federal Republic of Germany in specific individual cases. To this extent, the Federal Republic of Germany also reserves the right to make, in individual cases, mutual legal assistance on the basis of the Convention and its Protocols dependent on its limitation to a specific use or a special purpose. In this context, the Federal Republic of Germany makes reference to its declaration in respect of Article 12 (2) of the Convention for the Protection of Individuals with regard to Automatic Processing of Personal Data of 28 January 1981. According to this declaration, it is the understanding of the Federal Republic of Germany that Article 12 (2) of the Convention referred to above allows the Parties the freedom to make provisions in their national data protection law which may in certain cases, in consideration of the data protection interests of the persons concerned, rule out the transmission of data."

- "Notwithstanding the above reservations and declarations, the Federal Republic of Germany declares in accordance with Article 33 (1) first and second sentences that it upholds all the reservations und declarations made in respect of the Convention and the Protocol [...]."
- "In accordance with Article 4 (8) (b), the Federal Republic of Germany declares that requests, except urgent requests, are to be addressed to the Federal Office of Justice."
- "In accordance with Article 4 (8) (d), the Federal Republic of Germany declares that requests by administrative authorities are always to be addressed to the Federal Office of Justice, that is, also in urgent cases."
- "In accordance with Article 6 of the Second Additional Protocol, the Federal Republic of Germany up-dates its declaration in respect of Article 24 of the Convention and defines what authorities it will, for the purpose of the Convention, deem judicial authorities. These are as follows:
  - *das Bundesministerium der Justiz und für Verbraucherschutz* (Federal Ministry of Justice and Consumer Protection), Berlin
  - *das Bundesamt für Justiz* (*Federal* Office of Justice), Bonn
  - *der Bundesgerichtshof* (Federal Court of Justice), Karlsruhe
  - *der Generalbundesanwalt beim Bundesgerichtshof* (Federal Prosecutor-General at the Federal Court of Justice), Karlsruhe
  - *das Justizministerium Baden-Württemberg* (Ministry of Justice of Land Baden-Württemberg), Stuttgart
  - *das Bayerische Staatsministerium der Justiz* (Bavarian Ministry of Justice), Munich
  - *die Senatsverwaltung für Justiz und Verbraucherschutz* (Senate Department for Justice and Consumer Protection), Berlin

- *das Ministerium der Justiz und für Europa und Verbraucherschutz des Landes Brandenburg* (Ministry of Justice and for Europe and Consumer Protection of Land Brandenburg), Potsdam
- *der Senator für Justiz und Verfassung* (Senator of Justice and Constitution), Bremen
- *die Behörde für Justiz und Gleichstellung der Freien und Hansestadt Hamburg* (Free and Hanseatic City of Hamburg Ministry of Justice and Equalities)
- *das Hessische Ministerium der Justiz* (Hessian Ministry of Justice), Wiesbaden
- *das Justizministerium Mecklenburg-Vorpommern* (Ministry of Justice of Mecklenburg-Western Pomerania), Schwerin
- *das Niedersächsische Justizministerium* (Ministry of Justice of Lower Saxony), Hannover
- *das Justizministerium des Landes Nordrhein-Westfalen* (Ministry of Justice of North Rhine-Westphalia), Düsseldorf
- *das Ministerium der Justiz und für Verbraucherschutz des Landes Rheinland-Pfalz* (Ministry of Justice and Consumer Protection of the State of Rhineland-Palatinate), Mainz
- *das Ministerium der Justiz des Saarlandes* (Ministry of Justice of Saarland), Saarbrücken
- *das Sächsische Staatsministerium der Justiz* (Saxon State Ministry of Justice), Dresden
- *das Ministerium für Justiz und Gleichstellung des Landes Sachsen-Anhalt* (Ministry of Justice and Gender Equality, Saxony-Anhalt), Magdeburg
- *das Ministerium für Justiz, Kultur und Europa des Landes Schleswig-Holstein* (Ministry of Justice, Cultural and European Affairs Schleswig-Holstein), Kiel
- *Thüringer Ministerium für Justiz* (Thuringian Ministry of Justice), Erfurt
- *die Oberlandesgerichte* (the higher regional courts)
- *die Landgerichte* (the regional courts)
- *die Amtsgerichte* (the local courts)
- *die Generalstaatsanwaltschaften/die Staatsanwaltschaften bei den Oberlandesgerichten* (offices of the public prosecutors general)
- *die Staatsanwaltschaften/Staatsanwaltschaften bei den Landgerichten* (public prosecution offices)
- *die Zentrale Stelle der Landesjustizverwaltungen zur Aufklärung nationalsozialistischer Verbrechen* (Central Office of the Land Judicial Authorities for the Investigation of National Socialist Crimes), Ludwigsburg."

bb) EU level

Germany ratified the *Convention of 29 May 2000 on Mutual Assistance in Criminal Matters between the Member States of the European Union* (in the following MLA Convention EU) as well as its additional *Protocol to the Convention of 16 October 2001 on Mutual Assistance in Criminal Matters between the Member States of the European Union* (in the following: MLA Protocol EU). Both MLA Convention EU and MLA Protocol EU entered into force for Germany on 2 February 2006.[247] In relation to the specific rules on the interception of telecommunications, the Federal Republic of Germany declared with reference to Article 24(1)(e) of the MLA Convention EU "that the competent contact point in accordance with Article 20(4)(d) is the following: Bundeskriminalamt 65173 Wiesbaden Phone: 0049 (0) 611-55-13101 Fax: 0049 (0) 611-55-12141 e-Mail: mail@bka.bund.de."

Germany did not make declarations concerning the MLA Protocol EU.

It should be noted at this point that, in the future, mutual legal assistance with EU countries will be regulated by the German law implementing the *Directive 2014/41/EU regarding the European Investigation Order in criminal matters* (see also above and C. below). In July 2016, the Federal Government *(Bundesregierung)* agreed on a bill.[248] It will be discussed in the two chambers of the German Parliament. It is expected that the law can be passed before the parliamentary elections in 2017. It should further be noted here that Germany did not implement Framework Decision 2008/978/JHA on the European evidence warrant since, according to the German opinion, its regulations were overtaken by the negotiations on the Directive regarding the European Investigation Order that started in 2010.

cc) Global level

There is currently no general worldwide international convention on mutual legal assistance in criminal matters. Cooperation with non-European countries[249] not relating to a specific area of crime (cf. b.) is either based on bilateral treaties (in particular with the United States[250] and Canada[251]) or on the national German law

---

[247] Cf. https://www.ejn-crimjust.europa.eu/ejn/EJN_Library_RatificationsByCou.aspx and http://www.consilium.europa.eu/en/documents-publications/agreements-conventions/agreement/?aid=2001090

[248] Cf. https://www.bmjv.de/SharedDocs/Gesetzgebungsverfahren/DE/InternationaleRechtshilfeStrafsachen.html

[249] Except countries that ratified the European Convention on Mutual Legal Assistance of 1959 and/or its Protocols (cf. above).

[250] Cf. in particular Article 12 No. 1 of the Treaty of 14 October 2003 between the Federal Republic of Germany and the United States of America on Mutual Legal Assistance in Criminal Matters (MLA Treaty Germany-USA), according to which "[e]ach Party may at the request of the other Party, within its possibilities and under the conditions prescribed by its domestic law, take the necessary steps for the surveillance of telecommunications."

on international cooperation in criminal matters (non-treaty-based MLA – cf. 3. below).

b) Conventions regulating cooperation for a specific area of crime

Regarding the relevant international conventions that contain obligations on MLA for a specific area of crime, the following should be noted:

aa) Global level

On the global level, Germany ratified the *United Nations Convention against Transnational Organized Crime of 15 November 2000.* It entered into force for Germany on 14 June 2006. On the same date, the two additional protocols entered into force for Germany: (i) *The Protocol to Prevent, Suppress and Punish Trafficking in Persons, Especially Women and Children, supplementing the United Nations Convention against Transnational Organized Crime and the Protocol against the Smuggling of Migrants by Land, Sea and Air, supplementing the United Nations Convention against Transnational Organized Crime.* Germany has not yet ratified the Protocol against the Illicit Manufacturing of and Trafficking in Firearms, Their Parts and Components and Ammunition, supplementing the United Nations Convention against Transnational Organized Crime.[252]

bb) European level

Regarding the regional, European level, emphasis is placed on the ratification of the *Convention on Cybercrime of the Council of Europe* of 23 November 2001. It entered into force for Germany on 1 July 2009. Germany also ratified the Additional Protocol to the Convention on Cybercrime, concerning the criminalisation of acts of a racist and xenophobic nature committed through computer systems of 28 January 2003. It entered into force for Germany on 1 October 2011.

---

[251] Cf. Treaty of 13 May 2002 between Canada and the Federal Republic of Germany on Mutual Assistance in Criminal Matters (MLA Treaty Germany-Canada). The Treaty does not contain a specific provision on the surveillance of telecommunications. However, Article 1 para. 5 lit. h) contains a general clause according to which assistance shall include "other assistance consistent with the objects of this Treaty, which is not inconsistent with the law of the Requested State." This clause includes the possibility – provided that the further requirements of the Treaty, in particular the double criminality requirement, are met – to execute requests on the interception of telecommunications (see BT-Drs.. 15/2598, p. 18).

[252] For the status of ratification of the Convention and its protocols, consult the following website: https://www.unodc.org/unodc/en/treaties/CTOC/signatures.html

2. Bilateral treaties

As regards the "European level," Germany concluded bilateral treaties on MLA that supplement the 1959 European Convention on Mutual Assistance in Criminal Matters. These treaties aim at further developing the founding European Convention and thus facilitating and strengthening MLA with the corresponding countries. Such bilateral treaties were concluded with Austria (1972), France (1974), Israel (1977), Italy (1979), The Netherlands (1979), Switzerland (1969), the Czech Republic, and Poland. However, only the "more recent" bilateral supplementary treaties with the Czech Republic (2000) and Poland (2003) contain specific provisions on the interception of electronic communications.

The relevant provision in the *treaty with the Czech Republic (Article 17)* – entitled "interception of telecommunication" – reads as follows:[253]

> (1) The [European] Convention [on Mutual Assistance in Criminal Matters of 1959] and this [bilateral] treaty also apply to requests concerning the ordering of measures of interception of telecommunications.
>
> (2) Requests pursuant to Subsection 1 are only executed if:
>
> 1. an interception order or warrant is submitted by the competent court of the requesting contracting party, or it emanates from a declaration by such court that the requirements of the interception would be met if such measure were carried out on the territory of the requesting party;
> 2. the interception could also lawfully be ordered in accordance with the law of the requested party if the offence to which the request relates were to be prosecuted there;
> 3. the subject of the interception or telecommunications device that is to be intercepted and from which the identifier of the subject of interception is used is:
>   a) present in the territory of the requested state,
>   b) present in the territory of the requesting state and the requesting state needs the technical assistance of the requested state to intercept the communication, or
>   c) present in the territory of a third state and the requesting state needs the technical assistance of the requested state to intercept the communication, provided that the third state consented to the interception;
>
> (3) If the requested party claims reimbursement of the costs incurred through the interception of the telecommunications pursuant to Art. 13 Subsection 2 sentences 1 and 2 of this treaty, the interception may be terminated if the requesting party refuses to bear the costs or does not undertake to refund said costs within a time period specified by the requested party;
>
> (4) Personal data that were gained by a measure pursuant to Subsection 1 may only be used for other criminal proceedings with prior consent of the requested party. The requested party shall give its consent if the measure could also have been ordered in relation to the offence to which the criminal proceeding relates. The records must be destroyed once they are no longer needed for criminal proceedings. If the law of the requested state provides for a notification of the person concerned about the measure, the requesting party informs the requested party if the notification can be made without jeopardizing the purpose of the investigation or other important interests.

---

[253] Translation by the author. No official translation in English is currently available.

(5) Paragraphs 1, 2 (no. 1 and 2), and 4 shall apply *mutatis mutandis* to requests on the handing over of records that derive from measures on the interception of telecommunications relating to criminal investigations or proceedings on the territory of the requested state.

The provision of the bilateral treaty with the Czech Republic served as a model for the corresponding provision in the bilateral treaty with Poland (Article 16). However, the wording of this provision is slightly different in some respects. The differences are as follows:

- Article 16 of the bilateral treaty with Poland not only mentions "interception" *(Überwachung)* of telecommunication but also "recording" *(Aufzeichnung)* of telecommunication.
- The treaty with Poland does not contain the possibility for a court to submit a declaration as a replacement for the order of or warrant for an interception of telecommunications.[254]
- The provision on the notification of the person concerned by the measures stipulates that the requesting party inform the requested party when the notification can be made without "jeopardising important interests" and thus does not refer additionally to "jeopardising the purpose of investigation."[255]

The question arises as to whether the provisions on the interception of telecommunications in the bilateral treaty supplementing the 1959 MLA Convention remain applicable alongside the 2000 MLA Convention EU (particularly in view of its Article 18), to which the parties of the bilateral treaty also belong. The opinion in Germany is that, if the bilateral treaty enables MLA in a more efficient and favorable way than the 2000 MLA Convention EU, the bilateral treaty remains applicable.[256]

3. National regulation

The execution of requests relating to the interception/surveillance/recording of telecommunications that stem from countries with which Germany has no treaty-based relations is possible. In this case, the Act on International Cooperation in Criminal Matters (AICCM – *Internationales Rechtshilfegesetz*, IRG) applies. Although the AICCM does not contain specific provisions on the interception or surveillance of telecommunications, the execution of a respective request can be based on the general clause of Section 59 AICCM. It reads as follows:

(1) At the request of a competent authority of a foreign State, other legal assistance in a criminal matter may be provided.

---

254 Cf. Article 17 Subsection 2 No. 1 of the bilateral treaty with the Czech Republic.

255 Cf. Article 16 Subsection 6 of the bilateral treaty with Poland vs. Article 17 Subsection 4 sentence 4 of the bilateral treaty with the Czech Republic.

256 *Hackner/Schierholt*, Internationale Rechtshilfe in Strafsachen, mn. 215.

(2) Legal assistance within the meaning of subsection (1) above shall be any kind of support given for foreign criminal proceedings regardless of whether the foreign proceedings are conducted by a court or by an executive authority and whether the legal assistance is to be provided by a court or by an executive authority.

(3) Legal assistance may be provided only in those cases in which German courts and executive authorities could render mutual legal assistance to each other.

In the concrete case of a request from a foreign country that seeks the interception of telecommunications, the requirements of the respective provisions of the German Criminal Procedure Code (in the following: GCPC) must be met (Section 77 AICCM in connection with Sections 100a, 100b, 100g, 101 GCPC).

An important national regulation concerning the interception of telecommunications is contained in No. 77a of the Guidelines on Relations with Foreign Countries in Criminal Law Matters (*Richtlinien für den Verkehr mit dem Ausland in strafrechtlichen Angelegenheiten* – in the following: RiVASt).[257] The Guidelines were established by the Federal Government with the consent of the governments of the *Länder*. They are addressed to the courts, the prosecution services, and other executive authorities that deal with international cooperation in criminal matters and must be observed by them. Only if the judiciary takes decisions in its capacity as independent judges are the Guidelines not binding for them.[258]

No. 77a Subsection 1 RiVASt first confirms that the execution of requests on the interception of telecommunications in Germany is possible on the basis of both an international treaty/convention/agreement or on the basis of Section 59 Subsection 1 AICCM (non-treaty-based cooperation). Furthermore, No. 77a RiVASt confirms that the interception of the content of telecommunications is admissible only if it complies with the provisions of Sections 100a, 100b, 101 GCPC.

On the other hand, No. 77a contains important indications on the necessary assurances that must be provided for by the foreign country. It stipulates that – if not stated otherwise in an international agreement or if conditions as set in the context of handing over the records are not sufficient – the foreign authority must assure that

a) The requirements of the interception would be met, if such measure were carried out on the territory of the requesting state,

b) The obtained data are only used for the investigation and prosecution of the offense(s) to which the request relates to,

c) The recordings of the interception are destroyed when they are no longer needed for the criminal prosecution.

---

[257] The most recent version dates from 19 December 2012. The RiVASt is available (in German only) via the following link: http://www.bmjv.de/SiteGlobals/Forms/Suche/RiVaStsuche_Formular.html?nn=6428404&templateQueryString=Suchbegriff.

[258] No. 1 RiVASt.

In addition, No. 77a RiVASt deals with the issue of notification. The foreign authority must be informed that the German public prosecution office has to notify the participants in the telecommunication under surveillance of the surveillance measure pursuant to Section 101 GCPC if the surveillance measure is terminated and a notification is possible without jeopardizing the purpose of investigation, public security, or a person's life and limb. If the requesting state does not react within a specific time period (as set by the German authorities) or does not provide material facts that justify not making a notification, Germany assumes that the notification can be carried out.

No. 77a Subsection 2 RiVASt acknowledges that, under the conditions of Section 59 AICCM, German authorities can also provide a summary of the findings of a telecommunication interception, carried out for the purposes of a German criminal investigation, if this information is requested by the foreign state for the same offense or an offense that is listed in Section 100a GCPC (Sections 77 AICCM, 100b Subsection 5 GCPC). Under the same conditions, copies of surveillance protocols, comprehensive notes on the content of the conversation, or recording tapes can be handed over.

No. 77a Subsection 3 RiVASt acknowledges that mutual legal assistance to a foreign authority can also be provided for information on telecommunication connections (Section 100g GCPC) if the requirements of Section 66 AICCM are met.[259] Regarding the obligation of the German authorities to notify pursuant to Section 101 GCPC, the aforementioned rules apply *mutatis mutandis*.

No. 77a Subsection 4 contains procedural rules if a German authority is contacted within the framework of Article 20 Subsections 2 and 3 of the 2000 MLA Convention EU (interception of telecommunications without the need for technical assistance of another Member States).

---

259 Section 66 AICCM deals with the handing over of objects. In particular, the requirements of Section 66 Subsection 2 AICCM must be given. Accordingly, surrender shall not be admissible unless

1. the offence on which the request is based contains elements of the *actus reus* and *mens rea* of a criminal offence or of an offence permitting the imposition of a fine under German law or unless mutatis mutandis it would be such an offence under German law,

2. an order for seizure by a competent authority of the requesting State is submitted or a declaration of such an authority shows that the requirements for seizure would exist if the objects were located in the requesting State and

3. measures are in place to ensure that the rights of third parties will not be infringed and that objects handed over under a condition will be returned upon request without undue delay.

B. Requirements and Procedure (Including the Handling of Privileged Information)

1. Incoming requests

a) Regular procedure

As regards incoming requests, it is first worth mentioning that Germany distinguishes between two procedures that are fundamental to German mutual legal assistance law and are particularly relevant for the area of "other assistance." The first procedure concerns the question of whether the assistance requested can be provided to the foreign state or requested from it, that is, *whether* the conditions for mutual legal assistance are fulfilled and the request can be granted (procedure of approval – *Bewilligungsverfahren*). These conditions are mainly stipulated in the applicable international conventions and/or in the AICCM, respectively.

The second procedure deals with the question of the conditions and (coercive) measures that must be applied in order to enforce the request in domestic territory (enforcement procedure – *Vornahmeverfahren*). In this context, Article 59 Subsection 3 of the AICCM provides that legal assistance may be provided only under circumstances under which German courts and governmental authorities could render legal assistance to each other (cf. above). The question of *how* a request must be carried out is mainly a question of German procedural criminal law.[260] The procedure of granting a request is principally carried out prior to the procedure of enforcing the request. Both procedures are interconnected insofar as the request is not enforced if assistance cannot be provided, or assistance is not provided if the requested measure is not possible or illegal under German national law.[261]

Corresponding to the distinction between these two procedures, different authorities may also be involved in managing the request. Let us first look at the authorities who decide *whether* assistance can be provided. As a general rule, it is the Federation *(Bund)* which has jurisdiction over international legal assistance in criminal matters. In principle, the Federal Minister of Justice *(Bundesminister der Justiz)*, in consent with the Federal Foreign Office *(Auswärtiges Amt)*, decides on foreign requests and requests addressed to foreign states (Article 74 Subsection 1 AICCM). In 2007, the competence of the Federal Ministry of Justice was transferred to the Federal Office of Justice *(Bundesamt für Justiz)*, a subordinate authority of the

[260] For the distinction, see *Lagodny*, in: Schomburg/Lagodny/Hackner/Gleß, Internationale Rechtshilfe in Strafsachen, 5th ed., vor § 59, mn. 6 *et al.*

[261] *Ahlbrecht*, in: Ahlbrecht/Böhm/Esser/Hugger/Kirsch/Rosenthal, Internationales Strafrecht in der Praxis, mn. 1006.

Ministry, located in Bonn, and responsible, *inter alia*, for dealing with international cooperation in criminal matters on the federal level.[262]

However, the federation delegated its competences to the governments of the federal states *(Länder)* by the Agreement of Competences of 28 April 2004 *(Zuständigkeitsvereinbarung 2004)*.[263] The federal states in turn further transferred the competences by individual decrees, which vary from federal state to federal state. As a general rule, the (heads of the) prosecutors' offices at the Regional Courts *(Staatsanwalttschaften bei den Landgerichten)* are competent to decide on whether a request from an EU Member State can be granted. Some decrees of federal states stipulate that the competence of the prosecutors' offices is given only if an international agreement allows for the direct transmission of MLA requests. This is the case when the MLA Convention EU applies (cf. Article 6 Subsection 1).[264] The bilateral treaties with the Czech Republic and Poland, for instance, also foresee the direct transmission of MLA requests.

It is of note that the delegation to the prosecutors' offices does not mean that the federation loses its competence. The federal government (Federal Minister of Justice and Federal Office of Justice, respectively) remains legally responsible for issuing and executing requests for international legal assistance. It remains the "master" of the granting procedure and always has the possibility to appropriate a case. The judicial authorities of the federal states do not replace the competences of the federal government but act in its stead.

In general, it is important to note that international legal assistance, even if it is based on the EU instruments implementing the principle of mutual recognition in criminal matters (such as Directive EIO), is seen as a matter of foreign relations, which, according to constitutional law, lies within the competence of the Federation. The principal competence of the federal authorities is accompanied by certain reporting duties. If the request has "political, de facto, or legal importance" the federal state must act "in accordance with" the federal government (i.e., Federal Office of Justice).[265] Accordingly, the Guidelines on Relations with Foreign Countries in

---

262 Section 2 Subsection 2 No. 3 of the Act establishing the Federal Office of Justice (*Gesetz über die Errichtung des Bundesamts für Justiz*) in connection with the Decree of the Federal Ministry of Justice *(Erlass des Bundesministeriums der Justiz)* of 2 January 2007 – II B 6 – BfJ –, both published by *Schomburg/Lagodny/Hackner/Gleß*, Internationale Rechtshilfe in Strafsachen, Annex 7.

263 Published by *Schomburg/Lagodny/Hackner/Gleß*, Internationale Rechtshilfe in Strafsachen, Annex 8.

264 Germany did not make a declaration that a central authority would be competent to receive certain MLA requests (no declaration in this respect in accordance with Article 25 MLA Convention EU).

265 No. 8 of the Agreement of Competences of 28 April 2004. In such important cases, the Federal Office of Justice itself will regularly inform the Federal Minstry of Justice. It may also enquire a statement by the Federal Ministry of Justice in order to receive guidance.

Criminal Law Matters (RiVASt) and the individual decrees of the *Länder* foresee a corresponding reporting duty of the competent prosecutor's office in these cases.[266] It is further stipulated by the 2004 Agreement of Competences that the granting authority "take into account the concerns of the federal government" in the above-mentioned significant cases.

The granting authority examines the request as to whether there is an obligation to render MLA to the foreign (requesting) state, that is, whether the requirements of an international MLA agreement are met. If the answer is in the affirmative, the second stage of the procedure, the enforcement procedure, starts.

The authority which *enforces* the request ("how" of providing MLA) is the authority that would enforce the measure in purely domestic cases.[267] In a conventional criminal prosecution case of interception of telecommunications, the prosecutors' offices at the Regional Courts *(Staatsanwaltschaften bei den Landgerichten)* are competent to prepare the enforcement of the request.[268] As a result, the authority that normally grants the request and executes it by means of national law is identical (prosecutors' offices at the Regional Courts). The prosecutor must apply for an interception/surveillance order before the investigative judge at the local court *(Ermittlungsrichter beim Amtsgericht).*[269]

One of the particularities of the German procedure is that the investigative judge is not only obliged to examine whether the requested coercive measure complies with national German criminal procedure ("how" – enforcement procedure) but also whether the requirements for rendering MLA are met. That means the judge also examines *whether* the MLA request is admissible under the conditions of the international treaty, for example, whether the formal criteria as stipulated by the treaty are met or whether grounds for refusal (double criminality, proportionality, *ordre public*, etc.) are given, so that international assistance can be rendered or

---

266 Cf. No. 13 RiVASt.

267 *Lagodny*, in: Schomburg/Lagodny/Hackner/Gleß, Internationale Rechtshilfe in Strafsachen, vor § 59, mn. 14.

268 I.e., if a not very serious crime (such as offences against the security of the state, terrorism, or crimes against international law) is at issue, which – pursuant to Section 120 of the Courts Consititution Act (*Gerichtsverfassungsgesetz*, GVG) – establishes the special competence of the Federal Prosecutor General *(Generalbundesanwalt)* or of the public prosecution office at the Higher Regional Court (*Staatsanwaltschaften bei den Oberlandesgerichten*, also called *Generalstaatsanwaltschaften*). Whether the Federal Prosecutor General or the public prosecution office at the Higher Regional Court is responsible is subject to rather complicated rules. As a rule, the Federal Prosecutor General accroaches competence when a criminal act as listed in Section 120 Courts Constitution Act is deemed to be of special significance.

269 Section 162 GCPC. In case of responsibility on the part of the Federal Prosecutor General, the competent judge is the investigative judge at the Federal Court of Justice *(Ermittlungsrichter beim Bundesgerichtshof)*. If the crime at issue falls within the responsibility of the public prosecution office at the Higher Regional Court, the investigative judge at the Higher Regional Court is competent to decide on an interception order.

not.[270] If the investigative judge at the local court considers the requirements for providing legal assistance not met, he/she must give reasons for his/her opinion and request a ruling by the Higher Regional Court *(Oberlandesgericht)*.[271]

The Higher Regional Court is also competent after an application by public prosecution service at the Higher Regional Court *(Generalstaatsanwaltschaft)*.[272] The Higher Regional Court decides on the admissibility of the request, that is, whether legal assistance can be rendered. This corresponds to the German system that all questions relating to the admissibility of MLA are concentrated at the Higher Regional Court.

In sum, one can say that the Higher Regional Court decides on the admissibility of a MLA request by way of a preliminary ruling if (and only if) the investigative judge or the public prosecution service at the Higher Regional Court has doubts on the requirements of whether MLA can be rendered in accordance with the international agreements. The judgment of the Higher Regional Court regarding the admissibility of the MLA request is binding for the investigative judge at the local court and the enforcing authority.

The investigative judge at the local court, by contrast, always maintains its jurisdiction when it comes to the enforcement of the measure, which has to be assessed by German criminal procedural law.[273]

The prosecution service at the Regional Court *(Staatsanwaltschaften)*, which is primarily responsible for the incoming MLA request, has no right to apply for a preliminary ruling at the Higher Regional Court. However, it can recommend a respective application with its superior judicial authority, the prosecution service at the Higher Regional Court *(Generalstaatsanwaltschaft)*.

The Higher Regional Court itself can apply for a preliminary ruling on legal issues by the Federal Court of Justice *(Bundesgerichtshof)*. The Higher Regional Court shall request the decision of the Federal Court of Justice concerning a legal issue by means of a reasoned decision, if it deems a ruling by the Federal Court of Justice necessary for the clarification of a legal issue of fundamental significance or if it wishes to deviate from a decision of the Federal Court of Justice or from a decision taken after the coming into force of the AICCM by another Higher Regional Court concerning a legal issue (Section 61 Subsection 1 in connection with Section 42 Subsection 1 AICCM). Also the Federal Prosecutor General or the public

---

270 In case of non-treaty-based cooperation, the requirement of the AICCM must be fulfilled. However, it does not differ substantially from the international MLA agreements that Germany applies (cf. also No. 77a RiVASt for the specific case of interception of telecommunications).

271 Article 61 Subsection 1 sentence 1 AICCM.

272 Article 61 Subsection 1 sentence 2 AICCM.

273 Cf. *Lagodny*, in: Schomburg/Lagodny/Hackner/Gleß, Internationale Rechtshilfe in Strafsachen, vor § 59, mn. 45 et al. and § 61 IRG, mn. 2.

prosecution service at the Higher Regional Court can also make such a request to the Federal Court of Justice for the clarification of a legal issue.[274] Neither the investigating judge nor the public prosecution service at the Regional Court or the person concerned have rights to make such a request.

b) The rights of the individual for judicial review

The German law does not explicitly regulate how and to what extent an individual can proceed against any decisions to provide and to order MLA for the interception of telecommunications.[275] In other words, it has not been clarified which remedy applies in the two different stages of the MLA procedure (stage of the admissibility of the MLA request and stage of enforcement – cf. supra). In case of "open" coercive measures, such as search and seizure or the hearing of witnesses, the Federal Constitutional Court *(Bundesverfassungsgericht)* established the rule that the person concerned can seek legal remedies against the decision to order the investigative measure, that is, to enforce the MLA (enforcement procedure). As part of this remedy, the person concerned can also claim that the competent court assesses the admissibility of the MLA request, that is, whether the request complies with the requirements of the international treaty or, in case of non-treaty-based MLA, with the national MLA regulations (cf. A.1.–3. supra).[276] Thus, the remedy against the admissibility of the MLA request is integrated into the remedy against the ordering of the coercive measure, which follows the regular rules of the GCPC (so-called *Integrationslösung*).[277]

These rules must also apply accordingly in cases of the use of modern investigation techniques that are typically covert coercive measures, such as the interception of telecommunications. In these cases, the person concerned can regularly only seek subsequent legal protection *(nachträglicher Rechtsschutz)*, that is, he/she can apply for a legal review of the lawfulness as well as the manner and means of implementation of the interception of telecommunications[278] after the measure was granted, ordered, and enforced. In this context, the above-mentioned notification of the person concerned (cf. A.3.) is important to secure his/her rights of judicial review. The person concerned can proceed against the decision ordering the interception of telecommunications within two weeks after notification of the interception measure against him/her (Section 77 AICCM in connection with Section 101 Sub-

---

[274] Section 61 Subsection 1 in connection with Section 42 Subsection 2 AICCM.

[275] Section 61 AICCM only regulates the case of an application by a person claiming that his/her rights would be infringed if the return of an asset were ordered. This rule is not applied *mutatis mutandis* to other investigative/coercive measures at issue for rendering MLA.

[276] BVerfG, EzSt IRG § 61 Nr. 2; BVerfG, decision of 24 June 1997 – 2 BvR 1581/95.

[277] Cf. OLG Dresden, NStZ-RR 2011, 146.

[278] Section 101 Subsection 7 GCPC.

section 7 sentence 2 GCPC). In conventional cases,[279] the competent court for this judicial review is the investigative judge at the local court where the competent prosecution service is located (Section 77 AICCM in connection with Section 101 Subsection 7 sentence 1, 162 Subsection 1 sentence 1 GCPC).

The person concerned has no direct access to the Higher Regional Court in order to apply for a review of the admissibility of the MLA request. He/she is only able to ask the judge at the local court to apply for preliminary ruling at the Higher Regional Court as described above. If the Higher Regional Court takes a decision in the preliminary ruling procedure, its decision is final. There are no further ordinary remedies, such as a remedy to the Federal Court of Justice. However, the person concerned may file – as an extraordinary remedy – a constitutional complaint before the Federal Constitutional Court. In this case, the person concerned must substantiate that one of his/her fundamental rights as enshrined in the Basic Law was infringed by the decision of the Higher Regional Court or that the law on which the decision is based is unconstitutional.

2. Outgoing requests

In case of outgoing requests, two stages of the procedure must also principally be distinguished: In the first stage, it is the question of whether a MLA request for the interception of telecommunications should be issued to the foreign authorities. In the second stage, it is the question of whether the MLA request can be approved (procedure of approval – *Bewilligungsverfahren*).

In the first stage, the competent public prosecution service that investigates a criminal case decides whether an interception of telecommunications abroad is necessary in order to gather sufficient evidence.[280] The police or other law enforcement authorities may encourage the public prosecution service to file a MLA request, but cannot issue it themselves.

The competent public prosecutor can only issue a MLA request if the requirement(s) of the respective measure are fulfilled if it were to be enforced on German territory. Therefore, the competent public prosecutor must examine whether the lawfulness and appropriateness of the interception of telecommunications comply with the rules of the GCPC. In terms of substance, it is particularly necessary that (1) certain facts give rise to the suspicion that a person has committed a serious criminal offence referred to in subsection 2 of Section 100a GCPC; and (2) the offence is one of particular gravity in the individual case as well; and (3) other means

[279] Cf. supra V.B.1.b.

[280] It is commonly the public prosecution service at the Regional Courts. Within its competence, the general prosecutor (public prosecutor at the Higher Regional Court) or the Federal Prosecutor General may also be the responsible prosecution service (cf. footnote 268).

of establishing the facts or determining the accused's whereabouts would be much more difficult or offer no prospect of success. In formal terms, the public prosecution service must apply for an order to intercept telecommunications at the competent court.[281] The order of the court has no enforcement effects for the foreign authority, but corresponds to the relevant formal requirements in the international MLA treaties, such as Article 18 Subsection 3 lit. b) MLA Convention EU or Article 17 Subsection 2 No. 1 of the bilateral supplementary MLA Treaty between Germany and the Czech Republic (cf. supra).

The public prosecution service also prepares the MLA request. In particular, it must take into account all the formal requirements as stipulated in the applicable international agreement (e.g., Article 18 paras. 2 and 4 MLA Convention EU). The RiVASt contains general guidelines for the issuance of MLA requests to foreign countries (Nos. 25 et seq.).

At the beginning of the second stage of the procedure, the public prosecution service submits the drafted MLA request to the competent authority for approval. The authority responsible for approving the MLA request results from Section 74 AICCM in connection with the various decrees of the federal states (cf. supra). As a rule, the federal states delegated the competence for approving MLA requests addressed to EU Member States to the heads of the respective public prosecution service (commonly the chief public prosecutors).[282] Within the framework of the approval procedure, the competent authority (head of the public prosecution service) examines anew the lawfulness of the measure in accordance with the national law (code of criminal procedure) as well as the fulfillment of the requirements of the international MLA agreement that exists with the requested state at issue.

The approved/granted MLA request is transmitted to the competent foreign authorities via the foreseen channels (as stipulated in the international agreements, such as Article 6 MLA Convention EU).

The person concerned may proceed against the decision of the competent investigating public prosecution service to issue a MLA request after notification of the interception measure (Section 101 Subsection 7 sentence 2 GCPC). It has not yet been clarified whether the person concerned may also contest the decision of ap-

[281] Section 100b Subsection 1 GCPC. In a conventional case, it is the investigative judge at the local court. In cases involving the competence of the Federal Prosecutor General, the investigative judge at the Federal Court of Justice is responsible; in cases involving the competence of the general prosecutor at the Higher Regional Court, it is the investigative judge at the Higher Regional Court. In exigent circumstances, the public prosecution office may also issue an order. However, such an order must be confirmed by the court within three working days (Section 100b Subsection 2, sentences 2 and 3 GCPC).

[282] In case of the competence of the Federal Prosecutor General to investigate a criminal case, the authority responsible for approving the request is the Federal Office of Justice *(Bundesamt für Justiz)* according to Section 74 Subsection 1 AICCM in connection with No. 1 of the decree of the Federal Ministry of Justice of 2 January 2007 – II B 6 – BfJ –.

proval and claim that the admissibility of the outgoing MLA request was not given. The majority of legal scholars negate that the decision of approval is subject to judicial review.[283] However, this question is rather theoretical. In legal practice, the question instead is whether the information collected by means of an interception of telecommunications abroad can be used as evidence in criminal proceedings against the defendant in Germany. This question is further explored in the following section.

3. Technical regulations of "customary" interception of telecommunications

German criminal procedure law contains several restrictions and prohibitions when it comes to the taking of evidence in the form of an interception of telecommunications. These restrictions and prohibitions serve to safeguard the civil liberties of suspects and/or uninvolved persons. The question arises as to whether these restrictions/prohibitions must also be observed in transnational cases. The following part deals with the "customary" interception of telecommunications by which German authorities wiretap someone and transmit the records to a foreign country afterwards. In these cases, the German authorities may examine the records before transmission to the foreign authority. Part 4 examines possible specifics in cases of real-time transmission of intercepted data to a foreign country. In each case, a distinction is made between incoming and outgoing MLA requests for the surveillance of telecommunications.

a) Incoming requests

The German law does not contain an explicit rule that regulates the observance of the restrictions and prohibitions of the taking of evidence within the framework of MLA. Specific, settled case law does not exist either. Therefore, one must resort to the general rules. In this context, one should take note of Section 59 Subsection 3 AICCM:

> Legal assistance may be provided only in those cases in which German courts and executive authorities could render mutual legal assistance to each other.

This provision formulates a general rule that the requested MLA measure can only be implemented if it complies with German national law. It means that rendering mutual legal assistance in criminal matters cannot be further than is lawfully possible in purely national cases. In other words: the national rules that apply to the enforcement of the MLA measure also set the legal boundaries for MLA to foreign countries.

---

283 *Schomburg/Hackner*, in: Schomburg/Lagodny/Gleß/Hackner, Internationale Rechtshilfe in Strafsachen, Vor § 68 IRG, mn. 97.

The Federal Constitutional Court *(Bundesverfassungsgericht)* has established case law regarding the legal requirements for carrying out covert surveillance measures for purely national cases only. In a recent decision of 20 April 2016, which consolidated the established case law so far, the Federal Constitutional Court emphasised again that investigative powers, which lead to interference with the strictly protected core area of private life (including the interception of telecommunications), must be accompanied by particular protective rules.[284] These protective rules must be considered on two levels. First, at the level of data collection, precautionary measures must be established in order to exclude, as far as possible, the unintended acquisition of information on the core area of private life.[285] Second, at the level of the use of the data, it must be ensured that any unavoidably collected information relating to the core area of private life must be filtered out before use of the data.[286] This seems to back the viewpoint of legal scholars who deduce from Section 59 Subsection 3 that German rules restricting or prohibiting the taking of evidence *(Beweisverbote)* also block the transmission of the evidentiary result to a foreign state, at any rate if these rules implement constitutional safeguards of fundamental rights and civil liberties.[287] If a German authority is not entitled to use certain items of information for its own purposes, it is not even entitled to forward this information to other third parties in Germany, as a result of which it is not even possible to transfer information to foreign authorities.

Based on these statements, Germany would have filtering obligations if it comes to the transmission of "privileged information." In detail, this would mean:

i) The interception of telecommunications as a MLA measure for the foreign country must be denied, if there are factual indications for assuming that solely *(sic)* information concerning the core area of the private conduct of life would be acquired (Section 100a Subsection 4 sentence 1 GCPC).

ii) The records of the interception cannot be handed over if information concerning the core area of the private conduct of life is acquired during an interception of telecommunications (Section 100a Subsection 4 sentence 1 GCPC).

iii) The interception of telecommunications cannot be carried out if the interception is directed at a clergyman; defense counsel of the accused; members of the Federal Parliament, of the Federal Convention, of the European Parliament from the Federal Republic of Germany or of a *Land* parliament; an attorney; a person who has been admitted to a Bar Association pursuant to section 206 of the Fed-

---

284 BVerfG, judgment of 20 April 2016 – 1 BvR 966/09, 1 BvR 1140/09, NJW 2016, 1781, mn. 119. An English summary of the decision is available at: http://www.bundesverfassungsgericht.de/SharedDocs/Pressemitteilungen/EN/2016/bvg16-019.html

285 BVerfG, *op. cit.* (fn. 284), mn. 126.

286 BVerfG, *op. cit.* (fn. 284), mn. 129.

287 *Güntge*, in: Ambos/König/Rackow (eds.), Rechtshilferecht in Strafsachen, HT 4, mn. 2; *Lagodny*, in: Schomburg/Lagodny/Gleß/Hackner, Internationale Rechtshilfe in Strafsachen, § 59 IRG, mn. 34.

eral Regulations for Practising Lawyers or a non-attorney provider of legal services who has been admitted to a Bar Association if it is expected to produce information in respect of which such person would have the right to refuse to testify (Section 160a Subsection 1 sentence 1 GCPC).

iv) Records could not be handed over, if any information in the aforementioned cases iii) is obtained during the interception of telecommunications (Section 160a Subsection 1 sentence 2 GCPC) or if information about a person referred to in the first sentence of Section 160a Subsection 1 GCPC is obtained through an investigation measure that is not aimed at such person and in respect of which such person may refuse to testify (Section 160a Subsection 1 sentence 5 GCPC).

v) The interception of telecommunications cannot be carried out if a person named in Section 53 subsection (1), first sentence, numbers 3 to 3b or number 5 GCPC[288] might be affected by the investigation measure and it is to be expected that information would thereby be obtained in respect of which the person would have the right to refuse to testify, and an examination of the circumstances concludes that an interception is disproportionate (Section 160a Subsection 2 sentence 1 GCPC).

vi) The records cannot be handed over if one of the aforementioned constellations v) occurs during the interception of telecommunications or the factual basis for the examination of proportionality has changed (Section 160a Subsection 2 sentence 3 GCPC).[289]

As a consequence of these findings, the obligation to delete the obtained information as set by the law (Section 100a Subsection 4 sentence 3; Section 160a Subsection 1 sentence 2 GCPC) would also apply.

---

288 Section 53a (1) 1 No.
3: attorneys, patent attorneys, notaries, certified public accountants, sworn auditors, tax consultants and tax representatives, doctors, dentists, psychological psychotherapists, psychotherapists specializing in the treatment of children and juveniles, pharmacists, and midwives;
3a: members or representatives of a recognized counselling agency pursuant to Sections 3 and 8 of the Act on Pregnancies in Conflict Situations;
3b: drugs dependency counsellors in a counselling agency recognized or set up by an authority, a body, an institution or a foundation under public law, concerning the information that was entrusted to them or became known to them in this capacity;
5: individuals who are or have been professionally involved in the preparation, production or dissemination of periodically printed matter, radio broadcasts, film documentaries or in the information and communication services involved in instruction or in the formation of opinion.

289 Note: Section 160a GCPC does not apply where certain facts substantiate the suspicion that the person who is entitled to refuse to testify participated in the offence or in accessoryship after the fact, obstruction of justice or handling stolen goods (Section 160a Subsection 4 GCPC).

However, the strict application of the German rules on evidence gathering, even in MLA cases, leads to two inconsistencies. First, the Federal Constitutional Court regularly stresses that the Basic Law's alignment towards international cooperation encompasses the respect for foreign legal orders and conceptions.[290] This is also why own constitutional requirements become valid in the event of international cooperation. As a result, German fundamental rights standards prevailing the national legal order cannot be fully upheld if Germany enters into international cooperation in criminal matters, and they do not fundamentally prevent the transfer of evidence to third countries, although German state authorities remain bound to respect the Basic Law's fundamental rights.[291] Second, in the reverse case, that is, if Germany receives evidence obtained abroad on the basis of a German MLA request (see b. below), German courts principally ignore the rules on the gathering and use of evidence in the foreign country and apply the rule that the evidentiary law of the *forum* reigns if it comes to the use of evidence in Germany. An exception is made, however, if the gathering of evidence abroad contradicts the German public policy order *(ordre public)*, that is, basic principles of the German legal order. Therefore, it may be questioned why Germany does not accept the *forum regit actum* principle, also in cases when it comes to the transfer of evidence collected in Germany.

Against this background, it remains open whether the above-mentioned obligations and guidelines can be maintained and whether other more flexible solutions could even be found.[292] Comprehensive obligations on the part of German authorities to examine the records of the interception and to filter out unlawful content are one of the disadvantages of the above-mentioned guidelines. This could render MLA for the interception of telecommunications more or less impracticable. Furthermore, it could be doubted whether a stringent applicability of the German restrictions and prohibitions on the taking of evidence strike the right balance between the obligations from international agreements (e.g., Article 18 Subsection 5 MLA Convention EU), the protection of civil liberties, and the interests of the participating states.

It could be deliberated whether the public policy exception *(ordre public)* could not serve as a limit for rendering MLA for the interception of telecommunications. The *ordre public* limit means that legal assistance cannot be granted if it would conflict with basic principles of German law.[293] Whether a rule of German criminal procedure is a "basic principle of German law" is subject to determination by case law. If this approach is followed, the German authorities would still have certain obligations to examine the information obtained and not to transmit information

---

[290] BVerfGE 63, 343 (370).

[291] BVerfG, NJW 2016, 1781, mn. 325 et seq.

[292] *Gleß*, in: Samson (ed.), Festschrift Grünwald, p. 197 (199) remarks that international cooperation in criminal matters often requires pragmatic solutions.

[293] Cf. Article 2 lit. b) 1959 MLA Convention; Section 73 AICCM.

that contradicts the basic principles of German law. This would include information that affects the core area of the private conduct of life and information obtained from "privileged persons" (cf. supra). In contrast to the more stringent approach, the German authorities, however, may secure observance of the basic principles (in particular) by setting conditions (as foreseen in Article 18 Subsection 5 lit. b) MLA Convention EU and No. 77a RiVASt). These conditions would restrict the use of the privileged information in foreign criminal proceedings by the international rule of speciality. The setting of conditions would above all be necessary if the person concerned seeks subsequent judicial review by which a court could deem the transferred information not to be in line with the basic principles of German law.

In sum, the question of whether and to what extent there are obligations to filter out or delete "privileged information" is not easy to answer, since there is a lack of settled case law and clear statements in the literature for specific MLA cases of covert investigations by means of wiretapping. General statements so far seem to require a strict observance of the German criminal procedural rules that restrict or prohibit the taking of evidence by means of the interception of telecommunications. As a result, the German authorities would have comprehensive obligations to filter out and delete "privileged information", in particular information that concerns the "core area of the private conduct of life" or information that affects certain persons with the right to refuse testimony. Another approach, which is favored here, could be to assess first whether the German rule affects the German *ordre public*, that is, the basic principles of German law. In the affirmative and as a second step, German authorities could make the use of privileged information dependent on conditions vis-à-vis the requesting state.

b) Outgoing requests

There are no specific legal rules on whether German authorities have a duty to filter out or to delete information that could not be intercepted according to German laws (or even acc. to the law of the sending state) due to a legal privilege accorded to Germany if it is the requesting state and later receives the results of the requested interception measure. However, the problem in Germany is considered less a question of duties to filter out or to delete information but rather an issue of whether the received information can be used as evidence in the trial before the German criminal court. In this context, the Federal Court of Justice *(Bundesgerichtshof)* – Germany's highest court of civil and criminal jurisdiction – dealt with the use of evidence of intercepted telecommunication information in a decision of 2012.[294] Although the underlying facts of the decision did not concern the interception of

[294] BGH 1 StR 310/12 – decision of 21 November 2012 (LG Hamburg) = BGHSt 58, 32 = HRRS 2013, Nr. 314.

telecommunications of a person abroad on the basis of a targeted German MLA request, but instead the handing over of records by Czech authorities of intercepted data that had initially been obtained for the purpose of criminal proceedings in the Czech Republic (preserved data already in the possession of the Czech authorities), the Federal Court of Justice set important guidelines that also apply to other constellations. The Federal Court of Justice reiterated its standpoint that the question of the use of evidence obtained abroad must follow the rules of the requesting state, that is, German law in the case at issue. In other words: the Federal Court of Justice applies the *forum regit actum* principle when it comes to the use of evidence instead of the *locus regit actum* principle, which applies to the enforcement of a requested MLA measure in Germany (cf. B.1.).

The Federal Court of Justice further emphasised that – as far as judicial cooperation within the EU is concerned (and there are no indications of abusive actions of the public authorities) – the use of the evidence obtained abroad is independent of the lawfulness of the measure in the requested EU state (here: the law of the Czech Republic). The Federal Court of Justice mainly argues that, in an area like the EU, which is footed on the principle of mutual recognition of judicial decisions, Germany is not entitled to examine the compliance of the measure at issue with the law of the enforcing state. As a consequence, it is not relevant if the requested state does not comply with the protection of privileged information in accordance with its law or other substantive or formal requirements of its law. In contrast, the received information cannot be used as evidence in German criminal procedure if the content of the information is affected by an exclusionary rule of German (criminal procedural) law. This would be the case if, for example, the received information involves the core area of the private conduct of life or conversation with privileged persons pursuant to Section 160a GCPC.

4. Real-time transfer of communication data

a) Incoming requests

Real-time transfer of telecommunication data is possible in Germany. It is possible both on the basis of an international agreement, such as Article 18 MLA Convention EU and – upon individual agreement on details with the requesting state – on the basis of Article 59 AICCM. This is confirmed by No. 77a Subsection 1 and (implicitly) No. 2 RiVASt. By consenting to the MLA Convention EU in the form of federal law, Germany entered into an obligation to render MLA in the form of the real-time transfer of communication data with the other EU Member State to which the Convention is applicable.

Also in this case, however, the German authorities are obliged to observe the restrictions and prohibitions stipulated by German criminal procedure law and to secure their observance vis-à-vis the requesting state as is the case for the "customary" method of interception of telecommunications. The particularity with regard to the real-time transfer of communication data is that German authorities are only able to fulfill their duties by establishing conditions pursuant to Article 18 Subsection 5 MLA Convention EU, unless – at the moment of the enforcement of the MLA request – it is already clear that "privileged information" would be collected. An intervention before the transmission begins is hardly possible.

In purely national cases, the Federal Constitutional Court *(Bundesverfassungsgericht)* established various requirements that compensate interference into the civil liberties of the person concerned (in particular, Article 10 of the Basic Law [Privacy of correspondence, posts and telecommunications]), for example, labelling requirements for intercepted data, notification, deletion of no longer needed data, exclusionary rules for "privileged information," etc. It is still open whether the establishment of conditions in transnational cases (MLA cases) can be regarded as a sufficient compensation measure for interference into the civil liberties of the person concerned.[295] In the personal view of the author, conditions as foreseen in Article 18 Subsection 5 MLA Convention EU are possible in order to safeguard German fundamental rights standards, also vis-à-vis foreign EU states (cf. B.3.a. above). At the moment, however, this approach is not explicitly backed by law or case law.

b) Outgoing requests

As mentioned above (B.3.b.), the concrete question is whether received information can be used as evidence in the criminal proceedings. This question is mainly addressed to the public prosecutor who prepares the indictment and to the criminal court that sits in trial. Insofar, there are no peculiarities between the real-time transfer of intercepted communications data and the "customary" surveillance of telecommunication by which records are transmitted and analysed. The principles as established by the Federal Court of Justice apply (cf. B.3.b.).

C. European Investigation Order

Cross-border cooperation in the interception of telecommunications with most EU Member State will be based on the rules of Directive 2014/41/EU regarding the European Investigation Order (in the following: Directive EIO) if it is transposed by the Member States.[296] The legal basis for the handling by the German judicial authorities of MLA requests based on the EIO will be the German implementing law (Germany as the executing state). It will also regulate the outgoing requests of

295 See also B.3.a. above.

296 The United Kingdom, Ireland and Denmark will not take part in the Directive EIO.

German authorities (Germany as the issuing state). As mentioned above, the Federal Government drafted a corresponding bill in July 2016.[297] On the basis of this bill, the following section explains to what extent legal changes may affect Germany in comparison to the current conventional MLA system that is primarily based on the MLA Convention EU and bilateral treaties (regarding the interception of telecommunications, in particular Poland and the Czech Republic).

By the way of a preliminary remark, it should be noted that the German legislator will follow its approach of embedding EU rules into the AICCM. The bill foresees Secs. 91a et seq. as the main implementing rules of the Directive EIO. As for the relationship between the implementing national law and the existing provision of the AICCM as well as that between the law implementing EU secondary law and international agreements, please refer to the introductory remarks in Section A. above.

In general, the Federal Government does not see much difference to the conventional MLA scheme as regards the rules in substance. It does, however, consider the following points to be an added value of the EIO:[298]

- Strengthened duties on the part of the authorities of the issuing and executing states to communicate with one another, so that better planning of criminal proceedings is possible;
- Duty to carry out the investigative measure within certain time limits, which will accelerate MLA within the EU;
- Use of standard forms which is considered ensuring better quality of MLA requests.[299]

The bill also highlights that the Directive EIO stipulates the grounds for refusal (reasons why a MLA request is admissible or approvable) in an exclusive way. The most important part of the bill transposes these grounds for refusal or suspension, respectively.[300] Furthermore, the bill stresses that the provisions of the Directive EIO enable a number of clarifications in comparison to the previous MLA scheme. Some of these clarifications have also been transposed into the AICCM; others will be included into the RiVASt, which ought to be revised.

---

[297] Entwurf eines […] Gesetzes zur Änderung des Gesetzes über die internationale Rechtshilfe in Strafsachen (in the following: RegE EEA), BR-Drs. 421/16, also available at: https://www.bmjv.de/SharedDocs/Gesetzgebungsverfahren/Dokumente/RegE_EU_Ermittlungsanordnung.pdf;jsessionid=99E4C8B80707A8CF4263769E14B26535.1_cid324?__blob=publicationFile&v=3. In the following, the references made relate to the Internet document.

[298] Cf. Press Release of 20 July 2016: https://www.bmjv.de/SharedDocs/Artikel/DE/2016/07202016_EU_Ermittlungsanordnung.html?cms_app=true

[299] For the interception of telecommunications, see particularly Section H7 of the form, Annex A of the Directive EIO, Official Journal EU 2014 L 130, p. 29.

[300] Cf. Sections 91b, 91c, 91e, and 91f AICCM-Draft.

Regarding the specific rules on the interception of telecommunications, which require the technical assistance of another Member State (and which are largely aligned with Article 18 MLA Convention EU), the Federal Government principally sees no need for specific legal implementing provisions.[301] The bill refers to the already possible investigative measures on the surveillance of telecommunications, as described in No. 77a RiVASt (cf. supra). The bill confirms that Germany is not only able to render MLA in the form of the interception of the content of telecommunications but also in the form of obtaining[302] telecommunications traffic data. However, in both cases, the respective requirements of the national criminal procedural law must be fulfilled (Sections 100a, 100b, 100g, 101 and 101a GCPC).

In this context, the bill refers to the "special" grounds for refusal as stipulated in Article 30 Subsection 5 Directive EIO. According to this provision, and in addition to the grounds for non-execution referred to in Article 11 Directive EIO, the execution of an EIO for the interception of telecommunications, for which the technical assistance of a Member State is needed, may also be refused where the investigative measure would not have been authorized in a similar domestic case. This ground for refusal is going to be transposed explicitly. The draft text stipulates that, in case of requests for the interception of telecommunications, MLA can be provided only if assistance can be rendered to German courts and authorities under the conditions of Section 59 Subsection 3.[303] This will not entail a change compared to the current system. The new provision clarifies that Section 59 Subsection 3 AICCM (cf. supra) remains fully applicable for certain investigative measures that are requested on the basis of the Directive EIO.[304]

The text does not refer to the possibility of making conditions which would have to be observed in a similar domestic case (Article 30 Subsection 5 sentence 2 Directive EIO). However, the explanatory report of the bill clarifies that the making of conditions is included as *maiore ad minus* in the implementing norm. Thus, there will be no change to the current possibilities for the German authorities to make the consent of an interception of telecommunications subject to conditions, as

---

301 RegE EEA, *op. cit.*, (fn. 297), pp. 45 et seq.

302 The bill clarifies that, for telecommunications traffic data already in the possession of the German authorities (historic data), Article 30 Directive EIO does not apply. However, the handing over of these traffic data is regarded a coercive measure, as a consequence of which Article 10 Subsection 2 Directive EIO also does not apply. Therefore, Articles 10 Subsection 1 and 11 Directive EIO remain fully applicable. The handing over of historic traffic data is only possible if no refusal ground or no recourse to a different type of measure is given (Section 66 AICCM and Sections 91b, 91e, 91f AICCM-Draft).

303 Section 91c Subsection 2 No. 2 lit. c) dd) AICCM-Draft.

304 RegE EEA, *op. cit.*, (fn. 297), p. 70. The clarification is considered particularly necessary because Section 59 Subsection 3 AICCM is modified by Article 10 Subsection 2 Directive EIO.

already foreseen in Article 18 Subsection 5 MLA Convention EU and No. 77a Subsection 1 RiVASt (cf. supra).[305]

The explanatory report of the bill further points out that Article 30 Subsection 6 Directive EIO alters the system of Article 18 MLA Convention EU insofar as the immediate (real-time) transmission of telecommunications is no longer considered the rule. It is now up to the involved states to agree on whether the interception of telecommunications should be carried out in the form of immediate transmission or in the form of subsequent transmission of recorded telecommunications. The bill clarifies that there is no need for implementation because German MLA law already allows for both possibilities and also assumes that the technical details of the interception are subject to individual agreements between the competent authorities of the requesting and requested states. The bill indicates that the solution must be found on a case-by-case basis. It may be dependent on technical aspects, such as secure communication channels, as well as the presumably sufficient protection of the fundamental rights of the person concerned.[306]

There is also no need for implementation of Article 30 Subsection 7 Directive EIO, which foresees the possibility for the issuing state to request a transcription, decoding or decrypting of the recording subject to the agreement of the executing authority. Article 30 Subsection 7 largely corresponds to Article 18 Subsection 8 MLA Convention EU. Germany already assumes that the German authorities should comply with the formalities and procedures indicated by the requesting state unless they were to contradict contingent provisions of its national law (No. 22 Subsection 1 sentence 2 RiVASt).

Regarding the special provision on the costs resulting from the application of Article 30 Directive EIO (Article 30 Subsection 8 Directive EIO), the German law already complies with the EU requirements (Section 75 AICCM). However, the intention is to include clarifications in the RiVASt.

In contrast, the Federal Government considers certain amendments necessary in cases involving the interception of telecommunications pursuant to Article 31 Directive EIO in which no technical assistance from another Member State is needed. In particular, adaptations of the German law and the German guidelines need be made as far as the differences between Article 31 Directive EIO and Article 20 MLA Convention EU are concerned.[307]

In sum, the intricate legal questions remain to be solved with regard to the trans-border interception of telecommunications on the current basis of Article 18 MLA

[305] See also RegE EEA, *op. cit.* (fn. 297), p. 47.

[306] RegE EEA, *op. cit.* (fn. 297), p. 47.

[307] Cf. in more detail RegE EEA, *op. cit.* (fn. 297), pp. 48 et seq.

Convention EU. In particular, the bill will not fundamentally alter the current system of judicial review of the MLA request.[308]

D. Statistics

There are no official statistics available from the German executive authorities as far as "other" mutual legal assistance in criminal matters is concerned.

---

308 RegE EEA *op. cit.* (fn. 297), pp. 30 et seq. Amendments are necessary insofar as the bill foresees a distinction between refusal grounds which concern the admissibility of the request and grounds which concern the approvability of the request. Within the judicial review of Article 61 AICCM, the Higher Regional Court now also has to take a decision on the refusal grounds that concern the approvability of the request, i.e., it must decide on the correct use of the discretion as applied by the granting authority (cf. Section 91i Subsection 1 AICCM Draft).

Appendix

Serious criminal offences for the purpose of Section 100a subsection 1 number 1 StPO shall be:

1. Pursuant to the German Criminal Code:

a) crimes against peace, high treason, endangering the democratic state based on the rule of law, treason and endangering external security pursuant to sections 80 to 82, 84 to 86, 87 to 89a and 94 to 100a:
   - Section 80 Preparation of a war of aggression, Section 80a Incitement to a war of aggression, Section 81 High treason against the Federation, Section 82 High treason against a member state,
   - Section 84 Continuation of a political party declared unconstitutional, Section 85 Violation of a ban on forming an association, Section 86 Distribution of propaganda material of unconstitutional organisations,
   - Section 87 Acting as a secret agent with the aim of sabotage, Section 88 Sabotage against the constitution, Section 89 Exerting anti-constitutional influence on the Armed Forces and public security forces, Section 89a Preparation of a serious violent offence endangering the state,
   - Section 94 Treason, Section 95 Disclosure of state secrets with intent to cause damage, Section 96 Treasonous espionage, spying on state secrets, Section 97 Disclosure of state secrets and negligently causing danger, Section 97a Disclosure of illegal secrets, Section 97b Disclosure based on mistaken assumption that secret is illegal, Section 98 Treasonous activity as an agent, Section 99 Working as an agent for an intelligence service, Section 100 Engaging in relations that endanger peace, Section 100a Treasonous forgery;

b) taking of bribes by, and offering of bribes to, mandate holders pursuant to section 108e,

c) crimes against the national defence pursuant to sections 109d to 109h:
   - Section 109d Disruptive propaganda against the Armed Forces, Section 109e Sabotage against means of defence, Section 109f Intelligence activity endangering national security, Section 109g Taking or drawing pictures etc. endangering national security, Section 109h Recruiting for foreign armed forces;

d) crimes against public order pursuant to sections 129 to 130:
   - Section 129 Forming criminal organisations, Section 129a Forming terrorist organisations, Section 129b Criminal and terrorist organisations abroad; extended confiscation and deprivation, Section 130 Incitement to hatred;

e) counterfeiting money and official stamps pursuant to sections 146 and 151, in each case also in conjunction with section 152, as well as section 152a subsection (3) and section 152b subsections (1) to (4):
   - Section 146 Counterfeiting money, Section 151 Securities, Section 152 Foreign money, stamps and securities, Section 152a subsection (3) Commercial or gang counterfeiting of debit cards, etc., cheques, and promissory notes, Section 152b subsections (1) to (4) Counterfeiting of credit cards with guaranteed payment, etc., and blank eurocheque forms;

f) crimes against sexual self-determination in the cases referred to in sections 176a, 176b, 177 subsection (2), number 2, and section 179 subsection (5), number 2:

- Section 176a Aggravated child abuse, Section 176b Child abuse resulting in death, Section 177 subsection (2), number 2 Sexual assault committed jointly, Section 179 subsection (5), number 2 Abuse of persons incapable of resistance committed jointly.

g) distribution, acquisition and possession of pornographic writings involving children and involving juveniles, pursuant to section 184b subsections (1) to (3), section 184c subsection (3):

- Section 184b subsections (1) to (3) Distribution, acquisition and possession of pornographic writings involving children, Section 184c subsection (3) Distribution, acquisition and possession of pornographic writings involving juveniles reproducing an actual or realistic activity on a commercial basis or as a member of a gang;

h) murder and manslaughter pursuant to sections 211 and 212,

i) crimes against personal liberty pursuant to sections 232 to 233a, 234, 234a, 239a and 239b:

- Section 232 Trafficking in human beings for the purpose of sexual exploitation, Section 233 Trafficking in human beings for the purpose of exploitation of labour, Section 233a Assisting in trafficking in human beings, Section 234 Abduction, Section 234a Causing a danger of political persecution through use of force, threats or deception, Section 239a Abduction for the purpose of extortion, Section 239b Taking of hostages;

j) gang theft pursuant to section 244 subsection (1), number 2, and aggravated gang theft pursuant to section 244a,

k) crimes of robbery or extortion pursuant to sections 249 to 255:

- Section 249 Robbery, Section 250 Aggravated robbery, Section 251 Robbery resulting in death, Section 252 Theft and use of force to retain stolen goods, Section 253 Extortion, Section 255Extortion resembling robbery;

l) commercial handling of stolen goods, gang handling of stolen goods and commercial gang handling of stolen goods pursuant to sections 260 and 260a,

m) money laundering or concealment of unlawfully acquired assets pursuant to section 261 subsections (1), (2) and (4), under exclusion of the attempt and less serious cases.

n) fraud and computer fraud subject to the conditions set out in section 263 subsection (3), sentence 2, and in the case of section 263 subsection (5), each also in conjunction with section 263a subsection (2):

- Section 263 subsection (3), sentence 2 Particularly serious case of fraud resulting in major financial loss, Section 263 subsection (5) Commercial and gang fraud, also in conjunction with Section 263a Computer fraud;

o) subsidy fraud subject to the conditions set out in section 264 subsection (2), sentence 2, and in the case of section 264 subsection (3), in conjunction with section 263 subsection (5):

- Particularly serious cases of subsidy fraud/ Commercial and gang subsidy fraud;

p) criminal offences involving falsification of documents under the conditions set out in section 267 subsection (3), sentence 2, and in the case of section 267 subsection (4), in each case also in conjunction with section 268 subsection (5) or section 269 subsection (3), as well as pursuant to sections 275 subsection (2) and section 276 subsection (2):

- Section 267 subsection (3), sentence 2 Particularly serious case of falsification of documents, Section 267 subsection (4) Commercial and gang falsification of documents, Section 268 Falsification of technical records, Section 269 Falsification of data intended to provide proof, Section 275 Preparatory acts to tampering with official identity documents, Section 276 Acquisition of false official identity documents.

q) bankruptcy subject to the conditions set out in section 283a, sentence 2:
   – Particularly serious cases of bankruptcy.

r) crimes against competition pursuant to section 298 and, subject to the conditions set out in section 300, sentence 2, pursuant to section 299:
   – Section 298 Restricting competition through agreements in the context of public bids,
   – Sections 299, 300 sentence 2 Particularly serious cases of taking and offering bribes in commercial practice, i.e. if the offence relates to a major benefit or the offender acts on a commercial basis or as a member of a gang;

s) crimes endangering public safety in the cases referred to in sections 306 to 306c, section 307 subsections (1) to (3), section 308 subsections (1) to (3), section 309 subsections (1) to (4), section 310 subsection (1), sections 313, 314, 315 subsection (3), section 315b subsection (3), as well as sections 316a and 316c:
   – Section 306 Arson, Section 306a Aggravated arson, Section 306b Particularly aggravated arson, Section 306c Arson resulting in death,
   – Section 307 Inducing a nuclear explosion,
   – Section 308 Inducing an explosion, Section 309 Misuse of ionising radiation,
   – Section 310 subsection (1) Acts preparatory to inducing an explosion or radiation offence,
   – Section 313 Inducing flooding, Section 314 Inducing a common danger by poisoning, Section 315 subsection (3) Dangerous disruption of rail, ship and air traffic,
   – Section 315b subsection (3) Dangerous disruption of road traffic,
   – Section 316a Attacking a driver for the purpose of committing a robbery; Section 316c Attacks on air and maritime traffic;

t) taking and offering a bribe pursuant to sections 332 and 334.

Other serious offences pursuant to supplementary criminal statutes:

2. Pursuant to the Fiscal Code:

a) tax evasion under the conditions set out in section 370 subsection (3), sentence 2, number 5:
   – Particularly serious case of tax evasion where the perpetrator as a member of a gang formed for the purpose of repeatedly committing acts pursuant to section 370 subsection (1), understates value-added taxes or excise duties or derives unwarranted VAT or excise duty advantages.

b) commercial, violent and gang smuggling pursuant to section 373,

c) handling tax-evaded property as defined in section 374 subsection (2):
   – Commercial or gang handling tax-evaded property.

3. Pursuant to the Pharmaceutical Products Act:

   criminal offences pursuant to section 95 subsection (1), number 2a, subject to the conditions set out in section 95 subsection (3), sentence 2, number 2, letter b,
   – Placing on the market or prescribing medicinal products for doping purposes in the field of sport or administering such medicinal products to others commercially or as a member of a gang.

4. Pursuant to the Asylum Procedure Act:

a) inducement of an abusive application for asylum pursuant to section 84 subsection (3)
   – committed commercially or as a member of a gang;

b) commercial *and* gang inducement of an abusive application for asylum pursuant to section 84a.

5. Pursuant to the Residence Act:

a) smuggling of aliens pursuant to section 96 subsection (2):
   – in particularly serious cases: committed commercially or as a member of a gang, subjection of the smuggled persons to potentially fatal, inhumane or humiliating treatment or a risk of sustaining severe damage to their health.

b) smuggling resulting in death and commercial and gang smuggling pursuant to section 97.

6. Pursuant to the Foreign Trade and Payments Act:

wilful criminal offences pursuant to sections 17 and 18 of the Foreign Trade and Payments Act:

– Section 17 subsection (1) Violation of an ordinance serving to implement an economic sanction adopted by the Security Council of the United Nations under Chapter VII of the Charter of the United Nations or by the Council of the European Union in the field of Common Foreign and Security Policy related to weapons, ammunition and equipment goods, to the extent the ordinance provides for criminal punishment; Note that Section 17 subsections (2) et seqq. include both less serious as well as particularly serious cases of Section 17 subsection (1),

– Section 18 subsection (1) Violation of a prohibition on or a licensing requirement for the export, import, transit, transfer, sale, acquisition, delivery, provision, passing on, service or investment or prohibition on the disposal of frozen money and economic assets of a directly applicable act of the European Communities or the European Union published in the Official Journal of the European Communities or the European Union which serves to implement an economic sanction adopted by the Council of the European Union in the field of Common Foreign and Security Policy,

– Section 18 subsection (2) Violation of the Foreign Trade and Payments Ordinance by (e.g.)

  (a) exporting goods cited in it without a license – mostly again weapons, ammunition and equipment goods,

  (b) undertaking a trafficking and brokering transaction without a license,

  (c) providing technical support without a license;

– Section 18 subsection (3) et seqq. Violation of Council Regulation (EC) No. 2368/2002 of 20 December 2002 implementing the Kimberley Process certification scheme for the international trade in rough diamonds (OJ L 358 of 31 December 2002, p. 28), most recently amended by Regulation (EC) No. 1268/2008 (OJ L 338 of 17 December 2008), by importing rough diamonds in violation of Article 3 or exporting rough diamonds in violation of Article 11.

7. Pursuant to the Narcotics Act:

a) criminal offences pursuant to one of the provisions referred to in section 29 subsection (3), sentence 2, number 1, subject to the conditions set out therein:
   – i.e., commercial commission of certain narcotics-related offences;

b) criminal offences pursuant to section 29a, section 30 subsection (1), numbers 1, 2 and 4, as well as sections 30a and 30b:
   - Section 29a Particularly serious cases: illicitly supplying narcotic drugs to a person under the age of 18 as a person over the age of 21 or, in contravention of section 13 subsection 1, administering them to such a person or putting them at their disposal for immediate use; illicitly trading, producing or supplying narcotic drugs in quantities which are not small,
   - Section 30 subsection (1) number 1 illicitly trading, producing or cultivating narcotic drugs as a member of a gang, number 2 supplying narcotic drugs to a person under the age of 18 as a person over the age of 21 on a commercial basis, number 4 importing of narcotic drugs in quantities which are not small,
   - Section 30a illicitly trading, producing, cultivating or importing/exporting narcotic drugs in quantities which are not small, acting as a member of a gang; as a person over the age of 21 causing a person under the age of 18 to illicitly trade in narcotic drugs; illicitly trading in narcotic drugs in quantities, which are not small and so doing, carrying a firearm,
   - Section 30b criminal association for the purpose of unauthorised international distribution of narcotic drugs.

8. Pursuant to the Precursors Control Act:

   criminal offences pursuant to section 19 subsection (1), subject to the conditions set out in section 19 subsection (3), sentence 2:
   - Violation of the Precursors Control Act or of EU-Regulation No. 273/2004 or EU Regulation No. 111/2005, i.e. commercial or gang illegal handling of basic materials used for the production of narcotic drugs.

9. Pursuant to the War Weapons Control Act:

a) criminal offences pursuant to section 19 subsections (1) to (3) and section 20 subsections (1) and (2), as well as section 20a subsections (1) to (3), each also in conjunction with section 21,
   - illegal handling of weapons of mass destruction, mines and cluster ammunition, including the facilitation or enticement of such handling; this is also punishable when committed abroad, provided the perpetrator is a German citizen; exclusion of criminal liability based on negligence.

b) criminal offences pursuant to section 22a subsections (1) to (3),
   - illegal handling of war weapons under exclusion of liability based on negligence.

10. Pursuant to the Code of Crimes against International Law:

a) genocide pursuant to section 6,
b) crimes against humanity pursuant to section 7,
c) war crimes pursuant to sections 8 to 12.

11. Pursuant to the Weapons Act:

a) criminal offences pursuant to section 51 subsections (1) to (3):
   - illegal handling of guns for shooting fixed ammunition, both in particularly serious (commercial or gang commission) as well as in less serious cases;

b) criminal offences pursuant to section 52 subsection (1), number 1 and number 2, letters c and d, as well as section 52 subsections (5) and (6).

Bibliography*

Albrecht, Florian/Braun, Frank, Die strafprozessuale Überwachung des Surfverhaltens. HRRS 2013, 500 et seq.

Ahlbrecht, Heiko/Böhm, Klaus Michael/Esser, Robert/Hugger, Heiner/Rosenthal, Michael, Internationales Strafrecht in der Praxis. 2nd edition. Munich 2016.

Ambos, Kai/König, Stefan/Rackow, Peter (eds.), Rechtshilfe in Strafsachen. Baden-Baden 2015.

Arndt, Hans-Wolfgang, Telekommunikationsgesetz: Kommentar. 2nd edition. Berlin 2015.

Arndt, Hans-Wolfgang/Fademrecht, Thomas (eds.), Berliner Kommentar zum Telekommunikationsgesetz. 2nd edition. Berlin 2015 (cited as BerlKommTKG/*author*).

Bär, Wolfgang, Die Neuregelung des § 100j StPO zur Bestandsdatenauskunft – Auswirkungen auf die Praxis der Strafverfolgung. MMR 2013, 700 et seq.

Becker, Christian/Meinicke, Dirk, Die sog. Quellen-TKÜ und die StPO – von einer „herrschenden Meinung" und ihrer fragwürdigen Entstehung. StV 2011, 50 et seq.

Beck'scher Online-Kommentar zur Strafprozessordnung, see *Graf, Jürgen Peter*.

Beck'scher TKG-Kommentar zum Telekommunikationsgesetz, see *Geppert, Martin/Schütz, Raimund* (eds.).

Berliner Kommentar zum Telekommunikationsgesetz, see *Arndt, Hans-Wolfgang/Fademrecht, Thomas* (eds.).

Böckenförde, Thomas, Auf dem Weg zur elektronischen Privatsphäre. JZ 2008, 925 et seq.

Boehm, Franziska/Andrees, Markus, Zur Vereinbarkeit der Vorratsdatenspeicherung. CR 2016, 146 et seq.

Braun, Frank, Überwachung des Surfverhaltens nach den §§ 100a, 100b StPO zulässig. jurisPR-ITR 18/2013.

Brodowski, Dominik, Strafprozessualer Zugriff auf E-Mail-Kommunikation. JR 2009, 402 et seq.

– Anmerkung zum Urteil des LG Landshut, Beschluss vom 20.1.2011 – 4 Qs 346/10. JR 2011, 533 et seq.

Brunst, Phillip, Anonymität im Internet – rechtliche und tatsächliche Rahmenbedingungen. Berlin 2009.

Buermeyer, Ulf/Bäcker, Matthias, Zur Rechtswidrigkeit der Quellen-Telekommunikationsüberwachung auf Grundlage des § 100a StPO. HRRS 2009, 433 et seq.

---

* All URLs were last accessed in 10/2016.

Denninger, Erhard/Rachor, Frederik, Handbuch des Polizeirechts. 5th edition. Munich 2012.

Eisenberg, Ulrich/Singelnstein, Tobias, Zur Unzulässigkeit der heimlichen Ortung per „stiller SMS“. NStZ 2005, 62 et seq.

Erbs, Georg/Kohlhaas, Max, Strafrechtliche Nebengesetze. 183th supplement. Munich.

Geppert, Martin/Schütz, Raimund (eds.), Beck'scher TKG-Kommentar – Telekommunikationsgesetz. 4th edition. Munich 2013 (cited as BeckTKG-Komm/*author*).

Gleß, Sabine, Das Verhältnis von Beweiserhebungs- und Beweisverwertungsverboten und das Prinzip „locus regit actum“. In: Erich Samson (ed.), Festschrift für Gerald Grünwald zum 70. Geburtstag. Baden-Baden 1999, pp. 197 et seq.

Graf, Jürgen Peter, Beck'scher Online-Kommentar Strafprozessordnung. Munich (cited as Beck-OK/*author*).

Hackner, Thomas/Schierholt, Christian, Internationale Rechtshilfe in Strafsachen. 2th edition. Munich 2012.

Hannich, Rolf (ed.), Karlsruher Kommentar zur Strafprozessordnung. 7th edition. Munich 2013 (cited as KK/*author*).

Hiéramente, Mayeul, Legalität der strafprozessualen Überwachung des Surfverhaltens. StraFo 2013, 96 et seq.

Karlsruher Kommentar zur Strafprozessordnung, see *Hannich, Rolf* (ed.).

Kindhäuser, Urs/Neumann, Ulfried/Paeffgen, Hans-Ullrich (eds.), Strafgesetzbuch. 4th edition. Munich 2013 (cited as NK/*author*).

Klein, Oliver, Offen und (deshalb) einfach – Zur Sicherstellung und Beschlagnahme von E-Mails beim Provider. NJW 2009, 2996 et seqq.

Klesczewski, Diethelm, Straftataufklärung im Internet – Technische Möglichkeiten und rechtliche Grenzen von strafprozessualen Ermittlungseingriffen im Internet. ZStW 123 (2011), 737 et seqq.

Kudlich, Hans, Strafverfolgung im Internet – Bestandsaufnahme und aktuelle Probleme. GA 2011, 193 et seq.

Löwe, Ewald/Rosenberg, Werner, Die Strafprozessordnung und das Gerichtsverfassungsgesetz, 26th edition. Berlin/Boston 2014.

Maunz, Theodor/Dürig, Günther, Grundgesetz, 39. Ergänzungslieferung. Munich 2001.

Meinicke, Dirk, Anmerkung zum Urteil des AG Reutlingen, Beschluss vom 31.10.2011 – 5 Ds 43 JS 18155/10 jug. StV 2012, 463 et seq.

Meyer-Goßner, Lutz/Schmitt, Bertram, Strafprozessordnung. 58th edition. Munich 2015 (cited as Meyer-Goßner/*author*).

Nomos Kommentar zur Strafprozessordnung, see *Kindhäuser, Urs/Neumann, Ulfried/ Paeffgen, Hans-Ullrich* (eds.).

Park, Tido, Handbuch Durchsuchung und Beschlagnahme. 2nd edition. Munich 2009.

Pfeiffer, Gerd, Strafprozessordnung. 5th edition. Munich 2005

Roßnagel, Alexander, Die neue Vorratsdatenspeicherung. NJW 2016, 533 et seq.

Roxin, Claus/Schünemann, Bernd, Strafverfahrensrecht. 28th edition. Munich 2014.

Schenke, Wolf-Rüdiger, Polizei- und Ordnungsrecht. 8th edition. Heidelberg, Munich a.o. 2013.

Schomburg, Wolfgang/Lagodny, Otto/Gleß, Sabine/Hackner, Thomas (eds.), Internationale Rechtshilfe in Strafsachen. 5th edition. Munich 2012.

Schönke, Adolf/Schröder, Horst, Strafgesetzbuch. 29th edition. Munich 2014 (cited as Schönke/Schröder/*author*).

Sieber, Ulrich, Straftaten und Strafverfolgung im Internet – Gutachten zum 69. Deutschen Juristentag. Munich 2012.

Singelnstein, Tobias, Möglichkeiten und Grenzen neuerer strafprozessualer Ermittlungsmaßnahmen – Telekommunikation, Web 2.0, Datenbeschlagnahme, polizeiliche Datenverarbeitung & Co. NStZ 2012, 593 et seq.

Systematischer Kommentar zur Strafprozessordnung, see *Wolter, Jürgen* (ed.).

Wolter, Jürgen (ed.), Systematischer Kommentar zur Strafprozessordnung. 4th edition. Munich 2011 (cited as *author*, in: SK-StPO).

List of Abbreviations

AG	Amtsgericht
AICCM	Act on International Cooperation in Criminal Matters of 23 December 1982 (Gesetz über die international Rechtshilfe in Strafsachen)
BayLT	Bayrischer Landtag (Bavarian state parliament)
BayPAG	Bayrisches Polizeiaufgabengesetz (Bavarian police law)
BDSG	Bundesdatenschutzgesetz (Federal Data Protection Act)
Beck-OK StPO	Beck'scher Online-Kommentar zur Strafprozessordnung (legal commentary)
BeckTKG-Komm	Beck'scher Kommentar zum Telekommunikationsgesetz (legal commentary)
BerlKommTKG	Berliner Kommentar zum Telekommunikationsgesetz (legal commentary)
BfV	Bundesamt für Verfassungsschutz (German Domestic Intelligence Service)
BGH	Bundesgerichtshof (Federal Court of Justice)
BKAG	Bundeskriminalamtsgesetz (Federal Bureau of Investigation Act)
BND	Bundesnachrichtendienst (Federal Intelligence Agency)
BNDG	Bundesnachrichtendienstgesetz (Federal Intelligence Agency Act)

BMWi	Bundesministerium für Wirtschaft und Energie (Federal Ministry for Economic Affairs and Energy)
BT-Drs.	Bundestagsdrucksache (parliamentary document)
BVerfG	Bundesverfassungsgericht (Federal Constitutional Court)
BverfGE	Bundesverfassungsgerichtsentscheidung (Decision of the Federal Constitutional Court)
BVerfSchG	Bundesverfassungsschutzgesetz (domestic intelligence law)
BvR	Aktenzeichen einer Verfassungsbeschwerde zum Bundesverfassungsgericht (File number of the Constitutional Court)
BWPolG	Polizeigesetz Baden-Württemberg (Police law of Baden-Württemberg)
CR	Computer und Recht (law journal)
ECJ	European Court of Justice
EIO	European Investigation Order
ErmR	Ermittlungsrichter (investigating judge)
EuGH	Europäischer Gerichtshof (European Court of Justice)
G 10	Gesetz zur Beschränkung des Post-, Brief- und Fernmeldegeheimnisses (Act Restricting the Secrecy of the Post, of Letters, and of Telecommunication)
GA	Goltdammer's Archiv (law journal)
GCPC	German Criminal Procedure Code
GG	Grundgesetz
GVG	Gerichtsverfassungsgesetz (Courts Constitution Act)
HamPolG	Hamburger Polizeigesetz (Police law of Hamburg)
HessSOG	Hessisches Gesetz über die öffentliche Sicherheit und Ordnung (Police law of Hessen)
HRRS	Online-Zeitschrift für Höchstrichterliche Rechtsprechung im Strafrecht (law journal)
HSOG	Hessisches Sicherheits- und Ordnungsgesetz (Police law of Hesse)
IMEI	International Mobile Equipment Identity
IMSI	International Mobile Subscriber Identity
IRG	(see AICCM)
JR	Juristische Rundschau (law journal)
jurisPR-ITR	juris-Praxisreport IT-Recht (law journal)
JZ	Juristenzeitung (law journal)

KK	Karlsruher Kommentar zur Strafprozessordnung (legal commentary)
KG	Kammergericht
LG	Landgericht (District Court)
MLA	mutual legal assistance in criminal matters
MMR	Multimedia und Recht (law journal)
NdsSOG	Niedersächsisches Gesetz über die öffentliche Sicherheit und Ordnung (Police law of Lower Saxony)
NJOZ	Neue Juristische Online-Zeitschrift (law journal)
NJW	Neue Juristische Wochenschrift (law journal)
NK	Nomos Kommentar zur Strafprozessordnung (legal commentary)
NStZ	Neue Zeitschrift für Strafrecht (law journal)
OLG	Oberlandesgericht
POG RP	Polizeigesetz Rheinland-Pfalz (Police law of Rhineland-Palatinate)
RegE EEA	Entwurf eines […] Gesetzes zur Änderung des Gesetzes über die internationale Rechtshilfe in Strafsachen (Draft of the AICCM)
RiStBV	Richtlinien für das Strafverfahren und das Bußgeldverfahren
RiVASt	Richtlinien für den Verkehr mit dem Ausland in strafrechtlichen Angelegenheiten (Guidelines on Relations with Foreign Countries in Criminal Law Matters)
SaarPolG	Saarländisches Polizeigesetz (Police law of Saarland)
SK-StPO	Systematischer Kommentar zur Strafprozessordnung (legal commentary)
SOG LSA	Gesetz über die öffentliche Sicherheit und Ordnung Sachsen-Anhalt (Police law of Saxony-Anhalt)
SOG M-V	Gesetz über die öffentliche Sicherheit und Ordnung Mecklenburg-Vorpommern (Police law of Mecklenburg-Western Pomerania)
StGB	Strafgesetzbuch (Penal Code)
StPO	Strafprozessordnung (German Code of Criminal Procedure)
StraFo	StrafverteidigerForum (law journal)
StV	Strafverteidiger (law journal)
ThürPAG	Polizeiaufgabengesetz Thüringen (Police law of Thuringia)
TKG	Telekommunikationsgesetz (Telecommunications Act)

TKÜV	Telekommunikations-Überwachungsverordnung (Telecommunications Interceptions Ordinance)
TR TKÜV	Technische Richtlinie TKÜV (Technical Directive TKÜV)
VoIP	Voice over IP
ZStW	Zeitschrift für die gesamte Strafrechtswissenschaft (law journal)
ZUM-RD	Zeitschrift für Urheber- und Medienrecht – Rechtsprechungsdienst (law journal)

Sweden*

National Rapporteur:
Iain Cameron

* This report reflects legislation and case law as of September 2016.

Contents

Introductory Note

References to the Swedish statute book (SFS) are by year of enactment followed by the relevant number. I use the short form of citation of a provision in a statute which is otherwise rather cumbersome in English, thus, Chapter 2, section 1, paragraph 1, point 1 is cited as 2:1, para 1, p. 1. Where a section has only one paragraph but several points, the paragraph number is omitted.

As regards, interpretation of legal provisions, there is relatively little case law in this area. Cases from the Supreme Court are cited from the semi-official series *Nytt Juridisk Arkiv* (NJA). Unreported cases from courts of appeal – which have a low value as precedents – are cited by case number and date. There are some decisions from the Ombudsman, and more recently, from the oversight body, SIN (see below). In Swedish legal culture, the courts place considerable significance on the historical interpretative method, and so the *travaux préparatoires* are regarded as an authorative source. Having said this, in criminal law the textual method of interpretation (objective wording of the provision) is at least as important. References to *travaux préparatoires* are either to the number of the commission responsible for investigating the law, *Statens offentliga utredningar* (SOU) or *Departements serien* (Ds) and the year of its report, or the number of the bill (proposition) put before parliament in the parliamentary year in question. The majority of provisions are regulated in considerable detail in the Code of Judicial Procedure (*Rättegångsbalken,* CJP). A translation of this was produced in 1998, but so many provisions have changed, that all the translations used in the present report are my own.

I. Security Architecture and the Interception of Telecommunication

A. Law Enforcement Institutions and Security Services with Powers of Telecommunication Interception

1. National security architecture

Sweden has a national police force, administratively divided into seven regions and subdivided into smaller areas. There is a separate customs service, with responsibility for, *inter alia*, investigation of smuggling offences. Since 1 January 2015 the police and Security Police have been separate entities. The Security Police is now a largely civilian security agency, but it also has certain police powers. Sweden has a signals intelligence agency, *Försvarets radio anstalt* (FRA). All four of these administrative agencies can engage in interception of telecommunications. Thus, in Sweden communication interception is possible under three different legal regimes; (repressive) criminal law, (preventive/investigative) police law, and intelligence (or state security) law.

2. Powers for the interception of telecommunications

a) Law of criminal procedure

Interception of telecommunications by the police, and Security Police in the context of criminal investigations is regulated in the Code of Judicial Procedure (*Rättegångsbalken*, CJP) (1942:740). Relaxations of the normal rules in the CJP for the security police in certain circumstances are set out in the Act (2008:854) on measures to investigate certain societally dangerous crimes.

b) Preventive law

Proactive interception by the police or Security Police (which is rare) is provided for in the Act (2007:979) on measures to prevent particularly serious crimes. In addition, the police and security police, prior to opening a preliminary investigation, have access to metadata for intelligence purposes as regards investigating more serious offences. This is regulated under the Act (2012:278) on the collection of data on electronic communications in law enforcement intelligence.

c) Law of intelligence agencies

The signals intelligence agency, *Försvarets radio anstalt* (FRA) is permitted to intercept international communications (metadata and content data). This is permitted subject to certain conditions, but only for intelligence purposes under the Act on Communications Interception for Defence Intelligence Purposes (2008:717).

d) Customs Investigation Service

The customs service has access to interception of telecommunications under the same conditions as the police, i.e., interception for the investigation of criminal offences, regulated in CJP and of metadata for intelligence purposes, regulated in the Act (2012:278) on the collection of data on electronic communications in law enforcement intelligence.

3. Responsibility for the technical performance of interception measures

Telecommunications data is physically held by different telecommunications companies. The court where the criminal investigation is taking place issues a warrant requiring the telecommunications company to give the police or security police access to specified teleaddresses or specified historical or real-time telecommunications records. The prosecutorial authority is organised in the same way as the police, i.e., with a central unit in Stockholm and seven regional offices. The Security Police is also a national organisation, with regional offices. The Security Police has the technical expertise in this area, so it handles the technical aspects of interception even for the police, transferring the requested data to them. When the Security Police collects its own data, it applies for court warrants through a specialised prosecutorial chamber based in Stockholm.

For signals intelligence, the law requires telecommunications companies to route all international communications through certain connecting points which have been placed under the physical control of an independent oversight body, *Statens Inspektion för Underrättelsearbete* (SIUN). If the Defence Intelligence Court has issued a warrant for interception of particular cables for particular purposes, SIUN permits FRA access to the signal bearers in question, for the specified purposes.

4. Legitimacy of data transfers between different security agencies

Exchange of secret information between administrative authorities is governed by the Transparency and Secrecy Act (2009:400). This provides *inter alia* that an administrative agency can transfer secret information to another administrative agency if this is necessary in order for the transferring agency to fulfil its functions as set out in statute or subordinate legislation (Chapter 10, section 2). Thus, transfer is possible between customs, the police and the Security Police, and between these agencies and the signals intelligence agency. The Security Police has a more preventive role, and primacy when it comes to the investigation of specified security offences. FRA can be tasked by the police or Security Police to obtain strategic (i.e., on the general level) intelligence concerning international terrorism or organised crime, but the FRA is forbidden to engage in, or assist in, the investigation of specific offences.[1]

---

[1] This – relatively – clear dividing line has become less clear with the entry into force on 1 April 2016 of an amendment to the Act (2010: 299) on Punishment for Public incitement etc. of Terrorism which criminalizes travelling abroad for the purposes of joining at terrorist organisation. Signals intelligence will be one the prime means of investigating this offence.

B. Statistics on electronic communication interception

1. Obligation to collect statistics

There is an obligation on the police and Security Police to report statistics every year to Prosecutorial Authority, which produces a public report the year after (for 2014, on 22 May 2015, Report ÅM-A 2014/1569, for 2016 on 30 May 2016, Report ÅM-A 2016/0093). The signals intelligence agency reports statistics to the oversight body (SIUN) and the Security Police to the oversight body (the Commission on Security and Integrity Protection, SIN), although these are not published.

2. Current data

As noted, statistics are not publicly available for interceptions by the Security Police or the signals intelligence agency. As far as the police and customs are concerned, during 2014, 1235 people had the content of their telecommunications intercepted, and 2022 people had their metadata intercepted. During 2015, 1158 people had the content of their telecommunications intercepted, and 2104 people had their metadata intercepted There is overlap between these two figures, i.e., the same person could have been subjected to both (metadata interception is included in a warrant to intercept content, but not vice versa).

II. Principles of Telecommunication Interception in Constitutional and Criminal Procedural Law

A. Constitutional Safeguards of Telecommunication and the Constitutional Proportionality Principle Regarding Access to Data

Under the Swedish constitution (Instrument of Government (IG) 2:6 para 1), there is protection "against body searches, house searches and other such invasions of privacy, against examination of mail or other confidential correspondence, and against eavesdropping and the recording of telephone conversations or other confidential communications". Under 2:6 para 2 "everyone shall be protected in their relations with the public institutions against significant invasions of their personal privacy, if these occur without their consent and involve the surveillance or systematic monitoring of the individual's personal circumstances". The right under IG 2:6 para 2 is relative, meaning it can be limited by statute. There is no irreducible "core" and absolute right of privacy. The right under IG 2:6 para 2 is also comparatively new, dating from 2011. Historically, freedom of information and freedom of expression have been more strongly guaranteed than privacy and data protection.

There is no express constitutional right to informational self-determination, though it can be seen as an implicit part of the right to personal integrity.

Under IG 2:20 limitations in IG 2:6 and other relative rights (listed in IG 2:20), "may be imposed only to satisfy a purpose acceptable in a democratic society. The limitation must never go beyond what is necessary with regard to the purpose which occasioned it, nor may it be carried so far as to constitute a threat to the free shaping of opinion as one of the fundaments of democracy. No limitation may be imposed solely on grounds of a political, religious, cultural or other such opinion." This constitutional principle is mainly aimed at the legislature, in drafting legislation, however it has on occasion been applied by the courts. CJP 27:1 (below) is invoked much more frequently.

B. Statutory Protection of Personal Data, Oversight and Consequences for the Unlawful Infringement of Telecommunications

Personal data is generally protected by the principle of "purpose limitation of personal data", which is expressed in the Act on Personal Data (1998:204). As regards telecommunications companies and staff, the Electronic Communications Act (2003:389) (hereinafter, ECA) provides for duties of confidentiality and also for exceptions to this duty, as regards revealing data to law enforcement personnel (when this has been duly authorised). Where the police have obtained telecommunications data, or stored personal data, the police are themselves under obligations in the Police Data Act not to disclose this except where this is necessary for criminal investigation.

Seizure of a computer in order to access data stored upon it is governed by similar rules as the seizure of a physical document, meaning that CJP 27:2 applies. This provides that "If it can be assumed that a document contains information that an official or other person may not disclose under testimony under Chapter 36, Section 5, the document may not be seized from the possession of that person or the person who is owed the duty of confidentiality. Nor may from the person of the suspect or his relative, as defined in Chapter 36, Section 3, written communications between the suspect and his relative or between such relative be seized, except if the issue concerns an offence in respect of which a less severe penalty than imprisonment for two years is not prescribed."

As regards the consequences of these safeguards for the interception of (electronic) communication, the primary protection is preventive, in logging routines etc. The Data Protection Inspectorate has oversight of all data registers, including those of the police and Security Police. The police have been criticised on occasion for deficiencies in data registers (overlong retention of information, registering of information on ethnic origin etc which should not have been registered). In addition, a special body, the Commission on Security and Integrity Protection (*Säkerhets och integritetsskyddsnämnden*, or SIN) has oversight of both the police and Security Police registers and can receive complaints from the public. SIN also has a follow-up oversight of coercive measures and access to metadata. Criminal penalties for breach of confidentiality requirements by the police or telecommunications staff are to be found in the ECA and the Transparency and Secrecy Act (2009:400), which in turn makes reference to Criminal Code (CC) (1962:700). The offences in question are misuse of office (CC 20:1) and breach of official secrecy (CC 20:3). A few police every year are prosecuted for misuse of office, due to unauthorised access to information.

C. Powers in the Code of Criminal Procedure

Coercive powers in the Swedish criminal procedural law are based on differentiated, precise, and specific provisions. An analogous application of coercive powers is not possible. The principle of "legal security" *(rättssäkerhet)* is fundamental to Swedish criminal law and criminal procedure. It is only partially codified; the constitutional rights in IG 2 8–10 since the reform of 2010 have been grouped together in the Instrument of Government under the subheading *rättssäkerhet*, but there is no definitively agreed content to the concept and sections 8–10 in the Instrument of Government certainly do not exhaust it. It includes the need for criminalisation and coercive state measures to have clear support in law.

Having said this, the fact that interception and surveillance are both defined in technique neutral ways (see below) means that new techniques for obtaining data can be used within existing legal provisions. These new techniques, perhaps together with changed social habits (e.g. not turning off one's mobile phone, meaning that a "temporary" dynamic IP address "lasts longer") can mean that considerably more personal data becomes available, without the need for a change in the law. The CJP provides for a sliding scale of authorisation as regards what are called "coercive measures" *(tvångsmedel)*.[2] There is no definition of "coercive measures" in the CJP but it is often defined in doctrine and the *travaux préparatoires* as being a direct intervention against a person or property within the exercise of public authority and with the character of an intrusion in the personal integrity of the individual.[3]

---

[2] The interception of metadata has so far not been regarded as a sufficiently serious interference with personal integrity as to be seen as a "coercive measure", although analogous levels of safeguards apply (see further below).

[3] See for example SOU 1995:47, p. 137, Bill 2005/06:178 p. 21 and, generally, Lindberg, G., *Straffprocessuella Tvångsmedel [Coercive measures under the law of criminal*

Under CJP 27:1 there is a general rule of proportionality applying to all coercive measures:

> "The coercive measures described in this chapter may be imposed only if the reasons for the measure outweigh the consequent intrusion or other detriment to the suspect or to another adverse interest."

As regards specific categories of protected communications, under CJP 27:22

> "Telephone conversations or other telecommunications between the suspect and his defence counsel may not subject to secret wiretapping. If during the tapping it appears that it is such a conversation or communication, the surveillance shall be discontinued. Recordings or notes, to the extent that they are subject to the prohibition, shall immediately be destroyed."

Other privileged categories of communications are those between a priest or doctor and a suspect.

Which coercive measures can be used is dependent upon the seriousness of the material offences under investigation: where stiffer sanctions apply, more coercive measures are available.

A preliminary inquiry into a criminal offence is to be initiated, and led, by the police or a prosecutor if information is received that a crime has been committed (CJP 23:1). If an investigation has been initiated by the police and the matter is not of a simple nature, the prosecutor is to assume responsibility for conducting the investigation as soon as someone is reasonably suspected of the offence. The prosecutor is also to take over the conduct of the investigation if special reasons so require (CJP 23:3). In practice, the question of who shall lead the investigation in a particular case is often solved informally, although the prosecutor always has the last word. The percentage of investigations led by the prosecutor varies considerably according to the type of offence in question, with the majority of investigations into serious offences being led by the prosecutor.

III. Powers for Accessing Electronic Communications Data in the Law of Criminal Procedure

A. Overview of the Legal Framework and the Respective Provisions in Criminal Procedural Law

Most of the relevant provisions are set out in considerable detail in chapter 27 CJP. No additional general clauses are applicable.

---

procedure], 3 uppl. Karnov, 2013. Coercive measures can be open, such as search, seizure or body search, or covert, such as interception of telecommunications.

B. Interception of Content Data

1. Scope, object and temporal limits

The main provision in criminal procedural law dealing with the interception of the content of communication in transmission is CJP 27:20 which provides that:

> "Covert interception of electronic communications and covert surveillance of electronic communications shall, unless otherwise provided in the second paragraph, only occur if someone is reasonably suspected of the offence and the measure is of particular importance to the investigation. This measure may only relate to
>
> 1. a phone number or address, or a certain electronic communication during the time of the authorisation which is held or has been held by the suspect or which may otherwise be assumed to have been used or may be used by the suspect, or
> 2. a phone number or address, or a certain electronic communication if there is particular reason to assume that the suspect during the time of the authorisation has or will contact this number etc.
>
> Secret surveillance of electronic communication shall, in addition to what is stated in the first paragraph, be carried out in order to investigate who may reasonably be suspected of the crime, if this is of particular importance to the investigation. However, only data relating to the past may be collected."

As regards the object of interception, the definitional provisions are in two different Acts. CJP 27:18 provides that

> "Covert interception of an electronic communication means that the content of a message which in an electronic communications network is being or has been conveyed to or from a telephone number or other address, is covertly listened to or intercepted by technical means".

The ECA (2003:389) 6:1 defines electronic communication and provides:

> "electronic communication means any information exchanged or transmitted between a limited number of parties through a publicly available electronic communications service, except information which is transmitted as part of the broadcasting of radio and television programs that are targeted to the general public …".

This should be read together with the definition in 1:7 of the same Act, namely

> "electronic communications network means transmission systems and applicable equipment, switching or routing equipment and passive network elements and other resources which permit the transfer of signals, by wire or radio, by optical or by other electromagnetic means, independently of the type of information transmitted".

As regards temporal limits, warrants are for a maximum period of one month (CJP 27:21, para 2). This period can be renewed.

A warrant is not needed for the interception of communications which are purely by radio, but as mobile phones communicate partly by radio and partly by cable, the full body of legal safeguards applies to these.

All of the following contents of traffic can be captured under Swedish criminal procedural law:

– analog communication (voice and data) via landlines

– IP traffic of a person-to-person communication
– IP traffic between a person and an automated information system (such as communication with a webserver while downloading from a website)
– IP traffic between a person's computer and their data storage in a cloud or other remote storage of data processing systems
– IP traffic between two independent computer systems (e.g. between an automated machine and its computer-based automated control centre, especially in the "internet of things")

As regards the third of these, communication between a personal computer and the cloud, it should be added that the content of information which is stored on the cloud can only be accessed via a warrant for interception of electronic communication.[4]

Both stored data and data in communication are protected, meaning that a warrant is necessary to access both. If the email which the police wish to search has been received by and is stored on the suspect's computer, or if a text message (SMS, MMS) is retained on the suspect's mobile phone, an alternative method is to seize the computer or mobile phone and access the email or SMS/MMS message.

2. Special protection of confidential communication content

The CJP provides for specific safeguards excluding particular types of information from electronic communication interception. Under CJP 27:22 Covert interception of electronic communications must not refer to phone calls or other messages where someone expresses himself/herself if the person in question could not be heard as a witness (CJP 36:5) If the interception is ongoing it must be immediately interrupted. If recordings have been made, these must be immediately destroyed.

Where a person argues that privileged data is kept on a computer or a mobile phone (e.g. the suspect is a journalist), then the search must occur in the presence of the suspect's lawyer.[5]

The law regulating financial and banking secrecy does not contain special protection for communications.

There is no special protection for communication in a "core area of private life" (e.g. prayers, communication during sexual activities, diaries, etc) except where it falls under CJP 27:22/36:5 (above). The latter provision provides *inter alia* that:

---

4 Bill 2002/03:74, p. 88, and Lindberg, p. 500.

5 Ombudsman decision 1724-2011, 2012-04-25, see also Court of Appeal for Northern Norrland, Mål nr Ö 198-15, judgment 2015-03-26.

"Anyone who is a priest or performs a similar function in a religious community may not be heard as a witness concerning something he or she has learned during confession or individual counselling".

As regards communication during sexual activities, diaries etc, these communications would normally not be necessary for the investigation of the offence, and so would routinely be destroyed after the preliminary investigation is concluded (CJP 27:24).

There are a small number exceptions which are set out in CJP 36:5 detailing when people who have privileged communications nonetheless may be called upon to testify.

There are no legal differences between handling analogue and digital communication, but an important technical one in that real-time monitoring (and so switching off of interception) of some forms of digital communication is not possible.

The person leading the investigation determines whether a person is entitled or not to privileges. Such a decision is made under criminal responsibility (i.e., it will be misuse of office to take a unjustified decision in this respect, although having said this, the threshold for "misuse" is set relatively high). As noted already, it will usually depend on the seriousness of the case whether the person leading the investigation is a prosecutor or a senior police officer. In either case, this person determines which other people involved in the investigation are permitted to access the data collected (CJP 27:12). The court in the subsequent trial also has access to all data not immediately destroyed as irrelevant or as privileged. The internet provider simply receives the order to hand over specified data, without any explanation, and has no discretion to determine whether it may be handed over or not.

3. Execution of telecommunications interception

The standard mode of interception is for the police, customs or Security Police to order access providers to extract and surrender specific communication. The police, customs and Security Police do not intercept specific communication themselves and without recourse to third parties.

For signals intelligence collection (i.e., not applicable for the investigation of specific crimes) SIUN gives the signals intelligence agency access to the signal bearers (the fibre optic cables). Once this has been done, FRA can access the data without the participation of the telecommunications companies.

As has already been mentioned, the Security Police handle the technical aspects of interception on behalf of the police and customs. The Security Police do not have direct access to telecommunications companies' cables etc. Once a court order has been issued to the telecommunication companies, the Security Police instruct the company either to hand over requested data or to connect the listed numbers (IP addresses etc.) to the Security Police equipment.

As regards which types of accompanying investigative measures are permitted in Sweden, with court permission, clandestine access to plant a bug is permissible (although the expense and other technical difficulties involved means that this happens only rarely in practice). A by-product of this can be the interception of electronic communications. The Security Police do not have the right to use hacking techniques or key loggers as such, but have argued that the legislature should give them this explicit possibility.[6] This has also been recommended by Commissions of Inquiry.[7] If permission is given to plant a bug, then this could also cover a key logger, but as mentioned, bugging is rare.

The definition of "public communications network" in ECA 1:7 is:

> "an electronic communications network which is wholly or mainly used for the provision of publicly available electronic communications services and which supports the transfer of information between network connection points".

ECA 2:1 specifies that any person or company which provides public communications network services is obliged to seek a licence from the Post and Telecom Authority (*Post och telestyrelsen* (PTS)). This definition will presumably cover companies which provide services at a "deeper" level (IP transport level etc) even if it is assumed that it will be only rarely that such a provider will be ordered to implement electronic communications interception or electronic communications surveillance.

4. Duties of telecommunication service providers to cooperate

The cooperation duties of internet providers are set out in ECA 6:16a which provides that:

> "Anyone who conducts activities that are subject to notification under 2:1 is obliged to store such information as referred to in section 20 first paragraph 1 and 3 which is necessary to trace and identify the communication source, the destination of the communication, date, time and duration of the communication, type of communication, communication equipment and the location of mobile communication at the start and end of the communication.
>
> The retention requirement under the first paragraph includes data generated or processed in telephony, messaging, Internet access and the provision of capacity to get internet access (connection form). Even when a call is unsuccessful there is an obligation to retain data generated or processed.
>
> A person who is required to store the data under this section may instruct another person to carry out the storage."

The more detailed requirements are set out in the Ordinance (2003:396) on Electronic Communication (as amended by Ordinance 2012:128) – see also below.

---

6 http://www.dagensjuridik.se/2014/04/aklagare-och-sapo-vill-infora-nytt-tvangsmedel.

7 See, e.g., SOU 2012:44 p. 765–771.

There are provisions requiring communication providers to follow certain rules on interception capabilities in their networks. These are set out in administrative regulations from the Swedish body responsible for overseeing the ECA, the PTS (PTS regulation (2012:4)).

As regards norms which exist concerning the technical aspects of the internet providers' transfer of intercepted data to the police, e.g. with respect to formats and protocols, security measures and encryption, under section 37 of the Ordinance (2003:396) on Electronic Communication:

> "Any entity which is required to store data according to ECA 6:16 shall take the measures necessary to ensure that the stored data is of the same quality and subject to the same level of safety and protection as was the case for the data before it was stored.
>
> The entity under the storage obligation shall take the necessary measures to protect the data against accidental or unlawful destruction and the accidental loss or alteration. Such measures should also be taken to prevent unauthorised storage, processing or access, and unauthorised disclosure of data. The data may be made available only to specially authorised personnel."

More detailed duties relating to physical and data security, together with encryption requirements are set out in PTS regulation (2012:4).

As regards norms regulating technical aspects of the internet provider's transfer of intercepted data to authorities in a foreign country (e.g. in the context of mutual legal assistance), the general rule in Swedish mutual legal assistance is that the same data is made available for foreign police, courts and prosecutors as is available for their Swedish equivalents (Act on Mutual Legal Assistance (2000:562) 2:1). The same Act provides (4:25a) that direct transfer of data can occur to EU states, Iceland and Norway, if this can be done in a secure way. The same applies when Sweden is asked to assist technically another state to carry out an interception (4:25b). However, no special rules apply to technical aspects, meaning that what is available is only the same information available to the Swedish police/prosecutor, and only in the same form.

The telecommunications companies are to provide the requested data to the police, and this can presumably mean that the Security Police/police specify that only certain types of call are to be recorded. However, the Security Police/police do not usually wish to give away to the telecommunications company any operational details and so it is my understanding is that the police do the necessary refining afterwards. A general duty to provide data in a usable form (meaning inter alia, decrypted data) is to be found in ECA 6:19 which provides that

> "the provision of telecommunication services shall be conducted so that decisions on secret interception of electronic communications and covert surveillance of electronic communication can be executed … The content and information on intercepted or monitored communications must be made available in an easily accessible form".

5. Formal prerequisites of interception orders

The normal system is that the police, customs, or Security Police officer leading an investigation requests the prosecutor to bring an application before a court to approve telecommunications content interception. (CJP 27:21, para 1). In case of emergency, under CJP 27:21a (since 2014) it is provided that a prosecutor can give interim permission to intercept. The prosecutor must give reasons for his/her decision. If this emergency procedure is used, the case must immediately be brought before the responsible court which can confirm or terminate the interception order. This emergency procedure was previously only available under the 2008 Act, for listed security crimes, and was used rarely.[8]

The procedure is in writing. If the requesting prosecutor provides further oral information at the hearing, this must be documented. The court can request further information. It gives summary reasons for its decision. The application is a simple application before the court, not on oath. However, it is backed by the offence of misuse of office. In 2000, a prosecutor was convicted for having (negligently) applied for an interception warrant when the legal conditions were not fulfilled.[9]

6. Substantive prerequisites of interception orders

As regards the degree of suspicion for a past crime (or – in some countries – the degree of future danger or risk) necessary for an interception order, CJP 27:20 provides that:

> "Covert interception of electronic communications ... may only be conducted if someone is reasonably suspected of an offence ...".

Thus, reasonable suspicion of a specified, concrete, offence is necessary and there must normally be a suspected person. However, an amendment in 2012 now makes an exception to this rule, allowing interception of content in order to determine who may be reasonably suspected of a given, specific offence, where this is of particular importance to the investigation.[10]

The normal use of coercive powers is only permissible to investigate an offence which has already been committed, is in the process of being committed, or in specific cases set out in law, where attempt, preparation, or conspiracy to commit an offence is punishable. However, proactive surveillance is now allowed under the Act (2007:979) on measures to prevent particularly serious crimes, when, having regard to the circumstances, there is reason to believe that a person will perform

---

[8] It was used four times between 2009–2012, see SOU 2012:44, p. 326.

[9] Lindberg, p. 506.

[10] The text of the provision is set out above, section III.B.1. For the *travaux préparatoires* see Bill 2011/12:55, p. 130. Laxer requirements apply to the interception of traffic data, see below.

criminal acts in the future, including certain listed offences (such as sabotage, arson, terrorist offences, and murder). The 2007 Act moves the threshold for using interception of communications a little further forward in time for certain specified security-related offences. However, in practice the Act is not used much (not at all during 2014 or 2015). For particularly serious security-related offences, attempt, preparation, and conspiracy will also be punishable, and reach the statutory minimum sanction level for communications interception. Thus, where there are sufficient concrete indications to justify the application of the Act, there will almost invariably also be sufficient concrete indications to justify communications interception applying the normal rules in the CJP.

As regards which crimes or (dangers) can justify an interception order, CJP 27:18 provides that:

> "Covert interception may be used in the preliminary investigation of: (1) offences punishable by a minimum period of two or more years' imprisonment; or (2) offences set out in section 2 para 2, points 2–7 (3) attempt, preparation, or conspiracy to commit such an offence if such act is subject to punishment (4) other offences if, with regard to the circumstances, it can be assumed that the punishment imposed will exceed more than two years imprisonment."

In Sweden, only serious offences are punishable by a minimum of 2 years imprisonment. Having said this, the effect of the Act on penalties for terrorist offences (2003:148), implementing the EU Framework Decision on Terrorism is that the commission of a list of ordinary offences with a terrorist intent carries a minimum penalty of 4 years imprisonment. Thus, if a terrorist intent is suspected, a long list of offences can form the basis of an interception order.

As regards (2), the list of crimes set out in section 2, para 2–7 are offences with a wide spectrum of penalties. In the circumstances, these offences will often fall under point (1) but not always (e.g. where a terrorist intent within the meaning of the above act is missing). These offences are:

2. sabotage or aggravated sabotage according to CC 13:4 or 13:5;
3. arson, aggravated arson, devastation endangering the public, hijacking, or maritime, aircraft or airport sabotage, according to CC 13:1, 2, 3, 5 a or 5 b, if the offence involves sabotage according to 13:4;
4. rebellion, armed threats against the lawful order or crime against civil liberty under CC 18:1, 3 or 5;
5. treason, inciting wars, espionage, aggravated espionage, unauthorised dealing with secret information, aggravated unauthorised dealing with secret information, or illegal intelligence activities against Sweden, against a foreign power, or against persons pursuant to CC19:1, 2, 5, 6, 7, 8, 10, 10 a or 10 b;
6. industrial espionage according to section 3 of the Act (1990:409) on the protection of business secrets, if there is reason to believe that the offence has been committed on behalf of or has been supported by a foreign power or by someone who has acted for a foreign power;
7. terrorist offences according to section 2 of the Act (2003:148) on penalties for terrorist offenses, offences under section 3 of the Act (2002:444) for the financing of particularly serious crimes in some cases, or offences under the Act (2010:299) on pen-

alties for the public provocation, recruitment and training for terrorist offences and other particularly serious crime.

Point (4) is a "safety valve", introduced in 2004. It is mainly used for offences against property with a relatively wide sentencing scale.[11] It is stated in the *travaux préparatoires* that point (4) should be interpreted restrictively. It is only when there are good reasons for believing that the sentence will be more than 2 years imprisonment that the provision should be used as the basis for an interception order.

As regards who can be subject to an interception order (e.g. suspects, their intermediaries, their communication partners, specific devices), CJP 27:20 provides that:

> "Covert interception of electronic communications and covert surveillance of electronic communications shall, unless otherwise provided in the second paragraph, only occur if someone is reasonably suspected of the offence and the measure is of particular importance to the investigation. This measure may only relate to 1. a phone number or address, or a certain electronic communication during the time of the authorisation which is held or has been held by the suspect or which may otherwise be assumed to have been used or may be used by the suspect, or 2. a phone number or address, or a certain electronic communication if there is particular reason to assume that the suspect during the time of the authorisation has or will contact this number etc.
>
> Secret surveillance of electronic communication shall, in addition to what is stated in the first paragraph, be carried out in order to investigate who may reasonably be suspected of the crime, if this is of particular importance to the investigation. However, only data relating to the past may be collected."

Thus, it is possible to monitor a teleaddress other than that held or used by the suspect if there are "particular reasons" to suspect that s/he will contact that number.

The targeting of particular communication content (e.g. through the automated use of certain trigger words) is only possible within the context of a signals intelligence operation by FRA directed against international communications.

There is no specific statutory requirement that the anticipated evidence will actually be obtained by means of the requested interception, however, as noted above, the measure must be of "particular importance to the investigation".

Nor is there a specific requirement that other – less intrusive – means of investigation must first be tried unsuccessfully or be considered unlikely to be successful. However, the application of the principles of proportionality and necessity will often mean this in practice.[12] On the other hand, it is noted in the *travaux préparatoires* that it is not necessary first to have tried less intrusive means where it is obvious from the beginning that less intrusive measures will not be effective, or where this would involve the use of disproportionate police resources, would risk revealing the covert investigation or pose a risk to the lives of the investigators.

---

[11] Lindberg, p. 492.

[12] See Bill 1988/89:124, p. 66, Lindberg, p. 501.

Interception must be proportionate to the seriousness of the offence in the individual case. The principle of proportionality has a special role in protecting the interests of third parties. These can sometimes be secured by attaching special conditions, e.g. real-time monitoring and the possibility of only recording communications where it is clear that the suspect is one of the parties. A duty to specify conditions designed to protect individuals' personal integrity is now an explicit part of CJP 27:21. As regards situations in which proportionality will be precluded, in the *travaux préparatoires* it is stated specifically that there is very little room for ever covertly intercepting the communications of a media company.[13]

According to the leading authority, an interception order should be required even when one of the parties to the communication has consented to the interception.[14] The police force in one region allegedly interpreted the law up until 2010 so as to permit them to use hidden microphones to record a conversation if one party to the conversation consented to this (i.e., wearing a wire). The case law of the European Court of Human Rights clearly requires court-ordered approval of this kind of coercive measure, and this was noted by the Commission of Inquiry on Certain Police Methods (SOU 2010:103). On balance, it should be assumed that this police practice is no longer followed.

7. Validity of interception orders

As already mentioned, the maximum length of an interception order under both normal circumstances and emergencies is one month.

There is no limit set out in the law to prolongations, but the application of the principle of proportionality will often mean that limits will apply in practice. There were security cases in the 1960's when warrants were renewed every month for a period of 16 years. This would nowadays be regarded as quite unacceptable. However, security operations and organised crime investigations generally last longer than a month.

The renewal or prolongation of the interception warrant follows the same procedure as the initial application for an interception.

An interception order must be revoked when the circumstances show that it is no longer necessary. CJP 27:23 provides that

> "The prosecutor or the court shall immediately rescind an order authorising covert interception of electronic communications and covert surveillance of electronic communications once cause no longer exists for the order."

Interception does not need to be halted if it reveals information pointing to the commission of offences not anticipated by or not mentioned in the interception

---

13 See Bill 1988/89:124, p. 28.

14 Lindberg, p. 53–54.

order. The issue of whether such information ("surplus information") may be used is now regulated in the law. CJP 27:23a provides that

> "If, when covert interception of electronic communications… has produced details of an offence other than that which has been the basis of the decision permitting the interception … the resulting information may be used to investigate the offence in question if 1. imprisonment for one year or more is prescribed for the offence and it can be assumed that the offence does not result only in fines, or 2. there are special reasons for allowing this."

This provision was subject to considerable debate and only allowed after a detailed empirical study by a commission of inquiry (SOU 2012:44) revealed that there was no evidence that the police or prosecutor were deliberately circumventing the – relatively – demanding 2 year minimum sentence rule by initiating investigations into more serioius offence, in order to obtain information on less serious offences.

8. Recording, reporting and destruction requirements

There are protocol duties which apply to the person leading the preliminary investigation under section 7 of the Ordinance on Preliminary Investigation (1947:948), as well as, for prosecutors, under internal regulations issued by the Prosecuting Authority. However, the protocol duties are kept separate from the preliminary investigation file. The practice is only to note covert interception or covert monitoring of traffic data in the preliminary investigation file if this is likely to be relied upon as evidence in a subsequent trial.[15]

There is no requirement that reports on progress of interception and final reports have to be submitted to the court. However, the interception period is relatively short, meaning that the authorisation must be renewed regularly and the prosecutor will be obliged to inform the court of any new relevant information, and changed circumstances.

There are requirements to destroy the records which are not related to the aim of the interception warrant, or which are not needed as evidence. The prosecutor is responsible for these. The Commission on Security and Integrity Protection (SIN) has on occasion criticised prosecutors for not promptly ordering, and supervising, the destruction of records. New guidelines were therefore issued by the Chief Public Prosecutor in 2012.[16] SIN has also criticised the police for not promptly carrying out orders to destroy surplus information.

---

[15] Lindberg, p. 515.

[16] ÅM RättsPM 2012:8.

9. Notification requirements and remedies against interception orders

There is a duty of the investigative authorities to inform intercepted persons about an interception. CJP 27:31 provides:

> "Anyone who is or has been suspected of a crime shall, subject to section 33, notified of such covert interception or surveillance of electronic communications … as he or she has been subjected to.
>
> If interception or surveillance of electronic communications has concerned a phone number or address, or certain electronic communication equipment possessed by someone other than the suspect, this person shall also be notified. This does not apply if the provisions of section 33 apply or it has taken place with the support of section 20, para 2 and the infringement of the individual's privacy is likely to be minor.
>
> …
>
> A notification shall be submitted as soon as it can be without damaging the investigation, however, not later than one month after the investigation has been terminated.
>
> Notification need not be given to someone who already according to CJP 23:18 or otherwise has received access to the data. Notification is not required either if, with regard to the circumstances, it is obviously unnecessary."

CJP 27:32 provides

> "Notification pursuant to section 31 shall include information on which coercive measure has been used and when it occurred. The person who is or has been suspected of an offence should obtain information about any suspected offence which has been the basis for the measure, or which the measure has led to. Anyone who is not, or has not been, suspected of an offence should be informed of this.
>
> A notice of covert interception of electronic communications or covert surveillance of electronic communications should also include a statement of which phone number or other address or which electronic communications equipment has been the subject of a warrant."

CJP 27:33 provides

> "If secrecy applies under the Transparency and Secrecy Act (2009:400) 15:1 or 2, 18:1, 2 or 3 or 35:1 or 2, for information referred to in section 32, notification under section 31 may be postponed until the secrecy no longer applies.
>
> If one year elapses from the time of the completion of the investigation, and notification can still not be made because of secrecy requirements, the duty to notify expires."

The exception referred to in CJP 27:20, para 2 is for the relatively rare occasions when the police empty a mobile mast of metadata, in order to determine active mobile phones in the area (e.g. after a robbery).

The exceptions set out in Chapter 15 of the Transparency and Secrecy Act cover offences within the jurisdiction of the Security Police. Notification (almost) never occurs for these. Instead, the Commission on Security and Integrity Protection supervises all cases of non-notification.

The exceptions set out in Chapter 18 of the Transparency and Secrecy Act cover damage to ongoing criminal investigations. There is a specific exception in Chapter 18:17 covering mutual legal assistance.

The exceptions set out in Chapter 35 of the Transparency and Secrecy Act cover information potentially damaging to individuals' economic or personal integrity.

In theory: a person who receives notification can complain to the Commission on Security and Integrity Protection (SIN) and/or the chief government law officer (the Chancellor of Justice), or initiate a case before the civil courts (for damages). However, I know of no such cases since the late 1980's where this has occurred. There was a case concerning unlawful surveillance conducted by senior Security Police officers in the aftermath of the murder of Prime Minister Palme, where the people subjected to the unlawful surveillance attempted to secure full disclosure of methods etc and the prosecution demanded restrictions on the injured parties' right of access to the evidence. It is unclear how such a case would be resolved if it arose today. The Transparency and Secrecy Act applies, but so too does the right to a fair trial under IG and the ECHR. The issue has not been tested since the late 1980's and the situation is unclear.[17]

If SIN find that an offence (presumably misuse of office) has been committed in the course of surveillance operations it is to report this to the prosecutor with a view to prosecution. This has arisen only very rarely.

SIN is the independent monitoring authority which has the power to control, after the fact, the interception of communication and make sure that it is carried out in accordance with the legal requirements/legal authorisation. There were several reasons for creating SIN in 2007. Increased investigative powers had been, or were in the process of being, granted to the police and the Security Police. There was also a realisation that prosecutorial and judicial control only checked whether there was reasonable cause to initiate surveillance, and there was no *post hoc* monitoring. SIN was thus given a follow-up oversight function over surveillance. Having said this, the most important part of the work of SIN is still the function of monitoring personal data. SIN's mandate is 1) to ensure that surveillance activities by the police, and the Security Police, are conducted in accordance with laws and other regulations and 2) that the police and the Security Police filing of personal data is 'conducted in accordance with laws and other regulations'. These laws include the limits set out on the filing of sensitive data in the Constitution (Instrument of Government Chapter 2, Section 6; European Convention on Human Rights (ECHR) Article 8) and in the Police Data Act, as well as the police and the Security Police's own regulations on initiating, adding to, correcting and terminating personal files. Although the mandate is only framed in terms of ensuring compliance with the law, a proportionality test is a fundamental part of this.

---

[17] Lindberg, p. 512.

10. Confidentiality requirements on telecommunication providers and reliability requirements on those conducting telecommunication interceptions

There is a specific obligation for all service providers to keep their support measures confidential under ECA 6:20-23. Specific criminal sanctions for infringements of this obligation are set out in ECA 7:15, with a further reference to the CC (which in turn contains a reference to the content of a secrecy breach in the Act on Transparency and Secrecy).

There are also obligations for the person conducting the interception to maintain the integrity and reliability of the material obtained in CJP 27:24, and in Ordinance 1947:948. There is also a constitutional rule on impartiality and objectivity *(saklighet)* in IG 1:9.

B. Collection and Use of Traffic Data and Subscriber Data

1. Collection of traffic data and subscriber data

In Sweden, law enforcement access to metadata is regulated in a number of different laws. The actual duty on service providers to retain the metadata for a period of six months is in the Act on Electronic Communication (2003:389), primarily in section 16a (see also below, regarding subscriber information).

Access by law enforcement to more extensive metadata than the name of a subscriber is regulated in the Act (2007:979) on measures to prevent particularly serious crimes, the Act (2008:854) on measures to investigate certain societally dangerous crimes and the Act (2012:278) on the collection of data on electronic communications in law enforcement intelligence. The 2007 Act is used relatively rarely. The 2008 Act provides for less stringent rules in certain circumstances for Security Police investigations into security crime but is not particularly significant in the area of metadata.

CJP section 19 provides

> "Secret monitoring of electronic communication means that information is secretly gathered on
>
> 1. messages in an electronic communications which is or has been transferred to or from a phone number or other address, or
> 2. identifying which electronic communication equipment which has been present in a given geographical area, or
> 3. identifying the geographical area where specific electronic communications equipment has been present.
>
> Messages referred to in para 1 may also be prevented from reaching their destination through covert surveillance of electronic communications.

Secret surveillance of electronic communication may be used during a preliminary investigation of

1. Offences for which the penalty is at least six months in prison,
2. Computer hacking under CC 4:9c, child pornography offences under CC 16:10a which are not regarded as minor, drug offences under section 1 of the Narcotics Act (1968:64), drug trafficking according to section 6 para 1 of the Act (2000:1225) on Penalties for Smuggling,
3. The offences referred to in section 2, para 2 p. 2–7, or
4. Attempts, preparation or conspiracy to commit an offence referred to in p. 1–3 above, if such an offence is punishable.

In the cases referred to in section 20 para 2, secret surveillance of electronic communications may be used only in preliminary investigations concerning offences that may lead to secret interception of electronic communications according to section 18 para 2".

Giving the police or Security Police access to metadata is not seen as a "coercive measure". However it undoubtedly involves an interference with personal integrity within the meaning of the Swedish Constitution (above) and the ECHR. Because of this, access to metadata within the framework of a preliminary investigation requires court permission.

Although the main legal provision is in the CJP, the police and Security Police may, however, also access metadata if certain conditions are fulfilled, as part of their intelligence work under the above Act from 2012. The police and Security Police themselves decide whether or not to obtain this data, which can only be obtained if there is reasonable suspicion of "criminal activity" (but not sufficiently specified information so that one can say that they suspect that a particular criminal offence has been committed). Around 100-150 people are affected by such decisions taken by the police per year (SOU 2015:31, p. 263). The figure for the Security Police is not public, but probably double the figure than that for the open police (200-250 people). Some of these intelligence-based decisions later become preliminary investigations, and so there is overlap between these figures and those presented in chapter I.B.2. above.

2. Use of traffic data and subscriber data

As regards the requirements for accessing traffic data in Sweden, to begin with, this is not yet possible by way of an automated online procedure. The Security Police have on several occasions requested telecommunications operators agree voluntarily to such a system, but this has been resisted. Competition is rife in the Swedish telecommunications market, and several Swedish companies, partly in order to attract and keep customers, advertise themselves as maintaining a high level of data integrity, i.e., keeping it secret even from the police.

Under CJP 27:20, a person must normally be reasonably suspected of the offence. However, a change was made in 2012, allowing access to metadata, but only historical (i.e., not real-time) data, in order to investigate who can be reasonably suspected of having committed the offence. In all cases, the measure must be of particular importance for the investigation before it can be ordered.

Under CJP 27:21 the court has to determine on the application of the prosecutor, whether the conditions required for the acquisition of metadata are met, the phone numbers and other addresses to be monitored, and the period of time for which access is granted, which may not exceed one month.

CJP 27:20 provides

> "Covert interception of electronic communications and covert surveillance of electronic communications shall, unless otherwise provided in the second paragraph, only occur if someone is reasonably suspected of the offence and the measure is of particular importance to the investigation. This measure may only relate to
>
> 1. a phone number or address, or a certain electronic communication during the time of the authorisation which is held or has been held by the suspect or which may otherwise be assumed to have been used or may be used by the suspect, or
> 2. a phone number or address, or a certain electronic communication if there is particular reason to assume that the suspect during the time of the authorisation has or will contact this number etc.
>
> Secret surveillance of electronic communication shall, in addition to what is stated in the first paragraph, be carried out in order to investigate who may reasonably be suspected of the crime, if this is of particular importance to the investigation. However, only data relating to the past may be collected."

The provisions in the CJP, especially after the changes made in 2012, would seem to cover all the conceivable situations when law enforcement need access to metadata. However, under the CJP, a preliminary investigation cannot be started to find out if an offence has been committed. Thus, police and Security Police investigations into organised crime and security crime respectively need some other legal basis. The 2012 Act regulates the preconditions for the police, the Security Police and the Customs Service to collect metadata in the course of intelligence operations. Prior to the enactment of the act, the agencies in question simply directed telecommunications providers to provide them with specified historical records.

The information which may be collected in accordance with section 1 of the Act is both historical traffic data (i.e., not real-time data) and location data – both historical location data and real-time location data. Data may be accessed if the circumstances are such that the measure is of particular importance to detect or prevent criminal activity involving crimes which have a minimum punishment of imprisonment for at least two years and if the measure is proportionate (section 2). Data may also be accessed where there is criminal activity involving certain specified security crimes which have a lower penalty than the minimum of two years (section 3). Generally speaking, Swedish sentences are relatively low, meaning that only serious offences are punishable by a minimum of two years. Thus, the threshold for intelligence access to metadata is set significantly higher than the threshold for access to metadata within the context of a preliminary investigation.

Decisions on whether or not to require production of metadata are made by the agency itself and are not subject to any prior external review (section 4). Formally speaking, the head of the agency makes such decisions, but in practice this has been delegated down in the official hierarchy. However, no one actually participating in operational (intelligence gathering) activities is to take such a decision. Decisions shall be in writing, and the period covered by the order shall not exceed one month (section 5). If the metadata gathered indicates that criminal offences are being or have been committed, and the agency wishes to open a preliminary investigation, transfer of the metadata to the preliminary investigation requires court permission, applying the rules applicable for secret surveillance of electronic communications (section 8).

As regards the requirements for accessing subscriber data, the ECA provides for law enforcement access to information on who has a particular telephone number, or temporary IP address, *inter alia*, when this is necessary to investigate the commission of any offence. There is no requirement that the offence be punishable by a minimum sentence (unlike the case under the CJP or the 2012 Act). Minor offences can thus be investigated under the ECA, but only the name of the subscriber is available. This has, up to now, not been regarded as particularly serious from the perspective of personal integrity. As already mentioned, this is not possible by way of an automated online procedure.

Internet providers are required to retain subscriber information. Internet providers are also required to retain traffic data. The general duty of cooperation has already been mentioned. The more detailed requirements are set out in the Ordinance (2003:396) on Electronic Communication (as amended by Ordinance 2012:128). The relevant parts of this provide:

"**Section 39**. In terms of telephony, the following are to be stored:

1. The caller,
2. The dialled number and the number that call is passed on to,
3. Information about the calling and the called subscriber and, where appropriate, registered users,
4. Date and traceable time when communication began, and ended, and
5. Details of the service or services that have been used.

Section 40. When it comes to telephone service over a mobile network access point, in addition to those mentioned in § 39, the following is to be stored:

1. The caller and the called subscriber's subscription identity and equipment identity;
2. The location information for the start and end of the communication, and
3. The date, traceable time and location data for the initial activation of a prepaid anonymous service.

Section 41. In terms of telephony service that uses IP packets for transmission, in addition to those mentioned in §§ 39 and 40, the following information is to be stored:

1. The caller and the called subscriber's IP addresses,
2. Date and traceable time for log-on and log-off or the services used, and

3. Information identifying the equipment where the communication between the entity with the storage obligation and the individual subscriber is completed.

If the entity which finally relays the communication to the individual subscriber is not covered by ECA 6:16 a, the first paragraph 3 applies to the entity which relayed the communication to that entity.

Section 42. In terms of messaging, the following are to be stored:

1. Sender's and recipient's number, IP address, or other communication address,
2. Information on sending and receiving subscriber and, where appropriate, registered users,
3. Date and traceable time for log-on and log-off or the services used,
4. Date and traceable time of dispatch and receipt of message, and
5. Details of the service or services that have been used.

Section 43. In terms of Internet access and the provision of capacity to obtain internet access (connection form) the following should be stored:

1. The user's IP address,
2. Information on the subscriber and, where applicable, registered users,
3. Date and traceable time for log-on and log-off service providing Internet access;
4. The type of transmission capacity used, and
5. Information identifying the equipment where the communication between the entity with the storage obligation and the individual subscriber is completed.

If the entity which finally relays the communication to the individual subscriber is not covered by ECA 6:16 a, the first paragraph 5 applies to the entity which relayed the communication to that entity."

All the above data is to be made available on request to law enforcement agencies. Failure to do so is sanctioned by the PTS through administrative fines. It should be noted that after the Court of Justice of the EU (CJEU) declared the Data Retention Directive null and void, certain telecommunications companies refused to hand over data on request in cases where the police or Security Police requested this for intelligence operations under the 2012 Act (as opposed to a preliminary investigation into an offence, which had been authorised by a court). The PTS was unsure of whether the Swedish 2012 Act was in compliance with the CJEU's judgment and announced that, pending clarification, it would not enforce the duty to cooperate by issuing administrative fines. A commission of inquiry was appointed which analysed the judgment. It came to the conclusion that the 2012 Act (which *inter alia* provides for *post hoc* control by SIN) set out sufficient safeguards to be in compliance with the requirements of EU law (as clarified by the CJEU).[18] The PTS then resumed sanctioning non-compliance, and the telecom companies resumed their compliance. However, two telecom companies appealed the PTS decision. The district administrative court ruled against them, whereupon this in turn was appealed. The administrative court of appeal has recently requested a pre-

---

[18] Ds. 2014:23. A later, follow-up, inquiry made a detailed empirical study of police and Security Police use of metadata under the 2012 Act and came to the same conclusion. See SOU 2015:31.

liminary ruling from the CJEU on whether the Swedish system is in compliance with EU law or not. In the meantime, one of these companies has refused to comply with police orders to produce traffic data for intelligence purposes, and is facing administrative fines.[19]

3. Identification of the device ID (IMEI) and location of mobile terminal devices

The device ID (IMEI) is part of the information which must be stored and made available by the service provider. ISMI catchers are also in use in Sweden, although their use is apparently rare. This is not specifically regulated, apparently on the basis that this is not a significant infringement on privacy (IG 2:6 para. 2 above). This is not a strong argument, but in any event, the failure to regulate specifically the use of ISMI catchers means that their use will probably violate Article 8 ECHR.

C. Access to (Temporarily) Stored Communication Data

Access to (temporarily) stored communication data is possible for messages which have been delivered to the recipient and so stored in his/her mobile or computer.[20] This is not possible for data in the possession of the ISP. Instead, a warrant has to be issued for interception of electronic communications. Access to stored communication may only be performed as an open measure, not in a clandestine way. The principle of proportionality applies to seizure. This standard of proof means that there must be specific evidence of specific strength indicating that the property is of importance for the investigation of the offence.[21] The Chancellor of Justice and the Ombudsman have on occasion criticised the police and prosecutors for seizing a person or a company's computers – making their continued business activity impossible. The police and prosecutors have therefore adopted a more restrictive approach, copying data which is then destroyed to the extent it is not necessary for the investigation. There is, on the other hand, a greater degree of latitude

---

[19] For more discussion, see Cameron, I., Law enforcement access to metadata in Sweden, in Lind, A.S., Reichel, J., Österdahl I. (eds.), *Information and Law in Transition*, Liber, 2015. The Advocate-Generals opinion in Joined Cases C-203/15 Tele2 Sverige AB v. Post-och telestyrelsen and C-698/15 Secretary of State for Home Affaris was published on July 16 2016. Basically the Advocate-General considers that a general requirement of data retention is compatible with EU law, but that each of the safeguards set out by the ECJ in the Digital Rights Case must be satisfied (instead of making a general appraisal of the national system of safeguards as a whole). If upheld by the ECJ, this would mean making a change to the law, introducing a requirement of prior judicial or quasi-judicial approval before the police or Security Police may access metadata for intelligence purposes.

[20] SOU 1998:46, p. 373; Lindberg, p. 522.

[21] See, e.g., SOU 2011:45, p. 274; Lindberg, p. 45.

given when transferring such data abroad in execution of a request for mutual legal assistance.[22]

As regards the issue of cooperation duties for decoding encrypted data, in Sweden a witness can be obliged to witness under oath in court proceedings, but there is no possibility for the police or a prosecutor to insist that a suspect hand over a password.

IV. Use of Electronic Communication Data in Judicial Proceedings

As regards the issue whether there are specific rules for using intercepted electronic communication data in criminal procedure, Swedish procedural law is based on the principle of free evaluation and admissibility of evidence. It is the court which determines the value to be given to a particular piece of evidence, for example, a conviction could be based purely on circumstantial evidence.

Intercepted material can be introduced as evidence in criminal proceedings in the form of transcripts, audio recordings, and witness testimony. The principle of orality means that witness testimony is the primary method. Transcripts and the original recordings can be used if for some reason witness testimony is not available or if it assists the court in understanding the evidence.

Evidence which has been obtained in a fashion which is regarded as improper, or where the rights of the defence have not been properly safeguarded, is still admissible but will usually be given a low or very low evidential value. In a case where the court considers that the police have acted through an *agent provacteur*, the court will apply ECtHR case law and disregard the evidence.

As noted above intercepted data can be used for the prosecution of offences other than the offences mentioned or anticipated in the interception order. Moreover, intercepted data can be used for the prosecution of individuals who were not the subject of the underlying interception order, so long as the (relatively strict) conditions for use of surplus information are met.

Intercepted data obtained from outside the criminal justice system (e.g. intelligence services, non-judicial police forces) is at the present time not admissible as evidence in criminal proceedings. However, there has been a recent proposal by a commission of inquiry (SOU 2015:163) that it should be possible for the signals intelligence agency (FRA) to continue to monitor communications of suspected "foreign fighters" and collect, on behalf of the Security Police, evidence that these

---

22 See NJA 2013, s. 867.

people have committed offences. However, this evidence would not be directly admissible in subsequent trials. This proposal has been criticised, and it is unclear whether it will result in a legislative bill.

As far as transnational criminality is concerned, the principle of free admissibility of evidence means that evidence gathered by foreign police and prosecutors, in whatever form, can be presented. Nor is it essential that foreign witnesses physically attend the main hearing in Sweden. Although efforts are invariably made to allow such witnesses to give their evidence by means of live telephone or video links, where this is impracticable, written statements are usually admissible.

As regards the possibilities the accused has of challenging the probity of intercepted evidence, when a preliminary investigation has reached the point where a person is reasonably suspected of a crime, s/he should be informed of these suspicions (they will usually have been charged and arrested at this point anyway). There are two schools of thought as to whether such a suspect has the right to be informed of the results of the preliminary investigation. When a person has been formally accused of the offence (which usually occurs at the time of trial), it is clear that s/he has the right under CJP to be informed) of all relevant evidence and have access to the material gathered in the preliminary investigation. If this is refused, s/he can apply to the court to grant him/her access. Where a preliminary investigation is discontinued without leading to a formal accusation and trial, the person previously suspected has no explicit right to receive the preliminary investigation file. However, refusal to grant access to the file can be appealed to the administrative courts, and the Supreme Administrative Court has on occasion found that the person's interests in seeing the file outweigh the interests involved in keeping it secret. So far, none of these cases have involved covert surveillance.[23]

V. Exchange of Intercepted Electronic Communication Data between Foreign Countries

A. Legal Basis for Mutual Legal Assistance

Mutual legal assistance is governed by the Act on International Legal Assistance (2000:562).[24] The Act can form the basis of granting requests from other states, i.e., Sweden does not require that another state requesting mutual legal assistance has acceded to a treaty to which Sweden has also acceded. However, accession to

---

23 Lindberg, p. 513.

24 For more discussion, see Cameron, I., Thunberg Schunke, M. Påle-Bartes, C., Wong, K. and Asp, P., *International Criminal Law from Swedish Perspective*, Intersentia, Brussels, 2011, chapter 4.

such a treaty generally makes the provision of mutual legal assistance easier. Sweden has acceded to the following most central multilateral conventions concerning international legal assistance in criminal matters:

(1) the European Convention (1959) on Mutual Assistance in Criminal Matters (hereafter the "ECMLA"), including the two additional protocols of 1978 and 2001,[25]

(2) the European Convention (1977) on terrorism,[26]

(3) the United Nations Convention (1988) against Illicit Traffic in Narcotic Drugs and Psychotropic Substances,[27]

(4) the European Convention (1990) on Laundering, Search, Seizure and Confiscation of the Proceeds from Crime,[28]

(5) the Schengen Convention (1990),[29]

(6) the United Nations Convention (2000) against Transnational Organized Crime and its supplementing Protocols,[30]

(7) the EU Convention (2000) on Mutual Assistance in Criminal Matters (hereafter "EUCMLA"), and its Protocol of 16 October 2001,[31]

(8) the international Agreement of 19 December 2003 between the EU and Norway and Iceland.[32]

Apart from these most central conventions, Sweden has also ratified other treaties which are not primarily regulating international cooperation in criminal matters but still contain clauses on mutual assistance. Sweden also has a small number of bilateral treaties with states (e.g. with China, regarding Hong Kong).

B. Procedures and Execution of Requests

There are no special prerequisites concerning requests for interception of telecommunications in the Swedish Act on International Legal Assistance. The rules in

---

25 SÖ 1968:15, SÖ 1979:12, and Bills 1961:48 and 1978/79:80. The second additional protocol to the ECMLA has not yet been ratified by Sweden. However, most of the provisions of this protocol are already implemented into Swedish law mainly through the implementation of the EUCMLA 2000 and its Protocol of 16 October 2001.

26 SÖ 1977:12, and Bill 1976/77:124.

27 SÖ 1991:41, and Bill 1990/91:127.

28 SÖ 1996:19, and Bill 1995/96:49. The Council of Europe Convention on Laundering, Search, Seizure and Confiscation of the Proceeds from Crime and on the Financing of Terrorism, ETS 198, has been signed but not ratified by Sweden.

29 SÖ 1998:49, and Bills 1997/98:42, 1997/98:58 and 1999/2000:61.

30 SÖ 2004:21, and Bills 2002/03:146, 2003/04:111 and 2004/05:138.

31 SÖ 2005:42, SÖ 2005:43, and Bill 2004/05:144.

32 OJ L 26, 29.01.2004, p. 1, and Bill 2004/05:144.

the CJP are applicable also when the measures are taken upon request from a foreign state.

Foreign requests for interception of telecommunications are handled by the responsible prosecutor (who will often be attached to one of the three specialist international prosecution chambers). The prosecutor shall immediately consider if the prerequisites for the measure exist and in such a case apply to the court for permission to undertake the measure.[33]

Where a Swedish prosecutor has sought covert electronic interception or surveillance, s/he must apply the CJP rules on legal privilege to the data delivered and filter out or delete information which would have been privileged had it been gathered in Sweden.

A request to execute a cross-border interception of a person present in Sweden (or rather, a telecommunications address held or used in Sweden)[34] may only be made from an EU Member State or from Iceland or Norway and must concern a criminal investigation.[35]

The prerequisites for Swedish authorities to give consent to a foreign cross-border interception of telecommunications are identical to those which rule requests for the traditional forms of interception.[36] These stricter conditions, for example concerning the minimum penalty applicable to an offence before interception can be ordered, are due to the fact that the address to be intercepted in such a case is held or used in Sweden. Even though Sweden is in general positive to judicial cooperation based on the principle of mutual recognition, execution of decisions involving telecommunications interception is particularly sensitive.[37] There is a requirement of double criminality. Requests are handled by a prosecutor, who shall immediately consider if the prerequisites for the measure exist, and in such a case apply to the court for permission to undertake the measure.[38] Having set out the conditions, it is unclear if this measure is used in practice. The long land borders with Norway and Finland would indicate that there will be some situations in which these states might be able to intercept telecommunications in Sweden near the border. Separate statistics on this are however not available in Sweden.

Concerning the real-time transfer of communication data, Swedish communication providers are under a duty of confidentiality, which can only be waived in relation to Swedish police, prosecutors and courts: thus requests must go through the Swedish system.

---

33 Ch. 4 sec. 25 para. 1 ILA Act.

34 See Bill 2004/05:144 p. 206.

35 Ch. 4 sec. 26a para. 1 ILA Act.

36 Ch. 4 sec. 26a para. 3 ILA Act.

37 See Bill 2004/05:144 pp. 178–179.

38 Ch. 4 sec. 26a para. 1–2 ILA Act.

In my opinion, relatively few technical, legal, and organisational national reform measures would be necessary to enable "real time cooperation" in the field of interception measures or to increase its effectiveness, assuming there is mutual trust. This undoubtedly exists as regards other Nordic states and some EU states (including Germany), but almost certainly not for others. If such a possibility were introduced as a result of an EU measure, implemented into Swedish law, the likelihood is that Sweden, during the negotiations, would probably want to make it discretionary, rather than mandatory. Moreover, it is likely that it would be limited by reference to safeguards which could be adapted to fit individual cases, depending upon which EU state had requested the data etc.

I anticipate no challenges for mutual legal assistance in the implementation of the recently adopted European Investigation Order in the area of intercepted communications.

C. Statistics

International requests make up a small proportion of the whole: in 2007 these amounted to 42 of 996 warrants issued, in 2008, they were 28 of 990 issued.[39]

According to more recent figures, (in 2013, 72 applications were made on behalf of foreign states and granted for covert interception of electronic communications.[40] In 2014, the figure was 84 applications made and granted. Many of these concerned the same person(s), i.e., permission was extended for several periods of one month. In 2014, a total of 39 people were affected by these applications.

In 2013, 245 applications were made on behalf of foreign states and granted for covert surveillance of electronic communications. In 2014, the figures were 204 applications made and granted. Again, many of these concerned the same person(s), i.e., permission was extended for several periods of one month. In 2014, 85 people were affected.

Figures broken down by country are not available, however on the basis of questions put to the relevant prosecutors, a small proportion of these concerned requests from Germany.

---

[39] See respectively Rskr 2008/09:79, p. 16 and Rskr 2009/10:66, p. 8. A warrant can involve more than one teleaddress and can therefore concern more than one person.

[40] ÅM 2014/1569.

Bibliography

Lind, A.S., Reichel, J., Österdahl I. (eds.), *Information and Law in Transition*, Liber 2015.

Lindberg, G., *Straffprocessuella Tvångsmedel* (Coercive measures under the law of criminal procedure), 3 uppl. Karnov, 2013.

Cameron, I., Thunberg Schunke, M., Påle-Bartes, C., Wong, K. and Asp, P., *International Criminal Law from Swedish Perspective*, Intersentia, Brussels, 2011.

List of Abbreviations

CJEU	Court of Justice of the European Union
CJP	Code of Judicial Procedure
Ds	Departmental commissions of inquiry
ECA	Electronic Communications Act
ECHR	European Convention on Human Rights
ECJ	Court of Justice of the European Union
ECtHR	European Court of Human Rights
FRA	Defence Radio Establishment (signals intelligence agency)
NJA	Supreme Court reports
Rskr	Government report to parliament
SIN	Commission on Security and Integrity Protection
SIUN	Defence Intelligence Inspection
SÖ	Swedish treaty series
SOU	State Commissions of Inquiry

Spain*

National Rapporteur:
Lorena Bachmaier Winter

* This report reflects legislation and case law as of September 2016.

Contents

I. Security Architecture and the Interception of Telecommunication

A. Law Enforcement Institutions and Security Services with Powers of Telecommunication Interception

1. National security architecture

For understanding the gathering of information through the interception of telecommunications, it is not necessary to enter into details regarding the precise regulation of all the departments, bodies, and units that may be in some or another way involved in the national security field. The Spanish national security "architecture" follows a quite simple structural pattern:

- State Security intelligence service, the National Intelligence Centre (*Centro Nacional de Inteligencia*, CNI), and the criminal prosecution;
- Ministry of Interior: law enforcement, criminal policies and public security, and criminal prevention functions;
- Criminal Prosecution: Judiciary and public prosecution service.

The legal framework and their precise powers with regard to the interception of telecommunications will be explained below.

2. Powers for the interception of telecommunication

a) Law of criminal procedure

Article 588 of the Spanish Criminal Procedure Code (*Ley de Enjuiciamiento Criminal*, LECRIM), as of 5 October 2015 provides for the general legal framework on interception of telecommunications regarding the investigation of criminal offences within the criminal procedure. The general threshold for these interceptions is: offences sanctioned with a penalty higher than three years' imprisonment, or organised crime, terrorism, and cybercrime. The regulation will be explained in detail below.

b) Preventive law

The Spanish system does not allow for the interception of communications within the preventive law. So-called "pro-active" investigative measures are prohibited. This prohibition is now specifically stated under Article 588*bis* a LECRIM:

> 2. The principle of speciality requires that the investigative measure is related to the investigation of a specific offense. No IT investigative measures may be authorized aimed

at *preventing a crime* nor for discovering it or confirm suspicions that have not an objective foundation.

Prior to this rule, the Supreme Court had repeatedly stated that interception of communications without enough probable cause of a concrete offence, are unlawful (STS 1 December 1995, RJ 1995/9031, or 11 April 1997, RJ 1997/2802).

c) Law of intelligence agencies

The activities of the CNI (*Centro Nacional de Inteligencia*, National Intelligence Centre) are regulated by Law 11/2002.[1] Article 4 lists the functions of the CNI. For the fulfilment of its objectives, the CNI has the following functions (paragraph b):

> To prevent, detect, and enable the neutralization of those activities of foreign services, groups, or individuals that endanger, threaten, or violate the constitutional order, rights and freedoms of European citizens, sovereignty, integrity, and security of the state, the stability of its institutions, national economic interests, and welfare of the population.

The prevention of criminal offences such as terrorism, organised crime, and cybercrime fall within this provision.

Organic Law 2/2002[2] regulates the interception of communications by the CNI. Previously the Supreme Court had convicted several agents for illegal interception of communications in its judgment STS 367/2001, of 22 March. In this judgment the Supreme Court said: "The defence of national security cannot be used as an extra-legal reason to prevail upon the legal principles protected by the rule of law."

Following the Organic Law 2/2002, the interception of communications conducted by the CNI are subject to previous judicial control. This Organic Law, which has only one article, states:

> Within the development of its functions, the Director of National Intelligence shall request the competent Judge of the Supreme Court, according to the Organic Law of the Judiciary, authorisation for the adoption of measures affecting the inviolability of the home and the secrecy of communications, provided that such measures are necessary for the fulfilment of the functions assigned to the Centre. The decision shall be taken by reasoned order, which will remain secret.

No specific threshold or suspicion is set out for the decision on the interception of communications by the CNI. The judicial control is a requisite stemming directly from Article 18 of the Spanish Constitution (SC). But the criteria the Supreme Court Judge has to take into account when granting the authorisation for the CNI to carry out interception of communications are not laid out. The statutory provisions determine that the judicial warrant shall be founded, but as those decisions are secret, it is impossible to know what the grounds for them are. It is also unknown

---

[1] Law 11/2002, 6 May, reguladora del Centro Nacional de Inteligencia.

[2] Organic Law 2/2002, 6 May, reguladora del control judicial previo del Centro Nacional de Inteligencia.

how many requests are filed with the Supreme Court Judge, or how many of the requests are granted and/or denied.

d) Customs Investigation Service

There are no powers to intercept communications out of a criminal procedure and thus the powers are the same as regulated in the LECRIM.

3. Responsibility for the technical performance of interception measures

Within the investigation of criminal offences that fall under Article 588 LECRIM, the technical performance of the interception of telecommunications is done by the judicial police, with the aid of the telecommunications service providers, when needed. This issue will be developed more extensively below.

Within the CNI, this competence lies with the officers of the CNI.

4. Legitimacy of data transfers between different security agencies

There is no precise regulation on the transfer of information from the CNI to the law enforcement agents. The provisions in the law of the CNI are very general.

Article 4

[...]

c) To promote cooperative relations and cooperation with intelligence services of other countries or international organizations, to better fulfil its objectives.

[...]

e) Coordinate the action of different government bodies using means or procedures of encryption, ensure the safety of information technology in this field, inform on the coordinated acquisition of cryptology equipment and train their own personnel and staff from other administrations in this field to ensure the proper accomplishment of the tasks of the Centre.

According to the general rules, when the CNI detects possible elements of a criminal offence, like any other person and/or entity, it has the obligation to report to the police, the Public Prosecutor or the Investigation Judge. The general obligation to report facts related to a possible criminal offence are stated in Articles 259, 262 and 264 LECRIM. How this reporting activity is done in practice by the CNI is not public and there is no statutory regulation on it.

a) Exchange of data between law enforcement authorities and preventive police authorities

The structure and functions of the law enforcement authorities in Spain (mainly National Police and Guardia Civil) are regulated in Organic Law 2/1986, 13 March, last modified 29 July 2015 *(Ley Orgánica Fuerzas y Cuerpos de Seguridad del Estado)*. When listing the functions, the law mentions both prevention and investigation, without differentiating which authorities or units will carry out preventive functions and which ones investigation:

Article 11: Functions

[…]

f) prevent the commission of criminal acts.

g) investigate crimes, discover and detain suspects, secure the instruments, effects, and evidence of crime, making them available to the competent judge or court and prepare the necessary technical and expert reports.

h) detect, receive, and analyse any data of interest for public order and safety, and to study, plan, and implement methods and techniques of crime prevention.

Thus, one cannot speak of a "preventive police authority" different from the law enforcement authority. Within the organisational structure and internal division of departments those functions are more differentiated. The Royal Decree 769/1987, 19 June, on the regulation of the Judicial Police, states what the specific functions of the police are when acting within a criminal investigation as judicial police, and how each of the units of Judicial Police is composed. But every law enforcement agent can act as judicial police when required, even if he/she is not integrated in one of the specific Judicial Police units.

In sum, there is no legal provision on the exchange of data between criminal investigation units and prevention or police intelligence units. This has been pointed out by scholars,[3] highlighting the need for a more precise regulation on the exact scope of activities the police can carry out within their preventive functions and how the information gathered for that aim could be transferred to the criminal investigation.

b) Passing on of data by intelligence agencies

See above, under this same paragraph.

c) Passing on of data to intelligence agencies

There is no specific regulation on this.

[3] See, Bachmaier Winter, "Información de inteligencia y proceso penal" in *Terrorismo, proceso penal y derechos fundamentales*, ed. L. Bachmaier, Marcial Pons, pp. 45–101.

B. Statistics on Telecommunication Interception

There is no legal provision that requires collecting statistical data on the number and type of telecommunications interceptions carried out in the criminal investigation. If such data exist, they are not public and are not available.

II. Principles of Telecommunication Interception in Constitutional and Criminal Procedural Law

A. Constitutional Safeguards of Telecommunication

The relevant constitutional provision safeguarding the right to privacy, the right to secrecy of communications, and the *habeas data* is Article 18 SC, which reads as follows:

Article 18 SC

1. The right to honour, to personal and family privacy, and to the own image is guaranteed.

2. The home is inviolable. No entry or search may be made without the consent of the occupant or a legal warrant, except in cases of flagrante delicto.

3. Secrecy of communications is guaranteed, particularly of postal, telegraphic, and telephonic communications, except in the event of a court order to the contrary.

4. The law shall limit the use of data processing in order to guarantee the honour and personal and family privacy of citizens and the full exercise of their rights.

The precise scope of the concept of privacy, secrecy of communications, and definition of what should be considered as personal data has been established by the case law of the Constitutional Court and the Supreme Court.

The principles of proportionality and necessity are not expressly set out in the text of the SC when addressing the limits of fundamental rights. These principles were also not expressly stated in the Spanish Code of Criminal Procedure of 1882. However, despite the lack of a specific provision requiring that the principles of proportionality and necessity be respected when ordering and carrying out any coercive measure within the criminal investigation, these are elements that have been well elaborated by both Constitutional Court and Supreme Court in their jurisprudence, following the case law of the ECtHR on Article 8 ECHR.

Regarding the interception of communications (telephone), the Constitutional Court in its decision 49/1999, 5 April, stated that the principle of proportionality requires that both the legal provisions and the practice on telephone interceptions be limited to a constitutional legitimate aim[4] and such interference will only be

[4] See SSTC 48/1995; 108/1986; 90/1983.

justified if the restrictive measure is strictly necessary to achieve that aim and such sacrifice is proportionate.

The investigation of a serious criminal offence is considered a legitimate constitutional aim, without having to be stated expressly in the Constitution. In assessing the principle of necessity, the criterion to be followed is the possibility to achieve the same results through other measures less intrusive in the sphere of fundamental rights, taking into account the risks for securing the evidence and also the dangers for the law enforcement agents. In a strict sense, proportionality is understood as the relation between the encroachment on the fundamental right and the importance of the aim sought.[5]

To analyse the proportionality of telephone tapping the Constitutional Court mentions which criteria should be taken into account: not only the seriousness of the crime and the penalty foreseen for it, but also other elements like the legal values protected and the social relevance of those legal values, the degree of suspicion, and the possibility to obtain the evidence by other less intrusive means.

In general it can be stated that the Spanish courts have followed strictly the parameters set out in the case law of the ECtHR.[6]

However, Spain has had problems in complying with Articles 6 and 8 ECHR and has several times been found in violation of the ECHR, for lack of enough legal foreseeability as to telephone interceptions.[7]

Finally in its inadmissibility decision *Abdulkadir Coban*, 25 September 2006, the ECtHR considered that although the Spanish statutory rules were not sufficient to

---

[5] The principle of proportionality is not expressly mentioned in the Spanish Constitution of 1978, but Article 106.1 SC recognises it as a guiding principle of administrative law by stating: "1. The Courts control the power to issue regulations and to ensure that the rule of law prevails in administrative action, as well as to ensure that the *latter is subordinated to the ends which justify it.*" On the constitutional doctrine regarding the principle of proportionality, see, among others, González Beilfuss, *El principio de proporcionalidad en la jurisprudencia del Tribunal Constitucional*; Bernal Pulido, *El principio de proporcionalidad y los derechos fundamentales*; Pedraz Penalva and Ortega Benito, "El principio de proporcionalidad y su configuración en la jurisprudencia del Tribunal Constitucional y en literatura especializada alemana", *Rev. Poder Judicial* 17 (1990), pp. 69–100; Barnes Vázquez, "Introducción al principio de proporcionalidad en el derecho comparado y comunitario, *Rev. Actualidad Penal* 135 (1994), pp. 531 ff.; Vidal Fueyo, "El principio de proporcionalidad como parámetro de constitucionalidad de la actividad del juez," in *Anuario de Derecho Constitucional Latinoamericano* 2005, pp. 427–447.

[6] See, among others, ECtHR, *Klass and Others v. Germany*, 6.9.1978; *Malone v. United Kingdom*, 2.8.1984; *Kruslin v. France*, 24.4.1990, and *Huvig v. France*, 28.9.1995; *Kopp v. Switzerland*, 25.3.1998.

[7] ECtHR, *Valenzuela Contreras v. Spain*, 30.7.1998; *Prado Bugallo v. Spain*, 18.2.2003 See generally on the case law of the ECtHR against Spain regarding telephone interceptions, see L. Bachmaier, *Telephone tapping in the Spanish Criminal Procedure: An Analysis from the European Court of Human Right's Perspective*, Rev. JURA, 2007/2, Pécs, pp. 7–15.

comply with the standards on legal foreseeability, the Supreme Court case law provided enough guidance in this respect.[8]

Thus the situation until now has been the following: an insufficient legal provision completed with the criteria set out in the case law of Supreme Court and Constitutional Court.[9]

Besides the lack of sufficient legal rules on duration, requirements, remedies, etc., regarding telephone interceptions until the reform of 2015, the Spanish Code of Criminal Procedure neither provided for a list of offences or a penalty threshold where the interception of communications could be considered as proportional and thus could be ordered. In short, the statutory law did not define what the proportionality principle should be, and thus it had to be defined in each case by the courts. In general until reforming LECRIM in 2015, the courts considered that the interception of communications could only be ordered for the investigation of crimes sanctioned with a custodial penalty of at least three years, or if lower, to grant the interception if the crime involved a criminal organisation.

This situation has changed with the recent legal reform of the LECRIM of 5 October 2015, which will be reflected when addressing each of the questions below.

1. Core area of privacy

Following the case law of the Spanish Constitutional Court the right to privacy *(intimidad)* recognised under Article 18.1 SC is linked to the sphere of life a person wants to preserve from prying eyes, that area the individual wants to keep hidden from others because it belongs to his/her private sphere (SSTC 151/1997, 29 September). This right is closely linked to human dignity and the right to the free human personal development (Article 10.1 SC). Thus the right to an inaccessible core of privacy is granted even to those persons who are most exposed to public view (STC 134/1999, 15 July). The right to privacy, according to the constitutional provision, is recognised not only to the individual, but also to the family (SSTC 197/1991, 17 October, or 231/1988, 2 December).

---

[8] See Montón Redondo, "Las interceptaciones telefónicas constitucionalmente correctas," *La Ley* 1995-4, pp. 1043–1052; Gimeno Sendra, "Las intervenciones telefónicas en la jurisprudencia del Tribunal Constitucional y del Tribunal Supremo," *La Ley* 1996-2, pp. 1617–1624.

[9] See, for instance, the following decisions of the Spanish Constitutional Court: STC 239/1999, 20.12.1999; STC 47/2000, 17.2.2000; STC 126/2000, 16.5.2000; STC 299/2000, 11.12.2000; STC 202/2001, 15.10.2001; STC 87/2002, 22.4.2002; STC 167/2002, 18.9.2002; STC 184/2003, 23.10.2003; STC 165/2005, 20.6.2005; STC 205/2005, 18.7.2005; and STC 26/2006, 30.1.2006. See also the following decisions of the Supreme Court: STS 25.6.1993; STS 2.7.1993; STS 5.7.1993; STS 26.1.1994; STS 7.5.1994; STS 20.5.1994; STS 15.2.1996; STS 2.4.1996; STS 10.3.1997; STS 22.4.1998; STS 24.1.2000; STS 3.3.2000; STS 10.2.2001; STS 18.6.2001; STS 25.6.2001; STS 30.1.2002; STS 4.4.2002; STS 24.4.2002; STS 4.7.2003.

Based on this premise the extension and scope of the right depends on the particular circumstances of the case, the type of life of the person, and the specific aspect of his/her life that is affected (STC 115/2000, May 5, SSTC 83/2002 and 196/2004).

Within the criminal investigation, the protection of the right to privacy is always linked to the proportionality of the measure according to the judicial assessment. However, there is no sphere of privacy that is absolutely protected from being investigated within a criminal procedure (Spain has no "Tagebuch-doctrine").

2. Right to informational self-determination

In the landmark decision of the Constitutional Court 292/2000, 30 November, which decided the unconstitutionality challenge brought by the Ombudsman against several articles of the Law on Personal Data Protection, the Spanish Constitutional Court makes a clear and sharp distinction between the concepts of privacy and the protection of personal data, arguing that:

> "The peculiarity of the fundamental right to data protection, so close to that of privacy, lies in its distinct function, purpose, and content, differently from the function of the fundamental right to privacy of Art. 18.1 SC which is to grant protection against any interference in the area of personal and family life by third persons (e.g., STC 144/1999, 22 July, FJ 8).
>
> The fundamental right to data protection is intended to guarantee that the individual has the power of control over their personal data, its use and destination, in order to prevent any illicit and damaging transfer of those data, that may affect the dignity and the rights of the affected person."

In short, the judgment of the Constitutional Court states that the right to privacy aims to guarantee the individual an area of privacy, where the interference of third persons is excluded, whilst the right to informational self-determination recognises a power of control over the information regarding him/herself, about its use and destination, to avoid an illicit use of it.

It is important to add to the above that the fundamental right to privacy does not provide by itself sufficient protection for the new situation arising from technological progress and therefore, with the constitutional provision of Article 18 paragraph 4 SC, the right to *habeas data* and informational self-determination is given specific protection.

3. Proportionality of access to data

In general, proportionality is a prerequisite that has to be met for the constitutional validity of any investigative measure restrictive of fundamental rights, thus also to access to data.

Unlike what happens in other constitutions, the SC does not explicitly mention nor regulate the principle of proportionality as a guiding principle or parameter for the actions of public authorities. The Constitutional Court has based the application of the principle of proportionality on different articles: the rule of law clause (Article 1.1 SC), justice as higher value (Article 1.1 SC) or the principle of prohibition of arbitrariness (Article 9.3 SC), although, for example, the STC 160/1987 established a link between the proportionality principle and the dignity of the person (Article 10.1 SC). The Court has also recognised that Article 10.2 SC supports the adoption by the Spanish courts of the case law of the Strasbourg Court on proportionality and reasonableness for the valid restriction of fundamental rights.

In the very relevant STC 55/1996 the Constitutional Court stated that "the principle of proportionality in our constitutional system is not an autonomous constitutional principle which can be invoked separately from other constitutional rights. In the 90's the Spanish Constitutional Court started to fix the elements of the principle of proportionality under clear, although not explicitly recognized, German inspiration (e.g., SSTC 66/1995, 55/1996, 207/1996 and 136/1999)." Today it is established that the check of proportionality is comprised of: control of the adequacy or appropriateness of the measure under consideration (means-end relationship); an examination of the need for it (absence of a less intrusive alternative measure); and the strict proportionality control (the conflicting interests involved which are to be weighed to check if the advantages outweigh or at least offset the disadvantages).

Proportionality of every measure of telecommunications interception, until the legal reform of LECRIM of 5 October 2015, was assessed against those elements by the investigating judge competent to grant it. Generally it has been considered that the minimum threshold for authorising communications interception should be three years, although exceptions are to be found in the case law, justified by the presence of an organised group, or economic or social relevance of the act.

The proportionality and reasonableness of the interference in the fundamental right has to be clearly set out in the judicial warrant, although in practice many of these judicial warrants are quite sparse in their motivation. Generally, the gravity of the offence (penalty higher than three years' imprisonment) and the absence of less intrusive measures to reach the same result are the grounds invoked in the judicial warrants authorising any telecommunications interception.

The interception of content data needs to be more substantiated than access to traffic data, as the latter implies a less intrusive measure in the sphere of fundamental rights.[10]

---

[10] On the control of telecommunications and the right to data protection, see, Zoco Zabala, *Nuevas tecnologías y control de las comunicaciones*, pp. 102–109.

Since the legal reform of 5 October 2015 has entered into force,[11] the elements to be taken into account for assessing the proportionality of the measure of telecommunications interception are set out in

Article 588*bis* a LECRIM paragraph 5

The investigative measures covered in this chapter are only deemed proportional when taken into consideration all the circumstances of the case, the limitations of the rights and interests affected do not exceed the benefits of their adoption for the public interest or the interests of third parties. For the weighing of the conflicting interests, the public interest will be assessed taking into account the seriousness of the crime, its social significance or the technological sphere where it has been committed, the intensity of the existing evidence and the importance of the possible information or evidence sought by the measure restricting the right.

The new rules also establish a strict penalty threshold for the type of offences where telecommunications interceptions are allowed, and thus *sensu contrario*, if these requirements are not met, the measure would not be proportional, and is thus unlawful. These will be referred in more detail below.

Not meeting the proportionality test or not justifying the grounds for considering the measure restrictive of a fundamental right in compliance with the proportionality test, will render the investigative measure in breach of the constitutional right to the secrecy of communications and thus be void.

4. Statutory protection of personal data

Article 18.1 SC establishes the protection of the "right to honour, to personal and family privacy, and to the own image." Expressly Article 18.4 SC, within the protection of the right to privacy, states: "The law shall limit the use of data processing in order to guarantee the honour and personal and family privacy of citizens and the full exercise of their rights."

The SC was one of the first to establish the fundamental right to the protection of personal data and pursuant to the protection of this fundamental right there is a complete regulatory regime in the Spanish statutory provisions in accordance with the International and European Conventions. The general rules applicable to the protection of personal data are defined in Organic Law 5/1992, 29 October, on the Regulation of Automated Personal Data Processing, and Organic Law 15/1999, 13 December, on the Protection of Personal Data, but there are numerous other provisions that regulate data protection for each area.[12] There have been significant efforts made in Europe to guarantee adequate protection to the right to personal data, mainly the Convention 108, 28 January 1981, of the European Council on the automated processing of personal data; and the European Directive 95/46/CE of the European Parliament and Council, 24 October, on the protection of individuals

[11] The law entered into force on 6 December 2015.

[12] See Ortí Vallejo, *Derecho a la intimidad e informática*, pp. 20 ff.

with regard to the processing of personal data and on the free movement of such data.[13]

Spanish Organic Law 15/1999 largely follows the wording of Directive 95/46/CE,[14] but the scope of these legal instruments differs. While the Directive states that it shall not apply to the processing of personal data "concerning the public security, defence, State security and the activities of the State in areas of criminal law" (Article 3), the national regulation does not expressly exclude from the scope of the law activities in the criminal prevention or prosecution. Article 2 of Organic Law 15/1999 excludes from the application of the law files affecting classified information (mainly State security material) and files concerning the investigation of terrorism and serious forms of organised crime. In any case, the law provides that the controller of these files shall inform the supervising authority, the Data Protection agency, on the existence of this database, the general features of it and its purposes (Article 2.2.c) Organic law on Data Protection).[15]

For the protection of data linked to networks and communication services, the relevant statutory provision is Article 38 of the General Law on Telecommunications, which lists all the rights that assist consumers and users of telecommunications services.

a) Criminal liability for the unlawful interception of telecommunications

The criminal liability for unlawful interception of telecommunications within the criminal proceedings is provided under Article 539 of the Spanish Criminal Code (CC). I will mention here also the rules on unlawful interception of other communications and the unlawful entering of the home, as they may play some role when electronic data are collected.

The three provisions are enumerated under the heading "Of the offenses committed by public officials against the inviolability of the home and other privacy safeguards."

---

13 Extensively on this Directive see Heredero Higueras, "La Directiva Comunitaria de proteccion de datos de carácter personal."

14 Martín Casallo, "Implicaciones de la Directiva sobre protección de datos en la normativa española" in *X años de Encuentro sobre Informática y Derecho*, pp. 75–86. At the moment of writing this report the Spanish Law on Data Protection has not been yet adapted to the new EU Directive 2016/680 of 27 April 2016 on the protection of natural persons with regard to the processing of personal data by competent authorities for the purposes of the prevention, investigation, detection, or prosecution of criminal offences or the execution of criminal penalties, and on the free movement of such data, and repealing Council Framework Decision 2008/977/JHA.

15 On the exclusion of these data from the scope of application of the Law on Data Protection for reasons of national security, see Serrano Pérez, "El derecho fundamental a la protección de datos. Derecho español y derecho comparado," p. 405.

Article 534 CC

1. The authority or public officer who, within criminal proceedings, and without respecting the constitutional or legal guarantees:

1°- enters into a home without the consent of the occupant;

2°- records any papers or documents of a person or objects that are in his/her home, unless the owner has freely consented;

shall be punished with a fine of six to twelve months and disqualification from public office for two to six years.

If immediately after registration, the papers, documents and recorded effects are not returned to the owner, the penalty will be special disqualification from public office for six to twelve years and a fine of twelve to twenty four months, independently from the penalty corresponding to the offence of misappropriation.

2. The authority or public official who, during lawful registration of papers, documents or effects of a person commits any unjust harassment or unnecessary damage to the property, shall be punished with the penalties for these facts, imposed in the upper half and also with the penalty of special disqualification from public office for a period of two to six years.

Article 535 CC

The authority or public officer, who, within criminal proceedings, intercepts any kind of private postal or telegraphic correspondence with violation of constitutional or legal guarantees, shall incur into the penalty of disqualification from public employment or office for two to six years.

If the information obtained is divulged or distributed, the disqualification penalty shall be imposed in the upper half, as well as the fine from six to eighteen months.

Article 536 CC

The authority, public official, or agent who, within criminal proceedings, intercepts telecommunications or uses any technical devices for eavesdropping, transmission, recording, or reproduction of sound, image or any other communication signal, with violation of the constitutional or legal guarantees, shall be liable to a penalty of special disqualification from public office of two to six years.

If he/she reveals the information obtained, the disqualification penalty will be imposed in its upper half as well as the fine from six to eighteen months.

b) Protection of professional secrets in criminal procedural law

Professional secrets are protected in LECRIM through the privilege to refuse testimony, set out under Articles 416 and 417 LECRIM. These provisions, which have not been updated, read as follows:

Article 416 LECRIM

Following persons are exempted from the obligation to testify:

1. The relatives of the accused in direct ascending and descending lines, spouse or relationship analogous to marriage, their brothers or half blood and collateral blood relatives up to the second degree, and relatives referred number 3 of article 261.

   The investigating judge has to warn the witnesses of the preceding paragraph that they are not obliged to testify against the accused; but can make the statements they deem appropriate.

2. The lawyer of the accused, regarding the facts that he had trusted him in his capacity as defender.
3. The translators and interpreters with regard to the conversations and communications between the accused and the persons mentioned in the preceding paragraph, in relation to the facts to which he was referred for translation or interpretation.

Furthermore, Article 417 LECRIM states that the following persons may not be obliged to testify: 1) priests, pastors, or religious ministers, with regard to the facts entrusted them in the exercise of their pastoral functions; 2) public officials subject to state secrecy; and 3) morally or physically incapacitated persons.

No other provisions are included in LECRIM for protecting professional secrets. Spanish law is very sparse in this regard. It is understood that journalists cannot be obliged to give information or testify about their sources of information, as this professional secret is granted constitutional protection under Article 20.1 SC.

c) Principle of "purpose limitation of personal data"

This principle is set out in Article 4 Organic Law 15/1999 on Data Protection, together with the principle of consent, the right to be informed, and the right to rectification/deletion of data as well as the confidentiality of data processing. Although the principle of purpose limitation also applies to non-automatic data processing, given the fact that information technologies enable massive collection and storage of personal data and the cross-referencing of such data, special importance must be given to purpose limitation. Only data that is suitable and relevant for the purpose for which they were collected may be processed and used. Furthermore, the excessive storing of data or for an unjustified period of time, is unlawful.

The interconnection of national databases between public administrations basically affects the principle of consent and that of quality. Only databases that have compatible purposes may be interconnected without the consent of the data subject and those data could be processed without his/her previous consent (Article 21 OL 15/1999). However, the question has been raised whether the transfer of data amongst different public agencies – for esample, the Tax Agency and Social Security Administration – without common powers or purposes may occur, as this might be necessary and useful in practice for the efficiency of the Administration.[16] The Spanish Constitutional Court in the decision 292/2000, 30 November, stated that the interconnection of data amongst different public agencies for different purposes or matters is only legitimate and in accordance with the fundamental right to personal data protection if there is a specific legal provision that enables it, or if the affected person expressly consents. Although the interconnection is technically

16 See Troncoso Reigada, "Protection of data in e-government" in the foreword to the study coordinated by the Data Protection Agency of Madrid and published under the title e-Prodat: e-Government and Data Protection in European Regions and Cities, p. 23.

feasible, in order to be lawful, it must fulfil the conditions stated by the Constitutional Court.

The transfer of data to third countries is subject to the conditions stated in Article 25 of European Directive 95/46, that is, that the third country in question ensures an adequate level of protection. Spanish law requires, as a general rule, the consent of the data subject and the previous authorisation of the Director of the Data Protection Agency (Article 33). The data transfer to a third country will be registered in the Data Protection Agency, with indication of the country in question and the causes that motivated the transfer.[17] However, neither the authorisation of the supervising authority nor the consent of the data subject is needed in the following cases (only those affecting the criminal justice system are noted): 1) when the international transfer of personal data is allowed by an international treaty; 2) when the transfer of personal data is done at the request of a judicial authority within the field of international judicial cooperation; 3) when the transfer of data is needed for the protection of a public interest recognised by law, for example, for the fulfilment of the tasks of the tax and customs administration; and 4) when the data transfer is addressed to a Member State of the European Union and the Commission has declared that the third country in question has adequate safeguards to protect the right to personal data;[18] 5) for the transfer of data within the SIS, according to the Schengen Agreement; and 6) for the transfer of data recorded in police databases for a specific investigation, when the request comes from INTERPOL or other channels established in international treaties. In these cases the data will be transferred if it is needed for an actual criminal police investigation in a third country.[19]

d) Data protection of service providers' files and information gathered from interception of communications

The situation of data protection as regards files that have to be stored following Data Retention Law was clarified by the Royal Decree 1720/2007, 21 December, which approved the regulatory framework implementing the Organic Law on Data Protection (O.L. 15/1999 of 13 December on the protection of personal data). Title VIII develops in detail the regulation of various security levels, distinguishing between files and authorised and unauthorised processing. The regulation establishes a definition of the level of protection required for the files that are under the responsibility of telecommunication service providers, giving precise content to the requirement of guaranteeing the authenticity, confidentiality, and integrity of the

---

[17] Instruction 1/2000, 1st December of the Data Protection Agency, regarding the rules to be applied in the international transfer of personal data.

[18] Article 33 a), b), h) and k) Organic Law 15/1999.

[19] See Articles 3 and 4 R.D. 1332/1994, 20 June.

information obtained from the interception under Article 97 of the Telecommunication Law. Following the Regulation of 2007 these are the levels of protection to be ensured: Traffic data and location data undergo the basic and medium levels of protection, but the registry of accesses will be recorded according to the higher level of protection (Articles 103 and 81.4). The access log is certainly a crucial safeguard to ensure the authenticity and non-tampering of the different information stored by order of the data retention law.

The remaining data, in particular identification data of the user or subscriber, is subject to the basic level of protection, as long as it does not allow a user profile to be created, in which case it would also be subject to the middle level of protection (Article 81.1 and 2 f.).

Fourth paragraph of Article 81, paragraph b) states that the information provided to the authorised agent who carried out the interception of communications will be subject to the higher level of data protection. This higher level protection ensures a level of transparency in the management and the non-manipulation of the data obtained, dispelling doubts on the integrity of the evidence, and at the same time allowing the parties to test whether communications and data submitted by the operators concerned has been subject to manipulation or unauthorised access, and to what level.

e) Rules on cancelling data stored in police files

According to the Resolution of 30 June 1995 issued by the General Directorate of the Police a distinction must be made between three different categories of police activities:

a) Police actions carried out within State security or within the fight against serious forms of organised crime (terrorism, drug-trafficking money laundering, and all other criminal acts committed by organised groups). These data are not subject to the application of the safeguards and requirements established in the Organic Law for Data Protection.

b) Police actions aimed at the prevention of other real dangers, not included in the previous paragraph. The personal data obtained within these investigations shall be cancelled by the police within five years of the moment the last data was added.

c) The police actions developed in the field of criminal repression and investigation which have required the use and storage of personal data will be cancelled within five years when the criminal proceedings ended with a conviction sentence. The time limit will start to run the moment the penalty has been enforced.

B. Powers in the Code of Criminal Procedure

1. Requirement of (reasonable) clarity for powers in the law of criminal procedure

When it comes to the division of powers between the different actors that intervene in criminal procedure, there is no comprehensive regulation of all the investigative measures that can be adopted by the police, but rather a general rule of the powers of the judicial police within the criminal investigation.

The lack of a complete regulation of the powers of the judicial police in LECRIM is due to the idea underlying the whole structure of criminal proceedings in LECRIM: the investigating judge *(juez de instrucción)* directs the criminal investigation and gives precise instructions to the judicial police officers. Although this division of functions is no longer completely true in every case, the statutory rules still conform to that model. Generally, the police may carry out all the necessary investigative acts to find out the circumstances of the offence and the author or persons involved in it, except those measures that need a previous judicial warrant (Article 549.1 a) LOPJ and Article 282 LECRIM). Specifically, the Judicial Police Act (Royal Decree 769/1987, 19 June) states that at the crime scene the police shall observe the scene, try to reconstruct the facts, and collect all elements that could be used as evidence or that could help identity the offenders. To find out the identity of the offenders the police may perform DNA analysis, expert studies of voices, show photographs of possible perpetrators to the victims and the witnesses, and line-up identifications. They can make inquiries to find out where the suspects can be found and interrogate witnesses. The police are also empowered to carry out alcoholic tests and drug controls on drivers, regardless whether there has been an accident with possible criminal consequences or not. Furthermore they have to adopt those measures necessary to protect the victims and detain the suspect or suspects if possible.

Police cannot adopt any measure that restricts fundamental rights, without a previous judicial warrant, except the entering of a domicile when the action is urgent (Article 553 LECRIM).

The term "coercive measure" is not defined in LECRIM and it is not usually a concept that is used by scholars or courts. The usual classification distinguishes between "measures restrictive of fundamental rights" and the rest.

Although a majority of investigative methods interfere in some way with the fundamental rights of the person under investigation or even third persons, in LECRIM only those measures which are subject to a judicial authorisation fall within the category of "measure restrictive of fundamental rights." These are precisely: search of dwellings, interception of communications (postal, telephone or other), body searches other than external, and the investigation by an undercover agent. The controlled delivery of drugs requires a judicial warrant, but this measure may also be adopted by the Chief of the Judicial Police unit. In LECRIM there are no provisions concerning other investigative measures carried out by the police, like cross-referencing data or other kinds of surveillance, and thus the requisites to adopt these measures, which undoubtedly can interfere with the fundamental rights of citizens, are not clearly defined.

The Public Prosecutor may direct preliminary pre-trial police investigations in certain criminal proceedings, before the case is handed over to the investigating judge.[20] According to LECRIM the investigative stage is directed by the investigating judge under the direct supervision of the Public Prosecutor (Article 302 LECRIM). This has been the distribution of functions since LECRIM was enacted in 1882. However, since 1988 in the so-called abbreviated proceedings (proceedings for offences sanctioned with a penalty up to nine years, thus the majority of cases!) the preliminary investigation may be carried out by the Public Prosecutor (Article 773 LECRIM) before the judicial inquiry is started. The only investigative acts the Public Prosecutor cannot order are those measures "restrictive of fundamental rights," as stated above.

2. Differentiation and classification of powers in the law of criminal procedure

See answer under 1.

III. Powers for Accessing Telecommunication Data in the Law of Criminal Procedure

A. Overview

From 6 December 2015 onwards (date the reform of LECRIM by Organic Law 13/2015 enters into force), Article 588 LECRIM within the criminal procedure, allows telecommunications interception, under the conditions and requirements explained below.

For the interception of communications by the CNI, the Organic Law 2/2002 of 6 May – which only provides for the requirement of judicial control of the interception of communications by the CNI –, is still applicable.

[20] On the investigative powers of the Spanish public prosecutor during the pre-trial stage of the criminal proceedings, see Aguilera Morales, "Las diligencias de investigación fiscal," pp. 25 ff.

B. Interception of Content Data

1. Statutory provision

Until Law 13/2015, 5 October 2015, Article 579 LECRIM was the only provision regulating – in a very incomplete form – postal, telegraphic, and telephone communications interceptions.

If we focus on telephone interceptions, the regulation on telephone tapping was introduced quite late in the statutory provisions of LECRIM, mainly due to the judgments of the ECHR against Spain, stating that the lack of a specific regulation constituted a violation of Article 8 ECHR. As a consequence of the case law of the ECtHR, the law was changed to meet the ECHR requirements of "legal basis," but unfortunately in a very incomplete manner. Article 579.2 LECRIM, as reformed in 1988, stated that

> "a court may also authorise, in a reasoned decision, the monitoring of the telephone calls of a person charged if there is evidence to show that facts or circumstances material to the case may thereby be uncovered or verified."

This legal provision still did not comply with the requisite foreseeability standard, as declared in the cases *Prado Bugallo v. Spain*, of 18 February 2003 and *Valenzuela Contreras v. Spain*, of 30 July 1998. The *Naseiro* case before the Spanish Supreme Court (Decision of 8 June 1992) was the first judicial decision where the Supreme Court defined precisely and comprehensively the conditions that telephone interception must comply with. After this Supreme Court decision, the Constitutional Court rendered a judgment (STC 49/1999, 5 April), stating in full detail the legal and constitutional requirements telephone tapping should meet in order to be lawful. As had been explicitly recognised by the ECtHR in its decision *Abdulkadir Coban* already cited, the legislative reform of 1988, together with the well-established case law of the Spanish courts since 1992, constituted a body of law on telephone tapping that was adequate to provide a sufficient legal basis for the interception of telephone communications in Spain.

In addition to having a sufficient legal basis, according to Spanish law interception of telephone communications must meet the following requisites to be justified: the aim pursued must be consistent with the Constitution; the measure must be adequate to achieve the goal pursued, that is, to obtain data of substantial value that will elucidate the investigation of the crime at issue; it must be necessary, thus phone tapping has to be excluded if there is a different means to achieve the aim pursued; there must be a reasonable balance between the fundamental right at stake and the expected result that the measure should obtain. The Constitutional Court has affirmed that the proportionality of the measure must be considered "through an analysis of the circumstances existing at the time it was accorded" (STC 126/2000, 16 May).

The Spanish system, however, was still lacking a specific and complete regulation on the interception of electronic communications. Such measures were adopted by resorting to the rules provided for telephone tapping, rules that were not always apt to meet the needs of other telecommunications interceptions. Since the 90's scholars and practitioners have been requesting an adequate and comprehensive legal regulation of telecommunications interceptions.[21]

The insufficient regulation in LECRIM was to be interpreted and complemented with the regulation of Article 33 (paragraphs 1 and 2) of Law 32/2003 of Telecommunications *(Ley General de Telecomunicaciones)*, 3 November (BOE 264, 4 January 2003), as amended by the final provision of Law 25/2007, 18 October, on Retention of Data Relating to Electronic Communications (BOE 251, 19 October 2007), which recalled expressly that the restriction of the secrecy of electronic communications was in accordance with Article 18.3 of the Constitution and the organic laws developing its content.

Complete regulation has recently been provided by the legal amendment of LECRIM of 5 October 2015. The next subchapter will refer to the new regulation.

The main legal provision for telecommunications interception within criminal proceedings is the new lengthy Article 588 LECRIM, which covers all possible interceptions of communications: telephone and electronic communications (Article 588*ter* LECRIM); eavesdropping or interception of oral communications and recording of images through hidden devices (Article 588*quarter* LECRIM); the use of technical devices for surveillance and geo-location (Article 588*quinquies* LECRIM); the search of massive information storage devices (Article 588*sexies*); and the remote search of computers and computer systems (Article 588*septies*).

Within this paragraph a only with the interception of telephone or electronic telecommunications (content) are dealt with. The general provisions are set out under Article 588*bis* LECRIM and state:

> 1. During the investigation of the criminal case investigative measures covered by this chapter may be adopted provided that there is a judicial warrant issued with full respect for the principles of specialty, adequacy, exceptionality, necessity, and proportionality of the measure.
>
> 2. The principle of specialty requires that a measure is related to the investigation of a specific offense. No IT investigative measures shall be authorized which aims at preventing or discovering a crime, where there are no clear factual suspicions.
>
> 3. The principle of adequacy will define the objective and subjective scope of the measure as well as its duration, taking into account the usefulness of the measure.
>
> 4. In applying the principles of exceptionality and necessity, the IT investigative measure shall only be granted:

---

[21] See, among others, Montón Redondo, "Las interceptaciones telefónicas constitucionalmente correctas," *La Ley* 1995-4, pp. 1043–1052; Gimeno Sendra, "Las intervenciones telefónicas en la jurisprudencia del Tribunal Constitucional y del Tribunal Supremo", *La Ley* 1996-2, pp. 1617–1624.

a) when less restrictive measures for the fundamental rights of the investigated or prosecuted person which are equally useful to clarify the facts are not available, in view of their characteristics, or

b) when the discovery or verification of the investigated fact, the determination of its author, the investigation of his whereabouts, or the location of the effects of the crime would be severely hampered without resorting to this measure.

5. The investigative measures covered in this chapter are only deemed proportional when taken into consideration all the circumstances of the case, the limitations of the rights and interests affected does not exceed the benefits of their adoption for the public interest or the interests of third parties. For the weighing of the conflicting interests, the public interest will be assessed taking into account the seriousness of the crime, its social significance or the technological sphere where it has been committed, the intensity of the existing evidence, and the importance of the possible information or evidence sought by the measure restricting the right.

2. Scope of application

a) Object of interception

LECRIM uses the heading "Interception of telephone and electronic communications" *(Interceptación de las comunicaciones telefónicas y telemáticas)*. Article 588*ter* b LECRIM defines the scope, including also some definitions. It is worth reproducing the provision here:

1. The terminals or means of communication that can be intercepted must be those regularly or occasionally used by the investigated person.

2. The judicial warrant may authorize the access to content data and to electronic traffic data or data related to the electronic communication process, as well as those generated independently of the establishment of a particular communication, in which the person investigated is either sender or recipient, and may affect the terminals or means of communication the investigated person is owner or user.

Interception of terminals or means of the victim can also be authorized, when there is a serious risk to his/her life or integrity.

For the purposes of this article, electronic traffic data or related data, shall mean all those data that are generated as a result of conducting a communication through an electronic communications network, its making available to the user, as well as the provision of a service of the information society or a telematic communication of similar nature.

As to the interception of communication, Article 588*ter* b LECRIM covers all electronic communications data: during transmission or data stored before, after, or during the process of communication although it does not specifically distinguish the moment at which electronic communications can be intercepted.

As to stored traffic data, there is a specific provision regulating its access under Article 588*ter* j LECRIM, that will be explained later when discussing traffic data.

b) *Current matters of dispute*

The debates that took place during past decades caused by the lack of legal regulation of telephone and other telecommunications interceptions have lost much significance now that a specific provision has been adopted. There are still voices that criticise the extension of investigative powers within a criminal investigation, highlighting the risks of possible infringements of the right to privacy, or questioning the necessity of such measures for combating criminality.[22] These criticisms are focused mainly on the measure of eavesdropping and remote search of computers, but not so much on the interception of electronic communications, where the new regulation is generally welcomed,[23] as it provides legal certainty and clear limits and safeguards.

3. Special protection of confidential communication content

a) *Privileged communication*

Organic Law 13/2015, 4 October, amending LECRIM provides specific protection to communications between the defendant or suspect and his/her defence lawyer. Such communications were already protected by the case law of the Supreme Court (e.g., decision of 19 October 2010) and the Constitutional Court, on the basis of the constitutional right to defence envisaged in Article 24 SC. No communication between lawyer and client can be intercepted, save the exception made by the penitentiary rules.

Chapter VIII of Title II of the General Penitentiary Organic Law 1/1979, 26 September, regulates communications and visits in the prison system. Specifically, Article 51.2, concerning the right of communication of inmates, without specifying their status as remand prisoners or convicts, reads as follows:

> 2. Communications of prison inmates with the defence attorney, the duty appointed attorney for the precise criminal case, or the court representatives *(procuradores)*, will be held in appropriate rooms and may not be suspended or intercepted except by judicial order and in cases of terrorism.

The conditions for these exceptional interceptions are cumulative: a judicial order is needed and such authorisation can only be granted in cases of terrorism, for preventive reasons and for avoiding destroying of evidence. The well-known case of Judge Garzón, dismissed from his judicial career as a disciplinary measure for authorising the interception of communications of an inmate and his lawyer in a

---

22 See Bachmaier Winter, "Remote search of computers under the new Spanish Law of 2015. Has it got the right balance?," *Burgas University Law Review, special issue: Law and the Internet* (forthcoming).

23 See, for example, Marchena Gómez/González-Cuéllar, "La reforma de la Ley de Enjuiciamiento Criminal de 2015."

case of corruption, makes clear the seriousness with which infringements of these fundamental rights are treated.[24]

The amendment of LECRIM of 5 October 2015 gives statutory regulation to the protection of communications between lawyer and defendant. Article 118.4 LECRIM introduced following provision:

> All communications between the suspect or defendant and his lawyer are confidential.
>
> If these conversations or communications had been captured or intervened during the execution of some of the measures regulated by this law, the court shall order the removal of the recording or delivery to the recipient of the detained correspondence, noting this circumstance in the proceedings.
>
> The provisions in the first subparagraph shall not apply when there is objective evidence of the participation of the counsel in the offence investigated or his involvement together with the suspect or defendant in the commission of another criminal offense, notwithstanding the provisions of the Penitentiary Law.

The responsibility for ensuring the special protection of communications between defendant and defence lawyer lies with the investigating judge.

No other professional secrets are expressly protected within LECRIM, which has long been criticised by legal scholars. However, the protection of other professional secrets needs to be balanced by the investigating judge when deciding on the authorisation to intercept communications that may affect confidential relationships.

If it is clear that the judge will not authorise the interception of communications between the defendant and his/her lawyer (as this would constitute an offence of rendering willingly an illicit decision, which is sanctioned under Article 447 PC[25]) in practice it may occur, and occurs quite often, that conversations between client and lawyer are intercepted. The legal framework does not clearly state how to proceed in these cases. If the conversations are in another language or the interlocutors do not identify themselves, it may not be possible to know at the moment of recording of the conversation that the privileged lawyer-client relationship is being affected. In such cases, the interception will continue and the critical conversations shall be deleted by the investigating judge. This is however not specifically provided for in LECRIM.

---

[24] See the comprehensive study of Manso Porto, "Las escuchas telefónicas entre abogado defensor y cliente en una comparación internacional," *Estudios Penales y Criminológicos USC*, vol. XXXII (2012), pp. 39–95, in particular, pp. 64 ff.

[25] According to Article 447 PC, judges shall be held criminally liable for criminal offences committed in the exercise of their functions, in particular, knowingly passing an unjust judgment constitutes a criminal offence. The penalty varies, depending on whether the judgment has been rendered in a criminal procedure or not, and if the penalty has been executed or not. The penalty ranges from six months to four years imprisonment or a fine. In all cases, this criminal offence will entail the dismissal of the judge and the prohibition to exercise any public post up to a maximum of 20 years.

There is no legal provision that states that the police shall suspend immediately the recording of a communication when it appears that the client-lawyer privilege is being infringed.

The only clear rules are: such communications cannot be authorised and cannot be used as evidence, but precise instructions as how to proceed when such conversations are recorded by chance are not established by law. It has been expressly highlighted that the Spanish legal framework should regulate these situations and provide for clear action to ensure a stronger guarantee to the lawyer-client confidentiality.[26]

4. Execution of telecommunication interception

a) Execution by the authorities with or without the help of third parties

The execution of the interception of telecommunications will be carried out by the authorised officer of the judicial police, through the comprehensive system for intercepting electronic communications (*Sistema integrado de interceptación legal de las telecomunicaciones*, SITEL).

SITEL is an advanced software application that allows the interception not only of conversations but also of the data package that accompanies it, which is called "information associated to the communication." Thus, the geographical location of the caller or the type of contract of the subscriber is also made available by SITEL. Royal Decree 424/2005, approving the Regulation on conditions for the provision of electronic communications services, universal service, and protection of users (BOE 102, 20 April 2005) authorised the advanced technical process of interception of communications or SITEL to be installed on suppliers of telecommunications network services (ISP). Its functioning has not been without controversy as it allows all types of data regarding the communication to be accessed directly.[27]

The "spyware" is integrated into the networks of telecom operators, whether fixed or mobile. However, the system is only activated when there is a judicial authorisation. Upon receipt of the judicial warrant, the system sends via a secured connection the intercepted communication "point to point" to a central computer at the Directorate General of Police and Civil Guard, which in turn distributes it to peripheral terminals.

Only expressly authorised agents can access SITEL. To ensure full confidentiality and secrecy of the intercepted communications, SITEL has specific computers

---

26 Bachmaier Winter, "Intervenciones telefónicas y derechos de terceros en el proceso penal. La necesidad de una regulación legal del secreto profesional y de otras relaciones de confianza," *Revista de Derecho Procesal* (2004/1-3), pp. 41–82.

27 Rodríguez Laínz, "Consideraciones jurídicas en torno a la licitud constitucional de SITEL," *La Ley* n° 7344, Sección Doctrina, 17 February 2010, pp. 1–29.

in police investigation units connected in a "sealed" to the central SITEL server. The system works only "online" and no copies can be made of the intercepted material. Agents have to use special passwords and only have access to information related to the case under investigation. Only agents of the unit responsible for the relevant investigation can have access to the system.

SITEL is based on the Telecommunications Act of 2007, which established the requirements and legal prerequisites for applying and executing the interception of telecommunications, and is further developed in Regulation 425/2005, 15 April.

b) Accompanying powers for the execution of interception

Clandestine access to houses to place equipment to record conversations held in them is now allowed under Article 588*quater* a LECRIM. Clandestine recording of direct conversations is authorised in any public or private space, however, clandestine recording of images can, as a rule, only be carried out in public spaces (Article 588*quinquies* LECRIM).

The use of a false identity or "digital undercover" activities are also provided for in the newly amended Article 282*bis* LECRIM, upon judicial authorisation, if this is needed for the discovery and/or investigation of a cybercrime or by way of the internet (Article 588*ter* a LECRIM).

The use of spyware for conducting remote computer searches is explained below. It is unclear whether it shall be considered as an accompanying power for the execution of the interception or a special mode of executing the specific measure of remote computer search.

5. Duties of telecommunication service providers to cooperate

a) Possible addressees of duties of cooperation

The duty to cooperate is established in a very broad way, as according to the law the addressees are "all telecommunication service providers and any kind of person that plays a role in facilitating the communications. No differentiation is made between cloud-providers and others."

Article 588*ter* e LECRIM states that all telecommunications service providers and persons involved in the process of facilitating communications, are obliged to cooperate with and assist in the execution of a measure of telecommunications interception, including the judge, public prosecutor and the member of the judicial police named in the judicial warrant.

Paras. 2 and 3 of this article read:

> 2. The persons requested to provide cooperation will be required to maintain secrecy about the activities they were asked to perform by the authorities.

3. Those who fail to fulfil the above duties may incur in criminal liability for disobedience to a judicial order.

This provision of LECRIM reproduces almost exactly Article 85 of the R.D. 424/2005, 15 April, on the Regulation of the conditions for the provision of electronic communications services, universal service, and user protection.

b) Content of duties to cooperate

The duties of telecommunications service providers and others involved in the communication process to cooperate are also very broadly drafted: they are obliged to provide "assistance and cooperation necessary to execute the judicial order of interception of telecommunications" (Article 588*ter* e LECRIM). Not complying with this obligation constitutes an infringement of a judicial order, which can entail criminal liability. The offence of "disobedience" to the public authority applies also to deliberate non-compliance with a court order and is sanctioned with a custodial penalty from three months to one year and fine from six to 18 months (Article 556.1 PC, as amended by O.L. of 1 July 2015).

The service providers shall facilitate the access to all telecommunications data requested in the judicial warrant. The access shall cover all types of communications, also future communications. If urgent, this access should be provided as soon as possible. Otherwise, access shall be ensured within a day of the issuing of the order, starting from 12:00 a.m.

Expressly R.D. 424/2005 says that service providers are only obliged to cooperate in providing access to communications according to LECRIM and Organic Law 2/2002 on the National Centre of Intelligence.

According to Article 88 R.D. 424/2005:

1. The service providers obliged shall provide to the authorized agent, unless that due to the service characteristics they are not available, those data included in the following list and authorized in the judicial warrant granting the interception:

a) Identity or identities-in the sense defined in Article 84.i) – of the persons subject to the measure of interception.
b) Identity or identities-in the sense defined in Article 84.i) – of other parties involved in the electronic communication.
c) Basic services used.
d) Supplementary services used.
e) Address of communication.
f) Signal of response.
g) Cause of termination.
h) Duration.
i) Location Information.
j) Information exchanged through the control channel.

2. In addition to information concerning the interception under the preceding paragraph, entities shall provide the authorized agent – unless that due to the characteristics of the service they are not available – following data of any party involved in the communication that are clients of the obligated party:

a) Identification of the natural or legal person.

b) Address where the provider performs notifications.

And, even if they are not clients, if the service allows to access, they shall provide also the following data:

c) Number of service holder (both the directory number as all identifications of electronic communications subscriber).

d) Identification number of the terminal.

e) Account number assigned by the ISP.

f) E-mail address.

3. Along with the information specified in the preceding paragraphs, the service providers obliged shall provide, unless that the characteristics of the service does not allow it, information on the geographical location of the originating and terminating end points. In case of mobile services, it will provide the most accurate position possible to the point of communication and, in any case, the identification, location, and type of the affected base station.

c) Duties to provide technical and organisational infrastructure

R.D. 425/2005 sets out the obligation of service providers to adopt all technical measures to facilitate access to all kinds of communications (Articles 86 and 87.2), and is obliged to adopt technical measures to safeguard the right to secrecy of the communications (Article 91). The service provider obliged to cooperate shall ensure that only the authorised person is given access to communications (Article 92) and this authorised agent only has access to the communications identified in the judicial warrant, excluding any others (Article 87). The service providers shall keep the process confidential (Article 93).

d) Security requirements for data transfers by communication service providers

Article 91 R.D. 424/2005 states that all the technical measures to ensure the safety and the secrecy of communications, as well as the confidentiality of interceptions, shall be adopted.

In case of particular danger of breaches of the network security the Ministry of Interior and the clients shall be informed.

e) Checks, filtering, and decryption obligations of communication service providers

These issues are not specifically regulated. The practice is unknown.

6. Formal prerequisites of interception orders

a) Competent authorities

The competence to apply for a measure lies with the public prosecutor and the judicial police, but it can also be ordered *ex officio* by the investigating judge (Article 558*bis* b.1. LECRIM).

The competence for authorizing the interception of telecommunications lies with the investigating judge, Articles 588*bis* b, 588*bis* c, 588*ter* d LECRIM.

Exceptionally, in urgent cases, within the investigation of offences related to organised groups or terrorism and where there are reasonable grounds to consider that the measure is indispensable, the interception of the telecommunications can be ordered by the Ministry of Interior or, in his/her absence, by the Secretary of State for Security (immediate level below the Ministry of Interior).

The adoption of this measure shall be immediately notified to the competent investigating judge, within a maximum time period of 24 hours, expressing the reasons for its adoption, the acts undertaken, and the results obtained. The judge will grant or reject the adoption of the measure in a reasoned decision within a maximum time of 72 hours since it was adopted (Article 588*ter* d.3 LECRIM).

b) Formal requirements for applications

Requirements for the judicial application for all measures under chapter IV, Title VIII, Book II LECRIM (interception of telecommunications, interception of direct conversations, recording of images, use of geo-location devices, computer searches, and remote searches of computers and computer networks) are:

Article 588*bis* b 2) LECRIM

2.) When the public prosecutor or the judicial police request the judge an IT investigative measure *(medida de investigación tecnológica)*, the request shall contain:

1. The description of the facts under investigation and the identity of the subject or otherwise affected person by the measure, provided that such data are known.
2. The detailed statement of the reasons justifying the necessity of the measure according to the guiding principles set out in Article 588bis, as well as indications of the offence that have been found during the investigation prior to the application for authorization for the restrictive measure.
3. Identification data of the suspect or defendant under investigation and, if appropriate, the means of communication used by him that will allow the execution of the measure.
4. The extension of the measure specifying its content.
5. The investigative unit of the judicial police who will take over the interception.
6. The form of execution of the measure.
7. The duration of the measure sought.
8. The precise person obliged to execute the measure, if known.

For the measure of interception of telecommunications the additional requirements of the application are set out under:

Article 588*ter* d LECRIM

1. The request for authorization must contain, in addition to the requirements referred to in Article 588*bis* b, following:

a) Identification of the number of subscriber, the terminal or the technical label,

b) Identification of the connection which is subject of the interception or

c) Data necessary to identify the means of telecommunication to be intercepted

2. To determine the scope of the measure, the application for judicial authorization may concern one of the following objectives:

a) The registration and recording of the content of the communication, specifying the form or type of communications that are involved.

b) The data of origin or destination of the communication at the moment in which communication is taking place.

c) The geographical location of the origin or destination of the communication.

d) Other related traffic data linked or not, that may add value to the communication. In this case, the request shall specify the specific data to be obtained.

c) Formal requirements for orders

The judicial warrant, according to new Article 588*bis* c LECRIM shall be rendered in a maximum time of 24 hours after the request is filed, and shall have at least following content:

Article 588*bis* c paragraph 3 LECRIM

a) The punishable acts under investigation and their legal qualification, stating the reasonable suspicion to ground the measure.

b) The identity of the suspects/defendants and any other third person affected by the measure, if known.

c) The scope of the restrictive measure, specifying the extension and the compliance with the guiding principles established in Article 588bis.

d) The judicial police investigative unit that will take over the interception.

e) The duration of the measure.

f) The manner and frequency in which the requesting authority shall inform the judge about the results of the measure.

g) The aims sought by the measure.

h) The person obliged to execute the measure, if known, expressly stating his/her duty to cooperate and to keep the acts secret, where appropriate, being liable for the offence of disobedience of a court order."

7. Substantive prerequisites of interception orders

a) Degree of suspicion

Mere suspicion, conjecture, or guesses are not enough to order the interception of telecommunications. Spanish doctrine and jurisprudence do not differentiate clearly between "sufficient or justified grounds," "reasonable suspicion" and "probable cause" to qualify degrees of suspicion. The courts and the law use the term "sufficient indications of the existence of the criminal offence." What this means in practice is not easily defined, but has been considered to be "facts that rationally – objectively assessed – indicate the probability that some person is involved in a criminal act."[28]

The Spanish case law, interpreting previous Article 579 LECRIM on telephone tapping, has repeatedly stated that evidence must consist of external data, accessible to third parties, that provides a real basis from which it is possible to infer that a crime has been or is about to be committed; the mere appraisal of the behaviour or the quality of a person is not admissible.[29] The initial circumstantial evidence must refer to precise criminal facts and precise persons, and must be grounded on objective data. In addition, this circumstantial evidence must lead to the establishment of a connection between the people using the telephones to be intercepted and the criminal facts that are being investigated. These requirements are aimed at preventing the judge from issuing a warrant for phone tapping for the mere purpose of an exploratory search, without being linked to a concrete criminal fact.[30]

Moreover, the Supreme Court case law states that "the mere affirmation by the police on the existence of certain suspicions is not enough to order the interception of the communications" (Supreme Court Decision 18 June 1992, which is one of the landmark decisions), but precise facts and the origins of the information about those acts that form the basis of suspicion have to be substantiated for ordering the telecommunications interception. Anonymous information or information coming from a confidential source has usually been considered insufficient grounds for telecommunications interception.

In practice for obtaining a judicial order authorising telephone interception, police undertake surveillance activities to gather enough information to meet the standards of "probable cause."

The question has recently been raised in some Supreme Court judgments whether the information obtained from cooperation with foreign law enforcement or in-

---

28 On the reasonable suspicion required for granting the interception of communications, see, for example, the following judgments of the Constitutional Court, SSTC 136/2006; 220/2006; 219/2009 or 26/2010. See also Zoco Zabala, "Nuevas tecnologías y control de las comunicaciones," pp. 208–217.

29 STS 11 November 1996, STS 6 May 1997 or STS 10 October 1998. See also the Constitutional Court's decision STC 184/2003, 23 October 2003, §11, in which the Court held that it was unconstitutional to issue a warrant of phone tapping on the exclusive basis of an anonymous denunciation of a possible crime of corruption.

30 In the judgment 165/2005, 20 June 2005, the Constitutional Court stated that the fact that a person did not have a job, but spent great sums of money, was not sufficient grounds to issue a warrant, as this is not an objective fact that defines the necessity of the phone tapping.

telligence services (e.g., FBI or DEA), may be enough to meet the required degree of suspicion for authorising telephone interception.

One such case relates to telecommunications interception and confiscation of a significant amount of drugs based on information provided by the US Drugs Enforcement Agency (DEA). The defence lawyer contended that the telecommunications interceptions were unlawful, as the initial suspicion was not established by lawful means. The answer of the Supreme Court was that it cannot be presumed that the sources of information of the police are unlawful, and that since in the instant case there were no indications that the information came from an illegal interception of communications, their validity was presumed, and the evidence so obtained was considered admissible (STS 884/2012, 8 November, RJ 2012/11360).

b) Predicate offences

There is no closed list of offences where the measure of interception of communications can be ordered. Article 588*ter* a.1 LECRIM (that refers to Article 579) lists:

1. intentional offences punishable with a maximum imprisonment penalty of at least three years,
2. crimes committed within a group or criminal organisation,
3. Terrorist offences.

In addition to these offences, and not subject to the minimum of three years custodial penalty, telecommunications interception can be ordered with regard to the investigation of offences committed through computers or IT equipment *(instrumentos informáticos)*, or other information technology or communication or communication services.

c) Persons and connections under surveillance

Article 588*bis* h LECRIM provides for the possibility to authorise the investigative measures intercepting communications also when third persons are affected, in the cases and under the conditions set out in the regulation of each of the measures.

Additionally, for the interception of telecommunications, Article 588*ter* c LECRIM states:

> The interception of communications originating from terminals or electronic communication means belonging to a third person may be authorized, provided that:
>
> 1. there is evidence that the suspect or defendant under investigation uses them to transmit or receive information, or
> 2. the subscriber collaborates with the investigated person in their illicit acts or benefits from his activities.
>
> Such communication interceptions may also be authorized when the device which is the object of the surveillance is being used maliciously by others electronically *(por vía telemática)*, without the knowledge of its owner.

d) *Principle of subsidiarity*

As for any measure restrictive of fundamental rights, the interception of electronic communications must comply with the principle of subsidiarity, that is, that the same data are not reasonably accessible by less intrusive means. The assessment in each case of compliance with this requirement is to be done by the investigating authority who, in some cases will request that other means are tried first, and on other occasions they may accept that other means are likely to be unsuccessful. This is one of the points that requires a deep empirical analysis. Although most judges are very strict when it comes to ordering telecommunications interceptions others just resort to a general statement that reads "considering that the data needed for the investigation cannot be acceded through other less intrusive means [...]," without any further verification of whether such less intrusive means are really available or not.

e) *Proportionality of interception in individual cases*

The judge shall assess the proportionality of the measure in view of the seriousness of the offence to be investigated, although usually when the offence is sanctioned with more than three years custodial penalty, it is considered that it meets the proportionality principle. Usually the likelihood of obtaining the requested data is considered by the judge when ordering the interception of telecommunications. However, the likelihood does not exclude the need to comply with the requirements of necessity and proportionality.

f) *Consent by a communication participant to the measure*

Consent given by one of the interlocutors, according to the case law of the Supreme Court (STS 217/2014, 30 January 2014), excludes that there has been an unlawful interference of the State in the right to secrecy of communications. However, in a case where a person held in prison gave consent to the police officers to listen to his conversations, the ECtHR held that even in such case the legal requirements for the State to intercept communications have to be followed (ECtHR *M.M. v The Netherlands*, 8 April 2004, no. 39339/98).

8. Validity of interception order

a) *Maximum length of interception order*

The general rule is that any measure restrictive of fundamental rights shall not last longer than is absolutely necessary for the discovery of the facts (Article 588*bis* e LECRIM). For interception of telecommunications the period is three months, extendable for the same period, up to a maximum of 18 months (Article 588*ter* g LECRIM). The whole process of execution of the measure is subject to judicial control. The judicial police shall report on the progress of the investigation within the time periods established in the judicial warrant authorising the interception of telecommunications (Articles 588*ter* f and 588*bis* g LECRIM). To that end, the judge may request the integral records and/or transcripts of the recorded conversations.

b) Prolongation of authorisation

The duration of the measure may be prolonged, through a reasoned judicial decision, by the competent judges, *ex officio* or upon application of the public prosecutor or the judicial police. The judge may prolong the measure if the reasons that justified its adoption remain (Article 588*bis* e LECRIM). To authorise the prolongation of communications interception, the investigating judge has to check what information has been obtained and whether the need, adequacy, and proportionality of the measure still exist.

If the time for which the measure was authorised expires without granting the time extension, the measure will cease. Any evidence obtained after expiry of the period, even if there is no abuse on the side of the authorities, is unlawful and will not have any evidentiary value.

The request for prolongation of communications interceptions shall be filed with enough time left before the authorisation expires. The application for an extension shall be accompanied by: 1) a detailed report on the execution of the measure and its results; and 2) the reasons that may justify the need for an extension. The judge shall decide on this application within two days (Article 588*bis* f LECRIM).

c) Revocation of authorisation

The measure will cease once the conditions that led to its adoption disappear or it is made clear that no results are to be obtained through it, and in any event, once the timeframe has expired (Article 588*bis* j LECRIM).

The whole execution of the communication interception is subject to regular judicial control, with a frequency established by the judge. As a consequence of this periodical control, the Investigating Judge may revoke the initial authorisation, even if the maximum time period of three months has not lapsed. The frequency for judicial control is to be decided by each judge and will depend on the type of case. Until now, as prolongation could only be authorised for a period of one month, this was the usual frequency of judicial control of the measure.

9. Duties to record, report, and destroy

a) Duty to record and report

The reporting duties have been explained above. As to recording, Article 588*ter* f LECRIM provides:

The Judicial Police will make available to the judge, at intervals determined by it the transcription of the passages considered relevant and the complete recorded communications. The police shall indicate the origin and destination of each of the communications and shall ensure, through a sealing system or advanced electronic signature or sufficiently reliable system of authentication, the authenticity and integrity of the data dumped from the host computer to the digital files in which the communications were recorded.

b) Duty to destroy

Article 588*bis* k LECRIM provides for the destruction of records in the following way:

1. Once the criminal proceedings are terminated by a final ruling, the original records that are kept in the electronic and computer systems used in the execution of the measure shall be deleted and erased, upon order. A copy of those records will be kept under the custody of the court secretary (*secretario judicial*, kind of court notary).

2. The preserved copies will be destroyed after five years have elapsed since the penalty was executed or when the time for the statute of limitations of the offence or the prosecution has expired or the decision to put an end or sentence of acquittal is final, provided that the court does not order its conservation.

3. The Court shall instruct the Judicial Police to put into effect the destruction referred to in the preceding paragraphs.

10. Notification duties and remedies

a) Duty to notify persons affected by the measure

Until the amendment by Organic Law 13/2015 of 5 October 2015, there was no legal obligation to inform third persons that had been affected by the interception of telecommunications. This was repeatedly criticised by scholars, for non-compliance with the adequate protection of human rights. This flaw has been corrected with the new provision introduced recently in LECRIM, which reads:

Article 588*ter* i.3 LECRIM

The Investigating Judge shall notify the persons involved in intercepted communications the fact of the interference and shall inform them of the specific communications in which they have participated. This information shall take place, unless it should require a disproportionate effort or it could prejudice future investigations. If the notified person so requests he/she will be given a copy of the recording or the transcription of such communications, insofar as this does not affect the right to privacy of others or is contrary to the objectives of the proceedings under which the measure was adopted.

This new provision stating the obligation to notify the persons whose conversations have been recorded is to be welcomed. However, as the exceptions for complying with this duty are so broadly drafted, in practice it may lead to a generalised lack of information. It has to be noted that the notification of the conversations held by a third person in most cases will "affect the privacy of others," unless the conversation was with one of the defendants.

b) Remedies

If the third person affected by the telecommunications interception should consider that there has been an unlawful infringement of his/her fundamental rights, he/she could choose to file a criminal complaint (the victim has standing to press charges in criminal cases and become, independently from the public prosecutor, a private accuser) and also claim civil damages within the criminal procedure for violation of his/her right to secrecy of communications; or file a civil suit against the relevant authority claiming damages for the infringement; or claim damages from the State for malfunctioning of the administration of justice, a procedure where guilt does not need to be proven, as there is strict liability of the State for damages caused by miscarriage of justice or malfunctioning of justice.

As the obligation to notify third parties is new and is not yet in force, there is no practice on this issue.

c) Criminal consequences of unlawful interception measures

The precise criminal sanctions provided in the Criminal Code for unlawful interceptions of communications have been explained above. As to the frequency of such infringements, it is not easy to give any accurate information. The judicial police are very much aware that any telecommunications interception is subject to prior judicial warrant, and the strict evidentiary rule has a strong deterrence effect. Thus, there is no case law on unlawful actions of judicial police members in this regard. The main reasons for considering telecommunications interceptions unlawful, until now, have been the lack of adequate reasoning in the judicial warrant, no reasoning given for the need for prolongation, or for not providing the complete recorded conversations or the whole files granting authenticity, but not for illegal acts on the part of officers. There was a case were a telephone interception was declared void and inadmissible as evidence by the Constitutional Court, because the interception had lasted some days longer than authorised in the warrant, because the police had mistaken the moment from which to count the extension of 30 days.

If an officer were found to have carried out an illegal interception of the communication, he/she would not only be criminally liable for violation of the secrecy of the communications, but would also be subject to disciplinary sanctions as a public servant, with possible dismissal.

As to an independent monitoring authority with power to control the interception of communications, Spain has no such a body or authority. This is explained by the fact that it is considered sufficient guarantee to subject all telecommunications interceptions to the judicial authority, who has the strongest guarantees of independence according to the Constitution.

However, the absence of any statistics or external body controlling the use that is being made in practice of the powers to intercept telecommunications does not seem to ensure sufficiently the transparency of the whole system. The fact that a measure of interception of communication can be ordered *ex officio* by the investigating judges certainly is a deficit of the system of guarantees that in my opinion should be reviewed.

11. Confidentiality requirements

Article 588*ter* e LECRIM states that all telecommunications service providers and persons involved in the process of facilitating communications are obliged to cooperate with and assist the judge, public prosecutor, and the member of the judicial police designated with the execution of the measure of telecommunications interception. Paras. 2 and 3 of this article read:

> 2. The persons requested to provide cooperation will be required to maintain secrecy about the activities they were asked to perform by the authorities.
>
> 3. Those who fail to fulfil the above duties may incur in criminal liability for disobedience to a judicial order.

Furthermore the General Law 32/2003 of Telecommunications establishes sanctions for serious, less serious, and grave infringements of the legal provisions on telecommunications services. Those sanctions are administrative fines that may rank from up to a maximum of 30,000 euros for less serious infringements to proportionate fines according to the benefit obtained (Article 56).

C. Collection and Use of Traffic Data and Subscriber Data

1. Collection of traffic data and subscriber data

a) Collection of traffic data

Law 25/2007 of October 18 on Data Retention of Electronic Communications requires judicial authorisation to access not only traffic data (connected terminals, user identification, and dating of the communication), but also other data that may be classified as value added services.

Since the reform by Law 13/2005, there is also a omplete regulation of the access and transfer of traffic data by telecommunications service providers and other persons obliged to cooperate.

Article 588*ter* j LECRIM on data contained in automated files of service providers provides:

> 1. The electronic data held by service providers or individuals that facilitate the communication in compliance with the legislation on data retention regarding electronic communications – on its own initiative or for commercial reasons or otherwise – and which are linked to the processes of communication, can only be transferred for incorporation into the procedure upon judicial authorization.
>
> 2. When knowledge of these data is indispensable for the criminal investigation, a judicial warrant shall be applied for to the aim of collecting the information contained in the computerized files of service providers, including cross-linked searches or data mining *(búsqueda entrecruzada o inteligente de datos)*. The application shall indicate which kind of data are required and what are the reasons that justify the transfer of those data.

The formal and substantive prerequisites for the collection of traffic data are the same as for content data: no specific provisions are provided in the LECRIM for the application for the order, the content of the judicial order, or the duty of telecommunications service providers to cooperate with the criminal investigation. Therefore, what has been already stated with regard to telecommunications interception of content data, applies in general to traffic data. In practice, the main difference lies in the assessment of the proportionality of the measure and the required degree of suspicion. Although there are no precise standards or definitions in this regard, as the intrusiveness of this measure in the fundamental right to secrecy of communications and privacy is lower, courts and scientific scholarship consider that the standards for granting it could also be lowered. However, the general requisite of the type of offence and gravity of the penalty, set out in Article 588*ter* a LECRIM (offence sanctioned with penalty higher than three years' imprisonment, organised crime or terrorism, plus cybercrime offences or offences committed by using ITs) applies here equally.

In fact, until now, the same general authorisation for intercepting telephone conversations was used to access all traffic and other data associated to the communication. This is possible as long as the SITEL mechanism gives access to the whole "package" of communication data. Generally the Supreme Court has considered that the main authorisation for content data implies also access to the traffic and associated data. However, scholars have raised the issue of the proportionality principle, as it obviously has a different impact to only access the conversations, rather than also the accompanying names, addresses, and geographical location of the interlocutors.

b) Collection of subscriber data

If in the exercise of their preventive and investigative functions of offences committed through the internet, judicial officers have access to an IP that is being used to commit a crime, and neither the equipment or identity of the user is identified nor is the equipment located, the officers shall request from the judge an order to obtain the identification data from the telecommunications service provider in order to identify the suspect (Article 588*ter* k). The requirement of the judicial warrant is based on data protection law and not on the protection of the right to secrecy of communications.

In general, the identification of the subscriber of a telephone or other communication service, or otherwise, the identification of the telephone number of a person, can be directly requested by the public prosecution or by the judicial police from the company providing such service (Article 588*ter* m LECRIM).

The addressees are obliged to comply with the request, or face the penalty for the offence of disobedience. These data are provided in an automated way.

c) "Data retention"

Law 25/2007 of 18 October on Data Retention transposed into the domestic legal order EU Directive 2006/24/EU, later annulled. Article 3 of the Spanish law essentially reproduces Article 5 of the (annulled) Directive when listing the data that the service providers are obliged to retain. The data have to be retained for 12 months.

2. Identification of device ID (IMEI), card number (IMSI), and location of mobile terminal devices

a) Identification of device ID with the help of IMSI-catchers

IMSI-catchers are used by law enforcement agents in their investigative activities. The Supreme Court case law has declared that such devices to track the presence of mobile phones in a certain location do not need a judicial warrant, as such activity does not affect personal data: it only identifies the presence of an object in a certain place. The same applies to IP directions. In fact, such tracking devices and the information obtained therefrom has been used frequently in practice to underpin the judicial application for obtaining subscriber identification and later the authorisation for telecommunications interception. LECRIM does not specifically mention the use of IMSI-catchers.

It is unclear whether the new Article 588*quinquies* b LECRIM refers to these devices or not. The heading of this provision reads: "The use of devices or technical means for tracking and location." From the heading it is unclear whether IMSI-catchers are included among those devices or not: on one hand they do not track a certain person, but only a mobile terminal; but on the other hand, they could fall within the category of "location devices." The content of the article does not provide further clarity on this issue, however it may be worth reproducing it here:

Article 588*quinquies* b LECRIM

1. Where there are good reasons that show that the measure is necessary and proportionate, the judge may authorize the use of devices or technical means for tracking and tracing.

2. The authorization shall specify the technical means to be used.

3. Providers, officers, and persons referred to in Article 588*ter*, are required to provide the judge, the prosecutor, and the judicial police officers appointed to execute the measure the necessary assistance and collaboration to facilitate the execution of the judicial order authorizing the monitoring, under penalty of committing an offence of disobedience.

4. In urgent cases, where there are reasons to fear that if the devices are not put in place immediately, this will frustrate the investigation, the Judicial Police may proceed to their placement, informing as soon as possible and in any case within 24 hours to the judge, who may ratify the measure or order its ceasing also within 24 hours. In the latter case, the information obtained from the device in place will have no effects in the criminal proceedings.

According to my interpretation, this provision is related to other tracking devices and not to IMSI-catchers. However, as the provision is not yet in force, and there is no practice on it, my interpretation cannot be seen as conclusive.

b) Location determination via "silent SMS"

LECRIM does not mention either IMSI or IMEI identification or tracking devices. Location via silent SMS is used in practice in criminal investigation, being unclear in the case law if a judicial warrant is required for it or not. The same considerations that have been expressed above under the previous paragraph regarding the IMSI-catcher are applicable here.

D. Access to (Temporarily) Stored Communication Data

1. Online searches with the help of remote forensic software

The new Law 13/2015 of 5 October introduces the regulation of the remote search of computer equipment. In the Spanish system, as explained above, no measures restrictive of fundamental rights can be used for preventive purposes by law enforcement. Only within the criminal procedure and with prior judicial authorisation may the new measure of remote search of computer equipment be carried out.

The new Article 588*septies* a LECRIM sets out the requirements for this measure:

The judge may authorize the use of identification data and codes, as well as the installation of a software that allow the electronic remote search, without knowledge of the owner or user, of the contents of a computer, an electronic device, a computer system, or instruments for mass storage of computer data, or databases, for the aim of investigating one of the following offenses:

a) Crimes committed within criminal organizations.
b) Terrorist offenses.
c) Crimes committed against minors or persons with legal incapacity judicially declared.
d) Crimes against the Constitution, treason and related to national defence.
e) Crimes committed through computer tools or other information technology or telecommunications or communication service.

2. The court order authorizing the remote search shall specify:

a) the computers, the electronic devices, the computer systems or part of them, the data storage media or databases to be searched, and the data or other digital content targeted by the measure.
b) The scope of it, the way in which the access and the seizure of data or computer files relevant to the case will be done, and the software by which the access and control of the information will be done.
c) The officers authorized to execute the measure.
d) The authorization, if any, for making and retaining copies of the computer data.
e) The precise measures to preserve the integrity of the stored data as well as the measures for ensuring the inaccessibility or deletion of such data from the computer system that has been accessed.

3. When the officers who conduct the remote search have reasons to believe that the data sought are stored in another computer system or part of it, they will inform the judge about this matter, who may authorize an extension of the conditions of the search.

It has to be noted that the duration of this measure is much shorter than provided for other IT investigative measures. While all other IT measures may be authorised usually for three months, extendable for equal terms up to a maximum of 18 months, the remote search of computers can only be authorised for one month, with a maximum extension up to three months (Article 588*septies* c LECRIM).

2. Search and seizure of stored communication data

a) Special provisions

Until Law 13/2005 of 5 October there was no specific regulation for the search and seizure of stored communication data, although it was used in practice under the general rules on telephone tapping (Article 579 LECRIM) or search and seizure of documents and objects. The lengthy new Article 588*sexies* a to c LECRIM provides for a complete regulation of this measure, specifying the requisites for judicial authorisation, the restrictions to the seizure of computer hardware, the way to make copies of the relevant data seized and the need for a specific authorisation for this measure beyond the authorisation for searching premises.

Article 588*sexies* a – Need for specific motivation

1. When it is foreseeable that during a domicile search the apprehension of computers, telephone or electronic communications instruments, mass storage digital information devices, or the access to telematic data repositories will take place, the judicial warrant authorizing the search of dwellings shall extend its reasoning to express the reasons, if any, that authorize the agents to access the information contained in such devices.

2. The simple seizure of any of the devices to which the preceding paragraph refers, carried out during the house search, does not authorize to access to its content, notwithstanding the possibility that such access could be authorized later by the judge.

Article 588*sexies* b – Access to information of electronic devices seized outside the home of the suspect/defendant

The requirement set out in paragraph 1 of the preceding Article shall also apply to cases in which computers, communication instruments, or devices of mass data storage, and access to telematic data repositories, are seized independently from a house search. In such cases, officials shall inform the judge of the seizure of such devices. If the judge considers that the access to the information hosted in such devices, he may grant the corresponding authorization.

Article 588*sexies* c – Judicial authorization

1. The judicial warrant authorizing access to the information contained in the devices this section refers to, shall determine the conditions and scope of the search and may authorize the copying of the computer data found. It shall also determine the conditions necessary to ensure data integrity and preservation guarantees to enable, where appropriate, the examination by an expert for preparing an expert opinion.

2. Unless they constitute the object or instrument for committing the crime or there are other reasons that justify the seizure of hardware containing computer data or files, the confiscation of the hardware will be avoided, when this would cause serious damage to the user or owner and it is possible to secure the data by obtaining a copy of them in conditions that guarantee the authenticity and integrity of the data.

An extended search of other computers connected to those placed in the domicile under search is also regulated under paragraph 3 of this article, but it needs to be authorised specifically by the judge, if not authorised initially.

b) Different standards of protection for stored and for transmitted data

The new regulation on interception of telecommunications and access to stored data does not provide for different requisites, duration or formal requirements for real-time communications and stored communications.

What has been noted regarding the interception of content data of communications is applicable *mutatis mutandis* to access to stored electronic data. The new legal framework seems to consider stored data as communications and not documents. However, the regulation is unclear, because when regulating access to stored electronic data in computers or other electronic devices, it does not distinguish between ordinary files and stored communications.

c) *Open and clandestine access to stored data*

If the stored data are accessible via remote computer search (as explained below) they can also be accessed in a clandestine way, without the relevant person being aware of it. However, if the stored data are on a device or hard disk, which is not accessible via remote computer search, then in principle, the only way to access those data is by way of a search and seizure order. The execution of the home search requires the presence of the inhabitant or owner and thus it could not be carried out in a clandestine way.

3. Duties to cooperate: production and decryption orders

Article 588*sexies* 5. LECRIM

The authorities and officials responsible for the investigation may order any person who knows the operation of the computer system or is aware of the measures that protect the computer data, to provide the information necessary, provided that such cooperation does not entail a disproportionate burden for such person, under the penalty of committing an offence of disobedience.

This provision shall not apply to the suspect or defendant and persons who are exempted from the obligation to testify by reason of kinship and those that, in accordance with Article 416.2 LECRIM, cannot testify due to professional secrecy.

IV. Use of Electronic Communication Data in Judicial Proceedings

1. Use of electronic communication data in the law of criminal procedure

For the telecommunications interception to be assessed as evidence in criminal proceedings, the general principles on evidence production are to be respected: the evidence has to be introduced in a public hearing, and the parties must be granted the right for the defence to confront the evidence, granting the opportunity to challenge the authenticity, reliability, and integrity of the evidentiary materials.

The production of the evidence will vary depending on whether it is recorded conversations, recorded images, or other electronic data.

For telephone conversations, the jurisprudence has required the reproduction of the relevant conversations in the public hearing and/or the reading of the written transcripts (e.g., STS 14 July 2006, RJ 2006/6093; STS 9 April 2007, RJ 2007/2013), but has also admitted testimony of the person recording the conversations.

For other data, the reading of the transcripts or the reproduction on a computer before the trial court is the usual way to introduce the data into evidence, or by way of written transcripts. Expert evidence is usually in place, too, with the presence of an expert witness to explain the procedure for collecting data and how the integrity, authenticity, etc. has been secured.

For the admissibility of intercepted communications as evidence the courts have required (regarding telephone conversations): 1) that the original recordings are made available for the parties, so that they can listen to them; and 2) that the original recordings are complete. These have been considered essential safeguards to guarantee the integrity and authenticity of the evidence, declaring it inadmissible when the conversations were not presented as evidence on the original disks or recording media.

This stance had to be reviewed since the interception of communications by way of SITEL has by definition no "original disk" as the data are directly dumped into a central computer. This means all communications are presented to the court as copies or transcripts.

As to the need to present all the intercepted material, the case law is very clear: the police cannot select conversations or communications, but have to transfer all intercepted material to the investigating judge. All the tapes or disks with the recording of the intercepted conversations or electronic data must be conveyed to the court. For the purposes of using the recordings as evidence at trial, the investigating judge only, and not the police, is allowed to select conversations.[31] Therefore, the police must provide all the tapes with the totality of the conversations, no matter whether they are considered useful for the case or not. Otherwise, the tapes will not be admitted as evidence.

Until now, all the communications recorded were to be disclosed and made available to the defence. This rule has now been limited by the new Article 588*ter* i LECRIM, that provides that conversations affecting the intimacy of the parties will not be made available to the parties to the proceedings. The parties have to be informed that such parts have been excluded from the copies of the communications they have obtained. It is unclear how this provision will be interpreted and applied. It is to be welcomed that LECRIM has introduced this rule to better protect the core of the right to intimacy of persons whose communications have been intercepted, however, it will have to be balanced whether those communications affecting the intimacy are relevant as evidence or not. There is no exclusionary rule of evidence based on the protection of the core content of the right to privacy (or intimacy).

[31] See, e.g., the Supreme Court's decisions STS 23 January 1995; STS 4 February 1998, and STS 25 June 1993. In the same sense, J. Montero Aroca, "La intervención de las comunicaciones telefónicas en el proceso penal," pp. 246–247.

2. Inadmissibility of evidence as a consequence of inappropriate collection

The general rules and principles on exclusionary rules of evidence shall apply also to the evidence collected through an unlawful interception of communications. Spanish statutory rules provide for a very strict exclusionary rule. The key statutory provision regarding the exclusion of evidence is Article 11.1 of the Organic Law of the Judicial Power (*Ley Orgánica del Poder Judicial*, LOPJ). The LOPJ was enacted in 1985, one year after the Constitutional Court's landmark decision in STC 114/184, and this decision clearly influenced the wording of Article 11.1 LOPJ, which reads: "Evidence obtained, directly or indirectly, in violation of fundamental rights or liberties, shall have no effect."

The doctrine of the indirect or "reflex effects" (*fruit of the poisonous tree* doctrine) determines the exclusion not only of the main evidentiary elements but also of those other elements of evidence that derive from the originally illegal act. The Spanish courts have followed the doctrine of "reflex effects" in those cases where not applying it would result in leaving fundamental rights unprotected. Thus, for instance, recordings obtained through illegal phone tapping are not accepted, neither is the testimony of the officer in charge of the recording, for otherwise the meaning and purpose of the exclusionary rules would be circumvented and it would encourage the adoption of measures that are contrary to the constitutional right to the secrecy of communications.

It has been questioned whether the Constitution establishes a constitutional right to exclude illegally obtained evidence. Although initially the Constitutional Court considered that such right was not recognised in the SC, later it decided that a criminal conviction based on evidence gathered in violation of fundamental constitutional rights would undermine following constitutional safeguards:

The first is the fundamental right to a fair trial recognised under Article 24 SC. The second is the principle of equality of arms, because one of the parties, the prosecution, would be able to use illegally obtained evidence and benefit from the violation of the constitutional rights of the other, the defendant.[32] Finally, the admission of illegally gathered evidence would undermine the presumption of innocence, guaranteed by Article 24.2 SC. The presumption of innocence in the Spanish legal order not only implies the right to be treated as innocent until a judgment of conviction becomes final but has a wider scope. It also encompasses the right not to be held guilty if there has not been sufficient lawfully gathered evidence to prove the defendant's guilt.

---

[32] STC 114/1984, FJ 5. After this judgment, the close relation between the exclusionary rule and the right to a fair trial has been recognised in numerous Constitutional Court decisions.

3. Use of data outside the main proceedings

a) Data from other criminal investigations

If we focus on the question of accidental discoveries – data collected by chance during the interception of communications, relating to another criminal offence different to the one for which the judicial warrant was issued – until Law 13/2015 there was no express rule in LECRIM. The jurisprudence had developed a set of principles to be applied to casual findings or accidental discoveries, mainly within the realm of the execution of home searches, but also with regard to telephone interceptions.

If the facts discovered are not connected to the offence for which the investigative measure restrictive of fundamental rights was authorised, and those facts appear to be serious enough as to justify the adoption of the interception measure, they will serve as "notitia criminis." The authorities carrying out the measure will inform the competent judge about the facts discovered, and a new criminal procedure shall be opened (STS 940/2011, 27 September), so that the competent judge renders an ex-post judicial authorisation to cover the investigation of the newly discovered offence. However, the original investigating judge can also authorise the extension of the criminal investigation regarding the newly discovered offence.

If the newly discovered facts refer to a crime which would not allow the adoption of telecommunications interception, such offence may only be prosecuted on the basis of the accidental findings if it is connected to the principal offence.

Article 588*bis* i LECRIM as of 4 October 2015, provides for a special rule on accidental findings of another crime during the execution of a measure of telecommunications interception. This rule refers to the requisites set out under Article 579*bis* LECRIM. As a consequence, to proceed with the investigation of the newly discovered crime, a judicial warrant needs to be requested. And it will only be granted, if the newly discovered offence justifies the adoption of the measure of interception of communications (penalty higher than three years, or terrorism, or organised crime, or cybercrime or crime committed through internet). It is only by way of this subsequent judicial warrant that the communications can be used for the new procedure and the information obtained be used as evidence.

b) Data from preventive investigations

There are no preventive criminal investigations in the Spanish legal order. As to national security activities and their transfer to criminal proceedings, there are no legal provisions determining how and when this transfer should happen, as has been commented above. As to intelligence activity as evidence, there have been some controversial Supreme Court decisions admitting "intelligence reports" as expert evidence.

The judgment of the Criminal Chamber of the Supreme Court 2084/2001 of 13 December 2001 was the first to qualify intelligence reports issued by the Civil Guard officers on terrorism as "intelligence expert evidence." After this ruling, many more followed the same stance, as, for example, SSTS 985/2009, 13 October 2009, SSTS 480/2009, 22 May 2009, or SSTS 1097/2011, 25 October 2011.

However, the doctrine of the Supreme Court on this matter has not been uniform, as there are several rulings stating that the aforementioned "intelligence report" cannot be regarded as expert evidence. So the SSTS 1029/2005, 26 September 2005, SSTS 556/2006, 31 May 2006 and SSTS 1929/2007, 16 February 2007.

As far as we know since 2011 there have been no more decisions dealing with "intelligence expert evidence."

c) Data obtained from foreign jurisdictions

The traditional rule in international cooperation is that the execution of the requested measures will take place in accordance with the procedural rules of the executing state *(lex loci)*. This has been the rule according to Article 3.1 of the European Convention on Mutual Assistance in Criminal Matters of the Council of Europe of 20 April 1959. This same rule is found in most bilateral agreements on mutual legal assistance in criminal matters (e.g., Article 5.3 of the Convention with the United States in accordance with EU/US legal assistance agreement that was signed bilaterally with Spain and ratified on 17 December 2004; Article 7 of the Convention on Legal Cooperation and Mutual Assistance between Spain and Brazil of 22 May 2006; Article 10 of the Convention on Mutual Legal Assistance with the Mexico of September 29 2006).

Article 4 of the EU Convention on Criminal Judicial Assistance of 29 May 2000 introduces the possibility of requesting the compliance with certain formalities of the *lex fori*, which provides that in cases where mutual assistance is granted, the Member State shall comply with the formalities and procedures expressly indicated by the requesting Member State, unless otherwise provided in the Convention and provided that such formalities and procedures are not contrary to fundamental principles of law of the Member State addressed. Nevertheless, it basically retains the general principle of *lex loci* in the specific regulation of interception of communications contained in Articles 17–22.

The Spanish Supreme Court has repeatedly stated that evidence obtained abroad according to the rules of the executing state are valid in Spain.

Three general principles become evident when analysing the Supreme Court case law in this regard: 1) That the evidence obtained pursuant to the procedural rules in the state where it was collected should not be subjected to the test of compliance with the Spanish rules, for example, as in STS 340/2000, 3 March, or STS 1142/2005, 20 September, stating that it is not for the trial court to check whether the evidence obtained abroad complies with Spanish evidentiary rules; 2) It would be possible to check if the collecting of evidence complied with the rules of the executing state, but in such case the burden to prove the infringement of those rules would lie with the party claiming the inadmissibility of the evidence, for example, in STS 503/2008, 17 July; 3) The Spanish Supreme Court has held that for evidence collected in another EU Member State, a general principle of trust applies, for example, SSTS 18/2003, 10 January, SSTS 1345/2005, 14 October, and SSTS 886/2007, 2 November, may be mentioned.

There are, however, some comments to be made concerning this general doctrine: 1) the Supreme Court after recognising the admissibility of evidence obtained according to the *lex loci* of the executing state, states that this approach is applicable to states that share the same values and principles as Spain as enshrined in the Constitution, so that the requirements for restricting the rights of citizens are substantially similar. 2) for questioning the validity of the evidence obtained abroad it is necessary to provide some objective data suggestive of a possible breach of fundamental rights that is contrary to the constitutional values of the Spanish system (STS 1099/2005, 30 September).

It is important to note that the vast majority of these sentences analysed evidence obtained implementing the Convention on criminal judicial cooperation the Council of Europe of 1959.

Following the rules set out in the 2000 EU Convention and the aforementioned case law of the Supreme Court in the case of assessing the validity of the telecommunications interception practice abroad, the Spanish trial court has to look at the validity of the national warrant authorising a request of interception to a foreign authority and the content of the letter rogatory, as this has to comply with all requirements that would be necessary if the interception were to be executed in Spain: when the interception of communications is required through international judicial assistance, Article 18.3 of the 2000 Convention requires the inclusion of the national judicial warrant authorising this measure in the Spanish investigation.

It is different in a case in which evidence is presented as the result of interventions within a foreign criminal proceeding, upon their own initiative. In these cases the Spanish courts accept the use of such evidentiary elements obtained in compliance with the *lex loci*. It can be seen that the Spanish Supreme Court has long adopted the principle of mutual recognition, without checking the validity of the evidence obtained abroad, as long as there are no indications of fundamental rights infringements and as long as the foreign country shares equivalent legal values.

4. Challenging the probity of intercepted data

As has been pointed out already, Article 588*ter* I LECRIM provides for the full disclosure of communications intercepted, except parts that the investigating judge may exclude to protect the right to intimacy. The full disclosure shall allow the defence to listen to the recorded conversations as well as to analyse the intercepted data.

Defence lawyers in practice usually directly target the form and reasons for the judicial warrant authorising the interception, rather than its technical execution. The lack of enough initial suspicion, the lack of proportionality and in general the lack of sufficient formal motivation for the warrant are frequently invoked arguments against the validity of the interceptions and are also often accepted.

With regard to the technical requirements, defence lawyers do not often invoke such reasons against the admissibility of the evidence: first, because the system SITEL does not cast doubt as to the integrity of the communications intercepted and has been declared in conformity with the constitutional rights by the Supreme Court; and second, because the process of transferring information onto disks is to be done in the presence of the *secretario judicial* (court clerk acting as notary), and the IT expert witness is also usually involved, who can give information concerning the whole process relevant for the authenticity of the data.

A frequent argument against the admissibility of the evidence obtained by telecommunications interception has been also that the investigators did not present the original disk at court. However, the practice on this requirement differs greatly, some courts insisting on having an original disk and other courts being satisfied with copies of the data.

V. Exchange of Intercepted Electronic Communication Data between Foreign Countries

A. Legal Basis for Mutual Legal Assistance

1. International conventions

The European Convention on MLA in Criminal Matters of 20 April 1959 was ratified by Spain on 18 August 1982.

The Convention on MLA in Criminal Matters between the Member States of the EU of 29 May 2000, entered into force on 23 August 2005. However, Spain had previously agreed on the provisional implementation of the 2000 Convention, and it was therefore already applicable in Spain even before it had officially entered in force (BOE 15 October 2003).

The UN TOC Convention of 15 November 2000 was ratified by Spain in 2003 (BOE 29 September 2003).

The CoE Cybercrime Convention of 23 November 2001 has been ratified by Spain (BOE 17 September 2013).

2. Bilateral treaties

There are no bilateral treaties providing specific rules on interception of telecommunications (information provided by the international cooperation unit of the General Council of the Judiciary).

3. National regulation

The Law 23/2014 of 20 November on Mutual Recognition of Criminal Decisions in the European Union does provide specific rules on judicial cooperation in criminal matters in the EU. This law contains the domestic regulation of all mutual recognition instruments in criminal matters adopted until now, except the Directive on the European Investigation Order. None of the EU mutual recognition instruments provides for specific rules for the interception of communications, save for the Directive on the European Investigation Order. Therefore, in practice requests for international cooperation for a telecommunications interception are done via the EU Convention of 29 May 2000 or the MLA Convention of 1959, as far as this rapporteur has been able to confirm (information on bilateral conventions with EU Member States that might cover interceptions of telecommunications are unknown to us, but this data have not been definitively confirmed).

B. Requirements and Procedure (Including the Handling of Privileged Information)

1. Incoming requests

The main authorities that are involved in international judicial cooperation in Spain are three: 1) the judiciary; 2) the Ministry of Justice; and 3) the Public Prosecution Service.

Investigating judges will receive the legal assistance requests directly in all cases where the international conventions or the European instruments so provide.

Once the request has been received – either directly or through the central authority designated in the Conventions or through the National Court or Prosecutor's Office –, Spanish authorities are obliged to execute it. We must recall that the EU Convention of 1959 also allows the direct transmission of the requests in urgent cases (Article 15.2 of the Convention MLA in Criminal Matters 1959). In these urgent cases, the requests might be sent through Europol.

Under Spanish law, the competence to execute the legal assistance requests in criminal matters lies generally with the investigating judges. Requests coming from an EU Member State will be sent directly to the competent investigating Judge.

In order to determine the materially/territorially competent investigating judge, the contact points of the EJN shall be contacted or the assistance of Eurojust sought.

However, in practice it also occurs that when the requesting authority does not know the domicile of the person whose communications are to be intercepted and thus it is not possible to know which investigating judge is competent, the request is sent to the National Court, as it has jurisdiction over the whole territory of Spain. When the requesting state has contacted Eurojust, the national member of Eurojust will send the request for interception of telecommunications to the Public Prosecutor's Office, to its International Cooperation unit. This unit will then forward it to the competent investigating judge. It must be noted, however, that the members of the Prosecution Service are also competent to carry out the requests, except in those cases where coercive measures are requested. If the execution of an international request could entail the restriction of fundamental rights, only the judge can provide for its execution.

The General Council of the Judiciary *(Consejo General del Poder Judicial)* gives support in mutual legal assistance proceedings. Any Spanish judge that requires it, will be assisted by the General Council in the correct transmission, and effective execution of international legal assistance requests.[33] Furthermore, the Council has published an online guide which contains the complete regulation – listing all the bilateral and multilateral conventions, as well as the EU instruments and their transposition to Spanish domestic law –, practical explanations on how to manage legal assistance requests, standard forms, and information on how to communicate with the contact points of the European and the Spanish judicial networks.

2. Outgoing requests

The investigating judge carrying out the investigation of the offence is competent to issue the international cooperation request.

3. Technical regulation

There are no legal provisions on the filtering of incoming data or of outgoing data, or on the way the transfer of the information is to be carried out. Within the EU the secured intranet of the EJN could be used. In practice, the transfer takes place in different ways: it is not unfrequent that a member of the judicial police or even a member of the public prosecution travel abroad to fetch the disks and bring it to the Spanish investigating judge. This is often done when the Spanish officers have already travelled to the relevant country for purposes of the investigation, but there

[33] Articles 71 ff. of the Reglamento 5/1995, 7 June, *de los aspectos accesorios de las actuaciones judiciales*.

are also cases where the travel takes place only for bringing the elements of evidence, in particular, the disks with the intercepted communications. This is not, however, the only practice. For example, when it comes to judicial cooperation with France, as there is a liason magistrate in Madrid as well as in Paris, the transfer of the data is often done through them. The National Court reports of cases where the data have been transferred through the embassy (they refer to single cases of data transfer with USA). In investigations where several EU countries are involved and joint investigation teams have been set up, the disks sometimes are transferred through the heads of the respective joint investigation teams. In other cases, the disk is attached to the documents related to the request, and sent by ordinary channels.

In sum, there is no uniform practice.

4. Real-time transfer of communication data

As far as we know at present neither the current legal framework nor the technical setting allows for the judge from another EU Member State to have direct access to the data resulting from the telecommunications interception.

C. European Investigation Order

The EIO has not yet been transposed into the Spanish legal system. The Law 23/2014, 20 November 2014, on Mutual Recognition of Criminal Decisions in the European Union, sets out the general principles applicable to the mutual recognition principle in criminal matters in the EU. The main objective of this law is to bring together all the diverse legal provisions transposing the EU instruments on judicial cooperation in criminal matters. It provides for the domestic regulation of the EU evidence warrant, but does not include yet the rules regarding the EIO.

Although there is will to adopt the EIO without waiting for the expiry of the deadline for its transposition (22 May 2017), it cannot be predicted when the rules of Directive 2014/41/EU will be transposed into the Spanish legal order. However, the recent amendments of LECRIM on interception of communications will undoubtedly make the execution of EIO issued for interception of communications much easier.

D. Statistics

No statistics are available.

Bibliography

Aguilera Morales, "Las diligencias de investigación fiscal." Madrid 2014.

Bachmaier Winter, "Información de inteligencia y proceso penal" in *Terrorismo, proceso penal y derechos fundamentales*, ed. L. Bachmaier. Marcial Pons, Madrid 2012, pp. 45–101.

– "Intervenciones telefónicas y derechos de terceros en el proceso penal. La necesidad de una regulación legal del secreto profesional y de otras relaciones de confianza," in *Revista de Derecho Procesal* (2004/1-3), pp. 41–82.

– "Remote search of computers under the new Spanish Law of 2015. Has it got the right balance?," in *Burgas University Law Review, special issue: Law and the Internet.* Bulgaria 2016 (forthcoming).

Barnes Vázquez, "Introducción al principio de proporcionalidad en el derecho comparado y comunitario," in *Rev. Actualidad Penal* 135 (1994), pp. 531 ff.

Bernal Pulido, "El principio de proporcionalidad y los derechos fundamentales." Madrid 2003.

Gimeno Sendra, "Las intervenciones telefónicas en la jurisprudencia del Tribunal Constitucional y del Tribunal Supremo", in *La Ley* 1996-2, pp. 1617–1624.

González Beilfuss, "El principio de proporcionalidad en la jurisprudencia del Tribunal Constitucional." Cizur Menor, 2003.

Heredero Higueras, "La Directiva Comunitaria de proteccion de datos de carácter personal." Madrid 1998.

Manso Porto, "Las escuchas telefónicas entre abogado defensor y cliente en una comparación internacional," in *Estudios Penales y Criminológicos USC*, vol. XXXII (2012), pp. 39–95.

Marchena Gómez/González-Cuéllar Serrano, "La reforma de la Ley de Enjuiciamiento Criminal de 2015." Madrid 2015.

Martín Casallo, "Implicaciones de la Directiva sobre protección de datos en la normativa española," in *X años de Encuentro sobre Informática y Derecho*. Pamplona 1997.

Montero Aroca, "La intervención de las comunicaciones telefónicas en el proceso penal." Valencia 1999.

Montón Redondo, "Las interceptaciones telefónicas constitucionalmente correctas", in *La Ley* 1995-4, pp. 1043–1052.

Ortí Vallejo, "Derecho a la intimidad e informática." Granada 1994.

Pedraz Penalva/Ortega Benito, "El principio de proporcionalidad y su configuración en la jurisprudencia del Tribunal Constitucional y en literatura especializada alemana," in *Rev. Poder Judicial* 17 (1990), pp. 69–100.

Rodríguez Laínz, "Consideraciones jurídicas en torno a la licitud constitucional de SITEL," in *La Ley* nº 7344, Sección Doctrina, 17 Feb. 2010, pp. 1–29.

Serrano Pérez, "El derecho fundamental a la protecciónnd e datos. Derecho español y derecho comparado." Madrid 2003.

Troncoso Reigada, "Protection of data in e-government" in the foreword to the study coordinated by the Data Protection Agency of Madrid and published under the title e-Prodat: e-Government and Data Protection in European Regions and Cities. Madrid 2006.

Vidal Fueyo, "El principio de proporcionalidad como parámetro de constitucionalidad de la actividad del juez", in *Anuario de Derecho Constitucional Latinoamericano* 2005.

Zoco Zabala, "Nuevas tecnologías y control de las comunicaciones." Madrid 2015.

List of Abbreviations

BOE	Boletín Oficial del Estado
CC	Spanish Criminal Code
CNI	Centro Nacional de Inteligencia (National Intelligence Centre)
DEA	US Drugs Enforcement Agency
ECHR	European Convention on Human Rights
ECtHR	European Court of Human Rights
EIO	European Investigation Order
EJN	European Judicial Network
IMEI	International Mobile Equipment Identity
IMSI	International Mobile Subscriber Identity
LECRIM	Ley de Enjuiciamiento Criminal (Spanish Criminal Procedure Code)
LOPJ	Ley Orgánica del Poder Judicial (Organic Law of the Judicial Power)
MLA	Mutual Legal Assistance
O.L.	Organic Law
PC	Spanish Penal Code
RJ	Referencia Jurisprudencia
SC	Spanish Constitution
SIS	Schengen Information System
SITEL	Sistema integrado de interceptación legal de las telecomunicaciones (comprehensive system for intercepting electronic communications)
STC / SSTC	Sentencia/s Tribunal Constitucional

The United Kingdom*

National Rapporteur:
Ian Walden

* This report reflects legislation and case law as of September 2016.

Contents

I. Security Architecture and the Interception of Telecommunication

A. Law Enforcement Institutions and Security Services with Powers of Telecommunication Interception

1. National security architecture

In the UK, the key agencies responsible for national security are the Security Services (MI5)[1] and the Secret Intelligence Services (MI6).[2] The former has responsibility for domestic counter-intelligence, while the latter is responsible for foreign intelligence. The existence of MI5 was avowed by the government through the Security Service Act 1989 and MI6 by the Intelligence Services Act 1994. Both services have the functions of protecting national security, safeguarding the 'economic well-being of the United Kingdom' and 'the detection and prevention of serious crime'.[3] The agencies are supported by the Government Communications Headquarters (GCHQ),[4] which provides signals intelligence. Within the Ministry of Defence, there is also Defence Intelligence,[5] providing strategic defence intelligence to the Ministry and the armed forces.

The police are primarily responsible for criminal law enforcement. The structure of the UK police can be sub-divided into national and territorial bodies, the latter reflecting the different regions within England, Scotland, Wales and Northern Ireland. In addition to the police, we have the National Crime Agency (NCA)[6] with responsibility for tackling serious and organised crime through its 'crime reduction function' and its 'criminal intelligence function'.[7] The NCA is a non-ministerial government department, rather than a policing agency, and was established in 2013. Its remit includes the National Cyber Crime Unit.

---

1 https://www.mi5.gov.uk MI5 and MI6, as popularly known, refer to the respective sections of Military Intelligence established during the Second World War.

2 https://www.sis.gov.uk

3 Security Service Act 1989 (SSA), s 1 and Intelligence Services Act 1994 (ISA), s 1.

4 http://www.gchq.gov.uk/pages/homepage.aspx See also ISA, s 3.

5 https://www.gov.uk/government/groups/defence-intelligence

6 http://www.nationalcrimeagency.gov.uk

7 Crime and Courts Act 2013, s 1.

Obviously, the distinction between national security and criminal matters is often blurred. As such, the agencies regularly engage in joint operations,[8] while MI5 is specifically tasked with supporting the NCA and other law enforcement agencies.[9]

2. Powers for the interception of telecommunications

In *Malone v United Kingdom,*[10] the European Court of Human Rights (ECtHR) held that UK law was deficient with respect to the protection of Article 8(1) privacy rights for a failure to have a statutory framework governing the interception of communications in the course of a criminal investigation. In response to this ruling, the UK adopted the Interception of Communications Act 1985. However, in *Halford v United Kingdom,*[11] the ECtHR again held that UK law was deficient, by failing to adequately protect individuals against acts of interception. In the following year, the Human Rights Act 1998 incorporated the European Convention of Human Rights (ECHR) directly into UK domestic law. Taken together, these developments forced the government to reform its entire regime governing the interception of communications.

The Regulation of Investigatory Powers Act 2000 (RIPA) is the primary statute governing the coercive interception of communications, whether via telecommunications or postal services, for law enforcement purposes (Part I, Chapter I). In addition, however, there are legacy provisions in the Wireless Telegraphy Act 2006 (WTA),[12] and the Telecommunications Act 1984 (TA)[13] s 94, which can enable interception activities by law enforcement and supplement the RIPA. On 4 November 2015, the Government published its Investigatory Powers Bill (IPB), which is intended to establish a more consolidated regime for all law enforcement powers to intercept, as well as other covert investigative techniques, bringing together the three existing statutory regimes.[14]

There are also coercive powers to access stored data under various statutes, which can be used in certain circumstances to intercept communications when stored in the course of their transmission.[15] Two key examples are the Police and Criminal Evidence Act 1984 (PACE), in which a court may authorise access to

---

8 E.g. GCHQ and NCA join forces to ensure no hiding place online for criminals

9 SSA, s 1(4).

10 [1984] 7 EHRR 14.

11 (1997) IRLR 471.

12 Sections 48–49.

13 Section 94.

14 http://www.parliament.uk/business/bills-and-legislation/draft-bills/ The IPB contains powers for targeted interception, acquisition of communications data, equipment interference, bulk interception, acquisition and equipment interference, data retention and bulk personal data sets.

15 RIPA, s 1(5)(c).

material,[16] and the ISA, under which the Secret Intelligence Services can be authorised to interfere with property or wireless telegraphy, both domestic and foreign, which could result in the interception of a person's communications.[17]

3. Responsibility for the technical performance of interception measures

Technical implementation of an interception measure is generally carried out with the assistance of the telecommunications service provider (service provider), since they will need to identify the relevant equipment and the means by which the intercept can be carried out. The service provider has a duty to give all assistance that is 'reasonably practicable' (s 11(5)) or to have an 'intercept capability' with a government-defined minimum functionality. However, in certain circumstances, a law enforcement agency may be able to carry out the interception directly itself without the assistance of a service provider. Law enforcement agencies (LEAs) are given technical support by the National Technical Assistance Centre (NTAC), which is part of GCHQ.

4. Legitimacy of data transfers between different security agencies

Under RIPA, there are limitations on the disclosure of intercepted material both within and outside the agency that lawfully obtained the material. The number of persons to whom the material is disclosed; the extent of the disclosure; the extent to which the material is copied and the number of copies made is restricted to that which is necessary for the 'authorised purposes' (s 11(2)). These include the underlying purpose for which the intercept activity was authorised, to enable prosecutors to ensure a fair trail and for oversight purposes (s 11(3)). These safeguards are elaborated in a code of practice, adopted under RIPA (s 71) and applicable to all agencies exercising interception powers.[18]

B. Statistics on Telecommunication Interception

Under RIPA s 58(4), the number of interception warrants issued under the RIPA is reported to the Prime Minister every six months by the Interception of Communications Commissioner (IoCC).[19] This report is then laid before Parliament

[16] Section 9 and Schedule 1.

[17] Section 5 and 7.

[18] See Home Office, *Interception of Communications: Code of Practice*, January 2016, at sections 7 and 8, available at: https://www.gov.uk/government/publications/interception-of-communications-code-of-practice-2016.

[19] Prior to the Data Retention and Investigatory Act 2014, s 6, these reports were annual. See generally http://www.iocco-uk.info.

(s 58(6)). The two ministerial government departments that primarily issue warrants, the Home Office and the Foreign Office, supply the data; although all relevant LEAs and any telecommunications operator on whom a warrant has been served are required to disclose information to the IoCC, which is then used to generate statistics for the reports (s 58(1)). The numbers of interception warrants issued over the last 5 years are as follows:

Year	Number
2014	2795
2013	2760
2012	3372
2011	2911
2010	1865

The number of warrants granted under the ISA is reported every twelve months by the Intelligence Service Commissioner ('ISC').[20] The numbers of warrants over the past 4[21] years are as follows:

Year	Number
2014	2032
2013	1887
2012	2838
2011	2142
2010	1865

II. Principles of Telecommunication Interception in Constitutional and Criminal Procedural Law

1. Constitutional safeguards

The UK has no written constitution, but public bodies, including the courts, have an obligation to act in accordance with the ECHR, such as Article 8, as well as the jurisprudence of the ECtHR by virtue of the Human Rights Act 1998. The UK has been before the ECtHR on numerous occasions about the suitability of its domestic law on interception.[22]

20 http://intelligencecommissioner.com

21 Prior to 2011, the number of warrants issued was not published by the ISC 'because it would, I believe, assist those unfriendly to the UK' (Report for 2010, at para. 46).

22 E.g. *Malone* (1984), *Halford* (1997), *Liberty* (2008) and *Kennedy* (2010).

Since the entry into force of the Lisbon Treaty, on 1 December 2009, the EU Charter of Fundamental Rights (Charter) has also been applicable in the UK, but only where the UK is acting within the scope of EU law. Some of the rights confer a directly enforceable right, which would include Articles 7 (right to privacy) and 8 (right to protection of personal data).

The principles of necessity and proportionality are applicable in respect to considerations of compliance with both the ECHR and Charter rights.

2. Statutory safeguards

In terms of statutory protections, there are a number of provisions that provide potential criminal, administrative and/or civil law remedies against interception. As well as specifying circumstances in which acts of intercepting a person's communications are lawful (s 1(5)), the RIPA also contains provisions that either criminalise the unauthorised interception of communications; impose monetary penalties or give rise to a statutory tort (s 1). The maximum criminal penalty is two years imprisonment (s 1(7)), while the maximum monetary penalty is £50,000 (Sch A1, para 1(2)). Where an offence is committed by a legal person, such as a company, but with the consent, connivance or neglect of director, manager or similar officer, then that individual may also be personally liable (s 79).

The Computer Misuse Act 1990 criminalises unauthorised access to computer material (s 1) and unauthorised acts with intent to impair the operation of a computer (s 3), both of which could include computers involved in the transmission of communications. The maximum available penalties are 2 years and 10 years imprisonment respectively. The Act contains a general savings provision rendering any conduct by an 'enforcement officer' relating to powers of inspection, search or seizure or other authorised conduct immune from liability (s 10).

The Data Protection Act 1998 transposes Directive 95/46/EC and criminalises the unlawful obtaining of personal data without the consent of the data controller (s 55). This could include acts of interception. Currently, the maximum penalty is £5000. An amendment has been made to increase this to a maximum of 2 years imprisonment, although this has not yet been bought into force. Breach of the general obligations under the Act, such as processing personal data in breach of the data protection principles, does not give rise to criminal penalties directly.

The RIPA contains general safeguards concerning the use of intercepted material (s 15), which include limiting the disclosure of material to the minimum necessary for the authorised purpose and destroying any material as soon as there are no longer grounds for its retention. These safeguards are further specified in a Code of Practice on the Interception of Communications, adopted under s 71 of the RIPA.[23]

---

[23] See footnote no. 18 above.

However, breach of the safeguards detailed in the Code of Practice by a LEA does not give rise to any criminal or civil liability (s 72(2)).

3. Judicial oversight

A procedure for *ex post* judicial scrutiny of interception practices by LEAs exists through two different mechanisms. First, RIPA established the office of the Interception Commissioner (s 57),[24] currently the Rt. Hon. Sir Stanley Burnton, who reviews the exercise and performance of the powers and duties granted to persons under the RIPA and prepares a bi-annual report (s 58(4)). Over the years, the Commissioner has raised concerns about a range of matters; from the level of resources required to operate an effective oversight regime, to recommendations about the retention, storage, and destruction of intercept material.

The second scrutiny procedure is through persons having the right to bring proceedings (s 65(2)(a) or (d)), or make a complaint or reference (s 65(2)(b) or (c)) to the Investigatory Powers Tribunal (IPT).[25] The Tribunal has assumed responsibility for the jurisdiction previously held by the Interception of Communications Tribunal, the Security Service Tribunal and the Intelligence Services Tribunal. Of those cases dealt with by the IPT, to date, only a very small minority of decisions have found in favour of the complainant.[26] An appeal against a decision of the IPT would currently need to be made to the ECtHR, although the IPB would introduce a domestic right of appeal.

4. Parliamentary oversight

The Intelligence and Security Committee of Parliament (ISC) is a statutory committee of Parliament that has responsibility for oversight on behalf of the legislature of the UK intelligence community. The Committee was established by the Intelligence Services Act 1994, but Part I of the Justice and Security Act 2013 has recently reformed it, with enhanced powers.

The Committee oversees the activities of intelligence and security agencies, in particular MI5, MI6 and GCHQ (s 2(1)). The Committee also scrutinizes the work of other parts of the UK intelligence community, including the Joint Intelligence Organisation and the National Security Secretariat in the Cabinet Office; Defence Intelligence in the Ministry of Defence; and the Office for Security and Counter-Terrorism in the Home Office.

---

24 See generally www.iocco-uk.info

25 See generally www.ipt-uk.com

26 E.g. *Liberty and others v Secretary of State for Foreign and Commonwealth Affairs and others* [2015] UKIPTrib 13 77-H.

The Committee sets its own agenda and work programme, with an independent secretariat and investigator. It operates in accordance with a memorandum of understanding reached with the Prime Minister. It takes evidence from Government Ministers, the heads of the intelligence Agencies, officials from the intelligence community, and other witnesses as required. The Committee produces an Annual Report on the discharge of its functions. The Committee may also produce Reports on specific investigations. The most recent, *Privacy and Security: A modern and transparent legal framework*, fed into the reform process reflected in the IPB.[27] The Committee may also prepare confidential reports that it submits only to the Prime Minister (s 3(7)).

III. Powers for Accessing Telecommunications Data in the Law of Criminal Procedure

A. Overview of the Legal Framework

The RIPA addresses LEA access to electronic communications data obtained in different situations:

- Part I, Chapter I is concerned with the interception of communications content in the course of its transmission.
- Part I, Chapter II addresses the acquisition of 'communications data', which are the attributes of a communication, such as the address of the sender and recipient, but also includes details of the subscriber to the applicable telecommunication service.
- Part II governs surveillance activities. This could include, for example, a law enforcement investigator who regularly monitors a suspect's Facebook page, to gather information about his conduct and contacts.
- Part III is applicable to electronic communications data that has already been lawfully obtained, either through interception, surveillance or stored data access, but is protected by some form of protection mechanism, such as encryption, which renders the data unintelligible.

27 Intelligence and Security Committee of Parliament, *Privacy and Security: A modern and transparent legal framework*, HC 1075, March 2015, available at: http://isc.independent.gov.uk/committee-reports/special-reports

B. Interception of Content Data

1. Statutory provision

As noted above, the primary statute governing interception is RIPA, Part I. The default position under the Act is that interception conduct is unlawful, giving rise to either criminal or administrative penalties (s 1(1)-(2)) or civil remedies (s 1(3)). RIPA then specifies those circumstances in which an interception would have 'lawful authority'; these include where the parties to the communication have consented (s 3(1)); where it forms part of an authorised surveillance operation (s 3(2)),[28] or where it is carried out by a provider of telecommunication services for a purpose 'connected with the provision or operation of that service' or enforcement purposes (s 3(3)). In addition, provision is made for secondary regulations permitting interception, such as the 'Lawful Business Practice' Regulations,[29] which enable businesses to monitor the use of their telecommunication systems and transposes Article 5(2) of Directive 02/58/EC.[30]

Section 5 details a procedure for warranting interception for certain law enforcement purposes, outlined further below. Finally, any statutory powers, under other enactments, to obtain stored information or property may also constitute interception, but are recognised as permissible (s 1(5)(c)).

2. Scope of application

Under RIPA, the various constituent terms are defined. An act of 'interception' means:

> "a person intercepts a communication in the course of its transmission by means of a telecommunication system if, and only if, he–
>
> (a) so modifies or interferes with the system, or its operation,
>
> (b) so monitors transmissions made by means of the system, or
>
> (c) so monitors transmissions made by wireless telegraphy to or from apparatus comprised in the system,
>
> as to make some or all of the contents of the communication available, while being transmitted, to a person other than the sender or intended recipient of the communication." (s 2(2))

Where one party has consented to the interception, an interception warrant is not required, but it will be considered a form of surveillance that requires authorisation under Part II of the RIPA. The contents of the communication are made 'available' while being transmitted, even if it is recorded and made available for review at

---

[28] Surveillance is subject to a separate authorisation regime under Part II of RIPA.

[29] The Telecommunications (Interception of Communications) (Lawful Business Practice) Regulations 2000, SI No. 2699.

[30] OJ L 201/37, 31.7.2002.

some later point in time (s 2(8)). This definition does not include communications that are broadcast for general reception (s 2(3)). A 'communication' includes:

(a) (except in the definition of "postal service" in section 2(1)) anything transmitted by means of a postal service;
(b) anything comprising speech, music, sounds, visual images or data of any description; and
(c) signals serving either for the impartation of anything between persons, between a person and a thing or between things or for the actuation or control of any apparatus; (s 81(1))

A communication is therefore broadly defined to include content and other data, either related to the transmission of the communication itself or the operation of the telecommunication system over which the communication is transmitted. In terms of criminal procedure, a critically important distinction is made between the contents of a communication and its associated 'traffic data', defined in the following terms:

(a) any data identifying, or purporting to identify, any person, apparatus or location to or from which the communication is or may be transmitted,
(b) any data identifying or selecting, or purporting to identify or select, apparatus through which, or by means of which, the communication is or may be transmitted,
(c) any data comprising signals for the actuation of apparatus used for the purposes of a telecommunication system for effecting (in whole or in part) the transmission of any communication, and
(d) any data identifying the data or other data as data comprised in or attached to a particular communication,

but that expression includes data identifying a computer file or computer program access to which is obtained, or which is run, by means of the communication to the extent only that the file or program is identified by reference to the apparatus in which it is stored. (s 2(9))

The first sub-category would include the telephone number of a calling and called party, and the IP address of the sender and recipient of an Internet transmission. This category is exclusively concerned with the persons and apparatus[31] operating at the edges of a network. Such naming and addressing schemes may identify a person, but more usually will identify a CSP, IP holder and, or, an item of terminal equipment connected to the network. Reference is also made to the location to, or from, which a transmission may be made. Location data includes the latitude and longitude reference, where available, of the start and completion of a call, and the cell site data from the time the cell ceases to be used.

The second sub-category is concerned with the networks themselves. It would include the IP addresses of the routers or 'hops' taken by message packets transmitted over the Internet; as well as the networks over which traffic is carried, which may be required under interconnection arrangements.

---

[31] Defined as including "any equipment, machinery or device and any wire or cable" (*ibid.*, s 81(1)).

The third sub-category is intended to cover communications made between an end user and a network, rather than another end user. It is designed to address 'dial through fraud', where an end user manipulates a network to route his communication across the system. The final sub-category (d) was the subject of considerable controversy during the passage of the RIPA Bill. It was specifically included to address a feature present in packet-switched networks, rather than traditional circuit-switched networks. In order for the packets that comprise a transmission to be reassembled at the edge of a network, each and every packet will comprise data that enables them to be correctly associated with each other, such as a sequence number. However, each packet also contains the content of the communications, either in whole or part. The concern expressed at the time the Bill was going through Parliament was that law enforcement access to the former, communications data, should not inadvertently grant access to the latter content, which falls under the Interception regime, Part I, Chapter I of the RIPA. The provision, read in conjunction with the tailpiece, was intended to clearly distinguish between content and communications data.

What constitutes the content of a communication is not defined in RIPA, but it is presumed to be understood to include all possible types of content available over the Internet, such as the downloading of webpage, between a device and a cloud service and data transmitted by an IoT device.

A communication is not being intercepted if only the traffic data is being monitored or recorded. RIPA, Part I, Chapter II and the DRIPA govern the capture, retention and disclosure of such traffic data.

As noted above, the interception of communications generally requires an executive warrant under Part I, Chapter I of the RIPA. However, where communications content is being stored, including 'in the course of its transmission by means of a telecommunications system', then access may also be obtained through any other LEA power that grants access to stored information, which includes judicial authorisation. The uncertain nature of the line between these two states, i.e. of a communication being 'in transmission' and of it being stored or 'at rest', has been the subject of judicial consideration.

In *R (NTL Group Limited) v Ipswich Crown Court,*[32] the telecommunications provider, NTL, had been subject to a court order made under s 9 and Schedule 1 of PACE, after an application from the Chief Constable to access 'special procedure material'.[33] NTL applied for judicial review of the order on the grounds that compliance would require NTL to commit an interception offence under the RIPA. The issue arose due to the manner in which NTL's email system operated. In order to

[32] [2002] EWHC 1585 (Admin), [2003] 1 CrAppR 14.

[33] Under PACE, Sch 1, para 4, a court may grant access to material subject to certain access conditions (*ibid.,* para 2).

comply with the court order, and retain copies of the emails of the customer under investigation, the system would need to copy the targeted emails to a different address from that of the intended recipient. This, NTL argued, would result in an unlawful interception. The court agreed with NTL's characterisation of the process as one of interception, although expressing reservations as to whether this was the intention of the drafters of RIPA. The court then went on to consider whether such interception was lawful by virtue of s 1(5)(c), which permits access to stored data. NTL argued that since the conduct was theirs, they lacked the lawful authority granted to the police under the s 9 procedure. However, the court held that this police procedure would be rendered unworkable with such an interpretation and, therefore, an implicit power must exist to render NTL's conduct lawful.

Where a 'telecommunication system' stores the data for subsequent access or collection by the intended recipient, such as voice mailbox, then it is considered to still be 'in the course of transmission'.[34] The meaning of this provision was subject to extensive examination in *Edmondson*,[35] which concerned the phone hacking by journalists from the News of the World. The defendants argued that where a voice mail message residing on the service provider's server had been read by the intended recipient, it was no longer 'in the course of its transmission'. The court rejected this interpretation, finding that the 'natural meaning' of the provision does not support the proposition that "the first receipt of the communication should be considered as bringing the transmission to an end" (para 27). The court thought it significant that with voice mail, the intended recipient was 'totally dependent' on the service provider for access to the message. It would seem arguable, therefore, that a distinction could be made between voice mail, which is 'accessed' and email systems, where the intended recipient 'collects' messages on the intended recipient's device, whether a computer or smart phone. The court clearly stated that when interpreting RIPA provisions, they should be construed in compliance with Article 8 of the ECHR.

The power to authorise the interception of a person's communications resides with the executive branch of government, in the form of the Secretary of State at the Home Office or the Foreign Office.[36] The Secretary of State may only issue an interception warrant where he considers it necessary on the following grounds:

- in the interests of national security;
- prevention or detection of 'serious crime',[37] which represents the great majority of cases;

---

[34] RIPA, s 2(7).

[35] *Edmondson & ors v R* [2013] EWCA Crim 1026.

[36] RIPA, s 5(1). Other ministers also have the power, but very rarely exercise it.

[37] I.e. '(a) ... an offence for which a person who has attained the age of twenty-one and has no previous convictions could reasonably be expected to be sentenced to imprisonment for a term of three years or more; (b) that the conduct involves the use of violence, results

- safeguarding the 'economic well-being of the United Kingdom', where relevant to the interests of national security; or
- in response to a request under mutual legal assistance procedures.[38]

In addition, an application for a warrant to the Secretary of State may only be made by those persons listed on the face of the statute, such as the Director General of the National Crime Agency or the Commissioner of the Metropolitan Police.[39]

Under RIPA, the conduct authorised by the warrant must be proportionate to the objective being sought, including whether the information 'could reasonably be obtained by other means'.[40] Considerations of proportionality must not only be assessed by the Secretary of State when granting the warrant, but must also inform management of the implementation of the warrant, the implicit assumption being that interception is an investigative technique of last resort. To assist the Secretary of State in making a judgment on proportionality, the applicant is required to indicate any circumstances that should be taken into account, such as the extent of collateral intrusion likely to result, or where material relating to confidential, religious, medical, journalistic or legally privileged material may be involved.

Two forms of warrant may be issued under RIPA, under s 8(1) and 8(4). A section 8(1) warrant must identify a particular subject or a set of premises against which the interception is being carried out. This is commonly referred to as 'targeted' intercept and is primarily an investigative tool used by domestic law enforcement agencies against known threats or people. Where an individual is the subject of a s 8(1) warrant, interception may be carried out against any communication services used by that person, such as landline, mobile, and internet account, provided such services are detailed in the schedule to the warrant; in the form of 'addresses, numbers, apparatus or other factors ... used for identifying the communications' to be intercepted (s 8(2)).

Identity information does not need to appear in a s 8(4) warrant, where the interception is of an 'external communication' in the course of its transmission by a telecommunication system (s 8(4) and (5)). Instead of identifying persons or premises, a s 8(4) warrant will list 'selectors' that either relates to individual targets or more general enquiries, operating either through simple matching or more complex selection rules, against which flows of communications traffic will be monitored. This is commonly referred to as 'bulk' intercept and is primarily used by MI6 and GCHQ for foreign intelligence gathering purposes. An 'external communication' is defined as 'a communication sent or received outside the British Islands' (s 20),

in substantial financial gain or is conduct by a large number of persons in pursuit of a common purpose' (RIPA, s 81(3)).

38 RIPA, s 5(2)(a) and (3).

39 *Ibid.*, s 6(2). Any application made on behalf of the persons listed must be made by a person holding office under the Crown (s 6(3)).

40 RIPA, s 5(2)(b) and (4).

which would include communicating with a web server based in the US, but would not cover a communication sent and received in the UK, but which was routed via a foreign server or network, such as a Gmail account. This provision would enable, for example, a warrant to be issued in respect of traffic transiting through the UK where no identifiable person or premises were located here, triggered perhaps by the receipt of foreign intelligence.

Given the potential 'bulk' nature of s 8(4) warrants, they are subject to a second layer of procedure requiring a ministerial certificate, which governs the examination of the material collected under the warrant.[41] In essence they require the minister to certify that the material needs to be examined for one of the statutory purposes (s 8(4)(b)) and does not refer to a person known to be in the British Islands at the time (s 16(2)). The latter restriction is not absolute, however, since an examination may relate to a person known to be in the British Islands where either the minister certifies in respect of the 'individual in question' that it is necessary for the statutory purposes (s 16(3)), or a senior official authorises examination of the material for a short period in respect of a person who was thought to be abroad when he is in fact in the British Islands.[42]

For both a targeted and bulk warrant, the intercepting agency may choose whether to give effect to the warrant directly himself or request the assistance of another person, such as a telecommunication operator (s 11(1)). In the former case, direct obtaining, it may require the intercepting agency to interfere with the property of the suspect or a third party. The Security Service (MI5), the Intelligence Service (MI6) and the GCHQ can obtain a warrant to interfere directly with domestic property (e.g. a cable or computer) under the ISA, s 5. The police can obtain authorisation to interfere with property under the Police Act 1997, Part III.[43] In addition, the Computer Misuse Act 1990, s 10, was amended in April 2015, to grant immunity to any 'enforcement officer' involved in computer hacking or interference activities.

Under the IPB, the Government intends to introduce a consolidated regime for equipment inference, with two new warrants for targeted and bulk equipment interference.

3. Special protection of confidential communication content

The RIPA does not specifically protect privileged communications. However, the Interception Code of Practice, at Section 4, lays down specific procedures and safeguards when the communication or the intercept product is protected by privi-

---

41 RIPA, ss 8(4)(b) and 16.

42 *Ibid.*, s 16(4) and (5).

43 See also Home Office, *Code of Practice: Equipment Interference*, January 2016, available at https://www.gov.uk/government/publications/equipment-interference-code-of-practice

lege, such as legal privilege[44] or parliamentary, or some related form of confidential relationship, including with medical professionals or religious ministers. In general, the Code requires that greater consideration be given to the need to intercept such material, because of its special status under Article 8, but otherwise it can be obtained and used. The Secretary of State when granting the warrant should consider such matters, having been notified of any such possibility in the application for the warrant. In the Government's IPB, it is now proposed to address such protected communications directly on the face of the statute. This follows a number of cases and revelations by Edward Snowden that led to concerns that such communications were not given adequate protection.

4. Execution of telecommunication interception[45]

The implementation of a RIPA interceptions warrant is carried out by representatives of the law enforcement agencies ('LEAs') that are specified under RIPA, s 6(2), as being capable of requesting a warrant. Some of these are national agencies, such as the National Crime Agency, while others are regional police forces, such as the chief constable of the Police Service of Scotland. Finally, a non-UK entity may be issued with an interception warrant if it is the 'competent authority' under an international mutual legal assistance agreement. Sometimes one agency may apply for a warrant on behalf of another agency with whom it is engaged in a joint investigation. Intercept product may be disclosed to other LEAs as appropriate, although these agencies are required to minimise any such disclosure or usage to that necessary for an authorised purpose.

5. Duties of telecommunication service providers to cooperate

The obligation to comply with interception warrants issued under the RIPA are applicable to those that provide a 'public telecommunication service' or control the whole or part of a 'telecommunication system' located in the UK (s 11(4)). A 'telecommunication service' is defined in the following terms:

> any service that consists in the provision of access to, and of facilities for making use of, any telecommunication system (whether or not one provided by the person providing the service); (at s 2(1)) and
>
> For the purposes of the definition of "telecommunications service" in subsection (1), the cases in which a service is to be taken to consist in the provision of access to, and of facilities for making use of, a telecommunication system include any case where a service consists in or includes facilitating the creation, management or storage of communications transmitted, or that may be transmitted, by means of such a system. (at s 2(8A).

---

44 See Police Act 1997, s 98.

45 See also above at section I(A)(3).

The latter part of the definition was inserted into RIPA in 2014 specifically to clarify that the class of services extends beyond traditional telephone operators to include certain OTT communication services, such as Skype and FaceTime. As such, the concept of a 'telecommunication service' differs significantly from that of an 'electronic communication service' under EU law.[46]

A 'telecommunication system' is defined as follows:

> any system (including the apparatus comprised in it which exists (whether wholly or partly in the United Kingdom or elsewhere)) for the purpose of facilitating the transmission of communications by any means involving the use of electrical or electro-magnetic energy.

Under RIPA, a person has a duty to give effect to a warrant if they provide a 'public telecommunication service' to the public in the UK or where they 'control' a telecommunication system that is located in the UK (s 11(4)). In the first scenario, a person may provide a service, although the infrastructure relevant to effecting an interception warrant is located outside the United Kingdom. The territorial trigger in this case is the provision of services to the UK public, rather than the service provider's place of establishment or the use of equipment—an approach that is consistent with existing national, European, and international telecommunications law. In such a case, the obligation would have an extraterritorial effect and may give rise to a conflict with the laws of the jurisdiction where the infrastructure is located. In the second scenario, the obligation is applicable where part of a telecommunication system is located in the UK, such that a CSP established outside the UK would have compliance obligations were it to control a 'system' within the UK, even if it does not provide a public telecommunication service in the UK.

Uncertainties about the extraterritorial reach of the RIPA resulted in a series of amendments in 2014. First, it was expressly stated that an interception warrant could be served on a person 'outside the United Kingdom (and may relate to conduct outside the United Kingdom)' (s 2(2A)). Second, it was made explicit that a s 12 notice may be served on a person providing 'public telecommunications services' that is located 'outside the United Kingdom (and may be so imposed or given in relation to conduct outside the United Kingdom)' (s 12(3A)), Third, a request for communications data can be given to a person outside the United Kingdom (s 22(5A) and (5B)).

A person who receives a warrant has a statutory duty to give effect to the warrant, but is only required to take steps that are reasonably practicable (s 11(5) and (5A)). However, this includes anything required of an operator that has been subject to an order under s. 12 to build and maintain an intercept capability.

[46] Directive 2002/21/EC on a common regulatory framework for electronic communications networks and services (OJ L 108/33, 24 April 2002), at Art. 2(c).

A service provider may be subject to a notice under the RIPA, s 12. The Home Office will generally always discuss the notice with the service provider prior to its issuance, to agree the process by which its terms will be effected. However, if no agreement is reached and a notice is issued, the service provider has an opportunity, within a period of twenty-eight days from the date of the notice, to refer the notice to the Technical Advisory Board (TAB) for consideration (s 13). The TAB has the remit to examine only the 'technical requirements and the financial consequences' of the notice and report their conclusions to the Secretary of State (s 12(6)). It comprises balanced representation from industry and law enforcement interests (s 13(2)). After consideration, the Secretary of State is required to either withdraw the notice or give a further notice, although he is not bound to modify the terms of the initial notice.

Once a notice has been served, a service provider has a statutory duty to comply with the notice. Civil proceedings may be instigated by the Secretary of State to ensure compliance, for example through an order for specific performance (s 12(7)). To date, however, no such enforcement action has taken place, the Home Office preferring to negotiate arrangements with service providers.

The content of what may be required of a service provider is further detailed in the Regulation of Investigatory Powers (Maintenance of Interception Capability) Order 2002. Part II of the Schedule to the Order details those capabilities that are considered reasonable to impose on providers of public telecommunication services:

- To be able to implement an interception within one working day of being informed of an appropriately authorised request.
- To be able to obtain, in their entirety, all communications and related communications data[47] and be able to ensure their simultaneous (ie copied in near real time for stream-based services, while emails will need to be forwarded as soon as available within the service provider's infrastructure) transmission to a hand-over point within the service provider's network.
- The intercepted data should be capable of being transmitted in a manner in which it can be unambiguously correlated.
- The hand-over interface should comply with any standards notified to the service provider by the Secretary of State.
- To be able to filter out and supply only the 'traffic data'[48] associated with the warranted telecommunications identifier.
- To enable the removal of any electronic protection applied to the data by the service provider.

[47] I.e. attributes of the communications session, as defined in RIPA, s 21(4).
[48] As defined in RIPA, s 2(9).

- To enable the simultaneous interception of the communications of up to one in 10,000 persons to whom the service provider provides a service.
- To ensure that the reliability of the intercept capability matches that of the public telecommunication service.
- To ensure that the intercept capability may be audited to ensure that the intercepts were from or intended for the interception subject or premises specified in the warrant.
- To ensure that the capability is operated in a manner which prevents the interception subject or any other unauthorised person becoming aware of any interception.

These are agreed between service providers and the LEAs either on a case-by-case basis or, if the provider is subject to a Section 12 order, are set out in a service level agreement between the service provider and the Home Office, often accompanied by a financial commitment by the government to part fund the cost of building such facilities (s 13).

When responding to a LEA intercept request, the service provider will generally facilitate implementation of the facility and will either collect the data themselves and hand it over to the requesting agency, or enable the data to be collected directly by the agency.

6. Formal prerequisites of interception orders

Under RIPA, in normal circumstances, interception is authorised by a warrant granted by a relevant Secretary of State (s 5), generally either the Home or Foreign Secretary. In urgent cases, and for certain mutual legal assistance requests, this process may be fulfilled by a senior official (s 7(2)). A dossier is submitted to the Secretary of State, who either accepts the request, modifies it, returns it with questions or rejects it. The requesting agency does not orally present its case, the warrant granting process is done on the basis of a review of the documentation.

A RIPA warrant may only be granted where necessary in the interests of national security; the investigation and prevention of serious crime; to safeguard the economic well-being of the UK (where it relevant to the interests of national security)[49] or to give effect to an obligation under any international mutual legal assistance agreement (s 5(3)). The interests of national security or to safeguard the economic well-being of the UK are not defined in the legislation, but are for the Secretary of State to determine. A warrant for the investigation or detection of 'serious crime' means a crime that satisfies one of the following tests:

---

49 This qualification was inserted into RIPA by the Data Retention and Investigatory Powers Act 2014, s 3, to avoid accusations that a warrant would be issued for the purpose of state-sponsored economic espionage.

(a) that the offence or one of the offences that is or would be constituted by the conduct is an offence for which a person who has attained the age of twenty-one and has no previous convictions could reasonably be expected to be sentenced to imprisonment for a term of three years or more;
(b) that the conduct involves the use of violence, results in substantial financial gain or is conduct by a large number of persons in pursuit of a common purpose. (s 81(3)).

Under the WTA, an interception authority can be granted by a 'designated person', which includes the Secretary of State and the Commissioners for HM Revenue or Customs (s 48(5)). Such authority may be granted where it is necessary for a wider range of specified interests, including the interests of national security and the protection of public health (s 49(4)).

A 'direction' from the Secretary of State under the TA can require a telecommunications operator to do anything that is considered 'requisite or expedient' in the interests of national security or relations with another country (s 94(1)). An obligation imposed under a direction could therefore range from acts of interception to shutting down a network.

7. Warrant content

The content of a warrant is specified in the RIPA and the Code of Practice. For a s 8(1) warrant, it will include details of the person or premises subject to the interception; schedules listing the specific addresses, numbers and devices that will be subject to the interception; the threat which gives rise to the necessity to engage in such conduct (e.g. serious crime); the expected product for the interception; considerations of proportionality and any possible collateral intrusion; a justification for why other less intrusive techniques are not appropriate and identification of any potential privileged material.[50]

A warrant under s 8(4), will describe the communications to which the warrant applies, where the interception is of 'external communications' (defined at s 81(1)). Due to the extraterritorial impact of such warrants, the Foreign Secretary will also consider the technical and legal risks of carrying out such conduct.

8. Validity of interception order

The standard period for a warrant is three months for a serious crime and six months for national security matters (s 9). It can be renewed for further periods, under the same procedure, with no maximum duration. A warrant is regularly reviewed by the granting person and must be cancelled where it is no longer necessary for the specified purpose.

---

[50] For the warrant templates, see Annex C of the Intelligence and Security Committee report (see footnote no. 27 above).

9. Notification duties

There is no duty of the investigative authorities to notify the subject of an interception, either pre or post investigation. Any unauthorised disclosure of intercept product, such as by a service provider, would be an offence under the RIPA, s 19, with a maximum 5 year term of imprisonment. However, if a person becomes aware of the interception, then the person can bring a complaint to the Investigatory Powers Tribunal, established under the RIPA (see 2.4 above). In the event of such proceedings, the state can ask the Tribunal or courts for public-interest immunity, under which they can refrain from disclosing material to the other litigant.

C. Collection and Use of Traffic Data and Subscriber Data

1. Collection of 'Communications Data'

Part I, Chapter II of the RIPA details a regime that enables law enforcement agencies to *require* the disclosure of 'communications data' from a 'telecommunications operator' (CSP). Communications data comprises three types of data: (a) traffic data, as outlined above; (b) usage data, such as time and date of connection and (c) subscriber data, which includes any personal data held about a service subscriber (s 21(4)). The request may be made to any person who provides a 'telecommunication service', which would potentially include both publicly and privately provisioned services, as well as situations where the telecommunications service is simply a means for, or is incidental to, the provision of another type of service, such as an hotel, airport lounge, or web-based retail service (s 12(4)).

Under the provisions, the police, certain criminal and intelligence services, Inland Revenue and Customs and Excise, and other persons can, under an appropriate authorisation, give a 'notice' to a CSP requiring access to specified communications data. Such a notice shall only be issued by a 'designated person' (s 25(2)) within an authority where it is considered necessary for any of the public interest grounds set out in the Act: national security; preventing or detecting crime or preventing disorder; the economic well-being of the United Kingdom; public health and safety; the collection or assessing tax, duty, levy, or related payment, and preventing death or personal injury (s 22(2)). Considerations about whether requesting such data is proportionate to the purpose for which it is sought must include any collateral intrusion on the rights of third parties not under investigation.

2. Duties of telecommunication service providers to cooperate

It is a statutory duty of a CSP to comply with the requirements detailed in a notice (s 22(6)), which is enforceable through civil proceedings (s 22(8)). A refusal to comply with the provisions of a Code issued under RIPA would not render a CSP liable to civil or criminal proceedings (s 72(2)), so enabling a person to disagree with an interpretation adopted in the Code, although a court, tribunal, or Commissioner may have regard to the Code when determining any question (s 72(4)). As with interception, resort to a judicial remedy has not yet occurred, although problems have inevitably arisen where the request concerns a UK subscriber, using the services of a provider located in another jurisdiction, where the requested data is held. This was one reason for the insertion of the extraterritorial provisions by the Data Retention and Investigatory Powers Act 2014.

A request for communications data may include that which is already in the possession of the CSP, as well as data which the CSP is 'capable of obtaining' (s 22(4)). This latter gathering obligation is effectively limited to that which is 'reasonably practicable' for the CSP to do (s 22(7)). As well as detailing the communications data required, the notice will also indicate the time period for which such data is sought and the timescales within which a response is needed.

Where the issuance of a notice is inappropriate, communications data may be obtained directly by persons within the law enforcement agency under an 'authorisation' (s 22(3)). Possible circumstances where such conduct may be appropriate include where the CSP is not capable of obtaining or disclosing the requested data; the investigator believes notification to the CSP may prejudice an investigation or operation; or where arrangements exist with a CSP for direct law enforcement access to the relevant information. The latter arrangement exists with some CSPs in respect of subscriber checks, also referred to as 'reverse look ups', the most commonly requested information. Owing to the nature of an authorisation, it is not served on a CSP, although the CSP may request details as assurance that any such conduct is lawful.

3. Competent authorities

Under RIPA, the Secretary of State can determine which is a 'relevant public authority' under Part I, Chapter II as well as the types of communications data that may be accessed by a public authority and the purposes for which such data may be used (s 25). The current 2010 Order has been amended numerous times, both adding and removing public authorities from the list.[51] In 2012, Part I, Chapter II was amended to establish a separate judicial approvals regime for local authorities (s 23A). This was the result of a number of high profile cases of perceived abuse of the regime by local authorities. Currently, the vast majority of requests for data are made in respect of subscriber data, rather than traffic or usage data, therefore the

[51] Regulation of Investigatory Powers (Communications Data) Order 2010 (SI No 480).

right of access for the majority of authorities, specifically those designated persons within the authority, is limited to subscriber data falling within the third category of 'communications data'.

In order to rationalise and standardise requests for communications data from public authorities to CSPs, a system of accredited Single Points of Contact (SPoCs) has been established for public authorities exercising law enforcement functions, empowered to and responsible for making requests for information to CSPs. Each authority is required to have a trained individual, or group of individuals, through which any requests for information made under relevant powers must be made. The SPoCs are intended to 'help the public authority to regulate itself, by providing internal advice on quality assurance, and will also provide authentication of the pubic authority'; this is also referred to as a 'guardian and gatekeeper function'.[52] The latter issue is facilitated by the maintenance of a register by the Home Office, to which CSPs may refer when in receipt of a request for information from a person with a SPoC authentication identifier. In addition, under the applicable Code of Practice, a CSP may refuse to accept requests from a person not appropriately registered as a SPoC, and an authority should not try to acquire such data in the absence of an accredited SPoC.[53]

D. Access to (Temporarily) Stored Communications Data

1. Online searches with the help of remote forensic software

Under PACE, a constable may require 'any information which is stored in any electronic form and is accessible from the premises to be produced in a form in which it can be taken away …' (s 19(4)). On the face of it, this provision would appear to enable law enforcement officers to obtain information held on remote systems under a single search warrant, since information in electronic form will be accessible from a networked computer on the searched premises.

The exercise of police powers is, however, subject to the jurisdictional limitation placed on the police under the Police Act 1996: 'A member of a police force shall have all the powers and privileges of a constable throughout England and Wales and the adjacent United Kingdom waters' (s 30(1)). For other law enforcement

52 Statement made by Caroline Flint, Home Office Minister, at House of Commons Standing Committee on Delegated Legislation, Hansard, 4 November 2003, Col 024.

53 See the Home Office, *Code of Practice: Acquisition and Disclosure of Communications Data*, 2015, available at: https://www.gov.uk/government/uploads/system/uploads/attachment_data/file/426248/Acquisition_and_Disclosure_of_Communications_Data_Code_of_Practice_March_2015.pdf

agencies, similar jurisdictional limitations may be expressly provided for or implied.[54]

As a consequence of the jurisdictional limitation, a court would need to determine whether to characterise police access to a foreign online resource as being a territorial or extra-territorial exercise of power; then whether the activity is unlawful, under domestic or foreign law, either through breach of specific provisions, such as unauthorised access, or based on general principles of breach of national sovereignty and the comity of nations implied in the operation of such principles. A court, as outlined below, may exclude evidence obtained unlawfully from a foreign state.

2. Search and seizure of stored communications data

Search and seizure of stored material is permissible under a range of different statutory regimes, including:

- Proceeds of Crime Act 2002, s 345
- Police and Criminal Evidence Act 1984, s 9
- Terrorism Act 2000, Sch 5
- Social Security Administration Act 1992, s 109B

Under the PACE, s 20, powers of seizure can extend to any information 'accessible from the premises' being searched, which would include information held remotely, such as on a cloud storage service.

The provisions under the RIPA for interception do not supersede or replace other powers to obtained stored data (RIPA, s 1(5)(c)). The legal provisions for interception and access to stored data do differ, but also overlap. It is arguable whether a judicial or executive warrant offer the greater protection in terms of the rights of the target suspect.

Access to stored data can be performed without notification to the suspect, if it can be shown that such notification would prejudice the investigation due to a realistic threat that the evidence could be destroyed. The service provider who assists the LEA would normally be made aware of the order.

3. Duties to cooperate: production and decryption orders

Under Part I, Chapter I of the RIPA, a service provider subject to an interception obligation may be required to remove any encryption applied by the service provider (see further III(B)(5) above).

---

[54] E.g. in respect of the National Crime Agency, see Crime and Courts Act 2013, s 10, Sch 5, Pt 4, para 12.

Under Part III of the RIPA, a person may be subject to a notice requiring them to either provide information in an intelligible format or to disclose the 'key' to access the protected data.[55] Under RIPA, 'protected information' means:

any electronic data which, without the key to the data—

(a) cannot, or cannot readily, be accessed, or

(b) cannot, or cannot readily, be put into an intelligible form (s 56(1)).

A 'key' comprises 'any key, code, password, algorithm, or other data the use of which (with or without other keys):

(a) allows access to the electronic data, or

(b) facilitates the putting of the data into an intelligible form (s 56(1)).

A suspect in an investigation may be subject to a notice requiring them to disclose an encryption key. It is an offence if a person 'knowingly fails, in accordance with the notice, to make the disclosure required …', which carries a maximum two-year prison term (s 53). Under the Terrorism Act 2006, this penalty was increased in 'a national security case' to five years. A five-year term has also since been inserted in respect of 'child indecency' cases.

The validity of these provisions were examined in *R v S and A*.[56] The defendants were both arrested in connection with terrorist offences. *S* was detained in a room where an encryption key appeared to have been partially entered in the computer. In the case of *A*, computer materials seized subsequent to his arrest included a computer disc that contained an encrypted area. The defendants appealed against the notices issued under s 49 of the RIPA requiring that they disclose the encryption keys on the grounds of self-incrimination. The court noted that the legality of this process had to be addressed in two stages. The first question was to determine whether the principle was engaged at all. Relying upon the ECtHR decision in *Saunders*,[57] the court noted that the right not to self-incriminate does not extend to material that can be lawfully obtained by law enforcement and has 'an existence independent of the will of the suspect'. The key, irrelevant of the form in which it exists, was held to be such an independent fact, similar in nature to a urine sample taken from a driver suspected of driving under the influence. However, in addition, it was noted that the defendant's knowledge of the key could also be an incriminating fact. The second stage for the court, if it is assumed that the principle is engaged, is to consider whether the interference with the right consequent upon the issuance of the s 49 notice is necessary and proportionate. Here the court held that the procedural safeguards and limitations on usage detailed in the RIPA were sufficient to negate any claim of unfairness under the PACE, s 78 (see further 2.3 above).

---

55 See also the Home Office, Code of Practice: Investigation of Protected Electronic Information, 2007, available at: https://www.gov.uk/government/uploads/system/uploads/attachment_data/file/97959/code-practice-electronic-info.pdf

56 [2008] EWCA Crim 2177.

57 [1996] 23 EHRR 313.

IV. Use of Electronic Communications Data in Judicial Proceedings

1. Use of intercept material in the law of criminal procedure

Under RIPA, evidence obtained through a warranted intercept is considered to be inadmissible (s 17), subject to a series of very limited exceptions (s.18). The purpose of the exclusion is to protect from disclosure, forensic inquiry and defence counsel matters related to the operation of the warrant regime under s 5 of the RIPA, and the activities of the intelligence and law enforcement agencies. The provision is applicable in both criminal and civil proceedings.

By contrast, interception evidence *would* be admissible when it does not reveal anything about the activities of UK law enforcement agencies. So, for example, where a communication service provider engages in interception in the course of enforcing provisions of the Communications Act 2003, as provided for under the RIPA, s 3(3), the intercept product would be admissible.[58] Likewise, as stated by Lord Bingham: "there was no rule of law or practice which rendered inadmissible in criminal proceedings the product of any unofficial or private eavesdropping activity".[59]

Intercept evidence would also be admissible if it comes from an interception carried out in another country, even though it reveals information about the activities of foreign law enforcement agencies.[60]

In *Attorney-General's Reference (No 5 of 2002) sub nom R v W*,[61] the House of Lords was asked to consider the scope of the s 17 exclusion, specifically whether it prevented a court from investigating whether an interception had taken place on a private or public telecommunication system. The original case concerned the suspected disclosure of confidential and sensitive information by certain police officers to unauthorised persons, including journalists. The prosecution served evidence that the interception had taken place on a 'private telecommunication system', while defence asserted that it occurred on a 'public telecommunication system'. When the trial judged ruled that the defence were unable, by virtue of s 17, to make such an assertion, the defence asked for the prosecution's evidence to be excluded on the grounds of not being fair, under the Police and Criminal Evidence Act 1984, s 78, to which the judge agreed. As a consequence, the prosecution's case failed. On appeal by the Attorney-General, the Court of Appeal overturned the decision of

[58] E.g. Communications Act, s 125. Similar provisions were contained in IOCA, at s 1(3)(a), and were considered in *Morgans v DPP* [2001] 1 AC 315.

[59] In *Attorney-General's Reference (No 5 of 2002) sub nom R v W* (2005) 1 AC 167, at 174H. See also *Avocet Hardware plc v Morrison*, EAT, 17 February 2003 (re: incorrect exclusion of private intercept evidence); also *Senat* (1968) 52 Cr App R 282.

[60] See *R v P and others* [2001] 2 All ER 58.

[61] [2004] UKHL 40; [2005] 1 AC 167.

the trial judge,[62] but recognising the complexities of the issues referred it on to the House of Lords. The Lords noted that under the 1985 regime, the exclusion under s 9 had not prevented the courts from considering the public or private nature of the telecommunication system, a then particularly critical distinction as the 1985 Act only addressed interception when carried out over a public system.[63] Lord Bingham then went on to state: "Save where necessary to preserve the security of warranted interception, there is no reason why it should have been sought to exclude the product of any lawful interception where relevant evidence in any case whether civil or criminal".[64]

Following this decision, while s 17 potentially excludes evidence of an intercept carried out on either a public or private telecommunication system, where the intercept was lawful, by virtue of s 1(5) (i.e. under s 3, s 4 or s 1(5)(c)), the evidence would be admissible.[65] As a consequence, the courts must be able to inquire as to the lawfulness of the intercept in those circumstances, which would include establishing whether the interception has been carried out on a public or private system and, if private, whether it was carried out by, or on behalf of, the person 'with a right to control' the system.[66]

Communications data obtained in the course of obtaining content under an intercept warrant would also be inadmissible under s 17. However, communications data obtained under Part I, Chapter II would not be subject to any specific exclusionary provision, but may be excluded on general grounds, as outlined in the next section.

2. Inadmissibility of evidence as a consequence of inappropriate collection

Electronic communications data obtained other than under an interception warrant may be excluded from use in criminal proceedings in certain circumstances. The UK courts have jurisdiction, granted by statute or inherent to the court, to exclude evidence in certain circumstances if that evidence is considered to undermine or cause real prejudice to the defendant's right to a fair trial, as enshrined in article 6 of the ECHR.

The courts have an inherent jurisdiction to control their own proceedings to prevent an injustice occurring. By 'staying' criminal proceedings, the court effectively brings those proceedings to an end, without the need to consider fully the evidence being adduced by either side. Known as 'abuse of process', it involves the courts

---

62 [2003] EWCA Crim 1632, [2003] 1 WLR 2902.

63 See, e.g., *Ahmed (Iftikhar)* [1995] Crim LR 246; *Effik* [1994] 3 All ER 458, HL(E).

64 [2005] 1 AC 167, at 179E.

65 *Ibid.,* at 182G, interpreting s 18(4), an approach which is supported in the Explanatory Report, at para 142.

66 Which excludes the intercept conduct from criminal liability, see RIPA, s 1(6).

exercising indirect supervision of an investigative process. In *Grant*[67], for example, the use of a covert listening device in a police exercise yard to record conversations between the accused and his solicitor was held to be an abuse, rendering the conviction unsafe.

Alternatively, the courts have a general statutory power to exclude evidence on grounds of fairness. Section 78(1) PACE states:

> In any proceedings the court may refuse to allow evidence on which the prosecution proposes to rely to be given if it appears to the court that, having regard to all the circumstances, including the circumstances in which the evidence was obtained, the admission of the evidence would have such an adverse effect on the fairness of the proceedings that the court ought not to admit it.

The wording of the provision makes it clear that considerations of fairness include the manner in which the evidence was obtained, not just the trial itself. A determination to exclude under section 78 is not to be seen as an exercise of discretion in the same manner that occurs when a court orders a stay for abuse of process, engaging in a balancing exercise of the various interests present, since where a court holds that admission of a piece of evidence *would have* an adverse effect on the fairness of the proceedings, it is duty bound to exclude it.[68]

If obtained in breach of law, evidence gathered by an LEA may be excluded at the discretion of the court. Such a breach may result from the conduct of an LEA investigator exceeding the jurisdiction granted to the LEA, or the conduct itself being illegal under UK law. Where a procedural code is applicable to the actions of an LEA investigator, the code will be admissible as evidence in criminal proceedings for consideration by a court.[69] The more technical the breach, the less likely the courts will exclude the evidence;[70] conversely, where the rule breach causes a 'significant and substantial'[71] disadvantage to the defendant the evidence will be excluded. The sole consideration when deciding to exclude under section 78 is one of fairness; therefore, a court should not exclude simply to punish the investigating agency for its failure to comply with a code provision,[72] since it already has jurisdiction to order a stay for abuse of process.

The legality of conduct may of course differ between the foreign jurisdiction where the evidence was obtained, and the UK, where the evidence is being adduced and this may impact on the UK court's treatment of such evidence. In the UK, a breach of foreign legal procedures would only lead to the exclusion of real evi-

---

67 [2005] EWCA Crim 1089.

68 *Chalkley* [1998] QB 848.

69 PACE, s 67(11) and RIPA, s 72(3). They are also admissible in civil proceedings.

70 *Blackwell* [1995] 2 CrAppR 625, at 641.

71 *Quinn* [1990] Crim LR 581.

72 *Delaney* (1989) 88 CrAppR 338, at 341.

dence if the nature of the breach were considered to amount to an act of bad faith on behalf of the domestic LEA.[73]

As a general rule, evidence gathered under formal MLA procedures or through a 'letter rogatory' will be subject to the same rules of admissibility in the requesting state as evidence obtained domestically.[74] As a consequence, a defendant is generally only protected by the lowest threshold of admissibility; with evidential rules of the foreign state generally being ignored in the UK, even if they impose a higher admissibility threshold; while evidence obtained by unlawful means abroad, which would be inadmissible if the conduct occurred domestically, is admissible before the UK courts.[75]

V. Exchange of Intercepted Electronic Communication Data between Foreign Countries

The Crime (International Co-operation) Act 2003 details mechanisms for the mutual provision of evidence, either obtaining evidence from abroad for use in the UK or assisting overseas authorities to obtain evidence from the UK. In the former situation, a judge, on the application of a prosecuting authority (e.g. the CPS) or a person charged in the proceedings (i.e. the defendant), may issue requests for evidence from abroad.[76] Such a request, historically known as a 'letter rogatory' or '*commission rogatoire*', will only be made where it appears that an offence has been committed and that proceedings have been instituted or an investigation is underway (s 7(1)).

The request may be sent to a court in the relevant jurisdiction, to an authority designated in the jurisdiction for receipt of such requests or, in cases of urgency, the International Criminal Police Organisation (s 8). The evidence, once received, should then only be used for the purpose specified in the request, known as the 'specialty principle':

> Evidence obtained by virtue of a letter of request shall not without the consent of such an authority … be used for any purpose other than that specified in the letter: and when any document or other article obtained pursuant to a letter of request is no longer required for that purpose (or for any other purpose for which such consent has been ob-

---

73 Loof, R., 'Obtaining, adducing and contesting evidence from abroad: A defence perspective on cross-border evidence', *Crim LR*, 2011, No. 1, pp. 40–57.

74 E.g. CPS, Legal Guidance, 'International Enquiries – Using the evidence obtained and admissibility'.

75 Gane, C. and Mackarel, M., 'The admissibility of evidence obtained from abroad into criminal proceedings – The interpretation of mutual legal assistance treaties and use of evidence irregularly obtained', 4 *EurJCrime, CrimL&CrimJust* 98 (1996), at 116.

76 Crime (International Co-operation) Act 2003, Chapter 2, ss 7–12.

tained), it shall be returned to such an authority unless that authority indicates that the document or article need not be returned (s 3(7)).

Requests for UK-based evidence by overseas authorities must be sent to the Secretary of State at the Home Office, referred to as the 'territorial authority'.[77] The Secretary of State may then nominate a court to receive the requested evidence. As well as achieving the disclosure of particular evidence, the MLA procedure also provides for the obtaining of evidence. The Secretary of State may direct that a warrant be applied for from the courts in order that a search can be undertaken and evidence seized. Law enforcement agencies may also obtain a warrant to intercept communications, as discussed above. However, such coercive powers may only be exercised where the conduct constitutes an appropriate offence in both the requesting country and under the laws of England and Wales, the so-called 'double criminality' principle, as also required in extradition proceedings.

77 *Ibid.*, ss 13 and 28(9).

Bibliography*

Gane, C. and Mackarel, M., 'The admissibility of evidence obtained from abroad into criminal proceedings – The interpretation of mutual legal assistance treaties and use of evidence irregularly obtained', 4 *EurJCrime, CrimL&CrimJust* 98 (1996), pp. 98 ff.

Home Office, *Code of Practice: Equipment Interference*, January 2016, available at https://www.gov.uk/government/publications/equipment-interference-code-of-practice

Home Office, *Code of Practice: Investigation of Protected Electronic Information*, 2007, available at: https://www.gov.uk/government/uploads/system/uploads/attachment_data/file/97959/code-practice-electronic-info.pdf

Home Office, *Interception of Communications Code of Practice*, January 2016, available at: https://www.gov.uk/government/publications/interception-of-communications-code-of-practice-2016

Intelligence and Security Committee of Parliament, *Privacy and Security: A modern and transparent legal framework*, HC 1075, March 2015, available at: http://isc.independent.gov.uk/committee-reports/special-reports

Loof, R., 'Obtaining, adducing and contesting evidence from abroad: A defence perspective on cross-border evidence', *CrimLR*, 2011, No. 1, pp. 40 ff.

Walden, I., *Computer Crimes and Digital Investigations*, 2nd edition, Oxford University Press, 2016.

List of Abbreviations

All ER	All England Law Reports
CrAppR	Criminal Appeal Reports
CrimL&CrimJust	Criminal Law and Criminal Justice (law journal)
Crim LR	Criminal Law Review (law journal)
CSP	Communications service provider
DRIPA	Data Retention and Investigatory Powers Act
ECHR	European Convention of Human Rights
ECtHR	European Court of Human Rights
EHRR	European Human Rights Reports
EurJCrime	European Journal of Crime (law journal)

* All URLs were last accessed in 10/2016.

EWCA Crim	England and Wales Court of Appeal, Criminal Division
EWHC	High Court of England and Wales
GCHQ	Government Communications Headquarters
IOCA	Interception of Communications Act 1985
IoCC	Interception of Communications Commissioner
IP	Internet Protocol
IPB	Investigatory Powers Bill
IPT	Investigatory Powers Tribunal
'ISC'	Intelligence Service Commissioner
ISC	Intelligence and Security Committee of Parliament
ISSA	Intelligence Services Act 1994
LEA	Law Enforcement Agency
MI5	Military Intelligence, Section 5
MI6	Military Intelligence, Section 6
MLA	Mutual Legal Assistance
NCA	National Crime Agency
NTAC	National Technical Assistance Centre
PACE	Police and Criminal Evidence Act 1984
RIPA	Regulation of Investigatory Powers Act 2000
SPoC	Single Points of Contact
SSA	Security Service Act 1989
TA	Telecommunications Act 1984
UKHL	House of Lords
WTA	Wireless Telegraphy Act 2006

Appendix: Questionaires

Ulrich Sieber
Nicolas von zur Mühlen
Max Planck Institute for Foreign and International Criminal Law

Contents

Max Planck Institute for Foreign
and International Criminal Law
79100 Freiburg i.Br. / Germany
– Department for Criminal Law –
Prof. Dr. Dr. h.c. mult. Ulrich Sieber

International Legal Cooperation in the Interception of Telecommunication

– Guide for the Interviews with Representatives of LEAs and Government –

(INTLI-Research Doc. No. 2)

Function of this Document

The INTLI-study of the Max Planck Institute for Foreign and International Criminal Law in Freiburg/Germany aims to improve mutual legal assistance for the interception of telecommunication (INTernational Legal Interception – INTLI). Special focus lies on the question, whether and how intercepted data can be exchanged in real time between different national (esp. European) criminal justice systems, thus making investigation and prosecution of serious crimes more effective without undue limitations of the civil liberties of citizens.

The research is based on a study of the respective national laws and the relevant international instruments ("law in the books") and on the present practices in the various national criminal justice systems ("law in action"). This twofold approach is reflected in two questionnaires that focus on legal and practical aspects of lawful interception, and, thus, complement each other: **The practice of the law in action is investigated by interviews with practitioners (esp. from LEAs and Government) in the field of telecommunication interception; these interviews are structured and harmonized by the on hand interview guide draft INTLI-Doc. No. 2.** The law in the books is analyzed by country reports on the national legal situation following a common structure and common questions described in draft INTLI-Doc. No. 3.

Contents of INTLI Doc No. 2

Guide for the Interviews with Representatives of LEAs and Government

Guide for the Interviews with Representatives of LEAs and Government

I. General Information

1. [Acknowledgement for the invitation and the willingness to cooperate. Short presentation of the interviewer, the Max-Planck Institute for Foreign and International Criminal Law Freiburg, its experience with practice-oriented studies, its cooperation with German investigative authorities in the present project. Explanation of the aims and methods of the project.]

2. [Introductory questions for the interviewed person(s): Esp.:] What is your professional background and your present task? For how many years have you worked in the field of telecommunication interception and related fields? How many national and international interception procedures have you been involved in personally?

II. National Procedures

3. Which institutions deal with electronic interception in your country and what are the respective procedures in criminal matters? What is the relationship of telecommunication surveillance in criminal matters with interception procedures in preventive police activities, and with intelligence services and other institutions?
   Express note: All following questions will deal only with interception in *criminal* matters (criminal procedural law).

4. For which types of crimes (or dangers) is interception primarily used in practice? How important is electronic interception of content data for investigating crimes in your country? Can you compare the importance of analyzing content data with the importance of analyzing meta data (traffic data) for criminal investigations?

5. What is the procedure for interception in criminal justice matters in your country? Are there emergency procedures (e.g. not requiring a court order)?

6. Are there restrictions on the interception of telecommunications of specific persons (e.g. privileges for medical doctors, attorneys, journalists, priests)? To which extent do these privileges also apply if the said person is suspected of a serious crime? Do you also have a restriction on intercepting or analyzing data concerning the core area of privacy (e.g. communication on sexual activities, prayer).

7. How is the individual interception of electronic communication technically handled in your country?

   a) Are there centralized institutions (e.g. for the whole country) or different types of institutions?

   b) Is interception only executed through orders of state institutions given to service providers or also by state authorities acting on their own (e.g. by using IMSI-catchers)?

8. Most countries differentiate in their criminal procedural codes between criminal procedural provisions on telecommunication interception and / or provisions on search and seizure.

   a) Which of these provisions and which procedures (if any) are used in your country to access emails stored on a mail provider and data stored on an online storage service (e.g. a user's cloud)?

   b) Is there a difference if access to these data is attained by a single (possibly open) procedure or by permanent (clandestine) surveillance?

   c) What is the legal basis in these cases?

9. Interception of IP traffic (e.g. from internet access points, DSL routers, internet nodes, cable nodes, LTE or UMTS nodes) captures not only communication between persons but – in the same data stream - also communication between users and automated computer systems (e.g. user's access to websites, communication between a user's computer and his cloud, or communication between automated systems (e.g. in the "internet of things" such as connected home products).

   a) Do you usually intercept and collect *all* of these types of communication when you intercept IP-traffic?

   b) Are there any legal problems in collecting all these types of data under an interception order of your legal system (e.g. because they are not considered a communication between two persons)? Could you e.g. get an interception order for intercepting and analyzing the websites which are visited by the suspect? Is this question already being discussed in your country and is there any jurisprudence on this topic?

   c) Esp. if you are not entitled to intercept or use some types of these IP data: how, where and by whom are these data filtered out of the general IP-data stream and separated from the traditional telephone or telecommunication data?

   d) To what extent is it necessary to intercept and to collect all these types of communication between humans and machines (e.g. access of a user to visited websites) for an effective interception of electronic communication in order to capture possible communication between two persons which are using innovative information channels? What are you doing to capture hidden electronic communication using internet protocols and IP-ports that are not normally used for human communication?

10. For technical reasons interception of telecommunication data sometimes captures data which cannot be legally intercepted due to legal privileges protecting the professional secrecy of doctors, attorney, journalists, priests, etc. The same could apply if interception of data involves the core area of privacy (e.g. communication on sexual activities). How do you handle this problem of undue or excessive data collection including data which are not targeted for legal reasons? How, where and by whom are data streams which possibly contain such undue data analyzed and filtered out?

11. Is it technically possible for investigative agencies of your country to access encrypted telecommunication by (clandestine) remote access to the computers of the communicating partners (so called source telecommunication surveillance capturing specific communication data before encryption or after decryption) in the course of criminal investigations? Is this practiced? What is the legal basis for this procedure (e.g. traditional interception provision or a special provision)?

12. For criminal matters, do investigation agencies access or supervise in specific serious cases all other (general) data by covert remote access to the computers of suspects? If not: Could they do this under your criminal procedural law? What is the legal basis for this procedure? Is there a reform discussion on this issue in your country?

13. What are the main practical problems for intercepting electronic communication in your country? How does your country handle these practical problems (e.g. encrypted data, questions of retaining traffic data by the providers)? What should be changed (technically, organizationally or legally) for improving the situation?

14. Can data resulting from a legal interception of telecommunication in criminal matters be used in criminal (court) proceedings in general? In which cases of illegal interception is it not possible to use intercepted data (just give a short description, no details)?

15. Who controls the interception of electronic communication in criminal matters? Esp., how intensively are applications for an interception order scrutinized by a *judge* in practice and to which extent is the judge realistically able to verify the evidence submitted by the applicant? How much information/evidence do you need to submit in order to have your application approved? How often are applications rejected by the judge? Are there other independent bodies of oversight (other than a judge) and how do they function?

16. Did you have any court decisions limiting the interception of telecommunication on *constitutional* grounds?

17. Are there any specific concepts (best practices) for the interception of electronic communication in your country which are highly successful for investigations or which protect civil liberties in a very efficient way and which you would recommend to other countries?

18. In which laws and guidelines are the interception issues discussed in the present interview regulated? Is there a regulation or a technical protocol for the technical specifities of internet providers? Could we get copies or web-addresses of these national regulations (if possible in English, French or German)?

19. Are there any reform discussions (legislative or other) with respect to the discussed interception questions? What are the motives?

III. International Cooperation

20. How important is *transnational* electronic interception in foreign countries for your criminal justice system? Would a greater or a lesser extent or speed of foreign communication interception have a significant impact on the efficiency of your criminal justice system? Esp. for which types of cases?

21. a) What is the procedure for **obtaining** electronic interception in a foreign country? How often are applications for **obtaining** foreign interception successful, how often are they refused, and how often are they not answered? What are the grounds for refusal or for not answering the requests? Are there specific (legal, technical, organizational) obstacles for obtaining electronic interception in foreign countries (or in a specific foreign country)? Are your foreign partners filtering specific sensitive data out of the collected traffic before they transmit them to you (e.g. data on professional secrets, data on national security, specific types of data)? How effectively does international cooperation in electronic interception work in practice?

    b) What is the parallel situation for **granting** electronic interception in favor of a foreign country? Esp.: What are the reasons for which you deny, limit or delay requests for interception from other countries? If a request for legal interception is generally granted and you send the intercepted data from your country to the foreign police or judicial institution, do you check these data beforehand (for which purpose and with respect to which criteria?) or can you send the data unfiltered and unchecked as they are recorded?

22. a) How long does it take to initiate a procedure **for obtaining** interception in a foreign country?
    If the MLA-procedure is successful and data are gathered in the requested country, how long does it take to receive the respective data after the communication has been intercepted?

By which technical means (e.g. discs, Internet) are the data transmitted between the national police organizations?
Do you get direct (online) real-time access to interception equipment installed in the foreign country? If not, (why) is this (technically, organizationally or legally) not possible or problematic?

b) What is the parallel situation for **granting** electronic interception in favor of a foreign country, esp. regarding the duration of procedures and real-time access??

23. a) How do you handle the problem of data *obtained* from a foreign country which fall under legal privileges in your country (e.g. due to client-attorney privileges)?

    b) How do you handle the problem of *transmitting* data to a foreign country which fall under legal privileges in your country?

24. a) Under some mutual cooperation agreements (e.g. EU-MLA-requests for electronic interception), a *requested state* (who is asked to provide data for MLA) can make his consent subject to any condition which would have to be observed in a similar national case. Do you know about such demands? What demands have been made either by you or by a foreign state? Do they concern electronic data which are not subject to interception and which have to be separated and sorted out (in the requested or in the requesting state)? (see already above question 10)

    b) Have you otherwise asked or otherwise been asked to guarantee that the received data must be dealt with in a certain way (e.g. kept secret, used only for specific purposes, be deleted after a certain time period)? Did you demand such guarantees when you granted mutual assistance and transmitted intercepted data to a foreign country?

25. Under some mutual cooperation agreements (e.g. EU-MLA-requests for electronic interception), a requesting state can ask the requested country to comply with formalities and procedures of his law (e.g. demanded by his law for using the data in court) (as it is possible according to Art. 4 para. 1 MLA Convention EU)? Did you make or receive such demands when requesting mutual assistance for electronic interception? What types of requests have been made? Have these demands been fulfilled?

26. How effective is it to get communication intercepts by joint / parallel investigations in the foreign country?

27. What role do informal channels of cross border police and judicial cooperation play with regard to interception of communication?

28. Are the officials involved in interception sufficiently familiar with the applicable legal framework? Is there a significant discrepancy between the legal requirements and the interception practice?

29. Are there any specific problems with or restrictions on using data stemming from a foreign interception of communications in criminal *(court) proceedings* in your country? Does the use of this data depend on the legality of interception according to the foreign legal order or according to your own legal order?

30. Is the described MLA-system for the interception of telecommunications only used for the prosecution of past crimes or also for the prevention of future risks? If yes, on which basis is it done? If not, do you consider it necessary?

31. The internet enables a wide range of online interception and searches not only on a country's own territory but also with respect to computer and network nodes located in foreign countries. To what extent is it legally, technically, and practically possible in your country to access (communication) data in a foreign country without the involvement of foreign agencies? In which cases is this practiced in your country for criminal law purposes by the police or prosecution services (e.g. access to publicly available websites on a foreign sever, access to not publicly available services like e-mail accounts or Cloud services, cases where the location of a server is not known, emergency situations, other cases)? What types of cases have these been? Were these cases followed by a subsequent notice (e.g. as provided for specific cases by Art. 20 MLA convention EU)?

32. Did you have any court decisions limiting mutual legal assistance for *constitutional grounds* either in general or with respect to the interception of telecommunication?

33. In which laws and guidelines are the cooperation issues discussed in this interview regulated?

34. Are there any reform discussions (legislative or other) with respect to the current cooperation framework? What are the motives?

IV. Specifics of EU Cooperation

35. Are there practical differences between cooperation with EU and non-EU states?

36. To which extent are incoming MLA requests for electronic interception based on
    (a) Art. 18, 19, and 20 of the EU Convention on Mutual Assistance in Criminal Matters of 2000
    (b) the MLA Convention of the Council of Europe of 1959,
    (c) bilateral agreements, and
    (d) national law on international cooperation in criminal matters?
    Does the respective basis of MLA-requests play a role for your practical work?
    How is the situation with outgoing MLA-requests?

37. To which extent are the incoming MLA requests for electronic interception to your country executed by
    (a) direct and automated transfer of intercepted data ("immediate transmission" as e.g. foreseen in Art. 18 para. 1 lit. a MLA Convention EU), or
    (b) the traditional regime of interception, recording and subsequent transmission of data (lit. b)?
    How is the situation with outgoing MLA-requests?

38. To which extent do incoming MLA requests for electronic interception concern
    (a) subjects or access points in your country,
    (b) technical support for interception in the requesting state, or
    (c) technical support for interception in third countries
    (e.g. as foreseen in Art. 18 para 2 a – c MLA Convention EU)?
    How is the situation with outgoing MLA-requests?

39. What should be done – in general or within the EU - for making international interception procedures more efficient? What should be done in order to protect civil liberties in such procedures better?

V. Statistics

40. Are there any statistics on the use of electronic interception and/or the access to stored communication (esp. in the criminal justice system, but – if available – also in the other above regimes)?

41. a) Could you provide a rough estimation on the extent of requests for electronic telecommunication interception which your country **demands** from other countries? How many go to Germany?

    b) Could you provide a rough estimation on the extent of MLA-requests for interception of telecommunication which your country **receives** each year from abroad? How many are from Germany?

VI. Legal Regulation

Our study also requires a more detailed analysis of the legal framework of your country on electronic interception. Could you please help us later to go through our legal questionnaire (after a pause or tomorrow or even later in writing?). If time is short it is possible to deal only with the main questions (printed in bold).

Max Planck Institute for Foreign
and International Criminal Law
79100 Freiburg i.Br. / Germany
– Department for Criminal Law –
Prof. Dr. Dr. h.c. mult. Ulrich Sieber

International Legal Cooperation in the Interception of Telecommunication

– Structure and Questionnaire for the National Country Reports –

(INTLI-Research Doc. No. 3)

Function of this Document

The INTLI-study of the Max Planck Institute for Foreign and International Criminal Law in Freiburg/Germany aims to improve mutual legal assistance for the interception of telecommunication (INTernational Legal Interception – INTLI). Special focus lies on the question, whether and how intercepted data can be exchanged in real time between different national (esp. European) criminal justice systems, thus making investigation and prosecution of serious crimes more effective without undue limitations of the civil liberties of citizens.

The research is based on a study of the respective national laws and the relevant international instruments ("law in the books") and on the present practices in the various national criminal justice systems ("law in action"). This twofold approach is reflected in two questionnaires that focus on legal and practical aspects of lawful interception, and, thus, complement each other: The practice of the law in action is investigated by interviews with practitioners (esp. from LEAs and Government) in the field of telecommunication interception; these interviews are structured and harmonized by the on hand interview guide draft INTLI-Doc. No. 2. **The law in the books is analyzed by country reports on the national legal situation following a common structure and common questions described in draft INTLI-Doc. No. 3.**

Contents of INTLI Doc. No. 3:

Structure and Questionnaire for the National Country Reports

OBJECT, AIM, AND METHOD OF THE PROJECT

I. Object of Research

Technical and social changes in electronic communication and other internet services create new opportunities and new risks for *using computer data in criminal investigations*, esp. with respect to the interception of electronic communication and the access to stored communication data. This leads to new challenges for the traditional coercive powers in criminal procedural law, for the respective international cooperation, and for the protection of civil liberties of citizens. This is esp. the case for the subject matter of the present research in the field of criminal justice: the *interception of electronic communication in a global world*.

II. Aim of Research

The main practical aim of the present study and the following questionnaire is to analyze the chances of a *cooperation model* in the field of electronic interception, by which the judicial institutions of one country can directly access in real time electronic communication data in a foreign country. This practical goal requires two additional objectives in the area of more fundamental research: First, a comparative analysis of *national legal provisions on interception* of electronic communication and access to related data and services. And second, an analysis of the present *cooperation regime for transnational interception* of electronic evidence, esp. with respect to the results of telecommunication surveillance.[1]

III. Method of Research

The analysis of the legal questions to be solved will be based primarily on an investigation of the respective international instruments as well as a systematic comparative analysis of the national laws in the books. This normative analysis of the various national laws is based on the topics and questions described in this paper (INTLI Research Doc. No. 2). It will be amended by additional interviews with practitioners esp. from the law enforcement community which will also describe the existing problems and the law in action (INTLI Doc No. 3).

---

[1] Such a basic approach is necessary e.g. since countries can only provide legal assistance by activities permitted to them by their national laws and – in addition – can make their consent to mutual assistance subject to any condition which would have to be observed in a similar national case). Furthermore this information is needed as a basis for national and international law reform (esp. for the development of new internet-based international cooperation regimes).

IV. Scope of the Project

In the present questionnaire, the *definition of the object of interception*, i.e. electronic communication, is to be understood in a wide sense and *extended beyond the traditional concept* of communication between persons in order to obtain a broad working hypothesis especially to consider the two following developments:

(1) In today's information society, communication is no longer limited to communication between persons, but includes communication between persons and machines. Thus, when defining electronic communication for the purpose of this research, it is irrelevant whether the sender or the recipient of communication are persons or computer systems. The scope of this research includes – under the term of *electronic communication* – e.g. also communication between a person (behind a computer) and a website, a person and a server on which one's own data is stored (e.g. cloud servers), or between two machines (e.g. data transmitted within the "internet of things" e.g. between two cars). It also does not matter whether the object of transmission, i.e. data, represents audio or video content, tracking data, keystrokes, or any other kind of signals. Based on this broad working definition of "*electronic communication*" it is then up to each country report to explain, which of these broadly defined communication processes and data can be the object of the respective national legal provisions on the interception of telecommunication data.

(2) Furthermore, in IT-Systems the differentiation between *storage and communication* of data is losing its practical importance (as is illustrated by mail stored on the servers of a provider before being downloaded by the recipient). Since electronic communication is defined by the requirement of *transmission of data* between at least two persons or computer systems, this technical definition of communication does not directly apply to the access of investigation authorities to stored data e.g. by using the traditional provisions of search and seizure or remote forensic software (so-called online-search). However, since data of electronic communication can be often accessed "indirectly" by these traditional or new access-provisions before, during or after their transmission, these "access provisions" for stored data must also be considered in the following analysis (as far as they are directed to data which will be, are, or have been transmitted between two persons or computers, see below).

V. Special Emphasis

The following questions on the interception of electronic communication in European criminal justice include new topics, some of which are not yet clearly regulated or decided by criminal procedural law in many European States. For that reason, country reporters are asked, when responding to the following questions, to indicate also if questions are clearly decided or controversially disputed or not yet dealt with in their country; they should also refer to actual reform projects. If adequate, they should also indicate whether answers to the following questions are based on the wording of the respective laws, constitutional requirements, jurisprudence, literature, present practice (law in action) and/or on their own evaluation. It would also be helpful if country reporters would cite the decisive parts of relevant legal provisions in their answers in short and also collect the complete legal provisions and main decisions of jurisprudence in an appendix.

PROPOSED TOPICS AND COMMON STRUCTURE OF THE COUNTRY REPORTS

QUESTIONS TO BE ANSWERED WITHIN THE ABOVE STRUCTURE

A. Introduction: General Background of the National Legal System

Question 1: Basic architecture of the legal system

The Interception of electronic communication has become a major instrument for criminal investigation, prevention of future dangers, and information gathering of intelligence agencies. In many European countries, such an interception of electronic communication is possible under different legal regimes, esp.: (repressive) criminal law, (preventive) police law, and intelligence (or state security) law.

a) Which of these (or other) legal regimes exist and provide coercive powers for interception of electronic communication in your country?

b) What are the respective legal provisions for intercepting electronic communication in the above mentioned regimes? How far do the prerequisites for the interception of electronic communication differ between these regimes (please provide only a short overview, no details)?

c) Which authorities are technically enforcing the respective interception measures under the above regimes in your country? Is the technical implementation done by state agencies (also based on cooperation duties of IP-providers) or is it partly or completely outsourced to private companies? Are there centralized institutions, e.g. for the whole territory of the state or the country, either for one or for various of the above regimes?

d) Are the various institutions responsible for these regimes and functions separated from each other (as e.g. in Germany) or are the interceptions carried out by joint agencies (such as the English police being responsible for both prevention and repression, or the American FBI simultaneously performing duties as both a preventive and repressive police institution as well as an intelligence agency)? Can the results of interception measures under these different regimes be exchanged between the competent authorities and regimes within your country (e.g. from intelligence agencies to the police) (please provide only a short overview, no details)?

Question 2: Statistics on electronic communication interception

a) Scope of *national* interceptions in your country: Are there any statistics on the use of electronic interception and/or the access to stored communication (esp. in the criminal justice system, but – if available – also in the other above regimes)? If possible, please indicate the object of these statistics (esp. its definition of interception) and the number of interception incidents per year by providing absolute numbers and/or numbers per inhabitants and/or numbers per electronic communication-access points and/or electronic communication calls. Please be aware that a low number of interceptions under criminal law can be compensated to a certain degree by a high number of interceptions under intelligence or police law if there are no limitations on data flows between these systems.

b) Is there any obligation for enforcement agencies or courts to report statistics to a central institution, e.g. the Ministry of Justice?

B. Constitutional, Legal, and Doctrinal Safeguards for the Interception of Electronic Communication

Question 3: Specific constitutional and non-constitutional protection for electronic communication and for computer-stored data

a) Does your country have *constitutional* safeguards for the protection of telecommunication data (such as the secrecy of telecommunication[2]) and/or for personal data stored or transmitted in computer systems (e.g. the right to privacy, the right of informational self-determination on personal data",[3] or the integrity of information systems[4])?

b) Does your country provide a *constitutional* "principle of proportionality and necessity" and to what extent is it relevant for coercive powers in criminal procedural law, both in general and – especially – in the field of interception of electronic communication?

c) Are there other (non constitutional) legal safeguards for the protection of the secrecy of telecommunication (e.g. criminal laws), the protection of personal computer stored data (e.g. special protective rules for the *collection and transfer* of personal data by the principle of "purpose limitation of personal data."[5]) or special contents transmitted by telecommunication (such as professional secrets, business secrets)?

---

[2] The secrecy of telecommunication refers to a principle that aims at protecting the incorporeal transmission of information from a sender to an individual recipient using technical devices.

[3] In some countries, the principle of "self determination on personal data" requires that citizens have a right to decide on the collection, storage, use and disclosure of their data; the use of personal data must therefore be either regulated by law or be based on an informed consent of the respective person.

[4] The trust in the integrity of information systems is meant to protect information systems from impacts on their confidentiality, integrity or availability, esp. by means of the use of remote forensic software.

[5] In some countries, the principle of "purpose limitation of personal data" states that data can be collected by an agency for a specific purpose and be used by and transferred to another agency for another purpose only if this is permitted by law and if this is necessary.

d) What are the consequences of these safeguards for the interception of (electronic) communication? Are there legal safeguards to ensure effective protection of the intercepted data against the risk of abuse and against any unlawful access and use of that data?

Question 4: Principles for the definition of coercive powers in criminal procedural law

a) Are there any constitutional or doctrinal rules for the precise definition or interpretation of coercive powers in criminal procedural law (such as the nullum crimen sine lege principle in substantive criminal law,[6] or the principle of precise parliamentary enactment of public powers)[7]? Is an analogous application of coercive powers possible?[8]

b) Are coercive powers in your criminal procedural law based on differentiated, precise, and specific provisions? Or does your country have a general clause for coercive powers, either in general or for minor cases? Are there other important (esp. protective) aspects behind the systematization and definition of the coercive powers in your criminal procedural law?

C. Coercive Powers for Accessing Electronic Communications Data in Criminal Procedural Law

I. Overview of the legal framework and the respective provisions in criminal procedural law

Question 5: Framework for accessing electronic communications data in criminal justice

Please give a short overview on the system of criminal procedural laws which can be used for intercepting electronic communication and for otherwise accessing electronic communications data for the purpose of criminal investigations and which are described in more detail infra. Are additional general clauses applicable?[9]

---

[6] In substantive criminal law, the principle "no crime without legal definition" requires inter alia that criminal statutes must be defined precisely by the legislator before the commission of a criminal act can be assumed.

[7] The principle of precise parliamentary enactment of public powers requires that all infringements of civil liberties must be based on precise laws.

[8] This means that a provision can be applied to a situation that is not justified by the provision's wording, but by its purpose.

[9] Legal provisions of intelligence law (state security law) and preventive police laws should be mentioned only in question 1 above.

II. Interception of content of electronic communication data in criminal procedural law

Question 6: Respective provision

Most countries have one main provision in criminal procedural law (often specified by additional legal provisions) dealing with the interception of the content of communication in transmission. The following questions refer to this main provision (or - if available – to the main provisions), whereas provisions primarily concerning other specific purposes (e.g. search and seizure of stored data) should be dealt with in section D, questions 17 to 19 only. Please provide the provision and cite the wording of its core part (in English).

Question 7: Object of interception

a) How is the object of interception defined in the above provision of your criminal procedural law (e.g. as "telephone communication", "electronic communication", "electronic communication between persons", ...)?

b) Which of the following contents of traffic are covered by the respective provisions and can be captured under your criminal procedural law:
   - analogous communication (voice and data) via landlines?
   - IP-traffic of a person-to-person-communication?
   - IP-traffic between a person and an automated information system (such as communication with a webserver while downloading a website)?
   - IP-traffic between a person's computer and their data storage in a cloud or other remote storage of data processing systems (is this covered by "communication", as defined in the above main legal provision, between the user and the cloud provider or as an internal activity within the private storage devices of the user which is comparable with the use of a single internal storage device)?
   - IP-traffic between two independent computer systems (e.g. between an automated machine and its computer-based automated control center, esp. in the "internet of things")?
   - any other options?

c) Does the respective main provision for content interception cover electronic communication data only during their *transmission* or also when the respective data are *stored* before, during, or after this process of transmission (e.g. e-mail drafts or sent e-mails, e-mails stored by the provider, received e-mails stored by the recipient or completely web-based communication such as in social networks)? If so, are there any special criteria that stored e-mails or messages must fulfill in order to be covered by the main provision for content communication interception (is there e.g. a differentiation between read and unread e-mails or messages)?

d) If there are no explicit rules on these questions: Is there a discussion on respective constitutional requirements? Could constitutional reasoning influence these discussions in the future?

Question 8: Privileged information

a) Does your criminal procedural law (or any other law) provide specific safeguards excluding particular types of information from electronic communication interception, e.g.
   - communication under professional secrecy, such as communication between an attorney-at-law and a client, a medical practitioner and a patient, a priest and a parishioner, journalists' communication, etc.?
   - communication protected under the law regulating financial and banking secrecy?
   - communication in a "core area of private life" (e.g. prayers, communication during sexual activities, diaries, ...)?
   - any other type of communication?

b) If information is thus privileged, what consequences does this entail, e.g.
   - interception is not possible and has to be suspended immediately (and can be turned on later again?) by the police?
   - interception can be continued and critical records have to be checked and erased immediately or later by the police?
   - information can be used in certain cases (if so in which)?
   - any other options?
   - Are there (technical) differences between handling analogous and digital communication?

c) Who has to decide at which stage of the interception and in which way these privileges and/or the analysis of the respective captured information has to be conducted, e.g.,
   - the magistrate issuing the respective warrant?
   - the prosecutor?
   - the executive police agent or his technical assistants?
   - the internet provider before handing over the respective data?

d) If there are no explicit rules on these questions: Is there a discussion on respective constitutional requirements? Could constitutional reasoning influence these discussions in the future?

Question 9: Mode of interception

a) Which of the following *modes of interception* are state agencies *legally entitled* to use under criminal law in order to intercept the content of electronic communication?
   - Ordering access providers to extract and surrender specific communication?
   - Intercepting specific communication themselves and without recourse to third parties (e.g. by interception of cables, interception of a WLAN, use of remote forensic software)?

b) Which *types of accompanying investigative measures* are permitted in your country's main provision on electronic interception under your criminal law for the interception of electronic communication (e.g. clandestine access to houses in order to place equipment, hacking techniques, use of key loggers)?

Question 10: Specific cooperation duties of internet providers

a) Which internet providers can be ordered by judicial warrant to execute interception orders, e.g.,
   - access providers on the IP-transport level?
   - infrastructure providers working on the IP-transport level (such as central network nodes without direct contacts to the users)?
   - providers working on the IP-application level providing social interaction (e.g. e-mail or phone services, social networks) or data storing/processing services (e.g. cloud-providers) (see also question 18 below)?

b) How does your law describe and regulate the cooperation duties of internet providers?

c) Are there any provisions requiring communication providers to follow certain rules on interception capabilities in their networks, e.g. to purchase and install special equipment for intercepting communication, to ensure the technical capability to intercept communication, and/or to provide access to stored data for the police (not the powers to compel interception itself), protocolling duties, etc.?

d) Which norms exist concerning the technical aspects of the internet providers' transfer of intercepted data to the police, e.g. with respect to
   - formats and protocols?
   - transport channels?
   - security measures?
   - encryption?

e) Are there norms regulating technical aspects of the internet provider's transfer of intercepted data to authorities in a foreign country (e.g. in the context of mutual legal assistance)?

f) Are there any checks and filtering obligations which must be performed by the internet providers (automatically or manually) before or during the execution of the interception process, e.g.:
   - filtering out the traffic of specific persons, IP-numbers, devices (e.g. by deep packet inspection)?
   - filtering out specific protocols and or ports (e.g. phone, mail, access to websites, chat)
   - filtering out specific content (e.g. types of communication, content of communication, see questions above ....)?
   - Do the providers have a special duty to decrypt encoded data if possible?

Question 11: Formal prerequisites of interception orders

a) Which authority (e.g. judge, prosecutor, head of police) can authorize and which authorities can apply for interception orders
   - under normal circumstances;
   - in case of (which types of) emergency?

b) Are there any formal requirements for the application (e.g. oral presentation before the approving authority, written submission)? Which information must be contained in the order? Does it need to give a reason?

c) On grounds of what evidence is the applicant's case presented to the competent authority (e.g. simple application, oath, submission of investigative files)?

Question 12: Substantive prerequisites of interception orders

a) Which degree of suspicion for a past crime (or – in some countries – which degree of future danger or risk) is necessary for an interception order?

b) Which crimes or (dangers) can justify an interception order? Please also state whether the potential or the likely sentencing range serve as (additional?) limiting criteria.

c) In case of suspicion of crime, who can be subject to an interception order (e.g. suspects, their intermediaries, their communication partners, specific devices)?

d) Is it possible that an interception order, for the purpose of a *criminal investigation*, is not directed against a particular individual, against particular premises, or against a specific device, but instead targets particular communication content (e.g. through the automated use of certain trigger words)?

e) Is there a specific requirement regarding the likelihood that the anticipated evidence will actually be obtained by means of the requested interception?

f) For the admissibility of electronic communication interception does your law require that other - less intrusive – means of investigation first be tried unsuccessfully or be considered unlikely to be successful?

g) Besides consistency with the aforementioned requirements, is there an additional obligation for the authorizing authority to verify that the interception is proportionate to the seriousness of the offence in the individual case? Which particular factors will most likely preclude proportionality?

h) Is an interception order required when one of the parties to the communication has consented to the interception?

Question 13: Validity of interception orders

a) What is the maximum length of an interception order
   - under normal circumstances;
   - in case of emergency?

b) How often and to which maximum duration can it be prolonged?

c) Does the renewal or prolongation of the interception warrant follow the same procedure as the initial application for an interception?

d) Can an interception order be revoked and under which circumstances?

e) Is there an obligation for the relevant authority or any other body to revoke the authorization when a subsequent lack of substantive prerequisites becomes apparent?

f) Must the interception be halted if it reveals information pointing to the commission of offences not anticipated by or not mentioned in the interception order?

Question 14: Recording and reporting requirements

a) Are there protocolling duties?

b) Are there (obligatory) reports on progress of interception and final reports that have to be submitted to the judge/any other body (and at which time intervals)?

c) Are there any requirements to destroy the records which are not related to the aim of the interception warrant, or which are not needed as evidence (any more)? Who is responsible for the destruction of the records and what is the procedure?

Question 15: Notification requirements and remedies against interception orders

a) Is there a duty of the investigative authorities to inform intercepted persons about an interception, e.g. as soon as this is possible without endangerment of the investigation or after completion of the investigation? If so, to what extent is such notification practiced?

b) Does the person subject to an interception order have remedies against an illegal or illegally performed interception, in case he/she becomes aware of the interception?

c) In case of judicial review or other remedies: are there procedural particularities to such a review (e.g. *in camera* proceedings, limits on the state's disclosure obligations, need to give reasons for a dismissal)?

d) Are officials conducting interceptions illegally subject to particular sanctions? Can you state the frequency with which such cases arise or sanctions are imposed?

e) Is there any independent monitoring authority that has the power to control the interception of communication and make sure that it is carried out in accordance with the legal requirements/legal authorization?

Question 16: Confidentiality and reliability requirements

a) Is there a specific obligation for internet providers to keep their support measures confidential?

b) Are there specific (criminal?) sanctions for infringements of this obligation?

c) Are there particular obligations for the person conducting the interception to maintain the integrity and reliability of the material obtained (e.g. sealing the data storage medium, transmission of intercepted data to a judicial authority immediately following the interception, producing transcripts in the presence of defense lawyers)?

III. Interception of *traffic data* for criminal justice

Question 17: Interception of traffic data and subscriber data

a) Please provide the relevant provisions and, if possible, cite the wording of their core parts (in English).

b) What are the requirements (esp. safeguards) for accessing traffic data in your country? Is this possible by way of an automated on-line procedure?

c) What are the requirements for accessing subscriber data in your country? Is this possible by way of an automated on-line procedure?

d) Subject to which rules can the attribution of dynamic IP-addresses to specific users at a given time be obtained from internet providers? Is this possible by way of an automated on-line procedure?

e) Does your country require internet providers retain subscriber information?

f) Does your country require internet providers to retain traffic data? How long must data be stored? What kind of data must be stored (e.g. phone numbers, e-mail addresses, date and time of a connection, IP-addresses)?

Question 18: Identification of the device ID of a mobile end terminal and its card number

a) Does your country have such a provision? If yes, please give a short description of this provision, esp. with respect to the information to be obtained.

b) Or can such activities be justified by other provisions (e.g. the general provision on interception)? If so, please give a short description of this provision.

IV. Applying "access-to-stored-data provisions" to electronic communication processes

Question 19: Online-search by remote forensic software (including specialized norms on source electronic communication interception)

Does your country have such a provision or similar provisions? If so, please give a short description of this provision, esp. with respect to the activities permitted (e.g. hacking, keylogging), the data which can be accessed (all stored data or only electronic communication data), the option to use this measure without the knowledge of the persons concerned, the duties to disclose the measures at a later stage, the regional scope).

Question 20: Search and seizure for stored electronic communication data

a) To what extent is this approach possible in your legal system?

b) Is this option provided for in other ways than by using the general powers to intercept communication in form of the aforementioned central provisions for the interception of electronic communication or do the more restricted provisions on electronic communication interception (as the more specialized lex specialis) supersede or replace the provisions on search and seizure?

c) Do the safeguards and requirements for the interception of communication differ for interception and access to stored data? Does communication in transmission have a higher degree of legal protection (e.g. is information in transmission better protected than the same information the second after its transmission has terminated and it has been stored)?

d) Must the access to stored communication be performed as an open measure or can it be performed in a clandestine way? If it has to be performed openly, does it depend on the awareness of the suspect and/or on the awareness of the provider?

Question 21: Production order and decryption order

a) Does your country have a *special regulation* providing cooperation duties for decoding encrypted data or to hand over the necessary passwords in one or more of the following forms:
   - as an independent general provision?
   - in connection with the provisions on search and seizure and/or production orders?
   - in connection with the provisions on interception of electronic communication?

b) Who is the subject of the duty to provide the encryption key in the cases stated above (e.g. anybody, a communications provider, ...)? Are these provisions also applicable to the suspect of the investigation? If the suspect has a duty to decrypt or to provide a key, how does this correlate with the prohibition on self-incrimination in your legal doctrine? If possible, please make reference to any specific legal provision or court decision(s) on this matter.

Question 22: Others

Does your country have additional/other coercive powers which might be relevant for accessing electronic communication data either during transmission or in stored form before, during, or after transmission (e.g. a general clause)?

V. Use of electronic communication data in court proceedings

Question 23: Specific regulations on use

a) Are there specific rules for using intercepted electronic communication data in court proceedings (please only refer to rules especially designed for admissibility of intercepted or stored electronic communication data as evidence in the court and not to general rules)?

b) In which form is intercepted material introduced as evidence in criminal proceedings (transcripts, audio recordings, witness testimony)?

c) Which consequences does the non-observance of the aforementioned formal and substantive prerequisites have on the admissibility as evidence?

d) Can intercepted data be used for the prosecution of offences other than the offences mentioned or anticipated in the interception order?

e) Can intercepted data be used for the prosecution of individuals who were not subject of the underlying interception order?

f) Is intercepted data obtained from outside the criminal justice system (e.g. intelligence services, non-judicial police forces) admissible as evidence in criminal proceedings?

g) What are the rules on the admissibility of intercepted data obtained from foreign jurisdictions?

h) To what extent can the accused challenge the probity of intercepted evidence? Please also state relevant disclosure obligations of the prosecution (e.g. regarding the technical means used for the interception).

D. Exchange of Intercepted Electronic Communication Data between Foreign Countries

Question 24: Legal Basis for mutual legal assistance

a) Which *international conventions* on mutual assistance applicable for the interception of electronic communication are ratified and applicable in your country? E.g. the Convention on Mutual Assistance in Criminal Matters between the member States of the European Union of 2000 (esp. with Art. 17-21),[10] the European Convention on Mutual Assistance in Criminal Matters of 1959 (esp. with its general clause), the United Nations Transnational Organized Crime Convention of 2000 (esp. Article 18), etc. ?

b) Does your country have additional bilateral treaties on mutual legal assistance with Germany or with the EU covering interception of electronic communication? How is interception of electronic communication regulated therein (especially in comparison with the above mentioned EU Convention of 2000 or other conventions ratified by your country)?

c) Does your country have additional national regulation on mutual assistance and interception of electronic communication beyond the ratified treaties (e.g. in general national rules on mutual legal assistance)? What is the content of the respective national laws with respect to electronic interception (either in general rules on mutual assistance or in specific regulations on interception)? Does this legislation enable non-treaty based mutual assistance for the interception of electronic communication (e.g. for specific countries or in addition to the treaty-based legal regimes)?

Question 25: Procedures and execution of requests

a) If your country receives a foreign request for the interception of telecommunication: Which authorities are responsible for granting the request and which authorities are responsible for executing it? What is the respective procedure prescribed by your national law?

b) Is there a duty to filter out or to delete privileged information (see question 8) before your country transmits the results of an interception measure to a foreign country? Would this obligation also apply within a real-time transmission of intercepted data to a foreign country?

c) In the opposite case (if your state is requesting interception of electronic communication in a foreign country): Which authorities send out the requests? If you later receive the results of the requested interception measure, do you have a duty to filter out or to delete information which could not be intercepted according to the laws of your state (or even to the law of the sending state) due to a legal privilege (see question 8)?

[10] It should be noted that this convention has not yet been ratified by Greece, Italy, Croatia and Ireland.

Question 26: Real-time transfer of communications data

a) Looking at the current design of your national legal regime on telecommunications interception as well as at your national law on mutual legal assistance, to which extent is a *direct extraction and transfer* of intercepted electronic communications data among foreign police and judicial authorities already possible under your domestic law? Can a foreign police and judicial authority directly address communication providers in your country in view of requesting the extraction of communications data? Can communications providers in your country directly transfer communications data to a foreign authority without involvement of a domestic authority?

b) What technical, legal, and organizational reform measures (national and/or international) would be necessary to enable such "real time cooperation" in the field of interception measures or to increase its effectiveness?

c) If applicable, how will the recently adopted European Investigation Order affect MLA in the area of intercepted communication? Do you anticipate any challenges with regard to its domestic implementation?

Question 27: Statistics

Are there any statistics or information of your Ministry of Justice on the extent of MLA-requests for electronic telecommunication interception? If yes: How many MLA-requests for interception of telecommunication does your country receive each year from abroad? How many are from Germany?
How many of such requests does your country send to foreign countries / to Germany per year?

Authors and Co-authors

Mgr. *Tomáš Abelovský*	Masaryk University of Brno
Prof. Dr. Dr. h.c. *Lorena Bachmaier Winter*	*Complutense University* of Madrid
Gertjan Boulet, Ph.D. Candidate	Vrije Universiteit Brussel and Korea University Seoul
Prof. Dr. *Iain Cameron*	University of Uppsala
Prof. Dr. *Paul De Hert*	Vrije Universiteit Brussel and Tilburg University
Patrick Köppen	Max Planck Institute for Foreign and International Criminal Law
Dr. *Estelle De Marco*	InthemiS, Montpellier
JUDr. *Jakub Harašta*	Masaryk University of Brno
Mgr. *Pavel Loutocký*, BA (hons.)	Masaryk University of Brno
Mgr. MgA *Jakub Míšek*	Masaryk University of Brno
Nicolas von zur Mühlen	Max Planck Institute for Foreign and International Criminal Law
doc. JUDr. *Radim Polčák*, Ph.D.	Masaryk University of Brno
Prof. Dr. Dr. h.c. mult. *Ulrich Sieber*	Max Planck Institute for Foreign and International Criminal Law
Mgr. *Václav Stupka*	Masaryk University of Brno
Dr. *Tatiana Tropina*	Max Planck Institute for Foreign and International Criminal Law
Dr. *Benjamin Vogel*, LL.M. (Cantab.)	Max Planck Institute for Foreign and International Criminal Law
Thomas Wahl	Max Planck Institute for Foreign and International Criminal Law
Prof. Dr. *Ian Walden*	Queen Mary University of London

Schriftenreihe des Max-Planck-Instituts für ausländisches und internationales Strafrecht

The main research activities of the Max Planck Institute for Foreign and International Criminal Law are published in the following six subseries of the "Schriftenreihe des Max-Planck-Instituts für ausländisches und internationales Strafrecht" (Research Series of the Max Planck Institute for Foreign and International Criminal Law), which are distributed in cooperation with the publisher Duncker & Humblot:

- "Strafrechtliche Forschungsberichte" (Reports on Research in Criminal Law)
- "Kriminologische Forschungsberichte" (Reports on Research in Criminology)
- "Interdisziplinäre Forschungen aus Strafrecht und Kriminologie" (Reports on Interdisciplinary Research in Criminal Law and Criminology)
- "Publications of the Max Planck Partner Group for Balkan Criminology"
- "Series of the Max Planck Institute for Foreign and International Criminal Law and Bahçeşehir University Joint Research Group"
- "Sammlung ausländischer Strafgesetzbücher in deutscher Übersetzung" (Collection of Foreign Criminal Laws in German Translation)

These publications can be ordered from the Max Planck Institute at <www.mpicc.de> or from Duncker & Humblot at <www.duncker-humblot.de>. Two additional subseries are published: "research in brief" contains short reports on results of research activities, and "Arbeitsberichte" (working materials) present preliminary results of research projects. These publications are available at the Max Planck Institute.

Detailed information on all publications of the Max Planck Institute for Foreign and International Criminal Law can be found at <www.mpicc.de>.

Die zentralen Veröffentlichungen des Max-Planck-Instituts für ausländisches und internationales Strafrecht werden in Zusammenarbeit mit dem Verlag Duncker & Humblot in den folgenden sechs Unterreihen der „Schriftenreihe des Max-Planck-Instituts für ausländisches und internationales Strafrecht" vertrieben:

- „Strafrechtliche Forschungsberichte"
- „Kriminologische Forschungsberichte"
- „Interdisziplinäre Forschungen aus Strafrecht und Kriminologie"
- „Publications of the Max Planck Partner Group for Balkan Criminology"
- „Series of the Max Planck Institute for Foreign and International Criminal Law and Bahçeşehir University Joint Research Group"
- „Sammlung ausländischer Strafgesetzbücher in deutscher Übersetzung"

Diese Publikationen können direkt über das Max-Planck-Institut unter <www.mpicc.de> oder über den Verlag Duncker & Humblot unter <www.duncker-humblot.de> erworben werden. Darüber hinaus erscheinen in der Unterreihe „research in brief" zusammenfassende Kurzbeschreibungen von Forschungsergebnissen und in der Unterreihe „Arbeitsberichte" Veröffentlichungen vorläufiger Forschungsergebnisse. Diese Veröffentlichungen können über das Max-Planck-Institut bezogen werden.

Detaillierte Informationen zu den einzelnen Publikationen des Max-Planck-Instituts für ausländisches und internationales Strafrecht sind unter <www.mpicc.de> abrufbar.

Max-Planck-Institut für ausländisches und internationales Strafrecht

Selected criminal law publications:

S 154 *Carl-Wendelin Neubert*
Der Einsatz tödlicher Waffengewalt durch die deutsche auswärtige Gewalt
2016 • 391 Seiten • ISBN 978-3-86113-799-3 € 41,00

S 153 *Mehmet Arslan*
Die Aussagefreiheit des Beschuldigten in der polizeilichen Befragung
Ein Vergleich zwischen der EMRK, dem deutschen und dem türkischen Recht
2015 • 670 Seiten • ISBN 978-3-86113-801-3 € 55,00

S 152 *Albin Eser / Walter Perron* (Hrsg.)
Strukturvergleich strafrechtlicher Verantwortlichkeit und Sanktionierung in Europa
Zugleich ein Beitrag zur Theorie der Strafrechtsvergleichung
2015 • 1147 Seiten • ISBN 978-3-86113-802-0 € 66,00

S 151 *Emmanouil Billis*
Die Rolle des Richters im adversatorischen und im inquisitorischen Beweisverfahren
Modelltheoretische Ansätze, englisches und deutsches Beweisführungssystem, internationalrechtliche Dimensionen
2015 • 503 Seiten • ISBN 978-3-86113-804-4 € 44,00

S 150 *Ulrich Sieber / Benjamin Vogel*
Terrorismusfinanzierung
Prävention im Spannungsfeld von internationalen Vorgaben und nationalem Tatstrafrecht
2015 • 237 Seiten • ISBN 978-3-86113-805-1 € 35,00

S 149 *Stefan Drackert*
Die Risiken der Verarbeitung personenbezogener Daten
Eine Untersuchung zu den Grundlagen des Datenschutzrechts
2014 • 338 Seiten • ISBN 978-3-86113-806-8 € 35,00

S 148 *Harald Weiß*
Haft ohne Urteil
Strafprozessuale Freiheitsentziehungen im deutsch-französischen Vergleich
2015 • 891 Seiten • ISBN 978-3-86113-807-5 € 60,00

S 147 *Lennart M. Hügel*
Strafbarkeit der Anschlagsvorbereitung durch terroristische Einzeltäter und deren Unterstützer
Eine rechtsvergleichende Untersuchung anhand der deutschen und amerikanischen Rechtsordnung
2014 • 260 Seiten • ISBN 978-3-86113-808-2 € 35,00

Max-Planck-Institut für ausländisches
und internationales Strafrecht

Selected criminal law publications:

S 146 *Jon Petter Rui / Ulrich Sieber* (eds.)
Non-Conviction-Based Confiscation in Europe
Possibilities and Limitations on Rules Enabling Confiscation without a Criminal Conviction
2015 • 306 Seiten • ISBN 978-3-86113-809-9 € 40,00

S 145 *Xenia Lang*
Geheimdienstinformationen im deutschen und amerikanischen Strafprozess
2014 • 400 Seiten • ISBN 978-3-86113-811-2 € 41,00

S 140 *Ulrich Sieber / Marc Engelhart*
Compliance Programs for the Prevention of Economic Crimes
An Empirical Survey of German Companies
2014 • 312 Seiten • ISBN 978-3-86113-816-7 € 40,00

S 128.1.1 *Ulrich Sieber / Konstanze Jarvers / Emily Silverman* (eds.)
National Criminal Law in a Comparative Legal Context
Volume 1.1: Introduction to National Systems
2013 • 314 Seiten • ISBN 978-3-86113-822-8 € 40,00

S 128.1.2 Volume 1.2: Introduction to National Systems
2013 • 363 Seiten • ISBN 978-3-86113-826-6 € 43,00

S 128.1.3 Volume 1.3: Introduction to National Systems
2014 • 297 Seiten • ISBN 978-3-86113-818-1 € 40,00

S 128.1.4 Volume 1.4: Introduction to National Systems
2014 • 391 Seiten • ISBN 978-3-86113-810-5 € 43,00

S 128.2.1 *Ulrich Sieber / Susanne Forster / Konstanze Jarvers* (eds.)
Volume 2.1: General limitations on the application of criminal law
2011 • 399 Seiten • ISBN 978-3-86113-834-1 € 43,00

S 128.3.1 Volume 3.1: Defining criminal conduct
2011 • 519 Seiten • ISBN 978-3-86113-833-4 € 46,00

S 128.4.1 Volume 4.1: Special forms of criminal liability
2015 • 401 Seiten • ISBN 978-3-86113-803-7 € 43,00

S 128.5.1 Volume 5.1: Grounds for rejecting criminal liability
2016 • 410 Seiten • ISBN 978-3-86113-800-6 € 43,00